AN ENQUIRY CONCERNING HUMAN UNDERSTANDING

broadview editions
series editor: L.W. Conolly

AN ENQUIRY CONCERNING HUMAN UNDERSTANDING

David Hume

edited by Lorne Falkenstein

broadview editions

Library and Archives Canada Cataloguing in Publication

Hume, David, 1711-1776
    An enquiry concerning human understanding / David Hume ; edited by Lorne Falkenstein.

(Broadview editions)
Includes bibliographical references and index.
ISBN 978-1-55111-802-4

    1. Knowledge, Theory of. I. Falkenstein, Lorne, 1957- II. Title. III. Series: Broadview editions

B1481.F35 2011   121   C2011-903247-3

Broadview Editions
The Broadview Editions series represents the ever-changing canon of literature in English by bringing together texts long regarded as classics with valuable lesser-known works.

Advisory editor for this volume: Michel Pharand

Broadview Press is an independent, international publishing house, incorporated in 1985.

We welcome comments and suggestions regarding any aspect of our publications— please feel free to contact us at the addresses below or at broadview@broadviewpress.com.

North America
Post Office Box 1243, Peterborough, Ontario, Canada K9J 7H5
2215 Kenmore Avenue, Buffalo, NY, USA 14207
Tel: (705) 743-8990; Fax: (705) 743-8353
email: customerservice@broadviewpress.com

UK, Europe, Central Asia, Middle East, Africa, India, and Southeast Asia
Eurospan Group, 3 Henrietta St., London WC2E 8LU, United Kingdom
Tel: 44 (0) 1767 604972; Fax: 44 (0) 1767 601640
email: eurospan@turpin-distribution.com

Australia and New Zealand
NewSouth Books
c/o TL Distribution, 15-23 Helles Ave., Moorebank, NSW, Australia 2170
Tel: (02) 8778 9999; Fax: (02) 8778 9944
email: orders@tldistribution.com.au

www.broadviewpress.com

Broadview Press acknowledges the financial support of the Government of Canada through the Canada Book Fund for our publishing activities.

This book is printed on paper containing 100% post-consumer fibre.

Typesetting and assembly: True to Type Inc., Claremont, Canada.

PRINTED IN CANADA

Contents

Preface and Acknowledgements

This volume presents Hume's *Enquiry Concerning Human Understanding* in its historical context. A relatively early edition of the *Enquiry* has been chosen as the copy text for this edition (with notes on variants in other editions) and appendices present selections from the works of some of Hume's major contemporary critics. The Introduction briefly discusses the *Enquiry*'s origin and evolution, and its critical reception. Reactions to the *Enquiry* were voluminous, even during Hume's lifetime, making it impossible to present any but the most important—and even those at a loss.[1] The selection offered here aims to introduce the reader to works that were widely recognized at the time as among the most substantial and serious responses to Hume, and that have continued to be noticed. In making it, I have, with two exceptions, preferred works written early enough to have come to Hume's attention in time for him to have responded (whether he chose to do so or not). The two exceptions are Thomas Reid's analysis of Hume's argument for scepticism about the existence of an external world in Section 12 of the *Enquiry*, and Immanuel Kant's much-studied remarks on Hume in his *Prolegomena* and *Critique of Pure Reason*. These particular early responses to Hume are so serious, and have drawn so much attention, that they could not be excluded here on any principle.

Hume replied to two of the critics I have singled out for inclusion, George Campbell and Thomas Reid, though he did so only in correspondence with Hugh Blair. A third, James Beattie, was the victim of a notorious but well-deserved riposte. Hume's reactions to these critics are duly noted where appropriate. Because of the complexity of Reid's remarks on Hume, and the difficulty of Kant's, I have taken the liberty of expanding upon, abbreviating, and reordering their work. Vertical lines have been used to distinguish editorial commentary from the texts of the selected authors. As befits his status as Hume's most astute and far-reach-

---

1 It would in any case be impossible to improve on James Fieser's compendious, multi-volume collection of contemporary reactions to Hume's writings (see Bibliography, p. 299). I particularly regret lacking the space to include selections from Henry Home's *Essays on the Principles of Morality and Natural Religion*, William Adam's *Essay on Mr. Hume's Essay on Miracles*, and Richard Price's *Review of the Principal Difficulties and Questions in Morals* and *Four Dissertations*.

ing critic, the selections from Reid are considerably longer than those from other critics.

I would like to thank Brigitte Sassen for comments on my German translations and John Thorp for identifying unattributed Greek and Latin sources and for assistance in correcting Greek and Latin text. Paul Potter, Servanne Woodward, and Maité Cruz Tleugabulova helped with the background to some of Hume's, Reid's, and Beattie's literary references. Maité Cruz Tleugabulova assisted with final proofing of the primary texts. Special thanks to the copy editor for this edition, Michel Pharand. The idea for a modern edition of the philosophical works standardly collected to comprise a second volume of Hume's *Essays and Treatises on Several Subjects*, for which this volume is a preliminary exercise, is owing to Roger Emerson.

Abbreviations and References

Abbreviations

1758 etc.   Where called for, editions of Hume's works are referenced by date of publication in boldface.

Ab   [David Hume], *An Abstract of a Book lately Published; Entituled, A Treatise of Human Nature, &c. Wherein The Chief Argument of that Book is farther Illustrated and Explained* (London: C. Borbet, 1740; reprinted in *Treatise*).

Ab Pref   [David Hume], Preface to Ab.

Ax   David Hume, Appendix to *Treatise*.

B   Thomas Reid, *An Inquiry into the Human Mind on the Principles of Common Sense*, ed. Derek R. Brookes (University Park, PA: Pennsylvania State UP, 1997), and Thomas Reid, *Essays on the Intellectual Powers of Man*, ed. Derek R. Brookes (Edinburgh: Edinburgh UP, 2002).

Beauchamp   Tom L. Beauchamp, ed., *An Enquiry Concerning Human Understanding: A Critical Edition* (Oxford: Clarendon P, 2000).

DIS   David Hume, *A Dissertation on the Passions*, in ETSS and in Tom L. Beauchamp, ed., *A Dissertation on the Passions: The Natural History of Religion: A Critical Edition* (Oxford: Clarendon P, 2007).

DNR   David Hume, *Dialogues on Natural Religion*, ed. Norman Kemp Smith (Indianapolis: Bobbs-Merrill, 1947).

EHU   David Hume, *An Enquiry Concerning Human Understanding* in ETSS.

EPM   David Hume, *An Enquiry Concerning the Principles of Morals* in ETSS and as *An Enquiry Concerning the Principles of Morals: A Critical Edition*, ed. Tom L. Beauchamp (Oxford: Clarendon P, 2006).

ETSS   David Hume, *Essays and Treatises on Several Subjects* (London: A. Millar, 1758 and London: T. Cadell, 1777).

ETSS 1   David Hume, *Essays and Treatises on Several Subjects*, vol. 1 in *Essays, Moral, Political, and Literary*, revised edition, ed. Eugene F. Miller (Indianapolis: Liberty Fund, 1987).

HE	David Hume, *The History of England from the Invasion of Julius Caesar to the Revolution in 1688*, ed. William B. Todd (Indianapolis: Liberty Fund, 1983-85).
Letters	*The Letters of David Hume*, ed. J.Y.T. Grieg, 2 vols. (Oxford: Clarendon P, 1969).
MOL	David Hume, *My Own Life*, as published in *The Life of David Hume, esq., Written by Himself* (London: W. Strahan and T. Cadell, 1777).
New Letters	*New Letters of David Hume*, ed. Raymond Klibansky and Ernest C. Mossner (Oxford: Clarendon P, 1954).
NHR	David Hume, *The Natural History of Religion*, in ETSS and in Tom L. Beauchamp, ed., *A Dissertation on the Passions: The Natural History of Religion: a Critical Edition* (Oxford: Clarendon P, 2007).
S&E	David Hume, "Of Superstition and Enthusiasm," in ETSS 1.
Treatise	[David Hume], *A Treatise of Human Nature: a Critical Edition*, ed. David Fate Norton and Mary J. Norton (Oxford: Clarendon P, 2007).

References

Hume divided some of the sections of EHU into parts. References to EHU comprised of arabic numerals refer to sections and to paragraph numbers as assigned by Beauchamp. References comprised of arabic and roman numerals refer to sections and to part numbers as assigned by Hume. E.g., EHU 5.12 refers to section 5 paragraph 12; EHU 5.ii refers to section 5 part 2 (comprising paragraphs 10-22).

Introduction

David Hume was born on 26 April 1711 in Edinburgh, Scotland, during the reign of George I. He died there on 25 August 1776, at the start of the American Revolution, during the reign of George III. The Scotland of Hume's birth was an impoverished and backward country, only recently emerged from feudal government and strongly under the sway of its Presbyterian clerics, many of whom still adhered to the radical Calvinism that had been imported to that country in Elizabethan times by John Knox and other reformers. Hume was, by his own account, quite religious as a boy, but he lost his religious convictions early in life, perhaps as a consequence of the repeated failure of exercises involving attempts to argue in their support.[1] Hume considered the love of literary fame to be his governing passion, but a Socratic tendency to calmly and undogmatically follow an argument wherever it led him, even when it was to a conclusion opposed to his antecedent convictions or to the received opinions of his fellows, is a characteristic that strikes the student of his works much more strongly.

Hume's family were landed gentry, and he spent most of his early years on the family estate, Ninewells, near Berwick in southeastern Scotland. Though the family made efforts to have him trained for a career, first in law (frustrated when he left the University of Edinburgh without taking a degree) and then in business, he preferred to spend his time studying English, French, Latin, and Italian moral, literary, and philosophical classics. Hume's own independent reflections on the shortcomings of these works led him, at about the age of eighteen, to the discovery of what he called a "new scene of thought," possibly involving the insight that philosophical, moral, and aesthetic questions could be resolved by a preliminary study of human nature (perhaps specifically of the irrational or pre-rational workings of the imagination and the passions).[2] This discovery inspired him to pursue the career of a scholar and philosopher. But after an initial burst of enthusiasm he seems to have encountered writer's block, which he attributed to physical illness and variously sought to cure through medications; alcohol (a pint of claret a day had been prescribed by a physician); exercise; diversion (a possibly

---

1 Letter to Gilbert Elliot of Minto of 10 March 1751, *Letters* 1: 154.
2 Draft letter (possibly never sent or even addressed) to an unnamed physician in London or Bristol of March or April 1734, *Letters* 1: 12-18.

frivolous paternity suit was launched against him at this time); employment in the shipping industry in Bristol; and eventually a three-year sojourn in France. The last enabled him to at least partially recover his ability to integrate and express the scattered thoughts he had been accumulating, which he published anonymously in England under the title, *A Treatise of Human Nature*.

The *Treatise* (London: John Noon, 1739; Thomas Longman, 1740) is a long, systematic, and ambitious work in three parts, dealing with the understanding, the passions, and morals. Hume hoped that it would establish him as a major English thinker, and before he sent it to the press he spent some time attempting to facilitate that result by removing content that might be considered too irreligious.[3] His care did not extend, however, to excising deeply sceptical reflections on our knowledge of an external world, the existence of a persisting self, or the legitimacy of our inferences from effects to causes. Neither did it extend to an attempt to do anything more than offer an account of the psychological basis of human moral judgments, apart from any attempt to argue for the correctness of those judgments—a policy that led to the charge that he lacked "warmth in the cause of virtue."[4]

These sensational conclusions notwithstanding, the *Treatise* did not sell as well as Hume had hoped. He later declared that it had fallen "deadborn from the press,"[5] and came to view it as stylistically flawed. In addition to its convoluted presentation of core insights, it had tried the reader's patience by being "drawn out to a great length, and each part fortified with all the arguments, guarded against all the objections, and illustrated with all the views, which occur to a writer in the diligent survey of his subject" (Ab Pref 1). He also came to think that it had been too ambitious, attempting to "innovate in all the sublimist Parts of Philosophy" while at the same time failing to come up with any satisfactory solution to such basic questions as why we believe in the persistence of unperceived objects or the identity of a self over time. Yet at the same time it had exhibited an offensive "positive Air, which prevails in that Book, & which may be imputed to the Ardor of Youth."[6]

An attempt to puff up the work with an abstract (Ab), published anonymously in 1740, proved fruitless, and in 1741 Hume

---

3 Letter to Henry Home of 2 December 1737, corrected in *New Letters*: 2-3.

4 Letter to Francis Hutcheson of 17 September 1739, *Letters* 1: 32.

5 MOL: 7-8.

6 Letter to John Stewart of February 1754, *Letters* 1: 187.

made a very different attempt at winning literary fame by publishing, anonymously yet again, a collection of short essays on popular moral, political, and literary topics, *Essays, Moral and Political*.[7] An advertisement announced Hume's intentions.

> Most of these ESSAYS were wrote with a View of being publish'd as WEEKLY-PAPERS, and were intended to comprehend the Designs both of the SPECTATORS and CRAFTSMEN.[8] But having dropt that Undertaking, partly from LAZINESS, partly from WANT OF LEISURE, and being willing to make Trial of my Talents for Writing, before I ventur'd upon any more serious Compositions, I was induced to commit these Trifles to the Judgment of the Public.

Hume considered this effort to have been better received and published a second volume of essays, and a second edition of the first volume, within the year.

Hume's success with the *Essays* may have led him and his friends to believe that he would have a good chance of appointment to the chair of pneumatics[9] and moral philosophy, which opened at the University of Edinburgh in 1745. However, his candidacy was caught up in the struggle between the rival political factions of the day and, as is not unusual in such cases, members of the opposed faction proceeded to dig up what dirt they could on Hume. A manuscript appeared and was circulated among the Edinburgh clergy, charging that the author of the *Treatise* (known to have been Hume) had promoted atheism in various ways, denied the immateriality of the soul (and so, presumably, its immortality), and "sapp[ed] the Foundations of Morality, by denying the natural and essential Difference between Right and Wrong, Good and Evil, Justice and Injustice."[10] The project to have Hume appointed eventually failed.

---

7 Edinburgh: A. Kincaid, 1741.

8 The *Spectator* and *Craftsman* were widely read periodicals of the day.

9 "Pneumatics" was the term used at the time for the study of spirits, and of the human soul in particular, making it the cognate of what would today be called the philosophy of mind.

10 The manuscript containing this charge was eventually printed by Hume's friends under the title *A Letter From a Gentleman to his Friend in Edinburgh* (Edinburgh: 1745). It is cited here following the reprint in *Treatise*. The *Letter* contains a (possibly edited) response Hume had written (in the person of an anonymous gentleman writing to an anonymous friend), charging that the manuscript misrepresents the views of the author of the *Treatise*.

Those who worked so strenuously to scuttle Hume's appointment might have done more to advance their cause by abandoning their efforts. Feeling no more need to suppress his anti-religious sentiments now that he had been so summarily convicted of having them, he proceeded to "recast" the arguments of the first book of the *Treatise* in the form of short, popular essays, more like those he had found to be so successful. And this time he did not hesitate to say what he thought about religion. His *Philosophical Essays Concerning Human Understanding*, later entitled *An Enquiry Concerning Human Understanding*, appeared in 1748, and in that same year, he brought out a third edition of his *Essays, Moral and Political*, adding an essay on "national characters" that included a digression on professional characters and a long note sharply critical of the character that the profession of priest imposes on those who take it up. The 1748 edition of the *Essays, Moral and Political* was published under Hume's own name. That of the *Philosophical Essays* was identified as written by "the author of the *Essays, Moral and Political*." All subsequent editions of these works bore Hume's name.

In sharp contrast to the *Treatise*, the *Philosophical Essays* does not attempt to "innovate in all the sublimest Parts of Philosophy." It focuses on developing and applying a core thesis on what Hume considered to be a neglected but very important process of thought: the formation of beliefs about the existence of unperceived objects. It improves on the *Treatise*'s strikingly original treatment of this then neglected but central aspect of human cognition, both by making the argument more direct and by seeking to make it more entertaining—by "reconciling profound enquiry with clearness, and truth with novelty," as Hume put it (EHU 1.17). In the process, it articulates enduringly relevant positions on the role of experience in cognition, the nature and causes of belief, the nature of causality, and epistemological scepticism. But it is also a deeply disturbing work—one that challenges our confident assumption that we are "rational animals," possessed of knowledge of an external world and capable of freely choosing what reason tells us is the wisest or the best course of action. According to the *Philosophical Essays*, our choices are determined by our circumstances and our characters; it is instinct, rather than reason, that leads us to form the most important of our beliefs, such as those concerning the succession of causes and effects and the existence of an external world, and even in those cases where reason is able to give us at least some guidance, our beliefs will be formed in accord with instinctive mechanisms that are not necessarily in accord with reason and that, paradoxically, only the most determined scepticism can lead us to overcome.

The *Philosophical Essays* also contains a sustained and multi-faceted attack on religious belief. It picks many of its examples of skewed and extravagant beliefs from religious contexts. It suggests that moral judgments are grounded in naturally occurring sentiments rather than based on divinely revealed truths and raises uncomfortable questions about why God would permit moral evil. It argues that religious beliefs can have no role to play in inducing a reasonable person to be moral, and further suggests that God is either indifferent to natural evil and moral injustices or powerless to do anything about them. It also attacks the view that God has revealed that he intends a more perfect distribution of rewards and punishments in an afterlife.

This last project was undertaken in what was to become the most notorious and hotly-attacked section of the *Philosophical Essays*, that dealing with miracles. Barring knowledge by means of direct inspiration, the claims of a prophet to be delivering the revealed word of God can only be demonstrated by giving adequate signs to prove that the prophet really is speaking with divine authority. The only adequate sign of God's presence is a miracle, and the *Philosophical Essays* argues that stories of the occurrence of miracles ought not to be believed when appealed to in a religious context.

We might think that if an intelligent, benevolent creator exists, he would have wanted to tell us important things that we could not discover any other way, and would have done so sooner rather than later. Since he would have needed to perform miracles to prove his presence to us, miracles must have occurred in early times. But this line of reasoning depends on proving the antecedent that the creator is intelligent and benevolent. And the *Philosophical Essays* goes on to argue that because the universe is a unique effect, unlike any other, any attempt to draw a conclusion about the nature of its cause carries us beyond the bounds where we can argue from analogy with other cases. Considering the matter "a priori," or apart from any reference to or analogy with experience, on the other hand, leaves all options open. *A priori*, anything could cause anything.

As a final flourish, in a concluding delineation of those beliefs that we remain compelled to accept even after an encounter with sceptical arguments, Hume declared volumes of "divinity or school metaphysics" to contain "nothing but sophistry and illusion"—these being the final words of the *Philosophical Essays*.

The scepticism, the determinism, and the irreligion of the *Philosophical Essays* were decried by many of Hume's contemporaries, who tended to miss the positive messages that the work contained and see it as an attempt to subvert all human knowledge, and religious belief in particular. John Leland (1691-1766), a Presbyterian minister and author of numerous works contesting the views of those he took to be enemies of Christianity, wrote a comparatively temperate and generous assessment of EHU in the second volume of his *A View of the Principal Deistical Writers of the Last and Present Centuries*.[11]

> This Gentleman [Hume] must be acknowleged to be a subtil writer, of a very metaphysical genius, and has a neat and agreeable manner of expression. But it is obvious to every judicious reader, that he hath, in many instances, carried scepticism to an unreasonable height; and seemeth every-where to affect an air of making new observations and discoveries. His writings seem, for the most part, to be calculated rather to amuse, or even confound, than to instruct and enlighten the understanding: And there are not a few things in them, that strike at the foundation of natural, as well as the proofs and evidences of revealed religion. This appears to me to be, in a particular manner, the character of his *Philosophical Essays* [p. 2].

In fact, Hume had been careful to distance himself from both scepticism and atheism in the *Philosophical Essays*. Though he had offered sceptical arguments against the rationality of causal inference, he had also offered a "sceptical solution" to those arguments that identified more and less reliable natural causes of belief and culminated in the observation that the wise proportion their belief to the evidence. And though he had presented sceptical arguments against the belief in an external world, and suggested they are unanswerable, he had not done so in his own voice, but had affected an authorial disapproval while stressing that the natural causes responsible for the more stable of our instinctively formed beliefs will always prove stronger than the force of any argument. He was also careful to present his attacks on religion as if they were directed only against absurd practices and heretical doctrines, such as the attachment of Roman Catholics to rituals, relics, and the ongoing occurrence of miracles, or the attempts of the Deists to found religion on reason alone.

---

11 London: B. Dodd, 1755.

But it did not escape his contemporary readers that the principal effect of his arguments and insinuations was to undermine the rational basis for our most fundamental beliefs and to attack the rational foundations of religion, leaving only superstitious credulity and the "enthusiastic" conviction that one has been specially elected for inspiration as possible foundations for religious belief. Attempts to respond to Hume's perceived attack on knowledge and religion were made with increasing frequency in the years after the first publication of the *Philosophical Essays*, and were directed both against the obvious challenges to religious belief posed by what Hume had said against miracles and the design argument, and against the deeper and broader challenge to received opinions posed by his account of human understanding. Among the most notable of Hume's early critics were his own distant relative and friend, Henry Home (1696-1782), later Lord Kames, and William Adams (1706-89). Kames's anonymous *Essays on the Principles of Morality and Natural Religion*[12] attacked Hume's views on belief, personal identity, the authority of the senses, the idea of power, and providence and found fault with his claim that moral sentiments are not aroused by "remote" considerations. Adams offered a serious and sustained critique of Hume's essay on miracles.[13]

Hume was not idle, either. In 1750 he brought out a second edition of the *Philosophical Essays*, and in 1751 he published a similarly reworked version of the third book of the *Treatise*, entitled *An Enquiry Concerning the Principles of Morals*. In the following year he published another volume of essays, the *Political Discourses*, and in 1753 all of these works were integrated with the *Essays, Moral and Political* in the first edition of Hume's writings to bear the title, *Essays and Treatises on Several Subjects*. In this edition, the *Philosophical Essays* were retitled, *An Enquiry Concerning Human Understanding*, the title under which they have been recognized ever since.

With the publication of EHU and EPM, Hume had effectively "recast" the first and third books of his *Treatise*. He proceeded to do so for the second as well, writing a short piece that he entitled "A Dissertation on the Passions." In 1758 a new edition of ETSS appeared containing EHU, DIS, EPM, and a new work on the natural history of religion as four philosophical treatises following on an earlier collection of literary, moral, political, and economic essays.

---

12 Edinburgh: A. Kincaid and A. Donaldson, 1751.
13 *An Essay on Mr. Hume's Essay on Miracles* (London: E. Say, 1752).

With this edition, Hume had effectively re-edited his *Treatise*.[14]

In 1760 or 61 Hume was solicited by his friend, Hugh Blair (1718-1800), to review a manuscript that had been sent to him by the Aberdeen philosopher, George Campbell (1719-96). Campbell's subsequently published *Dissertation on Miracles*[15] was a sustained critique of almost everything Hume had said in his essay on miracles and many of Hume's contemporaries touted it as the definitive response to that essay. Then, in 1762, Blair forwarded a second Aberdeen manuscript, this time from Thomas Reid,[16] who presented some of the initial chapters from his forthcoming *Inquiry into the Human Mind on the Principles of Common Sense*—without a doubt the most serious and thoughtful set of criticisms of the fundamentals of Hume's philosophy that he was to receive in his lifetime. Hume commented on both Campbell's and Reid's performances in brief letters to Blair. These comments, contained in private correspondence, are almost the only responses he ever offered to critics of his work.

Hume remarked on a number of occasions that he had resolved never to reply to his critics, sometimes stating that a reply to one

---

14 It is worth noting that Hume fully intended to include his views on space, time, and geometry among the recastings of portions of the *Treatise* included in ETSS. In the mid-1750s he prepared a dissertation on the metaphysical principles of geometry, intended for publication along with DIS. Unfortunately, the mathematician, Philip Stanhope, convinced Hume to withdraw and likely destroy the essay. Hume wrote, some ten years later that this was on the grounds of "some Defect in the Argument or in its perspicuity; I forget which" (letter to William Strahan of 25 January 1772, *Letters* 2: 253). Hume's inability to remember what the problem was is telling, as is the fact that he continued to allude to the central doctrines of *Treatise* 1.2 throughout subsequent editions of EHU 12 (notes **kk** and **ll**, p. 203) and referred to those allusions twice in his sparse index to ETSS (once under the title, "Mathematics, their Foundation"). Stanhope's intervention was doubly unfortunate, as it precipitated one of the more stressful episodes in Hume's life. That story is omitted here as it has no bearing on the history of EHU, but see Ernest Campbell Mossner, *The Life of David Hume*, 2nd ed. (Oxford: Clarendon P, 1980), ch. 24.

15 Edinburgh: A. Kincaid and J. Bell, 1762.

16 Thomas Reid (1710-96) was at the time a regent and lecturer at King's College of the University of Aberdeen. He had previously been a minister in the town of New Machar, to the northwest of that city, and was later to succeed Adam Smith in the Chair of Moral Philosophy at the University of Glasgow. Scotland could not have given him a more prominent philosophical position.

would make it incumbent on him to reply to all, on pain of giving those who received no response a reason to fancy they had triumphed in the dispute.[17] However, between 1758 and his death in 1776, he revised ETSS eight times, bringing out new editions in 1760, 1764, 1767, 1768, 1770, 1772, and posthumously in 1777.[18] The history of the almost uniformly inconsequential nature of the changes Hume made on these occasions testifies to a kind of reply: one that took a reaffirmation of what he had already said, perhaps with greater attention to style and clarity, to be all that was required to make his case before the public. A further reply to his critics that makes precisely this point is to be found in another piece of correspondence connected with an advertisement he intended to be prefaced to the second volume of the 1770s editions of ETSS (reprinted in full below). Hume there chastised his critics for "[directing] all their batteries against that juvenile work, which the Author never acknowledged [i.e., the *Treatise*], and [affecting] to triumph in any advantages, which, they imagined, they had obtained over it," and he concluded by remarking, as noted above, that henceforth he desired the works contained in the second volume of ETSS to "alone be regarded as containing" his philosophical sentiments and principles. In a letter that accompanied the manuscript of the advertisement Hume remarked that he considered the advertisement to be "a compleat Answer to Dr Reid and to that bigotted silly Fellow, Beattie."[19]

James Beattie (1735-1803) was yet another Aberdeen philosopher and the author of *An Essay on the Nature and Immutability of Truth, in Opposition to Sophistry and Scepticism*,[20] an attack on Hume's philosophy that bears some affinity with Reid's earlier criticisms, but far exceeds them in asperity, and on that account alone more than merited Hume's riposte. Along with Beattie's

---

17 See, among other instances, his letter to George Campbell of 7 June 1762 (*Letters* 1: 360-61) and MOL: 15.

18 Catalogued in Beauchamp's editions.

19 Letter to William Strahan of 26 October 1775, *Letters* 2: 301. Later editions of ETSS were not consistent in how the various works were divided among volumes. However, the four philosophical treatises, EHU, DIS, EPM, and NHR were always collected together at the end of the series, most often to comprise a second volume. It is to this collection of works that I refer when I speak, here and elsewhere, of "the second volume of ETSS." Hume's authorial intentions notwithstanding, no similar collection has been produced in recent times.

20 Edinburgh: A. Kincaid and J. Bell, 1770. This work rapidly went through numerous editions.

own offensive style and a notorious later comment by Immanuel Kant (1724-1804),[21] Hume's often-quoted remark has done much to blacken Beattie's reputation. He was, for all that, not a furious bigot, but a sincere believer who, despite being appalled to the point of indignation by what he found in Hume's writings, insisted that only books and not persons were to be attacked, and that the proper means for dealing with objectionable opinions is not repression but "reason and ridicule chastised by decency and truth."[22] Though his objections are peppered with ridicule and sarcasm and punctuated by long rants on the pernicious consequences that accepting Hume's tenets would have on religion and morality, they are often challenging.

A challenge for readers wanting to respect Hume's injunction to consider the second volume of ETSS as solely containing his philosophical sentiments and principles, while still turning to the earlier *Treatise* for a fuller understanding of his thought, is to distinguish between parts of the *Treatise* that Hume omitted only because he considered them too "accurate and abstruse" to trust to the reader's patience, and parts that he omitted because he considered them to have gone too far in attempting to account for the operations of the understanding, the formation of the passions, or the causes of moral judgments. The evidence suggests that it would be better to err on the side of inclusion. As the twenty-year history of inconsequential emendations to EHU catalogued in this volume shows, Hume was not someone who was given to changing his mind about things. At the most, he might be persuaded to simply not talk about them while quietly persisting in the same opinions.[23] In some cases, as with DIS, he

---

21 "One cannot, without feeling a certain pain, see how completely and totally [Hume's] opponents: Reid, Oswald, Beattie and lastly also Priestly, missed the point of his work. By always taking for granted what he meant to call into doubt while emphatically, and often with great indignation demonstrating what he had never thought to question, they so completely mistook his hint for improvement [in metaphysics], as to leave everything in its previous state, as if nothing had happened." Immanuel Kant, *Prolegomena zur jeden künftigen Metaphysik* (Riga: Johann Friedrich Hartknoch, 1783), p. 258 in the standard pagination of vol. IV of the Prussian Academy edition of Kant's *Gesammelte Schriften* (Berlin: Reimer, 1903). My translation.

22 *Essay*, 5th ed. corrected (London: Edward and Charles Dilly; Edinburgh: William Creech, 1774), p. 349. For a further testament to a positive aspect of Beattie's character, see 463-68.

23 A case in point is Hume's views about space and time, alluded to earlier.

extensively recopied what he had said in the *Treatise*, largely confining his changes to a reorganization of materials, inconsequential stylistic alterations, and deletion of more intricate details.[24]

Nonetheless, it is important to consider whether doctrines contained in EHU, DIS, EPM, and NHR rigorously entail doctrines contained in the *Treatise* but not included in those works. Later scholars should do what they can to avoid the reproach of directing all their attention to the *Treatise*. The first step to doing so is to begin the study of Hume with a study of the works contained in the second volume of ETSS.

---

24 See the collation of passages from the *Treatise* and DIS in Tom L. Beauchamp's critical edition of DIS and NHR (Oxford: Clarendon Press, 2007).

David Hume: A Brief Chronology

1711   Birth of David Hume, 26 April (Old Style), in Edinburgh

1723-26   Studies at Edinburgh University; leaves without taking a degree

1726-34   Years spent in private study at the family estate near Berwick

1734   Brief attempt to start a career in business at Bristol

1734-37   First trip to France; time spent composing the *Treatise*

1739   *Treatise* 1 and 2 published anonymously

1740   *Treatise* 3 published anonymously

1740   Ab published anonymously

1741   Anonymous publication of the first part of *Essays, Moral and Political*, later incorporated into ETSS 1

1742   2nd part and 2nd edition of *Essays, Moral and Political* published anonymously

1745   Attempt at securing a position at the University of Edinburgh; anonymous publication (perhaps by Henry Home) of an edited letter written by Hume in response to criticisms of the *Treatise*, "A letter from a gentleman to his friend in Edinburgh"

1745-47   Years spent serving first as tutor to the Marquis of Annandale and then as aide-de-camp to General St. Clair; travel to Italy and Austria on diplomatic missions with St. Clair

1748   1st edition of EHU published under the title *Philosophical Essays Concerning Human Understanding*, by "the author of the *Essays, Moral and Political*"

1748   3rd part (including "Of national characters") and 3rd edition of *Essays, Moral and Political*, by "David Hume, esq."

1750   2nd edition of EHU, by "David Hume, esq."

1751   Publication of EPM, by "David Hume, esq."

1751   Anonymous publication of *Essays on the Principles of Morality and Natural Religion*, by Henry Home

1752   Takes up position as librarian to the Faculty of Advocates in Edinburgh; publication of *Political Discourses*

1752   Publication of *An Essay on Mr. Hume's Essay on Miracles* by William Adams

1753	1st edition of ETSS in four volumes, containing i) *Essays, Moral, Political, and Literary*; ii) EHU; iii) EPM; and iv) *Political Discourses*
1754-62	Publication of the *History of Great Britain* (later *History of England*) in multiple volumes beginning with the reigns of James I and Charles I, continuing with the period from the Interregnum to the Revolution of 1688, and then working backwards to the invasion by Caesar
1756	2nd edition of ETSS
1757	Publication of *Four Dissertations*, containing DIS and NHR
1758	3rd edition of ETSS, containing *Essays, Moral, Political, and Literary*; *Political Discourses* (as part 2 of *Essays, Moral, Political, and Literary*); EHU; DIS; EPM; and NHR
1758	Richard Price publishes *Review of the Principal Difficulties and Questions in Morals*
1760	4th edition of ETSS
1761	Correspondence with Hugh Blair concerning George Campbell's draft of his *Dissertation on Miracles*
1762	Publication of Campbell's *Dissertation*, subsequent correspondence between Hume and Campbell
1762	Correspondence with Hugh Blair and Thomas Reid concerning Thomas Reid's *Inquiry into the Human Mind*
1763-65	2nd trip to France, as secretary to Lord Hertford; affair with the Comtesse de Boufflers
1764	Publication of Reid's *Inquiry*
1764	5th edition of ETSS
1766	*Exposé succinct de la contestation qui s'est élevée entre Mr. Hume et M. Rousseau* published in response to Rousseau's charge of duplicity in Hume's attempts to secure a residence and pension for Rousseau in England
1766	2nd edition of Campbell's *Dissertation*
1767	6th edition of ETSS
1767	Richard Price publishes his *Four Dissertations*
1767-69	Serves as under-secretary of state for the Northern Department of the British government
1768	7th edition of ETSS
1770	8th edition of ETSS

1770	1st edition of James Beattie's *Essay on the Nature and Immutability of Truth*
1772	9th edition of ETSS
1775	First symptoms of terminal bowel disease
1775	Composition of the advertisement to the second volume of ETSS disowning the *Treatise* in answer to Reid and Beattie
1776	Death on 25 August, at Edinburgh
1777	Posthumous publication of a 10th edition of ETSS, the last to have been prepared by Hume
1777	Posthumous publication of Hume's autobiography, *My Own Life*
1779	Posthumous publication of DNR
1781	Publication of the 1st edition of Immanuel Kant's *Kritik der reinen Vernunft*
1782	Posthumous publication of essays on suicide and the immortality of the soul, originally intended for inclusion in *Four Dissertations* and ETSS
1783	Publication of Kant's *Prolegomena zu einer jeden künftigen Metaphysik*
1785	Publication of Reid's *Essays on the Intellectual Powers of Man*
1787	2nd edition of Kant's *Kritik der reinen Vernunft*
1797	Posthumous 3rd edition of Campbell's *Dissertation*

A Note on the Texts

This edition of EHU is based on the first edition to bear the title *An Enquiry Concerning Human Understanding*, that of 1758, as corrected by the errata to that edition.[1] Differences between **1758** and the final edition to have been prepared during Hume's lifetime, that appearing posthumously in 1777, have been noted.[2] Substantive differences between **1758** and the three earlier editions of what was then entitled *Philosophical Essays Concerning Human Understanding*, those of 1748, 1750, and 1756 have also been noted.[3] Hume's notes, which were printed as footnotes in **1758** and in other editions inserted either as footnotes or as endnotes depending on length, are gathered at the end of each section so as not to be confused with editorial footnotes.[4] To make reference to the notes easier, they have been sequentially assigned lower case letters (omitting "j"), a convention that was inconsistently adopted in **1758**. To further facilitate ease of reference, the text has been amended to include the numbers assigned to the paragraphs in Tom L. Beauchamp's critical edition.[5]

1758 was chosen as the copy text for this Broadview edition in preference to the first edition of 1748 because **1758** is the first edition that was bound together with DIS, EPM, and NHR to

---

1   A few blatant typographical errors have been corrected, though noted where they are corrected. Instances of missing or broken type have been silently corrected. This edition does not replicate eighteenth-century printing conventions such as the use of the long-s, setting the first word of each paragraph in small caps, or printing catch-words at the bottom of each page.

2   Differences in spelling (e.g., "betwixt," "between,") and formalities (e.g., substitution of "namely" and other equivalent expressions for "*viz.*") have not been noted. Differences in punctuation are too numerous to be represented, and also too numerous to make the job of distinguishing between substantive and inconsequential differences practical.

3   The notation of variant readings was greatly assisted by Beauchamp's register of emendations and variants to the different editions of ETSS 2.

4   Hume's note markers have been placed after his punctuation marks (**1758** places them before).

5   The paragraphing of **1758** is generally the same as that of **1772**, the copy text for Beauchamp's edition, but there are occasional divergences, so the reader will find that the paragraph numbers sometimes do not run without interruption or omission. Discrepancies are explained in the notes where they arise.

constitute a distinct, second part of ETSS. This makes it the first edition of EHU to appear in what was to become its canonical context, as the first of four "philosophical treatises"—the treatises Hume identified in the advertisement discussed earlier as "alone … containing [my] philosophical sentiments and principles." It is unfortunate that these works, which Hume intended to be read together as parts of a single volume, are now published separately and read with little attention to how that context affects their interpretation.[6] A companion volume to this one[7] aims to rectify this shortcoming by offering all four of the works together—a project that made it necessary that this volume also be based on **1758**. **1758** is still a comparatively early edition, so studying it along with notes on variants between this and **1777** gives the reader a good sense of how the text evolved over time. As Hume himself observed, "We always follow the succession of time in placing our ideas, and from the consideration of any object pass more easily to that, which follows immediately after it, than to that which went before it" (*Treatise* 2.3.7.7). And, as a matter of fact, it is much easier to appreciate the history of emendations to a text by starting with an earlier edition and proceeding in the forward rather than the backward direction.

An even more important reason for basing the text on **1758** is that this Broadview edition aims to present Hume's thought in its historical context, together with selections from the work of some of his critics. To this end, it makes more sense for the reader to see Hume's works in a version in which they would have been seen by critics writing in Hume's own time—and reciprocally to see his critics' works in a version in which those works would have been seen by him in time for him to have responded to them, whether he ultimately chose to do so or not. First editions of the works of Hume's critics have accordingly been preferred to later ones with one exception: Beattie's *Essay* went through multiple editions in such a short time after its first appearance that, in the absence of any compelling reason to identify any one of them as the one Hume might have consulted, I have made an arbitrary

---

6 The relation between EHU and NHR is particularly important, both with regard to ways in which the attack on religion in EHU is informed by NHR and on account of an apparent inconsistency in what the works have to say about the proper foundation of religious belief.

7 David Hume, *Philosophical Treatises (An Enquiry Concerning Human Understanding, A Dissertation on the Passions, An Enquiry Concerning the Principles of Morals, The Natural History of Religion)*, ed. Lorne Falkenstein and Neil McArthur (Broadview Press: forthcoming).

decision to select the fifth corrected edition of 1774 here—not too early to have been an edition that escaped Hume's notice, but not too late to have motivated his 1775 riposte to Strahan. Except for one historically interesting case I have not noted variants in the later editions of the works of any of Hume's critics.

Hume and his critics tended to cite their classical sources in the original Greek and Latin. Where available, contemporary (to them) translations of these passages have been supplied, to give the modern reader a sense of the idiom in which eighteenth-century readers would have understood these passages, and more of a context for appreciating the idiom they employed in their comments on one another's work. Their Greek and Latin have not been corrected.

This is not a critical edition or an edition intended for electronic searching. A critical edition should attempt to come up with a corrected text that seems, on the evidence of the various editions and other remains, to best represent the author's intentions. Such an edition already exists and the project here is not to produce another but to present the reader with a version of the text as it would have appeared to those reading and criticizing it at the time. In keeping with this project, this edition does not eliminate features that could frustrate an electronic search, such as inconsistencies (e.g., "connexion/connection," "color/colour"), idiosyncratic spellings (e.g., "knowlege," "falshood"), or all but the most obvious typographical errors. Though inelegant, such artefacts could conceivably illuminate a critic's comment. While a great deal of effort has been put into ensuring that the texts are accurate, limitations of time and resources mean that the methods employed have not been so rigorous as to avoid all possibility of error. Those concerned to cite exact editions should refer to the photocopies of the original pages available through the Eighteenth Century Collections Online (ECCO) database (http://www.gale. cengage.com/Digital Collections/products/ecco/index.htm)[8] and Beauchamp's text and register of variant readings. Those needing more background to the persons, events, and literary works mentioned by Hume should do likewise. An electronically searchable text (largely faithful to 1777) that removes inconsistencies in spelling can be obtained from www.nlx.com.

8　This database has also served as the source for many of the other eighteenth-century works cited in this volume. Because ECCO has made these rare books so widely available, they are cited here in their original editions, on the assumption that the reader will be more readily able to access them through that portal than by acquiring more recent editions.

Front Matter from the 1758 and 1777 Editions of Hume's Essays
and Treatises on Several Subjects

E S S A Y S

A N D

T R E A T I S E S

O N

S E V E R A L   S U B J E C T S.

B Y

D A V I D   H U M E, Efq;

K

A NEW EDITION.

L O N D O N:

Printed for A. MILLAR, in the STRAND;
AND
A. KINCAID and A. DONALDSON, at EDINBURGH.

M.DCC.LVIII.

ADVERTISEMENT[1]

Some Alterations are made on the Titles of the Treatises, contained in the following Volume. What in former Editions was called *Essays moral and political*, is here entitled *Essays, moral, political, and literary*, Part I. *The political Discourses* form the *second Part*. What in former Editions was called, *Philosophical Essays concerning human Understanding*, is here entitled *An Enquiry concerning human Understanding*.[2] The *four Dissertations* lately published[3] are dispersed thro' different Parts of this Volume.

---

1 This advertisement was placed in the front matter of **1758**.
2 **1758** collects all of Hume's essays in a single volume. The *Enquiry* follows the essays contained in Part II. Its title has the same prominence as the titles of parts I and II, though it is not assigned a distinct part number.
3 David Hume, *Four Dissertations* (London: A. Millar, 1757). This work contained "The Natural History of Religion," which became the last work included in the **1758** volume, "A Dissertation on the Passions," which was placed between the two enquiries in 1758, "Of Tragedy," and "Of the Standard of Taste," which became the last two essays in Part I of **1758**.

THE

CONTENTS.

ESSAYS, MORAL, POLITICAL, and LITERARY.

PART I.

ESSAYS, MORAL, POLITICAL, and LITERARY.

PART II.

An ENQUIRY concerning HUMAN UNDERSTANDING.

ESSAYS,

ESSAYS

AND

TREATISES

ON

SEVERAL SUBJECTS.

In TWO VOLUMES.

By DAVID HUME, Efq;

VOL. I.

CONTAINING

ESSAYS, MORAL, POLITICAL, and LITERARY.

A NEW EDITION.

LONDON:

Printed for T. CADELL, in the Strand: and
A. DONALDSON, and W. CREECH, at Edinburgh.
MDCCLXXVII.

THE

CONTENTS

OF THE

FIRST VOLUME.

ESSAYS, MORAL, POLITICAL, and LITERARY.

PART I.

Essay

CONTENTS.

PART II.

ESSAY

ESSAYS,

MORAL, POLITICAL,

AND

LITERARY.

PART I.*

*Published in 1742.

Vol. I.   B

ESSAYS

AND

TREATISES

ON

SEVERAL SUBJECTS.

By DAVID HUME, Esq;

VOL. II.

CONTAINING

An ENQUIRY concerning HUMAN
UNDERSTANDING;
A DISSERTATION on the PASSIONS;
An ENQUIRY concerning the PRINCIPLES
of MORALS;

AND *12 69*

The NATURAL HISTORY of RELIGION.

A NEW EDITION.

LONDON:
Printed for T. Cadell, in the Strand: and
A. Donaldson, and W. Creech, at Edinburgh.
MDCCLXXVII.

ADVERTISEMENT[4]

Most of the principles, and reasonings, contained in this volume, were published in a work in three volumes, called *A Treatise of Human Nature*: A work which the Author had projected before he left College, and which he wrote and published not long after. But not finding it successful, he was sensible of his error in going to the press too early, and he cast the whole anew in the following pieces, where some negligences in his former reasoning and more in the expression, are, he hopes, corrected. Yet several writers, who have honoured the Author's Philosophy with answers, have taken care to direct all their batteries against that juvenile work, which the Author never acknowledged, and have affected to triumph in any advantages, which, they imagined, they had obtained over it: A practice very contrary to all rules of candour and fair-dealing, and a strong instance of those polemical artifices, which a bigotted zeal thinks itself authorized to employ. Henceforth, the Author desires, that the following Pieces may alone be regarded as containing his philosophical sentiments and principles.[5]

---

4 As indicated here, this advertisement was placed between the title page of volume 2 and the contents. It serves as an advertisement to all the works contained in volume 2.

5 On 26 October 1775, ten months before his death, Hume wrote to his publisher, William Strahan, to request help in recommending a friend for a position at the University of Glasgow and to comment on affairs with the American colonies. Towards the close of this letter he wrote, "There is a short Advertisement, which I wish I had prefix'd to the second Volume of the Essays and Treatises in the last Edition. I send you a Copy of it. Please to enquire at the Warehouse, if any considerable Number of that Edition remain on hands; and if there do, I beg the favour of you, that you woud throw off an equal Number of this Advertisement, and give out no more Copies without prefixing it to the second volume. It is a compleat Answer to Dr Reid and to that bigotted silly Fellow, Beattie." *Letters* 2: 301.

THE

CONTENTS

OF THE

SECOND VOLUME.

An ENQUIRY concerning HUMAN UNDERSTANDING.

R   An

CONTENTS.

An ENQUIRY concerning the PRINCIPLES Of MORALS.

The NATURAL HISTORY of RELIGION.

CONTENTS.

AN

AN

ENQUIRY

CONCERNING

HUMAN

UNDERSTANDING.

AN ENQUIRY
CONCERNING
HUMAN UNDERSTANDING

SECTION 1
OF THE DIFFERENT SPECIES OF PHILOSOPHY

1. Moral philosophy,[1] or the science of human nature, may be treated after two different manners; each of which has its peculiar merit, and may contribute to the entertainment, instruction, and reformation of mankind. The one considers man chiefly as born for action; and as influenced in his actions[2] by taste and sentiment; pursuing one object and avoiding another, according to the value, which these objects seem to possess, and according to the light, in which they present themselves. Virtue, of all objects, is the most valuable and lovely; and accordingly[3] this species of philosophers paint her in the most amiable colors; borrowing all helps from poetry and eloquence, and treating their subject in an easy and obvious manner,[4] such as is best fitted to please the imagination, and engage the affections. They select the most striking observations and instances from common life; place opposite characters in a proper contrast; and alluring us into the paths of virtue, by the views of glory and happiness, direct our steps in these paths, by the soundest precepts and most illustrious examples. They make us *feel* the difference betwixt vice and virtue; they excite and regulate our sentiments; and so they can but bend our hearts to the love of probity and true honor, they think, that they have fully attained the end of all their labors.

2. The other species of philosophers treat man rather as a reasonable[5] than an active being, and endeavor to form his understanding more than cultivate his manners. They regard mankind[6]

---

1 Hume's use of the term "moral" is broader than current usage. "Moral philosophy" contrasts with "natural philosophy." The latter deals with what is now called natural science, the former with the social sciences and humanities. Psychology, logic, and aesthetics are included in "moral philosophy," as well as ethics, politics, and economics. Elsewhere, "moral reasoning" is used in contrast with demonstrative reasoning. Whereas the latter deals with whatever can be shown to necessarily follow from given premises, the former deals with all matters of probability.

2 1777: *measures* for *actions*

3 1777: *As virtue, of all objects, is allowed to be the most valuable,* for *Virtue, of all objects, is the most valuable and lovely; and accordingly*

4 1777: inserts *and*

5 1777: *consider man in the light of a reasonable rather* for *treat man rather as a reasonable*

6 1777: *human nature* for *mankind*

as a subject of speculation; and with a narrow scrutiny examine human nature,[7] in order to find those principles, which regulate our understanding, excite our sentiments, and make us approve or blame any particular object, action, or behavior. They think it a reproach to all literature, that philosophy should not yet have fixed, beyond controversy, the foundation of morals, reasoning, and criticism; and should for ever talk of truth and falsehood, vice and virtue, beauty and deformity, without being able to determine the source of these distinctions. While they attempt this arduous task, they are deterred by no difficulties; but proceeding from particular instances to general principles, they still push on their enquiries to principles more general, and rest not satisfied till they arrive at those original principles, by which, in every science, all human curiosity must be bounded. Tho' their speculations seem abstract and even unintelligible to common readers, they please themselves with[8] the approbation of the learned and the wise; and think themselves sufficiently compensated for the labors[9] of their whole lives, if they can discover some hidden truths, which may contribute to the instruction of posterity.

3. 'Tis certain, that the easy and obvious philosophy will always, with the generality of mankind, have the preference to[10] the accurate and abstruse; and by many will be recommended, not only as more agreeable, but more useful than the other. It enters more into common life; moulds the heart and affections; and by touching those principles, which actuate men, reforms their conduct, and brings them nearer[11] that model of perfection, which it describes. On the contrary, the abstruse philosophy, being founded on a turn of mind, which cannot enter into business and action, vanishes when the philosopher leaves the shade and comes into open day; nor can its principles easily retain any influence over our conduct and behavior. The feelings of our sentiments,[12] the agitations[13] of our passions, the vehemence of our affections, dissipate all its conclusions, and reduce the profound philosopher to a mere plebeian.

4. This also must be confessed, that the most durable, as well as justest fame has been acquired by the easy philosophy, and that

---

7 **1777**: *it* for *human nature*
8 **1777**: *aim at* for *please themselves with*
9 **1777**: *labour* for *labors*
10 **1777**: *above* for *to*
11 **1777**: inserts *to*
12 **1777**: *heart* for *sentiments*
13 **1777**: *agitation* for *agitations*

abstract reasoners seem hitherto to have enjoyed only a momentary reputation, from the caprice or ignorance of their own age, but have not been able to support their renown with more equitable posterity. 'Tis easy for a profound philosopher to commit a mistake in his subtile reasonings; and one mistake is the necessary parent of another, while he pushes on his consequences, and is not deterred from embracing any conclusion, by its unusual appearance, or its contradiction to popular opinion. But a philosopher, who proposes[14] only to represent the common sense of mankind in more beautiful and more engaging colors, if by accident he commits a mistake,[15] goes no farther; but renewing his appeal to common sense, and the natural sentiments of the mind, returns into the right path, and secures himself from any dangerous illusions. The fame of CICERO flourishes at present; but that of ARISTOTLE is utterly decayed. La BRUYERE passes the seas, and still maintains his reputation: But the glory of MALEBRANCHE is confined to his own nation and to his own age. And ADDISON, perhaps, will be read with pleasure, when LOCKE[16] shall be entirely forgotten.[17]

5. The mere philosopher is a character which is commonly but little acceptable in the world, as being supposed to contribute nothing either to the advantage or pleasure of society; while he lives remote from communication with mankind, and is wrapped

---

14 **1777:** *purposes* for *proposes*

15 **1777:** *falls into error* for *commits a mistake*

16 Drawing on examples from the ancient world, and from modern France and England, Hume here opposed the works of popular writers—the Roman statesman and orator Marcus Tullius Cicero (106-43 BCE), the French moralist, Jean de La Bruyère (1645-96), and the English essayist and co-founder of the *Spectator*, Joseph Addison (1672-1719, see p. 13, and p. 13, note 8)—with the work of the pre-eminent philosophers in each of those epochs: Aristotle (384-322 BCE), Nicolas Malebranche (1638-1715), and John Locke (1632-1704). In each case, the first member of the pair was a noted stylist as well as a highly popular commentator on human character and morals, whereas the second was a dry and often inelegant writer who wrote tediously long works on abstract philosophical topics (hence Hume's choice of Malebranche over Descartes as the representative French philosopher). Hume's assessment of which of the two would prove to have the most enduring reputation has yet to pass the test of time.

17 **1748-1750:** insert, as a note *This is not intended any way to detract from the Merit of Mr. _Locke_, who was really a great Philosopher, and a just and modest Reasoner. 'Tis only meant to shew the common Fate of such abstract Philosophy.*

up in principles and notions equally remote from their comprehension. On the other hand, the mere ignorant is still more despised; nor is any thing deemed a surer sign of an illiberal genius in an age and nation where the sciences flourish, than to be entirely void[18] of all relish for those noble entertainments. The most perfect character is supposed to lie between those extremes; retaining an equal ability and taste for books, company, and business; preserving in conversation that discernment and delicacy which arise from polite letters; and in business, that probity and accuracy which are the natural result of a just philosophy. In order to diffuse and cultivate so accomplished a character, nothing can be more useful than compositions of the easy style and manner, which draw not too much from life, require no deep application or retreat to be comprehended, and send back the student among mankind full of noble sentiments and wise precepts, applicable to every exigence of human life. By means of such compositions, virtue becomes amiable, science agreeable, company instructive, and retirement entertaining.

6. Man is a reasonable being; and as such, receives from science his proper food and nourishment: But so narrow are the bounds of human understanding, that little satisfaction can be hoped for in this particular, either from the extent or security of his acquisitions. Man is a sociable, no less than a reasonable being: But neither can he always enjoy company agreeable and amusing, or preserve the proper relish of[19] them. Man is also an active being; and from that disposition, as well as from the various necessities of human life, must submit to business and occupation: But the mind requires some relaxation, and cannot always support its bent to care and industry. It seems, then, that nature has pointed out a mixed kind of life as most suitable to human race, and secretly admonished them to allow none of these biasses to *draw* too much, so as to incapacitate them for other occupations and entertainments. Indulge your passion for science, says she, but let your science be human, and such as may have a direct reference to action and society. Abstruse thought and profound researches I prohibit, and will severely punish, by the pensive melancholy which they introduce, by the endless uncertainty in which they involve you, and by the cold reception which your pretended discoveries will[20] meet with, when communicated. Be a philosopher; but, amidst all your philosophy, be still a man.

---

18 **1777**: *destitute* for *void*
19 **1777**: *for* for *of*
20 **1777**: *will* for *shall*

7. Were the generality of mankind contented to prefer the easy philosophy to the abstract and profound, without throwing any blame or contempt on the latter, it might not be improper, perhaps, to comply with this general opinion, and allow every man to enjoy, without opposition, his own taste and sentiment. But as the matter is often carried farther, even to the absolute rejecting[21] all profound reasonings or what is commonly called *metaphysics*, we shall now proceed to consider what can reasonably be pleaded in their behalf.

8. We may begin with observing, that one considerable advantage which results from the accurate and abstract philosophy, is, its subserviency to the easy and humane; which, without the former, can never attain a sufficient degree of exactness in its sentiments, precepts, or reasonings. All polite letters are nothing but pictures of human life in various attitudes and situations; and inspire us with different sentiments, of praise or blame, admiration or ridicule, according to the qualities of the object which they set before us. An artist must be better qualified to succeed in this undertaking, who, besides a delicate taste and a quick apprehension, possesses an accurate knowlege of the internal fabric, the operations of the understanding, the workings of the passions, and the various species of sentiment, which discriminate vice and virtue. However painful[22] this inward search or enquiry may appear, it becomes, in some measure, requisite to those, who would describe with success the obvious and outward appearances of life and manners. The anatomist presents to the eye the most hideous and disagreeable objects; but his science is highly[23] useful to the painter in delineating even a VENUS or an HELEN. While the latter employs all the richest colours of his art, and gives his figures the most graceful and engaging airs; he must still carry his attention to the inward structure of the human body, the position of the muscles, the fabric of the bones, and the use and figure of every part or organ. Accuracy is, in every case, advantageous to beauty, and just reasoning to delicate sentiments.[24] In vain would we exalt the one by depreciating the other.

9. Besides, we may observe, in every art or profession, even those which most concern life or action, that a spirit of accuracy, however acquired, carries all of them nearer their perfection, and renders them more subservient to the interests of society. And tho'

---

21 1777: inserts *of*
22 1777: *How painful soever* for *however painful*
23 1777: omits *highly*
24 1777: *sentiment* for *sentiments*

a philosopher may live remote from business, the genius of philosophy, if carefully cultivated by several, must gradually diffuse itself thro' the whole society, and bestow a similar correctness on every art and calling. The politician will acquire greater foresight and subtilty, in the subdividing and ballancing of power; the lawyer more method and finer principles in his reasonings; and the general more regularity in his discipline, and more caution in his plans and operation.[25] The stability of modern governments above the antient, and the accuracy of modern philosophy, have improved, and probably will still improve, by similar gradations.

10. Were there no advantage to be reaped from these studies, beyond the gratification of an innocent curiosity, yet ought not even this to be despised; as being one accession to those few safe and harmless pleasures which are bestowed on human race. The sweetest and most inoffensive path of life leads thro' the avenues of science and learning; and whoever can either remove any obstructions in this way, or open up any new prospect, ought so far to be esteemed a benefactor to mankind. And tho' these researches may appear painful and fatiguing, 'tis with some minds as with some bodies, which being endowed with vigorous and florid health, require severe exercise, and reap a pleasure from what, to the generality of mankind, may seem burthensome and laborious. Obscurity, indeed, is painful to the mind as well as to the eye; but to bring light from obscurity, by whatever labor, must needs be delightful and rejoicing.

11. But this obscurity, in the profound and abstract philosophy, is objected to, not only as painful and fatiguing, but as the inevitable source of uncertainty and error. Here indeed lies the justest and most plausible objection against a considerable part of metaphysics, that they are not properly a science, but arise either from the fruitless efforts of human vanity, which would penetrate into subjects utterly inaccessible to the understanding, or from the craft of popular superstition,[26] which, being unable to defend themselves on fair ground, raise these intangling brambles to cover and protect their weakness.[27] Chaced from the open country, these robbers fly into the forest, and lie in wait to break

---

25 1777: *operations* for *operation*

26 1777: *superstitions* for *superstition*

27 For Hume "superstition" is a technical term, designating a prevalent and dangerous religious attitude. The attitude and its causes are described in S&E, and its bad effects on society are a principal focus of NHR. For more on how superstitious religion tends to incorporate philosophy and bend philosophy to serve its own purposes, see NHR 11.

in upon every unguarded avenue of the mind, and overwhelm it with religious fears and prejudices. The stoutest antagonist, if he remits[28] his watch a moment, is oppressed: And many, thro' cowardice and folly, open the gates to the enemies, and willingly receive them with reverence and submission, as their legal sovereigns.

12. But is this a just cause[29] why philosophers should desist from such researches, and leave superstition still in possession of her retreat? Is it not reasonable[30] to draw a direct contrary[31] conclusion, and perceive the necessity of carrying the war into the most secret recesses of the enemy? In vain do we hope, that men, from frequent disappointments,[32] will at last abandon such airy sciences, and discover the proper province of human reason. For besides, that many persons find too sensible an interest in perpetually recalling such topics; besides this, I say, the motive of blind despair can never reasonably have place in the sciences; since, however unsuccessful former attempts may have proved, there is still room to hope, that the industry, good fortune, or improved sagacity of succeeding generations may reach discoveries unknown to former ages. Each adventurous genius will still leap at the arduous prize, and find himself stimulated, rather than discouraged, by the failures of his predecessors; while he hopes, that the glory of atchieving so hard an adventure is reserved for him alone. The only method of freeing learning, at once, from these abstruse questions, is to enquire seriously into the nature of human understanding, and shew, from an exact analysis of its powers and capacity, that it is, by no means, fitted for such remote and abstruse subjects. We must submit to this fatigue, in order to live at ease for[33] ever after: And must cultivate true metaphysics with some care, in order to destroy the false and adulterate. Indolence, which, to some persons, affords a safeguard against this deceitful philosophy, is, with others, over-ballanced by curiosity; and despair, which, at some moments, prevails, may give place afterwards to sanguine hopes and expectations. Accurate and just reasoning is the only catholic remedy, fitted for all persons and all dispositions, and is alone able to subvert that abstruse philosophy and metaphysical jargon,

---

28 **1777**: *remit* for *remits*
29 **1777**: *sufficient reason* for *just cause*
30 **1777**: *proper* for *reasonable*
31 **1777**: *an opposite* for *a direct contrary*
32 **1777**: *disappointment* for *disappointments*
33 **1777**: omits *for*

which, being mixed up with popular superstition, renders it, in a manner, impenetrable to careless reasoners, and gives it the air of science and wisdom.

13. Besides this advantage of rejecting, after deliberate enquiry, the most uncertain and disagreeable part of learning, there are many positive advantages, which result from an accurate scrutiny into the powers and faculties of human nature. 'Tis remarkable concerning the operations of the mind, that tho' most intimately present to us, yet whenever they become the object of reflection, they seem involved in obscurity, nor can the eye readily find those lines and boundaries, which discriminate and distinguish them. The objects are too fine to remain long in the same aspect or situation; and must be apprehended, in an instant, by a superior penetration, derived from nature, and improved by habit and reflection. It becomes, therefore, no inconsiderable part of science barely to know the different operations of the mind, to separate them from each other, to class them under their proper divisions,[34] and to correct all that seeming disorder, in which they lie involved, when made the object of reflection and enquiry. This task of ordering and distinguishing, which has no merit, when performed with regard to external bodies, the objects of our senses, rises in its value, when directed towards the operations of the mind, in proportion to the difficulty and labor, which we meet with in performing it. And if we can go no farther than this mental geography, or delineation of the distinct parts and powers of the mind, 'tis at least a satisfaction to go so far; and the more obvious this science may appear (and it is by no means obvious) the more contemptible still must the ignorance of it be esteemed, in all pretenders to learning and philosophy.

14. Nor can there remain any suspicion, that this science is uncertain and chimerical; unless we should entertain such a scepticism as is entirely subversive of all speculation, and even action. It cannot be doubted, that the mind is endowed with several powers and faculties, that these powers are totally[35] distinct from each other, that what is really distinct to the immediate perception may be distinguished by reflection; and consequently, that there is a truth and falshood in all propositions on this subject, and a truth and falshood, which lie not beyond the compass of human understanding. There are many obvious distinctions of this kind, such as those betwixt the will and under-

---

34 1777: *heads* for *divisions*
35 1777: omits *totally*

standing, the imagination and passions, which fall within the comprehension of every human creature; and the finer and more philosophical distinctions are no less real and certain, tho' more difficult to be comprehended. Some instances, especially late ones, of success in these enquiries, may give us a juster notion of the certainty and solidity of this branch of learning. And shall we esteem it worthy the labor of a philosopher to give us a true system of the planets, and adjust the position and order of those remote bodies; while we affect to overlook those, who, with so much success, delineate the parts of the mind in which we are so intimately concerned?[36]

---

36 **1748-1750**: insert as note *That Faculty, by which we discern Truth and Falshood, and that by which we perceive Vice and Virtue had long been confounded with each other, and all Morality was suppos'd to be built on eternal and immutable Relations, which to every intelligent Mind were equally invariable as any Proposition concerning Quantity or Number. But a[*] late Philosopher has taught us, by the most convincing Arguments, that Morality is nothing in the abstract Nature of Things, but is entirely relative to the sentiment or mental Taste of each particular Being; in the same manner as the Distinctions of sweet and bitter, hot and cold, arise from the particular Feeling of each Sense or Organ. Moral Perceptions therefore, ought not to be class'd with the Operations of the Understanding, but with the Tastes or Sentiments.*

It has been usual with Philosophers to divide all the Passions of the Mind into two Classes, the selfish and benevolent, which were suppos'd to stand in constant Opposition and Contrareity; nor was it thought that the latter could ever attain their proper Object but at the Expence of the former. Among the selfish Passions were rank'd Avarice, Ambition, Revenge: Among the benevolent, natural Affection, Friendship, public Spirit. Philosophers may now[Ψ] perceive the Impropriety of this Division. It has been prov'd, beyond all Controversy, that even the Passions, commonly esteem'd selfish, carry the Mind beyond Self, directly to the Object; that tho' the Satisfaction of these Passions gives us Enjoyment, yet the Prospect of this Enjoyment is not the Cause of the Passion, but on the contrary the Passion is antecedent to the Enjoyment, and without the former, the latter could never possibly exist; that the Case is precisely the same with the Passions, denominated benevolent, and consequently that a Man is no more interested when he seeks his own Glory than when the Happiness of his Friend is the Object of his Wishes; nor is he any more disinterested when he sacrifices his Ease and Quiet to public Good than when he labours for the Gratification of Avarice and Ambition. Here therefore is a considerable Adjustment in the Boundaries of the Passions, which had been confounded by the Negligence or Inaccuracy of former Philosophers. These two Instances may suffice to show us the Nature and Importance of this Species of Philosophy.

---

* Mr. <u>Hutcheson</u>.
Ψ See <u>Butler</u>'s Sermons.

15. But may we not hope, that philosophy, if cultivated with care, and encouraged by the attention of the public, may carry its researches still farther, and discover, at least in some degree, the secret springs and principles, by which the human mind is actuated in its operations? Astronomers had long contented themselves with proving, from the phænomena, the true motions, order, and magnitude of the heavenly bodies: Till a philosopher, at last, arose, who seems from the happiest reasoning, to have also determined the laws and forces, by which the revolutions of the planets are governed and directed. The like has been performed with regard to other parts of nature. And there is no reason to despair of equal success in our enquiries concerning the mental powers and oeconomy, if prosecuted with equal capacity and caution. 'Tis probable, that one operation and principle of the mind depends on another; which, again, may be resolved into one more general and universal: And how far these researches may possibly be carried, it will be difficult for us, before, or even after, a careful trial, exactly to determine. This is certain, that attempts of this kind are every day made even by those who philosophize the most negligently; and nothing can be more requisite than to enter upon the enterprize with thorow care and attention; that, if it lie within the compass of human understanding, it may at last be happily atchieved; if not, it may, however, be rejected with some confidence and security. This last conclusion, surely, is not desireable, nor ought it to be embraced too rashly. For how much must we diminish from the beauty and value of this species of philosophy, upon such a supposition? Moralists have hitherto been accustomed, when they considered the vast multitude and diversity of[37] actions that excite our approbation or dislike, to search for some common principle, on which this variety of sentiments might depend. And tho' they have sometimes carried the matter too far, by their passion for some one general principle; it must, however, be confessed, that they are excusable, in expecting to find some general principles, into which all the vices and virtues were justly to be resolved. The like has been the endeavor of critics, logicians, and even politicians: Nor have their attempts been wholly unsuccessful; tho' perhaps longer time, greater accuracy, and more ardent application may bring these sciences still nearer their perfection. To throw up at once all pretensions of this kind may justly be deemed more rash, precipitate, and dogmatical, than even the boldest and most affir-

---

37 1777: inserts *those*

mative philosophy, which[38] has ever attempted to impose its crude dictates and principles on mankind.

16. What tho' these reasonings concerning human nature seem abstract, and of difficult comprehension? This affords no presumption of their falshood. On the contrary, it seems impossible, that what has hitherto escaped so many wise and profound philosophers can be very obvious and easy. And whatever pains these researches may cost us, we may think ourselves sufficiently rewarded, not only in point of profit but of pleasure, if, by that means, we can make any addition to our stock of knowlege, in subjects of such unspeakable importance.

17. But as, after all, the abstractedness of these speculations is no recommendation, but rather a disadvantage to them, and as this difficulty may perhaps be surmounted by care and art, and the avoiding[39] all unnecessary detail, we have, in the following enquiry, attempted to throw some light upon subjects, from which uncertainty has hitherto deterred the wise, and obscurity the ignorant. Happy, if we can unite the boundaries of the different species of philosophy, by reconciling profound enquiry with clearness, and truth with novelty! And still more happy, if, reasoning in this easy manner, we can undermine the foundations of an abstruse philosophy, which seems to have served hitherto[40] only as a shelter to superstition, and a cover to absurdity and error!

---

38 **1777**: *that* for *which*
39 **1777**: inserts *of*
40 **1777**: *hitherto served* for *served hitherto*

SECTION 2
OF THE ORIGIN OF IDEAS

1. Every one will readily allow, that there is a considerable difference between the perceptions of the mind, when a man feels the pain of excessive heat, or the pleasure of moderate warmth, and when he afterwards recalls to his memory this sensation, or anticipates it by his imagination. These faculties may mimic or copy the perceptions of the senses; but they never can reach entirely[1] the force and vivacity of the original sentiment. The utmost we say of them, even when they operate with greatest vigor, is, that they represent their object in so lively a manner, that we could *almost* say we feel or see it: But except the mind be disordered by disease or madness, they never can arrive at such a pitch of vivacity, as to render these perceptions altogether undistinguishable. All the colors of poetry, however splendid, can never paint natural objects in such a manner as to make the description be taken for a real landskip. The most lively thought is still inferior to the dullest sensation.

2. We may observe a like distinction to run thro' all the other perceptions of the mind. A man, in a fit of anger, is actuated in a very different manner from one who only thinks of that emotion. If you tell me, that any person is in love, I easily understand your meaning, and form a just conception of his situation; but never can mistake that conception for the real disorders and agitations of the passion. When we reflect on our past sentiments and affections, our thought is a faithful mirror, and copies its objects truly; but the colors which it employs are faint and dull, in comparison of those in which our original perceptions were clothed. It requires no nice discernment nor[2] metaphysical head to mark the distinction between them.

3. Here therefore we may divide all the perceptions of the mind into two classes or species, which are distinguished by their different degrees of force and vivacity.[3]

The less forcible and lively are commonly denominated THOUGHTS or IDEAS. The other species want a name in our language, and in most others; I suppose, because it was not requisite for any, but philosophical purposes, to rank them under a general term or appellation. Let us, therefore, use a little freedom, and call them IMPRESSIONS; employing that word in a sense somewhat

---

1   1777: *entirely reach* for *reach entirely*
2   1777: *or* for *nor*
3   1777: does not insert a paragraph break here

different from the usual. By the term *impression*, then, I mean all our more lively perceptions, when we hear, or see, or feel, or love, or hate, or desire, or will. And impressions are distinguished from ideas, which are the less lively perceptions of which we are conscious, when we reflect on any of those sensations or movements above mentioned.

4. Nothing, at first view, may seem more unbounded than the thought of man, which not only escapes all human power and authority, but is not even restrained within the limits of nature and reality. To form monsters, and join incongruous shapes and appearances, costs[4] no more trouble than to conceive the most natural and familiar objects. And while the body is confined to one planet, along which it creeps with pain and difficulty; the thought can in an instant transport us into the most distant regions of the universe; or even beyond the universe, into the unbounded chaos, where nature is supposed to lie in total confusion. What never was seen, nor[5] heard of, may yet be conceived; nor is any thing beyond the power of thought, except what implies an absolute contradiction.

5. But tho'[6] thought seems to possess this unbounded liberty, we shall find, upon a nearer examination, that it is really confined within very narrow limits, and that all this creative power of the mind amounts to no more than the[7] compounding, transposing, augmenting, or diminishing the materials afforded us by the senses and experience. When we think of a golden mountain, we only join two consistent ideas, *gold*, and *mountain*, with which we were formerly acquainted. A virtuous horse we can conceive; because, from our own feeling, we can conceive virtue, and this we may unite to the figure and shape of a horse, which is an animal familiar to us. In short, all the materials of thinking are derived either from our outward or inward sentiment: The mixture and composition of these belongs alone to the mind and will. Or, to express myself in philosophical language, all our ideas or more feeble perceptions are copies of our impressions or more lively ones.

6. To prove this, the two following arguments will, I hope, be sufficient. First, When we analyse our thoughts or ideas, however compounded or sublime, we always find, that they resolve them-

---

4 1777: inserts *the imagination*
5 1777: *or* for *nor*
6 1777: inserts *our*
7 1777: inserts *faculty of*

selves into such simple ideas as were copied from a precedent feeling or sentiment. Even those ideas, which, at first view, seem the most wide of this origin, are found, upon a narrower[8] scrutiny, to be derived from it. The idea of God, as meaning an infinitely intelligent, wise, and good Being, arises from reflecting on the operations of our own mind, and augmenting, without limit, those qualities of goodness and wisdom. We may prosecute this enquiry to what length we please; where we shall always find, that every idea[9] we examine is copied from a similar impression. Those who would assert, that this position is not absolutely universal and[10] without exception, have only one, and that an easy method of refuting it; by producing that idea, which, in their opinion, is not derived from this source. It will then be incumbent on us, if we would maintain our doctrine, to produce the impression or lively perception, which corresponds to it.

7. Secondly. If it happen, from a defect of the organ, that a man is not susceptible of any species of sensation, we always find, that he is as little susceptible of the correspondent ideas. A blind man can form no notion of colors; a deaf man of sounds. Restore either of them that sense, in which he is deficient; by opening this new inlet for his sensations, you also open an inlet for the ideas, and he finds no difficulty of[11] conceiving these objects. The case is the same, if the object, proper for exciting any sensation, has never been applied to the organ. A LAPLANDER or NEGROE has no notion of the relish of wine. And tho' there are few or no instances of a like deficiency in the mind, where a person has never felt or is wholly incapable of a sentiment or passion, that belongs to his species; yet we find the same observation to take place in a less degree. A man of mild manners can form no notion[12] of inveterate revenge or cruelty; nor can a selfish heart easily conceive the heights of friendship and generosity. 'Tis readily allowed, that other beings may possess many senses, of which we can have no conception; because the ideas of them have never been introduced to us in the only manner by which an idea can have access to the mind, *viz.* by the actual feeling and sensation.

8. There is, however, one contradictory phænomenon, which may prove, that 'tis not absolutely impossible for ideas to go

---

8 **1777**: inserts *nearer* for *narrower*
9 **1777**: inserts *which*
10 **1777**: *universally true nor* for *absolutely universal and*
11 **1777**: *in* for *of*
12 **1777**: *idea* for *notion*

before[13] their correspondent impressions. I believe it will readily be allowed, that the several distinct ideas of colors, which enter by the eyes, or those of sounds, which are conveyed by the hearing,[14] are really different from each other; tho', at the same time, resembling. Now if this be true of different colors, it must be no less so, of the different shades of the same color; and each shade produces a distinct idea, independent of the rest. For if this should be denied, 'tis possible, by the continual gradation of shades, to run a color insensibly into what is most remote from it; and if you will not allow any of the means to be different, you cannot, without absurdity, deny the extremes to be the same. Suppose, therefore, a person to have enjoyed his sight for thirty years, and to have become perfectly well[15] acquainted with colors of all kinds, except one particular shade of blue, for instance, which it never has been his fortune to meet with. Let all the different shades of that color, except that single one, be placed before him, descending gradually from the deepest to the lightest; 'tis plain, that he will perceive a blank, where that shade is wanting, and will be sensible, that there is a greater distance in that place betwixt the contiguous colors than in any other. Now I ask, whether 'tis[16] possible for him, from his own imagination, to supply this deficiency, and raise up to himself the idea of that particular shade, tho' it had never been conveyed to him by his senses? I believe there are few but will be of opinion that he can; and this may serve as a proof, that the simple ideas are not always, in every instance, derived from the correspondent impressions; tho' this instance is so singular, that 'tis scarce[17] worth our observing, and does not merit, that for it alone we should alter our general maxim.

9. Here, therefore, is a proposition, which not only seems, in itself, simple and intelligible; but, if a proper use were made of it, might render every dispute equally intelligible, and banish all that jargon, which has so long taken possession of metaphysical reasonings, and drawn such[18] disgrace upon them. All ideas,

---

13 **1777**: *arise, independent of* for *go before*
14 **1777**: *colour, which enter by the eye, or those of sound, which are conveyed by the ear* for *colors, which enter by the eyes, or those of sounds, which are conveyed by the hearing*
15 **1777**: omits *well*
16 **1777**: *it be* for *'tis*
17 **1777**: *scarcely* for *scarce*
18 **1777**: omits *such*

especially abstract ones, are naturally faint and obscure; the mind has but a slender hold of them: They are apt to be confounded with other resembling ideas: and when we have often employed any term, tho' without a distinct meaning, we are apt to imagine that[19] it has a determinate idea, annexed to it. On the contrary, all impressions, that is, all sensations, either outward or inward, are strong and sensible:[20] The limits between them are more exactly determined: Nor is it easy to fall into any error or mistake with regard to them. When we entertain therefore any suspicion, that a philosophical term is employed without any meaning or idea (as is but too frequent) we need but enquire, *from what impression is that supposed idea derived?* And if it be impossible to assign any, this will serve to confirm our suspicion. By bringing ideas into so clear a light, we may reasonably hope to remove all dispute, which may arise, concerning their nature and reality.[a]

NOTE

[a] 'Tis probable, that no more was meant by those, who denied innate ideas, than that all ideas were copies of our impressions; tho' it must be confessed, that the terms which they employed were not chosen with such caution, nor so exactly defined as to prevent all mistakes about their doctrine. For what is meant by *innate*? If innate be equivalent to natural, then all the perceptions and ideas of the mind must be allowed to be innate or natural, in whatever sense we take the latter word, whether in opposition to what is uncommon, artificial, or miraculous. If by innate be meant, cotemporary to our birth, the dispute seems to be frivolous; nor is it worth while to enquire at what time thinking begins, whether before, at, or after our birth. Again, the word, *idea*, seems to be commonly taken in a very loose sense, even by Mr. LOCKE[21] himself,[22] as standing for any of our perceptions, our sensations and passions, as well as thoughts. Now in this sense, I should desire to know, what can be meant by asserting, that self-love, or resentment of injuries, or the passion betwixt the sexes is not innate?

But admitting these terms, *impressions* and *ideas*, in the sense above explained, and understanding by *innate* what is original or copied from no precedent perception, then may we assert, that all our impressions are innate, and our ideas not innate.

---

19 1777: omits *that*
20 1777: *vivid* for *sensible*
21 See Section 1, note 16.
22 1777: *by* LOCKE *and others;* for *even by Mr* LOCKE *himself,*

To be ingenuous, I must own it to be my opinion, that Mr.[23] LOCKE was betrayed into this question by the schoolmen, who making use of undefined terms, draw out their disputes to a tedious length, without ever touching the point in question. A like ambiguity and circumlocution seem to run thro' all that great philosopher's reasonings on this subject.[24]

23 1777: omits *Mr.*
24 1777: *that philosopher's reasonings on this as well as most other subjects* for
    all that great philosopher's reasonings on this subject.

SECTION 3
OF THE ASSOCIATION[1] OF IDEAS

1. 'Tis evident, that there is a principle of connexion between the different thoughts or ideas of the mind, and that in their appearance to the memory or imagination, they introduce each other with a certain degree of method and regularity. In our more serious thinking or discourse, this is so observable, that any particular thought, which breaks in upon this[2] regular tract or chain of ideas, is immediately remarked and rejected. And even in our wildest and most wandering reveries, nay in our very dreams, we shall find, if we reflect, that the imagination ran not altogether at adventures, but that there was still a connexion upheld among the different ideas, which succeeded each other. Were the loosest and freest conversation to be transcribed, there would immediately be observed something, which connected it in all its transitions. Or where this is wanting, the person, who broke the thread of discourse, might still inform you, that there had secretly revolved in his mind a succession of thought, which had gradually led him away[3] from the subject of conversation. Among the languages of different nations,[4] even where we cannot suspect the least connexion or communication, 'tis found, that the words, expressive of ideas, the most compounded, do yet nearly correspond to each other: A certain proof, that the simple ideas, comprehended in the compound ones, were bound together by some universal principle, which had an equal influence on all mankind.

2. Tho' it be too obvious to escape observation, that different ideas are connected together; I do not find, that any philosopher has attempted to enumerate or class all the principles of association; a subject, however, that seems very[5] worthy of curiosity. To me, there appear to be only three principles of connexion among ideas, *viz. Resemblance, Contiguity* in time or place, and *Cause* or *Effect*.

3. That these principles serve to connect ideas will not, I believe, be much doubted. A picture naturally leads our thoughts to the original:[b] The mention of one apartment in a building naturally introduces an enquiry or discourse concerning the others:[c]

---

1 **1748-1750**: *CONNEXION* for *ASSOCIATION*
2 **1777**: *the* for *this*
3 **1777**: omits *away*
4 **1777**: *different languages* for *the languages of different nations*
5 **1777**: omits *very*

And if we think of a wound, we can scarce[6] forbear reflecting on the pain which follows it.[d] But that this enumeration is compleat, and that there are no other principles of association, except these, may be difficult to prove to the satisfaction of the reader, or even to a man's own satisfaction. All we can do, in such cases, is to run over several instances, and examine carefully the principle, which binds the different thoughts to each other, never stopping till we render the principle as general as possible.[7] The more instances we examine, and the more care we employ, the more assurance shall we acquire, that the enumeration, which we form from the whole, is compleat and entire.[8] Instead of entering into a detail of this kind, which would lead into many useless subtilties, we shall consider some of the effects of this connexion upon the passions and imagination; where we may open a field of speculation more entertaining, and perhaps more instructive, than the other.

4. As man is a reasonable being, and is continually in pursuit of happiness, which he hopes to attain by the gratification of some passion or affection, he seldom acts or speaks or thinks without a purpose and intention. He has still some object in view; and however improper the means may sometimes be, which he chuses for the attainment of his end, he never loses view of an end, nor will he so much as throw away his thoughts or reflections, where he hopes not to reap any satisfaction from them.

5. In all compositions of genius, therefore, 'tis requisite that the writer have some plan or object; and tho' he may be hurried from this plan by the vehemence of thought, as in an ode, or drop it carelesly, as in an epistle or essay, there must appear some aim or intention, in his first setting out, if not in the composition of the whole work. A production without a design would resemble more the ravings of a madman, than the sober efforts of genius and learning.

6. As this rule admits of no exception, it follows, that in narrative compositions, the events or actions, which the writer relates, must be connected together, by some bond or tye: They must be related to each other in the imagination, and form a kind of *Unity*, which may bring them under one plan or view, and which may be the object or end of the writer in his first undertaking.

7. This connecting principle among the several events, which form the subject of a poem or history, may be very different,

---

6 1777: *scarcely* for *scarce*
7 1777: moves note **f** here
8 1777: omits the remainder of the section from this point on.

according to the different designs of the poet or historian.[9] OVID[10] has formed his plan upon the connecting principle of resemblance. Every fabulous transformation, produced by the miraculous power of the gods, falls within the compass of his work. There needs but this one circumstance in any event to bring it under his original plan or intention.

8. An annalist or historian, who should undertake to write the history of EUROPE during any century, would be influenced by the connexion of contiguity in time and place. All events, which happen in that portion of space, and period of time, are comprehended in his design, tho' in other respects different and unconnected. They have still a species of unity, amidst all their diversity.

9. But the most usual species of connexion among the different events, which enter into any narrative composition, is that of cause and effect; while the historian traces the series of actions according to their natural order, remounts to their secret springs and principles, and delineates their most remote consequences. He chuses for his subject a certain portion of that great chain of events, which compose the history of mankind: Each link in this chain he endeavors to touch in his narration: Sometimes, unavoidable ignorance renders all his attempts fruitless: Sometimes, he supplies by conjecture what is wanting in knowlege: And always, he is sensible, that the more unbroken the chain is, which he presents to his readers, the more perfect is his production. He sees, that the knowlege of causes is not only the most satisfactory; this relation or connexion being the strongest of all others; but also the most instructive; since it is by this knowlege alone, we are enabled to control events, and govern futurity.

10. Here therefore we may attain some notion of that *Unity* of *Action*, about which all critics, after ARISTOTLE, have talked so much:[11] Perhaps, to little purpose, while they directed not their

---

9 Hume's use of "poem" is broader than current usage and covers all works of fiction. The only non-fictional works Hume is concerned with in this section are those that are narrative in character, such as history and biography.

10 Publius Ovidius Naso (43 BCE-17 CE) was a Roman poet and author of *Metamorphoses*, a collection of myths and stories related by the fact that they all involve transformations.

11 Aristotle's (see Section 1, note 16) *Poetics* draws a distinction between tragic and comic works of fiction and lays down the principle that in a successful tragic work one action or event must follow from another so that nothing happens by accident or by the sudden intervention of some novel and unanticipated cause.

taste or sentiment by the accuracy of philosophy. It appears, that in all productions, as well as in the epic and tragic, there is a certain unity required, and that, on no occasion, can our thoughts be allowed to run at adventures, if we would produce a work, which will give any lasting entertainment to mankind. It appears also, that even a biographer, who should write the life of ACHILLES,[12] would connect the events, by shewing their mutual dependence and relation, as much as a poet, who should make the anger of that hero, the subject of his narration.[e] Not only in any limited portion of life, a man's actions have a dependance on each other, but also during the whole period of his duration, from the cradle to the grave; nor is it possible to strike off one link, however minute, in this regular chain, without affecting the whole series of events, which follow. The unity of action, therefore, which is to be found in biography or history, differs from that of epic poetry, not in kind, but in degree. In epic poetry, the connexion among the events is more close and sensible: The narration is not carried on thro' such a length of time: And the actors hasten to some remarkable period, which satisfies the curiosity of the reader. This conduct of the epic poet depends on that particular situation of the *Imagination* and of the *Passions*, which is supposed in that production. The imagination, both of writer and reader, is more enlivened, and the passions more enflamed than in history, biography, or any species of narration, which confine themselves to strict truth and reality. Let us consider the effect of these two circumstances, an enlivened imagination and enflamed passions, circumstances, which belong to poetry, especially the epic kind, above any other species of composition; and let us examine the reason why they require a stricter and closer unity in the fable.[13]

11. First. All poetry, being a species of painting,[14] approaches us nearer to the objects than any other species of narration, throws a stronger light upon them, and delineates more distinctly those minute circumstances, which, tho' to the historian they seem superfluous, serve mightily to enliven the imagery, and

---

12 Achilles was a legendary warrior of superhuman abilities in Homer's (9th or 8th century BCE) *Illiad*, a poem that describes the events of the Trojan war, taking the wrath of Achilles as its guiding theme.

13 In other words, why a stricter and closer unity is required in fiction than in history.

14 Hume's use of "painting" was broader than current usage and refers to any representation of objects.

gratify the fancy. If it be not necessary, as in the *Iliad*, to inform us each time the hero buckles his shoes, and ties his garters, it will be requisite, perhaps, to enter into a greater detail than in the HENRIADE; where the events are run over with such rapidity, that we scarce have leisure to become acquainted with the scene or action.[15] Were a poet, therefore, to comprehend in his subject any great compass of time or series of events, and trace up the death of HECTOR to its remote causes, in the rape of HELEN, or the judgment of PARIS,[16] he must draw out his poem to an immeasurable length, in order to fill this large canvas with just painting and imagery. The reader's imagination, enflamed with such a series of poetical descriptions, and his passions, agitated by a continual sympathy with the actors, must flag long before the period of the narration, and must sink into lassitude and disgust, from the repeated violence of the same movements.

12. Secondly. That an epic poet must not trace the causes to any great distance, will farther appear, if we consider another reason, which is drawn from a property of the passions still more remarkable and singular. 'Tis evident, that in a just composition, all the affections, excited by the different events, described and represented, add mutual force to each other; and that while the heroes are all engaged in one common scene, and each action is strongly connected with the whole, the concern is continually awake, and the passions make an easy transition from one object to another. The strong connection of the events, as it facilitates the passage of the thought or imagination from one to another, facilitates also the transfusion of the passions, and preserves the affections still in the same channel and direction. Our sympathy and concern for EVE prepares the way for a like sympathy with ADAM: The affection is preserved almost entire in the transition; and the mind seizes immediately the new object as strongly related to that which formerly engaged its attention. But were the poet to make a total digression from his subject, and introduce a

---

15 See note 12 above for Homer's *Illiad*. The *Henriade* was a poem by Hume's contemporary Voltaire (1694-1778) that dealt with the life of Henry IV of France.

16 According to legend, Hector, the greatest of the Trojan warriors, was killed by Achilles during the Trojan war. The war had been caused by the abduction of Helen by Hector's brother, Paris, who had been asked to judge which of Aphrodite, Athena, and Hera was the most beautiful. Aphrodite had induced Paris to choose her by offering Helen as a reward.

new actor, no way connected with the personages, the imagination, feeling a breach in the transition, would enter coldly into the new scene; would kindle by slow degrees; and in returning to the main subject of the poem, would pass, as it were, upon foreign ground, and have its concern to excite anew, in order to take party with the principal actors. The same inconvenience follows in a less degree, where the poet traces his events to too great a distance, and binds together actions, which tho' not entirely disjoined, have not so strong a connexion as is requisite to forward the transition of the passions. Hence arises the artifice of the oblique narration, employed in the *Odyssey* and *Æneid*;[17] where the hero is introduced, at first, near the period of his designs, and afterwards shows us, as it were in perspective, the more distant events and causes. By this means, the reader's curiosity is immediately excited: The events follow with rapidity, and in a very close connexion: And the concern is preserved alive, and, by means of the near relation of the objects, continually increases, from the beginning to the end of the narration.

13. The same rule takes place in dramatic poetry; nor is it ever permitted, in a regular composition, to introduce an actor, who has no connexion, or but a small one, with the principal personages of the fable. The spectator's concern must not be diverted by any scenes, disjoined and separated from the rest. This breaks the course of the passions, and prevents that communication of the several emotions, by which one scene adds force to another, and transfuses the pity and terror, which it excites, upon each succeeding scene, 'till the whole produces that rapidity of movement, which is peculiar to the theatre. How must it extinguish this warmth of affection to be entertained, on a sudden, with a new action and new personages, no way related to the former; to find so sensible a breach or vacuity in the course of the passions, by means of this breach in the connexion of ideas; and instead of carrying the sympathy of one scene into the following, to be obliged, every moment, to excite a new concern, and take party in a new scene of action?[18]

---

17 Virgil's (70-19 BCE) *Aeneid*, describes the adventures of Aeneas, who is reputed to have escaped the sack of Troy to found the city of Rome. The work has long been supposed to have been modeled on Homer's *Odyssey*, which describes the adventures of Odysseus after the fall of Troy. Both works open just before the climax of the story and then review the events that led up to that climax.

18 **1764-1772**: omit the following paragraph

But tho' this rule of unity of action be common to dramatic and epic poetry; we may still observe a difference betwixt them, which may, perhaps, deserve our attention. In both these species of composition, 'tis requisite that the action be one and simple, in order to preserve the concern or sympathy entire and undiverted: But in epic or narrative poetry, this rule is also established upon another foundation, *viz.* the necessity, that is incumbent on every writer, to form some plan or design, before he enter on any discourse or narration, and to comprehend his subject in some general aspect or united view, which may be the constant object of his attention. As the author is entirely lost in dramatic compositions, and the spectator supposes himself to be really present at the actions represented; this reason has no place with regard to the stage; but any dialogue or conversation may be introduced, which, without improbability, might have passed in that determinate portion of space, represented by the theatre. Hence in all our ENGLISH comedies, even those of CONGREVE,[19] the unity of action is never strictly observed; but the poet thinks it sufficient, if his personages be any way related to each other, by blood, or by living in the same family; and he afterwards introduces them in particular scenes, where they display their humors and characters, without much forwarding the main action. The double plots of TERENCE[20] are licences of the same kind; but in a less degree. And tho' this conduct be not perfectly regular, it is not wholly unsuitable to the nature of comedy, where the movements and passions are not raised to such a height as in tragedy; at the same time, that the fiction or representation palliates, in some measure, such licences. In a narrative poem, the first proposition or design confines the author to one subject; and any digressions of this nature would, at first view, be rejected, as absurd and monstrous. Neither BOCCACE, LA FONTAINE,[21] nor any author of that kind, tho' pleasantry be their chief object, have ever indulged them.

---

19 William Congreve (1670-1729) was the most accomplished dramatist of the English Restoration. His plays were noted for their carefully constructed plot lines.

20 Publius Terentius Afer (195?-159 BCE) was a Roman playwright. A number of his comedies intertwine the separate stories of two pairs of lovers.

21 Both Giovanni Boccaccio (1313-75), and Jean de La Fontaine (1621-95), wrote compendia of fables that were intended to illustrate practical maxims or proverbs. Their stories were confined to that purpose and do not contain the sorts of digressions from the project found in dramatic comedy.

14. To return to the comparison of history and epic poetry, we may conclude, from the foregoing reasonings, that as a certain unity is requisite in all productions, it cannot be wanting to history more than to any other; that in history, the connexion among the several events, which unites them into one body, is the relation of cause and effect, the same which takes place in epic poetry; and that in the latter composition, this connexion is only required to be closer and more sensible, on account of the lively imagination and strong passions, which must be touched by the poet in his narration. The PELEPONNESIAN war is a proper subject for history, the siege of ATHENS for an epic poem, and the death of ALCIBIADES for a tragedy.[22]

15. As the difference, therefore, between history and epic poetry consists only in the degrees of connexion, which bind together those several events, of which their subject is composed, 'twill be difficult, if not impossible, by words, to determine exactly the bounds, which separate them from each other. That is a matter of taste more than of reasoning; and perhaps, this unity may often be discovered in a subject, where, at first view, and from an abstract consideration, we should least expect to find it.

16. 'Tis evident, that HOMER, in the course of his narration, exceeds the first proposition of his subject; and that the anger of ACHILLES, which caused the death of HECTOR, is not the same with that which produced so many ills to the GREEKS.[23] But the strong connexion between those two movements, the quick transition from one to another, the contraste[f] betwixt the effects of concord and discord among the princes, and the natural curiosity which we have to see ACHILLES in action, after such long repose; all these causes carry on the reader, and produce a sufficient unity in the subject.

17. It may be objected to MILTON,[24] that he has traced up his causes to too great a distance, and that the rebellion of the angels

---

22 The Peloponnesian war (431-404 BCE) was an on-again, off-again conflict between Athens and Sparta for Greek supremacy. The siege of Athens in 404 BCE ended the war. Alcibiades (c. 450-404 BCE) was a commander of the Athenian forces during the latter part of the war who made many enemies and was eventually assassinated. Aristotle remarked that epic differs from tragedy in the period of time it deals with, observing that tragedies tend to be confined to a period of about a day.

23 See note 12 above.

24 Though the principal theme of John Milton's (1608-74) *Paradise Lost* is the expulsion of Adam and Eve from the garden of Eden, he took the story back to the rebellion of Satan against God.

produces the fall of man by a train of events, which is both very long and very casual. Not to mention that the creation of the world, which he has related at length, is no more the cause of that catastrophe, than of the battle of PHARSALIA,[25] or any other event, that has ever happened. But if we consider, on the other hand, that all these events, the rebellion of the angels, the creation of the world, and the fall of man, *resemble* each other, in being miraculous and out of the common course of nature; that they are supposed to be *contiguous* in time; and that being detached from all other events, and being the only original facts, which revelation discovers, they strike the eye at once, and naturally recall each other to the thought or imagination: If we consider all these circumstances, I say, we shall find, that these parts of the action have a sufficient unity to make them be comprehended in one fable or narration. To which we may add, that the rebellion of the angels and the fall of man have a peculiar resemblance, as being counterparts to each other, and presenting to the reader the same moral, of obedience to our Creator.

18. These loose hints I have thrown together, in order to excite the curiosity of philosophers, and beget a suspicion at least, if not a full persuasion, that this subject is very copious, and that many operations of the human mind depend on the connexion or association of ideas, which is here explained. Particularly, the sympathy between the passions and imagination will, perhaps, appear remarkable; while we observe that the affections, excited by one object, pass easily to another connected with it; but transfuse themselves with difficulty, or not at all, along different objects, which have no manner of connexion together. By introducing, into any composition, personages and actions, foreign to each other, an injudicious author loses that communication of emotions, by which alone he can interest the heart, and raise the passions to their proper height and period. The full explication of this principle and all its consequences would lead us into reasonings too profound and too copious for this enquiry. 'Tis sufficient, at present, to have established this conclusion, that the three connecting principles of all ideas are the relations of *Resemblance, Contiguity,* and *Causation.*

---

25 Gaius Julius Caesar (100-44 BCE) defeated his main opponent of the time, Gnaeus Pompeius Magnus (Pompey, 106-48 BCE) at the battle of Pharsalia, in northern Greece, in 48 BCE.

NOTES

^b Resemblance.

^c Contiguity.

^d Cause and Effect.

^e Contrary to ARISTOTLE, Μῦθος δ'ἐστίν εἷς, οὐχ, ὥσπερ τινὲς οἴονται, ἐὰν περὶ θ'ἕνος[26] ἦ. Πολλὰ γὰρ, καὶ ἀπείρα τῶ γένει συμβαίνει, ἐξ ὧν ἐνίων[27] ἐστιν ἕν. Οὕτω δὲ καὶ πραξεῖς ἑνός πολλαί ἰστιν,[28] ἐξ ὧν μία ουδεμία γίνεται πρᾶξις &c.[29] Κεφ. η.[30]

^f Contraste[31] or contrariety is[32] a connexion among ideas, which[33] may, perhaps, be considered as a species of resemblance.[34] Where two objects are contrary, the one destroys the other, i.e. is the cause of its annihilation, and the idea of the annihilation of an object implies the idea of its former existence.

---

26 **Beauchamp**: ἕνα for θ'ἕνος
27 **1748-1756**: insert; οὐδέν
28 **1748-1756**: ἔσιν for ἰσιν; **Beauchamp**: εἴσιν for ἰσιν
29 "The Subject ought to be one, and not as many think, taken from one person *only:* For as we see every day an infinity of Accidents, of the greatest part of which, we can make nothing that is one; it happens also that the Actions of the same Man, are so many and different, that we can never *reduce them to this Unity,* and make of them one and the same Action." *Aristotle's Art of Poetry. Translated from the original Greek, according to Mr. Theodore Goulston's edition* (London: Daniel Browne, William Mears and Jonas Browne, 1714), 129. Gale Document CB3332842061.
30 *Poetics* 8: 1451a15-19.
31 **1777**: *For instance, contrast* for *Contraste*
32 **1777**: adds *also*
33 **1777**: *ideas: But it* for *ideas, which*
34 **1777**: *mixture of Causation and Resemblance* for *species of resemblance*

SECTION 4
SCEPTICAL DOUBTS CONCERNING THE
OPERATIONS OF THE UNDERSTANDING

PART I

1. All the objects of human reason or enquiry may naturally be divided into two kinds, *viz. Relations of Ideas* and *Matters of Fact*. Of the first kind are the sciences of Geometry, Algebra, and Arithmetic; and in short, every affirmation, which is either intuitively or demonstratively certain.[1] *That the square of the hypothenuse is equal to the squares[2] of the two sides*, is a proposition, which expresses a relation between these figures. *That three times five is equal to the half of thirty*, expresses a relation between these numbers. Propositions of this kind are discoverable by the mere operation of thought, without dependance on what is any where existent in the universe. Tho' there never were a true[3] circle or triangle in nature, the truths demonstrated by EUCLID,[4] would for ever retain their certainty and evidence.

2. Matters of fact, which are the second objects of human reason, are not ascertained in the same manner; nor is our evidence of their truth, however great, of a like nature with the foregoing. The contrary of every matter of fact is still possible; because it can never imply a contradiction, and is conceived by the mind with equal[5] facility and distinctness, as if ever so conformable to reality. *That the sun will not rise to-morrow* is no less intelligible a proposition, and implies no more contradiction, than the affirmation, *that it will rise*. We should in vain, therefore, attempt to demonstrate its falshood. Were it demonstratively false, it would imply a contradiction, and could never be distinctly conceived by the mind.

3. It may, therefore, be a subject, worthy[6] curiosity, to enquire what is the nature of that evidence, which assures us of any real

---

1 An affirmation is intuitively certain if it is known just by comparing ideas, so that the only way it could turn out to be false is if the ideas were to change. An affirmation is demonstratively certain if it is known by means of a chain of intuitively certain propositions.

2 **1777:** *square* for *squares*

3 **1777:** omits *true*

4 Euclid (4th-3rd century BCE) formalized geometry by presenting it as a system in which the entire body of knowledge is deduced from a few self-evident axioms.

5 **1777:** *the same* for *equal*

6 **1777:** inserts *of*

existence and matter of fact, beyond the present testimony of our senses, or the records of our memory. This part of philosophy, 'tis observable, has been little cultivated, either by the ancients or moderns; and therefore our doubts and errors, in the prosecution of so important an enquiry, may be the more excusable, while we march thro' such difficult paths, without any guide or direction. They may even prove useful, by exciting curiosity, and destroying that implicit faith and security, which is the bane of all reasoning and free enquiry. The discovery of defects in the common philosophy, if any such there be, will not, I presume, be a discouragement, but rather an incitement, as is usual, to attempt something more full and satisfactory, than has yet been proposed to the public.

4. All reasonings concerning matter of fact seem to be founded in[7] the relation of *Cause* and *Effect*. By means of that relation alone can we[8] go beyond the evidence of our memory and senses. If you were to ask a man, why he believes any matter of fact, which is absent; for instance, that his friend is in the country, or in FRANCE; he would give you a reason; and this reason would be some other fact; as a letter received from him, or the knowlege of his former resolutions and promises. A man, finding a watch or any other machine in a desert island, would conclude, that there had once been men in that island. All our reasonings concerning fact are of the same nature. And here 'tis constantly supposed, that there is a connexion between the present fact and that[9] inferred from it. Were there nothing to bind them together, the inference would be entirely precarious. The hearing of an articulate voice and rational discourse in the dark assures us of the presence of some person: Why? because these are the effects of the human make and fabric, and closely connected with it. If we anatomize all the other reasonings of this nature, we shall find, that they are founded in[10] the relation of cause and effect, and that this relation is either near or remote, direct or collateral. Heat and light are collateral effects of fire, and the one effect may justly be inferred from the other.

5. If we would satisfy ourselves, therefore, concerning the nature of that evidence, which assures us of all[11] matters of fact,

---

7 **1777:** *on* for *in*
8 **1777:** *we can* for *can we*
9 **1777:** inserts *which is*
10 **1777:** *on* for *in*
11 **1777:** omits *all*

we must enquire how we arrive at the knowlege of cause and effect.

6. I shall venture to affirm, as a general proposition, which admits of no exception, that the knowlege of this relation is not, in any instance, attained by reasonings *à priori*;[12] but arises entirely from experience, when we find, that any particular objects are constantly conjoined with each other. Let an object be presented to a man of ever so strong natural reason and abilities; if that object be entirely new to him, he will not be able, by the most accurate examination of its sensible qualities, to discover any of its causes or effects. ADAM, tho' his rational faculties be supposed, at the very first, entirely perfect, could not have inferred from the fluidity and transparency of water, that it would suffocate him, or from the light and warmth of fire, that it would consume him. No object ever discovers, by the qualities which appear to the senses, either the causes, which produced it, or the effects, which will arise from it; nor can our reason, unassisted by experience, ever draw any inferences[13] concerning real existence and matter of fact.

7. This proposition, *that causes and effects are discoverable, not by reason but by experience,* will readily be admitted with regard to such objects, as we remember to have been once[14] altogether unknown to us; since we must be conscious of the utter inability which we then lay under of foretelling what would arise from them. Present two smooth pieces of marble to a man, who has no tincture of natural philosophy;[15] he will never discover, that they will adhere together, in such a manner as to require great force to separate them in a direct line, while they make so small[16] resistance to a lateral pressure. Such events, as bear little analogy to the common course of nature, are also readily confessed to be known only by experience; nor does any man imagine that the explosion of gunpowder, or the attraction of a loadstone[17] could

---

12 "A priori" means "in advance" or "ahead of time." Hume's claim is that we cannot tell what an object's cause was or what its effect will be in advance, simply by inspecting that object. Instead, we need to try to find out what happened earlier, or wait to see what happens next. Indeed, we need to *repeatedly* see same sorts of things being preceded or followed by things of another sort.

13 1777: *inference* for *inferences*

14 1777: *once been* for *been once*

15 I.e., to someone who has no knowledge of the natural sciences.

16 1777: inserts *a*

17 Loadstone is a naturally magnetic stone.

ever be discovered by arguments *à priori*. In like manner, when an effect is supposed to depend upon an intricate machinery or secret structure of parts, we make no difficulty to attribute[18] all our knowlege of it to experience. Who will assert, that he can give the ultimate reason, why milk or bread is proper nourishment for a man, not for a lion or a tyger?

8. But the same truth may not appear, at first sight, to have the same evidence with regard to events, which have become familiar to us from our first appearance in the world, which bear a close analogy to the whole course of nature, and which are supposed to depend on the simple qualities of objects, without any secret structure of parts. We are apt to imagine, that we could discover these effects, by the mere operations[19] of our reason, without experience. We fancy, that, were we brought, on a sudden, into this world, we could at first have inferred, that one Billiard-ball would communicate motion to another upon impulse; and that we needed not to have waited for the event, in order to pronounce with certainty concerning it. Such is the influence of custom, that, where it is strongest, it not only covers our natural ignorance, but even conceals itself, and seems not to take place, merely because it is found in the highest degree.

9. But to convince us, that all the laws of nature and all the operations of bodies, without exception, are known only by experience, the following reflections may, perhaps, suffice. Were any object presented to us, and were we required to pronounce concerning the effect, which will result from it, without consulting past observation; after what manner, I beseech you, must the mind proceed in this operation? It must invent or imagine some event, which it ascribes to the object as its effect; and 'tis plain that this invention must be entirely arbitrary. The mind can never possibly find the effect in the supposed cause, by the most accurate scrutiny and examination. For the effect is totally different from the cause, and consequently can never be discovered in it. Motion in the second Billiard-ball is a quite distinct event from motion in the first; nor is there any thing in the one to suggest the smallest hint of the other. A stone or piece of metal raised into the air, and left without any support, immediately falls: But to consider the matter *à priori*; is there any thing we discover in this situation, which can beget the idea of a downward, rather than an upward, or any other motion, in the stone or metal?

18 1777: *in attributing* for *to attribute*
19 1777: *operation* for *operations*

10. And as the first imagination or invention of a particular effect, in all natural operations, is arbitrary, where we consult not experience; so must we also esteem the supposed tye or connexion between the cause and effect, which binds them together, and renders it impossible, that any other effect could result from the operation of that cause. When I see, for instance, a Billiard-ball moving in a strait line towards another; even suppose motion in the second ball should by accident be suggested to me, as the result of their contact or impulse; may I not conceive, that a hundred different events might as well follow from that cause? May not both these balls remain at absolute rest? May not the first ball return in a strait line, or leap off from the second in any line or direction? All these suppositions are consistent and conceivable. Why then should we give the preference to one, which is no more consistent nor[20] conceivable than the rest? All our reasonings *à priori* will never be able to shew us any foundation for this preference.

11. In a word, then, every effect is a distinct event from its cause. It could not, therefore, be discovered in the cause, and the first invention or conception of it, *à priori*, must be entirely arbitrary. And even after it is suggested, the conjunction of it with the cause must appear equally arbitrary; since there are always many other effects, which, to reason, must seem fully as consistent and natural. In vain, therefore, should we pretend to determine any single event, or infer any cause or effect, without the assistance of observation and experience.

12. Hence we may discover the reason, why no philosopher, who is rational and modest, has ever pretended to assign the ultimate cause of any natural operation, or to show distinctly the action of that power, which produces any single effect in the universe. 'Tis confessed, that the utmost effort of human reason is, to reduce the principles, productive of natural phænomena, to a greater simplicity, and to resolve the many particular effects into a few general causes, by means of reasonings from analogy, experience, and observation. But as to the causes of these general causes, we should in vain attempt their discovery; nor shall we ever be able to satisfy ourselves, by any particular explication of them. These ultimate springs and principles are totally shut up from human curiosity and enquiry. Elasticity, gravity, cohesion of parts, communication of motion by impulse; these are probably the ultimate causes and principles which we shall ever discover in

---

20 1777: *or* for *nor*

nature; and we may esteem ourselves sufficiently happy, if, by accurate enquiry and reasoning, we can trace up the particular phænomena to, or near to, these general principles. The most perfect philosophy of the natural kind only staves off our ignorance a little longer: As perhaps the most perfect philosophy of the moral or metaphysical kind serves only to discover larger portions of our ignorance.[21] Thus the observation of human blindness and weakness is the result of all philosophy, and meets us, at every turn, in spite of our endeavors to elude, or avoid it.

13. Nor is geometry, when taken into the assistance of natural philosophy, ever able to remedy this defect, or lead us into the knowlege of ultimate causes, by all that accuracy of reasoning, for which it is so justly celebrated. Every part of mixed mathematics[22] goes[23] upon the supposition, that certain laws are established by nature in her operations; and abstract reasonings are employed, either to assist experience in the discovery of these laws, or to determine their influence in particular instances, where it depends upon any precise degrees[24] of distance and quantity. Thus, 'tis a law of motion, discovered by experience, that the moment or force of any body in motion is in the compound ratio or proportion of its solid contents and its velocity; and consequently, that a small force may remove the greatest obstacle or raise the greatest weight, if by any contrivance or machinery we can encrease the velocity of that force, so as to make it an overmatch for its antagonist. Geometry assists us in the application of this law, by giving us the just dimensions of all the parts and figures, which can enter into any species of machine; but still the discovery of the law itself is owing merely to experience, and all the abstract reasonings in the world could never lead us one step towards the knowlege of it. When we reason *à priori*, and consider merely any object or cause, as it appears to the mind, independent of all observation, it never could suggest to us the notion of any distinct object, such as its effect; much less, shew us the inseparable and inviolable connection between them. A man must be very sagacious, who could discover by reasoning, that crystal is the effect of heat and ice of cold, without being previously acquainted with the operations[25] of these qualities.

---

21 **1777**: *it* for *our ignorance*
22 "Mixed mathematics" is what we would today call applied mathematics.
23 **1777**: *proceeds* for *goes*
24 **1777**: *degree* for *degrees*
25 **1777**: *operation* for *operations*

14. But we have not, as[26] yet, attained any tolerable satisfaction with regard to the question first proposed. Each solution still gives rise to a new question as difficult as the foregoing, and leads us on to farther enquiries. When it is asked, *What is the nature of all our reasonings concerning matter of fact?* The proper answer seems to be, that they are founded on the relation of cause and effect. When again it is asked, *What is the foundation of all our reasonings and conclusions concerning that relation?* it may be replied in one word, EXPERIENCE. But if we still carry on our sifting humor, and ask, *What is the foundation of all our[27] conclusions from experience?* this implies a new question, which may be of more difficult solution and explication. Philosophers, that give themselves airs of superior wisdom and sufficiency, have a hard task, when they encounter persons of inquisitive dispositions, who push them from every corner, to which they retreat, and who are sure at last to bring them to some dangerous dilemma. The best expedient to prevent this confusion, is to be modest in our pretensions; and even to discover the difficulty ourselves before it is objected to us. By this means, we may make a kind of merit of our very ignorance.

15. I shall content myself, in this section, with an easy task, and shall pretend only to give a negative answer to the question here proposed. I say then, that even after we have experience of the operations of cause and effect, our conclusions from that experience are *not* founded on reasoning, or any process of the understanding. This answer we must endeavor, both to explain and to defend.

16. It must certainly be allowed, that nature has kept us at a great distance from all her secrets, and has afforded us only the knowlege of a few superficial qualities of objects, while she conceals from us those powers and principles, on which the influence of these objects entirely depends. Our senses inform us of the color, weight, and consistence of bread; but neither senses[28] nor reason ever can[29] inform us of those qualities, which fit it for the nourishment and support of a human body. Sight or feeling conveys an idea of the actual motion of bodies; but as to that wonderful force or power, which would carry on a moving body

---

26 **1777**: omits *as*
27 **1777**: omits *our*
28 **1777**: *sense* for *senses*
29 **1777**: *can ever* for *ever can*

for ever in a continued change of place, and which bodies never lose but by communicating it to others; of this we cannot form the most distant conception. But notwithstanding this ignorance of natural powers[g][30] and principles, we always presume, where[31] we see like sensible qualities, that they have like secret powers, and lay our account,[32] that effects, similar to those, which we have experienced, will follow from them. If a body of like color and consistence with that bread, which we have formerly eat, be presented to us, we make no scruple of repeating the experiment, and expect,[33] with certainty, like nourishment and support. Now this is a process of the mind or thought, of which I would willingly know the foundation. 'Tis allowed on all hands, that there is no known connection between the sensible qualities and the secret powers; and consequently, that the mind is not led to form such a conclusion concerning their constant and regular conjunction, by any thing which it knows of their nature. As to past *Experience*, it can be allowed to give *direct* and *certain* information only of those precise objects,[34] and that precise period of time, which fell under its cognizance: But why this experience should be extended to future times, and to other objects, which, for aught we know, may be only in appearance similar; this is the main question on which I would insist. The bread, which I formerly eat, nourished me; that is, a body, of such sensible qualities, was, at that time, endued with such secret powers: But does it follow, that other bread must also nourish me at another time, and that like sensible qualities must always be attended with like secret powers? The consequence seems no way[35] necessary. At least, it must be acknowleged, that there is here a consequence drawn by the mind; that there is a certain step taken; a process of thought, and an inference, which wants to be explained. These two propositions are far from being the same, *I have found that such an object has always been attended with such an effect*, and, *I foresee, that other objects, which are, to*[36] *appearance, similar, will be attended with similar effects*. I shall allow, if you please, that the one proposition may justly be inferred from the

---

30 This note was first added in 1750.
31 1777: *when* for *where*
32 1777: *expect* for *lay our account*
33 1777: *forsee* for *expect*
34 1777: *of those precise objects only* for *only of those precise objects*
35 1777: *nowise* for *no way*
36 1777: *in* for *to*

other:[37] I know in fact, that it always is inferred. But if you insist, that the inference is made by a chain of reasoning, I desire you to produce that reasoning. The connection between these propositions is not intuitive. There is required a medium, which may enable the mind to draw such an inference, if indeed it be drawn by reasoning and argument. What that medium is, I must confess, passes my comprehension; and 'tis incumbent on those to produce it, who assert, that it really exists, and is the origin of all our conclusions concerning matter of fact.

17. This negative argument must certainly, in process of time, become altogether convincing, if many penetrating and able philosophers shall turn their inquiries this way; and no one be ever able to discover any connecting proposition or intermediate step, which supports the understanding in this conclusion. But as the question is yet new, every reader may not trust so far to his own penetration, as to conclude, because an argument escapes his research and[38] enquiry, that therefore it does not really exist. For this reason it may be requisite to venture upon a more difficult task; and enumerating all the branches of human knowlege, endeavor to shew, that none of them can afford such an argument.

18. All reasonings may be divided into two kinds, *viz.* demonstrative reasonings, or those[39] concerning relations of ideas, and moral[40] reasonings or those[41] concerning matter of fact and existence. That there are no demonstrative arguments in the case, seems evident; since it implies no contradiction, that the course of nature may change, and that an object seemingly like those which we have experienced, may be attended with different or contrary effects. May I not clearly and distinctly conceive, that a body falling from the clouds, and which, in all other respects, resembles snow, has yet the taste of salt or feeling of fire? Is there any more intelligible proposition than to affirm, that all the trees will florish in DECEMBER and JANUARY, and decay in MAY and JUNE? Now whatever is intelligible, and can be distinctly conceived, implies no contradiction, and can never be

---

37 For more on what Hume meant by "justly inferred" see the opening sentences of EHU 4.20 and the sentences towards the close of EHU 4.21, informed by EHU 5.15 and EHU 12.23.

38 **1777**: omits *research and*

39 **1777**: *reasoning, or that* for *reasonings, or those*

40 **1748–1750**: insert *or probable*

41 **1777**: *reasoning, or that* for *reasonings or those*

proved false by any demonstrative arguments[42] or abstract reasonings[43] *à priori.*

19. If we be, therefore, engaged by arguments to put trust in past experience, and make it the standard of our future judgment, these arguments must be probable only, or such as regard matter of fact and real existence, according to the division abovementioned. But that there are no arguments[44] of this kind, must appear, if our explication of that species of reasoning be admitted as solid and satisfactory. We have said, that all arguments concerning existence are founded on the relation of cause and effect; that our knowlege of that relation is derived entirely from experience, and that all our experimental conclusions proceed upon the supposition, that the future will be conformable to the past. To endeavor, therefore, the proof of this last supposition by probable arguments, or arguments regarding existence, must be evidently going in a circle, and taking that for granted, which is the very point in question.

20. In reality, all arguments from experience are founded on the similarity, which we discover among natural objects, and by which we are induced to expect effects similar to those, which we have found to follow from such objects. And tho' none but a fool or madman will ever pretend to dispute the authority of experience, or to reject that great guide of human life; it may surely be allowed a philosopher to have so much curiosity at least, as to examine the principle of human nature which gives this mighty authority to experience, and makes us draw advantage from that similarity, which nature has placed among different objects. From causes, which appear *similar,* we expect similar effects. This is the sum of all our experimental conclusions. Now it seems evident, that if this conclusion were formed by reason, it would be as perfect at first, and upon one instance, as after ever so long a course of experience. But the case is far otherwise. Nothing so like as eggs; yet no one, on account of this apparent[45] similarity, expects the same taste and relish in all of them.[46] 'Tis

---

42 **1777:** *argument* for *arguments*
43 **1777:** *reasoning* for *reasonings*
44 **1777:** *is no argument* for *are no arguments*
45 **1777:** *appearing* for *apparent*
46 This observation, which was particularly effective in an age when eggs were stored without refrigeration, still retains some of its force. The bare fact that one object is similar to another does not by itself lead us to suppose that it will have the same effect.

only after a long course of uniform experiments in any kind, that we attain a firm reliance and security with regard to a particular event. Now where is that process of reasoning, which from one instance draws a conclusion, so different from that which it infers from a hundred instances, that are no way[47] different from that single instance?[48] This question I propose as much for the sake of information, as with an intention of raising difficulties. I cannot find, I cannot imagine any such reasoning. But I keep my mind still open to instruction, if any one will vouchsafe to bestow it on me.

21. Should it be said, that from a number of uniform experiments, we *infer* a connection between the sensible qualities and the secret powers; this, I must confess, seems the same difficulty, couched in different terms. The question still recurs, On what process of argument this *inference* is founded? Where is the medium, the interposing ideas, which join propositions so very wide of each other? 'Tis confessed, that the color, consistence, and other sensible qualities of bread appear not, of themselves, to have any connexion with the secret powers of nourishment and support. For otherwise we could infer these secret powers from the first appearance of these sensible qualities, without the aid of experience; contrary to the sentiment of all philosophers, and contrary to plain matter of fact. Here then is our natural state of ignorance with regard to the powers and influence of all objects. How is this remedied by experience? It only shews us a number of uniform effects, resulting from certain objects, and teaches us, that those particular objects, at that particular time, were endowed with such powers and forces. When a new object, endowed with similar sensible qualities is produced, we expect similar powers and forces, and lay our account with[49] a like effect. From a body of like color and consistence with bread, we look for[50] like nourishment and support. But this surely is a step or progress of the mind, which wants to be explained. When a man says, *I have found, in all past instances, such sensible qualities, conjoined with such secret powers:* And when he says, *similar sensible qualities will always be conjoined with similar secret powers*; he is not guilty of a tautology, nor are these propositions in any respect the same. You say that the one proposition is an inference from

---

47 **1777:** *nowise* for *no way*
48 **1777:** *one* for *instance*
49 **1777:** *look for* for *lay our account with*
50 **1777:** *expect* for *look for*

another.[51] But you must confess, that the inference is not intuitive; neither is it demonstrative: Of what nature is it then? To say it is experimental is begging the question. For all inferences from experience suppose, as their foundation, that the future will resemble the past, and that similar powers will be conjoined with similar sensible qualities. If there be any suspicion, that the course of nature may change, and that the past may be no rule for the future, all experience becomes useless, and can give rise to no inference or conclusion. 'Tis impossible, therefore, that any arguments from experience can prove this resemblance of the past to the future; since all these arguments are founded on the supposition of that resemblance. Let the course of things be allowed hitherto ever so regular; that alone, without some new argument or inference, proves not, that, for the future, it will continue so. In vain do you pretend to have learnt the nature of bodies from your past experience. Their secret nature, and consequently, all their effects and influence may change, without any change in their sensible qualities. This happens sometimes, and with regard to some objects: Why may it not happen always, and with regard to all objects? What logic, what process of argument secures you against this supposition? My practice, you say, refutes my doubts. But you mistake the purport of my question. As an agent, I am quite satisfied in the point; but as a philosopher, who has some share of curiosity, I will not say scepticism, I want to learn the foundation of this inference. No reading, no enquiry has yet been able to remove my difficulty, or give me satisfaction in a matter of such vast[52] importance. Can I do better than propose the difficulty to the public, even tho', perhaps, I have small hopes of obtaining a solution? We shall at least, by this means, be sensible of our ignorance, if we do not augment our knowlege.

22. I must confess, that a man is guilty of unpardonable arrogance, who concludes, because an argument has escaped his own investigation, that therefore it does not really exist. I must also confess, that tho' all the learned, for several ages, should have employed their time[53] in fruitless search upon any subject, it may still, perhaps, be rash to conclude positively, that the subject must, therefore, pass all human comprehension. Even tho' we examine all the sources of our knowlege, and conclude them unfit

---

51 1777: *the other* for *another*
52 1777: omits *vast*
53 1777: *themselves* for *their time*

for such a subject, there may still remain a suspicion, that the enumeration is not compleat, or the examination not accurate. But with regard to the present subject, there are some considerations, which seem to remove all this accusation of arrogance or suspicion of mistake.

23. 'Tis certain, that the most ignorant and stupid peasants, nay infants, nay even brute beasts improve by experience, and learn the qualities of natural objects, by observing the effects, which result from them. When a child has felt the sensation of pain from touching the flame of a candle, he will be careful not to put his hand near any candle; but will expect a similar effect from a cause, which is similar in its sensible qualities and appearance. If you assert, therefore, that the understanding of the child is led into this conclusion by any process of argument or ratiocination, I may justly require you to produce that argument; nor have you any pretext[54] to refuse so equitable a demand. You cannot say, that the argument is abstruse, and may possibly escape your enquiry; since you confess, that it is obvious to the capacity of a mere infant. If you hesitate, therefore, a moment, or if, after reflection, you produce any intricate or profound argument, you, in a manner, give up the question, and confess, that it is not reasoning, which engages us to suppose the past resembling the future, and to expect similar effects from causes, which are, to appearance, similar. This is the proposition, which I intended to enforce in the present section. If I be right, I pretend to have made no[55] mighty discovery. And if I be wrong, I must acknowlege myself to be indeed a very backward scholar; since I cannot now discover an argument, which, it seems, was perfectly familiar to me, long before I was out of my cradle.

NOTE

g The word, Power, is here used in a loose and popular sense. The more accurate explication of it would give additional evidence to this argument. See Sect. 7.

---

54 1777: *pretence* for *pretext*
55 1777: *not to have made any* for *to have made no*

SECTION 5
SCEPTICAL SOLUTION OF THESE DOUBTS

PART I

1. The passion for philosophy, like that for religion, seems liable to this inconvenience, that, tho' it aims at the correction of our manners, and extirpation of our vices, it may only serve, by imprudent management, to foster a predominant inclination, and push the mind, with more determined resolution, towards that side, which already *draws* too much, by the byass and propensity of the natural temper. 'Tis certain, that, while we aspire to the magnanimous firmness of the philosophic sage, and endeavor to confine our pleasures altogether within our own minds, we may, at last, render our philosophy, like that of EPICTETUS, and other *Stoics*,[1] only a more refined system of self-ishness, and reason ourselves out of all virtue, as well as social enjoyment. While we study with attention the vanity of human life, and turn all our thoughts on[2] the empty and transitory nature of riches and honors, we are, perhaps, all the while flattering our natural indolence, which, hating the bustle of the world and drudgery of business, seeks a pretext[3] of reason, to give itself a full and uncontroled indulgence. There is, however, one species of philosophy, which seems little liable to this incon-venience, and that because it strikes in with no disorderly passion of the human mind, nor can mingle itself with any natural affection or propensity; and that is the ACADEMIC or

---

1 During the Hellenistic period in ancient Greece (3rd-2nd centuries BCE) three rival philosophical "schools," the Stoics, the Academics, and the Epicureans, were physically located on different premises, and led by generations of principal teachers promulgating characteristic and opposed doctrines. Philosophers in the Stoic school had a strong influence on many later Roman thinkers, including Epictetus (1st-2nd centuries CE). The Stoics were fatalists, who taught that a governing spirit has pre-ordained everything for the best and that the path to happiness lies with reconciling ourselves to the necessity of things and seeing how our own fate contributes to the greater good. They accord-ingly took virtue to consist in wisdom and resistance to passionate impulses, a feature that Hume, who based his theory of moral judg-ment on appeal to such passions as benevolence, found particularly objectionable. See "Of Moral Prejudices" in ETSS 1: 538-45.

2 1777: *towards* for *on*
3 1777: *pretence* for *pretext*

SCEPTICAL philosophy.[4] The academics talk always[5] of doubts,[6] and suspense of judgment, of danger in hasty determinations, of confining to very narrow bounds the enquiries of the understanding, and of renouncing all speculations which lie not within the limits of common life and practice. Nothing, therefore, can be more contrary than such a philosophy to the supine indolence of the mind, its rash arrogance, its lofty pretensions, and its superstitious credulity. Every passion is mortified by it, except the love of truth; and that passion never is, nor can be carried to too high a degree. 'Tis surprizing, therefore, that this philosophy, which, in almost every instance, must be harmless and innocent, should be the subject of so much groundless reproach and obloquy. But, perhaps, the very circumstance which renders it so innocent, is what chiefly exposes it to the public hatred, and resentment. By flattering no irregular passion, it gains few partizans: By opposing so many vices and follies, it raises to itself abundance of enemies, who stigmatize it as libertine, profane, and irreligious.

2. Nor need we fear, that this philosophy, while it endeavors to limit our enquiries to common life, should ever undermine the reasonings of common life, and carry its doubts so far as to destroy all action, as well as speculation. Nature will always maintain her rights, and prevail in the end over any abstract reasoning whatsoever. Tho' we should conclude, for instance, as in the foregoing section, that, in all reasonings from experience, there is a step taken by the mind, which is not supported by any argument or process of the understanding; there is no danger, that these reasonings, on which almost all knowlege depends, will ever be affected by such a discovery. If the mind be not engaged by argument to make this step, it must be induced by some other principle of equal weight and authority; and that principle will preserve its influence as long as human nature remains the same. What that principle is, may well be worth the pains of enquiry.

3. Suppose a person, tho' endowed with the strongest faculties of reason and reflection, to be brought on a sudden into this

---

4 The defense of "academic scepticism," with which this section opens, is continued in EHU 12.24-25. In sharp contrast to the Stoics, the Academics (successors to the chair in Plato's academy) sought to rehabilitate the purportedly Socratic view that we can have no certain knowledge of anything.

5 1777: *always talk* for *talk always*

6 1777: *doubt and* for *doubts, and*

world; he would, indeed, immediately observe a continual succession of objects, and one event following another; but he would not be able to discover any thing farther. He would not, at first, by any reasoning, be able to reach the idea of cause and effect; since the particular powers, by which all natural operations are performed, never appear to the senses; nor is it reasonable to conclude, merely because one event, in one instance, precedes another, that therefore the one is the cause, and[7] the other the effect. Their conjunction may be arbitrary and casual. There may be no reason to infer the existence of the[8] one from the appearance of the other. And in a word, such a person without more experience, could never employ his conjecture or reasoning concerning any matter of[9] fact, or be assured of any thing beyond what was immediately present to his memory and senses.

4. Suppose again, that he has acquired more experience, and has lived so long in the world as to have observed similar objects or events to be constantly conjoined together; what is the consequence of this experience? He immediately infers the existence of the[10] one object from the appearance of the other. Yet he has not, by all his experience, acquired any idea or knowlege of the secret power, by which the one object produces the other; nor is it, by any process of reasoning, he is engaged to draw this inference. But still he finds himself determined to draw it: And tho' he should be convinced, that his understanding has no part in the operation, he would nevertheless continue in the same course of thinking. There is some other principle, which determines him to form such a conclusion.

5. This principle is CUSTOM or HABIT. For wherever the repetition of any particular act or operation produces a propensity to renew the same act or operation, without being impelled by any reasoning or process of the understanding; we always say, that this propensity is the effect of *Custom*. By employing that word, we pretend not to have given the ultimate reason of such a propensity.[11] We only point out a principle of human nature, which is universally acknowleged, and which is well known by its effects. Perhaps, we can push our enquiries no farther, or pretend

---

7 1777: omits *and*

8 1777: omits *the*

9 Reading, with 1777, *of* for *or*

10 1777: omits *the*

11 The cause of our being creatures of habit is not one we can discover. But see EHU 5.21-22.

to give the cause of this cause; but must rest contented with it as the ultimate principle, which we can assign of all our conclusions from experience. 'Tis sufficient satisfaction, that we can go so far; without repining at the narrowness of our faculties, because they will carry us no farther. And 'tis certain we here advance a very intelligible proposition at least, if not a true one, when we assert, that, after the constant conjunction of two objects, heat and flame, for instance, weight and solidity, we are determined by custom alone to expect the one from the appearance of the other. This hypothesis seems even the only one, which explains the difficulty, why we draw, from a thousand instances, an inference, which we are not able to draw from one instance, that is, in no respect, different from them. Reason is incapable of any such variation. The conclusions, which it draws from considering one circle, are the same which it would form upon surveying all the circles in the universe. But no man, having seen only one body move after being impelled by another, could infer, that every other body will move after a like impulse. All inferences from experience, therefore, are effects of custom, not of reasoning.[h]

6. Custom, then, is the great guide of human life. 'Tis that principle alone, which renders our experience useful to us, and makes us expect for the future, a similar train of events with those which have appeared in the past. Without the influence of custom, we should be entirely ignorant of every matter of fact, beyond what is immediately present to the memory and senses. We should never know how to adjust means to ends, or to employ our natural powers in the production of any effect. There would be an end at once of all action, as well as of the chief part of speculation.

7. But here it may be proper to remark, that tho' our conclusions from experience carry us beyond our memory and senses, and assure us of matters of fact, which happened in the most distant places and most remote ages; yet some fact must always be present to the senses or memory, from which we may first proceed in drawing these conclusions. A man, who should find in a desert country the remains of pompous buildings, would conclude, that the country had, in antient times, been cultivated by civilized inhabitants; but did nothing of this nature occur to him, he could never form such an inference. We learn the events of former ages from history; but then we must peruse the volumes, in which this instruction is contained, and thence carry up our inferences from one testimony to another, till we arrive at the eye-witnesses and spectators of these distant events. In a word, if we

proceed not upon some fact, present to the memory or senses, our reasonings would be merely hypothetical; and however the particular links might be connected with each other, the whole chain of inferences would have nothing to support it, nor could we ever, by its means, arrive at the knowlege of any real existence. If I ask, why you believe any particular matter of fact, which you relate, you must tell me some reason; and this reason will be some other fact, connected with it: But as you cannot proceed after this manner, *in infinitum*, you must at last terminate in some fact, which is present to your memory or senses; or must allow, that your belief is entirely without foundation.

8. What then is the conclusion of the whole matter? A simple one; tho' it must be confessed, pretty remote from the common theories of philosophy. All belief of matter of fact or real existence is derived merely from some object, present to the memory or senses, and a customary conjunction betwixt that and any[12] other object. Or in other words; having found, in many instances, that any two kinds of objects, flame and heat, snow and cold, have always been conjoined together; if flame or snow be presented anew to our[13] senses; the mind is carried by custom to expect heat or cold, and to *believe*, that such a quality does exist, and will discover itself upon a nearer approach. This belief is the necessary result of placing the mind in such circumstances. 'Tis an operation of the soul, when we are so situated, as unavoidable as to feel the passion of love, when we receive benefits, or hatred, when we meet with injuries. All these operations are a species of natural instincts, which no reasoning or process of the thought and understanding is able, either to produce, or to prevent.

9. At this point, it would be very allowable for us to stop our philosophical researches. In most questions, we can never make a single step farther; and in all questions, we must terminate here at last, after our most restless and curious enquiries. But still our curiosity will be pardonable, perhaps commendable, if it carry us on to still farther researches, and make us examine more accurately the nature of this *belief*, and of the *customary conjunction*, whence it is derived. By this means we may meet[14] some explications and analogies, that will give satisfaction; at least to such as love the abstract sciences, and can be entertained with speculations, which, however accurate, may still retain a degree of

12 **1777:** *some* for *any*
13 **1777:** *the* for *our*
14 **1777:** inserts *with*

doubt and uncertainty. As to readers of a different taste; the remaining part of this section is not calculated for them, and the following enquiries may well be understood, tho' it be neglected.

PART II

10. There is nothing[15] more free than the imagination of man; and tho' it cannot exceed that original stock of ideas, which is[16] furnished by the internal and external senses, it has unlimited power of mixing, compounding, separating, and dividing these ideas, to[17] all the varieties of fiction and vision. It can feign a train of events, with all the appearance of reality, ascribe to them a particular time and place, conceive them as existent, and paint them out to itself with every circumstance, that belongs to any historical fact, which it believes with the greatest certainty. Wherein, therefore, consists the difference betwixt such a fiction and belief? It lies not merely in any peculiar idea, which is annexed to such a conception, as commands our assent, and which is wanting to every known fiction. For as the mind has authority over all its ideas, it could voluntarily annex this particular idea to any fiction, and consequently be able to believe whatever it pleases; contrary to what we find by daily experience. We can, in our conception, join the head of a man to the body of a horse; but it is not in our power to believe, that such an animal has ever really existed.

11. It follows, therefore, that the difference betwixt *fiction* and *belief* lies in some sentiment or feeling, which is annexed to the latter, not to the former, and which depends not on the will, nor can be commanded at pleasure.[18] It must be excited by nature, like all other sentiments; and must arise from the particular situation, in which the mind is placed at any particular juncture. Whenever any object is presented to the memory or senses, it immediately, by the force of custom, carries the imagination to conceive that object, which is usually conjoined to it; and this conception is attended with a feeling or sentiment, different from the loose reveries of the fancy. In this consists the whole nature of belief. For as there is no matter of fact which we believe so firmly, that we cannot conceive the contrary, there would be no difference betwixt the conception assented to, and that which is

---

15 1777: *Nothing is* for *There is nothing*
16 1777: omits *which is*
17 1777: *in* for *to*
18 Compare Ax 4.

rejected, were it not for some sentiment, which distinguishes the one from the other. If I see a billiard-ball moving towards another, on a smooth table, I can easily conceive it to stop upon contact. This conception implies no contradiction; but still it feels very differently from that conception, by which I represent to myself the impulse, and the communication of motion from one ball to another.

12. Were we to attempt a *definition* of this sentiment, we should, perhaps, find it a very difficult, if not an impossible task; in the same manner as if we should endeavor to define the feeling of cold or passion of anger, to a creature who never had an[19] experience of these sentiments. BELIEF is the true and proper name of this feeling; and no one is ever at a loss to know the meaning of that term; because every man is every moment conscious of the sentiment, represented by it. It may not, however, be improper to attempt a *description* of this sentiment; in hopes we may, by that means, arrive at some analogies, which may afford a more perfect explication of it. I say then, that belief is nothing but a more vivid, lively, forcible, firm, steady conception of an object, than what the imagination alone is ever able to attain. This variety of terms, which may seem so unphilosophical, is intended only to express that act of the mind, which renders realities, or what is taken for such, more present to us than fictions, causes them to weigh more in the thought, and gives them a superior influence on the passions and imagination. Provided we agree about the thing, 'tis needless to dispute about the terms. The imagination has the command over all its ideas, and can join and mix and vary them, in all the ways possible. It may conceive fictitious objects with all the circumstances of place and time. It may set them, in a manner, before our eyes, in their true colors, just as they might have existed. But as it is impossible, that that[20] faculty of imagination can ever, of itself, reach belief, 'tis evident, that belief consists not in the peculiar nature or order of ideas, but in the *manner* of their conception, and in their *feeling* to the mind. I confess, that 'tis impossible perfectly to explain this feeling or manner of conception. We may make use of words, which express something near it. But its true and proper name, as we observed before, is *belief*; which is a term, that every one sufficiently understands in common life. And in philosophy, we can go no farther than assert, that *belief* is something felt by the mind, which distin-

---

19 1777: *any* for *an*
20 1777: *this* for *that*

guishes the ideas of the judgment from the fictions of the imagination. It gives them more force[21] and influence; makes them appear of greater importance; inforces them in the mind; and renders them the governing principle of all[22] our actions. I hear at present, for instance, a person's voice, with whom I am acquainted; and the sound comes as from the next room. This impression of my senses immediately conveys my thought to the person, together with all the surrounding objects. I paint them out to myself as existing at present, with the same qualities and relations, of which I formerly knew them possest. These ideas take faster hold of my mind, than ideas of an inchanted castle. They are very different to the feeling, and have a much greater influence of every kind, either to give pleasure or pain, joy or sorrow.

13. Let us, then, take in the whole compass of this doctrine, and allow, that the sentiment of belief is nothing but a conception of an object[23] more intense and steady than what attends the mere fictions of the imagination, and that this *manner* of conception arises from a customary conjunction of the object with something present to the memory or senses: I believe that it will not be difficult, upon these suppositions, to find other operations of the mind analogous to it, and to trace up these phænomena to principles still more general.

14. We have already observed, that nature has established connexions among particular ideas, and that no sooner one idea occurs to our thoughts than it introduces its correlative, and carries our attention towards it, by a gentle and insensible movement. These principles of connexion or association we have reduced to three, *viz. Resemblance, Contiguity,* and *Causation;* which are the only bonds, that unite our thoughts together, and beget that regular train of reflection or discourse, which, in a greater or less degree, takes place among all mankind. Now here arises a question, on which the solution of the present difficulty will depend.[24] Does it happen, in all these relations, that, when one of the objects is presented to the senses or memory, the mind

---

21 1777: *weight* for *force*

22 1777: omits *all.*

23 1777: omits *of an object*

24 The "present difficulty" is the question why we should accept the hypothesis of EHU 5.13, that belief arises from a customary conjunction of the believed object with some object present in current sense experience or memory.

is not only carried to the conception of the correlative, but reaches a steadier and stronger conception of it than what otherwise it would have been able to attain? This seems to be the case with that belief, which arises from the relation of cause and effect. And if the case be the same with the other relations or principles of association, we may establish this[25] as a general law, which takes place in all the operations of the mind.

15. We may, therefore, observe, as the first experiment to our present purpose, that, upon the appearance of the picture of an absent friend, our idea of him is evidently enlivened by the *resemblance*, and that every passion, which that idea occasions, whether of joy or sorrow, acquires new force and vigor. In producing this effect, there concur both a relation and a present impression. Where the picture bears him no resemblance, or[26] at least was not intended for him, it never so much as conveys our thought to him: And where it is absent, as well as the person; tho' the mind may pass from the thought of the one to that of the other; it feels its idea to be rather weakened than enlivened by that transition. We take a pleasure in viewing the picture of a friend, when 'tis set before us; but when 'tis removed, rather chuse to consider him directly, than by reflection in an image, which is equally distant and obscure.

16. The ceremonies of the ROMAN CATHOLIC religion may be considered as experiments[27] of the same nature. The devotees of that[28] superstition usually plead in excuse of[29] the mummeries,[30] with which they are upbraided, that they feel the good effect of those external motions, and postures, and actions, in enlivening their devotion and quickening their fervor, which otherwise would decay, if directed entirely to distant and immaterial objects. We shadow out the objects of our faith, say they, in sensible types and images, and render them more present to us by the immediate presence of these types, than 'tis possible for us to do, merely by an intellectual view and contemplation. Sensible objects have always a greater influence on the fancy than any

---

25 1777: *this may be established* for *we may establish this*

26 1777: omits *or*

27 1777: *instances* for *experiments*

28 **1748-1750:** insert *strange*

29 1777: *for* for *of*

30 This term was originally used to refer to a performance by masked or hooded actors communicating by means of gestures. It was commonly used by Protestants to denigrate Catholic ceremonies, which they took to be extravagant and meaningless.

other; and this influence they readily convey to those ideas, to which they are related, and which they resemble. I shall only infer from these practices, and this reasoning, that the effect of resemblance in enlivening the ideas is very common; and as in every case a resemblance and a present impression must concur, we are abundantly supplied with experiments to prove the reality of the foregoing principle.

17. We may add force to these experiments by others of a different kind, in considering the effects of *contiguity* as well as of *resemblance*. 'Tis certain that distance diminishes the force of every idea, and that upon our approach to any object; tho' it does not discover itself to our senses; it operates upon the mind with an influence, which imitates an immediate impression. The thinking on any object readily transports the mind to what is contiguous; but 'tis only the actual presence of an object, that transports it with a superior vivacity. When I am a few miles from home, whatever relates to it touches me more nearly than when I am two hundred leagues distant; tho' even at that distance the reflecting on any thing in the neighborhood of my friends or family naturally produces an idea of them. But as in this latter case, both the objects of the mind are ideas; notwithstanding there is an easy transition betwixt them; that transition alone is not able to give a superior vivacity to any of the ideas, for want of some immediate impression.[i]

18. No one can doubt but causation has the same influence as the other two relations of resemblance and contiguity.[31] Superstitious people are fond of the relics of saints and holy men, for the same reason, that they seek after types or images, in order to enliven their devotion, and give them a more intimate and strong conception of those exemplary lives, which they desire to imitate. Now 'tis evident, that one of the best relics, which a devotee could procure, would be the handywork of a saint; and if his cloaths and furniture are ever to be considered in this light, 'tis because they were once at his disposal, and were moved and affected by him; in which respect they are to be considered as imperfect effects, and as connected with him by a shorter chain

---

31 Hume was not here invoking the phenomenon he was trying to explain. The influence of "causation" discussed in this paragraph is the influence of the causal relation in strengthening beliefs that have already been formed, not its influence in producing belief.

of consequences than any of those, by which we learn the reality of his existence.

19. Suppose, that the son of a friend, who had been long dead or absent were presented to us; 'tis evident, that this object would instantly revive its correlative idea, and recal to our thoughts all past intimacies and familiarities in more lively colors than they would otherwise have appeared to us. This is another phænomenon, which seems to prove the principle above-mentioned.

20. We may observe, that in these phænomena the belief of the correlative object is always pre-supposed; without which the relation could have no effect in enlivening the idea.[32] The influence of the picture supposes, that we *believe* our friend to have once existed. Contiguity to home can never excite our ideas of home, unless we *believe* that it really exists. Now I assert, that this belief, where it reaches beyond the memory or senses, is of a similar nature, and arises from similar causes, with the transition of thought and vivacity of conception here explained. When I throw a piece of dry wood into a fire, my mind is immediately carried to conceive, that it augments, not extinguishes the flame. This transition of thought from the cause to the effect proceeds not from reason. It derives its origin altogether from custom and experience. And as it first begins from an object, present to the senses, it renders the idea or conception of flame more strong and lively than any loose, floating reverie of the imagination. That idea arises immediately. The thought moves instantly towards it, and conveys to it all that force of conception, which is derived from the impression present to the senses. When a sword is levelled at my breast, does not the idea of wound and pain strike me more strongly, than when a glass of wine is presented to me, even tho' by accident this idea should occur after the appearance of the latter object? But what is there in this whole matter to cause such a strong conception, except only a present object and[33] customary transition to the idea of another object, which we have been accustomed to conjoin with the former? This is the whole operation of the mind in all our conclusions concerning matter of fact and existence; and 'tis a satisfaction to find some analogies, by which it may be explained. The transition from a present object does in all cases give strength and solidity to the related idea.

---

32 **1777**: omits *in enlivening the idea*
33 **1777**: inserts *a*

21. Here[34] is a kind of pre-established harmony betwixt the course of nature and the succession of our ideas; and tho' the powers and forces, by which the former is governed, be wholly unknown to us; yet our thoughts and conceptions have still, we find, gone on in the same train with the other works of nature. Custom is that admirable[35] principle, by which this correspondence has been effected; so necessary to the subsistence of our species, and the regulation of our conduct, in every circumstance and occurrence of human life. Had not the presence of an object instantly excited the idea of those objects, commonly conjoined with it, all our knowlege must have been limited to the narrow sphere of our memory and senses; and we should never have been able to adjust means to ends, nor[36] employ our natural powers, either to the producing of good, or avoiding of evil. Those, who delight in the discovery and contemplation of *final causes*, have here ample subject to employ their wonder and admiration.

22. I shall add, for a further confirmation of the foregoing theory, that as this operation of the mind, by which we infer like effects from like causes, and *vice versa*, is so essential to the subsistence of all human creatures, it is not probable that it could be trusted to the fallacious deductions of our reason, which is slow in its operations; appears not, in any degree, during the first years of infancy; and at best is, in every age and period of human life, extremely liable to error and mistake. 'Tis more conformable to the ordinary wisdom of nature to secure so necessary an act of the mind, by some instinct or mechanical tendency, which may be infallible in its operations, may discover itself at the first appearance of life and thought, and may be independent of all the labored deductions of the understanding. As nature has taught us the use of our limbs, without giving us the knowlege of the muscles and nerves, by which they are actuated; so has she implanted in us an instinct, which carries forward the thought in a correspondent course to that which she has established among external objects; tho' we are ignorant of those powers and forces, on which this regular course and succession of objects totally depends.

---

34 1777: inserts , *then,*
35 1777: omits *admirable*
36 1777: *or* for *nor*

ʰ Nothing is more usual than for writers even on *moral, political,* or *physical* subjects, to distinguish betwixt *reason* and *experience,* and to suppose, that these species of argumentation are entirely different from each other. The former are taken for the mere result of our intellectual faculties, which, by considering *à priori* the nature of things, and examining the effects, that must follow from their operation, establish particular principles of science and philosophy. The latter are supposed to be derived entirely from sense and observation, by which we learn what has actually resulted from the operation of particular objects, and are thence able to infer, what will, for the future, result from them. Thus, for instance, the limitations and restraints of civil government, and a legal constitution may be defended, either from *reason,* which, reflecting on the great frailty and corruption of human nature, teaches, that no man can safely be trusted with unlimited authority; or from *experience* and history, which inform us of the enormous abuses, that ambition, in every age and country, has been found to make of so imprudent a confidence.

The same distinction betwixt reason and experience is maintained in all our deliberations concerning the conduct of life; while the experienced statesman, general, physician or merchant is trusted and followed; and the unpractised novice, with whatever natural talents endowed, neglected and despised. Tho' it be allowed, that reason may form very plausible conjectures with regard to the consequences of such a particular conduct in such particular circumstances; 'tis still supposed imperfect, without the assistance of experience, which is alone able to give stability and certainty to the maxims, derived from study and reflection.

But notwithstanding that this distinction be thus universally received, both in the active and[37] speculative scenes of life, I shall not scruple to pronounce, that it is, at bottom, erroneous, or[38] at least, superficial.

If we examine those arguments, which, in any of the sciences abovementioned, are supposed to be the mere effects of reasoning and reflection, they will all[39] be found to terminate, at last, in some general principle or conclusion, for which we can assign no reason but observation and experience. The only difference betwixt them and those maxims, which are vulgarly esteemed the result of pure experience, is, that the former cannot be established without some process of thought, and some reflection on what we have observed, in order to distinguish its circumstances, and trace its consequences: Whereas in

---

37 **1777**: omits *and*
38 **1777**: omits *or*
39 **1777**: omits *all*

the latter, the experienced event is exactly and fully similar to that which we infer as the result of any particular situation. The history of a TIBERIUS or a NERO[40] makes us dread a like tyranny were our monarchs freed from the restraints of laws and senates: But the observation of any fraud or cruelty in private life is sufficient, with the aid of a little thought, to give us the same apprehension; while it serves as an instance of the general corruption of human nature, and shews us the danger which we must incur by reposing an entire confidence in mankind. In both cases, 'tis experience which is ultimately the foundation of our inference and conclusion.

There is no man so young and unexperienced, as not to have formed from observation, many general and just maxims concerning human affairs and the conduct of life; but it must be confessed, that, when a man comes to put these in practice, he will be extremely liable to error, till time and farther experience, both enlarge these maxims, and teach him their proper use and application. In every situation or incident, there are many particular and seemingly minute circumstances, which the man of greatest talents is, at first, apt to overlook, tho' on them the justness of his conclusions, and consequently the prudence of his conduct, entirely depend. Not to mention, that, to a young beginner, the general observations and maxims occur not always on the proper occasions, nor can be immediately applied with due calmness and distinction. The truth is, an unexperienced reasoner could be no reasoner at all, were he absolutely unexperienced; and when we assign that character to any one, we mean it only in a comparative sense, and suppose him possessed of experience in a smaller and more imperfect degree.

i "Naturane nobis, inquit, datum dicam, an errore quodam, ut, cum ea loca videamus,[41] in quibus memoria dignos viros acceperimus multum esse versatos, magis moveamur, quam siquando eorum ipsorum aut facta audiamus aut scriptum aliquod legamus? Velut ego nunc moveor. Venit enim mihi PLATONIS in mentem, quem accepimus primum hîc disputare solitum: Cujus etiam illi hortuli propinqui non memoriam solum mihi afferunt, sed ipsum videntur in conspectu meo hîc ponere. Hic SPEUSIPPUS, hîc XENOCRATES, hic ejus auditor POLEMO; cujus ipsa illa sessio suit, quam videamus. Equidem etiam curiam nostram, HOSTILIAM dico, non hanc novam, quæ mihi minor esse videtur postquam est major, solebam intuens, SCIPIONEM,

---

40 The Roman emperors Tiberius (42 BCE-37 CE) and Nero (37-68) were stock eighteenth-century examples of tyrants, much as Hitler and Stalin are today.

41 **Beauchamp**: *videmus* for *videamus*

CATONEM, LÆLIUM, nostrum vero in primis avum cogitare. Tanta vis admonitionis est[42] in locis; ut non sine causa ex his memoræ deducta[43] sit disciplina."[44] CICERO *de Finibus*. Lib. 5.[45]

---

42 **Beauchamp**: *inest* for *est*

43 **Beauchamp**: *ducta* for *deducta*

44 "... shall I attribute it to *Nature*, or to *Prejudice*, That when we behold any of the Places which have been frequented by Personages worthy of Renown, it makes a stronger Impression upon us, than the *hearing of their Actions*, or *reading their Writings*. I feel it now in my self; My Mind is filled with *Plato*, whom we understand used first to dispute in this Place; Those little Gardens hard by, not only bring the Idea of him to my *Memory*, but set him in Person before my *Eyes*. Here walks *Speusippus*, there *Xenocrates*, and here his Hearer *Polemo*; upon that very Spot he sate. And indeed when I used to look round our *Senate House*, I mean that of *Hostilius*, not the New One, which to me seems to be lessen'd by it's Enlargement, I had *Scipio*, *Cato*, *Laelius*, but, above all, my Grandfather before my Eyes. Such reverential Respect there is in *Places*, that it is not without some Reason the Art of Memory is drawn from them." William Guthrie (trans.), *The morals of Cicero* (London: T. Waller, 1744). Gale document CW3317450343.

45 Marcus Tullius Cicero, *De finibus bonorum et malorum* 5.1.2.

SECTION 6
OF PROBABILITY[k]

1. Tho' there be no such thing as *Chance* in the world; our ignorance of the real cause of any event has the same influence on the understanding, and begets a like species of belief or opinion.

2. There is certainly a probability, which arises from a superiority of chances on any side; and according as this superiority encreases, and surpasses the opposite chances, the probability receives a proportionable encrease, and begets still a higher degree of belief or assent to that side, in which we discover the superiority. If a dye were marked with one figure or number of spots on four sides, and with another figure or number of spots on the two remaining sides, it would be more probable, that the former should[1] turn up than the latter; tho' if it had a thousand sides marked in the same manner, and only one side different, the probability would be much higher, and our belief or expectation of the event more steady and secure. This process of the thought or reasoning may seem trivial and obvious; but to those, who consider it more narrowly, it may, perhaps, afford matter for very[2] curious speculations.[3]

3. It seems evident, that when the mind looks forward to discover the event, which may result from the throw of such a dye, it considers the turning up of each particular side as alike probable; and this is the very nature of chance, to render all the particular events, comprehended in it, entirely equal. But finding a greater number of sides concur in the one event than in the other, the mind is carried more frequently to that event, and meets it oftener, in revolving the various possibilities or chances, on which the ultimate result depends. This concurrence of several views in one particular event begets immediately, by an inexplicable contrivance of nature, the sentiment of belief, and gives that event the advantage over its antagonist, which is supported by a smaller number of views, and recurs less frequently to the mind. If we allow, that belief is nothing but a firmer and stronger conception of an object than what attends the mere fictions of the imagination, this operation may, perhaps, in some measure, be accounted for. The concurrence of these several views or glimpses imprints its[4] idea more strongly on the imagination; gives it superior force

---

1 1777: *would* for *should*
2 1777: omits *very*
3 1777: *speculation* for *speculations*
4 1777: *the* for *its*

and vigor; renders its influence on the passions and affections more sensible; and in a word, begets that reliance or security, which constitutes the nature of belief and opinion.

4. The case is the same with the probability of causes, as with that of chance. There are some causes, which are entirely uniform and constant in producing a particular effect; and no instance has ever yet been found of any failure or irregularity in their operation. Fire has always burnt, and water suffocated every human creature: The production of motion by impulse and gravity is an universal law, which has hitherto admitted of no exception. But there are other causes which have been found more irregular and uncertain; nor has rhubarb proved always[5] a purge, or opium a soporific to every one, who has taken these medicines. 'Tis true, when any cause fails of producing its usual effect, philosophers ascribe not this to any irregularity in nature; but suppose, that some secret causes, in the particular structure of parts, have prevented the operation.[6] Our reasonings, however, and conclusions concerning the event are the same as if this principle had no place. Being determined by custom to transfer the past to the future, in all our inferences; where the past has been entirely regular and uniform, we expect the event with the greatest assurance, and leave no room for any contrary supposition. But where different effects have been found to follow from causes, which are *to appearance* exactly similar, all these various effects must occur to the mind in transfering the past to the future, and enter into our consideration, when we determine the probability of the event. Tho' we give the preference to that which has been found most usual, and believe that this effect will exist, we must not overlook the other effects, but must give[7] each of them a particular weight and authority, in proportion as we have found it to be more or less frequent. 'Tis more probable, in[8] every place[9] of EUROPE, that there will be frost sometime in JANUARY, than that the weather will continue open thro' out that whole month; tho' this probability varies according to the different climates, and approaches to a certainty in the more northern kingdoms. Here then it seems evident, that when we transfer the past to the future, in order to determine the effect, which will result from any

---

5 1777: *always proved* for *proved always*
6 See EHU 8.13-14.
7 1777: *assign to* for *give*
8 1777: inserts *almost*
9 1777: *country* for *place*

cause, we transfer all the different events, in the same proportion as they have appeared in the past, and conceive one to have existed a hundred times, for instance, another ten times, and another once. As a great number of views do here concur in one event, they fortify and confirm it to the imagination, beget that sentiment which we call *belief*, and give it[10] the preference above its antagonist,[11] which is not supported by an equal number of experiments, and occurs[12] not so frequently to the thought in transferring the past to the future.[13] Let any one try to account for this operation of the mind upon any of the received systems of philosophy, and he will be sensible of the difficulty. For my part, I shall think it sufficient, if the present hints excite the curiosity of philosophers, and make them sensible how extremely[14] defective all common theories are, in treating of such curious and such sublime subjects.

NOTE

[k] Mr. LOCKE[15] divides all arguments into demonstrative and probable. In this view, we must say, that 'tis only probable all men must die, or that the sun will rise to-morrow. But to conform our language more to common use, we should[16] divide arguments into *demonstrations*, *proofs*, and *probabilities*. By proofs meaning such arguments from experience as leave no room for doubt or opposition.

---

10 **1777:** *its object* for *it*
11 **1777:** *the contrary event* for *its antagonist*
12 **1777:** *recurs* for *occurs*
13 This is discussed in more detail at EHU 10.4.
14 **1777:** omits *extremely*
15 See Section 1, note 16.
16 **1777:** *ought to* for *should*

SECTION 7
OF THE IDEA OF[1] NECESSARY CONNEXION

PART I

1. The great advantage of the mathematical sciences above the moral consists in this, that the ideas of the former, being sensible, are always clear and determinate, the smallest distinction between them is immediately perceptible, and the same terms are still expressive of the same ideas, without ambiguity or variation. An oval is never mistaken for a circle, nor an hyperbola for an ellipsis. The isosceles and scalenum are distinguished by boundaries more exact than vice and virtue, right and wrong. If any term be defined in geometry, the mind readily, of itself, substitutes, on all occasions, the definition for the term defined: Or even when no definition is employed, the object itself may be presented to the senses, and by that means be steadily and clearly apprehended. But the finer sentiments of the mind, the operations of the understanding, the various agitations of the passions, tho' really in themselves distinct, easily escape us, when surveyed by reflection; nor is it in our power to recall the original object, as often as we have occasion to contemplate it. Ambiguity, by this means, is gradually introduced into our reasonings: Similar objects are readily taken to be the same: And the conclusion becomes, at last, very wide of the premises.

2. One may safely, however, affirm, that, if we consider these sciences in a proper light, their advantages and disadvantages very[2] nearly compensate each other, and reduce both of them to a state of equality. If the mind with greater facility retains the ideas of geometry clear and determinate, it must carry on a much longer and more intricate chain of reasoning, and compare ideas much wider of each other, in order to reach the abstruser truths of that science. And if moral ideas are apt, without extreme care, to fall into obscurity and confusion, the inferences are always much shorter in these disquisitions, and the intermediate steps, which lead to the conclusion, much fewer than in the sciences, which treat of quantity and number. In reality, there is scarce[3] a proposition of[4] EUCLID[5] so simple as not to consist of more parts,

---

1 **1748-1750**: _Of the_ IDEA _of_ POWER _or_ _necessary_ CONNEXION for _OF THE IDEA OF NECESSARY CONNEXION_

2 1777: omits _very_

3 1777: _scarcely_ for _scarce_

4 1777: _in_ for _of_

5 See Section 4, note 4.

than are to be found in any moral reasoning, which runs not into chimera and conceit. Where we trace the principles of the human mind thro' a few steps, we may be very well satisfied with our progress; considering how soon nature throws a bar to all our enquiries concerning causes, and reduces us to an acknowlege-ment of our ignorance. The chief obstacle, therefore, to our improvement in the moral or metaphysical sciences is the obscu-rity of the ideas, and ambiguity of the terms. The principal diffi-culty in the mathematics is the length of inferences and compass of thought, requisite to the forming[6] any conclusion. And perhaps, our progress in natural philosophy is chiefly retarded by the want of proper experiments and phænomena, which often are[7] discovered by chance, and cannot always be found, when requisite, even by the most diligent and prudent enquiry. As moral philosophy seems hitherto to have received less improve-ments[8] than either geometry or physics, we may conclude, that, if there be any difference in this respect among these sciences, the difficulties, which obstruct the progress of the former, require superior care and capacity to be surmounted.

3.   There are no ideas, which occur in metaphysics, more obscure and uncertain, than those of *power, force, energy*, or *neces-sary connexion*, of which it is every moment necessary for us to treat in all our disquisitions. We shall, therefore, endeavor, in this section, to fix, if possible, the precise meaning of these terms, and thereby remove some part of that obscurity, which is so much complained of in this species of philosophy.

4.   It seems a proposition, which will not admit of much dispute, that all our ideas are nothing but copies of our impres-sions, or in other words, that 'tis impossible for us to *think* of any thing, which we have not antecedently *felt*, either by our external or internal senses. I have endeavored[1] to explain and prove this proposition, and have expressed my hopes, that, by a proper application of it, men may reach a greater clearness and precision in philosophical reasonings, than what they have hitherto been ever[9] able to attain. Complex ideas may, perhaps, be well known by definition, which is nothing but an enumeration of those parts or simple ideas, that compose them. But when we have pushed up definitions to the most simple ideas, and find still some ambi-

---

6 **1777**: inserts *of*
7 **1777**: *are often* for *often are*
8 **1777**: *improvement* for *improvements*
9 **1777**: omits *ever*

guity and obscurity; what resource are we then possessed of? By what invention can we throw light upon these ideas, and render them altogether precise and determinate to our intellectual view? Produce the impressions or original sentiments, from which the ideas are copied. These impressions are all strong and sensible. They admit not of ambiguity. They are not only placed in a full light themselves, but may throw light on their correspondent ideas, which lie in obscurity. And by this means, we may, perhaps, attain a new microscope or species of optics, by which, in the moral sciences, the most minute, and most simple ideas may be so enlarged as to fall readily under our apprehension, and be equally known with the grossest and most sensible ideas, which[10] can be the object of our enquiry.

5. To be fully acquainted therefore, with the idea of power or necessary connexion, let us examine its impression; and in order to find the impression with greater certainty, let us search for it in all the sources, from which it may possibly be derived.

6. When we look about us towards external objects, and consider the operation of causes, we are never able, in a single instance, to discover any power or necessary connexion; any quality, which binds the effect to the cause, and renders the one an infallible consequence of the other. We only find, that the one does actually, in fact, follow the other. The impulse of one billiard-ball is attended with motion in the second. This is the whole, that appears to the *outward* senses. The mind feels no sentiment or *inward* impression from this succession of objects: Consequently, there is not, in any single, particular instance of cause and effect, any thing which can suggest the idea of power or necessary connexion.

7. From the first appearance of an object, we never can conjecture what effect will result from it. But were the power or energy of any cause discoverable by the mind, we could foresee the effect, even without experience, and might, at first, pronounce with certainty concerning it, by the mere dint of thought and reasoning.

8. In reality, there is no part of matter, that does ever, by its sensible qualities, discover any power or energy, or give us ground to imagine, that it could produce any thing, or be followed by any other object, which we could denominate its effect. Solidity, extension, motion; these qualities are all compleat in themselves; and never point out any other event, which may result from them. The scenes of the universe are continually shifting, and one object

10 **1777:** *that* for *which*

follows another in an uninterrupted succession; but the power or force, which actuates the whole machine, is entirely concealed from us, and never discovers itself in any of the sensible qualities of body. We know, that, in fact, heat is a constant attendant of flame;[11] but what is the connexion between them, we have no room so much as to conjecture or imagine. 'Tis impossible, therefore, that the idea of power can be derived from the contemplation of bodies, in single instances of their operation; because no bodies ever discover any power, which can be the original of this idea.[m]

9. Since, therefore, external objects, as they appear to the senses, give us no idea of power or necessary connexion, by their operations[12] in particular instances, let us see, whether this idea be derived from reflection on the operations of our own minds, and be copied from any internal impression. It may be said, that we are every moment conscious of power in our own minds;[13] while we feel, that, by the simple command of our will, we can move the organs of our body, or direct the faculties of our minds, in their operation.[14] An act of volition produces motion in our limbs, or raises a new idea in our imagination. This influence of the will we know by consciousness. Hence we acquire the idea of power or energy; and are certain, that we ourselves and all other intelligent beings are possessed of power. This idea, then, is[15] an idea of reflection, since it arises from reflecting on the operations of our own minds,[16] and on the command, which is exercised by will, both over the organs of the body and faculties of the mind.[17]

10. We shall proceed to examine this pretension; and first with regard to the influence of volition over the organs of the body. This influence, we may observe,[18,19] is a fact, which, like all other

---

11 Reading, with **1777**, a semicolon for a question mark

12 **1777**: *operation* for *operations*

13 **1777**: *internal power* for *power in our own minds*

14 **1777**: *mind* for *minds, in their operation*

15 **1748-1750**: *The Operations and mutual Influence of Bodies are, perhaps, sufficient to prove, that they also are possess'd of it. However this may be, the Idea of Power must certainly be allow'd to be* for *This idea, then, is*

16 **1777**: *mind* for *minds*

17 **1777**: *soul* for *mind*

18 **1748**: *shall endeavour to avoid, as far as we are able, all Jargon and Confusion, in treating of such subtile and such profound Subjects.* [New Paragraph] *I assert, then in the first Place, that the Influence of Volition over the Organs of the Body* for *first with regard to the influence of volition over the organs of the body. This influence, we may observe,*

19 **1750**: omits *in the first Place* from the passage as it was in **1748**

natural operations,[20] can be known only by experience, and can never be foreseen from any apparent energy or power in the cause, which connects it with the effect, and renders the one an infallible consequence of the other. The motion of our body follows upon the command of our will. Of this we are every moment conscious: But the means, by which this is effected; the energy, by which the will performs so extraordinary an operation; of this we are so far from being immediately conscious, that it must for ever escape our most diligent enquiry.

11. For *first*; is there any principle in all nature more mysterious than the union of soul with body; by which a supposed spiritual substance acquires such an influence over a material one, that the most refined thought is able to actuate the grossest matter? Were we empowered, by a secret wish, to remove mountains, or control the planets in their orbit; this extensive authority would not be more extraordinary, nor more beyond our comprehension. But if by consciousness we perceived any power or energy in the will, we must know this power; we must know its connexion with the effect; we must know the secret union of soul and body, and the nature of both these substances; by which the one is able to operate, in so many instances, upon the other.

12. *Secondly*, We are not able to move all the organs of the body with a like authority; tho' we cannot assign any other[21] reason, besides experience, for so remarkable a difference betwixt one and the other. Why has the will an influence over the tongue and fingers, and[22] not over the heart or liver? This question would never embarrass us, were we conscious of a power in the former case, and[23] not in the latter. We should, then, perceive, independent of experience, why the authority of will over the organs of the body is circumscribed within such particular limits. Being in that case fully acquainted with the power or force, by which it operates, we should also know, why its influence reaches precisely to such boundaries, and no farther.

13. A man, struck suddenly[24] with a palsy in the leg or arm, or who had newly lost those members, frequently endeavors, at first, to move them, and employ them in their usual offices. Here he is as much conscious of power to command such limbs, as a

---

20 1777: *events* for *operations*
21 1777: omits *other*
22 1777: omits *and*
23 1777: omits *and*
24 1777: *suddenly struck* for *struck suddenly*

man in perfect health is conscious of power to actuate any member, which remains in its natural state and condition. But consciousness never deceives. Consequently, neither in the one case nor in the other, are we ever conscious of any power. We learn the influence of our will from experience alone. And experience only teaches us, how one event constantly follows another, without instructing us in the secret connexion, which binds them together, and renders them inseparable.

14. *Thirdly,* We learn from anatomy, that the immediate object of power in voluntary motion, is not the member itself, which is moved, but certain muscles, and nerves, and animal spirits,[25] and perhaps, something still more minute and more unknown, thro' which the motion is successively propagated, 'ere it reach the member itself, whose motion is the immediate object of volition. Can there be a more certain proof, that the power, by which this whole operation is performed, so far from being directly and fully known by an inward sentiment or consciousness, is, to the last degree, mysterious and unintelligible? Here the mind wills a certain event:[26] Immediately, another event, unknown to ourselves, and totally different from that[27] intended,[28] is produced: This event produces another, equally unknown: Till at last, thro' a long succession, the desired event is produced. But if the original power were felt it must be known: Were it known, its effect must also be known; since all power is relative to its effect. And *vice versa*, if the effect be not known, the power cannot be known or[29] felt. How, indeed, can we be conscious of a power to move our limbs, when we have no such power; but only that to move certain animal spirits, which, tho' they produce at last the motion of our limbs, yet operate in such a manner as is wholly beyond our comprehension?

15. We may, therefore, conclude from the whole; I hope, without any temerity, tho' with assurance; that our idea of power is not copied from any sentiment or consciousness of power within ourselves, when we give rise to animal motion, or apply our limbs to their proper use and office. That their motion follows the command of the will is a matter of common experience, like other natural events: But the power or energy, by which this is

---

25 Animal spirits were gaseous bodies supposed to flow through the nerves.
26 Namely, the motion of a limb.
27 1777: *the one* for *that*
28 Namely, the motion of the "animal spirits."
29 1777: *nor* for *or*

effected, like that in other natural events, is unknown and inconceivable.[n]

16. Shall we then assert, that we are conscious of a power or energy in our own minds, when, by an act or command of our will, we raise up a new idea, fix the mind to a[30] contemplation of it, turn it on all sides, and at last dismiss it for some other idea, when we think, that we have surveyed it with sufficient accuracy? I believe the same arguments will prove, that even this command of the will gives us no real idea of force or energy.

17. *First*, It must be allowed, that when we know a power, we know that very circumstance in the cause, by which it is enabled to produce the effect: For these are supposed to be synonimous. We must, therefore, know both the cause and effect, and the relation betwixt them. But do we pretend to be acquainted with the nature of the human soul and the nature of an idea, or the aptitude of the one to produce the other? This is a real creation; a production of something out of nothing: Which implies a power so great, that it may seem, at first sight, beyond the reach of any being, less than infinite. At least, it must be owned, that such a power is not felt, nor known, nor even conceivable by the mind. We only feel the event, *viz.* the existence of an idea, consequent to a command of the will: But the manner, in which this operation is performed; the power, by which it is produced; is entirely beyond our comprehension.

18. *Secondly*, The command of the mind over itself is limited, as well as its command over the body; and these limits are not known by reason, or any acquaintance with the nature of the[31] cause and effect; but only by experience and observation, as in all other natural events and in the operation of external objects. Our authority over our sentiments and passions is much weaker than that over our ideas; and even the latter authority is circumscribed within very narrow boundaries. Will any one pretend to assign the ultimate reason of these boundaries, or show why the power is deficient in one case and[32] not in another?

19. *Thirdly*, This self-command is very different at different times. A man in health possesses more of it, than one languishing with sickness. We are more master of our thoughts in the morning than in the evening: Fasting, than after a full meal. Can we give any reason for these variations, except experience?

---

30 **1777**: *the* for *a*

31 **1777**: omits *the*

32 **1777**: omits *and*

Where then is the power, of which we pretend to be conscious? Is there not here, either in a spiritual or material substance, or both, some secret mechanism or structure of parts, upon which the effect depends, and which being entirely unknown to us, renders the power or energy of the will equally unknown and incomprehensible?

20. Volition is surely an act of the mind, with which we are sufficiently acquainted. Reflect upon it. Consider it on all sides. Do you find any thing in it like this creative power, by which it raises from nothing a new idea, and with a kind of FIAT, imitates the omnipotence of its Maker, if I may be allowed so to speak, who called forth into existence all the various scenes of nature? So far from being conscious of this energy in the will, it requires as certain experience, as that of which we are possessed, to convince us, that such extraordinary effects do ever result from a simple act of volition.

21. The generality of mankind never find any difficulty in accounting for the more common and familiar operations of nature; such as the descent of heavy bodies, the growth of plants, the generation of animals, or the nourishment of bodies by food; but suppose, that, in all these cases, they perceive the very force and[33] energy of the cause, by which it is connected with its effect, and is for ever infallible in its operation. They acquire, by long habit, such a turn of mind, that, upon the appearance of the cause, they immediately expect with assurance its usual attendant, and hardly conceive it possible, that any other event could result from it. 'Tis only on the discovery of extraordinary phænomena, such as earthquakes, pestilence, and prodigies of any kind, that they find themselves at a loss to assign a proper cause, and to explain the manner, in which the effect is produced by it. 'Tis usual for men, in such difficulties, to have recourse to some invisible, intelligent principle,° as the immediate cause of that event, which surprises them, and which, they think, cannot be accounted for from the common powers of nature. But philosophers, who carry their scrutiny a little farther, immediately perceive, that, even in the most familiar events, the energy of the cause is as unintelligible as in the most unusual, and that we only learn by experience the frequent CONJUNCTION of objects, without being ever able to comprehend any thing like CONNEXION between them. Here then, many philosophers think themselves obliged by reason to have recourse, on all occasions,

---

33 1777: *or* for *and*

to the same principle, which the vulgar never appeal to but in cases, that appear miraculous and supernatural. They acknowlege mind and intelligence to be, not only the ultimate and original cause of all things, but the immediate and sole cause of every event, which appears in nature. They pretend, that those objects, which are commonly denominated *causes*, are in reality nothing but *occasions*; and that the true and direct principle of every effect is not any power or force in nature, but a volition of the supreme Being, who wills, that such particular objects should, for ever, be conjoined with each other. Instead of saying, that one billiard-ball moves another, by a force, which it has derived from the author of nature; 'tis the Deity himself, they say, who, by a particular volition, moves the second ball, being determined to this operation by the impulse of the first ball; in consequence of those general laws, which he has laid down to himself in the government of the universe. But philosophers, advancing still in their enquiries, discover, that, as we are totally ignorant of the power, on which depends the mutual operation of bodies, we are no less ignorant of that power, on which depends the operation of mind on body, or of body on mind; nor are we able, either from our senses or consciousness, to assign the ultimate principle, in one case more than in the other. The same ignorance, therefore, reduces them to the same conclusion. They assert, that the Deity is the immediate cause of the union betwixt soul and body, and that they are not the organs of sense, which, being agitated by external objects, produce sensations in the mind; but that 'tis a particular volition of our omnipotent Maker, which excites such a sensation, in consequence of such a motion in the organ. In like manner, it is not any energy in the will, that produces local motion in our members: 'Tis God himself, who is pleased to second our will, in itself impotent, and to command that motion, which we erroneously attribute to our own power and efficacy. Nor do philosophers stop at this conclusion. They sometimes extend the same inference to the mind itself, in its internal operations. Our mental vision or conception of ideas is nothing but a revelation made to us by our Maker. When we voluntarily turn our thoughts to any object, and raise up its image in the fancy; it is not the will, which creates that idea: 'Tis the universal Creator of all things,[34] who discovers it to the mind, and renders it present to us.

---

34 1777: omits *of all things*

22. Thus, according to these philosophers, every thing is full of God. Not contented[35] with the principle, that nothing exists but by his will, that nothing possesses any power but by his concession: They rob nature, and all created beings of every power, in order to render their dependance on the Deity still more sensible and immediate. They consider not, that by this theory they diminish, instead of magnifying, the grandeur of those attributes, which they affect so much to celebrate. It argues surely more power in the Deity to delegate a certain degree of power to inferior creatures, than to operate[36] every thing by his own immediate volition. It argues more wisdom to contrive at first the fabric of the world with such perfect foresight, that, of itself, and by its proper operation, it may serve all the purposes of providence, than if the great Creator were obliged every moment to adjust its parts, and animate by his breath all the wheels of that stupendous machine.

23. But if we would have a more philosophical confutation of this theory,[37] perhaps the two following reflections may suffice.

24. *First*, It seems to me, that this theory, of the universal energy and operation of the supreme Being, is too bold ever to carry conviction with it to a man, who is[38] sufficiently apprized of the weakness of human reason, and the narrow limits, to which it is confined in all its operations. Tho' the chain of arguments, which conduct to it, were ever so logical, there must arise a strong suspicion, if not an absolute assurance, that it has carried us quite beyond the reach of our faculties, when it leads to conclusions so extraordinary, and so remote from common life and experience. We are got into fairy-land, long ere we have reached the last steps of our theory; and *there* we have no reason to trust our common methods of argument, or[39] think that our usual analogies and probabilities have any authority. Our line is too short to fathom such immense abysses. And however we may flatter ourselves, that we are guided in every step, which we take, by a kind of verisimilitude and experience; we may be assured, that this

---

35 1777: *content* for *contented*
36 1777: *produce* for *operate*
37 The "confutation" offered in EHU 7.22 is not "philosophical" because it does not address the reason for thinking that God is the cause of everything, but instead appeals to a supposedly unacceptable consequence of that theory.
38 1777: omits *who is*
39 1777: inserts *to*

fancied experience has no authority when we thus apply it to subjects, that lie entirely out of the sphere of experience. But on this we shall have occasion to touch afterwards.[p]

25. *Secondly*, I cannot perceive any force in the arguments, on which this theory is founded. We are ignorant, 'tis true, of the manner, in which bodies operate on each other: Their force or energy is entirely incomprehensible. But are we not equally ignorant of the manner or force, by which a mind, even the supreme mind, operates either on itself or on body? Whence, I beseech you, do we acquire any idea of it? We have no sentiment or consciousness of this power in ourselves: We have no idea of the supreme Being but what we learn from reflection on our own faculties. Were our ignorance, therefore, a good reason for rejecting any thing, we should be led into that principle of denying all energy in the supreme Being as much as in the grossest matter. We surely comprehend as little the operations of one as of the other. Is it more difficult to conceive, that motion may arise from impulse, than that it may arise from volition? All we know is our profound ignorance in both cases.[q]

PART II

26. But to hasten to a conclusion of this argument, which is already drawn out to too great a length: We have sought in vain, for an idea of power or necessary connexion in all the sources, from which we could suppose it to be derived. It appears, that, in single instances of the operation of bodies, we never can, by our utmost scrutiny, discover any thing but one event following another; without being able to comprehend any force or power, by which the cause operates, or any connexion between it and its supposed effect. The same difficulty occurs in contemplating the operations of mind on body; where we observe the motion of the latter to follow upon the volition of the former; but are not able to observe nor[40] conceive the tye, which binds together the motion and volition, or the energy, by which the mind produces this effect. The authority of the will over our[41] own faculties and ideas is not a whit more comprehensible: So that upon the whole, there appears not, thro' all nature, any one instance of connexion, which is conceivable by us. All events seem entirely loose and separate. One event follows another; but we never can observe any tye betwixt them. They seem *conjoined*, but never *connected*.

---

40 **1777**: *or* for *nor*
41 **1777**: *its* for *our*

And as we can have no idea of any thing, which never appeared to our outward sense or inward sentiment, the necessary conclusion *seems* to be, that we have no idea of connexion or power at all, and that these words are absolutely without any meaning, when employed either in philosophical reasonings, or common life.

27. But there still remains one method of avoiding this conclusion, and one source, which we have not yet examined. When any natural object or event is presented, 'tis impossible for us, by any sagacity or penetration, to discover, or even conjecture, without experience, what event will result from it, or to carry our foresight beyond that object, which is immediately present to the memory and senses. Even after one instance or experiment, where we have observed a particular event to follow upon another, we are not entitled to form a general rule, or foretel what will happen in like cases; it being justly esteemed an unpardonable temerity to judge of the whole course of nature from one single experiment, however accurate or certain. But when one particular species of event has always, in all instances, been conjoined with another, we make no longer any scruple to foretel the[42] one upon the appearance of the other, and to employ[43] that reasoning, which can alone assure us of any matter of fact or existence. We then call the one object, *Cause*; and[44] the other, *Effect*. We suppose, that there is some connexion between them; some power in the one, by which it infallibly produces the other, and operates with the greatest certainty and strongest necessity.

28. It appears, then, that this idea of a necessary connexion among events arises from a number of similar instances, which occur, of the constant conjunction of these events; nor can that idea ever be suggested by any one of these instances, surveyed in all possible lights and positions. But there is nothing in a number of instances, different from every single instance, which is supposed to be exactly similar; except only, that after a repetition of similar instances, the mind is carried by habit, upon the appearance of one event, to expect its usual attendant, and to believe, that it will exist. This connexion, therefore, which we *feel* in the mind, or[45] customary transition of the imagination from one object to its usual attendant, is the sentiment or impression, from

---

42 **1777:** *of foretelling* for *to foretel the*
43 **1777:** *of employing* for *to employ*
44 **1777:** omits *and*
45 **1777:** *this* for *or*

which we form the idea of power or necessary connexion. Nothing farther is in the case. Contemplate the subject on all sides, you will never find any other origin of this[46] idea. This is the sole difference between one instance, from which we never can[47] receive the idea of connexion, and a number of similar instances, by which it is suggested. The first time a man saw the communication of motion by impulse, as by the shock of two billiard-balls, he could not pronounce that the one event was *connected*; but only that it was *conjoined* with the other. After he has observed several instances of this nature, he then pronounces them to be *connected*. What alteration has happened to give rise to this new idea of *connexion?* Nothing but that he now *feels* these events to be *connected* in his imagination, and can readily foretel the existence of one from the appearance of the other. When we say, therefore, that one object is connected with another, we mean only, that they have acquired a connexion in our thoughts,[48] and give rise to this inference, by which they become proofs of each other's existence. A conclusion, which is somewhat extraordinary; but which seems founded on sufficient evidence. Nor will its evidence be weakened[49] by any general diffidence of the understanding, or sceptical suspicion concerning every conclusion, which is new and extraordinary. No conclusions can be more agreeable to scepticism than such as make discoveries concerning the weakness and narrow limits of human reason and capacity.

29. And what stronger instance can be produced of the surprizing ignorance and weakness of the understanding, than the present? For surely, if there be any relation among objects, which it imports[50] us to know perfectly, 'tis that of cause and effect. On this are founded all our reasonings concerning matter of fact or existence. By means of it alone we attain any assurance concerning objects, which are removed from the present testimony of our memory and senses. The only immediate utility of all sciences, is to teach us, how to control and regulate future events by their causes. Our thoughts and enquiries, are, therefore, every moment, employed about this relation. And[51] yet so imperfect

---

46 **1777**: *that* for *this*
47 **1777**: *can never* for *never can*
48 **1777**: *thought* for *thoughts*
49 Reading, with 1777, *weakened* for *weakned*
50 **1777**: inserts *to*
51 **1777**: omits *And*

are the ideas which we form concerning it, that 'tis impossible to give any just definition of cause, except what is drawn from something extraneous and foreign to it.[52] Similar objects are always conjoined with similar. Of this we have experience. Suitable[53] to this experience, therefore, we may define a cause to be *an object, followed by another, and where all the objects, similar to the first, are followed by objects, similar to the second.* Or in other words, *where, if the first object had not been, the second never had existed.*[54] The appearance of a cause always conveys the mind, by a customary transition, to the idea of the effect. Of this also we have experience. We may, therefore, suitable[55] to this experience, form another definition of cause, and call it, *an object followed by another, and whose appearance always conveys the thought to that other.* But tho' both these definitions be drawn from circumstances foreign to the cause, we cannot remedy this inconvenience, or attain any more perfect definition, which may point out that circumstance in the cause, which gives it a connexion with its effect. We have no idea of this connexion; nor even any distinct notion what it is we desire to know, when we endeavor at a conception of it. We say, for instance, that the vibration of this string is the cause of this particular sound. But what do we mean by that affirmation? We either mean, *that this vibration is followed by this sound, and that all similar vibrations have been followed by similar sounds:* Or, *that this vibration is followed by this sound, and that upon the appearance of one, the mind anticipates the senses, and forms immediately an idea of the other.* We may consider the relation of cause and effect in either of these two lights; but beyond these, we have no idea of it [r][56].

30. To recapitulate, therefore, the reasonings of this section: Every idea is copied from some preceding impression or sentiment; and where we cannot find any impression, we may be certain that there is no idea. In all single instances of the opera-

---

52 A "just definition" of cause would "point out that circumstance ... which gives it a connexion with its effect" (as Hume puts it a few sentences later) or which serves to tie the two together. Since we can find no such circumstance or quality in causes we are left having to identify causes by their relation to other objects or their effects on our own minds—things that are "extraneous and foreign to it" in the sense that they are not grounded in any of its qualities.

53 1777: *Suitably* for *Suitable*

54 This sentence was added in 1756.

55 1777: *suitably* for *suitable.*

56 This note was added in 1750.

tion of bodies or minds, there is nothing that produces any impression, nor consequently can suggest any idea of power or necessary connexion. But when many uniform instances appear, and the same object is always followed by the same event; we then begin to entertain the notion of cause and connexion. We then *feel* a new sentiment or impression, *viz.* a customary connexion in the thought or imagination between one object and its usual attendant; and this sentiment is the original of that idea which we seek for. For as this idea arises from a number of similar instances, and not from any single instance; it must arise from that circumstance, in which the number of instances differ from every individual instance. But this customary connexion or transition of the imagination is the only circumstance, in which they differ. In every other particular they are alike. The first instance which we saw of motion, communicated by the shock of two billiard-balls (to return to this obvious instance[57]) is exactly similar to any instance that may, at present, occur to us; except only, that we could not, at first, *infer* one event from the other; which we are enabled to do at present, after so long a course of uniform experience. I know not, if[58] the reader will readily apprehend this reasoning. I am afraid, that, should I multiply words about it, or throw it into a greater variety of lights, it would only become more obscure and intricate. In all abstract reasonings, there is one point of view, which, if we can happily hit, we shall go farther towards illustrating the subject, than by all the eloquence and copious expression in the world. This[59] we should endeavor to attain,[60] and reserve the flowers of rhetoric for subjects, which are more adapted to them.

NOTES

[1] Section II.

m Mr. LOCKE,[61] in his chapter of power,[62] says, that finding from experience, that there are several new productions in matter, and concluding that there must somewhere be a power, capable of producing

---

57 **1777**: *illustration* for *instance*
58 **1777**: *whether* for *if*
59 **1777**: inserts *point of view*
60 **1777**: *reach* for *attain*
61 See Section 1, note 16.
62 *An Essay Concerning Human Understanding* 2.21.1.

them, we arrive at last by this reasoning at the idea of power. But no reasoning can ever give us a new, original, simple idea; as this philosopher himself confesses. This, therefore, can never be the origin of that idea.

ⁿ It may be pretended, that the resistance which we meet with in bodies, obliging us frequently to exert our force, and call up all our power; this gives us the idea of force, and power. 'Tis this *Nisus* or strong endeavor, of which we are conscious, that is the original impression, from which this idea is copied. But, *first,* we attribute power to a vast number of objects, where we never can suppose this resistance or exertion of force to take place: To the supreme Being, who never meets with any resistance; to the mind in its command over its ideas and limbs, in common thinking and motion, where the effect follows immediately upon the will, without any exertion or summoning up of force; to inanimate matter, which is not capable of this sentiment. *Secondly,* This sentiment of an endeavor to overcome resistance has no known connexion with any event: What follows it, we know by experience; but could not know it *à priori*. It must, however, be confessed, that the animal *Nisus*, which we experience, tho' it can afford no accurate precise idea of power, enters very much into that vulgar, inaccurate idea, which is formed of it.[63] See p. 326[64].[65]

ᵒ Θεος απο μηχανης.[66]

ᵖ Section XII.

ᑫ I need not examine at length the *vis inertiæ* which is so much talked of in the new philosophy, and which is ascribed to matter. We find by experience, that a body at rest or in motion continues for ever in its present state, till put from it by some new cause: And that a body impelled takes as much motion from the impelling body as it acquires itself. These are facts. When we call this a *vis inertiæ*, we only mark these facts, without pretending to have any idea of the inert power; in the same manner as when we talk of gravity, we mean certain effects, without comprehending that active power. It was never the meaning of

---

63 This sentence was added in **1756**.

64 p. 326 consists of the concluding lines of EHU 7.25, beginning "which seems founded on sufficient evidence," all of EHU 7.26, and the attached note.

65 **1777**: omits this sentence

66 **1748-1750**: *Quasi Deus ex machina* for Θεος απο μηχανης. **1748** places this remark in the text in parentheses. **1750** enters it as a footnote and adds *Cic. de Nat. Deorum* (Cicero, *De natura deorum*). A *deus ex machina* or Θεος απο μηχανης is a supernatural being who suddenly and arbitrarily intervenes to resolve a problem.

sir ISAAC NEWTON[67] to rob second causes[68] of all force or energy; tho'
some of his followers have endeavored to establish that theory upon his
authority. On the contrary, that great philosopher had recourse to an
etherial active fluid[69] to explain his universal attraction; tho' he was so
cautious and modest as to allow, that it was a mere hypothesis, not to
be insisted on, without more experiments: I must confess, that there is
something in the fate of opinions a little extraordinary. DES-CARTES[70]
insinuated that doctrine of the universal and sole efficacy of the Deity,
without insisting on it. MALEBRANCHE and other CARTESIANS made it
the foundation of all their philosophy.[71] It had, however, no authority
in ENGLAND. LOCKE, CLARKE, and CUDWORTH,[72] never so much as
take notice of it,[73] but supposed[74] all along, that matter has a real, tho'
subordinate and derived power. By what means has it become so
prevalent among our modern metaphysicians?[75]

---

67 In the "General Scholium" appended to the third book of his *Mathematical Principles of Natural Philosophy*, Isaac Newton (1642-1727) famously
declared that he meant to "frame no hypothesis" concerning the causes
of the gravitation of bodies, but went on to speculate that gravitation
might be the consequence of bodies being squeezed together by the
pressure of a surrounding, ether.

68 **1748-1750**: *Matter* for *second causes*

69 **1748-1750**: *Matter* for *fluid*

70 In the third part of his *Meditations on First Philosophy* and the first and
second parts of his *Principles of Philosophy*, René Descartes (1596-1650)
declared that God needs to recreate the entire universe from instant to
instant in order to preserve it in existence. Descartes went on to claim
that the laws of motion and collision describe the manner in which God
does this rather than the effects of physical forces operating on bodies.

71 This is the philosophy of occasionalism, discussed at EHU 7.21-25. For
Malebranche, see Section 1, note 16.

72 For Locke, see Section 1, note 16. Along with Locke, Samuel Clarke
(1675-1729) and Ralph Cudworth (1617-88) were the pre-eminent
English philosophers of the two generations before Hume. All had supposed that bodies possess powers to affect other bodies.

73 Reading, with **1777**, a comma for the period.

74 **1777**: *suppose* for *supposed*

75 This note should be read in the context of the analysis of vulgar and
philosophical views of the nature of force and causality that begins at
EHU 7.21. Hume's point is that whereas philosophers in France had
taken God to be the only cause, English philosophers had, up until
recently, entertained more vulgar or common views of force or power by
supposing, like the vulgar, that it resides in the events that regularly
precede effects. As a matter of fact, the inertial and gravitational forces
said to reside in matter are not forces at all. The laws of *(Continued)*

^{r} According to these explications and definitions, the idea of *power* is relative as much as that of *cause*; and both have a reference to an effect, or some other event constantly conjoined with the former. When we consider the *unknown* circumstance of an object, by which the degree or quantity of its effect is fixt and determined, we call that its power: And accordingly, 'tis allowed by all philosophers, that the effect is the measure of the power. But if they had any idea of power, as it is in itself, why could not they measure it in itself? The dispute, whether the force of a body in motion be as its velocity, or the square of its velocity;[76] this dispute, I say, needed not be decided by comparing its effects in equal or unequal times; but by a direct mensuration and comparison.

As to the frequent use of the words, Force, Power, Energy, &c. which every where occur in common conversation, as well as in philosophy; that is no proof, that we are acquainted, in any instance, with the connecting principle betwixt cause and effect, or can account ultimately for the production of one thing by another. These words, as commonly used, have very loose meanings annexed to them; and their ideas are very uncertain and confused. No animal can put external bodies in motion without the sentiment of a *Nisus* or endeavor; and

---

inertia and gravitation merely describe the ways in which bodies move, without giving us any insight into what makes them move that way, though even Newton seems to have thought, with the vulgar, that some kind of power resides in matter and might be invoked to explain gravitation. The principal "modern metaphysician" to have gone over from the English to the French side was George Berkeley. Given that we find no power anywhere and that both the vulgar English and the philosophical French views are equally groundless, there is something "extraordinary" in this study of their popularity.

76 Physicists of the early modern period were engaged in a heated debate over whether the force of a body in motion is measured by its momentum (the product of its mass and velocity), as Newton and his followers maintained, or instead by what Leibniz called *vis viva* or "living force" (the product of its mass and the square of its velocity). Mass and velocity are perceptible qualities of the body moved, but the dispute over which combination of these qualities is the moving force was carried out by appeal to the effects of the moving body, either in collision, or in raising weights contrary to the force of gravity. The dispute was resolved by remarking that Leibniz had been comparing effects of moving bodies over equal distances whereas Newton has been comparing them over equal times, so that the Leibnizian formulation was a correct description of the effects of moving force over distance and the Newtonian of its effects over time. Hume's point is that all that anyone had ever been measuring is the effects of the force, not the thing in the body that gives it the force.

every animal has a sentiment or feeling from the stroke or blow of an external object, that is in motion. These sensations, which are merely animal, and from which we can *à priori* draw no inference, we are apt to transfer to inanimate objects, and to suppose, that they have some such feelings, whenever they transfer or receive motion. With regard to energies, which are exerted, without our annexing to them any idea of communicated motion, we consider only the constant experienced conjunction of the events; and as we *feel* a customary connexion betwixt the ideas, we transfer that feeling to the objects; as nothing is more usual than to apply to external bodies every internal sensation, which they occasion.[77]

---

77 **1750**: replaces this entire paragraph with *A Cause is different from a Sign; as it implies Precedency and Contiguity in Time and Place, as well as constant Conjunction. A Sign is nothing but a correlative Effect from the same Cause.*

SECTION 8
OF LIBERTY AND NECESSITY

PART I

1. It might reasonably be expected, in questions, which have been canvassed and disputed with great eagerness since the first origin of science and philosophy, that the meaning of all the terms, at least, should have been agreed upon among the disputants; and our enquiries, in the course of two thousand years, been able to pass from words to the true and real subject of the controversy. For how easy may it seem to give exact definitions of the terms employed in reasoning, and make these definitions, not the mere sound of words, the object of future scrutiny and examination? But if we consider the matter more narrowly, we shall be apt to draw a quite opposite conclusion. From that[1] circumstance alone, that a controversy has been long kept on foot, and remains still undecided, we may presume, that there is some ambiguity in the expression, and that the disputants affix different ideas to the terms employed in the controversy. For as the faculties of the soul[2] are supposed to be naturally alike in every individual; otherwise nothing could be more fruitless than to reason or dispute together; it were impossible, if men affix the same ideas to their terms, that they could so long form different opinions of the same subject; especially when they communicate their views, and each party turn themselves on all sides, in search of arguments, which may give them the victory over their antagonists. 'Tis true; if men attempt the discussion of questions, which lie entirely beyond the reach of human capacity, such as those concerning the origin of worlds, or the œconomy of the intellectual system or region of spirits, they may long beat the air in their fruitless contests, and never arrive at any determinate conclusion. But if the question regard any subject of common life and experience; nothing, one would think, could preserve the dispute so long undecided, but some ambiguous expressions, which keep the antagonists still at a distance, and hinder them from grappling with each other.

2. This has been the case in the long disputed question concerning liberty and necessity; and to so remarkable a degree, that, if I be not much mistaken, we shall find[3] all mankind, both learned and ignorant, to have been always[4] of the same opinion

---

1 1777: *this* for *that*
2 1777: *mind* for *soul*
3 1777: inserts *, that*
4 1777: *have always been* for *to have been always*

with regard to that[5] subject, and that a few intelligible definitions would immediately have put an end to the whole controversy. I own, that this dispute has been so much canvassed on all hands, and has led philosophers into such a labyrinth of obscure sophistry, that 'tis no wonder, if a sensible and polite[6] reader indulge his ease so far as to turn a deaf ear to the proposal of such a question, from which he can expect neither instruction nor entertainment. But the state of the argument here proposed may, perhaps, serve to renew his attention; as it has more novelty, promises at least some decision of the controversy, and will not much disturb his ease, by any intricate or obscure reasoning.

3. I hope, therefore, to make it appear, that all men have ever agreed in the doctrines[7] both of necessity and of liberty, according to any reasonable sense, which can be put on these terms; and that the whole controversy has hitherto turned merely upon words. We shall begin with examining the doctrine of necessity.

4. 'Tis universally allowed, that matter, in all its operations, is actuated by a necessary force, and that every natural effect is so precisely determined by the energy of its cause, that no other effect, in such particular circumstances, could possibly have resulted from the operation of that cause.[8] The degree and direction of every motion is, by the laws of nature, prescribed with such exactness, that a living creature may as soon arise from the shock of two bodies, as motion in any other degree or direction, than what is actually produced by it. Would we, therefore, form a just and precise idea of *necessity*, we must consider, whence that idea arises, when we apply it to the operation of bodies.

5. It seems evident, that, if all the scenes of nature were shifted continually[9] in such a manner, that no two events bore any resemblance to each other, but every object was entirely new, without any similitude to whatever had been seen before, we should never, in that case, have attained the least idea of necessity, or of a connexion among these objects. We might say, upon such a supposition, that one object or event has followed another; not that one was produced by the other. The relation of cause and effect must be utterly unknown to mankind. Inference and reasoning concerning the operations of nature would, from that moment, be at an end; and the memory and senses remain the

---

5 1777: *this* for *that*
6 1777: omits *and polite*
7 1777: *doctrine* for *doctrines*
8 1777: *it* for *the operation of that cause*
9 1777: *continually shifted* for *shifted continually*

only canals, by which the knowlege of any real existence could possibly have access to the mind. Our idea, therefore, of necessity and causation arises entirely from that[10] uniformity, observable in the operations of nature; where similar objects are constantly conjoined together, and the mind is determined by custom to infer the one from the appearance of the other. These two circumstances form the whole of that necessity, which we ascribe to matter. Beyond the constant *conjunction* of similar objects, and the consequent *inference* from one to the other, we have no notion of any necessity, or connexion.[11]

6. If it appear, therefore, that all mankind have ever allowed, without any doubt or hesitation, that these two circumstances take place in the voluntary actions of men, and in the operations of the[12] mind; it must follow, that all mankind have ever agreed in the doctrine of necessity, and that they have hitherto disputed, merely for not understanding each other.

7. As to the first circumstance, the constant and regular conjunction of similar events; we may possibly satisfy ourselves by the following considerations. It is universally acknowleged, that there is a great uniformity among the actions of men, in all nations and ages, and that human nature remains still the same, in its principles and operations. The same motives produce always[13] the same actions: The same events follow from the same causes. Ambition, avarice, self-love, vanity, friendship, generosity, public spirit; these passions, mixed in various degrees, and distributed thro' society, have been, from the beginning of the world, and still are, the sources[14] of all the actions and enterprizes, which have ever been observed among mankind. Would you know the sentiments, inclinations, and course of life of the GREEKS and ROMANS? Study well the temper and actions of the FRENCH and ENGLISH. You cannot be much mistaken in transferring to the former *most* of the observations, which you have made with regard to the latter. Mankind are so much the same, in all times and places, that history informs us of nothing new or strange in this particular. Its chief use is only to discover the constant and universal principles of human nature, by shewing men in all varieties of circumstances and situations, and furnishing us with

---

10 **1777**: *the* for *that*
11 See EHU 7.29.
12 **1777**: omits *the*
13 **1777**: *always produce* for *produce always*
14 **1777**: *source* for *sources*

materials, from which we may form our observations, and become acquainted with the regular springs of human action and behavior. These records of wars, intrigues, factions, and revolutions, are so many collections of experiments, by which the politician or moral philosopher fixes the principles of his science; in the same manner as the physician or natural philosopher becomes acquainted with the nature of plants, minerals, and other external objects, by the experiments, which he forms concerning them. Nor are the earth, water, and other elements, examined by ARISTOTLE, and HIPPOCRATES,[15] more like to those, which at present lie under our observation, than the men, described by POLYBIUS and TACITUS,[16] are to those who now govern the world.

8. Should a traveller, returning from a far country, bring us an account of men, entirely[17] different from any, with whom we were ever acquainted; men, who were entirely divested of avarice, ambition, or revenge; who knew no pleasure but friendship, generosity, and public spirit; we should immediately, from these circumstances, detect the falshood, and prove him a liar, with the same certainty as if he had stuffed his narration with stories of centaurs and dragons, miracles and prodigies. And if we would explode any forgery in history, we cannot make use of a more convincing argument, than to prove, that the actions, ascribed to any person, are directly contrary to the course of nature, and that no human motives, in such circumstances, could ever induce him to such a conduct. The veracity of QUINTUS CURTIUS is as suspicious,[18] when he describes the supernatural courage of ALEXANDER,[19] by which he was hurried on singly to attack multitudes, as when he describes his supernatural force and activity, by which he was able to resist them. So readily and universally do we

---

15 Aristotle (see Section 1, note 16) in his physical works, and Hippocrates (early 4th-late 3rd centuries BCE) in his medical works, explained natural and medical phenomena by appeal to the four fundamental elements, earth, air, fire, and water, and the "humors" that are based on them.

16 Polybius (2nd century BCE) and Tacitus (56-117) were Roman historians who had a great deal to say about human nature, either as cause of historical events or as revealed by them.

17 1777: *wholly* for *entirely*

18 1777: *much to be suspected* for *suspicious*

19 Quintus Curtius Rufus (1st century) was a Roman historian who wrote a widely derided biography of the Greek conqueror, Alexander the Great (356-323 BCE).

acknowlege a uniformity in human motives and actions as well as in the operations of body.

9. Hence likewise the benefit of that experience, acquired by long life and a variety of business and company, in order to instruct us in the principles of human nature, and regulate our future conduct, as well as speculation. By means of this guide, we mount up to the knowlege of mens[20] inclinations and motives, from their actions, expressions, and even gestures; and again, descend to the interpretation of their actions from the[21] knowlege of their motives and inclinations. The general observations, treasured up by a course of experience, give us the clue of human nature, and teach[22] us to unravel all its intricacies. Pretexts and appearances no longer deceive us. Public declarations pass for the specious coloring of a cause. And tho' virtue and honor be allowed their proper weight and authority, that perfect disinterestedness, so often pretended,[23] is never expected in multitudes and parties; seldom in their leaders; and scarcely even in individuals of any rank or station. But were there no uniformity in human actions, and were every experiment which we could form of this kind irregular and anomolous, it were impossible to collect any general observations concerning mankind; and no experience, however accurately digested by reflection, would ever serve to any purpose. Why is the antient[24] husbandman more skilful in his calling than the young beginner, but because there is a certain uniformity in the operation of the sun, rain, and earth, towards the production of vegetables; and experience teaches the old practitioner the rules, by which this operation is governed and directed?

10. We must not, however, expect, that this uniformity of human actions should be carried to such a length, as that all men in the same circumstances, should[25] always act precisely in the same manner, without[26] any allowance for the diversity of characters, prejudices, and opinions. Such a uniformity, in every particular is found in no part of nature. On the contrary, from observing the variety of conduct in different men, we are enabled

---

20 1777: *men's* for *mens*
21 1777: *our* for *the*
22 Reading, with 1777, *teach* for *teaches*
23 1777: inserts *to*
24 1777: *aged* for *antient*
25 1777: *will* for *should*
26 1777: inserts *making*

to form a greater variety of maxims, which still suppose a degree of uniformity and regularity.

11. Are the manners of men different in different ages and countries? We learn thence the great force of custom and education, which mould the human mind from its infancy, and form it into a fixed and established character. Is the behavior and conduct of the one sex very unlike that of the other? 'Tis from[27] thence we become acquainted with the different characters, which nature has impressed upon the sexes, and which she preserves with constancy and regularity. Are the actions of the same person much diversified in the different periods of his life, from infancy to old age? This affords room for many general observations concerning the gradual change of our sentiments and inclinations, and the different maxims, which prevail in the different ages of human creatures. Even the characters which are peculiar to each individual, have a uniformity in their influence, otherwise our acquaintance with the persons, and our observation of their conduct could never teach us their dispositions, nor[28] serve to direct our behavior with regard to them.

12. I grant it possible to find some actions, which seem to have no regular connexion with any known motives, and are exceptions to all the measures of conduct, which have ever been established for the government of men. But if we would willingly know, what judgment should be formed of such irregular and extraordinary actions; we may consider the sentiments that are[29] commonly entertained with regard to those irregular events, which appear in the course of nature, and the operations of external objects. All causes are not conjoined to their usual effects, with like uniformity. An artificer, who handles only dead matter, may be disappointed of his aim as well as the politician, who directs the conduct of sensible and intelligent agents.

13. The vulgar, who take things according to their first appearance, attribute the uncertainty of events to such an uncertainty in the causes as makes the latter often fail of their usual influence; tho' they meet with no impediment in their operation. But philosophers, observing, that almost in every part of nature there is contained a vast variety of springs and principles, which are hid, by reason of their minuteness or remoteness, find, that 'tis at least possible the contrariety of events may not proceed

---

27 1777: omits *from*
28 1777: *or* for *nor*
29 1777: comma for *that are*

from any contingency in the cause, but from the secret operation of contrary causes. This possibility is converted into certainty by farther observation, when they remark, that, upon an exact scrutiny, a contrariety of effects always betrays a contrariety of causes, and proceeds from their mutual opposition. A peasant can give no better reason for the stopping of any clock or watch than to say that it commonly does not[30] go right: But an artizan[31] easily perceives, that the same force in the spring or pendulum has always the same influence on the wheels; but fails of its usual effect, perhaps by reason of a grain of dust, which puts a stop to the whole movement. From the observation of several parallel instances, philosophers form a maxim, that the connexion between all causes and effects is equally necessary, and that its seeming uncertainty in some instances proceeds from the secret opposition of contrary causes.

14. Thus for instance, in the human body, when the usual symptoms of health or sickness disappoint our expectation; when medicines operate not with their wonted powers; when irregular events follow from any particular causes;[32] the philosopher and physician are not surprized at the matter, nor are ever tempted to deny, in general, the necessity and uniformity of those principles, by which the animal œconomy is conducted. They know, that a human body is a mighty complicated machine: That many secret powers lurk in it, which are altogether beyond our comprehension: That to us it must often appear very uncertain in its operations: And that therefore the irregular events, which outwardly discover themselves, can be no proof, that the laws of nature are not observed with the greatest regularity in its internal operations and government.

15. The philosopher, if he be consistent, must apply the same reasonings[33] to the actions and volitions of intelligent agents. The most irregular and unexpected resolutions of men may frequently be accounted for by those who know every particular circumstance of their character and situation. A person of an obliging disposition gives a peevish answer: But he has the tooth-ake, or has not dined. A stupid fellow discovers an uncommon alacrity in his carriage: But he has met with a sudden piece of good-fortune. Or even when an action, as sometimes happens, cannot be par-

---

30 1777: *does not commonly* for *commonly does not*
31 1777: *artist* for *artizan*
32 1777: *cause* for *causes*
33 1777: *reasoning* for *reasonings*

ticularly accounted for, either by the person himself or by others; we know, in general, that the characters of men are, to a certain degree, inconstant and irregular. This is, in a manner, the constant character of human nature; tho' it be applicable, in a more particular manner, to some persons, who have no fixed rule for their conduct, but proceed in a continued course of caprice and inconstancy. The internal principles and motives may operate in a uniform manner, notwithstanding these seeming irregularities; in the same manner as the winds, rain, clouds, and other variations of the weather are supposed to be governed by steady principles; tho' not easily discoverable by human sagacity and enquiry.

16. Thus it appears, not only that the conjunction between motives and voluntary actions is as regular and uniform, as that between the cause and effect in any part of nature; but also that this regular conjunction has been universally acknowleged among mankind, and has never been the subject of dispute, either in philosophy or common life. Now as it is from past experience, that we draw all inferences concerning the future, and as we conclude, that objects will always be conjoined together, which we find always to have[34] been conjoined; it may seem superfluous to prove, that this experienced uniformity in human actions is the source of all the *inferences*, which we form[35] concerning them. But in order to throw the argument into a greater variety of lights, we shall also insist, tho' briefly, on this latter topic.

17. The mutual dependance of men is so great, in all societies, that scarce any human action is intirely compleat in itself, or is performed without some reference to the actions of others, which are requisite to make it answer fully the intention of the agent. The poorest artificer, who labours alone, expects at least the protection of the magistrate, to ensure[36] the enjoyment of the fruits of his labor. He also expects, that, when he carries his goods to market, and offers them at a reasonable price, he shall find buyers;[37] and shall be able, by the money he acquires, to engage others to supply him with those commodities, which are requisite for his subsistence. In proportion as mens dealings are more

---

34 **1777**: *to have always* for *always to have*

35 **1777**: *a source, whence we draw* *inferences* for *the source of all the* *inferences*, *which we form*

36 **1777**: *inserts* *him*

37 **1777**: *purchasers* for *buyers*

extensive,[38] and[39] their intercourse with others more complicated, they always comprehend, in their schemes of life, a greater variety of voluntary actions, which they expect, from their[40] proper motives, to co-operate with their own.[41] In all these conclusions, they take their measures from past experience, in the same manner as in their reasonings concerning external objects; and firmly believe, that men, as well as all the elements, are to continue, in their operations, the same, which[42] they have ever found them. A manufacturer reckons upon the labor of his servants, for the execution of any work, as much as upon the tools, which he employs, and would be equally surprized, were his expectations disappointed. In short, this experimental inference and reasoning concerning the actions of others enters so much into human life, that no man, while awake, is ever a moment without employing it. Have we not reason, therefore, to affirm, that all mankind have always agreed in the doctrine of necessity, according to the foregoing definition and explication of it?

18.   Nor have philosophers ever entertained a different opinion from the people in this particular. For not to mention, that almost every action of their life supposes that opinion; there are even few of the speculative parts of learning, to which it is not essential. What would become of *history*, had we not a dependence on the veracity of the historian, according to the experience, which we have had of mankind? How could *politics* be a science, if laws and forms of government had not a uniform influence upon society? Where would be the foundation of *morals*, if particular characters had no certain nor[43] determinate power to produce particular sentiments, and if these sentiments had no constant operation on actions? And with what pretext[44] could we employ our *criticism* upon any poet or polite author, if we could not pronounce the conduct and sentiments of his actors, either

---

38 **1777:** *men extend their dealings* for *mens dealings are more extensive*
39 **1777:** inserts *render*
40 **1777:** *the* for *their*
41 Hume's pronominal references are complex. "they expect" = men expect; "their proper motives" = the motives proper for the performance of those actions; "their own" = men's own intentions. Otherwise put, we rely on others to co-operate with us only insofar as we suppose them to be motivated to act conformably to our interests.
42 **1777:** *that* for *which*
43 **1777:** *or* for *nor*
44 **1777:** *pretence* for *pretext*

natural or unnatural, to such characters, and in such circumstances? It seems almost impossible, therefore, to engage, either in science or action of any kind, without acknowleging the doctrine of necessity, and this *inference* from motives to voluntary actions; from characters to conduct.

19. And indeed, when we consider how aptly *natural* and *moral* evidence link together, and form only one chain of argument, we shall make no scruple to allow, that they are of the same nature, and derived from the same principles. A prisoner, who has neither money nor interest,[45] discovers the impossibility of his escape, as well from[46] the obstinacy of the gaoler,[47] as from[48] the walls and bars, with which he is surrounded; and in all attempts for his freedom, chuses rather to work upon the stone and iron of the one, than upon the inflexible nature of the other. The same prisoner, when conducted to the scaffold, foresees his death as certainly from the constancy and fidelity of his guards, as from the operation of the ax or wheel.[49] His mind runs along a certain train of ideas: The refusal of the soldiers to consent to his escape; the action of the executioner; the separation of the head and body; bleeding, convulsive motions, and death. Here is a connected chain of natural causes and voluntary actions; but the mind feels no difference between them, in passing from one link to another: Nor is less certain of the future event than if it were connected with the objects present to the memory or senses, by a train of causes, cemented together by what we are pleased to call a *physical* necessity. The same experienced union has the same effect on the mind, whether the united objects be motives, volitions,[50] and actions; or figure and motion. We may change the names of things; but their nature and their operation on the understanding never change.[51]

---

45 In this context, to have no "interest" means to have no other means of interesting the jailer in facilitating an escape.

46 1777: *when he considers* for *from*

47 Reading, with 1777, *gaoler* for *goaler*

48 1777: omits *from*

49 The wheel is a device used to dismember a person.

50 1777: *volition* for *volitions*

51 1777: adds the following paragraph: [20.] *Were a man, whom I know to be honest and opulent, and with whom I live in intimate friendship, to come into my house, where I am surrounded with my servants, I rest assured, that he is not to stab me before he leaves it, in order to rob me of my silver standish; and I no more suspect this event, than the falling of the house itself* (Continued)

21. I have frequently considered, what could possibly be the reason, why all mankind, tho' they have ever, without hesitation, acknowleged the doctrine of necessity, in their whole practice and reasoning, have yet discovered such a reluctance to acknowlege it in words, and have rather shewn a propensity, in all ages, to profess the contrary opinion. The matter, I think, may be accounted for, after the following manner. If we examine the operations of bodies[52] and the production of effects from their causes, we shall find, that all our faculties can never carry us farther in our knowlege of this relation, than barely to observe, that particular objects are *constantly conjoined* together, and that the mind is carried, by a *customary transition*, from the appearance of one to the belief of the other. But tho' this conclusion concerning human ignorance be the result of the strictest scrutiny of this subject, men still entertain a strong propensity to believe, that they penetrate farther into the powers of nature, and perceive something like a necessary connexion between the cause and the effect. When again they turn their reflections towards the operations of their own minds, and *feel* no such connexion of the motive and the action; they are apt, from thence,[53] to suppose, that there is a difference betwixt the effects, resulting[54] from material force, and those which arise from thought and intelligence. But being once convinced, that we know nothing farther of causation of any kind, than merely the *constant conjunction* of objects, and the consequent *inference* of the mind from one to

---

which is new, and solidly built and founded.—But he may have been seized with a sudden and unknown frenzy.—So may a sudden earthquake arise, and shake and tumble my house about my ears*. I shall therefore change the suppositions. I shall say, that I know with certainty, that he is not to put his hand into the fire, and hold it there, till it be consumed: And this event, I think I can foretell with the same assurance, as that, if he throw himself out at the window, and meet with no obstruction, he will not remain a moment suspended in the air. No suspicion of an unknown frenzy can give the least possibility to the former event, which is so contrary to all the known principles of human nature. A man who at noon leaves his purse full of gold on the pavement at Charing-Cross, may as well expect that it will fly away like a feather, as that he will find it untouched an hour after. Above one half of human reasonings contain inferences of a similar nature, attended with more or less degrees of certainty, proportioned to our experience of the usual conduct of mankind in such particular situations.

52 1777: *body* for *bodies*
53 1777: *thence apt* for *apt, from thence,*
54 1777: *which result* for *resulting*

---

* 1777 misprints *years*.

another, and finding, that these two circumstances are universally acknowleged[55] to have place in voluntary actions; we may thence[56] be more easily led to own the same necessity common to all causes. And tho' this reasoning may contradict the systems of many philosophers, in ascribing necessity to the determinations of the will, we shall find, upon reflection, that they dissent from it in words only, not in their real sentiments.[57] Necessity, according to the sense, in which it is here taken, has never yet been rejected, nor can ever, I think, be rejected by any philosopher. It may only, perhaps, be pretended, that the mind can perceive, in the operations of matter, some farther connexion between the cause and effect; and a connexion which[58] has not place in the voluntary actions of intelligent beings. Now whether it be so or not, can only appear upon examination; and it is incumbent on these philosophers to make good their assertion, by defining or describing that necessity, and pointing it out to us, in the operations of material causes.

22. It would seem, indeed, that men begin at the wrong end of this question concerning liberty and necessity, when they enter upon it by examining the faculties of the soul, the influence of the understanding, and the operations of the will. Let them first discuss a more simple question, *viz.* the operations of body and of brute unintelligent matter; and try whether they can there form any idea of causation and necessity, except that of a constant conjunction of objects, and subsequent inference of the mind from one to another. If these circumstances form, in reality, the whole of that necessity, which we can[59] conceive in matter, and if these circumstances be also universally acknowleged to take place in the operations of the mind, the dispute is at an end; or,[60] at least, must be owned to be thenceforth merely verbal. But as long as we will rashly suppose, that we have some farther idea of necessity and causation in the operations of external objects; at the same time, that we can find nothing farther, in the voluntary actions of the mind; there is no possibility of bringing the dispute[61] to any determinate issue, while we proceed upon so erroneous a suppo-

---

55 1777: *allowed* for *acknowleged*
56 1777: omits *thence*
57 1777: *sentiment* for *sentiments*
58 1777: *that* for *which*
59 1777: omits *can*
60 1777: omits *or,*
61 1777: *question* for *dispute*

sition. The only method of undeceiving us, is, to mount up higher; to examine the narrow extent of science, when applied to material causes; and to convince ourselves, that all we know of them, is, the constant conjunction and inference above-mentioned. We may, perhaps, find, that 'tis with difficulty we are induced to fix such narrow limits to human understanding: But we can afterwards find no difficulty, when we come to apply this doctrine to the actions of the will. For as 'tis evident, that these have a regular conjunction with motives and circumstances and characters, and as we always draw inferences from the[62] one to the other, we must be obliged to acknowlege, in words, that necessity, which we have already avowed, in every deliberation of our lives, and in every step of our conduct and behavior.[s]

23. But to proceed in this reconciling project with regard to the question of liberty and necessity; the most contentious question, of metaphysics, the most contentious science; it will not require many words to prove, that all mankind have ever agreed in the doctrine of liberty as well as in that of necessity, and that the whole dispute, in this respect also, has been hitherto merely verbal. For what is meant by liberty, when applied to voluntary actions? We cannot surely mean, that actions have so little connexion with motives, inclinations, and circumstances, that the[63] one does not follow with a certain degree of uniformity from the other, and that the[64] one affords no inference, from[65] which we can conclude the existence of the other. For these are plain and acknowleged matters of fact. By liberty, then, we can only mean, *a power of acting or not acting, according to the determinations of the will*; that is, if we chuse to remain at rest, we may; if we chuse to[66] move, we also may. Now this hypothetical liberty[67] is universally

---

62 **1777**: omits *the*

63 **1777**: omits *the*

64 **1777**: omits *the*

65 **1777**: *by* for *from*

66 **1758**: prints *to* twice

67 By "hypothetical liberty" Hume means liberty defined in terms of hypothetical ("if ... then") propositions. To have hypothetical liberty means that *if* you will to do *x*, then *x* occurs, whereas *if* you will to refrain from doing *x*, then *x* does not occur. Hypothetical liberty is opposed to "constraint," which is the circumstance where you cannot move your body despite willing to move (as when bound) or prevent it from moving despite willing to prevent its motion (as when falling). It is consistent with supposing that acts of will are themselves caused or determined by motives, characters, and circumstances.

allowed to belong to every body,[68] who is not a prisoner and in chains. Here then is no subject of dispute.

24. Whatever definition we may give of liberty, we should be careful to observe two requisite circumstances; *first*, that it be consistent with plain matter of fact; *secondly*, that it be consistent with itself. If we observe these circumstances, and render our definition intelligible, I am persuaded that all mankind will be found of one opinion with regard to it.

25. 'Tis universally allowed, that nothing exists without a cause of its existence, and that chance, when strictly examined, is a mere negative word, and means not any real power, which has, any where, a being in nature. But 'tis pretended that some causes are necessary, and some are[69] not necessary. Here then is the admirable[70] advantage of definitions. Let any one *define* a cause, without comprehending, as a part of the definition, a *necessary connexion* with its effect; and let him shew distinctly the origin of the idea, expressed by the definition; and I shall frankly[71] give up the whole controversy. But if the foregoing explication of the matter be received, this must be absolutely impracticable. Had not objects a regular conjunction with each other, we should never have entertained any notion of cause and effect; and this regular conjunction produces that inference of the understanding, which is the only connexion, that we can have any comprehension of. Whoever attempts a definition of cause, exclusive of these circumstances, will be obliged, either to employ unintelligible terms, or such as are synonimous to the term, which he endeavors to define.[t] And if the definition above-mentioned, be admitted; liberty, when opposed to necessity, not to constraint, is the same thing with chance; which is universally allowed to have no existence.

PART II

26. There is no method of reasoning more common, and yet none more blameable, than in philosophical debates,[72] to endeavor the refutation of any hypothesis, by a pretext[73] of its dangerous consequences to religion and morality. When any

---

68 **1777**: *one* for *body*
69 **1777**: *some* for *and some are*
70 **1777**: omits *admirable*
71 **1777**: *readily* for *frankly*
72 **1777**: *disputes* for *debates*
73 **1777**: *pretence* for *pretext*

opinion leads into[74] absurdities, 'tis certainly false; but 'tis not certain that an opinion is false, because 'tis of dangerous consequence. Such topics, therefore, ought entirely to be forborne; as serving nothing to the discovery of truth, but only to make the person of an antagonist odious. This I observe in general, without pretending to draw any advantage from it. I submit frankly[75] to an examination of this kind, and shall venture to affirm, that the doctrines, both of necessity and of liberty, as above explained, are not only consistent with morality and religion, but are absolutely essential to the support of them.[76]

27. Necessity may be defined two ways, conformable[77] to the two definitions of *cause*, of which it makes an essential part.[78] It consists either in the constant conjunction of like objects, or in the inference of the understanding from one object to another. Now necessity, in both these senses, (which, indeed, are, at bottom, the same) has universally, tho' tacitly, in the schools, in the pulpit, and in common life, been allowed to belong to the will of man; and no man[79] has ever pretended to deny, that we can draw inferences concerning human actions, and that those inferences are founded in[80] the experienced union of like actions, with like motives, inclinations, and circumstances. The only particular, in which any one can differ, is, that either, perhaps, he will refuse to give the name of necessity to this property of human actions: But as long as the meaning is understood, I hope the word can do no harm: Or that he will maintain it possible to discover something farther in the operations of matter. But this, it must be acknowleged, can be of no consequence to morality or religion, whatever it may be to natural philosophy or metaphysics. We may here be mistaken in asserting, that there is no idea of any other necessity or connexion in the actions of body: But surely we ascribe nothing to the actions of the mind, but what every one does, and must readily allow of. We change no circumstance in the received orthodox system with regard to the will, but only in

---

74 **1777**: *to* for *into*

75 **1777**: *frankly submit* for *submit frankly*

76 **1777**: *are not only consistent with morality, but are absolutely essential to its support* for *are not only consistent with morality and religion, but are absolutely essential to the support of them*

77 **1777**: *conformably* for *conformable*

78 See EHU 7.29.

79 **1777**: *one* for *man*

80 **1777**: *on* for *in*

that with regard to material objects and causes. Nothing therefore can be more innocent, at least, than this doctrine.

28. All laws being founded on rewards and punishments, 'tis supposed as a fundamental principle, that these motives have a regular and uniform influence on the mind, and both produce the good and prevent the evil actions. We may give to this influence, what name we please; but as 'tis usually conjoined with the action, it must be esteemed a *cause*, and be looked upon as an instance of that necessity, which we would here establish.

29. The only proper object of hatred or vengeance, is a person or creature, endowed with thought and consciousness; and when any criminal or injurious actions excite that passion, 'tis only by their relation to the person, or connexion with him. Actions are, by their very nature, temporary and perishing; and where they proceed not from some *cause* in the character[81] and disposition of the person who performed them, they can neither redound to his honor, if good, nor infamy, if evil. The actions themselves may be blameable; they may be contrary to all the rules of morality and religion: But the person is not answerable for them; and as they proceeded from nothing in him, that is durable and constant, and leave nothing of that nature behind them, 'tis impossible he can, upon their account, become the object of punishment or vengeance. According to the principle, therefore, which denies necessity, and consequently causes, a man is as pure and untainted, after having committed the most horrid crime, as at the first moment of his birth, nor is his character any way[82] concerned in his actions; since they are not derived from it, and the wickedness of the one can never be used as a proof of the depravity of the other.

30. Men are not blamed for such actions as they perform ignorantly and casually, whatever may be the consequences. Why? but because the principles of these actions are only momentary, and terminate in them alone. Men are less blamed for such actions as they perform hastily and unpremeditately, than for such as proceed from deliberation. For what reason? but because a hasty temper, tho' a constant cause or principle in the mind, operates only by intervals, and infects not the whole character. Again, repentance wipes off every crime, if attended with a reformation of life and manners. How is this to be accounted for? but by asserting, that actions render a person criminal, merely as they

---

81 Reading, with 1777, *character* for *characters*
82 1777: *wise* for *way*

are proofs of criminal principles in the mind; and when, by any[83] alteration of these principles, they cease to be just proofs, they likewise cease to be criminal. But except upon the doctrine of necessity, they never were just proofs, and consequently never were criminal.

31. It will be equally easy to prove, and from the same arguments, that *liberty*, according to that definition above-mentioned,[84] in which all men agree, is also essential to morality, and that no human actions, where it is wanting, are susceptible of any moral qualities, or can be the objects either of approbation or dislike. For as actions are objects of our moral sentiments,[85] so far only as they are indications of the internal character, passions, and affections; 'tis impossible that they can give rise either to praise or blame, where they proceed not from these principles, but are derived altogether from external violence.

32. I pretend not to have obviated or removed all objections to this theory, with regard to necessity and liberty. I can foresee other objections, derived from topics, which have not here been treated of. It may be said, for instance, that if voluntary actions be subjected to the same laws of necessity with the operations of matter, there is a continued chain of necessary causes, pre-ordained and pre-determined, reaching from the original cause of all, to every single volition of every human creature. No contingency any where in the universe; no indifference; no liberty. While we act, we are, at the same time, acted upon. The ultimate Author of all our volitions is the Creator of the world, who first bestowed motion on this immense machine, and placed all beings in that particular position, whence every subsequent event, by an inevitable necessity, must result. Human actions, therefore, either can have no moral turpitude at all, as proceeding from so good a cause; or if they have any turpitude, they must involve our Creator in the same guilt, while he is acknowleged to be their ultimate cause and author. For as a man, who fired a mine,[86] is answerable for all the consequences, whether the train he employed be long or short:[87] so wherever a continued chain of necessary causes is[88] fixed, that Being, either finite or infinite,

---

83 1777: *an* for *any*
84 EHU 8.23.
85 1777: *sentiment* for *sentiments*
86 In other words, set off a land mine.
87 "Train" refers to a trail of gunpowder used to set off an explosive.
88 Reading, with 1777, *is* for *are*

who produces the first, is likewise the author of all the rest, and must both bear the blame, and acquire the praise, which belong to them. Our clearest and most[89] unalterable ideas of morality establish this rule, upon unquestionable reasons, when we examine the consequences of any human action; and these reasons must still have greater force, when applied to the volitions and intentions of a Being, infinitely wise and powerful. Ignorance or impotence may be pleaded for so limited a creature as man; but those imperfections have no place in our Creator. He foresaw, he ordained, he intended all those actions of men, which we so rashly pronounce criminal. And we must conclude, therefore,[90] either that they are not criminal, or that the Deity, not man, is accountable for them. But as either of these positions is absurd and impious, it follows, that the doctrine from which they are deduced, cannot possibly be true, as being liable to all the same objections. An absurd consequence, if necessary, proves the original doctrine to be absurd; in the same manner that[91] criminal actions render criminal the original cause, if the connexion between them be necessary and inevitable.

33. This objection consists of two parts, which we shall examine separately; *First*, that if human actions can be traced up, by a necessary chain, to the Deity, they can never be criminal; on account of the infinite perfection of that Being, from whom they are derived, and who can intend nothing but what is altogether good and laudable. Or *Secondly*, if they be criminal, we must retract the attribute of perfection, which we ascribe to the Deity, and must acknowlege him to be the ultimate author of guilt and moral turpitude in all his creatures.

34. The answer to the first objection seems obvious and convincing. There are many philosophers, who, after an exact scrutiny of all the phænomena of nature, conclude, that the WHOLE, considered as one system, is, in every period of its existence, ordered with perfect benevolence; and that the utmost possible happiness will, in the end, result to every created being,[92] without any mixture of positive or absolute ill and misery. Every physical ill, say they, makes an essential part of this benevolent system, and could not possibly be removed, even by

---

89 1777: *clear and* for *clearest and most*
90 1777: *therefore conclude,* for *conclude, therefore,*
91 1777: *as* for *that*
92 1777: *all created beings* for *every created being*

the Deity himself, considered as a wise agent, without giving entrance to greater ill, or excluding greater good, which will result from it. From this theory, some philosophers, and the antient *Stoics*[93] among the rest, derived a topic of consolation, under all afflictions, while they taught their pupils, that those ills, under which they labored, were, in reality, goods to the universe; and that to an enlarged view, which could comprehend the whole system of nature, every event became an object of joy and exultation. But tho' this topic be specious and sublime, it was soon found in practice weak and ineffectual. You would surely more irritate, than appease a man, lying under the racking pains of the gout, by preaching up to him the rectitude of those general laws, which produced the malignant humors in his body, and led them, thro' the proper canals, to the nerves and sinews,[94] where they now excite such acute torments. These enlarged views may, for a moment, please the imagination of a speculative man, who is placed in ease and security; but neither can they dwell with constancy on his mind, even tho' undisturbed by the emotions of pain or passion; much less can they maintain their ground, when attacked by such powerful antagonists. The affections take a narrower and more natural survey of their objects,[95] and by an oeconomy, more suitable to the infirmity of human minds, regard alone the beings around us, and are actuated by such events as appear good or ill to the private system. [35.][96] The case is the same with *moral* as with *physical* ill. It cannot reasonably be supposed, that those remote considerations, which are found of so little efficacy with regard to one, will have a more powerful influence with regard to the other. The mind of man is so formed by nature, that, upon the appearance of certain characters, dispositions, and actions, it immediately feels the sentiment of approbation or blame; nor are there any emotions more essential to its frame and constitution.[97]

The characters, which engage its[98] approbation, are chiefly such as contribute to the peace and security of human society; as the characters, which excite blame, are chiefly such as tend to

---

93 See Section 5, note 1.
94 **1777**: *sinews and nerves* for *nerves and sinews*
95 **1777**: *object* for *objects*
96 **1777**: inserts a paragraph break at this point
97 **1777**: omits the paragraph break at this point
98 **1777**: *our* for *its*

public detriment and disturbance: Whence we may reasonably presume,[99] that the moral sentiments arise, either mediately or immediately, from a reflection on these opposite interests. What tho' philosophical meditations establish a different opinion or conjecture; that every thing is right with regard to the WHOLE, and that the qualities, which disturb society, are, in the main, as beneficial, and are as suitable to the primary intention of nature, as those which more directly promote its happiness and welfare? Are such remote and uncertain speculations able to counterbalance the sentiments, which arise from the natural and immediate view of the objects? A man, who is robbed of a considerable sum; does he find his vexation for the loss any way[100] diminished by these sublime reflections? Why then should his moral resentment against the crime be supposed incompatible with them? Or why should not the acknowlegement of a real distinction between vice and virtue be reconcileable to all speculative systems of philosophy, as well as that of a real distinction between personal beauty and deformity? Both these distinctions are founded in the natural sentiments of the human mind: And these sentiments are not to be controled nor[101] altered by any philosophical theory or speculation whatsoever.

36. The *second* objection admits not of so easy and satisfactory an answer; nor is it possible to explain distinctly, how the Deity can be the mediate cause of all the actions of men, without being the author of sin and moral turpitude. These are mysteries, which mere natural and unassisted reason is very unfit to handle; and whatever system it[102] embraces, it[103] must find itself[104] involved in inextricable difficulties, and even contradictions, at every step which it[105] takes with regard to such subjects. To reconcile the indifference and contingency of human actions with prescience; or to defend absolute decrees, and yet free the Deity from being the author of sin, has been found hitherto to exceed all the skill[106]

---

99 **1777**: *whence it may reasonably be presumed* for *whence we may reasonably presume*

100 **1777**: *wise* for *way*

101 **1777**: *or* for *nor*

102 **1777**: *she* for *it*

103 **1777**: *she* for *it*

104 **1777**: *herself* for *itself*

105 **1777**: *she* for *it*

106 **1777**: *power* for *skill*

of philosophy.[107] Happy, if she be thence sensible of her temerity, when she pries into these sublime mysteries; and leaving a scene so full of obscurities and perplexities, return, with suitable modesty, to her true and proper province, the examination of common life; where she will find difficulties enow to employ her enquiries, without launching into so boundless an ocean of doubts, uncertainties and contradictions![108]

NOTES

ˢ The prevalence of the doctrine of liberty may be accounted for, from another cause, viz. a false sensation or seeming experience which we have, or may have of liberty or indifference, in many of our actions. The necessity of any action, whether of matter or of mind, is not, properly speaking, a quality in the agent, but in any thinking or intelligent being, who may consider the action; and it consists chiefly in the determination of his thoughts to infer the existence of that action from some preceding objects; as liberty, when opposed to necessity, is nothing but the want of that determination, and a certain looseness or indifference, which we feel, in passing, or not passing, from the idea of one object to that of any succeeding one. Now we may observe, that, tho' in *reflecting* on human actions we seldom feel such a looseness or indifference, but are commonly able to infer them with considerable certainty from their motives, and from the dispositions of the agent; yet it frequently happens, that, in *performing* the actions themselves, we are sensible of something like it: And as all resembling objects are readily taken for each other, this has been employed as a demonstrative and even an[109] intuitive proof of human liberty. We feel, that our actions are subject to our will, on most occasions; and imagine we feel, that the will itself is subject to nothing, because, when by a denial of it we are provoked to try, we feel that it moves easily every way, and produces an image of itself, (or a *Velleity*, as it is called in the schools) even on that side, on which it did not settle. This image, or faint motion, we persuade ourselves, could, at that time, have been compleated into the thing itself; because, should that be denied, we find, upon a second trial, that, at present, it can. We consider not, that the fantastical desire of shewing

---

107 By "prescience" Hume means the belief that God knew from the beginning of time what acts each human being would choose to perform. The doctrine of absolute decrees is the doctrine that God not only knew what would happen and permitted it, but himself decreed that certain souls would perform the wicked deeds on the basis of which they are damned to eternal punishment.

108 1777: *doubt, uncertainty, and contradiction* for *doubts, uncertainties and contradictions*

109 1777: omits *an*

liberty, is here the motive of our actions. And it seems certain, that however we may imagine we feel a liberty within ourselves, a spectator can commonly infer our actions from our motives and character; and even where he cannot, he concludes in general, that he might, were he perfectly acquainted with every circumstance of our situation · and temper, and the most secret springs of our complexion and disposition. Now this is the very essence of necessity, according to the foregoing doctrine.

ᵗ Thus if a cause be defined, *that which produces any thing*; 'tis easy to observe, that *producing* is synonimous to *causing*. In like manner, if a cause be defined, *that by which any thing exists*; this is liable to the same objection. For what is meant by these words, *by which?* Had it been said, that a cause is *that* after which *any thing constantly exists*; we should have understood the terms. For this is, indeed, all we know of the matter. And this constancy forms the very essence of necessity, nor have we any other idea of it.

SECTION 9
OF THE REASON OF ANIMALS

1. All our reasonings concerning matter of fact are founded on a species of ANALOGY, which leads us to expect from any cause the same events, which we have observed to result from similar causes. Where the causes are entirely similar, the analogy is perfect, and the inference, drawn from it, is regarded as certain and conclusive: Nor does any man ever entertain a doubt, where he sees a piece of iron, that it will have weight and cohesion of parts; as in all other instances, which have ever fallen under his observation. But where the objects have not so exact a similarity, the analogy is less perfect, and the inference is less conclusive; tho' still it has some force, in proportion to the degrees[1] of similarity and resemblance. The anatomical observations, formed upon one animal, are, by this species of reasoning, extended to all animals; and 'tis certain, that when the circulation of the blood, for instance, is proved clearly[2] to have place in one creature, as a frog or fish, it forms a strong presumption, that the same principle has place in all. These analogical observations may be carried farther, even to this science, of which we are now treating; and any theory, by which we explain the operations of the understanding, or the origin and connexion of the passions in man, will acquire additional authority, if we find, that the same theory is requisite to explain the same phænomena, in all other animals. We shall make trial of this, with regard to the hypothesis, by which, in the foregoing discourse,[3] we have[4] endeavored to account for all experimental reasonings; and 'tis hoped, that this new point of view will serve to confirm all our former observations.

2. *First*, It seems evident, that animals, as well as men, learn many things from experience, and infer, that the same events will always follow from the same causes. By this principle, they become acquainted with the more obvious properties of external objects, and gradually, from their birth, treasure up a knowlege of the nature of fire, water, earth, stones, heights, depths, &c. and of the effects, which result from their operation. The ignorance and

---

1   1777: *degree* for *degrees*
2   1777: *clearly proved* for *proved clearly*
3   EHU 5.
4   1777: *we have, in the foregoing discourse* for *in the foregoing discourse, we have*

inexperience of the young are here plainly distinguishable from the cunning and sagacity of the old, who have learned, by long observation, to avoid what hurt them, and to pursue what gave ease or pleasure. A horse, that has been accustomed to the field, becomes acquainted with the proper height, which he can leap, and will never attempt what exceeds his force and ability. An old greyhound will trust the more fatiguing part of the chace to the younger, and will place himself so as to meet the hare in her doubles;[5] nor are the conjectures, which he forms on this occasion, founded in any thing but his observation and experience.

3. This is still more evident from the effects of discipline and education on animals, who, by the proper application of rewards and punishments, may be taught any course of action, the most contrary to their natural instincts and propensities. Is it not experience, which renders a dog apprehensive of pain, when you menace him, or lift up the whip to beat him? Is it not even experience, which makes him answer to his name, and infer, from such an arbitrary sound, that you mean him, rather than any of his fellows, and intend to call him, when you pronounce it in a certain manner, and with a certain tone and accent?

4. In all these cases, we may observe, that the animal infers some fact beyond what immediately strikes his senses; and that this inference is altogether founded on past experience, while the creature expects from the present object the same events,[6] which it has always found in its observation to result from similar objects.

5. *Secondly*, 'Tis impossible, that this inference of the animal can be founded on any process of argument or reasoning, by which he concludes, that like events must follow like objects, and that the course of nature will always be regular in its operations. For if there be in reality any arguments of this nature, they surely lie too abstruse for the observation of such imperfect understandings; since it may well employ the utmost care and attention of a philosophic genius to discover and observe them. Animals, therefore, are not guided in these inferences by reasoning: Neither are children: Neither are the generality of mankind, in their ordinary actions and conclusions: Neither are philosophers themselves, who, in all the active parts of life are, in the main, the same with the vulgar, and are governed by the same maxims. Nature must have provided some other principle, of more ready,

---

5 That is, in her changes of course.
6 1777: *consequences* for *events*

and more general use and application; nor can an operation of such immense consequence in life, as that of inferring effects from causes, be trusted to the uncertain process of reasoning and argumentation. Were this doubtful with regard to men, it seems to admit of no question with regard to the brute-creation; and the conclusion being once firmly established in the one, we have a strong presumption, from all the rules of analogy, that it ought to be universally admitted, without any exception or reserve. 'Tis custom alone, which engages animals, from every object, that strikes their senses, to infer its usual attendant, and carries their imagination, from the appearance of the one, to conceive the other, in that strong and lively[7] manner, which we denominate *belief*. No other explication can be given of this operation, in all the higher, as well as lower classes of sensitive beings, which fall under our notice and observation.[u] [8]

6. But tho' animals learn many parts of their knowlege from observation, there are also many parts of it, which they derive from the original hand of nature, which much exceed the share of capacity they possess on ordinary occasions; and in which they improve, little or nothing, by the longest practice and experience. These we denominate INSTINCTS, and are so apt to admire, as something very extraordinary, and inexplicable by all the disquisitions of human understanding. But our wonder will, perhaps, cease or diminish; when we consider, that the experimental reasoning itself, which we possess in common with beasts, and on which the whole conduct of life depends, is nothing but a species of instinct or mechanical power, that acts in us unknown to ourselves; and in its chief operations, is not directed by any such relations or comparisons of ideas, as are the proper objects of our intellectual faculties. Tho' the instinct be different, yet still it is an instinct, which teaches a man to avoid the fire; as much as that, which teaches a bird, with such exactness, the art of incubation, and the whole oeconomy and order of its nursery.

NOTE

[u] Since all reasoning[9] concerning facts or causes is derived merely from custom, it may be asked how it happens, that men so much surpass animals in reasoning, and one man so much surpasses another? Has not the same custom the same influence on all?

---

7   1777: *particular* for *strong and lively*
8   This note was added in **1750**.
9   Reading, with **1767**, *reasoning* for *reasonings*

We shall here endeavor briefly to explain the great difference in human understanding:[10] After which, the reason of the difference betwixt men and animals will easily be comprehended.

1. When we have lived any time, and have been accustomed to the uniformity of nature, we acquire a general habit, by which we always transfer the known to the unknown, and conceive the latter to resemble the former. By means of this general habitual principle, we regard even one experiment as the foundation of reasoning, and expect a similar event with some degree of certainty, where the experiment has been made accurately, and free from all foreign circumstances.[11] 'Tis therefore considered as a matter of great importance to observe the consequences of things; and as one man may very much surpass another in attention and memory and observation, this will make a very great difference in their reasoning.

2. Where there is a complication of causes to produce any effect, one mind may be much larger than another, and better able to comprehend the whole system of objects, and to infer justly their consequences.

3. One man is able to carry on a chain of consequences to a greater length than another.

4. Few men can think long without running into a confusion of ideas, and mistaking one for another; and there are various degrees of this infirmity.

5. The circumstance, on which the effect depends, is frequently involved in other circumstances, which are foreign and extrinsic. The separation of it often requires great attention, accuracy, and subtilty.

6. The forming[12] general maxims from particular observation is a very nice operation; and nothing is more usual, from haste or a narrowness of mind, which sees not on all sides, than to commit mistakes in this particular.

7. When we reason from analogies, the man, who has the greater experience or the greater promptitude of suggesting analogies, will be the better reasoner.

8. Byasses from prejudice, education, passion, party, &c. hang more upon one mind than another.

9. After we have acquired a confidence in human testimony, books and conversation enlarge much more the sphere of one man's experience and thought than those of another.

'Twould be easy to discover many other circumstances that make a difference in the understandings of men.

---

10 **1777**: *understandings* for *understanding*

11 See *Treatise* 1.3.13.7-12 and 1.3.12.3.

12 **1777**: inserts *of*

SECTION 10
OF MIRACLES

PART I

1. There is in Dr. TILLOTSON'S writings an argument against the *real presence*,[1] which is as concise, and elegant, and strong as any argument can possibly be supposed against a doctrine, that is[2] so little worthy of a serious refutation.[3] 'Tis acknowledged on all hands, says that learned prelate, that the authority, either of the scripture or of tradition, is founded merely in the testimony of the apostles, who were eye-witnesses to those miracles of our Saviour, by which he proved his divine mission. Our evidence, then, for the truth of the *Christian* religion is less than the evidence for the truth of our senses; because, even in the first authors of our religion, it was no greater; and 'tis evident it must diminish in passing from them to their disciples; nor can any one be so certain of the truth of[4] their testimony, as of[5] the immediate object of his senses. But a weaker evidence can never destroy a stronger; and therefore, were the doctrine of the real presence ever so clearly revealed in scripture, it were directly contrary to the rules of just reasoning to give our assent to it. It contradicts sense, tho' both the scripture and tradition, on which it is supposed to be built, carry not such evidence with them as sense; when they are considered merely as external evidences, and are

---

1   This is a reference to the Roman Catholic doctrine that the body and blood of Christ are made to be really present in the bread and wine of the communion ceremony.

2   **1777**: omits *that is*

3   **Beauchamp**, 169, identifies Hume's source as John Tillotson, *The Hazard of being Saved in the Church of Rome*, 11th ed. (London: B. Tooke, J. Tonson, J. Round, et al., 1723). See pp. 15-16: "For the utmost assurance that the Apostles had of the truth of Christianity was the testimony of their own senses concerning our Saviour's miracles, and this testimony every man hath against *Transubstantiation*. From whence it plainly follows, that no man (no not the Apostles themselves) had more reason to believe *Christianity* to be true, than every man hath to believe *Transubstantiation* to be false. And we who did not see our Saviour's miracles (as the Apostles did) and have only a credible relation of them, but do see the *Sacrament*, have less evidence of the *truth of Christianity* than of the falshood of *Transubstantiation*." Gale document CB3326596043. A similar point had earlier been made by John Locke, *An Essay concerning Human Understanding*, IV.xviii.5.

4   **1777**: *rest such confidence in* for *be so certain of the truth of*

5   **1777**: *in* for *of*

not brought home to every one's breast, by the immediate operation of the Holy Spirit.

2. Nothing is so convenient as a decisive argument of this kind, which must at least *silence* the most arrogant bigotry and superstition, and free us from their impertinent sollicitations. I flatter myself, that I have discovered an argument of a like nature, which, if just, will, with the wise and learned, be an everlasting check to all kinds of superstitious delusion, and consequently, will be useful as long as the world endures. For so long, I presume, will the accounts of miracles and prodigies be found in all history, sacred and prophane.[6]

3. Tho' experience be our only guide in reasoning concerning matters of fact; it must be acknowleged, that this guide is not altogether infallible, but in some cases is apt to lead us into errors and mistakes.[7] One, who, in our climate, should expect better weather in any week of JUNE than in one of DECEMBER, would reason justly and conformable[8] to experience; but 'tis certain, that he may happen, in the event, to find himself mistaken. However, we may observe, that, in such a case, he would have no cause to complain of experience; because it commonly informs us beforehand of the uncertainty, by that contrariety of events, which we may learn from a diligent observation. All effects follow not with like certainty from their supposed causes. Some events are found, in all countries and all ages, to have been constantly conjoined together: Others are found to have been more variable, and sometimes to disappoint our expectations; so that in our reasonings concerning matter of fact, there are all imaginable degrees of assurance, from the highest certainty to the lowest species of moral evidence.

4. A wise man, therefore, proportions his belief to the evidence. In such conclusions as are founded on an infallible experience, he expects the event with the last[9] degree of assurance, and regards his past experience as a full *proof* of the future existence of that event. In other cases, he proceeds with more caution: He weighs the opposite experiments: He considers which side is supported by the greatest[10] number of experiments:

---

6 **1748-1750**: *prophane History* for *history, sacred and prophane*
7 1777: omits *and mistakes*
8 1777: *conformably* for *conformable*
9 That is, the highest.
10 1777: *greater* for *greatest*

To that side he inclines, with doubt and hesitation; and when at last he fixes his judgment, the evidence exceeds not what we properly call *probability*. All probability, then, supposes an opposition of experiments and observations; where the one side is found to over-balance the other, and to produce a degree of evidence, proportioned to the superiority. A hundred instances or experiments on one side, and fifty on another, afford a very[11] doubtful expectation of any event; tho' a hundred uniform experiments, with only one that is contradictory, reasonably beget a pretty strong degree of assurance. In all cases, we must balance the opposite experiments, where they are opposite, and deduct the smaller number from the greater, in order to know the exact force of the superior evidence.

5. To apply these principles to a particular instance; we may observe, that there is no species of reasoning more common, more useful, and even necessary to human life, than that[12] derived from the testimony of men, and the reports of eye-witnesses and spectators. This species of reasoning, perhaps, one may deny to be founded on the relation of cause and effect. I shall not dispute about a word. It will be sufficient to observe, that our assurance in any argument of this kind is derived from no other principle than our observation of the veracity of human testimony, and of the usual conformity of facts to the reports of witnesses. It being a general maxim, that no objects have any discoverable connexion together, and that all the inferences, which we can draw from one to another, are founded merely on our experience of their constant and regular conjunction; 'tis evident, that we ought not to make an exception to this maxim in favor of human testimony, whose connexion with any events[13] seems, in itself, as little necessary as any other. Were not the memory tenacious to a certain degree; had not men commonly an inclination to truth and a principle of probity; were they not sensible to shame, when detected in a falshood: were not these, I say, discovered by *experience* to be qualities, inherent in human nature, we should never repose the least confidence in human testimony. A man delirious, or noted for falshood and villany, has no manner of authority with us.

6. And as the evidence, derived from witnesses and human testimony, is founded on past experience, so it varies with the experience, and is regarded either as a *proof* or a *probability*, accord-

---

11 1777: omits *very*
12 1777: inserts *which is*
13 1777: *event* for *events*

ing as the conjunction between any particular kind of report and any kind of objects,[14] has been found to be constant or variable. There are a number of circumstances to be taken into consideration in all judgments of this kind; and the ultimate standard, by which we determine all disputes, that may arise concerning them, is always derived from experience and observation. Where this experience is not entirely uniform on any side, 'tis attended with an unavoidable contrariety in our judgments, and with the same opposition and mutual destruction of arguments[15] as in every other kind of evidence. We frequently hesitate concerning the reports of others. We balance the opposite circumstances, which cause any doubt or uncertainty; and when we discover a superiority on any side, we incline to it; but still with a diminution of assurance, in proportion to the force of its antagonist.

7. This contrariety of evidence, in the present case, may be derived from several different causes; from the opposition of contrary testimony; from the character or number of the witnesses; from the manner of their delivering their testimony; or from the union of all these circumstances. We entertain a suspicion concerning any matter of fact, when the witnesses contradict each other; when they are but few, or of a suspicious[16] character; when they have an interest in what they affirm; when they deliver their testimony with doubt and[17] hesitation, or on the contrary, with too violent asseverations. There are many other particulars of the same kind, which may diminish or destroy the force of any argument, derived from human testimony.

8. Suppose, for instance, that the fact, which the testimony endeavors to establish, partakes of the extraordinary and the marvellous; in that case, the evidence, resulting from the testimony, admits[18] a diminution, greater or less, in proportion as the fact is more or less unusual. The reason, why we place any credit in witnesses and historians is not[19] from any *connexion*, which we perceive *à priori* between testimony and reality, but because we are accustomed to find a conformity between them. But when the fact attested is such a one as has seldom fallen under our observation, here is a contest of two opposite experiences; of which the one

---

14 **1777**: *object* for *objects*
15 **1777**: *argument* for *arguments*
16 **1777**: *doubtful* for *suspicious*
17 **1777**: omits *doubt and*
18 **1777**: inserts *of*
19 **1777**: inserts *derived*

destroys the other as far as its force goes, and the superior can only operate on the mind by the force, which remains. The very same principle of experience, which gives us a certain degree of assurance in the testimony of witnesses, gives us also, in this case, another degree of assurance against the fact, which they endeavor to establish; from which contradiction there necessarily arise[20] a counterpoize, and mutual destruction of belief and authority.

9. *I should not believe such a story were it told me by* CATO;[21] was a proverbial saying in ROME, even during the life-time of that philosophical patriot.[v] The incredibility of a fact, it was allowed, might invalidate so great an authority.[22]

10. The INDIAN prince, who refused to believe the first relations concerning the effects of frost, reasoned justly; and it naturally required very strong testimony to engage his assent to facts, which[23] arose from a state of nature, with which he was unacquainted, and[24] bore so little analogy to those events, of which he had had constant and uniform experience. Tho' they were not contrary to his experience, they were not conformable to it.[w, 25]

11. But in order to increase the probability against the testimony of witnesses, let us suppose that the fact, which they affirm, instead of being only marvellous, is really miraculous;[26] and suppose also, that the testimony, considered apart, and in itself, amounts to an entire proof; in that case there is proof against proof, of which the strongest must prevail, but still with a diminution of its force, in proportion to that of its antagonist.

12. A miracle is a violation of the laws of nature; and as a firm and unalterable experience has established these laws, the proof[27] against a miracle, from the very nature of the fact, is as entire as

---

20 1777: *arises* for *arise*
21 Marcus Porcius Cato Uticensis (Cato the younger, 95-46 BCE) was a Roman statesman famed for his strict and austere morality.
22 This paragraph and the attached note were added in **1756.**
23 1777: *that* for *which*
24 1777: inserts *which*
25 This paragraph and the attached note were added in **1750.**
26 As explained more fully in Hume's note to the previous paragraph and at EHU 10.12, miracles are contrary to past experience of what happens in like circumstances, whereas marvels are merely contrary to what we would expect in circumstances that are analogous, but different in salient respects.
27 As used in this paragraph "proof" means "argument from experience." It does not mean "deductive demonstration." For another instance where Hume used "proved" in a more modest sense than it would be used today, see EHU note **bb.**

any argument from experience can possibly be imagined. Why is it more than probable, that all men must die; that lead cannot, of itself, remain suspended in the air; that fire consumes wood, and is extinguished by water; unless it be, that these events are found agreeable to the laws of nature, and there is required a violation of these laws, or in other words, a miracle to prevent them? Nothing is esteemed a miracle if it ever happen in the common course of nature. 'Tis no miracle that a man in seeming[28] good health should die on a sudden; because such a kind of death, tho' more unusual than any other, has yet been frequently observed to happen. But 'tis a miracle, that a dead man should come to life; because that has never been observed, in any age or country. There must, therefore, be an uniform experience against every miraculous event, otherwise the event would not merit that appellation. And as an uniform experience amounts to a proof, there is here a direct and full *proof*, from the nature of the fact, against the existence of any miracle; nor can such a proof be destroyed, or the miracle rendered credible, but by an opposite proof, which is superior.[x, 29]

13. The plain consequence is (and 'tis a general maxim worthy of our attention) "That no testimony is sufficient to establish a miracle, unless the testimony be of such a kind, that its falshood would be more miraculous, than the fact, which it endeavors to establish: And even in that case, there is a mutual destruction of arguments, and the superior only gives us an assurance suitable to that degree of force, which remains, after deducting the inferior." When any one tells me, that he saw a dead man restored to life, I immediately consider with myself, whether it be more probable, that this person should either deceive or be deceived, or that the fact which he relates, should really have happened. I weigh the one miracle against the other, and according to the superiority, which I discover, I pronounce my decision, and always reject the greater miracle. If the falshood of his testimony would be more miraculous, than the event which he relates; then, and not till then, can he pretend to command my belief or opinion.

---

28 **1777:** *seemingly in* for *in seeming*

29 In a letter of 1761 to Hugh Blair, Hume wrote: "The proof against a miracle, as it is founded on invariable experience, is of that *species* or *kind* of proof, which is full and certain *when taken alone*, because it implies no doubt, as is the case with all probabilities; *but there are degrees of this species*, and when a weaker proof is opposed to a stronger, it is overcome" (*Letters* 1: 350, my emphases). In the *Treatise* (1.3.12.2 and 1.3.13.19) Hume mentioned a number of cases in which a uniform experience can produce beliefs that fall short of conviction.

PART II

14. In the foregoing reasoning we have supposed, that the testimony, upon which a miracle is founded, may possibly amount to an entire proof, and that the falshood of that testimony would be a kind of[30] prodigy. But 'tis easy to shew, that we have been a great deal too liberal in our concessions,[31] and that there never was a miraculous event,[32] established on so full an evidence.

15. For *first*, there is not to be found, in all history, any miracle attested by a sufficient number of men, of such unquestioned good-sense, education, and learning as to secure us against all delusion in themselves; of such undoubted integrity, as to place them beyond all suspicion of any design to deceive others; of such credit and reputation in the eyes of mankind as to have a great deal to lose in case of[33] being detected in any falshood; and at the same time attesting facts, performed in such a public manner, and in so celebrated a part of the world, as to render the detection unavoidable: All which circumstances are requisite to give us a full assurance in the testimony of men.

16. Secondly. We may observe in human nature a principle, which, if strictly examined, will be found to diminish extremely the assurance, which we might have,[34] from human testimony,[35] in any kind of prodigy. The maxim, by which we commonly conduct ourselves in our reasonings, is, that the objects, of which we have no experience, resemble those, of which we have; that what we have found to be most usual is always most probable; and that where there is an opposition of arguments, we ought to give the preference to such of them[36] as are founded on the greatest number of past observations. But tho' in proceeding by this rule, we readily reject any fact, which is unusual and incredible in an ordinary degree; yet in advancing farther, the mind observes not always the same rule; but when any thing is affirmed utterly absurd and miraculous, it rather the more readily admits[37] such a fact, upon account of that very circumstance, which ought to destroy all its authority. The passion of *surprize* and *wonder*, arising from miracles, being an agreeable emotion, gives a sensi-

---

30 **1777**: *real* for *kind of*
31 **1777**: *concession* for *concessions*
32 **1748-1750**: insert *in any History*
33 **1777**: inserts *their*
34 **1777**: omits *have*
35 **1777**: inserts *have,*
36 **1777**: omits *of them*
37 **1777**: inserts *of*

ble tendency towards the belief of those events, from which it is derived. And this goes so far, that even those who cannot enjoy this pleasure immediately, nor can believe those miraculous events, of which they are informed, yet love to partake of the satisfaction at second-hand, or by rebound, and place a pride and delight in exciting the admiration of others.

17. With what greediness are the miraculous accounts of travellers received, their descriptions of sea and land monsters, their relations of wonderful adventures, strange men, and uncouth manners? But if the spirit of religion join itself to the love of wonder, there is an end of common sense; and human testimony, in these circumstances, loses all pretensions to authority. A religionist may be an enthusiast,[38] and imagine he sees what has no reality: He may know his narration[39] to be false, and yet persevere in it, with the best intentions in the world, for the sake of promoting so holy a cause: Or even where this delusion has no[40] place, vanity, excited by so strong a temptation, operates on him more powerfully than on the rest of mankind in any other circumstances; and self-interest with equal force. His auditors may not have, and commonly have not sufficient judgment to canvass his evidence: What judgment they have, they renounce by principle, in these sublime and mysterious subjects: Or if they were ever so willing to employ it, passion and a heated imagination disturb the regularity of its operations. Their credulity increases his impudence: And his impudence over-powers their credulity.

18. Eloquence, when in[41] its highest pitch, leaves little room for reason or reflection; but addressing itself entirely to the fancy or the affections, captivates the willing hearers, and subdues their understanding. Happily, this pitch it seldom attains. But what a CICERO[42] or a DEMOSTHENES[43] could scarcely operate[44] over a ROMAN or ATHENIAN audience, every *Capuchin*,[45] every itinerant or stationary teacher[46] can perform over the generality of

---

38 For more on "enthusiasm" see S&E.

39 1777: *narrative* for *narration*

40 1777: *not* for *no*

41 1777: *at* for *in*

42 1777: TULLY for CICERO

43 Marcus Tullius Cicero (106-43 BCE) and Demosthenes (384-322 BCE) were Roman and Greek statesmen noted for their oratorical skills.

44 1777: *effect* for *operate*

45 Capuchins were a sect of friars.

46 That is, every wandering preacher or priest assigned to a parish.

mankind, and in a higher degree, by touching such gross and vulgar passions.y[47]

20. Thirdly. It forms a very[48] strong presumption against all supernatural and miraculous relations, that they are observed chiefly to abound among ignorant and barbarous nations;[49] or if a civilized people has ever given admission to any of them, that people will be found to have received them from ignorant and barbarous ancestors, who transmitted them with that inviolable sanction and authority, which always attend antient and[50] received opinions.[51] When we peruse the first histories of all nations, we are apt to imagine ourselves transported into some new world, where the whole frame of nature is disjointed, and every element performs its operations in a different manner, from what it does at present. Battles, revolutions, pestilences, famines,[52] and death are never the effects[53] of those natural causes, which we experience. Prodigies, omens, oracles, judgments quite obscure the few natural events, that are intermingled with them. But as the former grow thinner every page, in proportion as we advance nearer the enlightened ages of science and knowlege,[54] we soon learn, that there is nothing mysterious or supernatural in the case, but that all proceeds from the usual propensity of mankind towards the marvellous, and that tho' this inclination may at intervals receive a check from sense and learning, it can never thoroughly be[55] extirpated from human nature.

21. 'Tis strange, a judicious reader is apt to say, upon the perusal of these wonderful historians, *that such prodigious events never happen in our days.* But 'tis nothing strange, I hope, that men should lie in all ages. You must surely have seen instances enow of that frailty. You have yourself heard many such marvellous relations started, which being treated with scorn by all the wise and judicious, have at last been abandoned, even by the vulgar. Be assured, that those renowned lies, which have spred and flourished to such a monstrous height, arose from like beginnings; but

---

47 This note was moved into the text in **1770**.
48 1777: omits *very*
49 See NHR 1-3 and 6.
50 1777: omits *antient and*
51 See *Treatise* 2.3.7-8.
52 1777: *pestilence, famine* for *pestilences, famines*
53 1777: *effect* for *effects*
54 1777: omits *of science and knowlege*
55 1777: *be thoroughly* for *thoroughly be*

being sown in a more proper soil, shot up at last into prodigies almost equal to those, which they relate.

22. 'Twas a wise policy in that cunning impostor,[56] ALEXANDER,[57] who, tho' now forgotten, was once so famous, to lay the first scene of his impostures in PAPHLAGONIA,[58] where, as LUCIAN[59] tells us, the people were extremely ignorant and stupid, and ready to swallow even the grossest delusion.[60] People at a distance, who are weak enough to think the matter at all worth enquiry, have no opportunity of receiving better information. The stories come magnified to them by a hundred circumstances. Fools are industrious to propagate the delusion;[61] while the wise and learned are contented, in general, to deride its absurdity, without informing themselves of the particular facts, by which it may be distinctly refuted. And thus the impostor above-mentioned was enabled to proceed, from his ignorant PAPHLAGONIANS, to the inlisting of votaries, even among the GRECIAN philosophers, and men of the most eminent rank and distinction in ROME. Nay could engage the attention of that sage emperor MARCUS AURELIUS;[62] so far as to make him trust the success of a military expedition to his delusive prophecies.

23. The advantages are so great of starting an imposture among an ignorant people, that even tho' the delusion should be too gross to impose on the generality of them *(which, tho' seldom, is sometimes the case)* it has a much better chance of[63] succeeding in remote countries, than if the first scene had been laid in a city renowned for arts and knowlege. The most ignorant and bar-

---

56 1777: *false prophet* for *cunning imposter*

57 Alexander of Abonoteichus (105-70) was a religious cult leader, charlatan, and thug who pretended to be what is today called a clairvoyant (in Hume's day, a "prophet," and in yet more ancient times an oracle).

58 Now the northern coast of Turkey, on the Black Sea.

59 Lucian of Samosata (125-80) was a Hellenic satirist. He exposed Alexander's tricks and wrote a book about him.

60 Lucian, "Alexander or the false prophet," Charles Blount, trans., in *The works of Lucian, translated from the Greek by several eminent hands*, 3 vols., vol. 1 (London: James Woodward, 1711), pp. 144-81. Gale document 3316585990. Lucian reported that Alexander had convinced the people that a snake that he had secreted in an egg-shell on temple grounds was a god.

61 1777: *in propagating the imposture* for *to propagate the delusion*

62 Marcus Aurelius (121-80) was emperor of Rome from 160 to 180. At one point Alexander encouraged the emperor to go into battle by prophesizing a great victory. A crushing defeat ensued.

63 1777: *for* for *of*

barous of these barbarians carry the report abroad. None of their countrymen have large enough[64] correspondence[65] or sufficient credit and authority to contradict and beat down the delusion. Mens inclination to the marvellous has full opportunity to display itself. And thus a story, which is universally exploded in the place where it was first started, shall pass for certain at a thousand miles distance. But had ALEXANDER fixed his residence at ATHENS, the philosophers of that renowned mart of learning, had immediately spred, thro'[66] the whole ROMAN empire, their sense of the matter, which, being supported by so great authority, and displayed by all the force of reason and eloquence, had entirely opened the eyes of mankind. 'Tis true; LUCIAN passing by chance thro' PAPHLAGONIA had an opportunity of performing this good office. But, tho' much to be wished, it does not always happen, that every ALEXANDER meets with a LUCIAN, ready to expose and detect his impostures.z[67]

24. I may add as a *fourth* reason, which diminishes the authority of prodigies, that there is no testimony for any, even those which have not been expressly detected,[68] that is not opposed by an infinite number of witnesses; so that not only the miracle destroys the credit of the[69] testimony, but even[70] the testimony destroys itself. To make this the better understood, let us consider that, in matters of religion, whatever is different is contrary, and that 'tis impossible the religions of antient ROME, of TURKEY, of SIAM, and of CHINA should, all of them, be established on any solid foundation. Every miracle, therefore, pretended to have been wrought in any of these religions (and all of them abound in miracles) as its direct scope is to establish the particular system, to which it is attributed; so has it the same force, tho' more indirectly, to overthrow every other system. In destroying a rival system, it likewise destroys the credit of those miracles, on which that system was established; so that all the prodigies of different religions are to be regarded as contrary facts, and the evidences of these prodigies, whether weak or strong, as opposite to

---

64 **1777:** *a large* for *large enough*
65 That is, have connections with people outside of their own small community.
66 **1777:** *throughout* for *thro'*
67 **1777:** omits this note
68 That is, expressly proven to be hoaxes.
69 **1777:** omits *the*
70 **1777:** omits *even*

each other. According to this method of reasoning, when we believe any miracle of MAHOMET[71] or any of[72] his successors, we have for our warrant the testimony of a few barbarous ARABIANS: And on the other hand, we are to regard the authority of TITUS LIVIUS, PLUTARCH, TACITUS,[73] and in short of all the authors and witnesses, GRECIAN, CHINESE, and ROMAN CATHOLIC, who have related any miracles[74] in their particular religion; I say, we are to regard their testimony in the same light as if they had mentioned that MAHOMETAN miracle, and had in express terms contradicted it, with the same certainty as they have for the miracles[75] they relate. This argument may appear over subtile and refined; but is not in reality different from the reasoning of a judge, who supposes, that the credit of two witnesses, maintaining a crime against any one, is destroyed by the testimony of two others, who affirm him to have been two hundred leagues distant, at the same instant when the crime is said to have been committed.

25. One of the best attested miracles in all prophane history, is that which TACITUS reports of VESPASIAN,[76] who cured a blind man in ALEXANDRIA, by means of his spittle, and a lame man by the mere touch of his foot; in obedience to a vision of the god, SERAPIS, who had enjoined them to have recourse to the emperor, for these miraculous and extraordinary[77] cures. The story may be seen in that fine historian;[aa] where every circumstance seems to add weight to the testimony, and might be displayed at large with all the force of argument and eloquence, if any one were now concerned to enforce the evidence of that exploded and idolatrous superstition. The gravity, solidity, age, and probity of so great an emperor, who, thro' the whole course of his life, conversed in a familiar way[78] with his friends and courtiers, and never affected those extraordinary airs of divinity, assumed by ALEXANDER and DEMETRIUS.[79] The historian, a cotemporary

---

71 Mohammed (c. 570-632), founder of Islam.

72 1777: omits *any of*

73 Titus Livius (Livy, 59 BCE-17 CE) and Plutarch (46-120) were Greco-Roman historians. For Tacitus, see Section 8, note 16. All three reported the occurrence of miracles attributed to pagan deities.

74 1777: *miracle* for *miracles*

75 1777: *miracle* for *miracles*

76 Titus Flavius Vespasianus (9-79) was emperor of Rome from 69 to 79.

77 1777: omits *and extraordinary*

78 1777: *manner* for *way*

79 Demetrius I (337-283 BCE) was a post-Alexandrian Macedonian king who allowed himself to be worshiped as a god.

writer, noted for candor and veracity, and withal, the greatest and most penetrating genius, perhaps of all antiquity; and so free from any tendency to superstition and[80] credulity, that he even lies under the contrary imputation, of atheism and prophaneness: The persons, from whose testimony[81] he related the miracle, of established character for judgment and veracity, as we may well presume; eye-witnesses of the fact, and confirming their verdict,[82] after the FLAVIAN family[83] were[84] despoiled of the empire, and could no longer give any reward, as the price of a lie. *Utrumque, qui interfuere, nunc quoque memorant, postquam nullum mendacio pretium.*[85] To which if we add the public nature of the facts, as related, it will appear, that no evidence can well be supposed stronger for so gross and so palpable a falshood.

26. There is also a very[86] memorable story related by Cardinal DE RETZ,[87] and[88] which may well deserve our consideration. When that intriguing politician fled into SPAIN, to avoid the persecution of his enemies, he passed thro' SARAGOSSA, the capital of ARRAGON, where he was shewn, in the cathedral, a man, who had served twenty[89] years as a door-keeper, and was well known to every body in town, that had ever paid their[90] devotions at that church. He had been seen, for so long a time, wanting a leg; but recovered that limb by the rubbing of holy oil upon the stump; and the cardinal assures us that he saw him with two legs.[91] This miracle was vouched by all the canons of the church;

---

80 **1777:** omits *superstition and*

81 **1777:** *authority* for *testimony*

82 **1777:** *testimony* for *verdict*

83 Members of the Flavian family, Vespasian, Titus, and Domitian, ruled Rome from 69 to 96.

84 **1777:** *was* for *were*

85 "Both events those who were present continue even now to recount, when from falsification [i.e., from perpetuating a falsehood] any gain is no longer to be hoped." Tacitus, *History*, Book IV, trans. Thomas Gordon, *The Works of Tacitus with Political Discourses upon that Author*, 3rd ed. (London: Longman, Hitch, Hawes, et al., 1753), Vol. 3, p. 354. Gale document CW3314974989.

86 **1777:** omits *very*

87 Jean François Paul de Gondi, Cardinal de Retz (1613-79) was a French churchman who wrote a widely read book of memoirs.

88 **1777:** omits *and*

89 **1777:** Beginning in **1764** this was corrected to seven.

90 **1777:** *his* for *their*

91 **1748-1750:** *when the Cardinal examin'd it, he found it to be a true natural Leg, like the other* for *the cardinal assures us that he saw him with two legs.*

and the whole company in town were appealed to for a confirmation of the fact; whom the cardinal found, by their zealous devotion, to be thorow believers of the miracle. Here the relater was also cotemporary to the supposed prodigy, of an incredulous and libertine character as well as of great genius, the miracle of so *singular* a nature as could scarce[92] admit of a counterfeit, and the witnesses very numerous, and all of them, in a manner, spectators of the fact, to which they gave their testimony. And what adds mightily to the force of the evidence, and may double our surprize on this occasion, is, that the cardinal himself, who relates the story, seems not to give any credit to it, and consequently cannot be suspected of any concurrence in the holy fraud. He considered justly, that it was not requisite, in order to reject a fact of this nature, to be able accurately to disprove the testimony, and to trace its falshood, thro' all the circumstances of knavery and credulity, which produced it. He knew, that as this was commonly altogether impossible at any small distance of time and place; so was it extremely difficult, even where one was immediately present, by reason of the bigotry, ignorance, cunning and roguery of a great part of mankind. He therefore concluded, like a just reasoner, that such an evidence carried falshood upon the very face of it, and that a miracle supported by any human testimony, was more properly a subject of derision than of argument.[93]

---

92 **1777:** *scarcely* for *scarce*

93 "I was shewed there a man who was employed to light the lamps, the number of which is prodigious, and I was told, that he had been seen at the door of that church for seven years together but with one leg, whereas now he had two [*avec une seule Jambe, je l'y vis avec deux*]. The dean and all the prehends assured me, that the whole town had seen it as well as they; and that if I would stay but two days longer, I might speak to above 20,000 persons from the neighbourhood, who had seen him, as well as those of the town. He had recovered his last leg (as he said) by anointing himself with some oil out of the lamps. They keep there a yearly holy day, in memory of that pretended miracle [*L'on celebre tous les ans la Fête de ce Miracle*], with an increadible concourse of people; and the truth is, that at the distance of a day's journey from Saragossa, I still met the roads full of persons of all qualities running to it [*couverts de gens de toutes sortes de qualitez qui y couroient*]." *Memoirs of the Cardinal De Retz*, vol. 3 (Dublin: R. Marchbank, 1777), 219. Gale Document CB3328485467. Original text from *Memoires du Cardinal De Retz*, vol. 3, expanded edition (Amsterdam, 1718), 294-95.

27. There surely never was so great a[94] number of miracles ascribed to one person, as[95] those, which were lately said to have been wrought in FRANCE upon the tomb of Abbé PARIS,[96] the famous JANSENIST,[97] with whose sanctity the people were so long deluded. The curing of the sick, giving hearing to the deaf, and sight to the blind, were every where talked of, as the usual effects of that holy sepulchre. But what is more extraordinary; many of the miracles were immediately proved, upon the spot, before judges of unquestioned integrity, attested by witnesses of credit and distinction, in a learned age, and on the most eminent theatre,[98] that is now in the world. Nor is this all: A relation of them was published, and dispersed every where; nor were the *Jesuits*, tho' a learned body, supported by the civil magistrate, and determined enemies to those opinions, in whose favor the miracles were said to have been wrought, ever able distinctly to refute or detect[99] them.[bb][100] Where shall we find such a number of circumstances, agreeing to the corroboration of one fact? And what have we to oppose to such a cloud of witnesses, but the absolute impossibility or miraculous nature of the events, which they relate? And this surely, in the eyes of all reasonable people, will alone be regarded as a sufficient refutation.

28. Is the consequence just, because some human testimony has the utmost force and authority in some cases, when it relates

---

94 1777: *a greater* for *so great a*

95 1777: *than* for *as*

96 François de Paris (1690-1727) was a Jansenist deacon who earned popularity through service to the poor and an austere lifestyle. After his death rumors of miraculous cures worked upon those who visited his tomb precipitated a frenzy.

97 The Jansenists were followers of the Catholic Bishop, Cornelius Jansen (1585-1638). Jansen's views on such topics as the possibility of salvation through the grace alone (downplaying the possibility of salvation through good works) revived an Augustinian strain of Christian theology that had also been emphasized by Protestants, and led Hume to declare that the Jansenists were only nominally Catholic (S&E: 79). The Jansenists were vigorously opposed by the Jesuits, a Catholic religious order that placed itself at the forefront of opposition to the Protestant Reformation.

98 I.e., in one of the most cosmopolitan cities.

99 I.e., expose them as forgeries.

100 This note was added in **1750**.

the battles[101] of PHILIPPI or PHARSALIA,[102] for instance; that therefore all kinds of testimony must, in all cases, have equal force and authority? Suppose that the CÆSAREAN and POMPEIAN factions had, each of them, claimed the victory in these battles, and that the historians of each party had uniformly ascribed the advantage to their own side; how could mankind, at this distance, have been able to determine between them? The contrariety is equally strong between the miracles related by HERODOTUS or PLUTARCH, and those delivered by MARIANA, BEDE, or any monkish historian.[103]

29. The wise lend a very academic faith[104] to every report, which favors the passion of the reporter; whether it magnifies his country, his family, or himself, or in any other way strikes in with his natural inclinations and propensities. But what greater temptation than to appear a missionary, a prophet, an ambassador from heaven? Who would not encounter many dangers and difficulties, in order to attain so sublime a character? Or if, by the help of vanity and a heated imagination, a man has first made a convert of himself and entered seriously into the delusion; who ever scruples to make use of pious frauds, in support of so holy and meritorious a cause?

30. The smallest spark may here kindle into the greatest flame; because the materials are always prepared for it. The *avidum genus auricularum,*[cc] the gazing populace receive greedily, without examination, whatever sooths superstition, and promotes wonder.

31. How many stories of this nature have, in all ages, been detected and exploded in their infancy? How many more have been celebrated for a time, and have afterwards sunk into neglect and oblivion? Where such reports, therefore, fly about, the solution of the phænomenon[105] is obvious; and we judge in conformity to

---

101 1777: *battle* for *battles*

102 These were decisive battles in Roman history. In 42 BCE Mark Anthony and Octavian defeated Caesar's assassins, Brutus and Cassius, at the battles of Philippi, marking an end to the Roman republic and the start of the empire. For the battle of Pharsalia, at which Pompey was defeated by Julius Caesar, see Section 3, note 25.

103 Herodotus of Halicarnassus lived in the mid-5th century BCE and wrote histories of Greece and Persia that contained a number of reports of marvelous events. For Plutarch, see note 73 above. Bede (c. 672-735) wrote a history of the Christian church in England. For Mariana, see Beauchamp's biographical appendix in **Beauchamp**: 277.

104 "Academic faith" is the sort of trust an academic sceptic would have in the truth of the story. See EHU 5.1 and p. 84 note 4.

105 That is, to the problem of whether to believe the testimony.

regular experience and observation, when we account for it by the known and natural principles of credulity and delusion. And shall we, rather than have a recourse to so natural a solution, allow of a miraculous violation of the most established laws of nature?

32. I need not mention the difficulty of detecting a falsehood in any private or even public history, at the time and[106] place, where it is said to happen; much more where[107] the scene is removed to ever so small a distance. Even a court of judicature, with all the authority, accuracy, and judgment, which they can employ, find themselves often at a loss to distinguish between truth and falsehood in the most recent actions. But the matter never comes to any issue, if trusted to the common method of altercation and debate and flying rumors; especially when men's passions have taken party[108] on either side.

33. In the infancy of new religions, the wise and learned commonly esteem the matter too inconsiderable to deserve their attention or regard. And when afterwards they would willingly detect the cheat, in order to undeceive the deluded multitude, the season is now gone,[109] and the records and witnesses, which might clear up the matter, have perished beyond recovery.

34. No means of detection remain, but those which must be drawn from the very testimony itself of the reporters: And these, tho' always sufficient with the judicious and knowing, are commonly too fine to fall under the comprehension of the vulgar.

35. Upon the whole, then, it appears, that no testimony for any kind of miracle has ever amounted[110] to a probability, much less to a proof; and that even supposing it amounted to a proof, it would be opposed by another proof, derived from the very nature of the fact, which it would endeavor to establish. 'Tis experience only, which gives authority to human testimony; and 'tis the same experience, which assures us of the laws of nature. When, therefore, these two kinds of experience are contrary, we have nothing to do but substract the one from the other, and embrace an opinion, either on one side or the other, with that assurance, which arises from the remainder. But according to the principle here explained, this substraction, with regard to all popular religions, amounts to an entire annihilation; and there-

---

106 **1777**: omits *time and*
107 **1777**: *when* for *where*
108 **1777**: *part* for *party*
109 **1777**: *past* for *gone*
110 **1748-50**: *can ever possibly amount* for *has ever amounted*

fore we may establish it as a maxim, that no human testimony can have such force as to prove a miracle, and make it a just foundation for any such system of religion.dd[111]

40. I am the better pleased with this method of reasoning,[112] as I think it may serve to confound those dangerous friends or disguised enemies to the *Christian Religion*, who have undertaken to defend it by the principles of human reason. Our most holy religion is founded on *Faith*, not on reason; and 'tis a sure method of exposing[113] it to put it to such a trial as it is, by no means, fitted to endure. To make this more evident, let us examine those miracles, related in scripture; and not to lose ourselves in too wide a field, let us confine ourselves to such as we find in the *Pentateuch*,[114] which we shall examine, according to the principles of these pretended Christians, not as the word or testimony of God himself, but as the production of a mere human writer and historian. Here then we are first to consider a book, presented to us by a barbarous and ignorant people, wrote[115] in an age when they were still more barbarous, and in all probability long after the facts which it relates; corroborated by no concurring testimony, and resembling those fabulous accounts, which every nation gives of its origin. Upon reading this book, we find it full of prodigies and miracles. It gives an account of a state of the world and of human nature entirely different from the present: Of our fall from that state: Of the age of man, extended to near a thousand years: Of the destruction of the world by a deluge: Of the arbitrary choice of one people, as the favorites of heaven; and that people, the countrymen of the author: Of their deliverance from bondage by prodigies the most astonishing imaginable: I desire any one to lay his hand upon his heart, and after[116] serious consideration declare, whether he

---

111 This note was moved into the text in **1770** as four successive paragraphs beginning at this point in the text, omitting the concluding reference to the passage cited from Bacon.

112 **1777**: *the method of reasoning here delivered* for *this method of reasoning*

113 "Expose" means attempt to kill by exposing to the elements, as when one abandons a newborn.

114 The five books of Moses which make up the early part of the "Old Testament" of the Christian Bible and are also recognized as sacred scriptures by Jews. By focusing on these books rather than the stories of the miracles of Jesus in the New Testament, Hume was softening what was otherwise a frontal attack on central Christian beliefs.

115 **1777**: *written* for *wrote*

116 **1777**: inserts *a*

thinks, that the falshood of such a book, supported by such a testimony, would be more extraordinary and miraculous than all the miracles it relates; which is, however, necessary to make it be received, according to the measures of probability above established.

41. What we have said of miracles may be applied, without any variation, to prophecies; and indeed, all prophecies are real miracles, and as such only, can be admitted as proofs of any revelation. If it did not exceed the capacity of human nature to foretel future events, it would be absurd to employ any prophecy as an argument for a divine mission or authority from heaven. So that, upon the whole, we may conclude, that the *Christian Religion*, not only was at first attended with miracles, but even at this day cannot be believed by any reasonable person without one. Mere reason is insufficient to convince us of its veracity: And whoever is moved by *Faith* to assent to it is conscious of a continued miracle in his own person, which subverts all the principles of his understanding, and gives him a determination to believe what is most contrary to custom and experience.

NOTES

ᵛ PLUTARCH. in vita CATONIS.[117]

ʷ No INDIAN, 'tis evident, could have experience that water did not freeze in cold climates. This is placing nature in a situation quite unknown to him; and 'tis impossible for him to tell *à priori* what will result from it. 'Tis making a new experiment, the consequence of which is always uncertain. One may sometimes conjecture from analogy what will follow; but still this is but conjecture. And it must be confest, that, in the present case of freezing, the event follows contrary to the rules of analogy, and is such as a rational INDIAN would not look for. The operations of cold upon water are not gradual, according to the degrees of cold; but whenever it comes to the freezing point, the water passes in a moment, from the utmost liquidity to perfect hardness. Such an event, therefore, may be denominated *extraordinary*, and requires a pretty strong testimony, to render it credible to people in a warm climate: But still it is not *miraculous*, nor contrary to uniform experience of the course of nature in cases where all the circum-

---

117 "And it was grown proverbial among the People, if any very unlikely or incredible thing were asserted, to say, *They would not believe it, though* Cato *Himself should affirm it*." Plutarch, "The life of Cato the younger," as translated in *Plutarch's Lives in eight volumes*, Vol. 6 (London: J. and R. Tonson and S. Draper, 1749), p. 241. Gale document CW3300254465.

stances[118] are the same. The inhabitants of SUMATRA have always seen water liquid[119] in their own climate, and the freezing of their rivers ought to be deemed a prodigy: But they never saw water in MUSCOVY during the winter; and therefore they cannot reasonably be positive what would there be the consequence.

ˣ Sometimes an event may not, *in itself*, *seem* to be contrary to the laws of nature, and yet, if it were real, it might, by reason of some circumstances, be denominated a miracle; because, in *fact*, it is contrary to these laws. Thus if a person, claiming a divine authority, should command a sick person to be well, a healthful man to fall down dead, the clouds to pour rain, the winds to blow, in short, should order many natural events, which immediately follow upon his command; these might justly be esteemed miracles, because they are really, in this case, contrary to the laws of nature. For if any suspicion remain, that the event and command concurred by accident, there is no miracle and no transgression of the laws of nature. If this suspicion be removed, there is evidently a miracle, and a transgression of these laws; because nothing can be more contrary to nature than that the voice or command of a man should have such an influence. *A miracle may be accurately defined, a transgression of a law of nature by a particular volition of the Deity, or by the interposal*[120] *of some invisible agent.* A miracle may either be discoverable by men or not. This alters not its nature and essence. The raising of a house or ship into the air is a visible miracle. The raising of a feather, when the wind wants ever so little of a force requisite for that purpose, is as real a miracle, tho' not so sensible with regard to us.

ʸ 19. The many instances of forged miracles, and prophecies and supernatural events, which, in all ages, have either been detected by contrary evidence, or which detect themselves by their absurdity, mark[121] sufficiently the strong propensity of mankind to the extraordinary and the marvellous, and ought reasonably to beget a suspicion against all relations of this kind. This is our natural way of thinking, even with regard to the most common and most credible events. For instance: There is no kind of report, which rises so easily, and spreads so quickly, especially in country places and provincial towns, as those concerning marriages; insomuch that two young persons of equal condition never see each other twice, but the whole neighborhood immediately join them together. The pleasure of telling a piece of news so interesting, of propagating it, and of being the first reporters of it,

---

118 Reading, with **1777**, *circumstances* for *circumstance*
119 **1777**: *fluid* for *liquid*
120 **1777**: *interposition* for *interposal*
121 **1777**: *prove* for *mark*

spreads the intelligence. And this is so well known, that no man of sense gives attention to these reports, till he finds[122] them confirmed by some greater evidence. Do not the same passions, and others still stronger, incline the generality of mankind to the believing and reporting,[123] with the greatest vehemence and assurance, all religious miracles?

z It may here, perhaps, be objected, that I proceed rashly, and form my notions of ALEXANDER merely from the account given of him by LUCIAN, a professed enemy. It were, indeed, to be wished, that some of the accounts published by his followers and accomplices had remained. The opposition and contrast betwixt the character and conduct of the same man, as drawn by a friend or an enemy is as strong, even in common life, much more in these religious matters, as that betwixt any two men in the world, betwixt ALEXANDER and St. PAUL,[124] for instance. See a letter to GILBERT WEST, Esq; on the conversion and apostleship of St. PAUL.[125]

aa Hist. Lib. 4.[126] Cap. 8. SUETONIUS gives[127] the same account *in vita* VESP.[128]

bb This book was wrote[129] by Mons. de[130] MONTGERON, counsellor or judge of the parliament of PARIS, a man of figure and character, who was also a martyr to the cause, and is now said to be somewhere in a dungeon on account of his book.[131]

---

122 **1777**: *find* for *finds*

123 **1777**: *believe and report* for *the believing and reporting*

124 The reference is to Paul of Tarsus (5-67), the pre-eminent figure in the establishment of the early Christian church.

125 [George, Lord Lyttelton], *Observations on the conversion and apostleship of St. Paul. In a letter to Gilbert West, esq.* (London: R. Dodsley, 1747). Gale document CB3326567773.

126 Reading, with **1748**, *4* for *5*. **Beauchamp**, 176, identifies 4.81 as the correct location. For a contemporary translation see Tacitus, *History*, Book IV, trans. Thomas Gordon, *The works of Tacitus with political discourses upon that author*, 3rd ed. (London: Longman, Hitch, Hawes, et al., 1753), Vol. 3, pp. 353-58. Gale document CW3314974988.

127 **1777**: inserts *nearly*

128 Suetonius, *The lives of the twelve Ceasars*, trans. Hughes, 2 Vols., 2nd ed., Vol. 2 (London: Theodore Sanders, 1726), pp. 456-57. Gale document CW3303610786.

129 **1777**: *writ* for *wrote*

130 **1777**: omits *de*

131 [Louis Basile Carré de Montgeron (1686-1754)], *La verité des miracles opérés par l'intercession de M. de Paris, démontrée contre M. l'Archêveque de Sens*, 3rd ed. (Cologne: Libraries de la Compagnie, 1739).

There is another book in three volumes (called *Recueil des Miracles de l'Abbé* PARIS)[132] giving an account of many of these miracles, and accompanied with prefatory discourses, which are very well wrote.[133] There runs, however, thro' the whole of these a ridiculous comparison betwixt the miracles of our Saviour and those of the Abbé; wherein 'tis asserted, that the evidence for the latter is equal to that for the former: As if the testimony of men could ever be put in the balance with that of God himself, who conducted the pen of the inspired writers. If these writers, indeed, were to be considered merely as human testimony, the FRENCH author is very moderate in his comparison; since he might, with some appearance of reason, pretend, that the JANSENIST miracles much surpass the others[134] in evidence and authority. The following circumstances are drawn from authentic papers, inserted in the above-mentioned book.

Many of the miracles of Abbé PARIS were proved[135] immediately by witnesses before the officiality or bishop's court of[136] PARIS, under the eye of cardinal NOAILLES,[137] whose character for integrity and capacity was never contested even by his enemies.

His successor in the archbishopric was an enemy to the JANSENISTS, and for that reason promoted to the see by the court. Yet 22 rectors or *cures* of PARIS, with infinite earnestness, press him to examine those miracles, which they assert to be known to the whole world, and indisputably certain: But he wisely forbore.[138]

---

132 *Recueil des miracles opérés au tombeau de M. de Paris Diacre. Avec les requêtes présentées à Monsieur de Vintimille Archevêque de Paris, par Messieurs les curés de cette ville; & un discours préliminaire sur les miracles.* 3 vols. (Utrecht: de la Compagnie, 1733).

133 **1777**: *written* for *wrote*

134 **1777**: *other* for *others*

135 Here "proved" is used in yet another sense more modest than what a modern reader would take it for. It merely means "testified to." Compare the modest sense of "proof" at EHU 12.

136 **1777**: *at* for *of*

137 Louis-Antoine de Noailles (1651-1729) was archbishop of Paris from 1695 to 1729 (two years after the death of Abbé Paris) and later named a Cardinal. He may have been sympathetic to the Jansenists.

138 The suggestion is that Vintimille, the new archbishop, refused to undertake the investigation because he appreciated that it would be impossible to expose the hoaxes, notwithstanding that he would have been strongly motivated to make the attempt and able to marshal considerable resources to ensure its success. The rectors, for their part, must have been so confident of their case that they were willing to gamble that even an investigation by a known opponent would fail to discredit the stories.

The MOLINIST[139] party had tried to discredit these miracles in one instance, that of Madamoiselle le FRANC. But besides, that their proceedings were in many respects the most irregular in the world, particularly in citing only a few of the JANSENIST[140] witnesses, whom they tampered with: Besides this, I say, they soon found themselves overwhelmed by a cloud of new witnesses, one hundred and twenty in number, most of them persons of credit and substance in PARIS, who gave oath for the miracle. This was accompanied with a solemn and earnest appeal to the parliament. But the parliament were forbid[141] by authority to meddle in the affair. It was at last observed that where men are heated by zeal and enthusiasm, there is no degree of human testimony so strong as may not be procured for the greatest absurdity: And those who will be so silly as to examine the affair by that medium,[142] and seek particular flaws in the testimony, are almost sure to be confounded. It must be a miserable imposture, indeed, that does not prevail in that contest.

All who have been in FRANCE about that time have heard of the great[143] reputation of Mons. HERAUT, the *lieutenant de Police*, whose vigilance, penetration, activity, and extensive intelligence have been much talked of. This magistrate, who by the nature of his office is almost absolute, was invested with full powers, on purpose to suppress or discredit these miracles; and he frequently seized immediately, and examined the witnesses and subjects of them: But never could reach any thing satisfactory against them.

In the case of Madamoiselle THIBAUT he sent the famous De SYLVA to examine her; whose evidence is very curious. The physician declares, that it was impossible she could have been so ill as was proved by witnesses; because it was impossible she could, in so short a time, have recovered so perfectly as he found her. He reasoned like a man of sense, from natural causes; but the opposite party told him, that the whole was a miracle, and that his evidence was the very best proof of it.

The MOLINISTS were in a sad dilemma. They durst not assert the absolute insufficiency of human evidence to prove a miracle: They were obliged to say, that these miracles were wrought by witchcraft and

---

139 "Molinist" is a synonym for "Jesuit." Luis de Molina (1535-1600) was a Jesuit theologian who attempted to reconcile Augustinian doctrines concerning salvation through grace alone with a strong position on the ability of human beings to freely choose to do good.

140 Reading, with **1777**, *JANSENIST* for *JANSENISTS*

141 **1777**: *forbidden* for *forbid*

142 That is, simply by considering the strength of the testimony in favour of the event, and trying to cast doubt on the occurrence of the event by attempting to show that the testimony is in some way flawed.

143 **1777**: omits *great*

the devil. But they were told, that this was the resource of the JEWS of old.

No JANSENIST was ever embarrassed to account for the cessation of the miracles, when the church-yard was shut up by the king's edict. It was the touch of the tomb, which operated[144] these extraordinary effects; and when no one could approach the tomb, no effects could be expected. God, indeed, could have thrown down the walls in a moment; but he is master of his own graces and works, and it belongs not to us to account for them. He did not throw down the walls of every city like those of JERICHO, on the sounding of the rams-horns, nor break up the prison of every apostle, like that of St. PAUL.[145]

No less a man, than the Duc de CHATILLON,[146] a duke and peer of FRANCE of the highest rank and family, gives evidence of a miraculous cure, performed upon a servant of his, who had lived several years in his house with a visible and palpable infirmity.

I shall conclude with observing, that no clergy are more celebrated for strictness of life and manners than the secular clergy of FRANCE, particularly the rectors or curés of PARIS, who bear such[147] testimony to these impostures.

The learning, genius, and probity of the gentlemen and the austerity of the nuns of PORT-ROYAL have been much celebrated all over EUROPE. Yet they all give evidence for a miracle, wrought on the niece of the famous PASCHAL,[148] whose sanctity of life, as well as extraordi-

---

144 **1777**: *produced* for *operated*
145 Compare EHU note **z** which contains another allusion to St. Paul with mention of Lyttleton's *Observations*. Lyttleton had asked why the miracles had ceased once a wall had been built around the church-yard, preventing entry to the tomb. "... if God had really worked any Miracles there, could this absurd Prohibition have taken Effect? Would He have suffered his Purpose to be defeated by building a Wall? When all the Apostles were shut up in Prison to hinder their working of Miracles, the Angel of the Lord opened the Prison Doors and let them out. But the Power of *Abbé Paris* could neither throw down the Wall that excluded his Votaries, nor operate through that Impediment. And yet his Miracles are often compared with, and opposed by Unbelievers to those of *Christ* and his Apostles, which is the reason of my having taken particular Notice of them here" (63). Gale document CB3326567837.
146 Perhaps Paul-Sigismond de Montmorency-Luxembourg (1663-1731), though he had resigned the title of Duc de Châtillon to his son, Charles-Paul-Sigismond (1697-1785) in 1713.
147 **1777**: omits *such*
148 Blaise Pascal (1623-62) along with Jean-Baptiste Racine (1639-99), Antoine Arnauld (1612-94), and Pierre Nicole (1625-95), mentioned below, were famous French intellectuals and literary figures (Pascal, a mathematician and philosopher; Racine, a dramatist; Arnauld and Nicole, theologians and philosophers) who were all Jansenists.

nary capacity, is well known.[149] The famous RACINE gives an account of this miracle in his famous history of PORT-ROYAL, and fortifies it with all the proofs, which a multitude of nuns, priests, physicians, and men of the world, all of them of undoubted credit, could bestow upon it. Several men of letters, particularly the bishop of TOURNAY,[150] thought this miracle so certain, as to employ it in the refutation of atheists and free-thinkers. The queen-regent of FRANCE,[151] who was extremely prejudiced against the PORT-ROYAL, sent her own physician to examine the miracle, who returned an absolute convert. In short, the supernatural cure was so uncontestable, that it saved, for a time, that famous monastery from the ruin with which it was threatened by the Jesuits. Had it been a cheat, it had certainly been detected by such sagacious and powerful antagonists, and must have hastened the ruin of the contrivers. Our divines, who can build up a formidable castle from such despicable materials; what a prodigious fabric could they have reared from these and many other circumstances, which I have not mentioned! How oft would the great names of PASCHAL, RACINE, ARNAUD, NICOLE,[152] have resounded in our ears? But if they be wise, they had better adopt the miracle, as being more worth, a thousand times, than all the rest of their collection. Besides, it may serve very much to their purpose. For that miracle was really performed by the touch of an authentic holy prickle of the holy thorn, which composed the holy crown, which, &c.[153]

ᶜᶜ LUCRET.[154]

---

149 She was reportedly cured of a facial ulcer by having it pricked with a thorn supposed to have been taken from the crown of thorns worn by Christ.

150 For information on the Bishop of Tournay, see Beauchamp's biographical appendix in **Beauchamp**: 273 and 274.

151 Anne of Austria (1601-66), consort to the late Louis XIII.

152 See note 147 above.

153 **1750**: *known; tho' he also was a Believer, in that and in many other Miracles, which he had less Opportunity of being inform'd of. See his Life.* for *known. The famous* RACINE ... *holy crown, which, &c.*

154 The text paraphrases Lucretius, *De rerum natura* 4.594, "humanum genus est auidum nimis auricularum" (T. Lucreti Cari, *De rerum Natura*, William Ellery Leonard and Stanley Barney Smith, eds. [Madison: University of Wisconsin Press, 1942]). "Mankind in general are mighty eager after Prodigies." T. Lucretius Carus, *Of the nature of things in six books illustrated with proper and useful notes. Adorned with copper plates curiously engraved by Guernier and others,* 2 Vols. (London: Daniel Browne, 1743) Vol. 2, p. 55. Gale document CW3319385938.

^{dd} 36. I beg the limitations here made may be remarked, when I say, that a miracle can never be proved, so as to be the foundation of a system of religion. For I own, that otherwise, there may possibly be miracles, or violations of the usual course of nature, of such a kind as to admit of proof from human testimony; tho', perhaps, it will be impossible to find any such in all the records of history. Thus, suppose, all authors, in all languages, agree, that from the first of JANUARY, 1600, there was a total darkness over the whole earth for eight days: Suppose that the tradition of this extraordinary event, is still strong and lively among the people: That all travellers, who return from foreign countries, bring us accounts of the same tradition, without the least variation or contradiction: 'Tis evident, that our present philosophers, instead of doubting of that[155] fact, ought to receive it for[156] certain, and ought to search for the causes, whence it might be derived. The decay, corruption, and dissolution of nature, is an event rendered probable by so many analogies, that any phænomenon, which seems to have a tendency towards that catastrophe, comes within the reach of human testimony, if that testimony be very extensive, and uniform.[157]

37. But suppose, that all the historians, who treat of ENGLAND, should agree, that on the first of JANUARY, 1600, queen ELIZABETH died; that both before and after her death she was seen by her physicians and the whole court, as is usual with persons of her rank; that her successor was acknowleged and proclaimed by the parliament; and that, after being interred a month, she again appeared, took possession of[158] the throne, and governed ENGLAND for three years: I must confess,[159] I should be surprized at the concurrence of so many odd circumstances, but should not have the least inclination to believe so miraculous an event. I should not doubt of her pretended death, and of those other public circumstances, that followed it: I should only assert it to have been pretended, and that it neither was, nor possibly could be real. You would in vain object to me the difficulty, and almost impossibility of deceiving the world in an affair of such consequence; the wisdom and integrity[160] of that renowned queen; with the little or no advantage which she could reap from so poor an artifice: All this might astonish me; but I would still reply, that the knavery and folly of men are such common phænomena, that I should rather believe the most extraordinary events to arise from their concurrence than admit[161] so signal a violation of the laws of nature.

---

155 1777: *the* for *of that*

156 1777: *as* for *for*

157 This sentence was added in **1756**.

158 1777: *resumed* for *took possession of*

159 1777: *that* for comma

160 1777: *solid judgment* for *integrity*

161 1777: inserts *of*

38. But should this miracle be ascribed to any new system of religion; men, in all ages, have been so much imposed on by ridiculous stories of that kind; that this very circumstance would be a full proof of a cheat, and sufficient, with all men of sense, not only to make them reject the fact, but even reject it without farther examination. Tho' the Being to whom the miracle is ascribed, be, in this case, Almighty, it does not, upon that account, become a whit more probable; since 'tis impossible for us to know the attributes or actions of such a being, otherwise than from the experience, which we have, of his productions, in the usual course of nature. This still reduces us to past observation, and obliges us to compare the instances of the violations[162] of truth in the testimony of men with those of the violation of the laws of nature by miracles, in order to judge which of them is most likely and probable. As the violations of truth are more common in the testimony concerning religious miracles than in that concerning any other matter of fact; this must diminish very much the authority of the former testimony, and make us form a general resolution never to lend any attention to it, with whatever specious pretext[163] it may be covered.

39. My[164] lord BACON[165] seems to have embraced the same principles of reasoning. "Facienda enim est congeries sive historia naturalis particularis omnium monstrorum & partuum naturæ prodigiosorum; omnis denique novitatis & raritatis & inconsueti in natura. Hoc vero faciendum est cum severissimo delectu, ut constet fides. Maxime autem habenda sunt pro suspectis quæ pendent quomodocunque ex religione, ut prodigia LIVII: Nec minus quæ inveniuntur in scriptoribus magiæ naturalis, aut etiam alchymiæ, & hujusmodi hominibus; qui tanquam proci sunt & amatores fabularum."[166]

Nov. Organ. Lib. 2. Aph. 29.[167]

---

162 1777: *violation* for *violations*

163 1777: *pretence* for *pretext*

164 1777: omits *My*

165 Francis Bacon (1561-1626) was Lord Chancellor of England from 1613 to 1621 during the reign of James I. He was also one of the founders of an inductivist program in natural philosophy that was inherited and further developed by Hobbes, Locke, and Hume himself.

166 1777 translates: *"We ought, says he, to make a collection or particular history of all monsters and prodigious births or productions, and in a word of every thing new, rare, and extraordinary in nature. But this must be done with the most severe scrutiny, lest we depart from truth. Above all, every relation must be considered as suspicious, which depends in any degree upon religion, as the prodigies of LIVY: And no less so, every thing that is to be found in the writers of natural magic or alchimy, or such authors, who seem, all of them, to have an unconquerable appetite for falsehood and fable."*

167 1777: enters "Nov. Org. lib. ii. aph. 29" as a footnote.

SECTION 11
OF A PARTICULAR PROVIDENCE[1]
AND OF A FUTURE STATE[2]

1. I was lately engaged in conversation with a friend who loves sceptical paradoxes; where, tho' he advanced many principles, of which I can by no means approve, yet as they seem to be curious, and to bear some relation to the chain of reasoning carried on thro' this Enquiry, I shall here copy them from my memory as accurately as I can, in order to submit them to the judgment of the reader.

2. Our conversation began with my admiring the singular good fortune of philosophy, which, as it requires intire liberty, above all other privileges, and flourishes chiefly[3] from the free opposition of sentiments and argumentation, received its first birth in an age and country of freedom and toleration, and was never cramped, even in its most extravagant principles, by any creeds, confessions, or penal statutes. For except the banishment of PROTAGORAS, and the death of SOCRATES,[4] which last event proceeded partly from other motives, there are scarce[5] any instances to be met with, in antient history, of this bigotted jealousy, with which the present age is so much infested. EPICURUS[6] lived at ATHENS to an advanced age, in peace and tranquility: EPICUREANS[ee] were even admitted to receive the sacerdotal charac-

---

1 According to NHR 6.2, particular providence consists of special acts performed by God to provide for particular human beings, by miraculous intervention in the course of nature. Extending the notion to include negative as well as positive providence would introduce fear of divine wrath, as well as hope for divine favour, as an inducement to serve God.

2 **1748**: *Of the* PRACTICAL CONSEQUENCES *of* NATURAL RELIGION for *OF A PARTICULAR PROVIDENCE AND OF A FUTURE STATE*

3 1777: *chiefly flourishes* for *florishes chiefly*

4 Protagoras (490-420 BCE) was reputedly banished from Athens and Socrates (469-399 BCE) offered the choice of exile from that city or death (he chose death). In both cases, the sentences were motivated by charges of impiety.

5 1777: *scarcely* for *scarce*

6 See Section 5, note 1. The Epicurean school was founded by Epicurus of Samos (341-270 BCE), who taught that there is no afterlife of any sort and that the gods did not create or design the universe and do not intervene in the course of nature to reward or punish human beings for service or violation of taboos.

ter,[7] and to officiate at the altar, in the most sacred rites of the established religion: And the public encouragement[ff] of pensions and sallaries was afforded equally, by the wisest of all the ROMAN emperors,[gg] to the professors of every sect of philosophy. How requisite such kind of treatment was to philosophy, in its first origin,[8] will easily be conceived, if we reflect, that even at present, when it[9] may be supposed more hardy and robust, it[10] bears with much difficulty the inclemency of the seasons, and those harsh winds of calumny and persecution, which blow upon it.[11]

3. You admire, says my friend, as the singular good-fortune of philosophy, what seems to result from the natural course of things, and to be unavoidable in every age and nation. This pertinacious bigotry, of which you complain, as so fatal to philosophy, is really her offspring, who, after allying with superstition, separates himself intirely from the interest of his parent, and becomes her most inveterate enemy and persecutor.[12] Speculative dogmas of religion, the present occasions of such furious dispute, could not possibly be conceived or admitted in the early ages of the world; when mankind, being wholly illiterate, formed an idea of religion, more suitable to their weak apprehension, and composed their sacred tenets chiefly of such tales[13] as were the objects of traditional belief, more than of argument or disputation.[14] After the first alarm, therefore, was over, which arose from the new paradoxes and principles of the philosophers; these teachers seem, ever after, during the ages of antiquity, to have lived in great harmony with the established superstitions,[15] and to have made a fair partition of mankind betwixt them; the former claiming all the learned and the[16] wise, and[17] the latter possessing all the vulgar and illiterate.

---

7 That is, they were allowed to serve as priests.

8 1777: *her early youth* for *its first origin*

9 1777: *she* for *it*

10 1777: *she* for *it*

11 1777: *her* for *it*

12 This is explained more fully in Hume's own voice at NHR 11, informed by NHR 1-7.

13 1777: *of such tales chiefly* for *chiefly of such tales*

14 See NHR 11.1 on the reasonableness of primitive polytheism and NHR 11.3 on the opposed "appetite" of monotheistic superstitions for absurdities.

15 1777: *superstition* for *superstitions*

16 1777: omits *the*

17 1777: omits *and*

4. It seems then, says[18] I, that you leave politics intirely out of the question, and never suppose, that a wise magistrate can justly be jealous[19] of certain tenets of philosophy, such as those of EPICURUS, which denying a divine existence, and consequently a providence and a future state, seem to loosen, in a great measure, the ties of morality, and may be supposed, for that reason, pernicious to the peace of civil society.

5. I know, replied he, that in fact these persecutions never, in any age, proceeded from calm reason, or any[20] experience of the pernicious consequences of philosophy; but arose entirely from passion and prejudice. But what if I should advance farther, and assert, that if EPICURUS had been accused before the people, by any of the *sycophants* or informers of those days, he could easily have defended his cause, and proved his principles of philosophy to be as salutary as those of his adversaries, who endeavored, with such zeal, to expose him to the public hatred and jealousy?

6. I wish, said I, you would try your eloquence upon so extraordinary a topic, and make a speech for EPICURUS, which might satisfy, not the mob of ATHENS, if you will allow that antient and polite city to have contained any mob, but the more philosophical part of his audience, such as might be supposed capable of comprehending his arguments.

7. The matter would not be difficult, upon such conditions, replied he: And if you please, I shall suppose myself EPICURUS for a moment, and make you stand for the ATHENIAN people, and shall deliver you such an harangue as will fill all the urn with white beans, and leave not a black one to gratify the malice of my adversaries.[21]

8. Very well: pray proceed upon these suppositions.

9. I come hither, O ye ATHENIANS, to justify in your assembly what I maintained in my school, and[22] find myself impeached by furious antagonists, instead of reasoning with calm and dispassionate enquirers. Your deliberations, which of right should be directed to questions of public good, and the interest of the com-

---

18 1777: *say* for *says*

19 Here "jealous" means "suspicious."

20 1777: *from* for *any*

21 In Athenian courts, the citizens assembled to hear the case would deliver their verdicts by placing either a black bean (for guilt) or a white bean (for innocence) in an urn. The case would be decided by the bean count.

22 1777: inserts *I*

monwealth, are diverted to the disquisitions of speculative philosophy; and these magnificent, but, perhaps, fruitless enquiries, take place of your more familiar but more useful occupations. But so far as in me lies, I will prevent this abuse. We shall not here dispute concerning the origin and government of worlds. We shall only enquire how far such questions concern the public interest. And if I can persuade you, that they are entirely indifferent to the peace of society and security of government, I hope that you will presently send us back to our schools, there to examine at leisure the question the most sublime, but, at the same time, the most speculative of all philosophy.

10. The religious philosophers, not satisfied with the traditions[23] of your forefathers, and doctrines[24] of your priests (in which I willingly acquiesce) indulge a rash curiosity, in trying how far they can establish religion upon the principles of reason; and they thereby excite, instead of satisfying the doubts, which naturally arise from a diligent and scrutinous enquiry. They paint, in the most magnificent colors, the order, beauty, and wise arrangement of the universe; and then ask, if such a glorious display of intelligence could proceed from the fortuitous concourse of atoms, or if chance could produce what the highest[25] genius can never sufficiently admire. I shall not examine the justness of this argument. I shall allow it to be as solid as my antagonists and accusers can desire. 'Tis sufficient, if I can prove, from this very reasoning, that the question[26] is entirely speculative,[27] and that when, in my philosophical disquisitions, I deny a providence and a future state, I undermine not the foundations of society, but advance principles,[28] which they themselves, upon their own topics, if they argue consistently, must allow to be solid and satisfactory.

11. You then, who are my accusers, have acknowleged, that the chief or sole argument for a divine existence (which I never questioned) is derived from the order of nature; where there

---

23 1777: *tradition* for *traditions*

24 1777: *doctrine* for *doctrines*

25 1777: *greatest* for *highest*

26 The question is whether the gods created or designed the universe.

27 See EHU 11.22 for a summary statement of why the question of whether the gods designed the universe is "entirely speculative," that is, has no practical implications for how people ought to comport themselves in society.

28 The principles advanced are scepticism about providence and an after life.

appear such marks of intelligence and design, that you think it extravagant to assign for its cause, either chance, or the blind and unguided force of matter. You allow, that this is an argument, drawn from effects to causes. From the order of the work, you infer, that there must have been project and forethought in the workman. If you cannot make out this point, you allow, that your conclusion fails; and you pretend not to establish the conclusion in a greater latitude than the phænomena of nature will justify. These are your concessions. I desire you to mark the consequences.

12. When we infer any particular cause from an effect, we must proportion the one to the other, and can never be allowed to ascribe to the cause any qualities, but what are exactly sufficient to produce the effect. A body of ten ounces raised in any scale may serve as a proof, that the counter-ballancing weight exceeds ten ounces; but can never afford a reason, that it exceeds a hundred. If the cause, assigned for any effect, be not sufficient to produce it, we must either reject that cause, or add to it such qualities as will give it a just proportion to the effect. But if we ascribe to it farther qualities, or affirm it capable of producing other effects, we can only indulge the licence of conjecture, and arbitrarily suppose the existence of qualities and energies, without reason or authority.

13. The same rule holds, whether the cause assigned be brute unconscious matter or a rational intelligent being. If the cause be known only by the effect, we never ought to assign[29] to it any qualities, beyond what are precisely requisite to produce the effect: nor can we, by any rules of just reasoning, return back from the cause, and infer other effects from it, beyond those by which alone it is known to us. No one, merely from the sight of one of ZEUXIS'S[30] pictures, could know, that he was also a statuary[31] or architect, and was an artist no less skilful in stone and marble than in colors.[32] The talents and taste displayed in the particular work before us; these we may safely conclude the workman to be possessed of.[33] The cause must be proportioned to the effect: And if we exactly and precisely proportion it, we shall never find in it any qualities that point farther, or afford an

---

29 1777: *ascribe* for *assign*

30 Zeuxis (c. 464–? BCE) was an ancient Greek artist.

31 That is, a sculptor.

32 Reading, with 1777, a sentence break at this point.

33 Reading this as a separate sentence, with 1777

inference concerning any other design or performance. Such qualities must be somewhat beyond what is merely requisite to produce[34] the effect, which we examine.

14. Allowing, therefore, the gods to be the authors of the existence or order of the universe; it follows, that they possess that precise degree of power, intelligence, and benevolence, which appears in their workmanship; but nothing farther can ever be proved, except we call in the assistance of exaggeration and flattery to supply the defects of argument and reasoning.[35] So far as the traces of any attributes, at present, appear, so far may we conclude these attributes to exist. The supposition of farther attributes is mere hypothesis; much more, the supposition, that, in distant periods of place and[36] time, there has been, or will be a more magnificent display of these attributes, and a scheme of administration more suitable to such imaginary virtues. We can never be allowed to mount up from the universe, the effect, to JUPITER, the cause; and then descend downwards, to infer any new effect from that cause; as if the present effects alone were not entirely worthy of the glorious attributes which we ascribe to that deity. The knowledge of the cause being derived solely from the effect, they must be exactly adjusted to each other, and the one can never point towards[37] any thing farther, or be the foundation of any new inference and conclusion.

15. You find certain phænomena in nature. You seek a cause or author. You imagine that you have found him. You afterwards become so enamoured of this offspring of your brain, that you imagine it impossible but he must produce something greater, and more perfect than the present scene of things, which is so full of ill and disorder. You forget, that this superlative intelligence and benevolence are entirely imaginary, or at least, without any foundation in reason; and that you have no ground to ascribe to him any qualities, but what you see he has actually exerted and displayed in his productions. Let your gods, therefore, O philosophers, be suited to the present appearances of nature: And presume not to alter these appearances by arbitrary suppositions, in order to suit them to the attributes, which you so fondly ascribe to your deities.

16. When priests and poets, supported by your authority, O ATHENIANS, talk of a golden or a[38] silver age, which preceded the

---

34 1777: *for producing* for *to produce*
35 See NHR 6.
36 1777: *regions of space and periods of* for *periods of place and*
37 1777: *refer to* for *point towards*
38 1777: omits *a*

present scene[39] of vice and misery, I hear them with attention and with reverence. But when philosophers, who pretend to neglect authority, and to cultivate reason, hold the same discourse, I pay them not, I own, the same obsequious submission and pious deference. I ask; Who carried them into the celestial regions, who admitted them into the councils of the gods, who opened to them the book of fate, that they thus rashly affirm that their deities have executed, or will execute, any purpose, beyond what has actually appeared? If they tell me, that they have mounted on the steps or by the gradual ascent of reason, and by drawing inferences from effects to causes, I still insist, that they have aided the ascent of reason by the wings of imagination; otherwise they could not thus change their manner of inference, and argue from causes to effects; presuming, that a more perfect production than the present world would be more suitable to such perfect beings as the gods, and forgetting, that they have no reason to ascribe to these celestial beings any perfection or any attribute, but what can be found in the present world.

17.   Hence all the fruitless industry to account for the ill appearances of nature, and save the honor of the gods; while we must acknowlege the reality of that evil and disorder, with which the world so much abounds. The obstinate and intractable qualities of matter, we are told, or the observance of general laws, or some such reason is the sole cause, which controlled the power and benevolence of JUPITER, and obliged him to create mankind and every sensible creature so imperfect and so unhappy.[40] These attributes, then, are, it seems, beforehand, taken for granted, in their greatest latitude. And upon that supposition, I own, that such conjectures may, perhaps, be admitted as plausible solutions of the ill phænomena. But still I ask; Why take these attributes for granted, or why ascribe to the cause any qualities but what actually appear in the effect? Why torture your brain to justify the course of nature upon suppositions, which, for aught you know,

---

39 1777: *state* for *scene*

40 "Epicurus" here alludes to two different explanations of why evil exists. According to the first, the gods did not create the world, but merely designed it out of pre-existent matter, and they did the best they could with the materials they had available—materials that are liable to various sorts of failure. According to the other, God has seen that it would be best if all events in nature occur in accord with laws that are never violated. He therefore refuses to work miracles, even if it means that misery occasionally results.

may be entirely imaginary, and of which there are to be found no traces in the course of nature?

18. The religious hypothesis, therefore, must be considered only as a particular method of accounting for the visible phænomena of the universe: But no just reasoner will ever presume to infer from it any single fact, and alter or add to the phænomena, in any single particular. If you think, that the appearances of things prove such causes, 'tis allowable for you to draw an inference concerning the existence of these causes. In such complicated and sublime subjects, every one should be indulged in the liberty of conjecture and argument. But here you ought to rest. If you come backward, and arguing from your inferred causes, conclude, that any other fact has existed, or will exist, in the course of nature, which may serve for[41] a fuller display of particular attributes; I must admonish you, that you have departed from the method of reasoning, attached to the present subject, and must certainly have[42] added something to the attributes of the cause, beyond what appears in the effect; otherwise you could never, with tolerable sense or propriety, add any thing to the effect, in order to render it more worthy of the cause.

19. Where, then, is the odiousness of that doctrine, which I teach in my school, or rather, which I examine in my gardens?[43] Or what do you find in this whole question, wherein the security of good morals, or the peace and order of society is in the least concerned?[44]

20. I deny a providence, you say, and supreme governor of the world, who guides the course of events, and punishes the vicious with infamy. and disappointment, and rewards the virtuous with honor and success, in all their undertakings. But surely, I deny not the course itself of events, which lies open to every one's enquiry and examination. I acknowlege, that, in the present order of things, virtue is attended with more peace of mind than vice; and meets with a more favorable reception from the world. I am sensible, that, according to the past experience of mankind, friendship is the chief joy of human life, and moderation the only

---

41 1777: *as* for *for*
42 1777: *have certainly* for *must certainly have*
43 Epicurus lectured in the gardens of his estate.
44 This question is answered in the next paragraph.

source of tranquility and happiness.[45] I never balance between the virtuous and the vicious course of life;[46] but am sensible, that, to a well disposed mind, every advantage is on the side of the former. And what can you say more, allowing all your suppositions and reasonings? You tell me, indeed, that this disposition of things proceeds from intelligence and design. But whatever it proceeds from, the disposition itself, on which depends our happiness or misery, and consequently our conduct and deportment in life, is still the same. 'Tis still open for me, as well as you, to regulate my behavior, by my experience of past events. And if you affirm, that, while a divine providence is allowed, and a supreme distributive justice in the universe, I ought to expect some more particular reward of the good, and punishment of the bad, beyond the ordinary course of events; I here find the same fallacy, which I have before endeavored to detect. You persist in imagining, that, if we grant that divine existence, for which you so earnestly contend, you may safely infer consequences from it, and add something to the experienced order of nature, by arguing from the attributes, which you ascribe to your gods. You seem not to remember, that all your reasonings on this subject can only be drawn from effects to causes; and that every argument, deduced from causes to effects, must of necessity be a gross sophism; since it is impossible for you to know any thing of the cause, but what you have antecedently, not inferred, but discovered to the full, in the effect.

21. But what must a philosopher judge[47] of those vain reasoners, who, instead of regarding the present scene of things, as the sole object of their contemplation, so far reverse the whole course of nature, as to render this life merely a passage to something farther; a porch, which leads to a greater, and vastly different building; a prologue, which serves only to introduce the piece, and give it more grace and propriety? Whence, do you think, can such philosophers derive their idea of the gods? From their own conceit and imagination surely. For if they derived it

---

45 These are in fact Epicurean ethical teachings. Contrary to the current meaning of "Epicurean," Epicurus taught that people ought to wean themselves from expensive tastes and take joy in a simple and self-sufficient lifestyle.

46 That is, I never pause to think about whether to behave virtuously or viciously.

47 1777: *think* for *judge*

from the present phænomena, it would never point to any thing farther, but must be exactly adjusted to them. That the divinity may *possibly* possess[48] attributes, which we have never seen exerted; may be governed by principles of action, which we cannot discover to be satisfied: All this will freely be allowed. But still this is mere *possibility* and hypothesis. We never can have reason to *infer* any attributes, or any principles of action in him, but so far as we know them to have been exerted and satisfied.

22. *Are there any marks of a distributive justice in the world?* If you answer in the affirmative, I conclude, that, since justice here exerts itself, it is satisfied. If you reply in the negative, I conclude, that you have then no reason to ascribe justice[49] to the gods. If you hold a medium between affirmation and negation, by saying, that the justice of the gods, at present, exerts itself in part, but not in its full extent; I answer, that you have no reason to give it any particular extent, but only so far as you see it, *at present,* exert itself.

23. Thus I bring the dispute, O ATHENIANS, to a short issue with my antagonists. The course of nature lies open to my contemplation as well as[50] theirs. The experienced train of events is the great standard by which we all regulate our conduct. Nothing else can be appealed to in the field, or in the senate. Nothing else ought ever to be heard of, in the school, or in the closet.[51] In vain, would our limited understandings[52] break thro' those boundaries, which are too narrow for our fond imaginations.[53] While we argue from the course of nature, and infer a particular intelligent cause, which first bestowed, and still preserves order in the universe, we embrace a principle, which is both uncertain and useless. 'Tis uncertain; because the subject lies entirely beyond the reach of human experience.[54] 'Tis useless; because our knowlege of this cause being derived entirely from the course of nature, we can never, according to the rules of just reasoning, return back from the cause with any new inferences,[55] or making additions to the common and expe-

---

48 **1777:** *be endowed with* for *possess*
49 **1777:** inserts *in our sense of it*
50 **1777:** inserts *to*
51 That is, in the home.
52 **1777:** *understanding* for *understandings*
53 **1777:** *imagination* for *imaginations*
54 This is more fully explained by Hume himself at EHU 11.30.
55 **1777:** *inference* for *inferences*

rienced course of nature, establish any new principles of conduct and behavior.

24. I observe (says[56] I, finding he had finished his harangue) that you neglect not the artifice of the demagogues of old; and as you was[57] pleased to make me stand for the people, you insinuate yourself into my favor, by embracing those principles, to which, you know, I have always expressed a particular attachment. But allowing you to make experience (as indeed I think you ought) the only standard of our judgment concerning this, and all other questions of fact; I doubt not but, from the very same experience, to which you appeal, it may be possible to refute this reasoning, which you have put into the mouth of EPICURUS. If you saw, for instance, a half-finished building surrounded with heaps of brick and stone and mortar, and all the instruments of masonry; could you not *infer* from the effect, that it was a work of design and contrivance? And could you not return again, from this inferred cause, to infer new additions to the effect, and conclude, that the building would soon be finished, and receive all the farther improvements, which art could bestow upon it? If you saw, upon the sea shore, the print of one human foot, you would conclude, that a man had passed that way, and that he had also left the traces of the other foot, tho' effaced by the rolling of the sands or inundation of the waters. Why then do you refuse to admit the same method of reasoning with regard to the order of nature? Consider the world and the present life only as an imperfect building, from which you can infer a superior intelligence; and arguing from that superior intelligence, which can leave nothing imperfect; why may you not infer a more finished scheme or plan, which will receive its completion in some distant period[58] of space or time? Are not these methods of reasoning exactly parallel?[59] And under what pretext[60] can you embrace the one while you reject the other?

25. The infinite difference of the subjects, replied he, is a sufficient foundation for this difference in my conclusions. In works of *human* art and contrivance, 'tis allowable to advance from the effect to the cause, and returning back from the cause,[61] form

---

56 1777: *said* for *says*
57 1777: *were* for *was*
58 1777: *point* for *period*
59 1777: *similar* for *parallel*
60 1777: *pretence* for *pretext*
61 1777: inserts *to*

new inferences concerning the effect, and examine the alterations, which it has probably undergone, or may still undergo. But what is the foundation of this method of reasoning? Plainly this; that man is a being, whom we know by experience, whose motives and designs we are acquainted with, and whose projects and inclinations have a certain connexion and coherence, according to the laws, which nature has established for the government of such a creature. When, therefore, we find, that any work has proceeded from the skill and industry of man; as we are otherwise acquainted with the nature of the animal; we can draw a hundred inferences concerning what may be expected from him; and these inferences will all be founded on[62] experience and observation. But did we know man only from the single work or production, which we examine, it were impossible for us to argue in this manner; because our knowlege of all the qualities, which we ascribe to him, being in that case derived from the production, 'tis impossible they could point to any thing farther, or be the foundation of any new inferences.[63] The print of a foot in the sand can only prove, when considered alone, that there was some figure adapted to it, by which it was produced: But the print of a human foot proves likewise, from our other experience, that there was probably another foot, which also left its impression, tho' effaced by time or other accidents. Here we mount from the effect to the cause; and descending again from the cause, infer alterations in the effect; but this is not a continuation of the same simple chain of reasoning. We comprehend in this case a hundred other experiences and observations, concerning the *usual* figure and members of that species of animal, without which this method of argument must be considered as fallacious and sophistical.

26. The case is not the same with our reasonings from the works of nature. The Deity is known to us only by his productions, and is a single being in the universe, not comprehended under any species or genus, from whose experienced attributes or qualities, we can, by analogy, infer any attribute or quality in him. As the universe shews wisdom and goodness, we infer wisdom and goodness: As it shows a particular degree of these perfections, we infer a particular degree of them, precisely adapted to the effect, which we examine. But farther attributes or farther degrees of the same attributes, we can never be authorized

---

62 1777: *in* for *on*

63 1777: *inference* for *inferences*

to infer or suppose, by any rules of just reasoning. Now without some such licence of supposition, 'tis impossible for us to argue from the cause, or infer any alteration in the effect, beyond what has immediately fallen under our observation. Greater good produced by this Being must still prove a greater degree of goodness: More[64] impartial distribution of rewards and punishments must proceed from a superior[65] regard to justice and equity. Every supposed addition to the works of nature makes an addition to the attributes of the author of nature; and consequently, being entirely unsupported by any reason or argument, can never be admitted but as mere conjecture and hypothesis.[hh]

27.[66] The great source of our mistake in this subject, and of the unbounded licence of conjecture, which we indulge, is, that we tacitly consider ourselves, as in the place of the supreme Being, and conclude, that he will, on every occasion, observe the same conduct, which we ourselves, in his situation, would have embraced as reasonable and eligible. But besides, that the ordinary course of nature may convince us, that almost every thing is regulated by principles and maxims very different from ours; besides this, I say, it must evidently appear contrary to all rule[67] of analogy to reason from the intentions and projects of men to those of a being so different, and so much superior. In human nature, there is a certain experienced coherence of designs and

---

64 **1777**: *A more* for *More*

65 **1777**: *greater* for *superior*

66 **1748-1750**: insert, as a new paragraph *In general, it may, I think, be estab-lish'd as a Maxim, that where any Cause is known only by its particular Effects, it must be impossible to infer any new Effects from that Cause; since the Qualities, which are requisite to produce these new Effects, along with the former, must either be different, or superior, or of more extensive Operation, than those which simply produc'd the Effect, whence alone the Cause is suppos'd to be known to us.* We can never, therefore, have any Reason to suppose the Existence of these Qualities.*

67 **1777**: *rules* for *rule*

---

* *To say that the new Effects proceed only from a Continuation of the same Energy, which is already known from the first Effects, will not remove the Difficulty. For even granting this to be the Case, (which can seldom be suppos'd) the very Continuation and Exertion of a like Energy (for 'tis impossible it can be absolutely the same) I say, this Exertion of a like Energy in a different Period of Space and Time is a very arbitrary Supposition, and what there cannot possibly be any Traces of in the Effects, from which all our Knowledge of the Cause is originally deriv'd. Let the infer'd Cause be exactly proportion'd (as it should be) to the known Effect; and 'tis impossible that it can possess any Qualities, from which new or different Effects can be infer'd.*

inclinations; so that when, from any facts,[68] we have discovered one intention of any man, it may often be reasonable, from experience, to infer another, and draw a long chain of conclusions concerning his past or future conduct. But this method of reasoning never can[69] have place with regard to a Being, so remote and incomprehensible, who bears[70] less analogy to any other being[71] in the universe than the sun to a waxen taper, and who discovers himself only by some faint traces or outlines, beyond which we have no authority to ascribe to him any attribute or perfection. What we imagine to be a superior perfection may really be a defect. Or were it ever so much a perfection, the ascribing[72] it to the supreme Being, where it appears not to have been really exerted, to the full, in his works, savors more of flattery and panegyric, than of just reasoning and sound philosophy. All the philosophy, therefore, in the world, and all the religion, which is nothing but a species of philosophy, will never be able to carry us beyond the usual course of experience, or give us measures of conduct and behavior, different from those which are furnished by reflections on common life. No new fact can ever be inferred from the religious hypothesis; no event foreseen or foretold; no reward or punishment expected or dreaded, beyond what is already known by practice and observation. So that my apology for EPICURUS will still appear solid and satisfactory; nor have the political interests of society any connexion with the philosophical disputes concerning metaphysics and religion.

28. There is still one circumstance, replied I, which you seem to have overlooked. Tho' I should allow your premises, I must still[73] deny your conclusion. You conclude, that religious doctrines and reasonings *can* have no influence on life, because they *ought* to have no influence; never considering, that men reason not in the same manner you do, but draw many consequences from the belief of a divine existence, and suppose that the Deity will inflict punishments on vice, and bestow rewards on virtue,[74] beyond what appear in the ordinary course of nature. Whether

---

68 1777: *fact* for *facts*
69 1777: *can never* for *never can*
70 1777: inserts *much*
71 Reading, with 1777, *being* for *Being*
72 1777: inserts *of*
73 1777: omits *still*
74 Reading with 1756 and 1760, a comma for the extra blank space present in 1758.

this reasoning of theirs be just or not, is no matter. Its influence on their life and conduct must still be the same. And those, who may[75] attempt to disabuse them of such prejudices, may, for aught I know, be good reasoners, but I cannot allow them to be good citizens and politicians; since they free men from one restraint upon their passions, and make the infringement of the laws of society, in one respect, more easy and secure.'

29. After all, I may, perhaps, agree to your general conclusion in favor of liberty, tho' upon different premises from those, on which you endeavor to found it. I think that the state ought to tolerate every principle of philosophy; nor is there an instance that any government has suffered in its political interests by such indulgence. There is no enthusiasm among philosophers; their doctrines are not very alluring to the people; and no restraint can be put upon their reasonings, but what must be of dangerous consequence to the sciences, and even to the state, by paving the way for persecution and oppression in points, where the generality of mankind are more deeply interested and concerned.

30. But there occurs to me (continued I) with regard to your main topic, a difficulty, which I shall just propose to you, without insisting on it; lest it lead into reasonings of too nice and delicate a nature. In a word, I much doubt whether it be possible for a cause to be known only by its effect (as you have all along supposed) or to be of so singular and particular a nature as to have no parallel and no similarity with any other cause or object, that has ever fallen under our observation. 'Tis only when two *species* of objects are found to be constantly conjoined, that we can infer the one from the other; and were an effect presented, which was entirely singular, and could not be comprehended under any known *species*; I do not see, that we could form any conjecture, or inference at all concerning its cause. If experience and observation and analogy be, indeed, the only guides which we can reasonably follow in inferences of this nature; both the effect and cause must bear a similarity and resemblance to other effects and causes which we know, and which we have found in many instances, to be conjoined with each other. I leave it to your own reflections[76] to prosecute[77] the consequences of this principle. I shall just observe, that as the antagonists of EPICURUS always suppose the universe, an effect quite singular and unparalleled, to

---

75 1777: omits *may*
76 1777: *reflection* for *reflections*
77 1777: *pursue* for *prosecute*

be the proof of a Deity, a cause no less singular and unparalleled; your reasonings, upon that supposition, seem, at least, to merit our attention. There is, I own, some difficulty, how we can ever return from the cause to the effect, and reasoning from our ideas of the former, infer any alteration on the latter, or any addition to it.

NOTES

ee Luciani συμπ. ἤ λαπιθαι.[78]

ff Id. ευνουχος.[79]

gg Id. & Dio.[80]

hh In general, it may, I think, be established as a maxim, that where any cause is known only by its particular effects, it must be impossible to infer any new effects from that cause; since the qualities, which are requisite to produce these new effects along with the former, must either be different, or superior, or of more extensive operation, than those which simply produced the effect, whence alone the cause is supposed to be known to us. We can never, therefore, have any reason to suppose the existence of these qualities. To say that the new effects proceed only from a continuation of the same energy, which is already known from the first effects, will not remove the difficulty. For even granting this to be the case, (which can seldom be supposed) the very continuation and exertion of a like energy (for 'tis impossible it can be absolutely the same) I say, this exertion of a like energy in a different period of space and time is a very arbitrary supposition, and what there cannot possibly be any traces of in the effects, from which all our knowlege of the cause is originally derived. Let the *inferred* cause be exactly proportioned (as it should be) to the known effect; and 'tis impossible that it can possess any qualities, from which new or different effects can be *inferred*.[81]

---

78 Lucian, "The lapithae: or, the drunken feast," trans. Thomas Brown, in *The works of Lucian, translated from the Greek by several eminent hands*, 3 Vols., Vol. 3 (London: James Woodward, 1711), p. 212. Gale document CW3312173289. One of the characters, Hermon, is described as both an Epicurean philosopher and a priest of Castor and Pollux.

79 Lucian, "The eunuch," trans. Thomas Brown, in *The works of Lucian, translated from the Greek by several eminent hands*, 3 Vols., Vol. 3 (London: James Woodward, 1711), pp. 3, 6. Gale document CW3312173078 and 81.

80 **Beauchamp**, 187, identifies this source.

81 **1748-1750**: reposition various parts of this note as described in note 66 above.

SECTION 12
OF THE ACADEMICAL OR SCEPTICAL PHILOSOPHY

PART I

1. There is not a greater number of philosophical reasonings, displayed upon any subject, than those, which prove the existence of a Deity, and refute the fallacies of *Atheists*; and yet the most religious philosophers still dispute whether any man can be so blinded as to be a speculative atheist. How shall we reconcile these contradictions? The knight-errants, who wandered about to clear the world of dragons and giants, never entertained the least doubt with regard to the existence of these monsters.

2. The *Sceptic* is another enemy of religion, who naturally provokes the indignation of all divines and graver philosophers; tho' 'tis certain, that no man ever met with any such absurd creature, or conversed with a man, who had no opinion or principle concerning any subject, either of action or speculation. This begets a very natural question; What is meant by a sceptic? And how far it is possible to push these philosophical principles of doubt and uncertainty?

3. There is a species of scepticism, *antecedent* to all study and philosophy, which is much inculcated by DES CARTES[1] and others, as a sovereign preservative against error and precipitate judgment.[2] It recommends an universal doubt, not only of all our former opinions and principles, but also of our very faculties; of whose veracity, say they, we must assure ourselves, by a chain of reasoning, deduced from some original principle, which cannot possibly be fallacious or deceitful. But neither is there any such original principle, which has a prerogative above others, that are self-evident and convincing: Or if there were, could we advance a step beyond it, but by the use of these[3] very faculties, of which we are supposed to be already diffident. The CARTESIAN doubt, therefore, were it ever possible to be attained by any human creature (as it plainly is not) would be entirely incurable; and no reasoning could ever bring us to a state of assurance and conviction upon any subject.

4. It must, however, be confessed, that this species of scepticism, when more moderate, may be understood in a very reason-

---

1   For Descartes, see Section 7, note 70.
2   See René Descartes, *Discourse on Method*, I-II, and *Meditations on First Philosophy* I.
3   **1777:** *those* for *these*

able sense, and is a necessary preparative to the study of philosophy, by preserving a proper impartiality in our judgments, and weaning our mind from all those prejudices, which we may have imbibed from education or rash opinion. To begin with clear and self-evident principles, to advance by timorous and sure steps, to review frequently our conclusions, and examine accurately all their consequences;[4] tho' by this[5] means we shall make both a slow and a short progress in our systems; are the only methods, by which we can ever hope to reach truth, and attain a proper stability and certainty in our determinations.

5. There is another species of scepticism, *consequent* to science and enquiry, where[6] men are supposed to have discovered, either the absolute fallaciousness of their mental faculties, or their unfitness to reach any fixed determination in all those curious subjects of speculation, about which they are commonly employed. Even our very senses are brought into dispute, by a certain species of philosophers; and the maxims of common life are subjected to the same doubt as the most profound principles or conclusions of metaphysics and theology. As these paradoxical tenets (if they may be called tenets) are to be met with in some philosophers, and the refutation of them in several, they naturally excite our curiosity, and make us enquire into the arguments, on which they may be founded.

6. I need not insist upon the more trite topics, employed by the sceptics in all ages, against the evidence of *sense*; such as those[7] derived from the imperfection and fallaciousness of our organs, on numberless occasions; the crooked appearance of an oar in water; the various aspects of objects, according to their different distances; the double images, which arise from the pressing one eye; with many other appearances of a like nature; these sceptical topics, indeed, are only sufficient to prove, that the senses alone are not implicitly to be depended on; but that we must correct their evidence by reason, and by considerations, derived from the nature of the medium, the distance of the object, and the disposition of the organ, in order to render them, within their sphere, the proper *criteria* of truth and falshood.

---

4 This is a summary of the four methodical rules Descartes presented in *Discourse* II.
5 1777: *these* for *this*
6 1777: *when* for *where*
7 1777: inserts *which are*

There are other more profound arguments against the senses, which admit not of so easy a solution.

7. It seems evident, that men are carried, by a natural instinct or prepossession, to repose faith in their senses; and that, without any reasoning, or even almost before the use of reason, we always suppose an external universe, which depends not on our perception, but would exist, tho' we and every sensible creature were absent or annihilated. Even the animal creation are governed by a like opinion, and preserve this belief of external objects, in all their thoughts, designs, and actions.

8. It seems also evident, that when men follow this blind and powerful instinct of nature, they always suppose the very images, presented by the senses, to be the external objects, and never entertain any suspicion, that the one are nothing but representations of the other. This very table, which we see white, and which we feel hard, is believed to exist, independent of our perception, and to be something external to our mind, which perceives it. Our presence bestows not being on it: Our absence annihilates it not.[8] It preserves its existence uniform and entire, independent of the situation of intelligent beings, who perceive or contemplate it.

9. But this universal and primary opinion of all men is soon destroyed by the slightest philosophy,[9] which teaches us, that nothing can ever be present to the mind but an image or perception, and that the senses are only the inlets, thro' which these images are received,[10] without being ever[11] able to produce any immediate intercourse between the mind and the object. The table, which we see, seems to diminish, as we remove farther from it: But the real table which exists independent of us, suffers no alteration: It was, therefore, nothing but its image, which was present to the mind. These are the obvious dictates of reason; and no man, who reflects, ever doubted, that the existences, which we consider, when we say, *this house* and *that tree* are nothing but perceptions in the mind, and fleeting copies or representations of other existences, which remain uniform and independent.

10. So far, then, are we necessitated by reasoning to contradict or depart from the primary instincts of nature, and to embrace a new system with regard to the evidence of our senses.

---

8 1777: *does not annihilate it* for *annihilates it not*

9 That is, by arguments grounded in the most basic and easily obtained experiences.

10 1777: *conveyed* for *received*

11 1777: omits *ever*

But here philosophy finds itself[12] extremely embarrassed, when it[13] would justify this new system, and obviate the cavils and objections of the sceptics. It[14] can no longer plead the infallible and irresistible instinct of nature: For that led us to a quite different system,[15] which is acknowleged fallible and even erroneous. And to justify this pretended philosophical system, by a chain of clear and convincing argument, or even any appearance of argument, exceeds the power of all human capacity.

11. By what argument can it be proved, that the perceptions of the mind must be caused by external objects, entirely different from them, tho' resembling them (if that be possible) and could not arise either from the energy of the mind itself, or from the suggestion of some invisible and unknown spirit, or from some other cause still more unknown to us? 'Tis acknowleged, that, in fact, many of these perceptions arise not from any thing external, as in dreams, madness, and other diseases. And nothing can be more inexplicable than the manner, in which body should so operate upon mind as ever to convey an image of itself to a substance supposed of so different, and even contrary a nature. .

12. 'Tis a question of fact, whether the perceptions of the senses be produced by external objects, resembling them: How shall this question be determined? By experience surely; as all other questions of a like nature. But here experience is, and must be entirely silent. The mind has never any thing present to it but the perceptions, and cannot possibly reach any experience of their connexion with objects. The supposition of such a connexion is, therefore, without any foundation in reasoning.

13. To have recourse to the veracity of the supreme Being, in order to prove the veracity of our senses, is surely making a very unexpected circuit.[16] If his veracity were at all concerned in this matter, our senses would be entirely infallible; because it is not possible that he can ever deceive. Not to mention, that if the external world be once called in doubt,[17] we shall be at a loss to

---

12 1777: *herself* for *itself*

13 1777: *she* for *it*

14 1777: *She* for *It*

15 Namely, to the view that external objects are directly encountered in sensory experience.

16 This is an allusion to Descartes' argument for the existence of an external world, which was well known and had been much discussed. See *Meditations* VI.

17 1777: *question* for *doubt*

find arguments, by which we may prove the existence of that Being or any of his attributes.

14. This is a topic, therefore, in which the profounder and more philosophical sceptics will always triumph, when they endeavor to introduce an universal doubt into all subjects of human knowlege and enquiry. Do you follow the instincts and propensities of nature, may they say, in assenting to the veracity of sense? But these lead you to believe, that the very perception or sensible image is the external object. Do you disclaim this principle, in order to embrace a more rational opinion, that the perceptions are only representations of something external? You here depart from your natural propensities and more obvious sentiments; and yet are not able to satisfy your reason, which can never find any convincing argument from experience to prove, that the perceptions are connected with any external objects.

15. There is another sceptical topic of a like nature, derived from the most profound philosophy; which might merit our attention, were it requisite to dive so deep, in order to discover arguments and reasonings, which can serve so little[18] any serious purpose. 'Tis universally allowed by modern enquirers, that all the sensible qualities of objects, such as hard, soft, hot, cold, white, black, &c. are merely secondary, and exist not in the objects themselves, but are perceptions of the mind, without any external archetype or model, which they represent. If this be allowed, with regard to secondary qualities, it must also follow with regard to the supposed primary qualities of extension and solidity; nor can the latter be any more entitled to that denomination than the former. The idea of extension is entirely acquired from the senses of sight and feeling; and if all the qualities, perceived by the senses, be in the mind, not in the object, the same conclusion must reach the idea of extension, which is wholly dependent on the sensible ideas or the ideas of secondary qualities. Nothing can save us from this conclusion, but the asserting, that the ideas of those primary qualities are attained by *Abstraction*;[19] which, if we examine[20] accurately, we shall find to be unintelligible, and even absurd. An extension, that is neither tangible nor visible, cannot possibly be conceived: And a tangible or visible extension, which is neither hard nor soft, black nor white, is equally beyond the reach of human conception. Let any man

---

18 **1777**: *so little serve to* for *serve so little*
19 **1777**: inserts *an opinion*
20 **1777**: inserts *it*

try to conceive a triangle in general, which is neither *Isosceles*, nor *Scalenum*, nor has any particular length nor[21] proportion of sides; and he will soon perceive the absurdity of all the scholastic notions with regard to abstraction and general ideas.[ii]

16. Thus the first philosophical objection[22] to the evidence of sense or to the opinion of external existence consists in this, that such an opinion, if rested on natural instinct, is contrary to reason, and if referred to reason, is contrary to natural instinct, and at the same time carries no rational evidence with it, to convince an impartial enquirer. The second objection[23] goes farther, and represents this opinion as contrary to reason; at least, if it be a principle of reason, that all sensible qualities are in the mind, not in the object.[24]

PART II

17. It may seem a very extravagant attempt of the sceptics to destroy *reason* by argument and ratiocination; yet is this the grand scope of all their enquiries and disputes. They endeavor to find objections, both to our abstract reasonings, and to those which regard matter of fact and existence.

18. The chief objection against all *abstract* reasonings is derived from the ideas of space and time; ideas, which, in common life and to a careless view, are very clear and intelligible, but when they pass thro' the scrutiny of the profound sciences (and they are the chief object of these sciences) afford principles which seem full of absurdity and contradiction. No priestly *dogmas*, invented on purpose to tame and subdue the rebellious reason of mankind, ever shocked common sense more than the doctrine of the infinite divisibility of extension, with its consequences; as they are pompously displayed by all geometricians and metaphysicians, with a kind of triumph and exultation. A real quantity, infinitely less than any finite quantity, containing quantities, infinitely less than itself, and so on, *in infinitum*; this is an edifice so bold and prodigious, that it is too weighty for any pretended demonstration

---

21 1777: *or* for *nor*

22 The one presented over EHU 12.7-14.

23 The one presented at EHU 12.15.

24 1777: inserts *Bereave matter of all its intelligible qualities, both primary and secondary, you in a manner annihilate it, and leave only a certain unknown, inexplicable* <u>something</u>, *as the cause of our perceptions; a notion so imperfect, that no sceptic will think it worth while to contend against it.*

to support, because it shocks the clearest and most natural principles of human reason.[kk] But what renders the matter more extraordinary, is, that these seemingly absurd opinions are supported by a chain of reasoning, the clearest and most natural; nor is it possible for us to allow the premises without admitting the consequences. Nothing can be more convincing and satisfactory than all the conclusions concerning the properties of circles and triangles; and yet, when these are once received, how can we deny, that the angle of contact betwixt a circle and its tangent is infinitely less than any rectilineal angle, that as you may encrease the diameter of the circle *in infinitum*, this angle of contact becomes still less, even *in infinitum*, and that the angle of contact between other curves and their tangents may be infinitely less than those between any circle and its tangent, and so on, *in infinitum?* The demonstration of these principles seems as unexceptionable as that which proves the three angles of a triangle to be equal to two right ones; tho' the latter opinion be natural and easy, and the former big with contradiction and absurdity. Reason here seems to be thrown into a kind of amazement and suspence, which, without the suggestions of any sceptic, gives her a diffidence of herself, and of the ground on which she[25] treads. She sees a full light, which illuminates certain places; but that light borders upon the most profound darkness. And betwixt these she is so dazzled and confounded, that she scarce[26] can pronounce with certainty and assurance concerning any one object.

19. The absurdity of these bold determinations of the abstract sciences seems to become, if possible, still more palpable with regard to time than extension. An infinite number of real parts of time, passing in succession, and exhausted one after another, appears so evident a contradiction,[27] that no man, one should think, whose judgment is not corrupted, instead of being improved, by the sciences, would ever be able to admit of it.

---

25 Reading, with **1777**, *she* for *he*

26 1777: *scarcely* for *scarce*

27 The idea seems to be that if there were infinitely many moments between any two given moments, say between 23:59:59.99 and midnight, a second hand of a clock would never be able to get from 23:59:59.99 to midnight, so that time would not pass. For, however quickly the second hand moves over the infinitely many moments between midnight and a hundredth of a second before midnight, as long as it takes one moment after another and never passes through multiple moments at once, it will never reach an end of the moments that must be passed over before reaching midnight.

20. Yet still reason must remain restless and unquiet, even with regard to that scepticism, to which she is led[28] by these seeming absurdities and contradictions. How any clear, distinct idea can contain circumstances, contradictory to itself, or to any other clear, distinct idea, is absolutely incomprehensible; and is, perhaps, as absurd as any proposition, which can be formed. So that nothing can be more sceptical, or more full of doubt and hesitation, than this scepticism itself, which arises from some of the paradoxical conclusions of geometry or the science of quantity.[II]

21. The sceptical objections to *moral* evidence or to the reasonings concerning matter of fact are either *popular* or *philosophical*. The popular objections are derived from the natural weakness of human understanding; the contradictory opinions, which have been entertained in different ages and nations; the variations of our judgment in sickness and health, youth and old age, prosperity and adversity; the perpetual contradiction of each particular man's opinions and sentiments; with many other topics of that kind. 'Tis needless to insist farther on this head. These objections are but weak. For as, in common life, we reason every moment concerning fact and existence, and cannot possibly subsist, without continually employing this species of argument, any popular objections, derived from thence, must be insufficient to destroy that evidence. The great subverter of *Pyrrhonism* or the excessive principles of scepticism,[29] is action, and employment, and the occupations of common life. These principles may florish and triumph in the schools; where it is, indeed, difficult, if not impossible to refute them. But as soon as they leave the shade,

---

28 1777: *driven* for *led*
29 The Pyrrhonians were followers of Pyrrho of Elis (360-270 BCE) and formed a minor Hellenic school. Like the Academics, they were sceptics, but they represented themselves as more thorough and consistent in their scepticism than the Academics. Hume, following that line, treated Pyrrhonian scepticism as a more extreme or excessive form of scepticism, but it is questionable whether his representation of Pyrrhonism is faithful to the actual teachings of the Pyrrhonists. Be that as it may, on Hume's account, Pyrrhonian scepticism denies not only all knowledge but also all probability and holds that nothing is any more likely than anything else, so that suspense of judgment is warranted on all things. In Hume's view, academic sceptics maintain that we can be warranted in forming beliefs on certain topics, though we must recognize that the beliefs are fallible and refrain from overstepping the bounds within which they are justified.

and by the presence of the real objects, which actuate our passions and sentiments, are put in opposition to the more powerful principles of our nature, they vanish like smoak, and leave the most determined sceptic in the same condition as other mortals.

22. The sceptic, therefore, had better keep in[30] his proper sphere, and display those *philosophical* objections, which arise from more profound researches. Here he seems to have ample matter of triumph; while he justly insists, that all our evidence for any matter of fact, which lies beyond the testimony of sense or memory, is derived entirely from the relation of cause and effect; that we have no other idea of this relation than that of two objects, which have been frequently *conjoined* together; that we have no arguments[31] to convince us, that objects, which have, in our experience, been frequently conjoined, will likewise, in other instances, be conjoined in the same manner; and that nothing leads us to this inference but custom or a certain instinct of our nature; which it is indeed difficult to resist, but which, like other instincts, may be fallacious and deceitful. While the sceptic insists upon these topics, he shews his force, or rather, indeed, his own and our weakness; and seems, for the time at least, to destroy all assurance and conviction. These arguments might be displayed at greater length, if any durable good or benefit to society could ever be expected to result from them.

23. For here is the chief and most confounding objection to *excessive* scepticism, that no durable good can ever result from it; while it remains in its full force and vigor. We need only ask such a sceptic, *What his meaning is? And what he proposes by all these curious researches?* He is immediately at a loss, and knows not what to answer. A COPERNICAN or PTOLEMAIC,[32] who supports each his different system of astronomy, may hope to produce a conviction, which will remain, constant and durable, with his audience. A STOIC or EPICUREAN displays principles, which may not only be durable, but which have a mighty[33] effect on conduct

---

30 1777: *within* for *in*

31 1777: *argument* for *arguments*

32 The reference is to the Copernican theory that the Sun is at rest and the Earth in orbit around it, and the Ptolemaic theory that the Earth at rest and the Sun in orbit around it. The theories are named after the Polish astronomer, Nicolas Copernicus (1473-1543) and the Alexandrian astronomer Ptolemy (late 1st to early 2nd centuries).

33 1777: *an* for *a mighty*

and behavior. But a PYRRHONIAN[34] cannot propose,[35] that his philosophy will have any constant influence on the mind: Or if it had, that its influence would be beneficial to society. On the contrary, he must acknowlege, if he will acknowlege any thing, that all human life must perish, were his principles universally and steadily to prevail. All discourse, all action would immediately cease; and men remain in a total lethargy, till the necessities of nature, unsatisfied, put an end to their miserable existence. 'Tis true; so fatal an event is very little to be dreaded. Nature is always too strong for principle. And tho' a PYRRHONIAN may throw himself or others into a momentary amazement and confusion by his profound reasonings; the first and most trivial event in life will put to flight all his doubts and scruples, and leave him the same, in every point of action and speculation, with the philosophers of every other sect, or with those who never concerned themselves in any philosophical researches. When he awakes from his dream, he will be the first to join in the laugh against himself, and to confess, that all his objections are mere amusements,[36] and can have no other tendency than to show the whimsical condition of mankind, who must act and reason and believe; tho' they are not able, by their most diligent enquiry, to satisfy themselves concerning the foundation of these operations, or to remove the objections, which may be raised against them.

PART III

24. There is, indeed, a more *mitigated* scepticism or *academical* philosophy, which may be both durable and useful, and which may, in part, be the result of this PYRRHONISM, or *excessive* scepticism, when its undistinguished doubts are, in some measure, corrected by common sense and reflexion. The greatest[37] part of mankind are naturally apt to be affirmative and dogmatical in their opinions; and while they see objects only on one side, and have no idea of any counterpoising arguments,[38] they throw

---

34 See Section 5, note 1 and Section 11, note 6. Like the Stoics, the Epicureans proposed to teach a way of life that would lead to happiness. It consists principally in weaning oneself of all strong desires, abandoning fear of death and of judgment or retribution by gods, and learning to take pleasure in simple things. For Pyrrhonism, see note 29 above.

35 1777: *expect* for *propose*

36 1777: *amusement* for *amusements*

37 1777: *greater* for *greatest*

38 1777: *argument* for *arguments*

themselves precipitately into the principles, to which they are inclined; nor have they any indulgence for those who entertain opposite sentiments. To hesitate or balance perplexes their understandings,[39] checks their passion, and suspends their actions.[40] They are, therefore, impatient till they escape from a state, which to them is so uneasy; and they think, that they can never remove themselves far enough from it, by the violence of their affirmations and obstinacy of their belief. But could such dogmatical reasoners become sensible of the strange infirmities of human understanding, even in its most perfect state, and when most accurate and cautious in its determinations; such a reflection would naturally inspire them with more modesty and reserve, and diminish their fond opinion of themselves, and their prejudice against antagonists. The illiterate may reflect on the disposition of the learned, who, amidst all the advantages of study and reflection, are commonly still diffident in their determinations: And if any of the learned are[41] inclined, from their natural temper, to haughtiness and obstinacy, a small tincture of PYRRHONISM may[42] abate their pride, by showing them, that the few advantages, which they may have attained over their fellows, are but inconsiderable, if compared with the universal perplexity and confusion, which is inherent in human nature. In general, there is a degree of doubt, and caution, and modesty, which, in all kinds of scrutiny and decision, ought for ever to accompany a just reasoner.

25. Another species of *mitigated* scepticism, which may be of advantage to mankind, and which may be the natural result of the PYRRHONIAN doubts and scruples, is the limitation of our enquiries to such subjects as are best adapted to the narrow capacity of human understanding. The *imagination* of man is naturally sublime, delighted with whatever is remote and extraordinary, and running, without control, into the most distant parts of space and time, in order to avoid the objects, which custom has rendered too familiar to it. A correct *Judgment* observes a contrary method; and avoiding all distant and high enquiries, confines itself to common life, and to such subjects as fall under daily practice and experience; leaving the more sublime topics to the embellishment of poets and orators, or to the arts of priests and

---

39 1777: *understanding* for *understandings*
40 1777: *action* for *actions*
41 1777: *be* for *are*
42 1777: *might* for *may*

politicians. To bring us to so salutary a determination, nothing can be more serviceable, than to be once thorowly convinced of the force of the PYRRHONIAN doubt, and of the impossibility that any thing but the strong power of natural instinct, could free us from it. Those who have a propensity to philosophy, will still continue their researches; because they reflect, that, besides the immediate pleasure, attending such an occupation, philosophical decisions are nothing but the reflections of common life, methodized and corrected. But they will never be tempted to go beyond common life, so long as they consider the imperfection of those faculties which they employ, their narrow reach, and their inaccurate operations. While we cannot give a satisfactory reason, why we believe after a thousand experiments, that a stone will fall, or fire burn; can we ever satisfy ourselves concerning any determinations[43] which we may form with regard to the origin of worlds, and the situation of nature, from, and to eternity?

26. This narrow limitation, indeed, of our enquiries, is, in every respect, so reasonable, that it suffices to make the slightest examination into the natural powers of the human mind,[44] and[45] compare them to[46] their objects, in order to recommend it to us.[47] We shall then find what are the proper subjects of science and enquiry.

27. It seems to me, that the only objects of the abstract sciences or of demonstration are quantity and number, and that all attempts to extend this more perfect species of knowlege beyond these bounds are mere sophistry and illusion. As the component parts of quantity and number are entirely similar, their relations become intricate and involved; and nothing can be more curious, as well as useful, than to trace, by a variety of mediums, their equality or inequality, thro' their different appearances. But as all other ideas are clearly distinct and different from each other, we can never advance farther, by all our[48] scrutiny, than to observe this diversity and, by an obvious reflection, pronounce one thing not to be another. Or if there be any difficulty in these decisions, it proceeds entirely from the undeterminate meaning of words,

---

43 1777: *determination* for *determinations*
44 Reading, with 1777, *mind* for *hind*
45 1777: inserts *to*
46 1777: *with* for *to*
47 This "slightest examination into the natural powers of the human mind" is undertaken over the paragraphs that follow.
48 1777: *our outmost* for *all our*

which is corrected by juster definitions. That *the square of the Hypotenuse is equal to the squares of the other two sides*, cannot be known, let the terms be ever so exactly defined, without a train of reasoning and enquiry. But to convince us of this proposition, *that where there is no property there can be no injustice*, 'tis only necessary to define the terms, and explain injustice to be a violation of property. This proposition is, indeed, nothing but a more imperfect definition. 'Tis the same case with all those pretended syllogistical reasonings, which may be found in every other branch of learning, except the sciences of quantity and number; and these may safely, I think, be pronounced the only proper objects of knowlege and demonstration.

28. All other enquiries of men regard only matter of fact and existence; and these are evidently incapable of demonstration. Whatever *is* may *not be*. No negation of a fact can involve a contradiction. The non-existence of any being, without exception,[49] is as clear and distinct an idea as its existence. The proposition, which affirms it not to be, however false, is no less conceivable and intelligible, than that which affirms it to be. The case is different with the sciences, properly so called. Every proposition, which is not true, is there confused and unintelligible. That the cube root of 64 is equal to the half of 10, is a false proposition, and can never be distinctly conceived. But that CÆSAR, or the angel GABRIEL, or any being never existed, may be a false proposition, but still is perfectly conceivable, and implies no contradiction.

29. The existence, therefore, of any being can only be proved by arguments from its cause or its effect; and these arguments are founded entirely on experience. If we reason *à priori*, any thing may appear able to produce any thing. The falling of a pebble may, for aught[50] we know, extinguish the sun; or the wish of a man control the planets in their orbits. 'Tis only experience, which teaches us the nature and bounds of cause and effect, and enables us to infer the existence of one object from that of another. **mm** Such is the foundation of moral reasoning,[51] which forms the greatest[52] part of human knowlege, and is the source of all human action and behavior.

---

49 By adding this clause Hume implicitly includes the existence of God in his claim.

50 1777: misprints *aught* as *ought*

51 Hume here and in the following paragraph used "moral" in the broad sense, to cover all non-demonstrative or probabilistic reasoning.

52 1777: *greater* for *greatest*

30. Moral reasonings are either concerning particular or general facts. All deliberations in life regard the former; as also all disquisitions in history, chronology, geography, and astronomy.

31. The sciences, which treat of general facts, are politics, natural philosophy, physic, chymistry, &c. where the qualities, causes, and effects of a whole species of objects are enquired into.

32. Divinity or Theology, as it proves the existence of a Deity, and the immortality of souls, is composed partly of reasonings concerning particular, partly concerning general facts. It has a foundation in *reason*, so far as it is supported by experience. But its best and most solid foundation is *faith* and divine revelation.

33. Morals[53] and criticism are not so properly objects of the understanding as of taste and sentiment. Beauty, whether moral or natural, is felt, more properly than perceived. Or if we reason concerning it, and endeavor to fix its standard, we regard a new fact, *viz.* the general taste of mankind, or of[54] some such fact, which may be the object of reasoning and enquiry.

34. When we run over libraries, persuaded of these principles, what havoc must we make? If we take in our hand any volume; of divinity or school metaphysics, for instance; let us ask, *Does it contain any abstract reasonings*[55] *concerning quantity or*[56] *number?* No. *Does it contain any experimental reasonings*[57] *concerning matters*[58] *of fact*[59] *or existence?* No. Commit it then to the flames: For it can contain nothing but sophistry and illusion.

NOTES

[ii] This argument is drawn from Dr. BERKLEY;[60] and indeed most of the writings of that very ingenious author form the best lessons of scepticism, which are to be found either among the antient or modern philosophers, BAYLE[61] not excepted. He professes, however, in his title-

---

53 Here "moral" is used in the narrow sense having to do with right and wrong behaviour.
54 1777: omits *of*
55 1777: *reasoning* for *reasonings*
56 Reading, with 1777 *or* for *of*
57 1777: *reasoning* for *reasonings*
58 1777: *matter* for *matters*
59 1777: *and* for *or*
60 George Berkeley (1685-1753), the great Irish idealist philosopher, who denied the existence of a material world. The reference is to *Principles* 9-10.
61 Pierre Bayle (1647-1706) was the outstanding sceptical philosopher of the generation before Hume.

page (and undoubtedly with great truth) to have composed his book against the sceptics as well as against the atheists and free-thinkers.[62] But that all his arguments, tho' otherwise intended, are, in reality, merely sceptical, appears from this, *that they admit of no answer and produce no conviction.* Their only effect is to cause that momentary amazement and irresolution and confusion, which is the result of scepticism.

kk Whatever disputes there may be about mathematical points, we must allow that there are physical points; that is, parts of extension, which cannot be divided or lessened, either by the eye or imagination. These images, then, which are present to the fancy or senses, are absolutely indivisible,[63] and consequently must be allowed by mathematicians to be infinitely less than any real part of extension; and yet nothing appears more certain to reason, than that an infinite number of them composes an infinite extension. How much more an infinite number of those infinitely small parts of extension, which are still supposed infinitely divisible.

ll It seems to me not impossible to avoid these absurdities and contradictions, if it be admitted, that there is no such thing as abstract or general ideas, properly speaking; but that all general ideas are, in reality, particular ones, attached to a general term, which recalls, upon occasion, other particular ones, that resemble, in certain circumstances, the idea, present to the mind.[64] Thus when the term Horse is pronounced, we immediately figure to ourselves the idea of a black or a white animal, of a particular size or figure: But as that term is also used to be[65] applied to animals of other colors, figures and sizes, these ideas, tho' not actually present to the imagination, are easily recalled, and our reasoning and conclusion proceed in the same way, as if they were actually present. If this be admitted (as seems reasonable) it follows that all the ideas of quantity, upon which mathematicians reason, are nothing but particular, and such as are suggested by the senses and imagination, and consequently, cannot be infinitely divisible.[66] 'Tis sufficient to have dropt this hint at present, without prose-

---

62 The subtitle of Berkeley's *Principles* was "Wherein the chief Causes of Error and Difficulty in the *Sciences*, with the Grounds of *Scepticism, Atheism,* and *Irreligion,* are inquir'd into." "Irreligion" was synonymous with "free thinking."

63 Reading, with **1777**, *indivisible* for *invisible*

64 See *Treatise* 1.1.7.

65 **1777**: *usually* for *used to be*

66 **1748-1750**: insert *In general, we may pronounce, that the Ideas of greater, less, or equal, which are the chief Objects of Geometry, are far from being so exact or determinate as to be the Foundation of such extraordinary Inferences. Ask a Mathematician what he means, when he pronounces* (Continued)

cuting it any farther. It certainly concerns all lovers of science not to expose themselves to the ridicule and contempt of the ignorant by their conclusions;[67] and this[68] seems the readiest solution of these difficulties.

mm That impious maxim of the antient philosophy, *Ex nihilo, nihil fit*,[69] by which the creation of matter was excluded, ceases to be a maxim, according to this philosophy. Not only the will of the supreme Being may create matter; but, for aught we know *à priori*, the will of any other being might create it, or any other cause, that the most whimsical imagination can assign.

---

two *Quantities to be equal, and he must say, that the Idea of* Equality *is one of those, which cannot be defin'd, and that 'tis sufficient to place two equal Quantities before any one, in order to suggest it. Now this is an Appeal to the general Appearances* [1750: *Appearance*] *of Objects to the Imagination or Senses, and consequently can never afford Conclusions so directly contrary to these Faculties.*

67 Which they do by insisting on infinite divisibility.

68 Taking mathematical terms to be general terms referring to particular sensible intervals, none of which can be infinitely divisible, rather than ideal entities.

69 Nothing comes from nothing.

Appendix A: *From George Campbell,*
A Dissertation on Miracles *(1762)*[1]

In what follows, editorial commentary on the selected texts is differentiated by vertical lines, as here.

[In a letter to Campbell of 7 June 1762 responding to Campbell's gift of a copy of his *Dissertation on Miracles* Hume wrote: "I own to you, that I never felt so violent an inclination to defend myself as at present, when I am thus fairly challenged by you, and I think I could find something specious at least to urge in my defence; but as I had fixed a resolution, in the beginning of my life, always to leave the public to judge between my adversaries and me, without making any reply. I must adhere inviolably to this resolution, otherways my silence on any future occasion would be construed as an inability to answer, and would be matter of triumph against me."[2]

In the following two excerpts, Campbell argues that our belief in testimony is not based on experience. Following on Hume's suggestion, I have made some comments on what he might have (or did) say in his defence.]

Dissertation 1.1: 14-17

That the evidence of testimony is derived solely from experience, which seems to be an axiom of this writer [Hume], is at least not so incontestable a truth, as he supposes it; that, on the contrary, testimony hath a natural and original influence on belief, antecedent to experience, will, I imagine, easily be evinced. For this purpose let it be remark'd, that the earliest assent, which is given to testimony by children, and which is previous to all experience, is in fact the most unlimited; that by a gradual experience of mankind, it is gradually contracted, and reduced to narrower bounds. To say therefore that our diffidence[3] in testimony is the result of experience, is more philosophical, because more consonant to truth, than to say that our faith in tes-

---

1 The selections that follow are drawn from Campbell's *A Dissertation on Miracles*, 1st ed. (Edinburgh: A. Kincaid & J. Bell, 1762). Gale document CW3320836635. The position of Campbell's note numbers has been shifted to conform to modern printing conventions.

2 *Letters* 1: 360-61.

3 That is, our distrust.

timony has this foundation. Accordingly youth, which is unexperienc'd, is credulous; age, on the contrary, is distrustful. Exactly the reverse would be the case, were this author's doctrine just.

Perhaps it will be said, If experience is allowed to be the only measure of a logical or reasonable faith in testimony, the question, *Whether the influence of testimony on belief, be original or deriv'd?* if 'tis not merely verbal, is at least of no importance in the present controversy. Far otherwise. The difference between us is by no means so inconsiderable, as to a careless view it may appear. According to his philosophy, the presumption lies against the testimony, or (which amounts to the same thing) there is not the smallest presumption in its favour, till properly supported by experience. According to the explication given above, there lies the strongest presumption in favour of the testimony, till properly refuted by experience.

If it be objected by the author, that such a faith in testimony as is prior to experience, must be unreasonable and unphilosophical, because unaccountable; I should reply, that there are, and must be, in human nature, some original grounds of belief, beyond which our researches cannot proceed, and of which therefore 'tis vain to attempt a rational account. I should desire the objector to give a reasonable account of his faith in this principle, that *similar causes always produce similar effects*; or in this, that *the course of nature will be the same to-morrow, that it was yesterday, and is to-day:* principles, which he himself acknowledges, are neither intuitively evident, nor deduced from premises; and which nevertheless we are under a necessity of presupposing, in all our reasonings from experience.[4]

Dissertation 1.2: 37-40

In the essay there is frequent mention of the word *experience*, and much use every where made of it. 'Tis strange that the author hath not favour'd us with the definition of a term, of so much moment to his argument. This defect I shall endeavour to supply; and the rather, as the word appears to be equivocal, and to be us'd by the essayist in two very different senses. The first and most proper signification of the word, which, for distinction's sake I shall call *personal* experience, is that given in the preceding section. 'It is,' as was observ'd, 'founded in *memory*, and consists solely of the general maxims or conclusions, that each individual hath form'd, from the comparison of the particular facts he hath remember'd.' In the other signification, in which the word is sometimes taken, and which I shall distinguish by the term

---

4 Campbell's note: Sceptical doubts. Part 2. [EHU 4.ii]

deriv'd, it may be thus defin'd. 'It is founded in *testimony*, and consists not only of all the experiences of others, which have thro' that channel been communicated to us, but of all the general maxims or conclusions we have form'd, from the comparison of particular facts attested.'

In proposing his argument, the author would surely be understood to mean only *personal* experience; otherwise, his making testimony derive its light from an experience which derives its light from testimony, would be introducing what logicians term a *circle in causes*. It would exhibit the same things alternately, as causes and effects of each other. Yet nothing can be more limited, than the sense which is convey'd under the term *experience*, in the first acceptation. The merest clown or peasant derives incomparably more knowledge from testimony, and the communicated experience of others, than in the longest life he could have amassed out of the treasure of his own memory. Nay, to such a scanty portion the savage himself is not confin'd. If that therefore must be the rule, the only rule, by which every testimony is ultimately to be judged, our belief in matters of fact must have very narrow bounds. No testimony ought to have any weight with us, that doth not relate an event, similar at least to some one observation, which we ourselves have had access to make ...

The author himself is aware of the consequences; and therefore, in whatever sense he uses the term *experience* in proposing his argument; in prosecuting it, he with great dexterity shifts the sense, and ere the reader is apprised, insinuates another.

[In a letter to Hugh Blair of 1761 commenting on a pre-publication draft of Campbell's *Dissertation*, Hume remarked that we have no more reason to look beyond experience for an account for our inferences from testimony than we do for our inferences from any other human actions.[5] Campbell thought that the only way to acquire confidence in testimony on the basis of experience is to hear people say things that you have already experienced for yourself. But that sort of experience cannot lead us to expect that, after we have heard people say something, subsequent experience will prove it to be true. It can at most lead us to expect that, after we have come across something, subsequent experience will lead us to hear people talking about it. We acquire confidence in testimony from the reverse sequence, where we hear them tell us about something that we know nothing about and then subsequently discover for ourselves that what they said was true. Repeated experience of this sort trains us to vividly anticipate subse-

---

5 *Letters* 1: 349.

quent confirmation upon hearing testimony. Accordingly, in a further remark on Campbell's effort, Hume claimed that while the only experience is personal experience, the experience of others becomes our own to the extent that we find their testimony trustworthy. "No man can have any other experience but his own. The experience of others becomes his only by the credit which he gives to their testimony; which proceeds from his own experience of human nature."[6] There is no circularity in this because we do not take experience of the way things are to justify a belief in what people tell us, which then justifies belief in the way things are. We take subsequent confirmation of what people have told us in the past to be a reason to trust what they say on future occasions.]

Dissertation 1.2: 42-46

I must once more ask the author, What is the precise meaning of the words *firm, unalterable, uniform?* An experience that admits no exception, is surely the only experience, which can with propriety be term'd *uniform, firm, unalterable.* Now since, as was remark'd above, the far greater part of this experience, which compriseth every age and every country, must be deriv'd to us from testimony; that the experience may be *firm, uniform, unalterable,* there must be no contrary testimony whatever. Yet by the author's own hypothesis, the miracles he would thus confute, are supported by testimony. At the same time to give strength to his argument, he is under a necessity of supposing, that there is no exception from the testimonies against them. Thus he falls into that parallogism, which is called *begging the question.* What he gives with one hand, he takes with the other. He admits, in opening his design, what in his argument he implicitly denies.

But that this, if possible, may be still more manifest, let us attend a little to some expressions, which one would imagine he had inadvertently dropt. "So long," says he, "as the world endures, I presume, will the accounts of miracles and prodigies be found in all profane history."[7] Why does he presume so? A man so much attach'd to experience, can hardly be suspected to have any other reason than this; because such accounts have hitherto been found in all the histories, profane as well as sacred, of times past. But we need not recur to an inference to obtain this acknowledgment. It is often to be met with in the essay. In one place we learn, that the witnesses for miracles are an

---

6 *Letters* 1: 349.
7 Campbell's note: p. 174. [Paraphrasing EHU 10.2]

infinite number;[8] in another, that all religious records of whatever kind abound with them.[9] I leave it therefore to the author to explain, with what consistency he can assert, that the laws of nature are establish'd by an uniform experience, (which experience is chiefly the result of testimony) and at the same time allow, that almost all human histories are full of the relations of miracles and prodigies, which are violations of those laws. Here is, by his own confession, testimony against testimony, and very ample on both sides. How then can one side claim a firm, uniform, and unalterable support from testimony?

It will be in vain to object, that the testimony for the laws of nature greatly exceeds the testimony for the violations ... I ask, Why are the testimonies much more numerous in the one case than in the other? The answer is obvious: Natural occurrences are much more frequent than such as are preternatural. But are all the accounts we have of the pestilence to be rejected as incredible, because, in this country, we hear not so often of that disease, as of the fever? Or, because the number of natural births is infinitely greater than that of monsters, shall the evidence of the former be regarded as a confutation of all that can be advanced in proof of the latter? Such an objector needs to be reminded of what was prov'd in the foregoing section; that the opposite testimonies relate to different facts, and are therefore not contradictory; that the conclusion founded on them, possesseth ... only such a presumptive evidence, as may be surmounted by the slightest positive proof. A general conclusion from experience is in comparison but presumptive and indirect; sufficient testimony for a particular fact is direct and positive evidence.

[Campbell's closing remarks are in reference to the following passage, in which he argues that Hume had been wrong to take our experience of the likelihood of the event reported to counterbalance the evidence of testimony.]

Dissertation 1.1: 18-32

But how, says Mr Hume, is testimony then to be refuted? Principally in one or other of these two ways: *first* and most directly by contradic-

---

8 Campbell's note: p. 190. [EHU 10.24. Hume's claim in this passage was actually that the witnesses *against* any given miracle are infinite in number, though he did take this to be only because they believe a variety of rival miracles. The term "infinite" is of course an exaggeration. Campbell used "infinite" in the same exaggerated sense when describing the number of normal births in the following paragraph.]

9 Campbell's note: p. 191. [EHU 10.24]

tory testimony; that is, when an equal or greater number of witnesses, equally or more credible, attest the contrary: *secondly*, by such evidence either of the incapacity or baseness of the witnesses, as is sufficient to discredit them. What, rejoins my antagonist, cannot then testimony be confuted by the extraordinary nature of the fact attested? Has this consideration no weight at all? That this consideration hath no weight at all, 'twas never my intention to maintain; that by itself it can very rarely, if ever, amount to a refutation against ample and unexceptionable testimony, I hope to make extremely plain ...

In his opinion, "When the fact attested is such as has seldom fallen under our observation, there is a contest of two opposite experiences, of which the one destroys the other, as far as its force goes, and the superior can only operate on the mind, by the force which remains."[10] There is a metaphysical, I had almost said, a magical *balance* and *arithmetic*, for the weighing and subtracting of evidence, which he frequently recurs to, and with which he seems to fancy he could perform wonders. I wish he had been a little more explicit in teaching us how these rare inventions must be us'd.

... I have liv'd for some years near a ferry. It consists with my knowledge that the passage-boat has a thousand times crossed the river, and as many times refurn'd safe. An unknown man, whom I have just now met, tells me in a serious manner, that it is lost; and affirms, that he himself standing on the bank, was a spectator of the scene; that he saw the passengers carried down the stream, and the boat overwhelm'd and dash'd to pieces ... how must I balance these opposite experiences, as you are pleas'd to term them? Must I set the thousand, or rather the two thousand[11] instances of the one side, against the single instance of the other? ... Or is it necessary, in order to make it credible, that the single instance have two thousand times as much evidence, as any of the opposite instances, supposing them equal among themselves; or supposing them unequal, as much as all the two thousand put together, that there may be at least an equilibrium? This is impossible. I had for some of those instances, the evidence of sense, which hardly any testimony can equal, much less exceed. Once more, must the evidence I have of the veracity of the witness, be a full equivalent to the two thousand instances, which oppose the fact attested? By the supposition, I have no positive evidence for or against his veracity, he being a person whom I never saw before. Yet if none of these be the balancing, which the essay writer means, I despair of being able to discover his meaning.

---

10 Campbell's note: p. 179. [Paraphrasing EHU 10.8]
11 Supposing each of the thousand is a round trip.

Is then so weak a proof from testimony incapable of being refuted? I am far from thinking so; tho' even so weak a proof could not be overturn'd by such a contrary experience.[12] How then may it be overturn'd? *First*, by contradictory testimony. Going homewards I meet another person, whom I know as little as I did the former; finding that he comes from the ferry, I ask him concerning the truth of the report. He affirms, that the whole is a fiction; that he saw the boat, and all in it, come safe to land. This would do more to turn the scale, than fifty thousand such contrary instances, as were suppos'd[13] ... I suppose *again*, that instead of meeting with any person who can inform me concerning the fact, I get from some, who are acquainted with the witness, information concerning his character. They tell me, he is notorious for lying; and that his lies are commonly forged, not with a view to interest, but merely to gratify a malicious pleasure, which he takes in alarming strangers ... In the former [case], where there is testimony contradicting testimony, the author's metaphor of a balance may be us'd with propriety. The things weighed are homogeneal: and when contradictory evidences are presented to the mind, tending to prove positions which cannot be both true, the mind must decide on the comparative strength of the opposite evidences, before it yield to either.

But is this the case in the supposition first made? By no means. The two thousand instances formerly known, and the single instance attested, as they relate to different facts, tho' of a contrary nature, are not contradictory. There is no inconsistency in believing both. There is no inconsistency in receiving the last on weaker evidence, (if it be sufficient evidence) not only than all the former together, but even than any of them singly ... 'Tis true, that the experienced frequency of the conjunction of any two events, leads the mind to infer a similar conjunction in time to come. But let it at the same time be remark'd, that no man considers this inference, as having equal evidence with any one of those past events, on which it is founded, and for the belief of which we have had sufficient testimony.[14] Before then the method

---

12 That is, by one's own past experience of the safe ferry transits.

13 That is, fifty thousand instances of safe ferry transits on other occasions.

14 Campbell's confidence that the eye-witness testimony of a single honest and competent judge could lead us to accept an extraordinary occurrence was not shared by Hume (EHU 8.8). It is one thing to accept testimony to as common and readily caused an event as the capsizing of a boat, and another to accept testimony to something that all our past experience tells us is contrary to what should have happened under the specified conditions. Had Campbell's witness testified that a passing bear had waded into the current to drag the drowning passengers one by one to safety, he would have come closer to describing the sort of case Hume had in mind.

recommended by this author can turn to any account, it will be necessary for him to compute and determine with precision, how many hundreds, how many thousands, I might say how many myriads of instances, will confer such evidence on the conclusion founded on them, as will prove an equipoize for the testimony of one ocular witness, a man of probity, in a case of which he is allow'd to be a competent judge.

There is in *arithmetic* a rule called REDUCTION, by which numbers of different denominations are brought to the same denomination. If this ingenious author shall invent a rule in *logic*, analogous to this, for reducing different classes of evidence to the same class, he will bless the world with a most important discovery ... But till this metaphysical *reduction* is discover'd, 'twill be impossible, where the evidences are of different orders, to ascertain by *subtraction* the superior evidence ...

'Tis an excellent observation, and much to the purpose, which the late learned and pious Bishop of Durham, in his admirable performance on the analogy of religion to the course of nature, hath made on this subject. "There is a very strong presumption," says he, "against the most ordinary facts, before the proof of them, which yet is overcome by almost any proof. There is a presumption of millions to one against the story of Cæsar, or of any other man"[15] ... to illustrate the observation above cited, suppose, first, one at random mentions, that at such an hour, of such a day, in such a part of the heavens, a comet *will* appear; the conclusion from experience would not be as millions, but as infinite to one, that the proposition is false. Instead of this, suppose you have the testimony of but one man of integrity, who is skill'd in astronomy, that at such an hour, of such a day, in such a part of the heavens, a comet *did* appear; you will not hesitate one moment to give him credit. Yet all the presumption that was against the truth of the first supposition, tho' almost as strong evidence as experience can afford, was also against the truth of the second, before it was thus attested.

[The following excerpts are drawn from a section of the *Dissertation*, entitled "Mr Hume himself gives up his favourite argument" and are critical of EHU note **dd** (EHU 10.36). In his letter to Blair, Hume commented on this section at greater length than on any other (which is to say, over five sentences).[16] While Campbell's criticism did not

---

15 Campbell's note: Part 2, chap. 2. § 3. [Joseph Butler, *The Analogy of Religion, Natural and Revealed to the Constitution and Course of Nature*, 5th ed. ([Glasgow]: 1754), p. 200, as cited by Campbell. Gale document CW3321885833.]

16 *Letters* 1: 349–50. Four of the five sentences are cited in notes below. The fifth is "There is very little more delicacy in telling a man he speaks nonsense by implication, than in saying so directly."

induce him to make any changes to the wording, he did, many years later, in **1770**, elevate the note Campbell had found so inconsistent into the body of the text (EHU 10.36-39).]

Dissertation 1.3: 62-65, 67-70

If to acknowledge, after all, that there may be miracles, which admit of proof from human testimony; if to acknowledge, that such miracles ought to be receiv'd, not as probable only, but as absolutely certain; or, in other words, that the proof from human testimony may be such, as that all the contrary uniform experience, should not only be overbalanced, but, to use the author's expression, should be annihilated; if such acknowledgments as these, are subversive of his own principles; if by making them, he abandons his darling argument; this strange part the essayist evidently acts.

[Campbell here accurately cited Hume's account of the days of darkness from EHU note **dd** / 10.36.]

Could one imagine, that the person who had made the above acknowledgment, a person too who is justly allow'd by all who are acquainted with his writings, to possess uncommon penetration and philosophical abilities, that this were the same individual, who had so short while before affirm'd, that "a miracle," or a violation of the usual course of nature, "supported by any human testimony, is more properly a subject of derision than of argument";[17] who had insisted, that "it is not requisite, in order to reject the fact, to be able accurately to disprove the testimony, and to trace its falsehood; that such an evidence carries falsehood on the very face of it";[18] that "we need but oppose even to a cloud of witnesses, the absolute impossibility, or," which is all one, "miraculous nature of the events, which they relate;

---

17 Campbell's note: p. 194. [EHU 10.26. Hume wrote "was" for Campbell's "is" and meant to describe a conclusion drawn by De Retz, though one he considered to be warranted in this case. His comments on the pre-publication draft sent to him by Blair include the remark that "There is no contradiction in saying, that all the testimony which ever was really given for any miracle, or ever will be given, is a subject of derision; and yet forming a fiction or supposition of a testimony for a particular miracle, which might not only merit attention, but amount to a full proof of it. For instance the absence of the sun during 48 hours; but reasonable men would only conclude from this fact, that the machine of the globe was disordered during that time." (*Letters* 1: 349-50.)]

18 Campbell's note: ibid. [Paraphrasing EHU 10.26. The reasons for the evident falsehood of the testimony are those given at EHU 10.19 (note **y**), 10.31, and 10.38 (note **dd**).]

that this in the eyes of all reasonable people, will alone be regarded as a sufficient refutation";[19] and who finally to put an end to all altercation on the subject, had pronounced this *oracle*. "NO TESTIMONY FOR ANY KIND OF MIRACLE CAN EVER POSSIBLY AMOUNT TO A PROBABILITY, MUCH LESS TO A PROOF."[20] Was there ever a more glaring contradiction?

... The proof then which the essayist admits from testimony [in the case of the days of darkness discussed in EHU note **dd**], is, by his own estimate, not only superior to a *direct* and *full* proof; but even superior to as *entire* a proof, as any argument from experience can possibly be imagin'd. Whence, I pray, doth testimony acquire such amazing evidence? 'Testimony,' says the author, 'hath no evidence, but what it derives from experience. These differ from each other only as the species from the genus.'[21] Put then for *testimony*, the word *experience*, which in this case is equivalent, and the conclusion will run thus: *Here is a proof from experience, which is superior to as entire a proof from expe-*

---

19 Campbell's note: p. 196. &c. [Paraphrasing EHU 10.27. The "cloud of witnesses" were those testifying to the miracles at the tomb of the Abbé de Paris.]

20 Campbell's note: p. 202. [EHU 10.35. While Campbell cited accurately from **1750**, his acknowledged source, Hume had already altered "can ever possibly amount" to "has ever amounted" in **1756**. This is consistent with the project of EHU 10.ii, which was just to show that there has yet to be any good testimony to the occurrence of miracles, not that there can be no such thing. In the Preface to the *Dissertation* (viii) Campbell stressed that while he had used **1750** when preparing the work for the publisher, he had checked his citations against a later edition (subsequently identified to have been **1760** [214n]). But he seems not to have noticed that the passage he shouted so loudly here had been altered in that edition. For his part, Hume never remarked on the misquotation, though the passage cited in note 17 above from his letter to Blair does comment that there is no contradiction in saying that all actual and future testimony is a subject of derision while envisioning possible cases that would not be. It apparently took Campbell until at least 1767 to notice that the edition of that year was changed from **1750**. In the Preface to the posthumous third edition (1797) of his *Dissertation* he wrote: "By this more moderate declaration, Mr Hume avoids the contradiction there was in the sentence to the concession he had subjoined in a note [i.e., note **dd**]. But no correction is given to many other sentences which needed correction, not less glaringly than this" (p. 3). Campbell nonetheless continued to shout the passage in the form in which it had appeared in **1750** in the third edition of *Dissertation* 1.3, merely adding a footnote that reads, "There is a small alteration made on this sentence in the edition of the Essays in 1767, which is posterior to the 2d. edition [1766] of this dissertation"—as if to say that Hume had only recently made the alteration in response to Campbell's criticisms.]

21 Paraphrasing EHU 10.5.

rience, as can possibly be imagined. This deduction from the author's words, the reader will perceive, is strictly logical. What the meaning of it is, I leave to himself to explain.[22]

What hath been above deduced, how much soever it be accounted, is not all that is implied in the concession made by the author [in note **dd**]. He further says, that the miraculous fact so attested, ought not only to be receiv'd, but to be receiv'd *for certain* ... does not this author remember, that he had oftener than once laid it down as a maxim, That when there is proof against proof, we must incline to the superior, still with a diminution of assurance, in proportion to the force of its antagonist?[23] But when a fact is received *for certain*, there can be no sensible diminution of assurance, such diminution always implying some doubt and *uncertainty*. Consequently the general proof from experience, tho' as entire as any argument from experience can possibly be imagin'd, is not only surmounted, but is really in comparison as nothing, or, in Mr Hume's phrase, undergoes annihilation, when balanced with the particular proof from testimony ... This conclusion, on the principles I have been endeavouring to establish, has nothing in it, but what is conceivable and just; but on the principles of the essay, which derive all the force of testimony from experience, serves only to confound the understanding, and to involve the subject in midnight darkness.

[In this final passage, drawn from a footnote, Campbell offers a passing criticism of Hume's account of probability in EHU 6.]

Dissertation 1.1: 34-35n

In matters of pure experience [balancing or numbering] hath often place. Hence the computations that have been made of the value of annuities, insurances, and several other commercial articles. In calculations concerning chances, the degree of probability may be deter-

---

22 Commenting on "p. 28" of Campbell's MS in his letter to Blair (likely this passage from p. 68 of Campbell's published work), Hume wrote: "I find no difficulty to explain my meaning, and yet shall not probably do it in any future edition. The proof against a miracle, as it is founded on invariable experience, is of that *species* or *kind* of proof, which is full and certain when taken alone, because it implies no doubt, as is the case with all probabilities; but there are degrees of this species, and when a weaker proof is opposed to a stronger, it is overcome" (*Letters* 1: 350). That the two proofs should have to cancel one another out is not obvious, for reasons Campbell himself gave in the passages from *Dissertation* 1.1: 18-37 printed above.
23 Campbell's note: p. 178. 180. [EHU 10.6, 10.11]

min'd with mathematical exactness. I shall here take the liberty, tho' the matter be not essential to the design of this tract, to correct an oversight in the essayist, who always supposes, that where contrary evidences must be balanced, the probability lies in the remainder or surplus, when the less number is subtracted from the greater. The probability doth not consist in the surplus, but in the ratio, or geometrical proportion, which the numbers on the opposite sides bear to each other. I explain myself thus. In favour of one suppos'd event, there are 100 similar instances, against it 50. In another case under consideration, the favourable instances are 60, and only 10 unfavourable. Tho' the difference, or arithmetical proportion, which is 50, be the same in both cases, the probability is by no means equal, as the author's way of reasoning implies. The probability of the first event is as 100 to 50 or 2 to 1. The probability of the second is as 60 to 10, or 6 to 1. Consequently on comparing the different examples, tho' both be probable, the second is thrice as probable as the first.[24]

---

24 Campbell did not appreciate that Hume was trying to provide a law for calculating the strength of belief in a proposition rather than the measure of its probability. He also did not appreciate that Hume's law does not just require subtracting numbers of contrary from numbers of confirming instances but also stipulates that we consider that result in proportion to the total number of trials. Witness EHU 6.4, where it is observed that we must give each of the contrary types of effects that have been observed to follow from a cause "a particular weight and authority, in proportion as we have found it to be more or less frequent." Where n is the number of confirming instances and x the number of contrary instances, the "weight and authority" of n is proportioned to its frequency, $n/n+x$. Likewise, the "weight and authority" of x is $x/n+x$. Strength of belief is the result of subtracting the lesser from the greater, $(n/n+x)-(x/n+x)$ or $n-x/n+x$. Strength of belief and measure of probability are related. Where probability is 100%, we ought to have a maximally strong belief, but where it is 0% we ought to have maximally strong disbelief. Suspension of both belief and disbelief (or 0 belief) is called for where the probability is 50%. Once this is appreciated, Hume's law can be seen to yield precisely those values for strength of belief that correspond to the related measure of probability. Where there are 100 similar instances and 50 contrary ones Hume's law would set the strength of belief at 50/150 (150 being the total number of cases, 50 the result of subtracting disconfirming from confirming cases) or one third of the way between no belief (=50% probability) and full conviction (=100% probability). But that value is 66.666...% probability, the same value yielded by Campbell's claim that the odds are 2:1 or 2/3 probability. Similarly, in the 60/10 case Hume's law determines a 50/70 degree of belief, which is 5/7ths of the way from 50% to 100% or 85.71% probability, the same value yielded by Campbell's calculation that the odds are 6:1 or 6/7 probability.

Appendix B: From Thomas Reid, An Inquiry into the Human Mind on the Principles of Common Sense *(1764) and* Essays on the Intellectual Powers of Man *(1785)*

[Thomas Reid was Hume's most astute and challenging contemporary critic, and among the most astute and challenging critics Hume has ever had. This brief excerpt from the letter of dedication to Reid's *Inquiry into the Human Mind*[1] contains an important autobiographical remark and a hint about what may have motivated him to be critical of Hume's work. A later passage from Reid's *Essays on the Intellectual Powers of Man*[2] only published after Hume's death, goes into more detail.]

Inquiry v and vii-viii/B 3-4

I acknowledge, my Lord, that I never thought of calling in question the principles commonly received with regard to the human understanding, until the *Treatise of human nature* was published, in the year 1739. The ingenious author of that treatise, upon the principles of Locke, who was no sceptic, hath built a system of scepticism, which leaves no ground to believe any one thing rather than its contrary. His reasoning appeared to me to be just: there was therefore a necessity to call in question the principles upon which it was founded, or to admit the conclusion.

...

[I] was not a little surprised to find, that it leans with its whole weight upon a hypothesis, which is ancient indeed, and hath been very generally received by philosophers, but of which I could find no solid proof. The hypothesis I mean is, That nothing is perceived but what is in the mind which perceives it: That we do not really perceive things

---

1   All citations are from the first original edition (Edinburgh: A. Kincaid & J. Bell, 1764). Gale document CW3317422497. Pages numbers for the corresponding text in the critical edition by Derek R. Brookes (University Park, PA: Pennsylvania State UP, 1997) are prefaced by "B."

2   All citations are from the first original edition (Edinburgh: John Bell, 1785). Gale document CW3307462279. Page references are also to the critical edition by Derek R. Brookes (Edinburgh: Edinburgh UP, 2002), cited as "B."

that are external, but only certain images and pictures of them imprinted upon the mind, which are called *impressions* and *ideas*.

If this be true; supposing certain impressions and ideas to exist presently in my mind, I cannot, from their existence, infer the existence of any thing else; my impressions and ideas are the only existences of which I can have any knowledge or conception: and they are such fleeting and transitory beings, that they can have no existence at all, any longer than I am conscious of them. So that, upon this hypothesis, the whole universe about me, bodies and spirits, sun, moon, stars, and earth, friends and relations, all things without exception, which I imagined to have a permanent existence whether I thought of them or not, vanish at once;

And, like the baseless fabric of a vision,
Leave not a track behind.[3]

I thought it unreasonable, my Lord, upon the authority of philosophers, to admit a hypothesis which, in my opinion, overturns all philosophy, all religion and virtue, and all common sense: and finding that all the systems concerning the human understanding which I was acquainted with, were built upon this hypothesis, I resolved to inquire into this subject anew, without regard to any hypothesis.

Intellectual Powers 2.10: 162/B 142

If I may presume to speak my own sentiments, I once believed this doctrine of ideas [that all the objects of knowledge are ideas in our own minds] so firmly, as to embrace the whole of BERKELEY'S system [rejecting the existence of a material world] in consequence of it; till, finding other consequences to follow from it, which gave me more uneasiness than the want of a material world, it came into my mind, more than forty years ago, to put the question, What evidence have I for this doctrine, that all the objects of my knowledge are ideas in my own mind? From that time to the present, I have been candidly and impartially, as I think, seeking for the evidence of this principle, but can find none, excepting the authority of Philosophers.

[The "other consequence" that gave Reid "more uneasiness than the want of a material world" was Hume's scepticism about the existence of minds or spirits—a doctrine that only appears in the *Treatise* and was not reaffirmed in EHU. In *Treatise* 1.4.5, Hume had argued that we cannot consistently suppose all of our perceptions to inhere in either a material or an immaterial substance, and in *Treatise* 1.4.6.1-.4

---

3 The passage is drawn from Shakespeare's *The Tempest*, act IV, scene i.

he had gone on to argue for the conclusion that we are "nothing but a bundle or collection of different perceptions," that there is "no simplicity in [the mind] at one time, nor identity in different," and that "They are the successive perceptions only, that constitute the mind; nor have we the most distant notion of the place where these scenes are represented, or of the materials of which it [the place where the scenes are represented] is composed." Hume reaffirmed these doctrines in the Appendix to that work, while at the same expressing great dissatisfaction with his attempts to explain why we are nonetheless so inclined to think of ourselves as single beings that persist over time.

Reid's strong aversion to Hume's position on the self in the *Treatise* is expressed in the following passage.]

Inquiry 2.6: 56-61, 63-66/B32-36

This might have been said without any apology before the *Treatise of human nature* appeared in the world. For till that time no man, as far as I know, ever thought either of calling in question that principle [that sensations cannot exist apart from a mind], or of giving a reason for his belief of it. Whether thinking beings were of an ethereal or igneous nature, whether material or immaterial, was variously disputed; but that thinking is an operation of some kind of being or other, was always taken for granted, as a principle that could not possibly admit of doubt.

However, since the author above mentioned, who is undoubtedly one of the most acute metaphysicians that this or any age hath produced, hath treated it as a vulgar prejudice, and maintained, that the mind is only a succession of ideas and impressions, without any subject; his opinion, however contrary to the common apprehensions of mankind, deserves respect. I beg therefore, once for all, that no offence may be taken at charging this or other metaphysical notions with absurdity, or with being contrary to the common sense of mankind. No disparagement is meant to the understandings of the authors or maintainers of such opinions.

...

Indeed, if it is true, and to be received as a principle of philosophy, That sensation and thought may be without a thinking being; it must be acknowledged to be the most wonderful discovery that this or any other age hath produced. The received doctrine of ideas is the principle from which it is deduced, and of which indeed it seems to be a just and natural consequence. And it is probable, that it would not have been so late a discovery, but that it is so shocking and repugnant to the common apprehensions of mankind, that it required an uncommon degree of philosophical intrepidity to usher it into the world. It is a fundamental principle of the ideal system, That every object of thought must be an impression, or an idea, that is, a faint copy of some preceding impression. This is a principle so commonly received, that the author above mentioned, although his whole system is built upon it, never offers the least proof of it. It is upon this principle, as a fixed point, that he erects his metaphysical engines, to overturn heaven and earth, body and spirit. And indeed, in my apprehension, it is altogether sufficient for the purpose. For if impressions and ideas are the only objects of thought, then heaven and earth, and body and spirit, and every thing you please, must signify only impressions and ideas, or they must be words without any meaning. It seems, therefore, that this notion, however strange, is closely connected with the received doctrine of ideas, and we must either admit the conclusion, or call in question the premises.

Ideas seem to have something in their nature unfriendly to other existences. They were first introduced into philosophy, in the humble character of images or representatives of things; and in this character they seemed not only to be inoffensive, but to serve admirably well for explaining the operations of the human understanding. But since men began to reason clearly and distinctly about them, they have by degrees supplanted their constituents,[4] and undermined the existence of every thing but themselves. First they discarded all secondary qualities of bodies; and it was found out by their means, that fire is not hot, nor snow cold, nor honey sweet; and, in a word, that heat and cold, sound, colour, taste, and smell, are nothing but ideas or impressions. Bishop Berkeley advanced them a step higher, and found out, by just reasoning, from the same principles, that extension, solidity, space, figure, and body, are ideas, and that there is nothing in nature but ideas and spirits. But the triumph of ideas was completed by the *Treatise of human nature*, which discards spirits also, and leaves ideas and impressions as the sole existences in the universe.

...

However this may be, it is certainly a most amazing discovery, that thought and ideas may be without any thinking being. A discovery big with consequences which cannot easily be traced by those deluded mortals who think and reason in the common track. We were always apt to imagine, that thought supposed a thinker, and love a lover, and treason a traitor: but this, it seems, was all a mistake; and it is found out, that there may be treason without a traitor, and love without a lover, laws without a legislator, and punishment without a sufferer,

---

4 I.e., the external objects they were originally supposed to represent. Reid was employing the metaphor of parliamentary representation.

succession without time, and motion without any thing moved, or space in which it may move: or if, in these cases, ideas are the lover, the sufferer, the traitor, it were to be wished that the author of this discovery had farther condescended to acquaint us, whether ideas can converse together, and be under obligations of duty or gratitude to each other; whether they can make promises and enter into leagues and covenants, and fulfil or break them, and be punished for the breach. If one set of ideas makes a covenant, another breaks it, and a third is punished for it, there is reason to think that justice is no natural virtue in this system.[5]

It seemed very natural to think, that the *Treatise of human nature* required an author, and a very ingenious one too; but now we learn, that it is only a set of ideas which came together, and arranged themselves by certain associations and attractions.

After all, this curious system appears not to be fitted to the present state of human nature. How far it may suit some choice spirits, who are refined from the dregs of common sense, I cannot say. It is acknowledged, I think, that even these can enter into this system only in their most speculative hours, when they soar so high in pursuit of those self-existent ideas, as to lose sight of all other things. But when they condescend to mingle again with the human race, and to converse with a friend, a companion, or a fellow-citizen, the ideal system vanishes; common sense, like an irresistible torrent, carries them along; and, in spite of all their reasoning and philosophy, they believe their own existence, and the existence of other things.[6]

Indeed it is happy they do so; for if they should carry their closet-belief into the world, the rest of mankind would consider them as diseased, and send them to an infirmary. Therefore, as Plato required certain previous qualifications of those who entered his school, I think it would be prudent for the doctors of this ideal philosophy to do the same, and to refuse admittance to every man who is so weak as to imagine that he ought to have the same belief in solitude and in company, or that his principles ought to have any influence upon his practice: for this philosophy is like a hobby horse, which a man in bad health may ride in his closet without hurting his reputation; but if he should take him abroad with him to church, or to the exchange, or to the playhouse, his heir would immediately call a jury, and seize his estate.

---

5   At *Treatise* 3.2.1 and again in EPM 3 Hume maintained that justice is not a natural virtue, instinctively felt by all, but an "artificial" one, created by what we would now call socialization.

6   This is an allusion to *Treatise* 1.4.7.9. See also *Treatise* 1.4.2.27 and EHU 12.23.

[Hume had retreated from making any comment on the self almost twenty years before these comments on *Treatise* 1.4.5-6 appeared, and it is doubtful that such objections would have motivated his reticence. An army can be invincible even though no one soldier in that army is invincible. A computer, while performing an operation, can be said to be "processing data" or even "thinking" even though none of the electrons flowing through its circuits can be said to be processing data or thinking. The question of whether operations of complex systems are reducible to simpler operations of component parts is not to be decided by appeals to the apparent absurdity of attributing the operations of the whole, such as committing treason or breaking promises, to the individual parts. And to worry about whether it is just to punish one set of ideas for what an earlier set of ideas has done is both to ignore that a bundle of ideas can at most be made to include ideas of pain and suffering (the other ideas in the bundle cannot be made to suffer) and to fail to engage Hume's serious arguments for the conclusion that our judgments of moral approbation and disapprobation, along with inclinations to attribute praise or blame or mete out rewards and punishments, are ultimately founded on feelings we are instinctively impelled to have upon contemplating the operations of those complex systems, human bodies supposed to act under the influence of character and motives.

Had Hume returned to the question of why we believe in a self in EHU, he would likely have given much the same answer that he gave to the question of why we believe in an external world: That just as we have a natural instinct or prepossession to mistake our sense impressions for external objects, so we have an natural instinct or prepossession to consider our thoughts and passions to be constitutive of a persisting self. This instinct or prepossession exists as a matter of brute fact, even though we may not be able to account for it by appeal to more basic mental operations. And while sceptics may raise unanswerable objections to following this instinct, no sceptical argument can overcome its influence.

Reid's charge that Hume had founded an absurd scepticism on the unexamined "hypothesis" that we only perceive mental images or pictures is misleading on more than one count. Hume had maintained that it is so far from being evident that we only perceive mental images or pictures, that we have, on the contrary, a "natural instinct or prepossession" to take our sensory experiences to be experiences of external objects (EHU 12.7-8). While he had gone on to say that "the slightest philosophy" teaches us that we do not in fact directly perceive external objects but only "fleeting images" (EHU 12.9), he had not simply assumed this to be the case or asserted it on the authority of philosophers. He had offered two arguments for it, one at EHU 12.9, involving an appeal to the fact that what we perceive changes as a consequence of causes that can only be supposed to affect us rather than things that exist independently of us, and the other, at EHU 12.15, resting on appeal to the fact that if we accept that sensible qualities like colour are merely sensations in us, then we will be left unable to ascribe any qualities whatsoever to external objects.[7] As he remarked in a letter to Blair commenting on a draft of Reid's dissertation,[8] he had offered two more arguments for the further proposition that we can form no ideas that go beyond what we find in our impressions: that we cannot find any examples of ideas that have not been copied from impressions (EHU 2.6), and that we cannot give new ideas to people otherwise than by putting them in situations where they can receive the impressions those ideas copy (EHU 2.7).[9] Moreover, Hume had been careful not to present the first set of arguments in his own voice. While he considered the arguments to be sound, he also maintained, like Reid, that we are naturally incapable of accepting their conclusions (EHU note **ii** and 12.23). The only sceptical conclusions he endorsed are that our reasoning, however necessary for practical purposes, is ultimately based on principles that are not further justifiable (EHU 12.23) and that we ought to restrict it to topics that can be continually verified by ongoing experience (EHU 12.25).

For Reid this was not enough. Where Hume took sceptical arguments, though ultimately unacceptable, to be useful for mitigating people's dogmatism and intolerance, and restraining their wilder speculations (EHU 12.24-25), Reid took them to be an intolerably humiliating insult to our intelligence and to the capacities of the being who endowed us with our cognitive powers.]

Inquiry 1.5: 27-28/B 21

It is a bold philosophy that rejects, without ceremony, principles which irresistibly govern the belief and the conduct of all mankind in the common concerns of life; and to which the philosopher himself must yield, after he imagines he hath confuted them.

... It can have no other tendency, than to show the acuteness of the sophist, at the expence of disgracing reason and human nature, and making mankind yahoos.[10]

---

7 These arguments were not original to EHU but had already been offered, in greater detail, over *Treatise* 1.4.2.44-45 and 1.4.4.6-15.

8 Discussed below, pp. 245-46.

9 These arguments are also found in *Treatise* 1.1.1.8-9.

10 The reference is to Jonathan Swift's (1667-1745) description of a fictional tribe of sub-human creatures. See Lemuel Gulliver [Jonathan Swift], *Travels into several Remote Nations of the World*. 2nd ed., vol. 2 (London: Benjamin Motte, 1726), part iv, esp. chs. 1 and 8. Gale document CW3309096271.

Inquiry 1.6: 31/B 22

... if [the mind] is indeed what the *Treatise of human nature* makes it, I find I have been only in an inchanted castle, imposed upon by specters and apparitions. I blush inwardly to think how I have been deluded; I am ashamed of my frame, and can hardly forbear expostulating with my destiny: Is this thy pastime, O Nature, to put such tricks upon a silly creature, and then to take off the mask, and shew him how he hath been befooled?

Inquiry 5.7: 146-47/B 68

This opposition betwixt philosophy and common sense, is apt to have a very unhappy influence upon the philosopher himself. He sees human nature in an odd, unamiable, and mortifying light. He considers himself, and the rest of his species, as born under a necessity of believing ten thousand absurdities and contradictions,[11] and endowed with such a pittance of reason, as is just sufficient to make this unhappy discovery: and this is all the fruit of his profound speculations. Such notions of human nature tend to slacken every nerve of the soul, to put every noble purpose and sentiment out of countenance, and spread a melancholy gloom over the whole face of things.

If this is wisdom, let me be deluded with the vulgar. I find something within me that recoils against it, and inspires more reverent sentiments of the human kind, and of the universal administration. Common sense and reason have both one author; that Almighty author, in all whose other works we observe a consistency, uniformity, and beauty, which charm and delight the understanding: there must therefore be some order and consistency in the human faculties, as well as in other parts of his workmanship. A man that thinks reverently of his own kind, and esteems true wisdom and philosophy, will not be fond, nay, will be very suspicious, of such strange and paradoxical opinions. If they are false, they disgrace philosophy; and if they are true, they degrade the human species, and make us justly ashamed of our frame.

[These opinions notwithstanding, Reid followed Hume in accepting that our belief in the existence of an external world cannot be demon-

---

11 In *Treatise* 1.4.2.24-43 Hume had argued that our belief in the continued existence of objects when not perceived results from an attempt to conceal multiple, deep contradictions in the way we view our experience. Over *Treatise* 1.4.2.46-55 he argued that the "philosophical" view that our impressions are representations of external objects is also caught up in inconsistencies and absurdities.

strated to be true, even though it is both irresistible and practically necessary.]

Inquiry 6.20: 410-15/B 168-70

I am aware, that this belief which I have in perception, stands exposed to the strongest batteries of scepticism. But they make no great impression upon it. The sceptic asks me, Why do you believe the existence of the external object which you perceive? This belief, Sir, is none of my manufacture; it came from the mint of nature; it bears her image and superscription; and if it is not right, the fault is not mine: I even took it upon trust, and without suspicion. Reason, says the sceptic, is the only judge of truth, and you ought to throw off every opinion and every belief that is not grounded on reason. Why, Sir, should I believe the faculty of reason more than that of perception; they came both out of the same shop, and were made by the same artist; and if he puts one piece of false ware into my hands, what should hinder him from putting another?

Perhaps the sceptic will agree to distrust reason, rather than give any credit to perception. For, says he, since by your own concession, the object which you perceive, and that act of your mind by which you perceive it, are quite different things, the one may exist without the other; and as the object may exist without being perceived, so the perception may be without an object. There is nothing so shameful in a philosopher as to be deceived and deluded; and therefore you ought to resolve firmly to with-hold assent, and to throw off this belief of external objects, which may be all delusion. For my part, I will never attempt to throw it off; and altho' the sober part of mankind will not be very anxious to know my reasons, yet if they can be of use to any sceptic, they are these.

First, Because it is not in my power ...

Secondly, I think it would not be prudent to throw off this belief, if it were in my power. ...

Thirdly, Although the two reasons already mentioned are perhaps two more than enough, I shall offer a third. I gave implicit belief to the informations of Nature by my senses, for a considerable part of my life, before I had learned so much logic as to be able to start a doubt concerning them. And now, when I reflect upon what is past, I do not find that I have been imposed upon by this belief. I find, that without it I must have perished by a thousand accidents. I find, that without it I should have been no wiser now than when I was born. I should not even have been able to acquire that logic which suggests these sceptical doubts with regard to my senses. Therefore, I consider this instinctive belief as one of the best gifts of Nature. I thank the author of my being who bestowed it upon me, before the eyes of my reason were opened, and still bestows it upon me to be my guide, where reason leaves me in the dark. And now I yield to the direction of my senses, not from instinct only, but from confidence and trust in a faithful and beneficent monitor, grounded upon the experience of his paternal care and goodness.

[Reid also accepted what Hume had said in EHU about the core issue of the basis of causal inference in a past experience of constant conjunction, uninformed by any discovery of a power in causes enabling them to bring about their effects.]

Inquiry 6.24: 482-85 and 488, 490/B 195-97 and 198-99

It is undeniable, and indeed is acknowledged by all, that when we have found two things to have been constantly conjoined in the course of nature, the appearance of one of them is immediately followed by the conception and belief of the other. The former becomes a natural sign of the latter; and the knowledge of their constant conjunction in time past, whether got by experience or otherwise, is sufficient to make us rely with assurance upon the continuance of that conjunction.

This process of the human mind is so familiar, that we never think of inquiring into the principles upon which it is founded. We are apt to conceive it as a self-evident truth, that what is to come must be similar to what is past. Thus, if a certain degree of cold freezes water to-day, and has been known to do so in all time past, we have no doubt but the same degree of cold will freeze water to-morrow, or a year hence. That this is a truth which all men believe as soon as they understand it, I readily admit; but the question is, Whence does its evidence arise? Not from comparing the ideas surely. For when I compare the idea of cold with that of water hardened into a transparent solid body, I can perceive no connection between them: no man can show the one to be the necessary effect of the other: no man can give a shadow of reason why nature hath conjoined them. But do we not learn their conjunction from experience? True; experience informs us that they have been conjoined in time *past:* but no man ever had any experience of what is *future:* and this is the very question to be resolved, How we come to believe that the *future* will be like the *past?* ... children and idiots have this belief as soon as they know that fire will burn them. It must therefore be the effect of instinct, not of reason.

The wise author of our nature intended, that a great and necessary part of our knowledge should be derived from experience, before we are capable of reasoning, and he hath provided means perfectly adequate to this intention. For, first, He governs nature by fixed laws, so that we find innumerable connections of things which continue from age to age. ... Secondly, He hath implanted in human minds an original principle by which we believe and expect the continuance of the course of nature, and the continuance of those connections which we have observed in time past. It is by this general principle of our nature, that when two things have been found connected in time past, the appearance of the one produces the belief of the other.

I think the ingenious author of the *Treatise of human nature* first observed, That our belief of the continuance of the laws of nature cannot be founded either upon knowledge or probability: but, far from conceiving it to be an original principle of the mind, he endeavours to account for it from his favourite hypothesis, That belief is nothing but a certain degree of vivacity in the idea of the thing believed. ...

...

However, we agree with the author of the *Treatise of human nature* in this, That our belief of the continuance of nature's laws is not derived from reason. It is an instinctive prescience of the operations of nature.

...

We perceive no proper causality or efficiency in any natural cause, but only a connection established by the course of nature between it and what is called its effect.[12] Antecedently to all reasoning, we have, by our constitution, an anticipation, that there is a fixed and steady course of nature; and we have an eager desire to discover this course of nature. We attend to every conjunction of things which presents itself, and expect the continuance of that conjunction. And when such a conjunction has been often observed, we conceive the things to be naturally connected, and the appearance of one, without any reasoning or reflection, carries along with it the belief of the other.

[To mount an effective critique of Hume's philosophy given these affinities, Reid needed to do what Kant was later to accuse him of failing to do: prove what Hume had called into question.[13] He needed to counter Hume's reasons at EHU 12.9 and 15 and the corresponding parts of the *Treatise* for concluding that we do not directly

---

12 Though Reid agreed that we do not perceive any necessary connection in external objects, he maintained that we do experience "active power" in ourselves and held that the term "cause" is not used in a "strict and philosophical sense" when taken to refer to events that regularly precede certain other events, apart from any reference to a productive power. However, while this doctrine is alluded to in the *Inquiry* (2.9: 78/B 40), it was only fully laid out in work published after Hume's death, and Reid was generally content to use the term "cause" in the looser, Humean sense.

13 See the opening passage in Appendix D, pp. 278-79.

or indirectly perceive external objects. He also needed to do something more than affirm what Hume had never proposed to call into doubt. He needed to offer some better alternative than simply insisting on points that Hume never denied, such as that we are innately so constituted as to believe our sensory experiences to be direct perceptions of external objects, that it is pragmatically necessary for us to do so, or that the supposition has so far proven to be useful for purposes of survival.

Kant's opinion, and Reid's repeated assertions that Hume's scepticism rests on an unjustified hypothesis notwithstanding, Reid did do both of these things. Though he did not address Hume's principal argument for scepticism about the existence of external objects at EHU 12.9 in work published during Hume's lifetime, he did engage Hume's second argument at EHU 12.15 at great length, and on the way to doing so he both challenged Hume's assertion that all ideas are copied from impressions and attempted to show that we are not just instinctively impelled to mistake sense impressions for external objects, but instead directly perceive them.

The key to Reid's response to Hume is a distinction he drew between sensation and perception.]

Inquiry 6.20: 407-08/B 167-68

Sensation, and the perception of external objects by the senses, though very different in their nature, have commonly been considered as one and the same thing. The purposes of common life do not make it necessary to distinguish them, and the received opinions of philosophers, tend rather to confound them: but without attending carefully to this distinction, it is impossible to have any just conception of the operations of our senses. The most simple operations of the mind, admit not of a logical definition: all we can do is to describe them, so as to lead those who are conscious of them in themselves, to attend to them, and reflect upon them: and it is often very difficult to describe them so as to answer this intention.

The same mode of expression is used to denote sensation and perception; and therefore we are apt to look upon them as things of the same nature. Thus, *I feel a pain*; *I see a tree:* the first denoteth a sensation, the last a perception. The grammatical analysis of both expressions is the same: for both consist of an active verb and an object. But, if we attend to the things signified by these expressions, we shall find, that in the first, the distinction between the act and the object is not real, but grammatical; in the second, the distinction is not only grammatical but real.

[Where Hume had claimed that sensory experience supplies us with "impressions," Reid claimed that it instead supplies us with two radically different kinds of things: sensations and perceptions, neither of which can be straightforwardly identified either with "impressions" or with "ideas" as Hume used those terms. In sensation the mind feels a certain way (even in smelling, tasting, hearing, and seeing, it experiences the way it feels to smell, taste, hear, and see). These feelings exist only in it, and only when felt by it. Importantly, these feelings should not be simply identified with smells, tastes, sounds, and colours. A sensation is the state the mind is in when it smells, tastes, hears, feels, or sees. A mind that feels heat or sees red is not hot or red in the sense that it takes on the qualities that cause objects to feel hot or red to minds. Nor is it engaged in an act of perceiving a hot impression or a red impression. It is in the sensory state we are in when we feel a hot object or see a red object.]

Inquiry 6.20: 408-09/B 168

The form of the expression, *I feel pain*, might seem to imply, that the feeling is something distinct from the pain felt; yet, in reality, there is no distinction. As *thinking a thought* is an expression which could signify no more than *thinking*, so *feeling a pain* signifies no more than *being pained*. What we have said of pain is applicable to every other mere sensation. It is difficult to give instances, very few of our sensations having names; and where they have, the name being common to the sensation, and to something else which is associated with it. But when we attend to the sensation by itself, and separate it from other things which are conjoined with it in the imagination, it appears to be something which can have no existence but in a sentient mind, no distinction from the act of the mind by which it is felt.

Inquiry 2.9: 83-84/B 42

... what is smelling? It is an act of the mind, but is never imagined to be a quality of the mind ... We say, This body smells sweet, that stinks; but we do not say, This mind smells sweet, and that stinks. Therefore smell in the rose, and the sensation which it causes, are not conceived, even by the vulgar, to be things of the same kind, although they have same name.

[In contrast to sensation, in perception the mind performs an act of conception with an attendant belief. These acts of conceiving and believing likewise exist only in the mind and only insofar as they are performed by the mind. But, Reid claimed, they give us an awareness of something other than themselves. In conceiving with belief, I am not just aware of conceiving with belief, as in feeling a certain way I am just aware of feeling a certain way. Instead, I am aware of an object distinct from my act of conception and belief. This object can exist whether or not I perform the acts of conceiving of it and believing it to exist.]

Inquiry 6.20: 409-10/B 168

Perception, as we here understand it, hath always an object distinct from the act by which it is perceived; an object which may exist whether it be perceived or not. I perceive a tree that grows before my window; there is here an object which is perceived, and an act of the mind by which it is perceived; and these two are not only distinguishable, but they are extremely unlike in their natures. The object is made up of a trunk, branches, and leaves; but the act of the mind by which it is perceived, hath neither trunk, branches, nor leaves. I am conscious of this act of my mind, and I can reflect upon it; but it is too simple to admit of an analysis, and I cannot find proper words to describe it. I find nothing that resembles it so much as the remembrance of the tree, or the imagination of it. Yet both these differ essentially from perception; they differ likewise one from another. It is in vain that a philosopher assures me, that the imagination of the tree, the remembrance of it, and the perception of it, are all one, and differ only in degree of vivacity. I know the contrary; for I am as well acquainted with all the three, as I am with the apartments of my own house. I know this also, that the perception of an object implies both a conception of its form, and a belief of its present existence. I know moreover, that this belief is not the effect of argumentation and reasoning; it is the immediate effect of my constitution.

[The analogy with memory and imagination is worth pursuing further. Reid considered that perception, memory, and imagination are all alike in being acts of the mind that refer to objects distinct from those acts. But whereas perception involves the conception of an object together with belief in its present existence, memory involves conception together with belief in its past existence, and imagination involves conception without any belief. It is the nature or presence of the attendant belief, rather than the manner of conceiving the object, that distinguishes these operations. Though the following discussion is built around the example of remembering a past *sensation* (the smell of a rose), the point to draw from the passage concerns the nature of the act of remembering and its relation to an object (which is in this case a sensation). Remembering an *object* such as the rose itself, or the pot in which it grew, would be accounted for in the same way.]

Inquiry 2.3: 44-45/B 28

Suppose that once, and only once, I smelled a tuberose in a certain room where it grew in a pot, and gave a very grateful perfume. Next day I relate what I saw and smelled. When I attend as carefully as I can to what passes in my mind in this case, it appears evident, that the very thing I saw yesterday, and the fragrance I smelled, are now the immediate objects of my mind when I remember it. Farther, I can imagine this pot and flower transported to the room where I now sit, and yielding the same perfume. Here likewise it appears, that the individual thing which I saw and smelled, is the object of my imagination.

Philosophers indeed tell me, that the immediate object of my memory and imagination in this case, is not the past sensation, but an idea of it, an image, phantasm, or species of the odour I smelled: that this idea presently exists in my mind, or in my sensorium; and the mind contemplating this present idea, finds it a representation of what is past, or of what may exist; and accordingly calls it memory, or imagination. This is the doctrine of the ideal philosophy ... Upon the strictest attention, memory appears to me to have things that are past, and not present ideas, for its object.

[The belief that is involved in conception and memory is very different from belief as understood by Hume. Reid criticized Hume's account of belief in the strongest terms. His criticisms are focused on the fourth and least significant of Hume's characterizations of belief at EHU 5.11-12 (a passage largely copied from *Treatise* 1.3.7.7, originally published in the appendix to the *Treatise*), one offered in terms of the "force and vivacity" of the way it feels to believe.]

Inquiry 2.5: 50-51/B 30

But what is this belief or knowledge which accompanies sensation and memory? Every man knows what it is, but no man can define it. Does any man pretend to define sensation, or to define consciousness? It is happy indeed that no man does. And if no philosopher had endeavoured to define and explain belief, we had wanted[14] some of those paradoxes of the ideal philosophy, which will always to sensible men appear as incredible as any thing that ever enthusiasm dreamed or

---

14 I.e., we would have lacked.

superstition swallowed.[15] Of this kind surely is that modern discovery of the ideal philosophy, that sensation, memory, belief, and imagination, where they have the same object, are only different degrees of strength and vivacity in the idea. Suppose the idea to be that of a future state after death; one man believes it firmly; this means no more than that he hath a strong and lively idea of it: Another neither believes nor disbelieves; that is, he has a weak and faint idea. Suppose now a third person believes firmly that there is no such thing; I am at a loss to know whether his idea be faint or lively: If it is faint, then there may be a firm belief where the idea is faint; if the idea is lively, then the belief of a future state and the belief of no future state must be one and the same ... may it not be said with equal reason, that in belief there is something more than an idea, to wit, an assent or persuasion of the mind?

Inquiry 6.24: 486-88/B 197-98

The belief which we have in perception, is a belief of the present existence of the object; that which we have in memory, is a belief of its past existence; the belief of which we are now speaking [that arising from causal inference], is a belief of its future existence, and in imagination there is no belief at all. Now, I would gladly know of this author [the author of the *Treatise*], how one degree of vivacity fixes the existence of the object to the present moment; another carries it back to time past; a third, taking a contrary direction, carries it into futurity; and a fourth, carries it out of existence altogether. Suppose, for instance, that I see the sun rising out of the sea; I remember to have seen him rise yesterday; I believe he will rise to-morrow near the same place; I can likewise imagine him rising in that place, without any belief at all. Now, according to this sceptical hypothesis, this perception, this memory, this foreknowledge, and this imagination, are all the same idea, diversified only by different degrees of vivacity. The perception of the sun rising, is the most lively idea; the memory of his rising yesterday, is the same idea a little more faint; the belief of his rising to-morrow, is the same idea yet fainter; and the imagination of his rising, is still the same idea, but faintest of all.[16] One is apt to think, that this idea might gradually pass through all possible degrees of vivacity, without stirring out of its place. But if we think so, we deceive ourselves; for no sooner does it begin to

---

15 The suggestion is that Hume was every bit as extravagant in his opinions as those caught up in the enthusiastic and superstitious forms of religious belief he so severely criticized.

16 Hume had graded the vivacity of ideas in this way at *Treatise* 1.3.13.19, though not in EHU.

grow languid, than it moves backward into time past. Supposing this to be granted, we expect at least that as it moves backward by the decay of its vivacity, the more that vivacity decays, it will go back the farther, until it remove quite out of sight. But here we are deceived again; for there is a certain period of this declining vivacity, when, as if it had met an elastic obstacle in its motion backward, it suddenly rebounds from the past to the future, without taking the present in its way. And now having got into the regions of futurity, we are apt to think, that it has room enough to spend all its remaining vigour: but still we are deceived; for, by another sprightly bound, it mounts up into the airy region of imagination. So that ideas, in the gradual declension of their vivacity, seem to imitate the inflection of verbs in grammar. They begin with the present, and proceed in order to the preterite, the future, and the indefinite. This article of the sceptical creed is indeed so full of mystery, on whatever side we view it, that they who hold that creed, are very injuriously charged with incredulity:[17] for to me it appears to require as much faith as that of Saint Athanasius.[18]

[Reid never explained how the mental act of conception can perform the trick of giving us an awareness of an object entirely distinct from that act itself. Attempting to illustrate the operation by appeal to how words or other signs lead us to think of objects[19] is not very helpful. Speaking in Humean terms, the connection between signs and signata is an association based on past experience of a conjunction between the two in virtue of which an encounter with the one leads us to form an idea (that is, a copy of a past experience) of the other. But what Reid was talking about was an operation that gives rise to an awareness of an object that may never before have been experienced—an awareness, moreover, that does not take the form of a copy of some past mental state or "impression" but does just the thing that is problematic: refer to something other than itself. This very radical form of reference, occurring without reviving a mental image of the object referred to as a consequence of association, is an achievement that Reid took to be beyond our abilities to further explain—but also something we are obviously able to do as a matter of fact.

17 A sarcastic reference to Hume's having been charged with not having any religious faith.
18 Athanasius (293-373) formulated a verbal agreement or "creed," the Athanasian creed, that took what came to be recognized as the orthodox stance on a number of highly contentious Christian doctrines concerning such matters as the Trinity and the nature of Christ. Hume's view of Athanasius's achievement is summed up in NHR 11.
19 See p. 240 below.

Supposing Reid was right about this, it would scuttle Hume's claim at EHU 12.12 that the only way we can come to know of the existence of external objects is by means of causal inferences based on a prior experience of both cause and effect. It would also scuttle his claim that all ideas are copied from impressions (supposing Reid to be right that the conceptions we come to form through perception are a kind of idea that is not copied from any sensation), and challenge his claim that our sensory experience only leads us to become aware of impressions (taking impressions to be sensations that only exist in us and only when perceived).

An obvious challenge to Reid's account is posed by the occurrence of illusions, hallucinations, and dreams, which has suggested to many that we must, at least sometimes, perceive something other than what actually exists outside of us.[20] Reid did not deny that these and other sorts of misperception occur, but he did not think this fact adequate to justify the inference that on these occasions (and perhaps on all occasions) we must be perceiving mental images. On Reid's account, even in misperception we perceive something distinct from ourselves and our mental states. It is just that this thing happens to not exist. This is not as absurd as it might seem and has attracted support from modern logicians.[21]

Reid maintained that our sense organs were designed by God to perform reliably in the normal circumstances we find ourselves in when engaged in the business of daily survival. An aspect of this design is that we are innately so constituted that, on the occasion of receiving certain sensations as a consequence of sensory stimulation, we form conceptions-with-belief of the figure and situation of the external objects that would normally have stimulated us in that fashion. We can sometimes be mistaken, in the sense that we might conceive an object

---

20 This argument from illusion should be distinguished from Hume's argument at EHU 12.9 which appeals to the relativity of perception.

21 Graham Priest, *Towards Non-Being* (Oxford: Clarendon Press, 2005). The standard objection is that to perceive what does not exist is either to perceive a currently existing mental image or to perceive nothing at all. Reid's response was that it is rather to perceive an object distinct from ourselves, just one that happens not to exist. The perception is an act of conception with belief, and that act of conception with belief does exist in the mind. But it is not the object conceived and it is not anything like the object. It manages to make us aware of the object even though the object does not exist just as an act of memory manages to make us aware of an object even though that object no longer exists. Reid's fascinating views on conceiving non-existent objects independently of forming mental pictures or images were only fully articulated in *Intellectual Powers* 4.1-2, published after Hume's death.

that does not exist or that is differently situated or configured from the object that in fact affected us. But these are isolated instances that most often result from using the sense organs outside of the normal circumstances in which they were designed to function reliably. There is no systematic error in sensory experience. We do not experience only our own internal states, which we mistake for external things, and we are not confronted with a question of how we could know that there is any such thing as an external world. Instead, we are instinctively led to conceive external objects, and the external objects we conceive are generally the ones that actually do exist, and they have at least the qualities that we conceive them to have. In conceiving these objects we do not perceive a "conception" or picture or impression or idea that exists only in our minds. Instead, an act of conceiving that exists only in our minds leads us to be directly aware of an object entirely distinct from us and anything we find within ourselves. In the case of veridical perception, we are directly aware of an object that actually exists in space outside of us; in the case of memory, of an object that no longer exists; and in the case of misperception, of an object that does not exist.

This critique of Hume presumes, however, that Reid was in fact right to draw a distinction between sensation and perception, in the terms that have been described. Reid's argument for the distinction was based on an appeal to introspection, backed up by a tacit and seldom acknowledged, but very crucial supposition that no mental state could be extended or disposed in space. The following selections, from Reid's discussions of the senses of smell and touch, are illustrative of the most important introspective conclusions he wanted to bring his readers to see. The first examines a case of sensation.]

Inquiry 2.2: 40-42/B 26-27

... let us now attend carefully to what the mind is conscious of when we smell a rose or a lily; and since our language affords no other name for this sensation, we shall call it a *smell* or *odour*, carefully excluding from the meaning of those names every thing but the sensation itself, at least till we have examined it.

Suppose a person who never had this sense before, to receive it all at once, and to smell a rose; can he perceive any similitude or agreement between the smell and the rose? or indeed between it and any other object whatsoever? Certainly he cannot. He finds himself affected in a new way, he knows not why or from what cause. Like a man that feels some pain or pleasure formerly unknown to him, he is conscious that he is not the cause of it himself; but cannot, from the nature of the thing, determine whether it is caused by body or spirit, by something near, or by something at a distance. It has no similitude to any thing else, so as to admit of a comparison; and therefore he can conclude nothing from it, unless perhaps that there must be some unknown cause of it.

It is evidently ridiculous, to ascribe to it figure, colour, extension, or any other quality of bodies. He cannot give it a place, any more than he can give a place to melancholy or joy: nor can he conceive it to have any existence, but when it is smelled. So that it appears to be a simple and original affection or feeling of the mind, altogether inexplicable and unaccountable. It is indeed impossible that it can be in any body: it is a sensation, and a sensation can only be in a sentient thing.

[In Reid's account, the sensation of smell "suggests" the conception of and belief in certain objects. Importantly, these objects are nothing like the smell sensation. They are certainly not copies of it nor does it represent them. As a nudge or an act of pointing leads us to look in a certain direction and see for ourselves what lies there, so a smell sensation nudges us to conceive certain objects and believe in their present existence. Our conception of these objects is appropriately described as direct or immediate because we conceive these objects by conceiving these objects rather than by conceiving something else distinct from them that is at best a representation or sign of them.]

Inquiry 2.6: 56 [misnumbered 36] and 58/B 32 and 33

It is certain, no man can conceive or believe smelling to exist of itself, without a mind, or something that has the power of smelling, of which it is called a sensation, an operation, or feeling. Yet if any man should demand a proof, that sensation cannot be without a mind, or sentient being, I confess that I can give none; and that to pretend to prove it, seems to me almost as absurd as to deny it.

...

If there are certain principles, as I think there are, which the constitution of our nature leads us to believe, and which we are under a necessity to take for granted in the common concerns of life, without being able to give a reason for them; these are what we call the principles of common sense; and what is manifestly contrary to them, is what we call absurd.

Inquiry 2.7: 68-69 and 71/B 37 and 38

It appears then to be an undeniable fact, that from thought or sensation, all mankind, constantly and invariably, from the first dawning of reflection, do infer a power or faculty of thinking, and a permanent being or mind to which that faculty belongs; and that we as invariably ascribe all the various kinds of sensation and thought we are conscious of, to one individual mind or self.

By what rules of logic we make these inferences, it is impossible to show; nay, it is impossible to show how our sensations and thoughts can give us the very notion and conception either of a mind or of a faculty. The faculty of smelling is something very different from the actual sensation of smelling; for the faculty may remain when we have no sensation. And the mind is no less different from the faculty; for it continues the same individual being when that faculty is lost. Yet this sensation suggests to us both a faculty and a mind; and not only suggests the notion of them, but creates a belief of their existence; although it is impossible to discover, by reason, any tie or connection between one and the other.

...

I beg leave to make use of the word *suggestion*, because I know not one more proper, to express a power of the mind, which seems entirely to have escaped the notice of philosophers, and to which we owe many of our simple notions which are neither impressions nor ideas, as well as many original principles of belief.

Inquiry 2.9: 77-78 and 84/B 40 and 42-43

The smell of a rose is a certain affection or feeling of the mind; and as it is not constant, but comes and goes, we want to know when and where we may expect it, and are uneasy till we find something, which being present, brings this feeling along with it, and being removed, removes it. This, when found, we call the cause of it ... Having found the smell thus constantly conjoined with the rose, the mind is at rest, without inquiring whether this conjunction is owing to a real efficiency or not; that being a philosophical inquiry, which does not concern human life.

...

By the original constitution of our nature, we are both led to believe, that there is a permanent cause of the [smell] sensation, and prompted to seek after it; and experience determines us to place it in the rose.

[Reid considered smell to "suggest" a direct perception of the existence of some external object, but to suggest nothing more about this object. It is left to experience to discover what the object is like and what it is about the object that produces the sensation. This is common to all of what Reid called the "secondary qualities" of bodies. All we immediately perceive concerning them is that they exist, and that they cause our sensations. The features that cause those sensations are not evident to perception.]

Inquiry 5.1: 110-13/B 54-55

[Sounds, tastes, and odours] are all likewise of one order, being all secondary qualities ...

As to heat and cold, it will easily be allowed that they are secondary qualities, of the same order with smell, taste, and sound ...

The sensations of heat and cold are perfectly known; for they neither are, nor can be, any thing else than what we feel them to be; but the qualities in bodies which we call *heat* and *cold*, are unknown. They are only conceived by us, as unknown causes or occasions of the sensations to which we give the same names. But though common sense says nothing of the nature of these qualities, it plainly dictates the existence of them; and to deny that there can be heat and cold[22] when they are not felt,[23] is an absurdity too gross to merit confutation ...

It is the business of philosophers to investigate, by proper experiments, and induction, what heat and cold are in bodies. And whether they make heat a particular element diffused through nature, and accumulated in the heated body, or whether they make it a certain vibration of the parts of the heated body; whether they determine that heat and cold are contrary qualities, as the sensations undoubtedly are contrary, or that heat only is a quality, and cold its privation; these questions are within the province of philosophy; for common sense says nothing on the one side or the other.

But whatever be the nature of that quality in bodies which we call *heat*, we certainly know this, that it cannot in the least resemble the sensation of heat. It is no less absurd to suppose a likeness between the sensation and the quality, than it would be to suppose, that the pain of the gout resembles a square, or a triangle.

[Reid's commitment to this last point is a legacy of his early attachment to Berkeley, who had maintained that nothing can be like an idea but another idea—specifically, that no material thing could be in any way like a mental state.]

Inquiry 5.8: 163/B 74

Bishop Berkeley gave new light to this subject, by showing, that the qualities of an inanimate thing, such as matter is conceived to be, cannot resemble any sensation; that it is impossible to conceive any

---

22 I.e., to deny the existence of those unknown qualities in bodies that cause our sensations of heat and cold.

23 I.e., when those qualities do not cause us to have sensations of heat and cold.

thing like the sensations of our minds, but the sensations of other minds. Every one that attends properly to his sensations must assent to this; yet it had escaped all the philosophers that came before Berkeley ... So difficult it is to attend properly even to our own feelings ... when we think we have acquired this power, perhaps the mind still fluctuates between the sensation and its associated quality, so that they mix together, and present something to the imagination that is compounded of both.

[Given that it is so difficult to attend to our sensations, we might wonder what made Reid so sure that a sensation could not be anything like an inanimate object. But setting this worry aside for the moment, Reid's position as thus far presented poses another problem: if sensations of smell, taste, hearing, and heat and cold only suggest that some cause or "occasion" of those sensations exists outside of us, and it is left to "experience" to tell us what that object is and what it is like, then what is the nature of this experience? How do we obtain any information about where the object (in the mind or outside of it) is and what it is like?

Reid's answer comes with the claim that the senses of touch and sight lead us to perceive something more than just the bare existence of some cause of our sensations.]

Inquiry 5.2: 114-17 and 119-22/B 55-58

Let us next consider hardness and softness; by which words we always understand real properties or qualities of bodies, of which we have a distinct conception.

When the parts of a body adhere so firmly, that it cannot easily be made to change its figure, we call it *hard*; when its parts are easily displaced, we call it *soft*. This is the notion which all mankind have of hardness and softness: they are neither sensations, nor like any sensation; they were real qualities before they were perceived by touch, and continue to be so when they are not perceived ...

There is, no doubt, a sensation by which we perceive a body to be hard or soft. This sensation of hardness may easily be had, by pressing one's hand against the table, and attending to the feeling that ensues, setting aside, as much as possible, all thought of the table and its qualities, or of any external thing. But it is one thing to have the sensation, and another to attend to it, and make it a distinct object of reflection. The first is very easy; the last, in most cases, extremely difficult.

We are so accustomed to use the sensation as a sign, and to pass immediately to the hardness signified, that, as far as appears, it was never made an object of thought, either by the vulgar or philosophers; nor has it a name in any language ...

There are indeed some cases, wherein it is no difficult matter to attend to the sensation occasioned by the hardness of a body; for instance, when it is so violent as to occasion considerable pain ... If a man runs his head with violence against a pillar, I appeal to him, whether the pain he feels resembles the hardness of the stone; or if he can conceive any thing like what he feels, to be in an inanimate piece of matter.

... It is quite otherwise when he leans his head gently against the pillar; for then he will tell you that he feels nothing in his head, but feels hardness in the stone. Hath he not a sensation in this case as well as in the other? Undoubtedly he hath: but it is a sensation which nature intended only as a sign of something in the stone; and, accordingly, he instantly fixes his attention upon the thing signified; and cannot, without great difficulty, attend so much to the sensation, as to be persuaded that there is any such thing, distinct from the hardness it signifies.

But however difficult it may be to attend to this fugitive sensation, to stop its rapid progress, and to disjoin it from the external quality of hardness, in whose shadow it is apt immediately to hide itself; this is what a philosopher by pains and practice must attain, otherwise it will be impossible for him to reason justly upon this subject, or even to understand what is here advanced. For the last appeal in subjects of this nature, must be to what a man feels and perceives in his own mind.

...

The firm cohesion of the parts of a body, is no more like that sensation by which I perceive it to be hard, than the vibration of a sonorous body is like the sound I hear: nor can I possibly perceive, by my reason, any connection between the one and the other. No man can give a reason, why the vibration of a body might not have given the sensation of smelling, and the effluvia of bodies affected our hearing, if it had so pleased our maker. In like manner, no man can give a reason, why the sensations of smell, or taste, or sound, might not have indicated hardness, as well as that sensation which, by our constitution, does indicate it ...

Here then is a phenomenon of human nature, which comes to be resolved. Hardness of bodies is a thing that we conceive as distinctly, and believe as firmly, as any thing in nature. We have no way of coming at this conception and belief, but by means of a certain sensation of touch, to which hardness hath not the least similitude; nor can we, by any rules of reasoning, infer the one from the other. The question is, How we come by this conception and belief?

First, as to the conception: Shall we call it an idea of sensation, or of reflection? The last will not be affirmed; and as little can the first, unless we will call that an idea of sensation, which hath no resemblance to any sensation. So that the origin of this idea of hardness, one of the most common and most distinct we have, is not to be found in all our systems of the mind: not even in those which have so copiously endeavoured to deduce all our notions from sensation and reflection.[24]

But, secondly, supposing we have got the conception of hardness, how come we by the belief of it? Is it self-evident, from comparing the ideas, that such a sensation could not be felt, unless such a quality of bodies existed? No. Can it be proved by probable or certain arguments? No, it cannot. Have we got this belief then by tradition, by education, or by experience? No, it is not got in any of these ways.[25]

... I see nothing left, but to conclude, that, by an original principle of our constitution, a certain sensation of touch both suggests to the mind the conception of hardness, and creates the belief of it ...

---

24 In writing this, Reid was ignoring *Treatise* 1.4.4 (where Hume elaborated on the claim of EHU 12.15 that the primary qualities cannot be conceived apart from the secondary qualities), esp. 1.4.4.9-14, where Hume had offered an account of the related notion of solidity. Like Reid, Hume had distinguished between a sensation of pressure that we feel when we touch a solid (or hard) body and solidity considered as the quality of resisting penetration by another body. But unlike Reid, who had claimed that hardness can only be conceived and cannot resemble any sensation, Hume had claimed that, since our sensations of vision and touch are disposed in space, we can perceive solidity (and by parity of example hardness) simply by observing how collections of coloured or tangible sensations behave over time through motion and collision. If they resist interpenetration (or deformation) they are solid (or hard). To suppose otherwise is to confuse the pressure sensation we feel when we touch a solid body with the quality of solidity understood as a complex relation obtaining between multiple, spatially disposed sensations of pressure or colour. Understood in this way, solidity and hardness are things that can not only be felt but seen. As Hume put it, a person with palsy (no sensation) in one hand, can sense the solidity of a table as well by seeing that hand rest on the table top as by touching it with the other hand. By implication, dropping the hand on the table top and seeing it fail to deform the table top upon collision would constitute seeing hardness. But all we are really seeing in this case is how collections of spatially disposed visual sensations of colour points or tangible sensations of pressure points remain disposed relative to one another in space over time.

25 Supposing the conception was formed on the basis of the experiences described in the previous note, the belief would be acquired from experience.

Further I observe, that hardness is a quality, of which we have as clear and distinct a conception as of any thing whatsoever. The cohesion of the parts of a body with more or less force, is perfectly understood, though its cause is not: we know what it is, as well as how it affects the touch. It is therefore a quality of a quite different order from those secondary qualities we have already taken notice of, whereof we know no more naturally, than that they are adapted to raise certain sensations in us. If hardness were a quality of the same kind, it would be a proper inquiry for philosophers, What hardness in bodies is? and we should have had various hypotheses about it, as well as about colour and heat ... we all know, that if the parts of a body adhere strongly, it is hard.

...

What hath been said of hardness, is so easily applicable, not only to its opposite, softness, but likewise to roughness and smoothness, to figure and motion, that we may be excused from making the application ... All these, by means of certain corresponding sensations of touch, are presented to the mind as real external qualities; the conception and belief of them are invariably connected with the corresponding sensations, by an original principle of human nature.

...

It is further to be observed, that hardness and softness, roughness and smoothness, figure and motion, do all suppose extension, and cannot be conceived without it; yet I think it must, on the other hand, be allowed, that if we had never felt any thing hard or soft, rough or smooth, figured or moved, we should never have had a conception of extension: so that as there is good ground to believe, that the notion of extension could not be prior to that of other primary qualities; so it is certain that it could not be posterior to the notion of any of them, being necessarily implied in them all.

Extension, therefore, seems to be a quality suggested to us, by the very same sensations which suggest the other qualities above mentioned.

[Reid went on to claim that vision also provides us with perceptions of primary qualities of bodies, though there are a number of disanalogies and complexities.[26]

---

26 Most notably, visual perceptions of figure and position are not "suggested" by visual sensations, of which we are conscious, but instead directly suggested by physiological stimulation of particular parts of the retina, of which we are entirely unconscious; and colour terminology is therefore not ambiguous in the way that smell and other secondary quality terminology is ambiguous. Colour terminology *never* refers to the sensations we experience in vision,

Despite the elaborate and detailed tour of the workings of the five senses that Reid led his readers along, his introspective argument for a distinction between sensation and perception rests on two bald assertions: that a sensation, being a mental state of feeling, can be like nothing but another sensation and can share no property in common with any physical object, and that the primary qualities of extension and its modes (figure, position, motion, hardness) can only be qualities of physical objects, not of mental states.

Reid charged anyone who would question these two assertions with conceptual and linguistic confusion.]

Inquiry 6.8: 159-60/B 72-73

All the systems of philosophers about our senses and their objects have split upon this rock, of not distinguishing properly sensations, which can have no existence but when they are felt, from the things suggested by them. Aristotle ... confounds these two; and makes every sensation to be the form, without the matter, of the thing perceived by it ... Aristotle made no distinction between primary and secondary qualities of bodies, although that distinction was made by Democritus, Epicurus, and others of the ancients.

Des Cartes, Malebranch, and Locke, revived the distinction between primary and secondary qualities. But ... They maintained, that colour, sound and heat, are not any thing in bodies, but sensations of the mind: At the same time, they acknowledged some particular texture or modification of the body, to be the cause or occasion of those sensations; but to this modification they gave no name. Whereas, by the vulgar, the names of colour, heat, and sound, are but rarely applied to the sensations, and most commonly to those unknown causes of them.

---

according to Reid (in passages to be cited below), but only ever to the unperceived qualities in bodies that we take to be causes of these sensations. The efforts of painters, cosmeticians, and interior decorators notwithstanding, our visual sensations are supposed to be so insignificant that people have not so much as bothered to give them names in any language. Vision also supplies us with direct perceptions only of the left/right and upward/downward directions in which objects or their parts lie relative to the centre of the eye, not of the distance at which objects are placed away from us in these directions. As a result, our perceptions of the size and figure of objects are only projections of their apparent size and figure, resulting from the fact that what we visually perceive is the position of the parts of the objects with reference to the position of the eye rather than with reference to one another.

Inquiry 2.8: 74/B 39

Suppose that such a man [a "sensible day-labourer"] meets with a modern philosopher, and wants to be informed, what smell in plants is. The philosopher tells him, that there is no smell in plants, nor in any thing, but in the mind; that it is impossible there can be smell but in a mind; and that all this hath been demonstrated by modern philosophy. The plain man will, no doubt, be apt to think him merry:[27] but if he finds that he is serious, his next conclusion will be, that he is mad; or that philosophy, like magic, puts men into a new world, and gives them different faculties from common men. And thus philosophy and common sense are set at variance. But who is to blame for it? In my opinion the philosopher is to blame. For if he means by smell, what the rest of mankind most commonly mean,[28] he is certainly mad. But if he puts a different meaning upon the word,[29] without observing it himself, or giving warning to others; he abuses language, and disgraces philosophy, without doing any service to truth.

Inquiry 2.9: 83-85/B 42-43

The vulgar are commonly charged by philosophers, with the absurdity of imagining the smell in the rose to be something like to the sensation of smelling: but I think, unjustly; for they neither give the same epithets to both, nor do they reason in the same manner from them ... smell in the rose, and the sensation which it causes, are not conceived, even by the vulgar, to be things of the same kind, although they have the same name.

From what hath been said we may learn, that the smell of a rose signifies two things. *First*, A sensation, which can have no existence but when it is perceived, and can only be in a sentient being or mind. *Secondly*, It signifies some power, quality, or virtue, in the rose, or in effluvia proceeding from it, which hath a permanent existence, independent of the mind, and which, by the constitution of nature, produces the sensation in us ... The names of all smells, tastes, sounds, as well as heat and cold,[30] have a like ambiguity in all languages: but it deserves our attention, that these names are but rarely, in common language, used to signify the sensations; for the most part, they signify the external qualities which are indicated by the sensations.

---

27 I.e., joking.

28 Namely, some unperceived quality in external objects that is responsible for causing our smell sensations.

29 I.e., if he takes the word, "smell," to refer to the sensation we feel when we smell rather than the quality in the object that causes this sensation.

30 The omission of colour from this list is deliberate.

With regard to primary qualities, these philosophers [Descartes, Malebranche, and Locke] erred more grossly: they indeed believed the existence of those qualities; but they did not at all attend to the sensations that suggest them, which having no names, have been as little considered as if they had no existence. They were aware, that figure, extension, and hardness, are perceived by means of sensations of touch; whence they rashly concluded, that these sensations must be images and resemblances of figure, extension, and hardness.

The received hypothesis of ideas naturally led them to this conclusion: and indeed could not consist with any other; for according to that hypothesis, external things must be perceived by means of images of them in the mind; and what can those images of external things in the mind be, but the sensations by which we perceive them?

This however was to draw a conclusion from a hypothesis against fact. We need not have recourse to any hypothesis to know what our sensations are, or what they are like. By a proper degree of reflection and attention we may understand them perfectly, and be as certain that they are not like any quality of body, as we can be, that a toothach is not like a triangle.

[Hume was unimpressed by these charges. Responding to a pre-publication draft of portions of the *Inquiry* (likely chapters 2-5) that Reid had sent to him by way of Hugh Blair, he insisted that if we were to ask ordinary people what heat or red are, they would not respond that they don't know what they are, that it is the business of scientists and not of ordinary people to find out what they are, and that all that they know is that they are some unperceived, hidden qualities in fire that cause them to feel certain tactile and visual sensations when they approach it. They would instead say that heat and red are the perfectly evident qualities they perceive when they approach a fire. And if we were to further ask them where this evident heat that they feel and red that they see are, they would say that they permeate the extension of the fire. To suppose them to think otherwise would be to suppose them to be "Philosophers & Corpuscularians from their Infancy," and to fail to recognize that, when they are shocked to be told that heat and red are not really in fire but only sensations in us, it is not because they understand you to be saying, absurdly, that the hidden qualities that cause our sensations are only sensations, but rather because they understand you to be saying that those things that they had all along supposed to be perceptually evident qualities inhering in the fire are in fact only sensations in us.]

David Hume, Letter to Hugh Blair of 4 July 1762

The Author supposes, that the Vulgar do not believe the sensible Qualities of Heat, Smell, Sound, & probably Colour[31] to be really in the Bodies, but only their Causes or something capable of producing them in the Mind. But this is imagining the Vulgar to be Philosophers & Corpuscularians from their Infancy. You know what pains it cost Malebranche & Locke to establish that Principle ... And indeed Philosophy scarce ever advances a greater Paradox in the Eyes of the People, than when it affirms that Snow is neither cold nor white: Fire hot nor red.[32]

[Philosophers not only grew up as common folk, but (notably in the opinion of EHU 12.23) relapse back into the views of the common folk as soon as they leave the study. Each of us is therefore in as privileged a position to say what the common folk think as anyone else. It is a serious question whether Reid's conviction (that common folk suppose red and heat, as they are in bodies, to be unperceived hidden causes rather than perceptually evident qualities) was actually based on introspection or was rather a position he was forced to develop as a consequence of other commitments.

Reid's second claim, that extension, figure, motion, hardness or softness, etc., could not be qualities of any mental state, is no more obvious to introspection than his first. Even his paradigm cases of the sensation of pain resulting from a rotting tooth, a gouty toe, or the point of a sword are unconvincing. Common sense takes heat to be in the fire but the pain of a burn or a stab to be in me because when I retreat from the fire or the sword I carry the pain away with me whereas the heat remains behind in the fire. But though I take the pain to be in me, I do not take it to be in my mind, but in my wounded hand or in my rotting tooth. Many pains are tactile sensations that occur at particular locations relative to other tactile sensations. The pain of a toothache, the pain of a stab wound in the left hand, and the pain of gout in the right toe are experienced as disposed in space in

---

31 Colour was only discussed in the sixth chapter of Reid's *Inquiry*, and in his abstract (B 262, referenced below) Reid made an allusion to Hume's having only been presented with the evidence of four of the five witnesses for Reid's position, i.e., four of the five senses, in the MS passed on to him by Blair.

32 Aberdeen University Library MS 2814/1/39, transcribed in Paul B. Wood, "David Hume on Thomas Reid's *An Inquiry into the Human Mind on the Principles of Common Sense*: A New Letter to Hugh Blair from July 1762," *Mind* 95 (1986): 411-16, and in B 256-57.

much the way that the three vertices of a triangle are felt or seen to be disposed in space.

Reid insisted otherwise.]

Inquiry 6.12: 295-96/B 125

The sensation of pain is, no doubt, in the mind, and cannot be said to have any relation from its own nature to any part of the body: but this sensation, by our constitution, gives a perception of some particular part of the body, whose disorder causes the uneasy sensation. If it were not so, a man who never before felt either the gout or the toothach, when he is first seized with the gout in his toe, might mistake it for the toothach.

[On Hume's contrary account, tactile sensations are immediately perceived as disposed relative to one another in space. Since they are not unordered, aspatial events like passions or thoughts, there is no problem accounting for how we come to assign them to one place rather than another. We feel the pain of gout in the toe because that is where it is disposed.

Introspection is not as opposed to this view as Reid claimed. When I go to scratch an itch, I do not think of myself as reaching out to touch a remote part of my body in a way that is magically going to remove some unknown cause of an unpleasant sensation that I feel only in my mind. I reach to scratch where I feel the itch. And I have never felt tempted to try to reach into my mind to scratch an itch I feel there.

In an abstract further detailing the course of his argument in response to Hume's criticisms, and likely forwarded to Hume by Hugh Blair, Reid admitted that the introspective evidence for his claims is far from obvious. But he insisted that it is ultimately unambiguous.[33]]

Thomas Reid, Abstract of the *Inquiry*

Ever since the treatise of human Nature was published I respected Mr Hume as the greatest Metaphysician of the Age, and have learned more from his writings in matters of that kind than from all others put together. I read that treatise over and over with

---

33 Aberdeen University Library MS 2131/2/iii/1, pp. 1-4, transcribed from .jpg images currently available from the library at http://www.abdn.ac.uk/diss /historic/Thomas_Reid/MS_2131/. A transcription can also be found in David Fate Norton, "Reid's Abstract of the *Inquiry into the Human Mind*," *Philosophical Monographs* 3 (1976): 125-32, and B 257-60.

great care, made an abstract of it and wrote my observations upon it. I perceived that his System is all founded upon one principle, from which his conclusions, however extraordinary, are deduced with irresistible Evidence. The principle I mean is, That all the objects of human thought are either Impressions or Ideas: which I was very much disposed to believe untill I read that Treatise; but finding that if this is true I must be an absolute Sceptic, I thought that it deserved a carefull Examination.

For this purpose I entered into a Strict Examination of my Impressions that I might know whether all my Thoughts & Conceptions were images and copies of them or not; taking for granted that if any object of thought was not like any impression it could not be an Idea, because Ideas in his System are faint copies of preceeding impressions.

I have perhaps taken more pains in this Enquiry than perhaps any man ever did, being heartily concerned to know whether there was any such thing as truth within the reach of the human faculties, and imagining that the examination of this principle upon which that System of Scepticism depended would not be very difficult.

... But however easy this task of attending to my sensations appeared in Theory, I found it very difficult in the Practice.

Indeed it is easy to attend to those Sensations which are either very painfull or very pleasant, and it is acknowledged on all hands that they are not like any of those things that we call external objects. But it is extreamly difficult to attend to the sensations that are neither pleasant nor painfull, such as those we have when we feel a body hard or soft, rough or smooth of this or the other figure.

This difficulty arises from our being determined by our Constitution to pass instantaneously from the sensation to the quality which corresponds to it, and to attend onely to the latter. One that attends carefully to such sensations will soon be sensible that the most painfull abstraction is not more difficult. And therefore as no philosopher as far as I know hath taken notice of this difficulty, it is probable they never attended to their sensations with sufficient care.

...

When I had acquired the power of thus attending to my Sensations, I was soon perswaded that I had never made them objects of thought before & that those Sensations which I had felt every day, perhaps every hour of my life, had notwithstanding been as much unknown to me as if I had never felt them, because I had never given any attention to them. I found in a word that hardness and softness, roughness and smoothness, figure extention and motion had not the least resemblance to those sensations that correspond to them & by which we are made acquainted with them.

This enquiry into the fundamental Article of Mr Humes System led me gradually into my present way of thinking with regard to the human Mind: And in what I have wrote concerning the five Senses, I have always had Mr Humes System and particularly this fundamental Article of it in my View.

In treating of the several Senses my Intentions are ...

3 To compare our Sensations with the sensible qualities corresponding: and in this comparison I always find a total dissimilitude ... I have ... proposed this as an *Experimentum Crucis* ... If what we call Extension, Figure, Motion, Hardness or Softness, Roughness or Smoothness have any Resemblance to the Sensations that correspond to them, then I must Subscribe to Mr Humes Creed and cannot avoid it. But if there is no such resemblance then his System falls to pieces ... and we are to seek for a new one. The last Appeal in a Question of this kind must be to a mans own Perceptions. He that can attend to his sensations[34] so far as to make them an object of thought, and can compare them with sensible qualities can be at no loss to judge in this question. And if he is at any loss this is an evident proof that he has not clear and distinct notions of the things he would compare. After taking much pains to attend to my Sensations and to form clear and distinct conceptions of them, it appears to me as clear and as certain that they are not like to sensible qualities, as that the pain of the toothach is not like to a triangle.

[Reid set great store by this *experimentum crucis*, which is repeated in the published *Inquiry*.]

Inquiry 5.7: 152/B 70

This I would therefore humbly propose as an *experimentum crucis*, by which the ideal system must stand or fall; and it brings the matter to a short issue: Extension, figure, motion, may, any one, or all of them, be taken for the subject of this experiment. Either they are ideas of sensation, or they are not. If any one of them can be shown to be an idea of sensation, or to have the least resemblance to any sensation, I lay my hand upon my mouth, and give up all pretence to reconcile reason to common sense in this matter, and must suffer the ideal scepticism to triumph.

[In Reid's estimation, the experiment turns out in his favour, because the contrary view, that visual and tactile sensations have location, and

---

34 MS inserts *sensations*

constitute extended, shaped aggregates that can be said to be hard or solid because of the way they are observed to behave in collision, is justified neither by argument nor by introspection.]

Inquiry 5.7: 149–50/B 69

Have those philosophers then given any solid proof of this hypothesis [that the material world "must be the express image of our sensations" and that "the sensations of touch are images of extension, hardness, figure, and motion"], upon which the whole weight of so strange a system rests? No. They have not so much as attempted to do it. But, because ancient and modern philosophers have agreed in this opinion, they have taken it for granted. But let us, as becomes philosophers, lay aside authority; we need not surely consult Aristotle or Locke, to know whether pain be like the point of a sword. I have as clear a conception of extension, hardness, and motion, as I have of the point of a sword; and, with some pains and practice, I can form as clear a notion of the other sensations of touch, as I have of pain. When I do so, and compare them together, it appears to me clear as daylight, that the former are not of kin to the latter, nor resemble them in any one feature.

[Hume's contrary position is far from being unjustified by argument or by introspection. At EHU 12.15 Hume had argued that extension, figure, and motion cannot be separated from our sensations of vision and touch. "An extension, that is neither tangible nor visible, cannot possibly be conceived: And a tangible or visible extension, which is neither hard nor soft, black nor white, is equally beyond the reach of human conception." In arguing that extension can only be visible or tangible Hume was appealing to introspective evidence at least as strong and compelling as any Reid was able to invoke. I cannot perceive or imagine a triangle or a circle, without perceiving or imagining contrasting colours or tactile sensations, disposed in such a way as to define edges and lines. And whatever we might think of Reid's attempt to argue that tactile sensations are locationless feelings that only suggest the conception of some unperceived disturbance in some body part, few things are as obvious to introspection as that colours—which all were agreed do not exist in the external world but are visual sensations—are disposed in space to constitute figures like triangles and circles. To establish that the *experimentum crucis* in fact turns out his way, and that extension, figure, and motion do not have any resemblance to any of our sensations, Reid would have had to show that it is introspectively obvious that, when I look at a stop sign or a traffic signal, the red and green colour sensations I experience are not disposed in the configuration of an octagon or a circle, but are no more located in space than passions of joy or surprise, or sensations of smell; while the traffic signals are perceived as colourless shapes that are believed to contain perceptually non-evident qualities that cause these locationless colour sensations. Confronted with this challenge, Reid's response was not to produce introspective evidence that might convince us that his view of the phenomenology of visual experience is correct, but to instead attempt to deprive people of the vocabulary needed to contest his opinion. He questioned the ordinary meaning of our colour terminology, attempting to define these terms in such a way as to make it impossible for anyone to say, using words like "colour," "red," or "green," that the evident qualities they experience in vision are disposed in space.]

Inquiry 6.2: 175/B 79

To those who see, a scarlet colour signifies an unknown quality in bodies, that makes to the eye an appearance, which they are well acquainted with ...

Inquiry 6.4: 190-95/B 85-87

By colour, all men, who have not been tutored by modern philosophy, understand, not a sensation of the mind, which can have no existence when it is not perceived, but a quality or modification of bodies, which continues to be the same, whether it is seen or not ... when I view this scarlet rose through a pair of green spectacles, the appearance is changed, but I do not conceive the colour of the rose changed. To a person in the jaundice, it has still another appearance; but he is easily convinced, that the change is in his eye, and not in the colour of the object ...

The common language of mankind shows evidently, that we ought to distinguish between the colour of a body, which is conceived to be a fixed and permanent quality in the body, and the appearance of that colour to the eye ... The permanent colour of the body is the cause, which, by the mediation of various kinds or degrees of light, and of various transparent bodies interposed, produces all this variety of appearances. When a coloured body is presented, there is a certain apparition to the eye, or to the mind, which we have called *the appearance of colour*. Mr Locke calls it *an idea*; and indeed it may be called so with the greatest propriety. This idea can have no existence but when it is perceived. It is a kind of thought, and can only be the act of a percipient or thinking being.[35] By the constitution of our nature, we are led to conceive this idea as a sign of something external, and are impatient till we learn its meaning. A thousand experiments for this purpose are made every day by children ... The ideas of sight, by these means, come to be associated with, and readily to suggest, things external, and altogether unlike them. In particular, that idea which we have called *the appearance of colour*, suggests the conception and belief of some unknown quality in the body, which occasions the idea; and it is to this quality, and not to the idea, that we give the name of *colour* ...

When we think or speak of any particular colour, however simple the notion may seem to be, which is presented to the imagination, it is really in some sort compounded. It involves an unknown cause, and a known effect. The name of *colour* belongs indeed to the cause only, and not to the effect. But as the cause is unknown, we can form no distinct conception of it, but by its relation to the known effect. And therefore both go together in the imagination, and are so closely united, that they are mistaken for one simple object of thought. When I would conceive those colours of bodies which we call *scarlet* and *blue*; if I conceived them only as unknown qualities, I could perceive no distinction between the one and the other. I must therefore, for the sake of distinction, join to each of them in my imagination some effect or some relation that is peculiar. And the most obvious distinction is, the appearance which one and the other makes to the eye ...

I conclude then, that colour is not a sensation, but a secondary quality of bodies, in the sense we have already explained; that it is a certain power or virtue in bodies, that in fair day-light exhibits to the eye an appearance, which is very familiar to us, although it hath no name. Colour differs from other secondary qualities in this, that whereas the name of the quality is sometimes given to the sensation which indicates it, and is occasioned by it, we never, as far as I can judge, give the name

---

35 Up to this point, Reid has said nothing that is in conflict with common sense. According to common sense, the colour of a body is not "an unknown quality in bodies" but a quality that is immediately evident in visual perception. Though it is distinct from the "appearances of colour" that Reid rightly drew our attention to, it is not unlike them. Common sense takes appearances of colour to be different tints, tones, or shades of the actual colour, produced by various sorts of interference, and the actual colour to be immediately evident when perceiving the object under ideal circumstances. This, however, is emphatically not Reid's view. As the ensuing sentences make clear, Reid wanted to insist that colours are not perceptually evident, that we need to learn what they are, that they are "altogether unlike" appearances of colour, and that they are in fact "unknown qualities" that cause our visual sensations.

of *colour* to the sensation, but to the quality only ... And indeed they [the sensations] are so little interesting, that they are never attended to, but serve only as signs to introduce the things signified by them.[36]

Inquiry 6.5: 196-99/B 87-89

We have shown, that the word *colour*, as used by the vulgar, cannot signify an idea in the mind, but a permanent quality of body ... If it should be said, that this quality to which we give the name of *colour*, is unknown to the vulgar, and therefore can have no name among them; I answer, it is indeed known only by its effects; that is, by its exciting a certain idea in us: but are there not numberless qualities of bodies which are known only by their effects, to which, notwithstanding, we find it necessary to give names? Medicine alone might furnish us with an hundred instances of this kind. Do not the words *astringent, narcotic, epispastic, caustic*, and innumerable others, signify qualities of bodies which are known only by their effects upon animal bodies? ... Philosophers have thought fit to leave that quality of bodies which the vulgar call *colour*, without a name, and to give the name of *colour* to the idea or appearance, to which, as we have shown, the vulgar give no name, because they never make it an object of thought or reflection. Hence it appears, that when philosophers affirm that colour is not in bodies, but in the mind; and the vulgar affirm, that colour is not in the mind, but is a quality of bodies; there is no difference between them about things, but only about the meaning of a word.[37]

...

---

36 This last claim completes Reid's inversion of the common sense phenomenology of visual perception. According to Reid, not only do terms like "coloured," "scarlet," and "blue" not name anything that is evident in visual experience, being instead only the names of perceptually non-evident causes of our visual sensations, but the visual sensations themselves have no names and are never talked about by anybody. The efforts of painters, cosmeticians, and interior decorators notwithstanding, all anybody ever talks about when they name colours, according to Reid, is perceptually non-evident causes of visual sensations and the sensations themselves are so "uninteresting" as not to even deserve to be named. In putting forward this doctrine Reid did not so much refute Hume as attempt to gag him—to deprive him of the words to describe the phenomenology of our visual experience.

37 The determination of the meaning of the word is far from trivial, for it puts Reid in a position to claim that when someone ascribes position, shape, or size to a "colour" they are only ascribing these qualities to a non-evident quality of bodies, not to the evident quality experienced in vision that philosophers argue is only a sensation. Those wishing to disagree are gagged by being deprived of a vocabulary that they can use to describe their introspective experience.

If you ask a man that is no philosopher, what colour is? or, what makes one body appear white, another scarlet? he cannot tell. He leaves that inquiry to philosophers, and can embrace any hypothesis about it, except that of our modern philosophers, who affirm, that colour is not in body, but only in the mind.

Nothing appears more shocking to his apprehension, than that visible objects should have no colour, and that colour should be in that which he conceives to be invisible.[38]

[Reid's ruminations on the meaning of colour terminology notwithstanding, it is introspectively evident that what Reid would call the nameless sensations that we experience when we look at objects are experienced by us as disposed alongside one another in space to constitute extended and variously located figures. The shapes I perceive are filled with and bounded by the evident visual sensations I feel. When I say that the stoplight is red, I do not mean that the round object I perceive contains some non-evident quality that causes a nameless visual sensation. I take the term "red" to name the sensation and I take that sensation to be round and disposed at a certain location relative to other colour sensations on my visual field.

As the following passage indicates, what made Reid so convinced that sensations of colour cannot be located in space and cannot constitute extended, figured, hard, or soft compounds was not introspective evidence, but a tacit commitment to a "hypothesis" of his own: the dualist hypothesis that the mind is an immaterial substance. It is this tacit commitment, rather than the introspective evidence, that led Reid to be convinced that no mental state could be disposed in space.]

---

38 This sentence expresses the triumph of Reid's word-game. If anyone could be accused of propounding the shocking view that visible objects have no colour, it was Reid. His claims notwithstanding, most of us use colour terminology to refer to qualities that are evident to us in visual perception—qualities that we take to be extended over the surfaces of the objects that we see and to define the visual boundaries of those surfaces, so that apart from colour contrasts, shapes become invisible. The philosophers Reid criticized denied that these colours exist on the surfaces of external objects, but they at least took mental images to be coloured. Reid, in contrast, wanted to maintain that the located, extended, and shaped objects that we immediately perceive in vision are not perceived to have any evident colour qualities on their surfaces but are merely conceived to be frames containing perceptually non-evident qualities that cause aspatial colour sensations. The shocking claim that visible objects have no colour (in the truly ordinary sense of that term) is his.

But Locke seems to place the ideas of sensible things in the mind: and that Berkeley, and the author of the *Treatise of human nature*, were of the same opinion, is evident. The last makes a very curious application of this doctrine, by endeavouring to prove from it, That the mind either is no substance, or that it is an extended and divisible substance; because the ideas of extension cannot be in a subject which is indivisible and unextended.[39]

I confess I think his reasoning in this, as in most cases, is clear and strong. For whether the idea of extension be only another name for extension itself, as Berkeley and this author assert; or whether the idea of extension be an image and resemblance of extension, as Locke conceived; I appeal it to any man of common sense, whether extension, or any image of extension, can be in an unextended and indivisible subject. But while I agree with him in his reasoning, I would make a different application of it. He takes it for granted, that there are ideas of extension in the mind; and thence infers, that if it is at all a substance, it must be an extended and divisible substance.[40] On the contrary, I take it for granted, upon the testimony of common sense, that my mind is a substance, that is, a permanent subject of thought; and my reason convinces me, that it is an unextended and indivisible substance;[41] and hence I infer, that there cannot be in it any thing that resembles extension. If this reasoning had occurred to Berkeley, it would probably have led him to acknowledge, that we may think and reason concerning bodies, without having ideas of them in the mind, as well as concerning spirits.

[As it was a visceral reaction to Hume's scepticism about the self that motivated Reid to reject the traditional views about mental representation he took to have culminated in Hume's work, so it was that same

---

39 Reid is alluding to *Treatise* 1.4.5, where Hume argued that because some of our perceptions, those of vision and touch, are extended, whereas others, such as our passions and perceptions of smell, taste, and hearing, do not exist in space at all, all of our perceptions cannot be conjoined with or contained in either a material or an immaterial substance.

40 This is not quite what Hume said in *Treatise* 1.4.5. His conclusion was that the mind could no more be a material than it could be an immaterial substance.

41 Though Reid said that reason convinces us that the mind is unextended and indivisible, he never actually produced such a demonstration. Even explicit references to a commitment to the doctrine of the immateriality of the soul are rare and ambivalent in his published works.

commitment to the existence of an immaterial soul that served as the ultimate justification for his opposed account of sensation and perception. But Reid's seldom acknowledged and never justified dualism was no less a "hypothesis" than the imagism he found in Hume. Indeed, it was more of a hypothesis, since EHU at least argued for imagism while Reid never argued for dualism. The same charge that Reid levelled against his opponents might therefore be levelled against him.]

Inquiry 5.8: 165-67/B 75-76

We may here again observe, that this acute writer [Berkeley] argues from a hypothesis against fact, and against the common sense of mankind. That we can have no conception of any thing, unless there is some impression, sensation, or idea, in our minds which resembles it, is indeed an opinion which hath been very generally received among philosophers; but it is neither self-evident, nor hath it been clearly proved.

...

That we have clear and distinct conceptions of extension, figure, motion, and other attributes of body, which are neither sensations, nor like any sensation, is a fact of which we may be as certain, as that we have sensations. And that all mankind have a fixed belief of an external material world ... is likewise a fact, for which we have all the evidence that the nature of the thing admits. These facts are phenomena of human nature, from which we may justly argue against any hypothesis, however generally received. But to argue from a hypothesis against facts, is contrary to the rules of true philosophy.

[As Berkeley argued from a hypothesis, imagism, against the supposed fact that extension, figure and motion are neither sensations nor like any sensation, so Reid argued from a hypothesis, dualism, against the fact that colours (in the ordinary sense, where that word is taken to refer to the evident qualities experienced in visual sensation) have location, shape, and extension. Since we have learned that colours (again in the ordinary sense of that word) are merely phenomenal, it follows that some phenomenal properties are extended. Thus, Reid's *experimentum crucis* turns out against him.

This collection of selections from Reid concludes with Reid's critique of Hume's first argument (at EHU 12.9) for concluding that our sensory experience is not a direct experience of external objects but only of our own perceptions. Though only published after Hume's death, the critique grows out of the account of visual perception of position, figure, and magnitude presented over *Inquiry* 6.7-19.]

There remains only one other argument that I have been able to find urged against our perceiving external objects immediately. It is proposed by Mr HUME, who, in the Essay already quoted, after acknowledging that it is an universal and primary opinion of all men, that we perceive external objects immediately, subjoins what follows.

But this universal and primary opinion of all men is soon destroyed by the slightest philosophy, which teaches us, that nothing can ever be present to the mind but an image or perception; and that the senses are only the inlets through which these images are received, without being ever able to produce any immediate intercourse between the mind and the object. The table, which we see, seems to diminish as we remove farther from it: But the real table, which exists independent of us, suffers no alteration. It was therefore nothing but its image which was present to the mind. These are the obvious dictates of reason; and no man who reflects, ever doubted that the existences which we consider, when we say *this house*, and *that tree*, are nothing but perceptions in the mind, and fleeting copies and representations of other existences, which remain uniform and independent. So far then, we are necessitated, by reasoning, to depart from the primary instincts of nature, and to embrace a new system with regard to the evidence of our senses.[42]

We have here a remarkable conflict between two contradictory opinions, wherein all mankind are engaged. On the one side stand all the vulgar, who are unpractised in philosophical researches, and guided by the uncorrupted primary instincts of nature. On the other side, stand all the Philosophers ancient and modern; every man without exception who reflects. In this division, to my great humiliation, I find myself classed with the vulgar.

The passage now quoted is all I have found in Mr HUME's writings upon this point;[43] and indeed there is more reasoning in it than I have found in any other author; I shall therefore examine it minutely.

---

42 Paraphrasing EHU 12.9-10.

43 As a matter of fact, this passage is not all Reid would have found in Hume's writings on this point. Not to mention the argument at EHU 12.15, which has been considered at great length, he would have found an argument at *Treatise* 1.4.2.45 that appeals to double vision. Over a sixth of Reid's *Inquiry* was devoted to a painstaking account of single and double vision. It is an interesting question whether he could have applied that account to mount a response to Hume's appeal to double vision along the lines of the one presented here to Hume's appeal to variations in visible magnitude. In the event, he did not.

...

The argument, the only argument follows:[44]

The table which we see, seems to diminish as we remove farther from it; but the real table which exists independent of us suffers no alteration: It was therefore nothing but its image which was presented to the mind. These are the obvious dictates of reason.

To judge of the strength of this argument, it is necessary to attend to a distinction which is familiar to those who are conversant in the mathematical sciences, I mean the distinction between real and apparent magnitude.[45] The real magnitude of a line is measured by some known measure of length, as inches, feet, or miles: The real magnitude of a surface or solid, by known measures of surface or of capacity. This magnitude is an object of touch only, and not of sight; nor could we even have had any conception of it, without the sense of touch; and Bishop BERKELEY, on that account, calls it *tangible magnitude*.

Apparent magnitude is measured by the angle which an object subtends at the eye. Supposing two right lines drawn from the eye to the

---

44 Over the omitted paragraphs Reid attacked Hume for illustrating his point by talking about images conveyed through the senses, a metaphor that is indeed ill-considered. He also took Hume to task for stating his conclusion at the outset, rather than first giving the argument for it.

45 The term "apparent" notwithstanding, Reid did not mean to suggest that apparent magnitude is merely an "appearance" in the sense of being something that exists only in the mind of the perceiver. Apparent magnitude is a real quality of bodies. It could just as well be described as angular magnitude. Like any magnitude, it is relative. "Real" or better tangible magnitude is relative to the size of other bodies, often our own bodies, which are the standards we generally appeal to in assessing whether something is large or small. Angular magnitude is relative to the position from which the angle subtended by objects is measured. In both cases there can be variation. The same object can be called great or small depending on whether it is compared to a greater or smaller unit of measure, or depending on whether its angular magnitude is measured from a greater or a smaller distance. But in neither case is the variation due to any change in the object itself. As Reid went on to point out, it only makes sense that the angular magnitude of an object should diminish as it is measured from greater and greater distances, even though the object itself does not change in tangible magnitude. Insofar as vision tells us about the angular magnitude of objects, it tells us about a relation between objects and ourselves; not about an invariant property of those objects. It is only to be expected that changes in our position should bring about changes in this relation. But this is not because, as Hume claimed, the thing we perceive is dependent on us and existent only in our minds, but rather because it is dependent on the position in space we happen to occupy. For Reid, that ambient space exists independently of us and the object has varying angular magnitudes at each point in that ambient space, whether we perceive them or not.

extremities of the object making an angle, of which the object is the subtense, the apparent magnitude is measured by this angle. This apparent magnitude is an object of sight, and not of touch. Bishop BERKELEY calls it *visible magnitude*.

If it is asked, what is the apparent magnitude of the sun's diameter? the answer is, that it is about thirty-one minutes of a degree. But if it is asked, what is the real magnitude of the sun's diameter? the answer must be, so many thousand miles, or so many diameters of the earth. From which it is evident, that real magnitude, and apparent magnitude, are things of a different nature, though the name of magnitude is given to both. The first has three dimensions, the last only two. The first is measured by a line, the last by an angle.

From what has been said, it is evident that the real magnitude of a body must continue unchanged, while the body is unchanged. This we grant. But is it likewise evident, that the apparent magnitude must continue the same while the body is unchanged? So far otherwise, that every man who knows any thing of mathematics can easily demonstrate, that the same individual object, remaining in the same place, and unchanged, must necessarily vary in its apparent magnitude, according as the point from which it is seen is more or less distant; and that its apparent length or breadth will be nearly in a reciprocal proportion to the distance of the spectator. This is as certain as the principles of geometry.

We must likewise attend to this, that though the real magnitude of a body is not originally an object of sight, but of touch, yet we learn by experience to judge of the real magnitude in many cases by sight. We learn by experience to judge of the distance of a body from the eye within certain limits; and from its distance and apparent magnitude taken together, we learn to judge of its real magnitude.

And this kind of judgment, by being repeated every hour, and almost every minute of our lives, becomes, when we are grown up, so ready and so habitual, that it very much resembles the original perceptions of our senses, and may not improperly be called *acquired perception*.

Whether we call it judgment or acquired perception is a verbal difference. But it is evident, that, by means of it, we often discover by one sense things which are properly and naturally the objects of another. Thus I can say without impropriety, I hear a drum, I hear a great bell, or I hear a small bell; though it is certain that the figure or size of the sounding body is not originally an object of hearing. In like manner, we learn by experience how a body of such a real magnitude, and at such a distance appears to the eye: But neither its real magnitude, nor its distance from the eye, are properly objects of sight, any more than the form of a drum, or the size of a bell, are properly objects of hearing.

If these things be considered, it will appear, that Mr HUME'S argument hath no force to support his conclusion, nay, that it leads to a contrary conclusion. The argument is this, the table we see seems to diminish as we remove farther from it; that is, its apparent magnitude is diminished; but the real table suffers no alteration, to wit, in its real magnitude; therefore it is not the real table we see: I admit both the premises in this syllogism, but I deny the conclusion. The syllogism has what the Logicians call two middle terms: Apparent magnitude is the middle term in the first premise; real magnitude in the second. Therefore, according to the rules of logic, the conclusion is not justly drawn from the premises; but, laying aside the rules of logic, let us examine it by the light of common sense.[46]

Let us suppose, for a moment, that it is the real table we see: Must not this real table seem to diminish as we remove farther from it? It is demonstrable that it must. How then can this apparent diminution be an argument that it is not the real table? When that which must happen to the real table, as we remove farther from it, does actually happen to the table we see, it is absurd to conclude from this, that it is not the real table we see. It is evident therefore, that this ingenious author has imposed upon himself by confounding real magnitude with apparent magnitude, and that his argument is a mere sophism.[47]

---

46 It is just as well that Reid laid aside this appeal to the rules of logic, because he did not do justice to Hume's argument. Hume's argument at least entails that the magnitude that we see diminishing as we retreat from the table could not be the real or tangible magnitude of the table. This is a conclusion that Reid endorsed. Reid went on to object that the magnitude that we see diminishing is actually an angular magnitude. But granting that point, a diminution in angular magnitude can have one of two causes: an increase in distance from the object, or a decrease in size of the object. If we accept that distance is not immediately perceived (as Reid did at, for instance, *Inquiry* 6.22, and Hume did in his letter to Blair on Reid's *Inquiry*), then it follows that the only way to immediately perceive a diminution in angular magnitude is by perceiving a diminution in the object that subtends the angle. The object itself must appear to shrink and lose parts, by way of the parts becoming increasingly confused and melding into one another. In Hume's terms, it must come to occupy fewer minimally visible points on the visual field. But if the real object is not diminishing or losing parts, then what we see diminishing must be distinct from the real object.

47 The charge might be retorted. Reid imposed on himself by confounding an idealized mathematical situation in which the existence of an external object in an ambient space is taken for granted with the phenomenological circumstances of visual perception. We cannot simply "suppose for a moment that we see the real table." Starting from the phenomenological facts, one of which (for both Reid and Hume) is that we do not immediately perceive distance, we need to offer a reason for supposing that we directly perceive real objects, retaining an invariant number of parts, set at a distance from us in ambient space—rather than shrinking and expanding mental images.

[Over the remainder of this passage, Reid improved on his objection to Hume by offering a transcendental argument for the existence of an external world—one that rivals Kant's more famous "refutation of idealism."

A transcendental argument proceeds by showing that something that we all do, and need to do, cannot be done without tacitly accepting something else. In this case, what we all do and need to do is, according to Reid, draw inferences about how objects will look in advance of actually seeing them, by referring to their "real" or tangible size, shape, and position, and then calculating how they will appear when viewed from different distances and angles. There is a constant, mathematical relation between the objective facts and the visual appearances that we rely upon in doing this. We assume the positions, figures, and magnitudes that we will see will look like projections or mappings of the real figures onto the inner surface of a sphere (effectively, the inner surface of the back of the eye). But this relation between the objects of touch and vision, on the basis of which our inferences from the former to the latter are made, presupposes the existence of an external ambient space, in which lines of projection can be drawn.

Visual theorists commonly consider only the reverse procedure, where we infer the real or tangible properties from the apparent or visual ones, and since Berkeley it has been supposed that this is an effect of associations learned from past experience rather than any sort of reasoning. But this does not seem to be the case when we go in the other direction and attempt to anticipate of how things will look based on prior knowledge of their real or tangible properties—something that is nonetheless an important part of such enterprises as drawing from perspective, architecture, astronomy, or marshalling troops to present a terrifying appearance to the opponent. Rather than read signs, we are conscious of deliberately and laboriously calculating how things will look in different circumstances. In making those calculations we tacitly assume the existence of an external space, and so of an external world.]

I observed that Mr HUME'S argument not only has no strength to support his conclusion, but that it leads to the contrary conclusion; to wit, that it is the real table we see; for this plain reason, that the table we see has precisely that apparent magnitude which it is demonstrable the real table must have when placed at that distance.

This argument is made much stronger by considering, that the real table may be placed successively at a thousand different distances; and in every distance, in a thousand different positions; and it can be determined demonstratively, by the rules of geometry and perspective, what must be its apparent magnitude, and apparent figure, in each of those distances and positions. Let the table be placed successively in as many of those different distances, and different positions, as you will, or in them all; open your eyes and you shall see a table precisely of that apparent magnitude, and that apparent figure, which the real table must have in that distance, and in that position. Is not this a strong argument that it is the real table you see?

In a word, the appearance of a visible object is infinitely diversified, according to its distance and position. The visible appearances are innumerable, when we confine ourselves to one object, and they are multiplied according to the variety of objects. Those appearances have been matter of speculation to ingenious men, at least since the time of EUCLID. They have accounted for all this variety, on the supposition, that the objects we see are external, and not in the mind itself. The rules they have demonstrated about the various projections of the sphere, about the appearances of the planets in their progressions, stations, and retrogradations, and all the rules of perspective, are built on the supposition that the objects of sight are external. They can each of them be tried in thousands of instances. In many arts and professions innumerable trials are daily made; nor were they ever found to fail in a single instance. Shall we say that a false supposition, invented by the rude vulgar, has been so lucky in solving an infinite number of phænomena of nature? This surely would be a greater prodigy than philosophy ever exhibited: Add to this, that upon the contrary hypothesis, to wit, that the objects of sight are internal, no account can be given of any one of those appearances, nor any physical cause assigned why a visible object should, in any one case, have one apparent figure and magnitude rather than another.

Appendix C: From James Beattie, An Essay on the Nature and Immutability of Truth *(1774)*[1]

[James Beattie was a harsh critic of Hume, whose often challenging objections are peppered with ridicule and sarcasm and punctuated by long rants on the pernicious consequences that accepting Hume's tenets would have on religion and morality. In order to present his work in the best light, I have largely excised merely abusive and rhetorical remarks to focus on philosophically substantive objections to doctrines that Hume continued to maintain in EHU—though something of the flavour of Beattie's full text has occasionally been preserved. The following passage rejects Hume's position on the value of sceptical arguments in a characteristically sarcastic style.]

Essay 1.9: 143-46

The end of all science, and indeed of every useful pursuit, is to make men happier, by improving them in wisdom and virtue. I beg leave to ask, whether the present race of men owe any part of their virtue, wisdom, or happiness, to what metaphysicians have written in proof of the non-existence of matter, and the necessity of human actions? ...

It is ... said, that such controversies make us sensible of the weakness of human reason, and the imperfection of human knowledge; and for the sanguinary[2] principles of bigotry and enthusiasm, substitute the milky ones of scepticism and moderation. And this is conceived to be of prodigious emolument to mankind; because a firm attachment to religion, which a man may call bigotry if he pleases, doth often give rise to a persecuting spirit; whereas a perfect indifference about it, which some men are good-natured enough to call moderation, is a principle of great good-breeding, and gives no sort of disturbance, either in private or public life. This is a plea on which our modern sceptics plume themselves not a little. And who will venture to arraign the virtue or the sagacity of these projectors?[3] To accomplish so great

---

1 *Essays on the Nature and Immutability of Truth, in Opposition to Sophistry and Scepticism,* 5th ed. corrected (London: Edward and Charles Dilly; Edinburgh: William Creech, 1774). Gale document CW3315618340. I have repositioned Beattie's note numbers to reflect modern printing conventions.

2 That is, bloody.

3 That is, of these charlatans.

effects by means so simple; to prevent such dreadful calamities by so innocent an artifice,—does it not display the perfection of benevolence and wisdom? Truly I can hardly imagine such another scheme, except perhaps the following. Suppose a physician of the Sangrado school,[4] out of zeal for the interest of the faculty, and the public good, to prepare a bill to be laid before the parliament, in these words:

> That whereas good health, especially when of long standing, has a tendency to prepare the human frame for acute and inflammatory distempers, which have been known to give extreme pain to the unhappy patient, and sometimes even bring him to the grave; and whereas the said health, by making us brisk, and hearty, and happy, is apt also, on some occasions, to make us disorderly and licentious, to the great detriment of glass windows, lanthorns, and watchmen: Be it therefore enacted, that all the inhabitants of these realms, for the peace of government, and the repose of the subject, be compelled, on pain of death, to bring their bodies down to a consumptive habit;[5] and that henceforth no person presume to walk abroad with a cane, on pain of having his head broke with it, and being set in the stocks for six months; nor to walk at all, except with crutches, to be delivered at the public charge to each person who makes affidavit, that he is no longer able to walk without them, &c.

—He who can eradicate conviction from the human heart, may doubtless prevent all the fatal effects of enthusiasm and bigotry; and if all human bodies were thrown into a consumption, I believe there would be an end of riot, as well as of inflammatory diseases. Whether the inconveniences, or the remedies, be the greater grievance, might perhaps bear a question. Bigotry, enthusiasm, and a persecuting spirit, are very dangerous and destructive; universal scepticism, would, I am sure, be equally so, if it were to infect the generality of mankind.

[Like Reid, Beattie considered Hume's scepticism to be founded in a mistaken theory of ideas, which Beattie attacked in his own way.]

---

4 See [Alain René Le Sage] *The Adventures of Gil Blas of Santillane. A new translation by the author of Roderick Random* [Tobias Smollet] (London: T. Osborne, W. Strahan, J. Rivington, et al., 1764), bk. 2, chs. 3-4, "Gil Blas engages himself in the service of Dr. Sangrado, and becomes a celebrated physician," etc. Gale document CB3328975083.

5 I.e., to acquire the symptoms of tuberculosis.

The whole of this author's [Hume's] system is founded on a false hypothesis taken for granted; and whenever a fact contradictory to that false hypothesis occurs to his observation, he either denies it, or labours hard to explain it away. This, it seems, in his judgment, is experimental reasoning: in mine, it is just the reverse.

He begins his book[6] with affirming, That all the perceptions of the human mind resolve themselves into two classes, impressions and ideas; that the latter are all copied from the former; and that an idea differs from its correspondent impression only in being a weaker perception. Thus, when I sit by the fire, I have an impression of heat, and I can form an idea of heat when I am shivering with cold; in the one case I have a stronger perception of heat, in the other a weaker. Is there any warmth in this idea of heat? There must, according to Mr. HUME's doctrine; only the warmth of the idea is not quite so strong as that of the impression. For this profound author repeats it again and again, that an idea is by its nature weaker and fainter than an impression, but is in every other respect (not only similar, but) the same.[7] Nay, he goes further, and says, that whatever is true of the one must be acknowledged concerning the other;[8] and he is so confident of the truth of this maxim, that he makes it one of the pillars of his philosophy. To those who may be inclined to admit this maxim on his authority, I would propose a few plain questions. Do you feel any, even the least, warmth, in the idea of a bonfire, a burning mountain, or the general conflagration? Do you feel more real cold in Virgil's Sycthian winter, than in Milton's description of the flames of hell? Do you acknowledge that to be true of the idea of eating, which is certainly true of the impression of it, that it alleviates hunger, fills the belly, and contributes to the support of human life? If you answer these questions in the negative, you deny one of the fundamental principles of Mr. HUME's philosophy. We have, it is true, a livelier perception of a friend when we see him, than when we think of him in his absence. But this is not all: every person of a sound mind knows, that in the one case we believe, and are certain, that the object exists, and is present with us; in the other we believe, and are certain, that the object is not present: which, however, Mr. HUME must deny; for he maintains, that an idea differs from an impression only in being weaker, and in no other respect whatsoever.

---

6   Beattie meant the *Treatise*, though the same points are made in EHU 2.
7   Beattie's note: Treatise of Human Nature, vol. 1. p. 131. [*Treatise* 1.3.1.7; similar claims are made at EHU 2.5-7.]
8   Beattie's note: Ibid. p. 41. [*Treatise* 1.1.7.5; this claim is not made in EHU.]

That every idea should be a copy and resemblance of the impression whence it is derived;—that, for example, the idea of red should be a red idea; the idea of a roaring lion a roaring idea; the idea of an ass, a hairy, long-eared, sluggish idea, patient of labour, and much addicted to thistles; that the idea of extension should be extended, and that of solidity solid;—that a thought of the mind should be endued with all, or any, of the qualities of matter,—is, in my judgment, inconceivable and impossible. Yet Mr. HUME takes it for granted; and it is another of his fundamental maxims. Such is the credulity of Scepticism![9]

If every idea be an exact resemblance of its correspondent impression, (or object; for these terms according to this author, amount to the same thing);[10]—if the idea of whiteness be white, of solidity solid, and of extension extended, as the same author allows;[11]—then the idea of a line, the shortest that sense can perceive, must be equal in length to the line itself; for if shorter, it would be imperceptible; and it will not be said, either that an imperceptible idea can be perceived, or that the idea of an imperceptible object can be formed:—consequently the idea of a line a hundred times as long, must be a hundred times as long as the former idea; for if shorter, it would be the idea, not of this, but of some other shorter line. And so it clearly follows, nay it admits of mathematical demonstration, that the idea of an inch is really an inch long; and that of a mile, a mile long.[12] In a word, every idea of any particular extension is equal in length to the extended object.[13] The same reasoning holds good in regard to the other dimensions of

---

9 EHU 12.9-15 offers two arguments for the claims that Beattie charged Hume with taking for granted.

10 Beattie's note: Treatise of Human Nature, vol. 1. p. 1, 2, 362. [The first two references are to the first two pages of the Introduction to the *Treatise*, which do not discuss this topic. The same references occur in the original, 1770 edition. The remaining reference is to Treatise 1.4.2.40. At EHU 12.14, Hume went so far as to say that the vulgar identify perceptions and objects and that philosophers have no justification for affirming the existence of objects distinct from perceptions—but stopped short of declaring the notion of an object distinct from our perceptions to be meaningless.]

11 Beattie's note: Ibid. p. 416, 417. [*Treatise* 1.4.5.15. The closest EHU comes to a similar assertion is note **kk**, though the assertion is implied by the arguments of EHU 12.9-15.]

12 At *Treatise* 1.1.7.12 Hume noted that where comparisons between large numbers are concerned (as in the comparison between an inch and a mile) we seldom form adequate ideas of the objects compared, but instead work with symbols.

13 Beattie neglected to consider that size is not an absolute quality but a relation between objects, determined by juxtaposition. In the case where the size of ideas is in question, the only juxtaposition that is possible is that with other ideas, not that with external objects, and so not with those external objects taken to define standard units of measurement.

breadth and thickness. All ideas, therefore, of solid objects, must be (according to Mr. HUME's philosophy) equal in magnitude and solidity to the objects themselves. Now mark the consequence. I am just now in an apartment containing a thousand cubic feet, being ten feet square, and ten high; the door and windows are shut, as well as my eyes and ears. Mr. HUME will allow, that, in this situation, I may form ideas, not only of the visible appearance, but also of the real tangible magnitude of the whole house, of a first-rate man of war, of St. Paul's cathedral, or even of a much larger object. But the solid magnitude of these ideas is equal to the solid magnitude of the objects from which they are copied: therefore I have now present with me an idea, that is, a solid extended thing, whose dimensions extend to a million of cubic feet at least. The question now is, where is this thing placed? for a place it certainly must have, and a pretty large one too. I should answer, in my mind; for I know not where else the ideas of my mind can be so conveniently deposited. Now my mind is lodged in a body of no extraordinary dimensions, and my body is contained in a room ten feet square and ten feet high.[14] It seems then, that, into this room, I have it in my power at pleasure to introduce a solid object a thousand, or ten thousand, times larger than the room itself. I contemplate it a while, and then, by another volition, send it packing, to make way for another object of equal or superior magnitude.

...

This author's method of investigation is no less extraordinary than his fundamental principles. There are many notions in the human mind, of which it is not easy perhaps to explain the origin. If you can describe in words what were the circumstances in which you received an impression of any particular notion, it is well; Mr. HUME will allow that you may form an idea of it. But if you cannot do this, then says he, there is no such notion in your mind; for all perceptions are either impressions or ideas, and it is not possible for us so much as to conceive any thing specifically different from ideas and impressions:[15] now all ideas are copied from impressions: therefore you can have no idea nor conception of any thing of which you have not received an impression.—All mankind have a notion of power or energy. No says Mr. HUME; an impression of power or energy was never received by any man, and therefore an idea of it can never be formed in the human mind. If you insist on your experience and consciousness of power, it

---

14 At *Treatise* 1.4.6.2-3 Hume claimed that we have no perception of the thing that contains our perceptions. Accordingly, we have no means of measuring its size, either relative to perceptions or relative to physical objects.

15 Beattie's note: Treatise of Human Nature, vol. 1. p. 123. [*Treatise* 1.2.6.8. An analogous claim was inserted at the close of EHU 12.16 in 1777.]

is all a mistake: his hypothesis admits not the idea of power,[16] and therefore there is no such idea.[17] ... This, it seems, is experimental reasoning!

[In the following passages, Beattie objected to Hume's position on freedom and determinism in EHU 8 (and its foundations in the theory of power and causality of EHU 7), and Hume's concluding critique of the cosmological argument in EHU 11.]

Essay 2.2.3: 293 [misnumbered 393]-98, 300, 303-09, 311, 331, 354-55, 360-61

The second instance to which I purpose to apply the principles of this discourse, by showing the danger of carrying any investigation beyond the dictates of common sense, is no other than the celebrated question concerning liberty and necessity ...[18]

1. That certain intentions and actions are in themselves, and previous to all consideration of their consequences, good, laudable, and meritorious; and that other actions and intentions are bad, blameable, and worthy of punishment,—has been felt and acknowledged by all reasonable creatures in all ages and nations ...

2. That we cannot do some things, but have it in our power to do others, is what no man in his senses will hesitate to affirm.
...

But this idea has had the misfortune to come under the examination of Mr. HUME, who, according to custom, has found means so to darken and disfigure it, that, till we have cleared it of his misrepresentations, we cannot proceed any further in the present subject.[19] And

---

16 Beattie neglected to notice that at EHU 7.i, Hume did not just draw a conclusion from an hypothesis, but gave a number of specific reasons for concluding that even though we may think we have an idea of a quality in causes in virtue of which they are enabled to bring their effects about, we really do not.

17 Beattie's note: Ibid. p. 282. [*Treatise* 1.3.14.11. EHU 7.26 notes that the conclusion of EHU 7.i "*seems* to be, that we have no idea of connexion or power at all," but Hume went on to dismiss this inference in favour of a different analysis of what the idea of power is really an idea of. However, Beattie would not have been satisfied with the substitute. The power he was referring to is a quality in causes in virtue of which they are enabled to bring about their effects.]

18 The first instance is the question of whether there is an external world. Beattie's target on that topic was Berkeley rather than Hume.

19 Beattie's distinction between what lies within and without our power is one that Hume provided for in his own terms at EHU 8.23.

we are the more inclined to digress on this occasion, that he has made his theory of power the ground of some atheistical inferences, which we should not scruple at any time to step out of our way to overturn ...

All ideas, according to Mr. HUME's fundamental hypothesis, are copied from and represent impressions: But we have never any impression that contains any power or efficacy: We never, therefore, have any idea of power.[20] In proof of the minor proposition of this syllogism, he remarks, That

> when we think we perceive our mind acting on matter, or one piece of matter acting upon another, we do in fact perceive only two objects or events contiguous and successive, the second of which is always found in experience to follow the first; but that we never perceive, either by external sense, or by consciousness, that power, energy, or efficacy, which connects the one event with the other. By observing that the two events do always accompany each other, the imagination acquires a habit of going readily from the first to the second, and from the second to the first; and hence we are led to conceive a kind of necessary connexion between them. But in fact there is neither necessity nor power in the objects we consider, but only in the mind that considers them; and even in the mind, this power or[21] necessity is nothing but a determination of the fancy, acquired by habit, to pass from the idea of an object to that of its usual attendant.[22]

—So that what we call the efficacy of a cause to produce an effect, is neither in the cause nor in the effect, but only in the imagination, which has contracted a habit of passing from the object called the cause, to the object called the effect, and thus associating them together. Has the fire a power to melt lead? No; but the fancy is determined by habit to pass from the idea of fire to that of melted lead, on account of our having always perceived them contiguous and succes-

---

20 Beattie's note: Treatise of Human Nature, vol. 1. p. 282. [*Treatise* 1.3.14.11. EHU makes no such claim, though it does argue that such an idea of power as we have is not an idea of a quality in causes that enables them to bring about their effects.]

21 Reading, with the 1770 edition, *or* for *of*.

22 Beattie's note: Treatise of Human Nature, vol. 1. p. 272-300. [The pages cited range from *Treatise* 1.3.14.1-11. Beattie's use of quotation marks, represented here in block, is meant only to signify that he was not speaking in his own voice but representing Hume's position. The passage is a fair representation of what Hume said over the entire course of EHU 7.]

sive—and this is the whole matter. Have I a power to move my arm? No; the volition that precedes the motion of my arm has no connexion with that motion; but the motion having been always observed to follow the volition, comes to be associated with it in the fancy; and what we call the power, or necessary connexion, has nothing to do, either with the volition or with the motion, but is merely a determination of my fancy, ... to associate the idea or impression of my volition with the impression or idea of the motion of my arm.

   ...

It is one of Mr. HUME'S maxims, That we can never have reason to believe that any object, or quality of an object, exists, of which we cannot form an idea.[23] But, according to this astonishing theory of power, and causation, we can form *no idea* of power, nor of any being endowed with any power, MUCH LESS of one endowed with infinite power.[24] The inference is—what I do not chuse to commit to paper. But our elegant author is not so superstitious. He often puts his readers in mind, that this inference, or something very like it, is deducible from his doctrine:[25]—for which, no doubt, every friend to truth, virtue, and human nature, is infinitely obliged to him!

   ...

If a man can reconcile himself to atheism, which is the greatest of all absurdities, I fear, I shall hardly put him out of conceit with his doctrine, when I show him that other less enormous absurdities are implied in it. We may make the trial however. Gentlemen are sometimes pleased to entertain unaccountable prejudices against their Maker; who yet, in other matters, where neither fashion nor hypothesis interfere, condescend to acknowledge, that the good old distinction between truth and falsehood is not altogether without foundation.

On the supposition that we have no idea of power or energy, and that the preceding theory of causation is just, our author gives the following definition of a cause; which seems to be fairly enough deduced from his theory, and which he says is the best that he can give. "A cause is an object precedent and contiguous to another, and so united with it, that the idea of the one determines the mind to form the idea of the other, and the impression of the one to form a more lively idea

---

23 Beattie's note: Treatise of Human Nature, vol. 1. p. 302. [*Treatise* 1.3.14.36. As noted earlier, an analogous claim was inserted at the close of EHU 12.16, though only in 1777.]

24 Beattie's note: Some readers will smile, perhaps, at the phraseology of this sentence; but I quote the author's own words. See Treatise of Human Nature, vol. 1. p. 432. [*Treatise* 1.4.5.31. EHU 7.25 makes a similar claim.]

25 Beattie's note: Ibid. p. 284, 291, 306, 431. &c. [*Treatise* 1.3.14.14, 1.3.14.23, 1.3.15.10, 1.4.5.31. EHU 7.25 makes a similar claim.]

of the other."[26] There are now in my view two contiguous houses, one of which was built last summer, and the other two years ago. By seeing them constantly together for several months, I find, that the idea of the one determines my mind to form the idea of the other, and the impression of the one to form a more lively idea of the other. So that, according to our author's definition, the one house is the cause, and the other the effect![27]—Again, day and night have always been contiguous and successive; the imagination naturally runs from the idea or impression of the one to the idea of the other: consequently, according to the same profound theory and definition, either day is the cause of night, or night the cause of day, just as we consider the one or the other to have been originally prior in time ...

Causation[28] implies more than priority and contiguity of the cause to the effect. This relation cannot be conceived at all, without a supposition of power or energy in the cause ...

When, therefore, Mr. HUME says, that the efficacy or energy of causes is not placed in the causes themselves, he says neither less nor more than this, that what is essential to a cause is not in a cause; or, in other words,—that a cause is not a cause.

... I maintain, that though it could be shown, that all simple ideas are derived from impressions, or intimations of sense, it is true, notwithstanding, that all men have an idea of power. They get it by experience, that is, by intimations of sense, both external and internal. Their mind acting upon their body gives them this notion or idea; their body acting on other bodies, and acted on by other bodies, gives them the same idea; which is also suggested by all the effects and changes they see produced in the universe ...[29]

---

26 Beattie's note: Treatise of Human Nature, vol. 1. p. 298. [*Treatise* 1.3.14.35. A similar claim occurs at EHU 7.29.]

27 Beattie is right that inferences to the existence of unobserved objects are often made on the basis of the past experience of a constant conjunction in space, as well as of a constant succession in time. However, this sort of "geographical reasoning" is consistent with Hume's general account of the role played by custom in our inferences to the unobserved, though he never recognized it, despite occasionally employing it (e.g., the inference from one human body part to another described at Ax 4).

28 Beattie's note: *Causation*, in Mr. HUME's style, denotes *the relation of cause and effect*. In English authors, the word rarely occurs, and never, I think, in this sense. It properly signifies, *The act or power of causing*.

29 Claims like these would have motivated Hume's complaint that his critics had neglected to consider what he said in EHU—in this case over the course of EHU 7.i.

3. By attending to my own internal feelings, and to the evidence given by other men of theirs, I am sensible, that I deserve reward or punishment for those actions only which are in my own power.[30] ...

This is the doctrine of common sense; and this doctrine has in all ages been supported by some of the most powerful principles of our nature; by principles which, in the common affairs of life, no man dares suppose to be equivocal or fallacious ...

But some philosophers, not satisfied with this view of it, are for bringing the sentiment of moral liberty to the test of reason.

...

Mr. HUME, in an essay on this subject, maintains, that the appearances in the moral and material world are equally uniform, and equally necessary; nay, and acknowledged to be so, both by philosophers and by the vulgar.[31] In proof of this, he prudently confines himself to general topics, on which he declaims with some plausibility. Had he descended to particular instances ... the fallacy of his reasoning would have appeared at once. Human nature has been nearly the same in all ages. True. For all men possess nearly the same faculties, which are employed about nearly the same objects, and destined to operate within the same narrow sphere. And if a man have power to chuse one of two things, to act or not to act, he has all the liberty we contend for. How is it possible, then, that human nature, taken in the gross, should not be found nearly the same in all ages! But if we come to particulars, we shall not perhaps find two human minds exactly alike. In two of the most congenial characters on earth, the same causes will not produce the same effects; nay, the same causes will not always produce the same effects even in the same character.[32]

...

The asserters of human liberty have always maintained, that to believe all actions and intentions necessary, is the same thing as to believe, that man is not an accountable being, or, in other words, no moral agent. And indeed this notion is natural to every person who has the courage to trust his own experience, without seeking to puzzle plain matter of fact with verbal distinctions and metaphysical refinement. But, it is said, the sense of moral beauty and turpitude still remains with us, even after we are convinced, that all actions and intentions are necessary; that this sense maketh us moral agents; and, therefore, that our moral agency is perfectly consistent with our necessary agency.[33]

---

30 By substituting "consequent upon my will" for "in my own power" Hume accommodated this principle.

31 EHU 8.20.

32 EHU 8.12-15 does "descend" to consider these "particulars."

33 EHU 8.35.

But this is nothing to the purpose; it is putting us off with mere words. For what is moral agency, and what is implied in it? This at least must be implied in it, that we ought to do some things, and not to do others. But if every intention and action of my life is fixed by eternal laws, which I can neither elude nor alter, it is absurd to say to me, You ought to be honest to-morrow, as to say, You ought to stop the motion of the planets to-morrow. Unless some events depend upon my determination, *ought*, and *ought not*, have no meaning when applied to me. Moral agency further implies, that we are accountable for our conduct; and that if we do what we ought not to do, we deserve blame and punishment. My conscience tells me, that I am accountable for those actions only that are in my own power; and neither blames nor approves, in myself or in others, that conduct which is the effect, not of choice, but of necessity. Convince me, that all my actions are equally necessary, and you silence my conscience for ever, or at least prove it to be a fallacious and impertinent monitor: you will then convince me, that all circumspection is unnecessary, and all remorse absurd.

...

It would lead us too far from our present purpose, to enter upon a logical examination of the argument for necessity. Our design is only to explain, by what marks one may distinguish the principles of common sense, that is, intuitive or self-evident notions, from those deceitful and inveterate opinions that have sometimes assumed the same appearance. If I have satisfied the reader, that the free agency of men is a self-evident fact, I have also satisfied him, that all reasoning on the side of necessity, though accounted unanswerable, is, in its very nature, and previously to all confutation, absurd and irrational, and contrary to the practice and principles of all true philosophers.

[In a footnote placed well after his principal attack on Hume's treatment of the cosmological argument at the close of EHU 11, Beattie complained that Hume had attempted to conceal his atheistic intentions. The note is placed after the following sentence: "This obscurity is sometimes ... affected; as when a philosopher, from prudential considerations, thinks fit to disguise any occasional attack on the religion or laws of his country, by some artful equivocation, in the form of allegory, dialogue, or fable."]

Essay 3.3: 470-71n

Mr. HUME is not unacquainted with this piece of policy. His apology for Atheism he delivers by the mouth of a *friend*, in the way of conference, prefaced with a declaration, that though he cannot by any means approve many of the sentiments of that friend, yet he thinks they bear some relation to the chain of reasoning carried on in his Inquiry concerning Human Nature. He had something, it seems, to say against his Maker, which he modestly acknowledges to be curious, and worthy of attention, and which he thought, no doubt, to be mighty smart and clever. To call it what it really is, An attempt to vindicate Atheism, or what he probably thought it, A vindication of Atheism, seemed dangerous, and might disgust many of his well-meaning readers. He calls it, therefore, *An Essay on a Particular Providence and a Future State*, and puts his capital arguments in the mouth of another person: thus providing, by the same generous, candid, and manly expedient, a snare for the unwary reader, and an evasion for himself.

[Beattie's attack on the conclusion of EHU 11 takes off from a consideration of the principle that every object must have some cause. EHU does not discuss this principle, but in the *Treatise* (1.3.3) Hume had maintained that our belief in it is not based on intuition or demonstration, but rather on experience. Beattie instead maintained that the principle is intuitively obvious,[34] and his critique picks up from there.]

Essay 1.2.5: 112-15, 118-20

The axiom now before us is the foundation of the most important argument that ever employed human reason; I mean that which, from the works that are created, evinces the eternal power and godhead of the Creator. That argument, as far as it resolves itself into this axiom, is properly a demonstration, being a clear deduction from a self-evident principle; and therefore no man can pretend to understand it without feeling it to be conclusive ...

That many of the objects in nature have had a beginning, is obvious to our own senses and memory, or confirmed by unquestionable testimony: these, therefore, according to the axiom we are here considering, must be believed to have proceeded from a cause adequate at least to the effects produced. That the whole sensible universe hath to us the appearance of an effect, of something which once was not, and

---

34 Beattie's critique of Hume's contrary position rests principally on an appeal to the apparent beliefs of children and an attack on the premises of Hume's argument for denying that the principle might be intuitive. It is omitted here because it addresses arguments Hume only clearly endorsed in the *Treatise*. In addition to sensation, memory, causal inference, intuition of relations between ideas, and demonstration by appeal to chains of intuitions, EHU 12.7 recognizes the existence of at least some beliefs based on natural instincts or prepossessions.

which exists not by any necessity of nature, but by the arbitrary appointment of some powerful and intelligent cause different from and independent on it;—that the universe, I say, has this appearance, cannot be denied: and that it is what it appears to be, an effect; that it had a beginning, and was not from eternity, is proved by every sort of evidence the subject will admit. And if so, we offer violence to our understanding, when we attempt to believe that the whole universe does not proceed from some cause; and we argue unphilosophically and irrationally, when we endeavour to disprove this natural and universal suggestion of the human mind.

It is true, the universe is, as one may say, a work *sui generis*, altogether singular, and such as we cannot properly compare to other works; because indeed all works are comprehended in it. But that natural dictate of the mind by which we believe the universe to have proceeded from a cause, arises from our considering it as an effect; a circumstance in which it is perfectly similar to all works whatsoever. The singularity of the effect rather confirms (if that be possible) than weakens our belief of the necessity of a cause; at least it makes us more attentive to the cause, and interests us more deeply in it. What is the universe, but a vast system of works or effects, some of them great, and others small; some more and some less considerable? If each of these works, the least as well as the greatest, require a cause for its production; is it not in the highest degree absurd and unnatural to say, that the whole is not the effect of a cause?—Each link of a great chain must be supported by something, but the whole chain may be supported by nothing:—Nothing less than an ounce can be a counterpoise to an ounce, nothing less than a pound to a pound; but the wing of a gnat, or nothing at all, may be a sufficient counterpoise to ten hundred thousand pounds:—are not these assertions too absurd to deserve an answer?[35]

The reader, if he has the misfortune to be acquainted with Mr. HUME'S *Essay on a particular providence and a future state*, will see, that these remarks are intended as an answer to a very strange argument there advanced against the belief of a Deity. "The universe," we are told, "is an object quite singular and unparalleled; no other object that has fallen under our observation bears any similarity to it; neither it nor its cause can be comprehended under any known species; and therefore concerning the cause of the universe we can form no rational conclusion at all."[36]—I appeal to any man of sound judgment, whether that suggestion of his understanding, which prompts him to infer a cause from an effect, has any dependence upon a prior opera-

35 Hume was to consider these objections in DNR 9.
36 Paraphrasing EHU 11.30.

tion of his mind, by which the effect in question is referred to its genus and species.

...

If Mr. HUME's argument be found to turn to so little account, from the simple consideration of the universe, as existing, and as having had a beginning, it will appear (if possible) still more irrational, when we take a view of the universe, and its parts, as of works curiously adapted to certain ends. Their existence displays the necessity of a powerful cause; their frame proves the cause to be intelligent, good, and wise. The meanest of the works of nature, (if any of Nature's works may be called mean),—the arrangement necessary for the production of the smallest plant, requires in the cause a degree of power, intelligence, and wisdom, which infinitely transcends the sublimest exertions of human ability. What then shall we say of the cause that produces an animal, a rational soul, a world, a system of worlds, an universe? Shall we say, that infinite power and wisdom are not necessary attributes of that universal cause, though they be necessary attributes of the cause that produces a plant? ...

For an answer to the other cavils thrown out by Mr. HUME, in this flimsy essay, against the divine attributes, the reader is referred to the first part of Butler's Analogy of Natural and Revealed Religion.[37] It needs not be matter of any surprise, that we name, on this occasion, a book which was published before Mr. HUME's essay was written. With infidel writers it has long been the fashion, (less frequently indeed with this author than with many others), to deliver as their own, and as entirely new, objections against religion, which have been repeatedly and unanswerably confuted. This piece of craft gives no offence to their disciples; these gentlemen, if they read at all, generally chusing to confine their inquiries to one side of the controversy: to themselves it is a considerable saving in the articles of time and invention.

---

37 See Appendix A, p. 212 note 15.

Appendix D: From Immanuel Kant, Prolegomena to Any Future Metaphysics (1784) and The Critique of Pure Reason (1781/1787)

[Like Thomas Reid, Immanuel Kant[1] was profoundly influenced by Hume's work. In addition to containing an important autobiographical remark, the following selection from Kant's *Prolegomena zu einer jeden künftigen Metaphysik*,[2] contains a notorious comment on Reid, Oswald, Beattie, and Priestly, as well as a summation of what Kant took to be Hume's greatest insight. Though Kant's comments on Hume's philosophy were published after Hume's death, their importance in the history of philosophy merits their inclusion here.]

Prolegomena: 257-60

HUME proceeded principally from a single but important metaphysical concept, namely that of the CONNECTION OF CAUSE AND EFFECT (and consequently also its derivative concepts of force and action, etc.). He demanded that reason, which claims to have generated this concept in her womb, explain to him with what right she thinks that something could be so made that, when it is given, something else must necessarily be given—for that is what is stated by the concept of cause. He proved incontestably that it is quite impossible for reason to

---

1 In his *Critique of Pure Reason* and *Prolegomena to any Future Metaphysics* Kant (1724-1804) sought, like Reid, to find a way around the scepticism that he took to be a consequence of Hume's empiricist philosophy. But rather than reject the "way of ideas" and seek to provide for direct perception of an external world by appeal to a theory of principles of common sense, as Reid had done, Kant sought to isolate quasi-logical ("transcendental" in his terminology) principles governing the possibility of the experience of beings like us and sought on this basis to provide for knowledge of things "as they appear to us" rather than "as they are in themselves."

2 Riga: Johann Friedrich Hartknoch, 1783. The translation that follows is my own, and, as Hume did not live to see the original edition, I have based it on the text as published in Karl Vorländer's edition, corrected by Norbert Hinske (Hamburg: Meiner, 1976). References are to the standard pagination, that of volume 4 of the Prussian Academy edition of Kant's *Gesammelte Schriften* (Berlin: Georg Reimer, 1910).

think such a connection by means of concepts and a priori,[3] for it involves necessity. And it is simply impossible to see why, because something is, something else must also necessarily be the case, or how the concept of such a connection could be introduced a priori. From this he inferred that reason was completely mistaken about this concept, which she mistakenly took for her own child, though it was nothing other than a bastard of the imagination who, impregnated by experience, had brought certain representations together under the law of association and presented the resulting subjective necessity (that is, custom) as if it were an objective necessity based on insight. From this he inferred that reason has absolutely no capacity to think such connections, even in only general terms,[4] because its concepts would in that case be mere fictions, and all its cognitions, purportedly arising a priori, would be nothing but falsely labelled general experiences—which is as much as to say as: there just is no metaphysics nor could there be any.[5]

As hasty and mistaken as his inference was, it was at least grounded on study. And this study more than merited that the best minds of his time would have united in the enterprise of trying to come up with a more satisfactory solution of the problem, in the sense in which he had presented it. This would have completely reformed the science of metaphysics.

But, unfortunately for metaphysics, Hume was not understood by anyone. One cannot, without feeling a certain pain, see how completely and totally his opponents: REID, OSWALD, BEATTIE and lastly also PRIESTLY, missed the point of his work. By always taking for granted what he meant to call into doubt while emphatically, and often with great indignation demonstrating what he had never thought to question, they so completely mistook his hint for improvement, as to leave everything in its previous state, as if nothing had happened. The question was not whether the concept of cause is correct, useful, or unavoidable in all of our knowledge of nature, for HUME had not doubted that. The question was whether it is thought a priori through reason and in this way has an intrinsic truth independent of all experience and a considerably broader applicability—one that is not

---

3 By "a priori" Kant meant independently of experience. Hume used the term in the subtly, but importantly different sense of being prior to experience.

4 As a passage to be cited later shows, Kant was willing to grant that we require experience to discover the connection between particular causes and particular effects. But he wanted to maintain that we can be assured, in advance of experience, of the general rule that every event must be necessitated by *some* cause or other, even if we can't tell precisely what it is. See pp. 283-84.

5 Kant inserted a note at this point which is omitted here.

limited just to objects of experience. That was what HUME wanted to have explained.

...

I freely admit that it was the recollection of DAVID HUME that, many years ago, first broke my dogmatic slumber, and gave a quite different direction to my investigations in the field of speculative philosophy. I was quite far from giving an ear to him in respect of his conclusions, which only arose because he did not conceive the whole of his problem, but fell only on a part of it which, without taking the whole into account, can provide no illumination.

[Kant expanded on where Hume went wrong in the following passages from the *Prolegomena* and the *Kritik der reinen Vernunft*.[6]]

Prolegomena: 272-73

But I cannot refrain from remarking on the harm that the neglect of this apparently simple and insignificant observation [that mathematical knowledge is not based on the analysis of concepts] has done to philosophy. HUME ... heedlessly separated a large and indeed the most valuable province, namely pure mathematics, from the realm of pure a priori knowledge in the conviction that its nature and so to speak its principles of government are quite different, resting on just the principle of non-contradiction. Though he did not divide propositions as formally or universally as I have here, or do so in the same terms, it was as if he had said that pure mathematics only contains ANALYTIC propositions, but metaphysics synthetic a priori ones.[7] This was a major mistake, and this mistake had decidedly adverse consequences for his entire outlook. Had he not committed it, he would have broadened his question about the origin of our synthetic judgments well beyond his metaphysical concept of causality, and extended it to the a priori possibility of mathematics, for he would have had to take this to be synthetic as well. But then he could not have grounded his metaphysical principles on bare experience, because he would have likewise had to subsume the axioms of pure mathematics under experience, which he was far too discerning to do.

---

6 The translation that follows is my own, based on the text as published in Jens Timmerman's edition (Hamburg: Meiner, 1998). References are to the standard pagination, that of the first and second original editions (Riga: Johann Friedrich Hartknoch, 1781 and 1787), cited as "A" and "B" respectively.

7 This is an allusion to Hume's distinction between relations of ideas and matters of fact in EHU 4.1-2, and his declaration there that geometry, algebra, and arithmetic affirm relations of ideas.

David Hume came closest of all philosophers to taking on this task [of explaining how synthetic a priori judgments are possible]. But he was far from thinking of it definitely enough and in its most general form. Focusing just on the synthetic principle of the connection of an effect with its cause (Principium causalitatis), he believed he had shown that such a principle is completely impossible a priori. And according to his conclusions everything that we call metaphysics became a mere delusion of taking what is in fact obtained merely from experience and has acquired the appearance of necessity through custom to instead arise from purported rational insight. But he would have never fallen into this opinion, which destroys all pure philosophy, if he had had our problem before his eyes in all its universality. For in that case he would have seen that, according to his arguments, there could also be no pure mathematics, since this certainly contains synthetic a priori principles. And his sound understanding would have prevented him from such an assertion.

[Kant was wrong that Hume treated mathematics as containing only principles that are "analytic" in the sense of being based on the principle of non-contradiction, though he can be forgiven for making this mistake because Hume's views were only made explicit in *Treatise* 1.3.1 and 1.2.4. Had he reviewed those passages, Kant would have learned that, for Hume, the propositions of geometry, arithmetic, and algebra are known by comparing ideas and "intuiting" the presence or absence of relations between them. While these relations depend just on the ideas compared and so are "necessary" in the sense that they cannot change without a change in the ideas, they are not based simply on an analysis of what is contained in the ideas being compared and an appeal to the principle of non-contradiction. I can simply intuit that orange stands in a greater relation of resemblance to red than it does to green, a fact that it would be very hard to discover from an analysis of what is contained in the concepts of orange, red, and green, or an attempt to show that there is a contradiction in asserting that orange is not more like red than green. I can also simply intuit that one line is longer than another, in advance of measurement and simply on the basis of the appearance of these lines. Indeed, for Hume this is so far the case that relations of exact equality, depending on a precise numeration or juxtaposition of parts, are indiscernible. We can only intuit notable differences in magnitude, and when we do so it is on the basis of the general appearance of the objects. The same holds for the straightness of lines, which for Hume is something that is indefinable (so not subject to further analysis) and that cannot be divorced from the appearance. And, as a consequence, the same holds for geometry as a whole, which for Hume has a far "fuzzier" metric than Kant countenanced. Had Hume's lamentable chance meeting with Stanhope not taken place,[8] his drafted essay on considerations "previous" to geometry and mathematics would have made it into *Four Dissertations* (which was translated into German in 1759), where it could have given Kant a more serious awakening than the one he got from Hume's views on causality.

This having been said, a more general version of Kant's criticism is that Hume erred in focusing just on causality and not considering other principles, at least some of which (according to Kant) ought to be recognized as resting neither on intuition of relations of ideas nor on experience of matters of fact.]

Kritik: A 767/B 795

The sceptical errors of this otherwise exceptionally astute man [Hume] sprang principally from a shortcoming that he shared in common with all dogmatists, namely, that he did not systematically review all the forms of a priori synthesis of the understanding. Had he done so he would have found ... for example, that THE PRINCIPLE OF PERMANENCE is one that, just like that of causality, anticipates experience.

[According to Kant, had Hume grasped his problem in its widest extent he would have seen that there are necessary connections in other synthetic judgments than just those involving causes and effects. There are necessary connections in space and time, having to do with limitations that the topology and the metric of space and time impose on the way objects can be disposed, putting us in a position to affirm such things as that no two straight lines can enclose a figure. There are also necessary connections involved with the persistence of substances, putting us in a position to affirm that for any given object there is exactly one object that is its later state and exactly one object that is its earlier state at any given earlier or later time, ruling out emergence and destruction *ex nihilo*, and splitting or joining over time.[9] Had Hume noticed these further instances, he would (so Kant supposed) have questioned whether the connections are only apparently necessary and would have looked for some other solution to the

---

8 This incident is discussed in the Introduction to this volume, p. 18 note 14.

9 Kant's many attempts to come up with additional examples were not very effective, notwithstanding his attempt to construct an elaborate "architectonic" or scheme of the structure of the understanding that created places for such examples.

general problem of synthetic a priori judgments than his preferred appeal to the influence of custom on the imagination.[10] Kant's own solution, alluded to in the passage above, was to claim that there are certain conditions that have to be satisfied in order for beings like us to be able to experience any sort of object whatsoever. Importantly, these conditions are not merely logical, following from the law of non-contradiction, but have to do with contingent, but very fundamental features of our make-up (such as, for instance, that we can only experience the manner in which objects are disposed in time successively). Not every thinking being would necessarily have to share these features (e.g., God would not), and conceivably we ourselves could change so radically that we would cease to share them. The *Kritik der reinen Vernunft* was not, however, written for such beings or with an eye to such eventualities. Setting them aside, Kant maintained that meditation on the conditions of the possibility of experience of beings like us could bring us to see why any object of our experience would necessarily have to have certain features in addition to those that can be intuited or demonstrated, and independently of those that are discovered by experience.

Turning to Hume's paradigm case of the connection between cause and effect, Kant charged that while Hume was right that we cannot identify causes or effects in advance of experience of a constant conjunction, a reflection on the conditions of the possibility of experience could lead us to be assured, in advance of all experience, that every event must have some cause or other—that it is not simply a matter of fact that nothing happens without a cause, but something that necessarily has to be the case because our experience would become unintelligible to us unless we make that presupposition.[11]]

Kritik: A 764-67/B 792-95

Hume probably had the idea, though he never fully developed it, that in judgments of a certain sort we go beyond our concept of an object.

---

10 In addition to offering an account of mathematical knowledge in *Treatise* 1.2.4, Hume had attempted to explain our identity attributions in *Treatise* 1.4.2, taking them to be effects of the imagination, much like causal relations. Kant did not read English and the *Treatise* was not translated into German until 1790.

11 That conditions of the possibility of our experience should also be taken by us to be conditions of the possibility of objects is something Kant accounted for by stipulating that the only objects that we can ever talk about are those that can appear to us. Other things (or things as they are in themselves and independently of how they appear to us) are in no way subject to the conditions that make our experience of things possible.

I have called these sorts of judgments SYNTHETIC. It requires no reflection to say how I can go beyond a previously given concept by means of experience. Experience is itself a kind of synthesis of perceptions that augments the concept given through a perception with others given along with it. But we also think that we can go beyond our concepts and expand our knowledge a priori. We try to do this either by means of pure understanding, with regard to that which can be at least AN OBJECT OF EXPERIENCE, or even by means of pure reason, with regard to certain properties of things, or even the existence of certain things which could never be given in experience. Our sceptic never distinguished these two kinds of judgment, though he should have,[12] and consequently took these expansions of concepts beyond themselves, and so to speak, this act of spontaneous generation on the part of an understanding (likewise a reason) that has not been impregnated by experience to be impossible. Consequently, he took all the purportedly a priori principles of understanding (and reason) to be merely imaginary and found that they are nothing but custom arising out of experience and its laws. This meant taking them to be merely empirical, that is, intrinsically contingent rules, to which we attribute a pretended universality and necessity. In maintaining this uncommon assertion he appealed to the universally recognized principle of the relation of cause and effect. Since no faculty of the understanding can lead us from the concept of one thing to the necessary and universal existence of something else, he thought he could infer that, apart from experience, we have nothing that can augment our concept and that could justify us in making judgments that extend themselves a priori. Based on the concepts that we have in advance, no understanding could judge that the sunlight that shines on wax should also melt it, while at the same time it hardens clay, much less could it infer these things in accord with a rule. Only experience could teach us such a law. In opposition to this, it was seen in the Transcendental Logic[13] that, though we can never go IMMEDIATELY beyond the content of a concept that has been given to us, we can do this completely a priori with reference to a third thing, namely POSSIBLE experience, and thus really can know, a priori, the law of its connection with other things. If previously firm wax melts, I can know a priori that something (for instance, the warmth of the Sun) must have preceded it, upon which it follows in accord with an abiding law, even though, a priori and

---

12 In Kant's opinion the former kind of judgment, which is based on considering what any object would have to be like in order to be an object of a possible experience, is legitimate, whereas the latter, which seeks to extend our knowledge beyond the sphere of possible experience, is not.
13 This is a reference to an earlier part of the *Kritik*.

without the benefit of instruction from experience, I could neither know the SPECIFIC cause by considering just the effect, nor the SPECIFIC effect by considering just the cause. He [Hume] drew a false inference from the contingency of our determination IN ACCORD WITH THE LAW to the contingency of THE LAW itself, and confused the act of going beyond the concept of a thing by appeal to possible experience (which occurs a priori and establishes the objective reality of the concept) with the synthesis of the objects of actual experience, which is admittedly always empirical. As a consequence he converted a principle of affinity, which has its place in the understanding and expresses necessary connection, into a rule of association that is only to be found in reproductive imagination and can only present contingent, not objective connections.

[Kant's allusion to an earlier part of the *Kritik* that actually explains how the causal principle is founded in the possibility of experience was to A 188-211/B 232-56, entitled the "Second Analogy." Over the course of these pages Kant appears to have given multiple, successive versions of the same short argument. The excerpt that follows reconstitutes one of those arguments, that of A 189-94/B 234-39, informed by some prior passages.]

Kritik: B 219

Perceptions are only haphazardly presented together in experience, so that the perception itself neither reveals nor can reveal any necessity in their connection.... But insofar as experience is a knowledge of objects by means of perception, the existence relations holding between the many things presented in perception have to be represented as they objectively are in time, and not just as they happen to be set together in time ... Consequently, the determination of the existence of objects in time can only take place by means of ... concepts that produce an a priori connection.

[This poses a question: Why shouldn't we simply suppose that the order in which perceptions are originally presented in experience is the correct, objective order of those perceptions—that the reason we see one thing first is because it occurred first, it being impossible to see earlier what only comes to exist later? In that case no special act of determining how objects are located in time would be required, particularly not one involving concepts that produce a connection a priori or independently of experience. The following passages attempt to give an answer.]

Kritik: B 232-33

The previous principle[14] has established that all appearances in the temporal sequence are only ALTERATIONS, that is, a successive being and not being of the determinations of a persisting substance.... ALL CHANGE (SUCCESSION) OF APPEARANCES IS ONLY ALTERATION ...

Kritik: B 233-34

I perceive that appearances follow one another, that is, that at one time a thing is in a state that is contrary to a prior state it was in. I am therefore in effect connecting two perceptions in time. But connection is not the work of the bare senses and intuition but here the work of a synthetic capacity of the imagination, which determines inner sense with respect to temporal relations. However, these two states can be thought to be connected in two different ways, so that either the one or the other precedes in time. For, time cannot be perceived in itself, and what precedes or follows in the object cannot be determined empirically, through reference to it.[15] I am therefore only conscious that my imagination places one earlier and the other later, not that the one state or the other is precedent in the object. In other words, mere perception leaves the OBJECTIVE RELATION of the successive appearances undetermined.

[Kant's claims that temporal connection "is not the work of the bare senses or intuition," and that "I am only conscious that my imagination places one earlier and the other later," might be taken to involve a tacit commitment to the notion that we are only conscious of what exists at the present moment. We cannot come to think of two things as successive in time by first perceiving the one and then perceiving the other, but only by thinking of both at one and the same moment (requiring replication of the earlier one in imagination) and then

---

14 This is a reference to an earlier argument, the "First Analogy," which purports to establish that all change must be conceived as an alteration in something that persists throughout the change.

15 The assertion that time cannot be perceived in itself is either irrelevant (since what is at issue is not the perception of an empty time, but of temporal relations between things) or else it sits uneasily with an earlier claim Kant made about time being the form of sensory intuition. However, a point might still be made if we were to jettison this problematic assertion and focus on another idea floated in this passage, that having perceptions successively is one thing and perceiving those perceptions to be successive is another that may require something more than just having the perceptions.

imagining them to stand in a temporal relation of succession—something we could do incorrectly because both are in fact only simultaneously present in consciousness. Though Hume did not discuss time cognition in EHU, he did present a very different account in *Treatise* 1.2.3. On that account, a perception of succession reduces to a succession of perceptions. I perceive that things are successive in time by first perceiving the one and then perceiving the other, and I subsequently remember or imagine successions by forming sequences of ideas that themselves take time to occur and that copy the original sequence of impressions (perhaps with jumps over some of the intermediate events, or an employment of general terms and symbols to stand for entire sequences, facilitating a review that occurs more quickly than the original events took to occur). Thus, for Hume, the "connection" involved in temporal succession is in fact directly perceived just by "sense and intuition" and subsequently remembered by re-enactment. It requires no imaginative reproduction of all the successively presented perceptions in an instant, and no acts of judgment concerning which perception ought to be placed where relative to the others, to be perceived or remembered or rendered "objective." Kant's contrary suggestion—supposing he intended to make it—rests on theoretical and phenomenological commitments that are not obviously true. Theoretically, it rests on the view that the only kind of image or copy that can be made of a temporally extended sequence of events is one consisting of parts that all exist at once, at the present moment. But we make temporally extended copies of temporally extended events all the time. Echoes, musical performances, and theatrical productions are such copies. Phenomenologically, the suggestion rests on the view that my idea of a temporally extended event, like the playing of the first four notes of Beethoven's Fifth Symphony, consists of simultaneously occurring memories of all four notes that I somehow come to judge to belong to successive locations in time. But try as I might, I find it impossible to remember or think of the first four notes of Beethoven's Fifth Symphony all at once, or to hear the fourth note while simultaneously remembering or thinking of the previous three. The only way I can think of or remember the first four notes of Beethoven's Fifth is successively. My idea of the four notes is an idea that takes time to occur and that consists of four parts playing in my imagination in succession. And to the extent that I worry that I am remembering the four notes in the right order, I address that worry not by appealing to a causal law that dictates that the notes must have been played in that order and no other, but by trusting that I was well enough trained by past experience to have that ear-worm more or less correctly burned into my brain, like a visual after-image.

The version of the argument that follows does not, however, depend on this questionable position on the phenomenology of time-consciousness (which it is possible that Kant may not have intended to take in any case). It instead appears to allow that a "subjective succession," or an order in which my imagination places objects, may be directly apprehended.]

Kritik: A 189-94/B 234-49

The apprehension of the manifold of appearance is always successive. The representations of the parts follow one another. Whether they also follow one another in the object is a second point for reflection, which is not decided by the first ... Thus, for example, the apprehension of the manifold in the appearance of a house that stands before me is successive.[16] Now the question is whether the manifold of this house itself is also in itself successive, which obviously no one will accept.... That something should happen, that is, that something or some state should come to be which previously did not exist, cannot be empirically perceived unless it is preceded by some earlier appearance that does not contain this state.... Every apprehension of an event is accordingly a perception that follows upon another perception. But since this is the way things are in all ... apprehension, as I earlier showed in the appearance of a house, an apprehension of an event is, by this means, not yet distinguished from other apprehensions. But let us also note that in an appearance that contains a happening the following state of perception, call it B, can only follow the prior state of perception, call it A, and not precede it. I see, for example, a ship floating downstream.[17] My perception of its position further downstream follows on my perception of its position higher upstream, and it is impossible that, in the apprehension of this appearance the ship should first be perceived lower downstream and only subsequently higher upstream. The order in the sequence of perceptions in apprehension is here determined and

---

16 Kant was thinking of standing too close to the house to see the whole thing at once and so having to move to see the different parts one after another.

17 To parallel the comparison with the case of the house imagine standing so close as not to be able to see the whole ship at once, but to instead experience different parts of the ship to move successively across your visual field. Whereas in the case of the house we think of the object as motionless, and so as persisting over time without changing, in the case of the ship we think of the object as in motion, and so as changing over time in the sense of coming to occupy successively different positions.

the apprehension is bound to this order.[18] In the previous example of a house my perceptions could have begun with the apprehension of the roof and ended with the foundation, but could just as well have begun from below and ended on top. Likewise, the manifold of the empirical intuition could have been apprehended from the right or the left. There was no determinate order in the sequence of these perceptions that made it necessary where I would have to begin the apprehension in order to empirically connect the manifold. But this rule is always to be found in the perception of an event, and it makes the order of the successively occurring perceptions (in the apprehension of this appearance) NECESSARY.[19]

In this case I must therefore derive[20] the SUBJECTIVE SEQUENCE of apprehension from the OBJECTIVE SEQUENCE of appearance because the former is completely undetermined and does not distinguish one appearance from the other. By itself, the former proves nothing about the connection of the manifold in the object because it is completely arbitrary. The latter consists of the order of the manifold of appearance in accord with which the apprehension of one thing (the thing that happens) follows IN ACCORD WITH A RULE after the other (which precedes). Only by that means can I be justified in saying that there is a succession to be found in the appearance itself, and not just in my

---

18 Another way to put this is to say that the subjective sequence of perceptions is in this case determined by the objective fact that one of the things perceived (one of the positions of the ship) did not exist earlier and so could not possibly have been perceived earlier. Compare Kant's statement at the outset of the next paragraph.

19 Note that it is one thing to say that, if an event occurs, then *the order of appearances constitutive of the event* (namely, the earlier and later appearances of the object that undergoes change) *is necessary*, and another to say either that *in all similar cases the same order must be observed* or that *there must have been some prior cause that necessitated the change*. At this point, Kant was only making the first of these three claims. But the third claim is made at the outset of the concluding paragraph of this selection. The move from the one to the other is justified (if it is justified at all) by the penultimate paragraph.

20 *ableiten.* The obvious meaning of Kant's German term notwithstanding, it would be pointless to go to the trouble of "deriving" a haphazard, subjective succession that contributes nothing to the knowledge of the object from a prior knowledge of an objective succession. Kant's point may rather have been that we do not so much *derive* the subjective succession of perceptions from the objective succession of states constitutive of an event as take the more directly and immediately known subjective succession to have been *determined* by the objective succession. In the case of the perception of the manifold of a house, the subjective succession is not so determined.

apprehension, which is so much as to say that I could not otherwise employ the apprehension than in this sequence.

What I mean by this reference to a rule is that included in what precedes an event, considered in general, there must be the condition of a rule, in accord with which this event must always and necessarily follow. But it is not possible to go in the reverse direction back from the happening to determine (through apprehension) what precedes it. ... Since there is nonetheless something that occurs only subsequently, it must be necessarily related to something else in general that precedes it, and upon which it follows in accord with a rule, that is, necessarily. In this way the event, as the conditioned, gives a sure indication of some condition, whereas the latter determines the former.

[Whereas Hume claimed that we cannot, simply by inspecting an effect, say anything in advance of experience about what its cause must have been, Kant tried to argue that if we pause to consider the conditions of the possibility of there being any such thing as an event in the experience of beings like us, we will uncover a reason for thinking, even in advance of experience, that every event must have been necessitated by some cause. We will not be able to say, in advance of experience, what this cause must have been or what it was like. But we can be assured it must have existed.

In brief, the argument is that for me to experience an event there must be some change in my experience. But this is only a necessary and not a sufficient condition for the possibility of the experience of an event. A change in my experience might arise from something new coming into being, but it might also arise from my encountering something old, that has existed all along, though it was previously unnoticed by me. To be justified in choosing the former alternative, I have to suppose that, among all the things that existed at the prior time, there is one that determined the event I now witness to only just now occur. This is tantamount to saying that the event must be conceived to have had a cause if it is to be conceived as an event at all.

Importantly, in drawing this inference, I understand this determining condition or cause as something that must have been followed by the event, and not merely as something that, so far as we have up to now observed, has just so happened to have always occurred first.[21]

---

21 It is not clear that Kant would have considered a proof that every event must have some cause to be an answer to Hume's scepticism about the causal principle. As the passage initially cited from the *Prolegomena* indicates, what he found provocative about Hume's position was not that it questioned the existence of a cause for every effect, but that it questioned the *(Continued)*

Before we can notice regularities, we need to have sorted out which changes in our experience are due to changes in the objects and which are due to perceiving unchanged, but previously unnoticed objects, and we already need to presume the existence of a necessitating cause to do so—otherwise, the prior occurrence of the cause could give us no assurance that the effect has only just now come to be. This is not to say that we understand the ground of this necessity. We need have no insight into the existence of any quality or power in the cause that forces the effect to occur. But we do have to assume that, for whatever reason, occurrences of the cause must always be followed by occurrences of the effect. The necessity in the connection between causes and effects is thus only nomological necessity—but it is necessity and not just hitherto observed regularity.

However, Hume would have had no problem dismissing Kant's reason for thinking that necessitating causes are required for events, and accounting for the distinction between the perception of a newly occurrent event and the perception of something that has existed unnoticed for some time on his own terms, without needing to presuppose that causes are anything more than empirically discovered, regular antecedents. On Hume's account, any change in experience is as much a change as any other, and those changes that arise from the discovery of something that was previously unnoticed are as much the regular consequences of antecedent perceptions as those changes that result from the emergence of something new. Standing in front of a house (too close to see the whole thing at once), there is either no change in my experience at all or, if there is, my perceptions of the roof are constantly conjoined with an immediately prior volition to raise my eyes or head up, my perceptions of the left side of the house are constantly conjoined with an immediately prior volition to turn my eyes or head to the left or to move my body to the left, and so on. *Pace* Kant, who was invested in claiming that there is some sort of "reversibility" in my perceptions of the parts of a house, when we take

---

necessity of the connection between causes and effects, substituting a brute factual regularity in its place, and that seems to be what he was principally concerned to establish in the Second Analogy. He was even more explicit in the *Kritik*. "The concept of cause so obviously contains the concept of necessity in the connection with an effect, and of the strict universality of the rule [of their succession], that it would be completely lost if one attempted to derive it, as Hume did, from a frequent conjunction of that which happens with that which precedes it, and the custom (that is, merely subjective necessity) to connect representations that arise from that conjunction" (B 5). In EHU, Hume did not question that every event must have a cause, though he did go so far as to note that, in principle, anything could be the cause of anything (a possibility Kant did not question).

our antecedent volitions to move into account there is as much regularity in the succession of earlier and later events in the one case as in the other.

In the empirical world nothing is certain, and we can imagine weird cases such as wearing inverting spectacles, but as a rule, the sight of upper portions of the house follows upon the experience of a volition to move the eyes up, rather than the reverse, and I find by experience that there is nothing I can do to put myself in a position where I will experience the reverse—a view of the roof that precedes rather than follows a volition to move my eyes up. Consequently, upon experiencing a volition to raise my eyes, I anticipate that colour points I now see on the upper periphery will reappear at the centre. I may even anticipate that many of the objects that I last saw to be above those I now see on the upper periphery will reappear on the upper periphery.

The case of the ship is analogous. Standing in front of a ship (too close to see the whole thing at once), I either experience no succession of the parts of the ship at all or, if I do, my perceptions of the successive parts are constantly conjoined with such things as the feeling of the wind, or a view of the current in the water, or the hearing of the sound of the engines. Just as, had I moved my eyes from top to bottom rather than from bottom to top, I would have experienced a reverse sequence, so, had the wind been blowing or the water flowing from the opposite side, or the propellers turning in the opposite direction, I would have experienced a reverse sequence.

We do all think that there is a difference between these cases—that the one involves a merely "apparent" or "subjective" change whereas the other involves a "real" or "objective" change. According to Kant, we ought to think that the parts of the house are really coexistent and consequently could have been perceived in either direction, from foundation to roof or roof to foundation. But we ought to think that the positions of the ship were successive and could therefore only have been experienced in one order. And we can only do that, Kant claimed, if we also suppose that the ship is an enduring object that changed from one state (or situation) to another at just the time it did because at the previous time something else happened, and it is a rule that happenings of the one sort are necessarily followed by alterations of the other sort. This ignores the fact that when volitions to move eyes or body parts are taken into account, the succession in the experience of a house is as irreversible as that of the ship, and that if we set aside references to antecedent volitions to move in the case of the house then, by parity of example, we ought to set aside references to antecedent motions of air or water or propeller parts in the case of the ship, in which case my perceptions of it are as reversible as my perceptions of the house.

For Hume the difference between real and apparent change reduces to the difference between change caused by object change and change caused by perceiver (or subject) motion, where the latter is distinguished from the former by the fact that its causes are volitions to move. We have learned that volitions to perform upward motions are regularly followed by the tracking of the entire visual or tangible field from the upward periphery towards the centre, and from the centre towards the bottom. We have also learned that, sometimes, isolated portions of these fields, or even the fields as a whole, move as a consequence of other causes than volition on our part. We denominate the effects of the one cause voluntary perceiver motion and those of the other causes object motion. All that remains is to appeal to the natural instinct or prepossession of EHU 12.7 to believe in the continued existence of impressions outside of the bounds of the visual and tangible fields in order to explain why we think of the former as moving the window of the visual or tangible field over a larger, continually existing field of objects, leading us to notice things that have existed all along (hence as involving a merely "apparent" change) and the latter as leading us to encounter newly emergent position-states of an object. And even if that attempt were judged a failure, the only casualty would be our belief in the continued existence of objects beyond the periphery of the visual and tangible fields. We would still, even in the absence of any commitment to the continued existence of unperceived objects, be in a position to draw the more primitive distinction between subjective changes due to perceiver motion and objective changes due to object motion.

There are ambiguous cases such as those of perceived motions of my own body parts, perceptions resulting from involuntary perceiver motion, and volitions to move that are restrained. But we learn to sort these things out over the course of experience. Perceived motions of body parts are tagged by the fact that the volition results in a motion of only a part of the sensory field relative to other parts, rather than a tracking of all parts across the field as a whole. And fuller experience teaches us whether we should treat this sort of ambiguous case as a case of object motion or of perceiver motion. Likewise, involuntary motion and restrained volition are both tagged by pressure sensations, in the one case accompanying acceleration and in the other accompanying restraint. In the cases where these tags are absent, such as experiences on trains moving past other trains or cases of paralysis, we are appropriately confused until further experience can disambiguate the circumstances. In all of these cases we do not impose an interpretation on our experience guided by a priori rules. We instead inspect the experience for analogies to previously encountered cases and treat it as an experience of the one sort or the other depending on the degree of analogy. Sitting in a train, seeing another train pass on the adjacent track, I am genuinely confused about whether it is a house case or a ship case—whether I am moving to see new parts of the train or the train is changing position—and it is only when I can catch a glimpse of the ground or feel an acceleration or get some other such information about the causes of the motion that I reach a decision.

Seen from this perspective, Kant's account leaves us saddled with a problem. It tells us that *if* we are to understand our experience as the experience of a newly occurrent event then we must suppose that, at the prior moment of time, some condition existed that necessitated the occurrence of the event. But it does not tell us *why* we should make the choice of interpreting our experience as the experience of an event rather than as the consequence of an encounter with a previously unnoticed object. The answer to that more fundamental question is guided by observations of regularities in the succession of kinds of impressions, such as volitions and pressure sensations, in the absence of which decisions about whether we are experiencing a changed object or a previously unnoticed object become mysterious. With those regularities, no appeal to necessitating conditions and rules is necessary. Without them, none will give us any guidance in how to interpret the data presented to us by our senses.]

Select Bibliography

Principal Works

Original editions of most of Hume's works are now electronically available through the "Eighteenth Century Collections Online" database. Gale document numbers for title pages of initial volumes are given here to facilitate locating these works.

[Hume, David. "Early memoranda."] In Ernest C. Mossner, "Hume's early memoranda, 1729-40: The Complete Text." *Journal of the History of Ideas* 9 (1948): 492-518. http://www.jstor.org/stable/2707220.

[Hume, David.] *A Treatise of Human Nature: Being an Attempt to Introduce the Experimental Method of Reasoning into Moral Subjects.* 3 vols. London: John Noon, 1739 and 1740. Gale document CW3317501541, CW3318260513, and CW3318260844. Critical edition by David Fate Norton and Mary J. Norton. Oxford: Clarendon P, 2007.

———. *An Abstract of a Book Lately Published; Entituled, A Treatise of Human Nature, &c. wherein the chief argument of that book is farther illustrated and explained.* London: C. Borbet, 1740. Gale document CW3318060774. Critical edition in David Fate Norton and Mary J. Norton (eds), *A Treatise of Human Nature.* Oxford: Clarendon P, 2007.

———. *Essays Moral and Political.* Edinburgh: A. Kincaid, 1741. Gale document CW3319526115. Subsequent editions in 1742 (CW3310979827) and 1748 (CB3326726447). Incorporated into *Essays and Treatises on Several Subjects* in 1753 and appearing after 1758 under the title *Essays Moral, Political, and Literary.* Scholarly editions in Eugene F. Millar (ed) *Essays Moral, Political, and Literary.* Indianapolis: Liberty Fund, 1985.

———. *A Letter from a Gentleman to his Friend in Edinburgh: containing some observations on a specimen of the principles concerning religion and morality, said to be manitain'd in a book lately publish'd, intituled, A treatise of human nature, &c.* [Henry Home (ed).] Edinburgh: no publisher identified, 1745. Critical edition in David Fate Norton and Mary J. Norton (eds), *A Treatise of Human Nature.* Oxford: Clarendon P, 2007.

———. *Philosophical Essays Concerning Human Understanding.* London: A. Millar, 1748. Gale document CW3319914515. Subsequent edition in 1750 by "David Hume, esq." (CW3317501541). Incor-

porated into *Essays and Treatises on Several Subjects* in 1753 and
retitled *An Enquiry Concerning Human Understanding* in 1758. Crit-
ical edition by Tom L. Beauchamp. Oxford: Clarendon P, 2000.
Hume, David. *Three Essays Moral and Political* ["Of national charac-
ters," "Of the original contract," and "Of passive obedience"].
London: A. Millar, 1748. Gale document CW3320755077. Incorporated into *Essays moral and political* in 1748.
——. *An Enquiry Concerning the Principles of Morals*. London: A.
Millar, 1751. Gale document CW3319331114. Incorporated into
Essays and treatises on several subjects in 1753. Critical edition by
Tom L. Beauchamp. Oxford: Clarendon P, 2006.
——. *Political Discourses*. Edinburgh: A. Kincaid and A. Donaldson,
1751. Gale document CW3304527312. Subsequent editions in
1752 (CW3305568536) and 1754 (CB3327115596). Incorpo-
rated into *Essays and Treatises on Several Subjects* in 1758. Scholarly
editions in Eugene F. Millar (ed) *Essays Moral, Political, and Liter-
ary*. Indianapolis: Liberty Fund, 1985.
——. *Essays and Treatises on Several Subjects*. London: A. Millar,
1753. Gale document CB3332074441. Subsequent lifetime editions in 1756 (partial at CW3316636588), 1758
(CW3317720363), 1760 (CW3317566941), 1764
(CW3319224902), 1767 (CB3329144106), 1768
(CW3320008206), 1770 (CW417565559), 1772
(CW3316422417), and 1777 (CW3322000944).
——. *The History of Great Britain. Volume 1. Containing the Reigns of
James I. and Charles I.* Edinburgh: Hamilton, Balfour, and Neill,
1754. Gale document CW3300385629. Subsequently incorporated into *The History of England from the Invasion of Julius Caesar
to the Revolution in 1688*. The multiple lifetime editions are not
further noted here. However, note the important changes in the
second edition of 1759, Gale document CW3300981012. Scholarly edition by William B. Todd. 6 vols. Indianapolis: Liberty
Fund, 1983.
——. *The History of Great Britain. Volume 2. Containing the Commonwealth and the Reigns of Charles II. and James II.* London: A.
Millar, 1757. Gale document CW3301494465. Subsequently
incorporated into *The History of England from the Invasion of Julius
Caesar to the Revolution in 1688*. The multiple lifetime editions are
not further noted here. Scholarly edition by William B. Todd. 6
vols. Indianapolis: Liberty Fund, 1983.
——. *Four Dissertations* ["The natural history of religion," "A dissertation of the passions," "Of tragedy," and "Of the standard of
taste"]. London: A. Millar, 1757. Gale document
CW3325288869. Incorporated into *Essays and Treatises on Several*

Subjects in 1758. Critical/scholarly editions in Tom L. Beauchamp (ed), *A Dissertation on the Passions/The Natural History of Religion.* Oxford: Clarendon P, 2007; and Eugene F. Millar (ed), *Essays Moral, Political, and Literary.* Indianapolis: Liberty Fund, 1985.

——. *The History of England Under the House of Tudor.* 2 vols. London: A. Millar, 1759. Subsequently incorporated into *The History of England from the Invasion of Julius Caesar to the Revolution in 1688.* Gale document CW3302194813. The multiple lifetime editions are not further noted here. Scholarly edition by William B. Todd. 6 vols. Indianapolis: Liberty Fund, 1983.

——. *The History of England from the Invasion of Julius Caesar to the Accession of Henry VII.* 2 vols. London: A. Millar, 1762. Gale document CW3304009046. Subsequently incorporated into *The History of England from the Invasion of Julius Caesar to the Revolution in 1688.* The multiple lifetime editions are not further noted here. Scholarly edition by William B. Todd. 6 vols. Indianapolis: Liberty Fund, 1983.

——. *Exposé succinct de la contestation qui s'est élevée entre M. Hume et M. Rousseau, avec les pièces justificatives.* Londres: 1766. Gale document CW3322603127.

[Hume, David.] *Two essays* ["Of suicide" and "Of the immortality of the soul"]. London: no publisher identified, 1777. Gale document CW3322575757. Scholarly edition in Eugene F. Millar (ed), *Essays Moral, Political, and Literary.* Indianapolis: Liberty Fund, 1985.

Hume, David. *My Own Life.* In *The Life of David Hume, esq., written by himself.* London: W. Strahan and T. Cadell, 1777. Gale document CB3329349118. Scholarly edition in Eugene F. Millar (ed), *Essays Moral, Political, and Literary.* Indianapolis: Liberty Fund, 1985.

——. *Dialogues concerning natural religion.* No place or publisher identified: 1779. Gale document CW3320013570. Scholarly edition by Norman Kemp Smith. 2nd ed. London: T. Nelson, 1947.

——. *The Letters of David Hume,* J.Y.T. Grieg (ed). 2 vols. Oxford: Clarendon P, 1969.

——. *New Letters of David Hume,* Raymond Klibansky and Ernest C. Mossner (eds). Oxford: Clarendon P, 1954.

Biography

Beauchamp, Tom L. "A history of the *Enquiry Concerning Human Understanding.*" In Tom L. Beauchamp (ed), *An Enquiry Concerning Human Understanding: A Critical Edition.* Oxford: Clarendon P, 2000. xi-civ.

Hume, David. *My Own Life.* In *The Life of David Hume, esq., written by himself.* London: W. Strahan and T. Cadell, 1777. Scholarly edition in Eugene F. Millar (ed), *Essays Moral, Political, and Literary*. Indianapolis: Liberty Fund, 1985.

Mossner, Ernest Campbell. *The Life of David Hume*. 2nd ed. Oxford: Clarendon P, 1980.

Norton, David Fate. "Historical Account of *A Treatise of Human Nature* from Its Beginnings to the Time of Hume's death." In David Fate Norton and Mary J. Norton (eds), *A Treatise of Human Nature: A Critical Edition*. 2 vols. Oxford: Clarendon P, 2007. 2: 433-588.

Stewart, M.A. "Hume's Intellectual Development," in Marina Frasca-Spada and P.J.E. Kail (eds), *Impressions of Hume*. Oxford: Clarendon P, 2005. 11-58.

Bibliography

Jessop, T.E. *A Bibliography of David Hume and of Scottish Philosophy from Francis Hutcheson to Lord Balfour*. London: A. Brown & Sons, 1938.

Hall, Roland. *Fifty Years of Hume Scholarship: A Bibliographical Guide*. Edinburgh: Edinburgh UP, 1978.

Hall, Roland, subsequently Morris, William E., subsequently Fieser, James. Annual bibliographies of Hume literature published in *Hume Studies*.

Annotated Bibliography

Yalden-Thompson, D.C. "Recent Work on Hume." *American Philosophical Quarterly* 20 (1983): 1-22.

Capaldi, Nicholas, James T. King, and Donald W. Livingston, "The Hume literature of the 1980's." *American Philosophical Quarterly* 28 (1991): 255-72.

Beauchamp, Tom L. "Supplementary Reading." In Tom L. Beauchamp (ed), *An Enquiry Concerning Human Understanding*. Oxford Philosophical Texts (not to be confused with the critical edition referenced elsewhere). Oxford: Oxford UP, 1999.

Millican, Peter. "Critical Survey of the Literature on Hume and the First *Enquiry*." In Peter Millican (ed), *Reading Hume on Human Understanding*. Oxford: Clarendon P, 2002.

Important Early Reactions to Hume's Philosophy

Adams, William. *An Essay on Mr. Hume's Essay on Miracles*. London: E. Say, 1752. Gale document CW3319965850. Later editions in

1762 (CB3332803494), 1767 (CW3305769505), and 1776 (CW3304783453).

[Balfour, James, of Pilrig]. *A Delineation of the Nature and Obligation of Morality. With Reflections upon Mr. Hume's Book, Intitled, An Inquiry Concerning the Principles of Morals.* Edinburgh: Hamilton, Balfour, and Neill, 1753. Gale document CW3322003910. Later edition in 1763 (CW3317429767).

——. *Philosophical essays.* Edinburgh: John Balfour, 1768.

Beattie, James. *An Essay on the Nature and Immutability of Truth; in Opposition to Sophistry and Scepticism.* Edinburgh: A. Kincaid and J. Bell, 1770. Gale document CW3321716300. Later editions in 1771 (CW3316259841), 1772 (CW3316250684), 1773 (CW3314135570), 1774 (CW3315618340), and 1777 (CW3316013797).

Campbell, George. *A Dissertation on Miracles.* Edinburgh: A. Kincaid and J. Bell, 1762. Gale document CW3320836635. Later editions in 1766 (CW3322180998) and 1796 (CB3329621927).

Fieser, James. *Early Responses to Hume,* 10 vols. 2nd ed. Bristol: Thoemmes, 2005.

[Home, Henry, Lord Kames]. *Essays on the Principles of Morality and Natural Religion.* Edinburgh: A. Kincaid and A. Donaldson, 1751. Gale document CW3317480883. Later editions in 1758 (CW3320098703) and 1779 (CW3323434100).

Jacobi, Friedrich Heinrich. *David Hume über den Glauben oder Idealismus und Realismus. Ein Gespräch.* Breslau: Gottl. Loewe, 1787. Reprinted in facsimile, New York: Garland, 1983.

Kant, Immanuel. *Kritik der reinen Vernunft.* Riga: Johann Friedrich Hartknoch, 1781. Later edition in 1787. Scholarly edition by Jens Timmermans. Hamburg: Meiner, 1998. Translation by Norman Kemp Smith. New York: Macmillan, 1965.

——. *Prolegomena zu einer jeden künftigen Metaphysik, die als Wissenschaft wird auftreten können.* Riga: Johann Friedrich Hartknoch, 1783. Scholarly edition by Karl Vorländer, corrected by Norbert Hinske. Hamburg: Meiner, 1976. Translation by Gary Hatfield. Cambridge: Cambridge UP, 1997.

Leland, John. *A View of the Principal Deistical Writers of the Last and Present Century. Volume II. Containing Observations on Mr. Hume's Philosophical Essays,* etc. London: B. Dod, 1755. Gale document CW3318862419. Earlier edition with no reference to Hume in 1754 (CW3318861911). Later editions in 1764 (CW3305859929) and 1766 (CW3315699352).

Price, Richard. *A Review of the Principal Questions and Difficulties in*

Morals. London: A. Millar, 1758. Later editions in 1769 (CW3321462020) and 1787 (CW3321510273).

———. *Four Dissertations*. London: A. Millar and T. Cadell, 1767. Gale document CW3320428628. Later editions in 1768 (CB3327574528), 1772 (CW3319077836), and 1777 (CW3314479417).

Reid, Thomas. *An Inquiry into the Human Mind on the Principles of Common Sense*. Edinburgh: A. Millar, A. Kincaid, and J. Bell, 1764. Gale document CW3317422497. Later editions in 1765 (CW3318428193), 1769 (CW3324955573), and 1785 (CW3321414118).

———. *Essays on the Intellectual Powers of Man*. Edinburgh: John Bell, 1785. Gale document CW3307462279.

———. *Essays on the Active Powers of Man*. Edinburgh: John Bell, 1788. Gale document CW3314158322.

Tetens, Johann Nicholas. *Über die allgemeine speculativische Philosophie*. Available in Wilhelm Uebele (ed) *Über die allgemeine speculativische Philosophie. Philosophische Versuche über die menschliche Natur und iher Entwicklung Bd. 1*. Berlin: Kantgesellschaft Neudrucke seltener philosophischer Werke, 1911.

———. *Philosophische Versuche über die menschliche Natur und iher Entwicklung*. 2 vols. Leipzig: M.G. Weidmans, 1777. (Complete volumes available in Google books.)

[Warburton, William.] *Remarks on Mr. David Hume's Essay on the Natural History of Religion*. [Richard Hurd (ed).] London: M. Cooper, 1757. Gale document CW3320371652. Later edition in 1777 (CW3321438110).

Classic Works on Hume's Philosophy

Beck, Lewis White. *Essays on Kant and Hume*. New Haven: Yale UP, 1978.

Brown, Thomas. *Observations on the Nature and Tendency of the Doctrine of Mr. Hume Concerning the Relation of Cause and Effect*. 2nd ed. Edinburgh: Mundell and Son, 1806. (Complete edition available in Google books.)

Green, T.H. "General Introduction," and "Introduction to the Moral Part of the *Treatise*." In T.H. Green and T.H. Grose (eds), *A Treatise of Human Nature*. 2 vols. London: 1874. 1: 1-299, 2: 1-71. Reprinted as *Hume and Locke*. New York: Thomas Crowell, 1968.

Kemp Smith, Norman. "The Naturalism of Hume." *Mind* 14 (1905): 149-73, 335-47.

Kuypers, Mary S. *Studies in the Eighteenth Century Background of Hume's Empiricism*. Minneapolis: U of Minnesota P, 1930.

Price, H.H. *Hume's Theory of the External World.* Oxford: Clarendon P, 1940.

Kemp Smith, Norman. *The Philosophy of David Hume.* London: Macmillan, 1941.

Popkin, Richard H. "David Hume: His Pyrrhonism and His Critique of Pyrrhonism." *Philosophical Quarterly* 1 (1951): 385-407.

Hendel, Charles W. *Studies in the Philosophy of David Hume.* Indianapolis: Bobbs-Merrill, 1963.

Hearn, Thomas K., Jr. "General rules in Hume's *Treatise.*" *Journal of the History of Philosophy* 8 (1970): 405-22.

Stove, David C. *Probability and Hume's Inductive Scepticism.* Oxford: Clarendon P, 1973.

Norton, David Fate, Nicholas Capaldi, and Wade Robison, (eds). *McGill Hume Studies.* San Diego: Austin Hill P, 1976.

Pike, Nelson. "Hume's Bundle Theory of the Self: A Limited Defense." *American Philosophical Quarterly* 4 (1976): 159-65.

Stroud, Barry. *Hume.* London: Routledge and Kegan Paul, 1977.

Work Specifically on Hume's *Enquiry*

Beauchamp, Tom L. (ed). *An Enquiry Concerning Human Understanding: A Critical Edition.* Oxford: Clarendon P, 2000.

Buckle, Stephen. *Hume's Enlightenment Tract: The Unity and Purpose of An Enquiry Concerning Human Understanding.* Oxford: Clarendon P, 2001.

Earman, John. *Hume's Abject Failure: The Argument Against Miracles.* Oxford: Oxford UP, 2000.

Flew, Anthony. *Hume's Philosophy of Belief: A Study of his First Enquiry.* London: Routledge, [1961].

Fogelin, Robert. *A Defense of Hume on Miracles.* Princeton, NJ: Princeton UP, 2003.

Millican, Peter (ed). *Reading Hume on Human Understanding: Essays on the First Enquiry.* Oxford: Oxford UP, 2000.

Penelhum, Terence. *David Hume: An Introduction to his Philosophical System.* West Lafayette, IN: Purdue UP, 1992.

Selected Recent Books and Articles

This list emphasizes work with bearing on Hume's philosophy in ETSS 2 that has been published since 1998. For earlier work, see "Bibliography" and "Annotated Bibliography" above.

Abramson, Kate. "Hume's Distinction Between Philosophical Anatomy and Painting." *Philosophy Compass* 2 (2007): 680-98.

——. "Sympathy and the Project of Hume's Second Enquiry." *Archiv für Geschichte der Philosophie* 83 (2001): 45-80.

Allison, Henry. *Custom and Reason in Hume. A Kantian Reading of the First Book of the Treatise*. Oxford: Clarendon P, 2008.

Annas, Julia. "Hume and Ancient Scepticism." *Acta Philosophica Fennica* 66 (2000): 271-85.

Batitsky, Vadim. "From Inexactness to Certainty: The Change in Hume's Conception of Geometry." *Journal for General Philosophy of Science* 29 (1998): 1-20.

Bayne, Steven M. "Kant's Answer to Hume: How Kant Should Have Tried to Stand Hume's Copy Thesis on Its Head." *British Journal for the History of Philosophy* 8 (2000): 207-24.

Baier, Annette. *A Progress of the Sentiments: Reflections on Hume's Treatise*. Cambridge, MA: Harvard UP, 1991.

Beaudoin, Paul. "On Some Criticisms of Hume's Principle of Proportioning Cause to Effect." *Philo* 2 (1999): 26-40.

Beebee, Helen. "The Two Definitions and the Doctrine of Causation." *Proceedings of the Aristotelian Society* 107 (2007): 413-31.

——. *Hume on Causation*. New York: Routledge, 2006.

Bell, Martin. "The 'Natural History of Religion'." In Emanuele Ronchetti and Emilio Mazza (eds), *New Essays on David Hume*. Milan: FrancoAngeli, 2007. 389-410.

Bitzer, Lloyd F. "The Indian Prince in Miracle Arguments of Hume and His Predecessors and Early Critics." *Philosophy and Rhetoric* 31 (1998): 175-230.

Bricke, John. "Hume, Freedom to Act, and Personal Evaluation." *History of Philosophy Quarterly* 5 (1988): 141-56.

——. *Mind and Morality*. Oxford: Clarendon P, 1996.

Box, M.A. *The Suasive Art of David Hume*. Princeton: Princeton UP, 1990.

Buckle, Stephen. "Marvels, Miracles, and Mundane Order: Hume's Critique of Religion in *An Enquiry Concerning Human Understanding*." *Australasian Journal of Philosophy* 79 (2001): 1-31.

Butler, Annemarie. "Natural Instinct, Perceptual Relativity, and Belief in the External World in Hume's *Enquiry*." *Hume Studies* 34 (2008): 115-58.

Craig, Edward. "Hume on Thought and Belief." In Godfrey Vesey (ed), *Philosophers Ancient and Modern*. Cambridge: Cambridge UP, 1986. 93-110.

Cohon, Rachel. *Hume's Morality: Feeling and Fabrication*. Oxford: Oxford UP, 2008.

Coleman, Dorothy. "Baconian Probability and Hume's Theory of Testimony." *Hume Studies* 27 (2001): 195-226.

Coventry, Angela. *Hume's Theory of Causation: A Quasi-Realist Interpretation.* New York: Continuum, 2006.

Costelloe, Timothy M. *Aesthetics and Morals in the Philosophy of David Hume.* New York: Routledge, 2007.

Crooks, Shelagh. "Hume, Images and the Mental Object Problem." *Dialogue* 39 (2000): 3-24.

Dauer, Francis W. "Force and Vivacity in the *Treatise* and the *Enquiry*." *Hume Studies* 25 (1999): 83-99.

Debes, Remy. "Humanity, Sympathy and the Puzzle of Hume's Second *Enquiry*." *British Journal for the History of Philosophy* 15 (2007): 27-57.

——. "Has Anything Changed? Hume's Theory of Association and Sympathy after the *Treatise*." *British Journal for the History of Philosophy* 15 (2007): 313-38.

Falkenstein, Lorne. "Hume's Answer to Kant." *Noûs* 32 (1998): 331-60.

——. "Hume and Reid on the Perception of Hardness," *Hume Studies* 28 (2002): 27-48.

——. "Condillac's Paradox," *Journal of the History of Philosophy* 43 (2005): 403-35.

——. "Hume on 'Genuine,' 'True,' and 'Rational' Religion." *Eighteenth Century Thought* 4 (2009): 171-201.

Faulkner, Paul. "David Hume's Reductionist Epistemology of Testimony." *Pacific Philosophical Quarterly* 79 (1998): 302-13.

Fieser, James. "Hume's Classification of the Passions and its Precursors." *Hume Studies* 18: 1992.

Frasca-Spada, Maria, and P.J.E. Kail, (eds). *Impressions of Hume.* Oxford: Oxford UP, 2005.

Fogelin, Robert J. *Hume's Sceptical Crisis, a Textual Study.* Oxford: Oxford UP, 2009.

Foster, Peter S. "Reid's Response to Hume on Double Vision." *Journal of Scottish Philosophy* 6 (2008): 189-94.

Garrett, Don. *Cognition and Commitment in Hume's Philosophy.* New York: Oxford UP, 1997.

——. "Hume's Naturalistic Theory of Representation." *Synthese* 152 (2006): 301-19.

——. "Should Hume Have Been a Transcendental Idealist?" In Daniel Garber and Béatrice Longunesse (eds), *Kant and the Early Moderns.* Princeton: Princeton UP, 2008. 193-208.

Gaskin, J.C.A. *Hume's Philosophy of Religion.* 2nd ed. New York: Macmillan, 1988.

Gill, Michael B. "Moral Rationalism vs. Moral Sentimentalism: Is Morality More Like Math or Beauty?" *Philosophy Compass* 2 (2007): 16-30.

Guyer, Paul. *Knowledge, Reason, and Taste: Kant's Response to Hume.* Princeton: Princeton UP, 2008.

Harris, James A. *Of Liberty and Necessity: The Free Will Debate in Eighteenth-Century British Philosophy.* Oxford: Clarendon P, 2005.

Harrison, Peter. "Prophecy, Early Modern Apologetics, and Hume's Argument Against Miracles." *Journal of the History of Ideas* 60 (1999): 241-56.

Herdt, Jennifer A. *Religion and Faction in Hume's Moral Philosophy.* Cambridge: Cambridge UP, 1996.

Holden, Thomas. *Spectres of False Divinity. Hume's Moral Atheism.* Oxford: Oxford UP, 2010.

Humber, James M. "Hume on Liberty, Necessity, Morality and Religion." *Philosophical Inquiry* 21 (1999): 17-31.

Kail, P.J.E. *Projection and Realism in Hume's Philosophy.* New York: Oxford UP, 2007.

——. "Understanding Hume's 'Natural History of Religion'." *Philosophical Quarterly* 57 (2007): 190-211.

Landy, David. "Hume's Impression/Idea Distinction." *Hume Studies* 32 (2006): 119-39.

Larmer, Robert A. "Interpreting Hume on Miracles." *Religious Studies* 45 (2009): 325-38.

Livingston, Donald W. *Philosophical Melancholy and Delirium. Hume's Pathology of Philosophy.* Chicago: U of Chicago P, 1998.

Loeb, Louis E. *Stability and Justification in Hume's Treatise.* New York: Oxford UP, 2002.

Loptson, Peter. "Memory, Skepticism, and Time in the First *Enquiry.*" *Iyyun* 48 (1999): 89-115.

McCormick, Miriam. "A Change in Manner: Hume's Scepticism in the *Treatise* and the FSirst *Enquiry.*" *Canadian Journal of Philosophy* 29 (1999): 431-47.

Millican, Peter. "Humes Old and New: Four Fashionable Falsehoods, and One Unfashionable Truth." *Aristotelian Society Supplementary Volume* 81 (2007): 163-99.

——. "Hume, Causal Realism, and Causal Science." *Mind* 118 (2009): 647-712.

Merivale, Amyas. "Hume's Mature Account of the Indirect Passions." *Hume Studies* 35 (2009): 185-210.

Morris, William Edward. "Meaning(fullness) Without Metaphysics: Another Look at Hume's Meaning Empiricism." *Philosophia* 37 (2009): 441-54.

Murdoch, Dugald. "Induction, Hume, and Probability." *Journal of Philosophy* 99 (2002): 185-99.

Norton, David Fate, and Jacqueline Taylor. *The Cambridge Companion to Hume.* 2nd ed. Cambridge: Cambridge UP, 2009.

Noonan, Harold W. *Hume on Knowledge*. London: Routledge, 1999.

Nichols, Ryan. "Visible Figure and Reid's Theory of Visual Perception." *Hume Studies* 28 (2002): 273-89.

Osborne, Gregg. "Does Kant Refute Hume's Derivation of the Concept of Cause?" *Journal of Philosophical Research* 32 (2007): 293-318.

Ott, Walter. "What Can Causal Claims Mean?" *Philosophia* 37 (2009): 459-70.

Owen, David. *Hume's Reason*. Oxford: Oxford UP, 1999.

—— (ed). *Hume: General Philosophy*. Aldershot, UK: Ashgate, 2000.

——. "Locke and Hume on Belief, Judgment and Assent." *Topoi* 22 (2003): 15-28.

Pears, David. *Hume's System*. Oxford: Oxford UP, 1990.

Pehelhum, Terence. *Themes in Hume: The Self, Will, Religion*. Oxford: Clarendon P, 2000.

Read, Rupert, and Kenneth A. Richman, (eds). *The New Hume Debate*. Revised edition. London: Routledge, 2008.

Ronchetti, Emanuele, and Emilio Mazza, (ed). *New Essays on David Hume*. Milan: FrancoAngeli, 2007.

Russell, Paul. *The Riddle of Hume's Treatise: Skepticism, Naturalism and Irreligion*. New York: Oxford UP, 2008.

Schnall, Ira M. "Hume on Popular and Philosophical Skeptical Arguments." *Hume Studies* 33 (2007): 41-66.

Schmidt, Claudia M. *David Hume: Reason in History*. University Park, PA: Pennsylvania State UP, 2003.

Sinclair, Alistair. "The Failure of Thomas Reid's Attack of David Hume." *British Journal for the History of Philosophy* 3 (1995): 389-98.

Spencer, Mark G. *David Hume and Eighteenth-Century America*. Rochester, NY: U of Rochester P, 2005.

Stern, Robert. "On Kant's Response to Hume: The Second Analogy as a Transcendental Argument." In Robert Stern (ed), *Transcendental Arguments: Problems and Prospects*. Oxford: Clarendon P, 1999. 47-66.

Stewart, John B. *Opinion and Reform in Hume's Political Philosophy*. Princeton, NJ: Princeton UP, 1992.

Stewart, M.A. (ed). *Studies in the Philosophy of the Scottish Enlightenment*. Oxford: Clarendon P, 1990.

——, and John P. Wright, (eds). *Hume and Hume's Connexions*. Edinburgh: Edinburgh UP, 1994.

Strawson, Galen. *The Secret Connexion: Causation, Realism, and David Hume*. Oxford: Clarendon P, 1989.

Stroud, Barry. "Gilding or Staining the World with Sentiments and Phantasms." *Hume Studies* 19 (1993): 253-72.

Somerville, James. *The Enigmatic Parting Shot: What was Hume's "compleat answer to Dr Reid and to that bigotted silly fellow, Beattie"?* Aldershot, UK: Avebury, 1995.

——. "Whose Failure? Reid's or Hume's?" *British Journal for the History of Philosophy* 6 (1998): 247-60.

——. "'The Table, Which We See': An Irresolvable Ambiguity." *Philosophy* 81 (2006): 33-63.

Suderman, Jeffrey M. *Orthodoxy and Enlightenment: George Campbell in the Eighteenth Century.* Montreal: McGill-Queen's UP, 2001.

Taylor, Jacqueline. "Humean Ethics and the Politics of Sentiment." *Topoi* 21 (2002): 175-86.

——. "Hume on the Standard of Virtue." *Journal of Ethics* 6 (2002): 43-62.

Traiger, Saul (ed). *The Blackwell Guide to Hume's Treatise.* Oxford: Blackwell, 2006.

——. "Experience and Testimony in Hume's Philosophy." *Episteme* 7 (2010): 42-57.

Tweyman, Stanley (ed). *David Hume: Critical Assessments.* 6 vols. New York: Routledge, 1995.

Van Cleve, James. "Reid on Single and Double Vision: Mechanics and Morals." *The Journal of Scottish Philosophy* 6 (2008): 1-20.

——. "Double Appearances Are Double Trouble." *The Journal of Scottish Philosophy* 6 (2008): 195-96.

Vesey, Godfrey. "Hume on Liberty and Necessity." In Godfrey Vesey (ed), *Philosophers Ancient and Modern.* Cambridge: Cambridge UP, 1986.

Vitz, Rico. "Sympathy and Benevolence in Hume's Moral Psychology." *Journal of the History of Philosophy* 42 (2004): 261-75.

Waxman, Wayne. *Hume's Theory of Consciousness.* Cambridge: Cambridge UP, 1994.

Wright, John P. *The Sceptical Realism of David Hume.* Manchester: Manchester UP, 1983.

Wilson, Fred. *Hume's Defence of Causal Inference.* Toronto: U of Toronto P, 1997.

——. *The External World and Our Knowledge of It. Hume's Critical Realism, an Exposition and a Defence.* Toronto: U of Toronto P, 2008.

——. "Hume and the Role of Testimony in Knowledge." *Episteme* 7 (2010): 58-78.

Winkler, Kenneth. "Hume's Inductive Scepticism." In Margaret Atherton (ed), *The Empiricists.* Lanham, MD: Rowman & Littlefield, 1999. 183-212.

Hume's Index to the Enquiry

[Hume prepared an index for the first edition of ETSS, writing to Andrew Millar on 3 September, 1757 that it had "cost me more Trouble than I was aware of when I begun it." The entries that follow have been culled from that index. They represent all the entries that refer to pages 283-375 of the second volume of 1758, the pages over which *An Enquiry Concerning Human Understanding* was printed. In some cases, Hume's index contains entries that name subjects that come up over these pages, but that were not referred to them. Those entries have been included here in square brackets in order to give the reader a better sense, not just of what Hume decided to include, but also of what he chose to omit, whether deliberately or inadvertently. Beyond that, and decisions made to resolve the inevitable ambiguity arising from overlapping page numbers, no attempt has been made to supplement or correct Hume's index. Apart from one case where Hume's reference appears inconsistent (noted below), this version of Hume's index has not been collated with other editions. (Readers interested in variants to the index should consult **Beauchamp**, p. 271.) This Broadview edition of Hume's index preserves Hume's inconsistent use of small capitals and his neglect of inclusive page numbers or ornaments such as "ff." (Where inclusive page numbers appear it is because the pages of this Broadview edition overlap the 1758 pages Hume referenced.) No attempt has been made to render Hume's references more precise than they appear to be from 1758, though decisions have been made about where Hume intended a reference to start (or, more rarely, stop) and about whether he intended to refer to body or footnotes. Readers interested in consulting the complete 1758 index may find it in ECCO beginning with Gale Document CW3317720906.]

A

Abstraction, what, 203.
[Addison.]
Alexander the Impostor in Lucian, his Artifice, 155.
[Analogies.]
Animals, their Reason, 142, 143, &c.
ARISTOTLE quoted, 69.
Atheism, whether possible, 189.

B

BACON, quoted, 172
[Bayle.]
BELIEF, what, 88, 89, &c.
Berkeley, Dr. a real Sceptic, 202-03.
[Boccace.]

C

Cartes, Des, quoted, 117.
CAUSE and EFFECT its Idea, whence, 71, 72, &c. Its Definition, 114, 133.
Causation, a Reason of Association, 60-61, 92, 93, &c.
Chance, what, 98.
Christian Religion founded in Faith, not in Reason, 163, 164.
CICERO quoted, 96-97.
[Cold. See "Ice."]
[Congreve.]
CONJUNCTION frequent, constant, the only Circumstance from which we know Cause and Effect, 108, 112, 121-22, &c.
CONNEXION necessary, our Idea of it, 101, 102, &c.
Contiguity, a Reason of Association, 60-61, 90.
[CURTIS, Quintus.]
CUSTOM or Habit the Source of experimental reasoning, 85-86.
_____ The great Guide of Life, 86.

D

[Descartes. See "Cartes, Des."]

E

Elizabeth, Queen, whether her Resurrection could be proved, 171.
Energy, its Idea, 102, 103.
[Enthusiasm, defended and explained.]
[Epictetus.]
Epicurus, his Apology, 175, 176.
Evidence, natural and moral, of the same Kind, 129.
EXPERIENCE, Source of all our Reasoning with Regard to Fact, 72, &c.
_____ Why we reason from Experience, 76, 77, 126-27.
_____ Often the same with what we call reason, 95-96.

F

FACT, Matters of, one Object of Reason, 70, 71.
[Fontaine, la.]

G

[General Rules, their Influence.]

H

HOMER, Unity of his Fable, 67.

I

JANSENISTS,[1] their Genius, 167-70.
Ice, Reports of it not credible to an Indian, 150, 164-65.
Ideas, their Association, 60, 61, &c. 90.
_____ their Origin, 54, 55, &c.
Immortality of the Soul, on what founded, 180, 181, 182.
Impressions, what, 54-55.
Indian justly incredulous with Regard to Ice, 150, 164-65.
[Interest.]

L

LIBERTY and NECESSITY, a Dispute of Words, 120, 121.
LOCKE, Mr. quoted, 58, 100, 115-16, 117.
LUCIAN quoted, 155, 188.
LUCRETIUS, quoted, 170.

M

Malebranche, quoted, 117.
Mathematics, their Foundation, 203, their Advantages, 101.
Metaphysics, what, 47, 48, 49.
Milton, the Unity of his Fable, 67-68.
MIRACLES, on what their Evidence is founded, 146, 147, 148.
_____ defined, 150-51, one mentioned by De Retz, 158-59.
Molinists, their Genius, 168-69.

---

1 In keeping with convention at the time, Hume treated words beginning with "i" and "j" as having the same initial letter.

N

NECESSITY, its Definition, 102, 103, 134.
[Newton, Sir Isaac.]
Nisus, or strong Endeavor, not the Origin of the Idea of Power, 116.

O

[OVID.]

P

[Painters.]
Paris, L'Abbe de, his Miracles, 159-60, 166-69.
Pascal, quoted, 169-70.
Philosophy the two Kinds of it, the obvious and abstruse, 43-44.
POWER, what its Idea, 102, 114.
[Presence, real.]
Probability, what, 98, 147-48.
Proof, what, 98, 147-48.
Providence, particular, on what founded, 180-81.

R

RACINE, quoted, 170.
[Reason.]
Relations of Ideas, one Object of Reason, 70.
[Religion.]
Resemblance, a Source of Association, 60, 90-91.
RETZ, Cardinal de, quoted, 158-59.

S

SCEPTICISM, 70, 83-84, excessive, 189 &c. moderate, 189, with regard to the Senses, [190][2], with Regard to Reason, 194.
Sciences, their Division, 201-02.
Stoics, their Idea of Providence, 138.
SUETONIUS quoted, 166.
[Superstition.]

---

2   **1758** refers to "365," the last page of section 11. The page reference given above conforms to the reference given in the next edition of Hume's index, **1764**, to p. 169 (approximately corresponding to p. 367 of **1758**, p. 190 in this Broadview edition).

T

U

V

W

FINIS

LIST
of products used:

1,228 lb(s) of Rolland Enviro100 Print
100% post-consumer .

Generated by : www.cascades.com/calculator

Sources : Environmental Paper Network (EPN)
www.papercalculator.org

RESULTS
Based on the Cascades products you selected
compared to products in the industry made with
100% virgin fiber, your savings are:

 10 trees

 10,159 gal. US of water
110 days of water consumption

 1,284 lbs of waste
12 waste containers

 3,338 lbs CO2
6,330 miles driven

 16 MMBTU
79,174 60W light bulbs for one hour

 10 lbs NOx
**emissions of one truck during 14
days**

FAIRY TAIL

フェアリーテイル

24

HIRO MASHIMA

What's inside!

Chapter 197: Bye-Bye Fairy Tail

KABOOM

Let 'im be.

Natsu-san, you're going too far!

Stop !!

Is this magic ...?!!

Such destructive power!!

Kyaa!

...will face a challenge from a hero without any magic.

This way the villain with great magic powers...

6

Y TE ATH!!!

Hang in there!!!

Take him down!!!

Way to go, Prince!

Right!

If you're faking this, why don't you take your fall now?

You idiot!!

The audience is getting into it.

You bastard, he's our prince...

Prince!!

Nooo!!

KA!!

Don't wanna!!!!

This is a Fairy Tail send-off party done my way!

Lemme tell you the three rules for anybody who wants to leave Fairy Tail.

PLUT!!

9

WHAM

As long as you got the guild spirit, there ain't nothing you can't do!!

WOBBLE

You got it?

Amazing!!

Prince!!!

I'm in love! ♡

Our Prince won!!!

All right!!!

eeeeen

What is this...

What?! What's that?!

SHIMMER

The demons' bodies are...

It's started!

Guess we gotta act like it hurts.

SHIMMER

Your body... It's...

KEEEEEEN

!

SHUDDER SHUDDER

With the anima in reverse, all the magic is being pulled out of Edolas.

In other words, since we have magic inside of us, the Exceed and the dragon slayers together...

What?!

I suspect Her Majesty knows about it too.

...will be pulled into Earth-land.

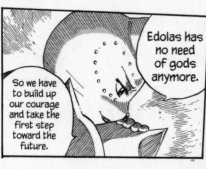

So we have to build up our courage and take the first step toward the future.

Edolas has no need of gods anymore.

It's all right... There's nothing to be afraid of.

My body...

Queen...!!

The anima is sucking us back!

You're...

Wh-What...?

Uwaah!

KEEEEEEN

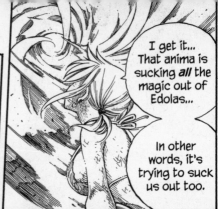

I get it... That anima is sucking *all* the magic out of Edolas...

In other words, it's trying to suck us out too.

So you're saying that all the magic is really being sucked out of our world...?

Every little bit...?

Don't look so glum!

Are you saying that without magic, you can't have a guild?

THUNK

CLENCH

It's the friends you got...

...that make a guild!

Night-walker!

No...

Take care...

WHFF

Scarlet!

...Erza.

Long live the Prince !!!!

Prince !!!!

The Prince saved us all!!!

The Demon King is being blown away!!!

Ohhh!

It's pulling *people* up with it...? I didn't expect that!

There's no need to adapt to change too quickly.

You can take your time.

Your highness...

Yes...

Even at a walking pace, people can still take that first step forward...

...as they tread down the road to their future.

And everybody from the other Fairy Tail!!!!

Bye-bye, Edo-Lucy!!!!

Bye-bye, Princess!

Waaaah!! Goodbye!!!

What are you saying?! You will never see them again!

See you later, everybody!!!

19

Pathetic. Now's no time to cry.

Then we all returned to Earth-land.

Farewell, Lily.

Farewell, Your Highness.

And
Natsu...
Gajeel...
Wendy...

*Farewell
to Fairy
Tail, my
family.*

I can't
say what
happened to
Edolas after
that...

WHOOSH

FAIRY TAIL
フェアリーテイル

Chapter 198: The Wings to Tomorrow

Everybody in both the guild and the town are just fine!

We've been doing a bit of flying.

We got to Earth-land a short time before you did, so...

They're fine!

It's still too early to celebrate! We have to make sure all the people are safe!

WHEE

わ WHEE い

WHEE

わ WHEE い

Earth-land is overflowing with magic! It's amazing!

I don't think anybody even knew they were turned into lacrima!

Why are all the Exceed in Earth-land?!!!

Why...

26

This is no laughing matter!

These creatures are dangerous! We have to send them back to Edolas!

Extalia has been destroyed. Why don't you let them stay?

Now, now...

No!

HUSH

We apologize for throwing those rocks!

But we've got no place to go back to!

We're going to change our ways!

We're sorry!

Please forgive us!

27

You people gave me an *order* to murder a dragon slayer and sent me to Earthland!!!

I don't care about that!!!

CLAMOR CLAMOR CLAMOR CLAMOR CLAMOR

Ah! Mister...

I won't let you forget about that!!

She's right!! The Queen went and stole our egg!!

We did mention that the Queen can see bits of the future, correct?

It happened six years ago.

I suppose we haven't explained that yet, have we?

28

In hindsight, it was caused naturally by the extraction of all the magic from Edolas...

...but at the time, we were convinced that the humans were the cause.

One day, Chagot foresaw that Extalia would crash to the ground.

SMASH

KABMBM...

...and devised a plan that would allow 100 children to escape from Edolas.

We knew who the victor would be if we went to war with the humans...

...so we held a conference.

We executed the plan in secret, hiding it even from the people of Extalia.

Did you say *escape* ?!!

Publicly, we said it was a plan to eliminate the threat of the monstrous, otherworldly dragon slayers.

QUEEN LOVE

And if the real reason got out, it would probably have caused a panic.

I see. You're saying that the excuse was necessary, right?

Of course we had no quarrel with the dragon slayers.

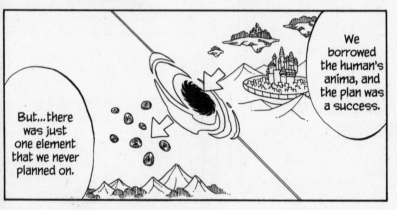

But...there was just one element that we never planned on.

We borrowed the human's anima, and the plan was a success.

What?

Like me, you have the power of foresight.

?!

That was your ability, Carla.

Of the hundred Exceed who were evacuated to Earth-land...

...Only you had that power.

However, for you it works subconsciously, which wreaked havoc with your memory.

You're kidding...

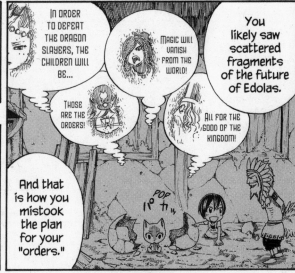

IN ORDER TO DEFEAT THE DRAGON SLAYERS, THE CHILDREN WILL BE...

MAGIC WILL VANISH FROM THE WORLD!

THOSE ARE THE ORDERS!

ALL FOR THE GOOD OF THE KINGDOM!

You likely saw scattered fragments of the future of Edolas.

POP

Were never ordered to do anything.

You mean we...

And that is how you mistook the plan for your "orders."

It was bad luck upon bad luck that caused you to create your own *fraudulent orders.*

It was a clumsy lie meant to build up the mystery surrounding the Queen. I have to apologize.

...so we made it sound as if we were manipulating you.

I'm so sorry!

We decided it was best if you didn't know of your power...

Ever since I came to Edolas, some geographical information has come to me little by little.

I don't know it either. Pieces of information just come up one after the next.

I don't know what's behind all this, but you've been a really big help, Carla.

There is a way to get close to the King.

So all of that was foresight?

No... I made all the families I took eggs from six years ago unhappy.

You were made to suffer through a combination of bad luck and my attempt to look powerful in front of our people and the humans.

It is my fault alone.

The Exceed are not to blame in this.

That is why I passed the sword to you.

CHATTER CHATTER

Hnn...

.....

We did a lot to delude ourselves too!

And now that we've finally made it to Earth-land, let's go find those children who came here six years ago!

That isn't true, Your Majesty!!

Everything you did as Queen, you did for us!

Ha ha!

They're sure forward-looking, huh?

It's a new beginning!

And let's try to make *friends* with the humans in the process this time!

Hey!!! I think we just got ourselves a new goal!!!

All right.

I'll accept it.

My people...

Let's see... Um...

H—hm, I wonder...

AHEM AHEM

Something's up!

But why do you and I have the same power?

Carla...

Move the same...?

Aye! Look... They move the same too...

Think so?

Don't you think that Carla and the Queen look kind of alike?

Huh?

Say, Mister...

You too, Gray.

Hey! You've picked up his habit, Natsu!

Yes, sir!

Anyway, I'm glad you all made it through this okay.

SHUM SHUM SHUM SHUM SHUM SHUM

Kaah!! What do you mean, "there?!"

See, right there!

TEE HEE

34

Yes...

For the present, we're thinking of living close to here.

Then we can see each other anytime!

What are you so happy about?

SHIVER SHIVER

Th-This guy is...

Mmm! Such a wonderful perfume!

But I must say, you are quite the beauty!

SNIFF SNIFF

HUG

We can see each other anytime, Carla!

Wait...

Warm...

But we can't stay silent about what happened to Mystogan.

Maybe... I mean nobody's even noticed what happened this time, right?

We have to report this to everybody!

Now let's get back to the guild!

SHUM SHUM SHUM

SHUM SHUM SHUM

SHUM SHUM SHUM

Every-body, your arms...

Where is Lily?

I haven't seen Panther Lily any-where!!!

Is there any *reason* to?!!

What's wrong, Gajeel...? You gonna pick up this habit too?

SHUM SHUM

W-Wait just a minute!

!!!

F+*O WHAM

I'm right here!

SPLASH

39

Not at present.

And...that doesn't bother you at all?

It seems my body type wasn't suited to Earth-land.

You've gotten a lot cuter!

HE'S TINY!!!!

And I assume you'll get me in just like you promised, Gajeel!

I desire to enter the guild that cared for my Prince!

?!

Then... on a different subject, I took this suspicious person into custody.

YANK

Of course I will!!!!

My cat!!!!

Whoa... He's crying.

YANKK

...call myself suspi- cious...

GASHAA

I wouldn't...

Hey...

Move!

GASHAK *PWING*

Kyaa!

SPLSH

41

...especially since I'm a member of Fairy Tail too...

Lisanna ...

Chapter 199: Lisanna

HIP FSSHHH

What?! You dissin' my cat, huh?!

I am Panther Lily!

Wait! You're Exceed?

And what's with this cat?!!

Hold it... She can't be...

Lisanna ...

Lisanna ?!

!

Someone from there ended up here?!

Wh-What do we do?

Could it be Edolas Lisanna?

Why...?

NATSU !!!!

It's Erza and Gray too! Long time no see!!

Wow, it's all coming back to me!

GNNF

HUG

Happy!!

It's me!! Lisanna!!

...the Earth-land Lisanna?!

Hold it... You...

'''can't be...

Wait, let me guess. Lucy and a young version of Wendy?

So are these girls new guild members?

...

Yeah.

YAAAY!!!

WHOOSH

You came back to life?!!

EHHH ?!

No way !!

WHA...?! !!!

GAGGH!

W-Wait!!

You should have been dead for two years!

ガッ GTCH!

Two years ago, I went out on a job with Mira and Elf.

Then I lost consciousness.

I...never died at all.

Back then there were a lot of small anima all over Earth-land.

I can only guess that I was sucked through the anima.

After I woke up on Edolas, I was surprised to find Fairy Tail there.

Ohh!

Lisanna has come back!

Lis-anna!

Everyone there mistook me for the Edolas Lisanna.

My guess is the Lisanna of Edolas...

A guild?

Everyone there seemed a little different than I expected, but there were a lot of familiar faces.

YAAAAAAAA!!

...might have been dead already.

I just got that impression from the mood of the guild.

Lisanna ...!!!

Don't ever leave us again...

No... Um...

After you fell from that height... we were so sure that you had...

WAAAAAH

Mira, Lisanna is alive!!!

So I pretended to be the Edolas Lisanna.

I'm home.

...

I wasn't able to tell them the truth.

...

I couldn't...

So you're saying what? That you're from another world called *Earth-land?*

So there's a Fairy Tail in that world too...

And in your world, Erza's an *ally?*

That'll do as a rough summation.

Aye.

And you've come to *this world* to try to rescue your friends?

SHHHHH!!!

Earth-land, Kardia Cathedral.

SHHHHHHH

Mirajane, think we should head back?

Just a bit longer...

Mira !!!

Elfman !!!

SPLASH

PLIP

PLIP

PLIP

It
can't
be...

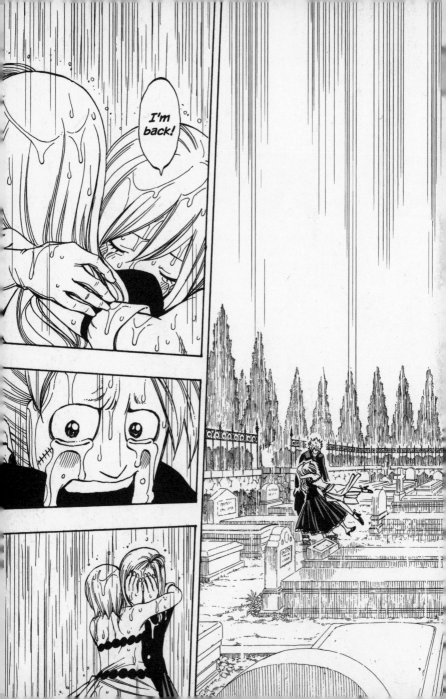

Welcome home!

What a...

...sorrowful sky that is.

I think she changed her hair style.

After all, I'm the ultimate fairy!

That isn't true.

The Raijin Tribe in the guild? That's rare!

Whoa!! Her too!!!

Rain?

GLOOOOM

Maybe it's her hair style.

What did you say?!!

In Edolas, it's Gray who's desperately in love with Juvia.

She isn't as lively as usual.

I wonder what happened to Juvia?

So *that's* it...?

Juvia wants to go to Edolas!!

KRAK キ

Oh, just say it!! I can't enjoy my liquor until you do!!

The "you" over there was... Pbt! Forget it. I can't say it without laughing.

Yeah, this guild is the absolute best!!!!

TMP TMP TMP TMP TMP!! TMP!!

Don't go on a rampage, Natsu!!

Aw, shut up!!

Was the Natsu over there like this guy?

If so, my deepest sympathies for them...

GYA HA HA HA

YEAH YEAH

CLAMOR CLAMOR

わい わい ぎゃ は は は

GYA HA HA HA

I wanna see that! I really wanna see that!!

Bwa ha ha ha ha!

And things like that!

He'd say, "L-Lucy keeps picking on me..."

Ah ha ha! About that...

He's really cute! ♡

And all of these members have some kind of magic within them...?

GULP

CLAMOR CLAMOR YEAH YEAH

It's fun!

Everyone has that first impression.

A... A *lively* guild, isn't it?

.....

CRASH BAMM KRATCH

But the magic isn't the important part.

It's the hearts of those who wield it.

Come to think of it, you were a part of Erza's group in Edolas, weren't you?

And you're together again.

Erza!!

Exactly. That is what Earth-land wizards are.

CHIN-SUKOU

You may be a different Erza...

...but it relaxes me to see such a familiar face.

Isn't that true, Lily?

Huh?

Let's have a big battle between my Lily and your blue and white cats!!!

Hey!!! Salamander!!!! Little girl!!!

Gee hee!

It's not so great...

That's a great idea!!!

Wah.

It looks like some dangerous guys have their eye on you.

Stop... I may not be much to look at now, but I commanded a division of wizards.

Meaningless battles only result in injury.

That's just pitiful... How can you give up so easily?

You think I've got a shot?!

Well when I say Happy is a cat, he's a cat, period! you jerk!!

Listen... I wouldn't last a second, you know...

Just to warn you, when I say my Lily is the strongest, he's the strongest, period!

71

KRAK

DONK WHUK

"KRAK

KAPLOT

WHAK

Goodness' sake.

He's doing fine.

...but we can only hope he's doing well in that Edolas place.

It's too bad about Mystogan...

So he's gotta be!

This guild raised him.

Gildarts ...

...are you going to be in town for a while?

Hmm... I don't know...

FWAF

Explain this pile of incident reports !!!

I refuse to accept this!!!!

74

All of these problems were caused by only *one* guild?!!

Fairy Tail!

They're a headache we inherited from the last group.

And technically, it's forbidden for any guild to go into battle with any other guild – even a dark guild!

It was set up independently by some regional guilds' alliance.

There is no record of the council approving that mission!

There's no need to be too harsh on them.

They're the ones who took down the Oración Seis of the Balam Alliance.

FLIP FLIP

But what I find disturbing is how some of them called Jellal a "friend!" They even said so in their reports!

That's a dangerous way to think!

No... I don't see that happening. They may call it an alliance, but it's really nothing more than a non-aggression pact.

And worse, this incident could cause reprisals from the Balam Alliance against official guilds!

.....

...we have to correct the problem guilds with strict punishment!

Chairman...

We have to regain the trust the old council squandered!

We'll have to show the people just what's *new* about us!!!!

We are the council reformed anew!!!!

BAM

This is it for Fairy Tail!

One more problem and the guild is disbanded!!!

GRAN DOMA
NEW CHAIRMAN OF THE MAGIC COUNCIL

I guess even Natsu gets lonely every so often.

He can be cute when he's sleeping.

MUMBLE MUMBLE

Ka...

Ka...

Hmm?

K...

KARYÛ NO TEKKEN!* ♥

* Fire Dragon's Iron Fist!

GYAH!!

FWHAK

Give up, Gray?! Mrbl

Ka ha ha ha!!!

WHACRASH

FYOOO

I knew it.

......

Haahhh
...

CHUP

GULP
GULP

You must not come near me.

RUSTLE

RUSTLE

GRAA

AHH-P

I am not your enemy.

Don't try it.

GRRRRRR

82

WHUD！！！

...tried to come close to me.

You shouldn't have...

WHUD！！！
WHUD

WHUD！！！
WHUD

But the world rejects me.

SHUM
SHUM

I never wanted to take anybody's life...

I'm sorry...

FAIRY TAIL

FAIRY TAIL

Name: **Lisanna**   Age: **17 yrs.**

Magic: **Takeover: Animal Soul**

Likes: **Animals (especially cats)**   Dislikes: **Studying**

Remarks

The younger sister of Mirajane and Elfman, and a childhood friend of Natsu's. She and Natsu together helped keep Happy's egg warm. Two years ago, everyone thought she had lost her life on a job, but actually she was transported and had to live in Edolas. Even though people like Lucy and Juvia entered the guild while Lisanna was gone, she knew versions of them in Edolas, so she was quick to adapt. Basically an upbeat person, she opened up to everyone in the guild soon after her return.

Chapter 201: Trial

Are you getting along with your father since you last saw him?

?!

No... Not really...

What's wrong? You seem a little down.

Do you normally take baths with other people?

Do you normally go to people's houses uninvited?

Hmmm...

Umm... I don't really know... I can't say we're not getting along... I mean, I haven't heard from him since.

AH!!!

SSSSH!

.....

What's up? If something's troubling you, you can tell me.

SIGH...

I'm thinking...

...about maybe quitting the guild.

Wha?

WHAAAAT ?!!!

91

HEE!

SQUIK
SQUIK

..... That's what she said, Mira-san!!!

And Cana wouldn't say why!!!

It'll soon be about half a year since I entered Fairy Tail.

Huh?!!

It's all right. She always says something like that around this time of year.

Sorry!! At this time of year, we work alone!!

Wait!! If you're going on a job, count me in...

Aye, Sir !!

Gotta get jobs done!! Gotta get jobs done!!!

But I never expected such a big event to come up at the year's end.

VOOOM

Mira!! I need a job for a **man**!!

Forget that!! I need another job!!!

Welcome back, Gray. Where are your clothes?

I'm back !!!!

Team Shadow Gear is disbanded for now!!!

Outta my way, you oaf!!

Who cares?!!

Hey, you jerk! I was here first!!

Rrrah !!!

I'll take this job!! This one!!

You'll find out soon enough!

What's going on?

94

Very soon, Wakaba will come in, and they're going to start talking about the young people of the guild.

GULP

For example, Macao is over there, right?

But let's see...

We sure set the place on fire, huh?

Now when we were young...

Sort of brings back memories.

That time of year has come around again, huh?

THUNK

Oh!

Yo, Macao!

GWA HA HA HA!!

L—legs...? I'd want 'em draped all over me!!! They can walk on me if they want!!!

Then what about legs?

I got kids of my own! Why would I look at those girls' butts?

What? Then you're a chest man?

You're talking about their butts?!!

But the young people today... They got great rear-end action going on!

That's amazing!! That's exactly what they're talking about!!

It's a pretty frightening conversation, but...

SHAKKA SHAKKA

BP BP

95

CLAMOR

CLAMOR

CLAMOR

CLAMOR

Nearly all the guild members are here.

Whoa... Look at all the people!

The next day...

Heh.

CROWD
CROWD
CROWD
CROWD

Natsu, calm down!

I hear there's a big announcement by the Master!

Doesn't interest me.

CHATTER
CHATTER

What's all the noise about?

Beats me.

Why don't you just go home!

Every time I see Gray-sama!

Juvia's heart pounds...

So we finally get to hear the secret.

98

Who's it going to be this year?!

Hurry up and make the announce-ment!

This is what we've been waiting for!!

Master!!!!

AHEM

In an ancient tradition of Fairy Tail....

I present...

And the location of this year's test...

Sirius Island!!!

OOOHHHHH!!!!!!

おお

Sacred ground for our guild.

There will be eight eligible wizards!!

I have spent this past year trying to discern each wizard's power, heart and soul...

After all, anybody who passes becomes an S-Class wizard!

The only thing the same is that it's always really hard.

It's different every year.

How do they do this test?

Huh?

Wow!! Everybody, go get 'em! ♡

I get it. Everybody wanted to make the eligibility cut, and that's why they were doing their best to stand out.

Ya-hooo!

Levy was chosen!

So was Gray's.

Natsu's name was finally called.

There's always next year, Alzack.

Aww... I missed it again this year!

This was the reason Cana wanted to quit the guild?

Come to think of it...

The test will take place in one week! Go make sure you are in top shape!

This time, only one will be allowed to pass the qualification test.

I've been hearing about how the guild sees you.

It's probably because not many people trust you, right?

Wh-Why wasn't my name in there...?

Even though Juvia is...

No, Mest, right?

Natsu and Gray are in there, too!

Fried is the favorite, right?

Just one?!!

104

Dammit!!!

Heh heh. Too soon for you!

Nobody suspects I'm a double agent. But you'd better worry about Laxus. Ivan's after his lacrima.

No, that can't be it!!! I can't tell you why, but that can't be it!!!

I heard it from Erza.

What was that? For just a moment...

N-Nothing...

What is it, Carla?

WHOM

WHOM

WHOM

I didn't know at the time, but...

Who...?!!

And I'd find myself taking part.

...this event would take an unexpected turn.

FAIRY TAIL

Name: Panther Lily   **Age:** ? yrs.

Magic: Aera & Battle Mode Shift

Likes: Kiwi Fruit   **Dislikes:** Thunder

Remarks

Born in Extalia on the other world, Edolas, he belongs to the same race as Happy, the Exceed. He was born larger than most Exceed, and it could be that difference that made him more interested in the humans than any of his fellow Exceed. One day, he found and saved the life of a human child (Mystogan), but when he brought him home to Extalia, that act got Panther Lily banished from his home country. From then on, he lived in the human world raising Mystogan, and with his military skills, he became a division commander in the Royal Forces.

Now in the world of Earth-land, his body has become very small. He can revert to his original body for very short periods of time, but he also seems quite fond of his new body.

Chapter 202: Best Partner

It tests a wizard's bonds to his or her friends.

They've always had two-man teams in the test.

Part- ner ?!!

During the one-week-long preparation time, each of the eight chosen wizards...

...must pick a single *partner*.

First, your partner must be a Fairy Tail member.

Second, you may not partner with an S-Class wizard.

There are two rules when choosing a partner.

.....

I imagine any team with Erza on it would be the strongest ever.

In other words, it's against the rules to partner with Erza, Mirajane, or Gildarts, right?

WHAAA?!!

And this time too, Erza herself will be blocking your path.

We will explain the details of the test once we've arrived on Sirius Island.

So now you see how hard this test can be?!

Well... I hope they'd be willing to go easy on me when I get my chance...

S-So does that mean if we don't take down Erza or Mirajane we'll never become S-Class?

WHAAAA?!!

And I'll be one of your obstacles too.

You're *happy* about that?!!

You're going to be in the mix too, Gildarts?!!

You can't mean...

Wait a second...

Everybody who's ever gotten to be an S-Class wizard has walked this same road!

Cut the complaining!

110

I want each of the chosen wizards and their partners...

...all gathered together in Hargeon Port in one week!

That is all!!!!

Ngaah! The road to S-Class will be long and hard for a *man!*

It seems very hard.

The hurdles this year are especially high!

I didn't expect that! So this is the *first* test for everybody at this table?

I'm rooting for you all!

I'm fired up!!! I am gonna make S-Class this year for sure!!!!

Aye!

Well my partner is Happy, of course.

Come to think of it, has everybody decided on partners?

I see...

He's probably more revved up for this test than anybody.

You know, Natsu thinks that when he becomes a full-fledged wizard, he'll be able to see Igneel again.

Ehh?! Why?!

Um... Juvia would like to pull out of this test.

Give it your best, Natsu!!

What I said... Um...

...was that Juvia...

What was that?

MUMBLE MUMBLE

Well... I want... to partner... with.........-sama...

Juvia knew it!! Lucy wants to be Gray-sama's partner!!!!

No, I don't.

Huh?

Somebody really wants to be *your* partner!

Long time, no see...

... every-one.

Sorry. I've already got a partner.

Sorry, Lucy, but I have to call a halt to our contract while the test is going on.

It was a promise from last year.

Loke?!!

But do you still fit the rules as a member of the guild?

For a spirit, you really act on your own a lot!

But never fear. I passed through my gate using my own magic.

So it shouldn't impede your use of magic in the slightest.

I am still a Fairy Tail wizard.

And I'm going to make Gray an S-Class Wizard for the pride of the guild!

I'm counting on you!

Leave it to me!

Hot...

!

I look forward to a hot one-on-one with you!

Oh, and I want you to come at us with everything you got.

When did those two get so chummy?

115

Maybe I'll team up with Juvia!!

Earth-land to Juvia...

A hot one-on-one?!!!

Lisanna-san...

And the Juvia here seems to have a really cute side!

I... got along really well with the Juvia on Edolas.

Are you serious, Lisanna?!

Think so? I've noticed somebody staring daggers at you from over there.

Wait a minute, Lisanna!! If you do that, I won't have a partner!!!

But maybe this girl is after Gray-sama too, and...

MUMBLE MUMBLE

So it's decided, right?!

Just how warped can you get?!

I hear that Fried has already chosen Bickslow as his partner.

Ever-green...

STAAAARE

Huh?

And I'll be the one to help her get there!!!

That's just amazing!!! You could become an S-Class wizard!!

Levy was chosen!!

BAAANG

Daggers? It feels more like she's ready to turn me into stone!!

You're the one after her!!

You may *say* that, but you're just trying to get alone with Levy!!!

But my magic is much better suited to battle!!!

I'm way faster than you, after all!!

Don't be stupid!! Of course it's going to be me!!!

Wait!!

You're obviously going to pick me as your partner, right?!

SIGH

117

...then I'll give you a hand.

If you're serious about being an S-Class Wizard...

GONNNG!

It means that I get to bust up people who annoy me, right?

Gajeel!!

Ahh!!

Stop... Let me down!!

POP

What's the good of being that weak-willed before you even try?

I'm... small, and I'm not much use to any- body...

...so I think I'm going to lose pretty quickly.

I'll make you big!

SLUMP
SLUMP

Nobody wants to partner with me, so you've got nothing to worry about there.

I absolutely forbid you to take part, Wendy!

I've got a bad feeling about this... About this test thing...

I'm just a little worried.

What's wrong, Carla? You've been quiet all morning.

Ah...

Um...

You are...

Miss Priestess of the Sky.

I wouldn't say that.

I'm Mest.

I was a disciple of Mystogan.

Natsu & Happy →

What's wrong, Natsu?

Natsu! Dinner is ready!

It's finally come! My chance!

And I'm gonna be sure to be an S-Class Wizard!!!!

Hm?

So snow falls in Magnolia too, huh?

Pu-puuun!

Whoa! Snow!!

This will be my fifth time.

Mmm...

So this has something to do with why you were talking about quitting the guild?

After four failures, I've sort of become the also-ran wizard.

Wait a second...!! There's no reason to be so uptight about being an S-Class wizard...

If I don't become an S-Class Wizard this time, I'll leave the guild.

That's why I decided this is the last time.

I'm the only one who has ever failed four times.

What's wrong? It doesn't matter how many times you fail a test like that, right?

I have to...

...or I'll have no right to talk to him.

I **have** to become an S-Class Wizard!!!

...

I...

...

...

...

... And that's the story...

I've already decided.

If I don't make S-Class Wizard this time...

...I'm leaving the guild.

Then I'll be your partner, Cana!!!!

I'll make sure you never leave the guild!!!!

I'll see that you become an S-Class Wizard, Cana!!!!

Lucy...

With everyone tense for their own reasons...

...the day came for the Qualification Test for S-Class Wizards.

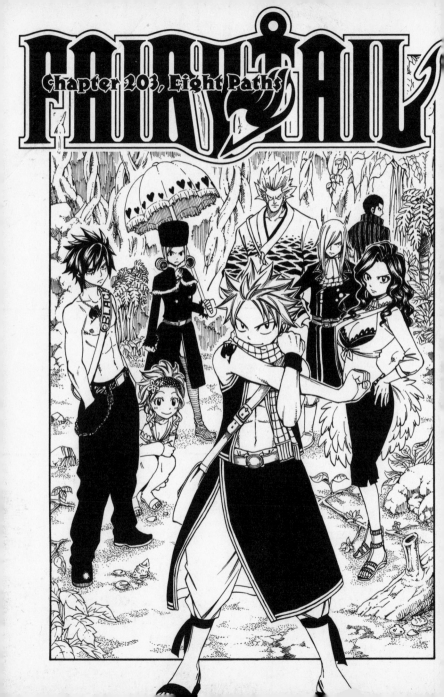

Chapter 203, Eight Paths

Wendy refuses to cast Troia on me...

BLEaaaGH

Gotta expect it. She's Mest's partner after all.

Natsu, keep your distance, okay?

URPS

WOBBLE

I'm gonna hurl...

I'm cooking!

Juvia would answer – Gray-sama's naked body!!

Ah!

So hot!

I don't like this! We're all about to be enemies, but here we're being so chummy!

FLAPPA FLAPPAS

*Loincloth: "Man"

Whoa!

Land ho!

oooo

Now I shall reveal the nature of the first test.

Well, it's hot!

What's with those clothes?!

A nude guy has no right to complain!

The *first* test?!

Pretty much every year, there are several different levels.

Your first order of business is to make your way there.

You see where that stream of smoke is rising from the shore?

Once you get there, there will be *eight paths*.

You will only be allowed one path per pair.

!!!

VEEEEN

And the paths will proceed like this.

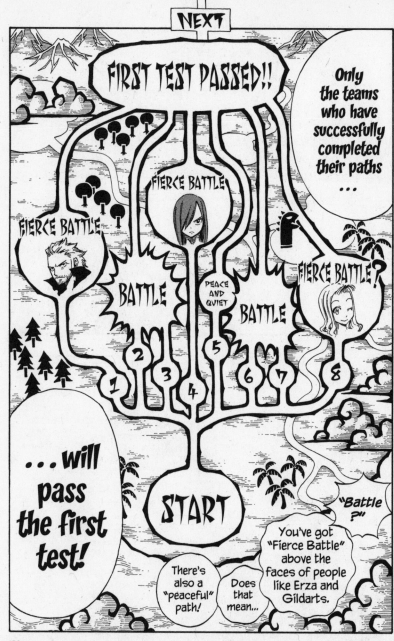

Gray and Loke Team

MANAGE

Natsu and Happy Team

Of the eight paths, the "Battle" routes are where two teams will bump into each other. Only one team can pass through to the end.

Elfman and Evergreen Team

Juvia and Lisanna Team

Where it says "Fierce Battle," you won't be able to advance unless you defeat an S-Class wizard. Those are the toughest routes.

Cana and Lucy Team

◎Fried and Bickslow Team

The "peace and quiet" path is one where there will be no battles. It's an automatic pass to the second test.

Mest and...

Levy and Gajeel Team

GONNNG

Did he just say... Luck?

VWAAN

The aims of the first test are fighting power and luck!!!

N-Not a chance!! I don't think anybody can get past Gildarts or Erza!!

So in theory, six teams could pass at most.

The chances of hitting the "peace and quiet" path are 8-to-1.

I think we can do the luck part!

The test starts now!!!!

Now begin!!!!

Sounds like fun!

And at worst, only three teams may pass...

Why didn't you just lock them up inside there for the length of the test?

Relax! It's due to come down after I get my five minute head start!

That wouldn't have been a test.

Fried !!!

You creep!!

GAM GAM GAM

HYAAH! DAMMIT !!!

I know!! Levy can...

But if you let him go like that, he'll set up Jutsu-shiki all over the island, right?

Well... It's not a race.

Hey, old man!! You gonna let him do that?!!

あおっ!! OHHH!!

KEEEEEN

Yep!

I can overwrite it!!

137

Now, let's go, Elfman !!!!

Ohhhh! Maaaan!

CAAW

CAAW

SPLAAAASH

Then Levy was able to overwrite that in only a minute...?!

Still four more minutes.

How many minutes left?

Dammit!!

It's come down!!

Five minutes later

EEEE!!!

If we don't hurry, we won't be able to choose a path!

SPLASH

SPLASH

DMP

I feel a whole lot of magic coming up from the ground on this island!

Yeah!

Yeah.

Thanks, Lucy.

Let's be sure to make you an S-Class wizard, okay, Cana?

And one thing I got is luck!

C-Route

Spirit-luminescent bugs. You usually see them in summer.

Bugs whose bodies glow.

It's a lot brighter than I'd expect.

!! DONG

Sign: Battle

闘

...Battle ?!!!

This can't be a...

Who's there ?!

!!

Hey, I hear voices!

RUMBLE

Then our *battle* is with you two?

I knew it!! It's Cana and costume girl...

That's *Lucy!!!*

The Raijin Tribe...

COULDN'T BEAT BICKSLOW WITHOUT LOKE.

What was that about the last being first?

COULDN'T LAY A FINGER ON FRIED.

Chapter 204: Who Is the Lucky One

Sorry, but you're done here, Cana.

That door!

They say that only the team that wins can pass through that door!

...will be me!

Because the one to follow after Laxus...

I'll take that challenge!!

I've got to become an S-Class wizard too!!

FWISH

So let's fight!!

"R"!

"R" is for my relentless service to Lucy-sama!

"Vi"!

Give me a "Vi"!

"Vi" is for my vigilance in cleaning the bath-room!

"GO"!

"Go" is for my goal of properly separated recyclables!

I kind of thought a girl would be best...

Why did you call that one?!!

YOU STINK!!!!

AHH!

!!

GYUUUM

THWAM!!!

BOOM

BAFF

BAM

You've got a lot to learn!!

Humph!

You think you can lure a man with *swim-wear?*

All you little girls are my enemies!! I'll bet you think smooth, tight skin is all there is in life, right?!!

Can't you tell the difference between friend and enemy?!

AHH...

Listen, you!! What was *that*?!!

Huh?

Wait... Cana...

You know, those two are kind of... alike.

What a classless, shallow...

Looking down your nose just because you have a boyfriend?

You're a zero! Zero as a woman!

Ah... That's probably why you can't keep a boyfriend!

You mean we did it?

Both Fried and Bickslow are down!

...Then... that means...?

Look!! The gate to the path has opened!!

159

But I owe a debt to those two.

If it had been any other team, I'd have gone full out.

I decided from the start to do this if it came to a battle with them.

That isn't what's important.

It's that Fairy Tail be Fairy Tail.

What about all that talk about inheriting Laxus' position?

Probably.

Don't you think you overdid that stupid "weak with women" concept?

... But the last thing I expected...

...was to go up against Lucy and Cana...

If it is, then Laxus will definitely come back.

...and that's when I get to be an S-Class Wizard!!!!

So I just go over there and take down Erza...

Somebody's here!

Who can it be?

Natsu!! The road opened into a clearing.

Oh!

FWOOOSH

CHANK

Afterword

あとがき

And it's the start of, "Let the S-Class Test Begin!!" Just when I couldn't come up with a good, exciting plot, my editor made a suggestion, and it turned into this "hot" new story! I had thought of doing an S-Class test story for a while, but I had always thought of it as a contest between Natsu and Gray. But since we're here, I thought it would be a lot more fun if we got the guild into the series. So it's turned into a story that includes a lot of the guild members. But at the same time, with the huge cast, it makes both drawing and story plotting a lot more difficult. Figuring out who gets put up against who and what's going to happen in the end... It isn't the hardest thing I've ever done, but it took me a long time to work the whole thing through. Now, you can see the chaos that is my thought process, on the inside covers of the book. I mean, everything is all messed up! (By the way, my initial plan for this story and the story you will read are going to be very different.) So in the next volume, you'll find out who that mysterious man who appeared in Chapter 200 was, but I'll bet it's impossible to predict. I know that since I haven't even placed a single hint of it in the book because I want it to be a complete surprise to the readers.

Lucy: They're always getting ripped to shreds, and later they're right back to normal, huh?

Mira: Those clothes are a special type that doesn't burn.

 : Wha?! Is that right?!!

Mira: Sure! They were made special for him by a Magnolia tailor.

Lucy: He could get a different design now and again.

: Face it. It's a pain to come up with things like that. For the author...

: You shouldn't be saying things like that...

How was Mystogan able to close the anima?

RUMBLE   RUMBLE

Mira: Before we try to answer that, first we have to reveal a bit of Mystogan's back story.

Lucy: His real name is Jellal. He's the Jellal from Edolas.

Mira: A long time ago, when Laxus said, "Another..." that's what he was talking about. "Another Jellal," was what he was about to say.

Lucy: How Laxus knew about it is a mystery though.

Mira: And six years ago, he came to Earth-land to close the anima.

Lucy: Anima are those holes in the sky, remember?

Mira: Right! Mystogan used those rods of his to close the holes in the sky. He'd go, "Unf!" and do it.

 : Really...? But Mystogan was originally from Edolas, so he doesn't have any magic inside him...

 : All of his magic came from those rods he always carried around with him.

Lucy: I wonder if everybody from there is doing okay...

Mira: They're fine! I'm sure they're all doing just great! After all, Mystogan is a member of the Fairy Tail guild!

: That's true, huh?

: Mira!

Mira: Lisanna!!

Lisanna: Lucy's here too!! We have to go!! The party's about to start!!

Lucy: Party?

Lisanna: The party celebrating my coming back to life!! Yaay!

Mira: You're right. Shall we go?

 : (Great! It looks like Mira's happy and not sighing anymore!)

EMERGENCY REQUEST!

EXPLAIN THE MYSTERIES OF FAIRY TAIL!

The lake behind the guild...

Mira: Sigh...

Lucy: What's wrong? What's with the sighs all of a sudden?

Mira: There were suddenly a lot of questions without anybody asking permission...

Lucy: But that means this corner is getting popular! That's a good thing, right?

Mira: It also means that there is a lot to complain about with this book.

 . Now, now. Let's not overthink it. Let's pick up our game and get to the first question.

> In the side story in Volume 19, Lucy said she had been in the guild for a year, but in the continuing story, it's only half a year. What is that about?

It's been exactly a year since you born as a Fairy Tail Wizard, right?

It is your birthday!

 : That question...comes up a lot.

Lucy: I guess it can be a little hard to follow.

Mira: The truth is the side stories take place a little while ahead of the main story.

 : But you know... About now the author will be having a few problems.

Mira: True. It seems that he thought the guild of a year from now would be pretty much the same as the guild is now.

Lucy: Yeah, the whole thing is beginning to look a little suspicious...

 : So I'll clear it all up right now. From now on, if there are any discrepancies between the side stories and the continuing story line, those side stories all become **LUCY'S DREAM,** and we'll leave it at that.

 : You're going to actually use the old, "It was all a dream" cliché?!!

Mira: Next question.

> Just how many sets of the same clothes does Natsu have?

Continued on the right-hand page.

TAIL d'ART

The Fairy Tail Guild d'Art is looking for illustrations! Please send in your art on a post card or at post-card size, and do it in black pen, okay? Those chosen to be published will get a signed mini poster! ♪ Make sure you write your real name and address on the back of your illustration!

Saitama Prefecture, Love ♡ PT

▲ Look at all those characters! Thanks for all the work!

Nagasaki Prefecture, Endō Mame

▲ It's Natsu and Lisanna, friends since childhood.

Kagawa Prefecture, Ōkawa

▲ What's this?! Someone who has been reading me ever since my debut work? Wait, that's good!

Nagano Prefecture, Yūki Itō

▲ Whoa!! Everybody's suddenly grown fangs!

Saitama Prefecture, Rina Maruyama

FAIRTAIL

▲ A rather sad Carla. It's a good thing that she made it back safely!

Hiroshima Prefecture, Rinatsu

▲ Now this is amazing!! I'm sure it was a hard thing to draw!! Good job!!

Gunma Prefecture, Mai Shimizu

▲ For some reason Coco is immensely popular. Will she show up again sometime?

Oita Prefecture, Black-and-White Bunny

▲ Oh, hey! That's good! This person draws Carla better than I do!

FAIRY GUILD

Gifu Prefecture, Rina Kato

Shizuoka Prefecture, Baboon

Miyagi Prefecture, Tomota

Shizuoka Prefecture, Sixth-Grade Clover

▲ There are a lot of Wendy postcards!! Thanks!!

▲ A sexy Erza. She's putting in her work helping to oversee the test!

▲ This one's kind of cool! This Natsu!

私は、FAIRY TAILが好きです。応援しているので連載がんばって下さい。

▲ Lisanna's popularity is on the rise too! Celebrate! She's come back to life!

REJECTION CORNER

ボツ

唐揚げにしようあいしてる

Hokkaido, Kentaro Fujitani

▲ And there it is... Yeah, I thought something like this could come. This guy. And a whole lot of him...

▲ The best combination!! These guys are tough!

Saitama Prefecture, G-Oen

最強コンビ

Shizuoka Prefecture, OSK

▲ So what's going to happen between these two?

Mest's real identity, ~~Grimoire Tartaros,~~ guild man, ~~Council Member~~

Mysterious Man → | Tôma | Mafuyu |
| Inberu | Fuyuki |

Death Magic

Think of a name

He appears before Natsu.

Cana's person.
Reason for going off alone?

Lucy → Searches for Cana

Gray → Goes on to Second Test.
(His promise with Loke)

The Highest Level Battle!!!!

Makarov ~~Tora moriko~~

The Island's Secret
↓
A secret that Fairy Tail must not reveal
about Fairy Tail's past.

( )

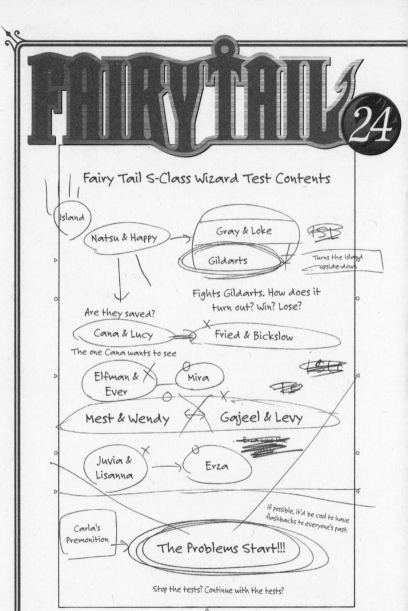

FROM HIRO MASHIMA

I've got too much to do lately.
But it's all things I can't tell you
about yet!
I had to think about *that*.
I had to get to work drawing *that*.
I had to check *that* thoroughly.
I had to…
I had to…
You get the picture.
I just have too much to do that isn't
connected with putting out my
weekly installments in *Magazine*!
My head is in chaos!
I want you all to know about it now!

Original Jacket Design: Hisao Ogawa

Translation Notes:

Japanese is a tricky language for most Westerners, and translation is often more art than science. For your edification and reading pleasure, here are notes on some of the places where we could have gone in a different direction with our translation of the work, or where a Japanese cultural reference is used.

Page 37, Blue
In Japanese, the word for "blue," *ao*, covers a range of colors from pale green to deep blue. So when someone is "green," (as in inexperienced), they use the term, *ao*, instead of "green." Unfortunately the pun doesn't work well in English considering Happy's deep blue coloring, so I left the sentence as a literal translation.

Page 101, Sirius Island
The Japanese name for this island is Tenrō-jima ("Heaven Wolf Island,") but Tenrō is also the name for the Dog Star of the heavens, Sirius.

Page 144, The last shall be first

In the original, this was a common Japanese phrase, *"Nokorimono ni wa fuku ga aru,"* meaning that those who are left behind have special providence.

Seven X-marks.

So we *were* the last here after all.

It's all right!! As they say, "The last shall be first!"

Page 145, Spirit-luminescent

The original Japanese was, *riekōmushi*, which, using different kanji, is the same Japanese word for bioluminescence. In bioluminescence, the first *kanji* is *rei* and means, "cold" (referring to a light source other than fire or incandescence). In the Fairy Tail world, the first *kanji* is also pronounced *rei*, but it means "ghost" or "spirit."

Spirit-luminescent bugs. You usually see them in summer.

Bugs whose bodies glow.

It's a lot brighter than I'd expect.

Page 153, "Vi" is for vigilant cleaning

The Japanese version was pretty much the same, only it used the Japanese syllabery rather than the alphabet. So Virgo, which is spelled *Barugo* in Japanese, used the same "Vi is for" pattern, but instead did it for "ba," "ru," and "go."

"Vi"!

Give me a "Vi"!

"Vi" is for my vigilance in cleaning the bathroom!

Preview of *Fairy Tail*, volume 25

We're pleased to present a preview from Fairy Tail Vol. 25,
due out in April 2013 from Kodansha Comics. Check out
our Web site (www.kodanshacomics.com) for more details!

D
Route

She's
strong
...!!!

Armor of
the Sea
King!

Has she
always
been...this
strong?

It protects
her completely
against your
attacks,
Juvia!

Well,
Juvia?

You'll
never be an
S-Class
wizard at
this rate.

KZWOOMP

Waahh!

Uhn...

Ouch...

A Route

WIGGLE WIGGLE

We're facing *her*.

So in the end...

...S-Class wizard !!!!

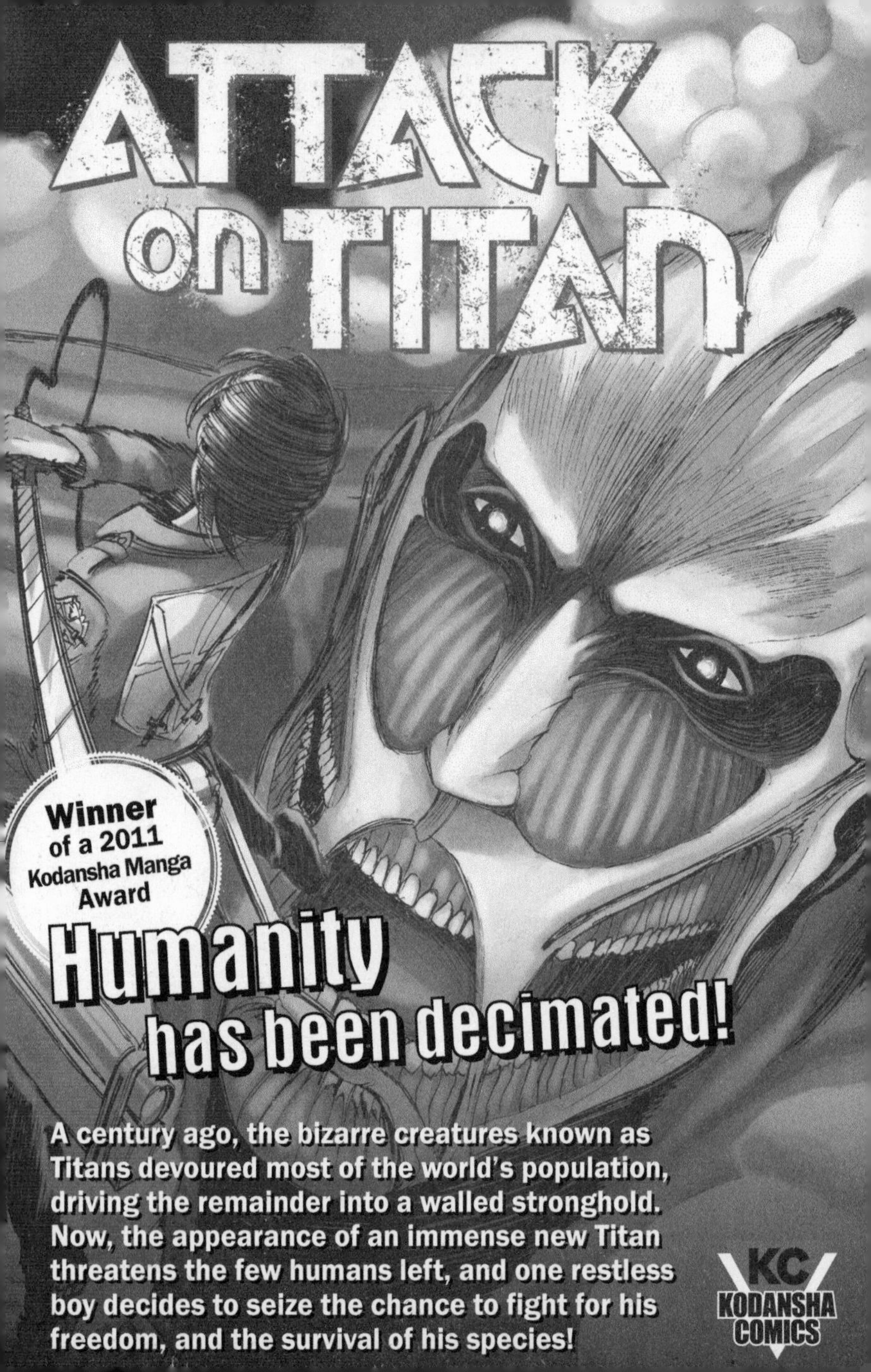
ATTACK on TITAN
Winner of a 2011 Kodansha Manga Award
Humanity has been decimated!
A century ago, the bizarre creatures known as Titans devoured most of the world's population, driving the remainder into a walled stronghold. Now, the appearance of an immense new Titan threatens the few humans left, and one restless boy decides to seize the chance to fight for his freedom, and the survival of his species!
KC KODANSHA COMICS

The Editor

MICHAEL PATRICK GILLESPIE is Louise Edna Goeden Professor of English at Marquette University. He is the author of *Oscar Wilde and the Poetics of Ambiguity*, *The Aesthetics of Chaos: Nonlinear Thinking and Contemporary Literary Criticism*, *Inverted Volumes Improperly Arranged: James Joyce and His Trieste Library*, *Reading the Book of Himself: Narrative Strategies in the Works of James Joyce*, and *Reading William Kennedy*, among others. His edited works include *James Joyce and The Fabrication of an Irish Identity* and *Joyce through the Ages: A Nonlinear View*.

W. W. NORTON & COMPANY, INC.
Also Publishes

THE NORTON ANTHOLOGY OF AFRICAN AMERICAN LITERATURE
edited by Henry Louis Gates Jr. and Nellie Y. McKay et al.

THE NORTON ANTHOLOGY OF AMERICAN LITERATURE
edited by Nina Baym et al.

THE NORTON ANTHOLOGY OF ENGLISH LITERATURE
edited by M. H. Abrams and Stephen Greenblatt et al.

THE NORTON ANTHOLOGY OF LITERATURE BY WOMEN
edited by Sandra M. Gilbert and Susan Gubar

THE NORTON ANTHOLOGY OF MODERN AND CONTEMPORARY POETRY
edited by Jahan Ramazani, Richard Ellmann, and Robert O'Clair

THE NORTON ANTHOLOGY OF POETRY
edited by Margaret Ferguson, Mary Jo Salter, and Jon Stallworthy

THE NORTON ANTHOLOGY OF SHORT FICTION
edited by R. V. Cassill and Richard Bausch

THE NORTON ANTHOLOGY OF THEORY AND CRITICISM
erdited by Vincent B. Leitch et al.

THE NORTON ANTHOLOGY OF WORLD LITERATURE
edited by Sarah Lawall et al.

THE NORTON FACSIMILE OF THE FIRST FOLIO OF SHAKESPEARE
prepared by Charlton Hinman

THE NORTON INTRODUCTION TO LITERATURE
edited by Jerome Beaty, Alison Booth, J. Paul Hunter, and Kelly J. Mays

THE NORTON INTRODUCTION TO THE SHORT NOVEL
edited by Jerome Beaty

THE NORTON READER
edited by Linda H. Peterson and John C. Brereton

THE NORTON SAMPLER
edited by Thomas Cooley

THE NORTON SHAKESPEARE, BASED ON THE OXFORD EDITION
edited by Stephen Greenblatt et al.

ENGLISH RENAISSANCE DRAMA
*edited by David Bevington, Lars Engle, Katharine Eisaman Maus,
and Eric Rasmussen*

For a complete list of Norton Critical Editions, visit
www.wwnorton.com/college/english/nce

A NORTON CRITICAL EDITION

Oscar Wilde

THE IMPORTANCE OF BEING EARNEST

AUTHORITATIVE TEXT
BACKGROUNDS
CRITICISM

Edited by

MICHAEL PATRICK GILLESPIE

MARQUETTE UNIVERSITY

W. W. NORTON & COMPANY

New York • London

W. W. Norton & Company has been independent since its founding in 1923, when William Warder Norton and Mary D. Herter Norton first published lectures delivered at the People's Institute, the adult education division of New York City's Cooper Union. The Nortons soon expanded their program beyond the Institute, publishing books by celebrated academics from America and abroad. By mid-century, the two major pillars of Norton's publishing program— trade books and college texts—were firmly established. In the 1950s, the Norton family transferred control of the company to its employees, and today—with a staff of four hundred and a comparable number of trade, college, and professional titles published each year—W. W. Norton & Company stands as the largest and oldest publishing house owned wholly by its employees.

Every effort has been made to contact the copyright holders of each of the selections in this volume. Rights holders of any selections not credited should contact W. W. Norton & Company, Inc., for a correction to be made in the next printing of our work.

The text of this book is composed in Fairfield Medium
with the display set in Bernhard Modern.
Composition by PennSet, Inc.
Manufacturing by the Maple-Vail Book Group, Binghamton.
Production manager: Benjamin Reynolds.

Library of Congress Cataloging-in-Publication Data
Wilde, Oscar, 1854–1900.
    The importance of being Earnest : authoritative text, backgrounds, criticism / Oscar Wilde ; edited by Michael Patrick Gillespie.
        p. cm. — (A Norton critical edition)
    Includes bibliographical references.

ISBN 0-393-92753-9 (pbk.)

    1. Identity (Psychology)—Drama. 2. Wilde, Oscar, 1854–1900. Importance of being Earnest. 3. Foundlings—Drama. 4. England—Drama. I. Gillespie, Michael Patrick. II. Title. III. Series.

PR5818.I4 2005
822'.8—dc22

2005052741

W. W. Norton & Company, Inc., 500 Fifth Avenue, New York, NY 10110-0017
www.wwnorton.com

W. W. Norton & Company Ltd., Castle House,
75/76 Wells Street, London W1T 3QT

3   4   5   6   7   8   9   0

This book is dedicated to the memory of Chavalah Madeline Pilmaier, a precious child to all who knew and loved her.

Contents

Preface

Oscar Fingal O'Flahertie Wills Wilde was born in Dublin in 1854 (though later in life he would claim 1856 as the year of his birth). He attended the exclusive Portora Royal School in Enniskillen (as did Samuel Beckett half a century later), and in 1874, after three years at Trinity College, Dublin, he received a scholarship to Magdalen College, Oxford. While there, Wilde distinguished himself academically, earning a rare double first in his final exams; artistically, winning the Newdigate Prize for his poem *Ravenna*; and socially, becoming notorious around the campus for his "art for art's sake" credo.

After leaving Oxford in 1878, Wilde quickly established himself in London, first as a personality and gradually as an author. Early in the 1880s, Wilde's charm and wit made him a favorite at dinner parties, and his friendships with notables such as Lillie Langtry and James A. McNeill Whistler and his association with people caricatured in *Punch* and the Gilbert and Sullivan operetta *Patience* provided broader notoriety. By the end of the decade, he had become a man with a growing reputation as a successful lecturer in America and England, as the editor of *Woman's World*, and as an engaging author of fairy tales, short stories, and critical essays.

Wilde's greatest creative period was from 1890 to 1895. His two best known works, *The Picture of Dorian Gray* (1890–91) and *The Importance of Being Earnest* (1895), bracketed a number of commercially and critically successful West End plays—*Lady Windermere's Fan* (1893), *A Woman of No Importance* (1893), and *An Ideal Husband* (1895)—as well as a stylized drama—*Salomé* (1892)—written in French. Wilde's writings were in demand, and his popularity was at its zenith. When Wilde's last play, *The Importance of Being Earnest*, opened on Valentine's Day 1895 at the St. James's Theatre in London's West End, it achieved immediate critical and popular acclaim. However, within a short time, events in Wilde's personal life produced a radical change in his professional career.

Early in 1895 Wilde brought an unsuccessful libel suit against the Marquess of Queensberry, the father of Wilde's lover, Lord Alfred Douglas. After Queensberry's acquittal, Wilde was arrested for homosexual offenses reported during the course of Queensberry's

trial. Despite an initial mistrial, Wilde was eventually convicted and sentenced on May 25 to two years at hard labor. The consequent scandal led to a premature cancellation of the run of *Earnest*, Wilde's financial ruin, and the virtual disappearance of his writings from booksellers' stocks.

During his time in prison, Wilde wrote *De Profundis*, and upon his release he left England for the Continent. For the next three years, he lived a transient and often impoverished existence, mainly in France. During this time of financial strain, poor health, and social ostracism, Wilde's creative abilities were at a near standstill. Though he spoke of several creative projects, he actually wrote only *The Ballad of Reading Gaol*, brought out by Leonard Smithers in 1898. The next year Smithers published *The Importance of Being Earnest* in an edition for which Wilde corrected the proofs. For the most part, however, Wilde subsisted on the charity of friends. He died in Paris on December 30, 1900, and is buried in Père Lachaise Cemetery.

Despite the sad circumstances of Wilde's final years, the ebullient *Earnest* remains one of the most frequently performed works in contemporary repertory. This durability comes by and large from the range of interpretive possibilities that the play continues to sustain. Although characters, plotlines, and settings appear at first glance both familiar and predictable, many productions have highlighted subtle features of its structure. The 1993 West End revival of the play offered a memorable instance of this quality. Maggie Smith's portrayal of Lady Bracknell as a woman whose domineering manner only partially masks her *nouvelle venue* insecurities brought to the foreground the elements of the play that presented sophisticated critiques of the foibles of humanity, as relevant today as they were a century ago.

Despite this variability, some readers and views continue to pigeon-hole *Earnest* as simply a charming and whimsical farce. Certainly, the play's humorously effective use of highly improbable plot situations, exaggerated characters, and often slapstick elements evokes justifiable praise of its farcical qualities. Nonetheless, cataloging it in this fashion and looking no further into the intricacies of its structure overlooks its considerable insights on the human condition.

Gently but persistently, *The Importance of Being Earnest* takes up large issues of class, gender, sexuality, identity, and other topics that engage the interest of contemporary readers. Like any great work of art, despite the specificity of its context, the rich and often sardonic representations of human nature allow *Earnest* to transcend its setting, time period, and local features, and to create broad resonance with its readers' and viewers' experiences.

One sees this trait neatly illustrated in the opening exchange of the play, between a smug and self-satisfied young man, Algernon Moncrieff, and his worldly-wise servant Lane (see pp. 5–6). Their discussion runs from Algy's abilities as a pianist, to the amount of wine young men and their servants consume, to the state of married life. In every instance wit dominates, but a dark undercurrent gives deeper meaning to the dialogue.

The flippancy of Algernon and the languor of Lane combine to comment profoundly on the complacency of the financially secure and the callousness of those who must make their own way in the world. On the surface, both Algernon and Lane understand the game being played—the master and servant match wits with the implicit understanding that the master must always win the contest. However, the sophistication and cynicism of Lane's responses go well beyond Algernon's ability to articulate a picture of the world he inhabits, and the deft manner of the butler does more than deflect and then undercut the attempted witticisms of the young man. Without trumpeting a heavy-handed didactic message, Lane's responses call attention to a range of social issues and class restraints that condition ordinary life.

Such intricate exchanges animate every scene of *Earnest*, and they extend interpretive possibilities that ensure ongoing pleasures in viewing and reading. The complexity of Wilde's characters and the suppleness of his plots continue to emerge with every encounter with the play. The material assembled in this volume, especially the critical essays, aims to highlight the interpretive potential of the play from textual, biographical, cultural, and personal perspectives.

The structure of the edition is fairly straightforward. Although Wilde originally wrote the play in four acts, he cut it to three at the urging of George Alexander, who owned St. James's Theatre and who played the part of the original Jack Worthing. The text here is the three-act version first published by Smithers in 1899, with a few typographical errors silently corrected. Following the play are excised portions, originally from Acts II and III, which Wilde combined into Act II. The three-act form of *Earnest* now dominates productions and editions, and the juxtaposition of deleted scenes offers students the opportunity to judge whether this approach is the best representation of the play. Additional scholarly materials follow these texts to stimulate further discussions of Wilde's work.

"Backgrounds" consists of selections from prominent cultural commentators—Karl Beckson, Joseph Donohue, and Regenia Gagnier—who have written about Wilde and the 1890s. Their essays provide a context for the period from the perspective of contemporary literary critics. This approach does double duty: It not only gives students a grounding in the period, but it also provides

sources that will support classroom discussions centered on interpretations based upon cultural criticism.

"Criticism" is comprised of two parts. The first, "Reviews and Reactions," contains a selection of contemporary responses to the play. It features prominent reviewers—among them William Archer, George Bernard Shaw, and H. G. Wells—reacting to the play's premiere. Most are positive, though Shaw's well-known dissenting view gives a sense of how difficult it is to discern the complex narrative patterns of *Earnest* in a single viewing. The second part, "Essays in Criticism," samples a variety of approaches to interpreting the work. It is weighted toward analyses appearing over the last few decades, with diversity standing as the key feature of this collection. After E. H. Mikhail's discussion of the four-act version of the play, Eva Thienpont offers a convincing argument for using the three-act version as the standard text. Camille Paglia and Christopher Craft offer contrasting views of the sexual dynamics animating the play. The pieces by Peter Raby and myself highlight alternative, though in the end complementary, conceptions of the function of wit in *Earnest*. Richard Haslam addresses the implications of Wilde's Irish identity in the interpretive process. In making these selections, I sought to reflect the changes in critical theory that have accrued over the past few years and to use the companion essays to the text to make readers aware of the range of valid interpretive approaches that make Wilde's work accessible.

While I sincerely believe that these essays provide a solid basis for students to begin to grasp the complexities of *The Importance of Being Earnest*, I must emphasize that this volume marks the initiation of analysis rather than offering the final words on the topic. The energy and enthusiasm Wilde's play continues to generate comes from its ability to engage and surprise us with every reading or viewing. The words of Enobarbus, describing Cleopatra in Shakespeare's *Antony and Cleopatra*, prove equally applicable to Wilde's play: "Age cannot wither her, nor custom stale her infinite variety." It is the infinite variety of *The Importance of Being Earnest* that inspires continuing discussions and ever new interpretations.

A great many people have contributed to this project, and I realize that to a great extent whatever success it enjoys relates directly to their efforts. I wish particularly to thank Brian Baker, Carol Bemis, Joseph Donohue, Darcy Dupree, A. Nicholas Fargnoli, Paula Gillespie, Warwick Gould, Richard Haslam, Merlin Holland, Tim Machan, Russell Maylone and the Special Collections staff at Northwestern Library, Michael McKinney, Donald Mead, Valerie Murrenus, John Navarre, Ben Reynolds, Albert Rivero, David Rose, and Joan Sommers and the Inter-Library Loan staff at Marquette University.

The Text of
THE IMPORTANCE OF
BEING EARNEST
A Trivial Comedy
for Serious People

To
Robert Baldwin Ross
In Appreciation
In Affection

The Persons of the Play

JOHN WORTHING, J.P.,[1] of the Manor House, Woolton, Hertfordshire
ALGERNON MONCRIEFF, his friend
REV. CANON CHAUSBLE, D.D.,[2] Rector of Woolton
MERRIMAN, butler to Mr. Worthing
LANE, Mr. Moncrieff's manservant
LADY BRACKNELL
HON. GWENDOLEN FAIRFAX, her daughter
CECILY CARDEW, John Worthing's ward
MISS PRISM, her governess

The Scenes of the Play

Act I   *Algernon Moncrieff's Flat in Half-Moon Street, W.*
Act II   *The Garden at the Manor House, Woolton*
Act III   *Morning-Room at the Manor House, Woolton*

Time: The Present

First Act

Scene— Morning-room in ALGERNON's *flat in Half-Moon Street.*[1] *The room is luxuriously and artistically furnished. The sound of a piano is heard in the adjoining room.*

(LANE *is arranging afternoon tea on the table, and after the music has ceased,* ALGERNON *enters.*)

ALGERNON   Did you hear what I was playing, Lane?   *emotion vs. logic*
LANE   I didn't think it polite to listen, sir.
ALGERNON   I'm sorry for that, for your sake. I don't play accurately—anyone can play accurately—but I play with wonderful expression. As far as the piano is concerned, sentiment is my forte. I keep science for Life.   *plays w/ wonderful expression*
LANE   Yes, sir.
ALGERNON   And, speaking of the science of Life, have you got the cucumber sandwiches cut for Lady Bracknell?

---

1. Justice of the Peace.
2. Doctor of Divinity.
1. Located in the fashionable West End of London.

5

LANE   Yes, sir. (*Hands them on a salver.*[2])

ALGERNON   (*Inspects them, takes two, and sits down on the sofa.*) Oh! . . . by the way, Lane, I see from your book that on Thursday night, when Lord Shoreman and Mr. Worthing were dining with me, eight bottles of champagne are entered as having been consumed.

LANE   Yes, sir; eight bottles and a pint.

ALGERNON   Why is it that at a bachelor's establishment the servants invariably drink the champagne? I ask merely for information.

LANE   I attribute it to the superior quality of the wine, sir. I have often observed that in married households the champagne is rarely of a first-rate brand.

ALGERNON   Good heavens! Is marriage so demoralizing as that?

LANE   I believe it *is* a very pleasant state, sir. I have had very little experience of it myself up to the present. I have only been married once. That was in consequence of a misunderstanding between myself and a young person.   *Lane's been married once*

ALGERNON   (*Languidly.*) I don't know that I am much interested in your family life, Lane.

LANE   No, sir; it is not a very interesting subject. I never think of it myself.

ALGERNON   Very natural, I am sure. That will do, Lane, thank you.

LANE   Thank you, sir. (LANE *goes out.*)

ALGERNON   Lane's views on marriage seem somewhat lax. Really, if the lower orders[3] don't set us a good example, what on earth is the use of them? They seem, as a class, to have absolutely no sense of moral responsibility.

(*Enter* LANE.)

LANE   Mr. Ernest Worthing.

(*Enter* JACK.)

(LANE *goes out.*)

ALGERNON   How are you, my dear Ernest? What brings you up to town?

JACK   Oh, pleasure, pleasure! What else should bring one anywhere? Eating as usual, I see, Algy!

ALGERNON   (*Stiffly.*) I believe it is customary in good society to take some slight refreshment at five o'clock.[4] Where have you been since last Thursday?

JACK   (*Sitting down on the sofa.*) In the country.

ALGERNON   What on earth do you do there?

---

2. A small tray commonly used for serving refreshments or for presenting letters, visiting cards, or similar items.

3. A vague designation referring to anyone not included in the refined social circles in which Algernon travels.

4. Typically the time to take a light meal of tea and sandwiches or cakes.

JACK   (*Pulling off his gloves.*) When one is in town one amuses oneself. When one is in the country one amuses other people. It is excessively boring.

ALGERNON   And who are the people you amuse?

JACK   (*Airily.*) Oh, neighbours, neighbours.

ALGERNON   Got nice neighbours in your part of Shropshire?[5]

JACK   Perfectly horrid! Never speak to one of them.

ALGERNON   How immensely you must amuse them! (*Goes over and takes sandwich.*) By the way, Shropshire is your county, is it not?

JACK   Eh? Shropshire? Yes, of course. Hallo! Why all these cups? Why cucumber sandwiches? Why such reckless extravagance in one so young? Who is coming to tea?

ALGERNON   Oh! merely Aunt Augusta and Gwendolen.

JACK   How perfectly delightful!

ALGERNON   Yes, that is all very well; but I am afraid Aunt Augusta won't quite approve of your being here.

JACK   May I ask why?

ALGERNON   My dear fellow, the way you flirt with Gwendolen is perfectly disgraceful. It is almost as bad as the way Gwendolen flirts with you.

JACK   I am in love with Gwendolen. I have come up to town expressly to propose to her.

ALGERNON   I thought you had come up for pleasure? . . . I call that business.

JACK   How utterly unromantic you are!

ALGERNON   I really don't see anything romantic in proposing. It is very romantic to be in love. But there is nothing romantic about a definite proposal. Why, one may be accepted. One usually is, I believe. Then the excitement is all over. The very essence of romance is uncertainty. If ever I get married, I'll certainly try to forget the fact.

JACK   I have no doubt about that, dear Algy. The Divorce Court[6] was specially invented for people whose memories are so curiously constituted.

ALGERNON   Oh! there is no use speculating on that subject. Divorces are made in Heaven— (JACK *puts out his hand to take a sandwich.* ALGERNON *at once interferes.*) Please don't touch the cucumber sandwiches. They are ordered specially for Aunt Augusta. (*Takes one and eats it.*)

JACK   Well, you have been eating them all the time.

ALGERNON   That is quite a different matter. She is my aunt. (*Takes*

---

5. A county in England located in the west midlands.
6. Established in 1857, the Court for Divorce and Matrimonial Causes, based in London, heard pleas for divorce that had previously come before the church courts. At the time of the play, men could obtain divorce for adultery, but women had to prove cruelty or desertion in addition to their husband's adultery.

plate from below.) Have some bread and butter. The bread and butter is for Gwendolen. Gwendolen is devoted to bread and butter.

JACK   (*Advancing to table and helping himself.*) And very good bread and butter it is too.

ALGERNON   Well, my dear fellow, you need not eat as if you were going to eat it all. You behave as if you were married to her already. You are not married to her already, and I don't think you ever will be.

JACK   Why on earth do you say that?

ALGERNON   Well, in the first place, girls never marry the men they flirt with. Girls don't think it right.

JACK   Oh, that is nonsense!

ALGERNON   It isn't. It is a great truth. It accounts for the extraordinary number of bachelors that one sees all over the place. In the second place, I don't give my consent.

JACK   Your consent!

ALGERNON   My dear fellow, Gwendolen is my first cousin. And before I allow you to marry her, you will have to clear up the whole question of Cecily. (*Rings bell.*)

JACK   Cecily! What on earth do you mean? What do you mean, Algy, by Cecily! I don't know anyone of the name of Cecily.
(*Enter* LANE.)

ALGERNON   Bring me that cigarette case Mr. Worthing left in the smoking-room[7] the last time he dined here.

LANE   Yes, sir. (LANE *goes out.*)

JACK   Do you mean to say you have had my cigarette case all this time? I wish to goodness you had let me know. I have been writing frantic letters to Scotland Yard[8] about it. I was very nearly offering a large reward.

ALGERNON   Well, I wish you would offer one. I happen to be more than usually hard up.

JACK   There is no good offering a large reward now that the thing is found.
(*Enter* LANE *with the cigarette case on a salver.* ALGERNON *takes it at once.* LANE *goes out.*)

ALGERNON   I think that is rather mean of you, Ernest, I must say. (*Opens case and examines it.*) However, it makes no matter, for, now that I look at the inscription inside, I find that the thing isn't yours after all.

7. Because of the lingering aroma of tobacco smoke, rooms in houses, hotels, and clubs were often set apart as places for smoking.
8. This is a shorthand designation for the location of the Metropolitan (i.e., London) police headquarters and a synonym for the force. At the time of the play, Scotland Yard was located on a tiny street off Whitehall called New Scotland Yard; it occupied the entire street.

JACK   Of course it's mine. (*Moving to him.*) You have seen me with it a hundred times, and you have no right whatsoever to read what is written inside. It is a very ungentlemanly thing to read a private cigarette case.

ALGERNON   Oh! it is absurd to have a hard-and-fast rule about what one should read and what one shouldn't. More than half of modern culture depends on what one shouldn't read.

JACK   I am quite aware of the fact, and I don't propose to discuss modern culture. It isn't the sort of thing one should talk of in private. I simply want my cigarette case back.

ALGERNON   Yes; but this isn't your cigarette case. This cigarette case is a present from someone of the name of Cecily, and you said you didn't know anyone of that name.

JACK   Well, if you want to know, Cecily happens to be my aunt.

ALGERNON   Your aunt!

JACK   Yes. Charming old lady she is, too. Lives at Tunbridge Wells.[9] Just give it back to me, Algy.

ALGERNON   (*Retreating to back of sofa.*) But why does she call herself little Cecily if she is your aunt and lives at Tunbridge Wells? (*Reading.*) "From little Cecily with her fondest love."

JACK   (*Moving to sofa and kneeling upon it.*) My dear fellow, what on earth is there in that? Some aunts are tall, some aunts are not tall. That is a matter that surely an aunt may be allowed to decide for herself. You seem to think that every aunt should be exactly like your aunt! That is absurd! For Heaven's sake give me back my cigarette case. (*Follows* ALGERNON *round the room.*)

ALGERNON   Yes. But why does your aunt call you her uncle? "From little Cecily, with her fondest love to her dear Uncle Jack." There is no objection, I admit, to an aunt being a small aunt, but why an aunt, no matter what her size may be, should call her own nephew her uncle, I can't quite make out. Besides, your name isn't Jack at all; it is Ernest.

JACK   It isn't Ernest; it's Jack.

ALGERNON   You have always told me it was Ernest. I have introduced you to everyone as Ernest. You answer to the name of Ernest. You look as if your name was Ernest. You are the most earnest looking person I ever saw in my life. It is perfectly absurd your saying that your name isn't Ernest. It's on your cards. Here is one of them. (*Taking it from case.*) "Mr. Ernest Worthing, B. 4, The Albany." I'll keep this as a proof that your name is Ernest if ever you attempt to deny it to me, or to Gwendolen, or to anyone else. (*Puts the card in his pocket.*)

9. Located in the county of Kent, Tunbridge Wells is southeast of London.

JACK   Well, my name is Ernest in town and Jack in the country, and the cigarette case was given to me in the country.

ALGERNON   Yes, but that does not account for the fact that your small Aunt Cecily, who lives at Tunbridge Wells, calls you her dear uncle. Come, old boy, you had much better have the thing out at once.

JACK   My dear Algy, you talk exactly as if you were a dentist. It is very vulgar to talk like a dentist when one isn't a dentist. It produces a false impression.

ALGERNON   Well, that is exactly what dentists always do. Now, go on! Tell me the whole thing. I may mention that I have always suspected you of being a confirmed and secret Bunburyist; and I am quite sure of it now.

JACK   Bunburyist? What on earth do you mean by a Bunburyist?

ALGERNON   I'll reveal to you the meaning of that incomparable expression as soon as you are kind enough to inform me why you are Ernest in town and Jack in the country.

JACK   Well, produce my cigarette case first.

ALGERNON   Here it is. (*Hands cigarette case.*) Now produce your explanation, and pray make it improbable. (*Sits on sofa.*)

JACK   My dear fellow, there is nothing improbable about my explanation at all. In fact it's perfectly ordinary. Old Mr. Thomas Cardew, who adopted me when I was a little boy, made me in his will guardian to his grand-daughter, Miss Cecily Cardew. Cecily, who addresses me as her uncle from motives of respect that you could not possibly appreciate, lives at my place in the country under the charge of her admirable governess, Miss Prism.

ALGERNON   Where is that place in the country, by the way?

JACK   That is nothing to you, dear boy. You are not going to be invited. . . . I may tell you candidly that the place is not in Shropshire.

ALGERNON   I suspected that, my dear fellow! I have Bunburyed all over Shropshire on two separate occasions. Now, go on. Why are you Ernest in town and Jack in the country?

JACK   My dear Algy, I don't know whether you will be able to understand my real motives. You are hardly serious enough. When one is placed in the position of guardian, one has to adopt a very high moral tone on all subjects. It's one's duty to do so. And as a high moral tone can hardly be said to conduce very much to either one's health or one's happiness, in order to get up to town I have always pretended to have a younger brother of the name of Ernest, who lives in the Albany, and gets into the most dreadful scrapes. That, my dear Algy, is the whole truth pure and simple.

ALGERNON   The truth is rarely pure and never simple. Modern life would be very tedious if it were either, and modern literature a complete impossibility!

JACK That wouldn't be at all a bad thing.

ALGERNON Literary criticism is not your forte, my dear fellow. Don't try it. You should leave that to people who haven't been at a University. They do it so well in the daily papers. What you really are is a Bunburyist. I was quite right in saying you were a Bunburyist. You are one of the most advanced Bunburyists I know.

JACK What on earth do you mean?

ALGERNON You have invented a very useful younger brother called Ernest, in order that you may be able to come up to town as often as you like. I have invented an invaluable permanent invalid called Bunbury, in order that I may be able to go down into the country whenever I choose. Bunbury is perfectly invaluable. If it wasn't for Bunbury's extraordinary bad health, for instance, I wouldn't be able to dine with you at Willis's[1] to-night, for I have been really engaged to Aunt Augusta for more than a week.

JACK I haven't asked you to dine with me anywhere to-night.

ALGERNON I know. You are absurdly careless about sending out invitations. It is very foolish of you. Nothing annoys people so much as not receiving invitations.

JACK You had much better dine with your Aunt Augusta.

ALGERNON I haven't the smallest intention of doing anything of the kind. To begin with, I dined there on Monday, and once a week is quite enough to dine with one's own relations. In the second place, whenever I do dine there I am always treated as a member of the family, and sent down[2] with either no woman at all, or two. In the third place, I know perfectly well whom she will place me next to, to-night. She will place me next Mary Farquhar, who always flirts with her own husband across the dinner-table. That is not very pleasant. Indeed, it is not even decent . . . and that sort of thing is enormously on the increase. The amount of women in London who flirt with their own husbands is perfectly scandalous. It looks so bad. It is simply washing one's clean linen in public. Besides, now that I know you to be a confirmed Bunburyist I naturally want to talk to you about Bunburying. I want to tell you the rules.

JACK I'm not a Bunburyist at all. If Gwendolen accepts me, I am going to kill my brother, indeed I think I'll kill him in any case. Cecily is a little too much interested in him. It is rather a bore. So I am going to get rid of Ernest. And I strongly advise you to do the same with Mr. . . . with your invalid friend who has the absurd name.

---

1. A shortened form of Willis's Rooms, a fashionable London restaurant where one could see celebrities dining.
2. Processing formally to dinner.

ALGERNON   Nothing will induce me to part with Bunbury, and if you ever get married, which seems to me extremely problematic, you will be very glad to know Bunbury. A man who marries without knowing Bunbury has a very tedious time of it.

JACK   That is nonsense. If I marry a charming girl like Gwendolen, and she is the only girl I ever saw in my life that I would marry, I certainly won't want to know Bunbury.

ALGERNON   Then your wife will. You don't seem to realize, that in married life three is company and two is none.

JACK   (*Sententiously.*) That, my dear young friend, is the theory that the corrupt French Drama has been propounding for the last fifty years.

ALGERNON   Yes; and that the happy English home has proved in half the time.

JACK   For heaven's sake, don't try to be cynical. It's perfectly easy to be cynical.

ALGERNON   My dear fellow, it isn't easy to be anything now-a-days. There's such a lot of beastly competition about. (*The sound of an electric bell is heard.*) Ah! that must be Aunt Augusta. Only relatives, or creditors, ever ring in that Wagnerian[3] manner. Now, if I get her out of the way for ten minutes, so that you can have an opportunity for proposing to Gwendolen, may I dine with you to-night at Willis's?

JACK   I suppose so, if you want to.

ALGERNON   Yes, but you must be serious about it. I hate people who are not serious about meals. It is so shallow of them.

(*Enter* LANE.)

LANE   Lady Bracknell and Miss Fairfax.

(ALGERNON *goes forward to meet them. Enter* LADY BRACKNELL *and* GWENDOLEN.)

LADY BRACKNELL   Good afternoon, dear Algernon, I hope you are behaving very well.

ALGERNON   I'm feeling very well, Aunt Augusta.

LADY BRACKNELL   That's not quite the same thing. In fact the two things rarely go together. (*Sees* JACK *and bows to him with icy coldness.*)

ALGERNON   (*To* GWENDOLEN.) Dear me, you are smart!

GWENDOLEN   I am always smart! Aren't I, Mr. Worthing?

JACK   You're quite perfect, Miss Fairfax.

GWENDOLEN   Oh! I hope I am not that. It would leave no room for developments, and I intend to develop in many directions.

(GWENDOLEN *and* JACK *sit down together in the corner.*)

3. Relating to the German operatic composer Richard Wagner (1813–1883), his music, and his theories of musical and dramatic composition. Wagner's music had a reputation for being bombastic and overblown.

LADY BRACKNELL   I'm sorry if we are a little late, Algernon, but I
  was obliged to call on dear Lady Harbury. I hadn't been there
  since her poor husband's death. I never saw a woman so altered;
  she looks quite twenty years younger. And now I'll have a cup of
  tea, and one of those nice cucumber sandwiches you promised
  me.

ALGERNON   Certainly, Aunt Augusta. (*Goes over to tea-table.*)

LADY BRACKNELL   Won't you come and sit here, Gwendolen?

GWENDOLEN   Thanks, mamma, I'm quite comfortable where I am.

ALGERNON   (*Picking up empty plate in horror.*) Good heavens!
  Lane! Why are there no cucumber sandwiches? I ordered them
  specially.

LANE   (*Gravely.*) There were no cucumbers in the market this
  morning, sir. I went down twice.

ALGERNON   No cucumbers!

LANE   No, sir. Not even for ready money.[4]

ALGERNON   That will do, Lane, thank you.

LANE   Thank you, sir. (*Goes out.*)

ALGERNON   I am greatly distressed, Aunt Augusta, about there being no cucumbers, not even for ready money.

LADY BRACKNELL   It really makes no matter, Algernon. I had some
  crumpets[5] with Lady Harbury, who seems to me to be living entirely for pleasure now.

ALGERNON   I hear her hair has turned quite gold from grief.

LADY BRACKNELL   It certainly has changed its colour. From what
  cause I, of course, cannot say. (ALGERNON *crosses and hands tea.*)
  Thank you. I've quite a treat for you to-night, Algernon. I am going
  to send you down with Mary Farquhar. She is such a nice woman,
  and so attentive to her husband. It's delightful to watch them.

ALGERNON   I am afraid, Aunt Augusta, I shall have to give up the
  pleasure of dining with you to-night after all.

LADY BRACKNELL   (*Frowning.*) I hope not, Algernon. It would put
  my table completely out. Your uncle would have to dine upstairs.
  Fortunately he is accustomed to that.

ALGERNON   It is a great bore, and I need hardly say, a terrible disappointment to me, but the fact is I have just had a telegram to
  say that my poor friend Bunbury is very ill again. (*Exchanges
  glances with* JACK.) They seem to think I should be with him.

LADY BRACKNELL   It is very strange. This Mr. Bunbury seems to
  suffer from curiously bad health.

---

4. The term denotes cash available for immediate payment for anything bought. Lane sar-
   donically indicates that he would have gone so far as actually to pay for the cucumbers
   rather than acquire them through credit.
5. A soft, round cake made of flour, beaten egg, milk, and barm or baking powder, mixed
   into batter, and baked on a griddle, and usually eaten toasted with butter.

ALGERNON   Yes; poor Bunbury is a dreadful invalid.

LADY BRACKNELL   Well, I must say, Algernon, that I think it is high time that Mr. Bunbury made up his mind whether he was going to live or to die. This shilly-shallying with the question is absurd. Nor do I in any way approve of the modern sympathy with invalids. I consider it morbid. Illness of any kind is hardly a thing to be encouraged in others. Health is the primary duty of life. I am always telling that to your poor uncle, but he never seems to take much notice . . . as far as any improvement in his ailment goes. I should be much obliged if you would ask Mr. Bunbury, from me, to be kind enough not to have a relapse on Saturday, for I rely on you to arrange my music for me. It is my last reception, and one wants something that will encourage conversation, particularly at the end of the season when everyone has practically said whatever they had to say, which, in most cases, was probably not much.

ALGERNON   I'll speak to Bunbury, Aunt Augusta, if he is still conscious, and I think I can promise you he'll be all right by Saturday. Of course the music is a great difficulty. You see, if one plays good music, people don't listen, and if one plays bad music people don't talk. But I'll run over the programme I've drawn out, if you will kindly come into the next room for a moment.

LADY BRACKNELL   Thank you, Algernon. It is very thoughtful of you. (*Rising, and following* ALGERNON.) I'm sure the programme will be delightful, after a few expurgations. French songs I cannot possibly allow. People always seem to think that they are improper, and either look shocked, which is vulgar, or laugh, which is worse. But German sounds a thoroughly respectable language, and indeed, I believe is so. Gwendolen, you will accompany me.

GWENDOLEN   Certainly, mamma.

(LADY BRACKNELL *and* ALGERNON *go into the music-room,* GWENDOLEN *remains behind.*)

JACK   Charming day it has been, Miss Fairfax.

GWENDOLEN   Pray don't talk to me about the weather, Mr. Worthing. Whenever people talk to me about the weather, I always feel quite certain that they mean something else. And that makes me so nervous.

JACK   I do mean something else.

GWENDOLEN   I thought so. In fact, I am never wrong.

JACK   And I would like to be allowed to take advantage of Lady Bracknell's temporary absence . . .

GWENDOLEN   I would certainly advise you to do so. Mamma has a way of coming back suddenly into a room that I have often had to speak to her about.

JACK (*Nervously.*) Miss Fairfax, ever since I met you I have admired you more than any girl . . . I have ever met since . . . I met you.

GWENDOLEN Yes, I am quite well aware of the fact. And I often wish that in public, at any rate, you had been more demonstrative. For me you have always had an irresistible fascination. Even before I met you I was far from indifferent to you. (JACK *looks at her in amazement.*) We live, as I hope you know, Mr. Worthing, in an age of ideals. The fact is constantly mentioned in the more expensive monthly magazines, and has reached the provincial pulpits I am told: and my ideal has always been to love someone of the name of Ernest. There is something in that name that inspires absolute confidence. The moment Algernon first mentioned to me that he had a friend called Ernest, I knew I was destined to love you.

JACK You really love me, Gwendolen?

GWENDOLEN Passionately!

JACK Darling! You don't know how happy you've made me.

GWENDOLEN My own Ernest!

JACK But you don't really mean to say that you couldn't love me if my name wasn't Ernest?

GWENDOLEN But your name is Ernest.

JACK Yes, I know it is. But supposing it was something else? Do you mean to say you couldn't love me then?

GWENDOLEN (*Glibly.*) Ah! that is clearly a metaphysical speculation, and like most metaphysical speculations has very little reference at all to the actual facts of real life, as we know them.

JACK Personally, darling, to speak quite candidly, I don't much care about the name of Ernest . . . I don't think the name suits me at all.

GWENDOLEN It suits you perfectly. It is a divine name. It has a music of its own. It produces vibrations.

JACK Well, really, Gwendolen, I must say that I think there are lots of other much nicer names. I think Jack, for instance, a charming name.

GWENDOLEN Jack? . . . No, there is very little music in the name Jack, if any at all, indeed. It does not thrill. It produces absolutely no vibrations. . . . I have known several Jacks, and they all, without exception, were more than usually plain. Besides, Jack is a notorious domesticity for John! And I pity any woman who is married to a man called John. She would probably never be allowed to know the entrancing pleasure of a single moment's solitude. The only really safe name is Ernest.

JACK Gwendolen, I must get christened at once—I mean we must get married at once. There is no time to be lost.

GWENDOLEN   Married, Mr. Worthing?

JACK   (*Astounded.*) Well . . . surely. You know that I love you, and you led me to believe, Miss Fairfax, that you were not absolutely indifferent to me.

GWENDOLEN   I adore you. But you haven't proposed to me yet. Nothing has been said at all about marriage. The subject has not even been touched on.

JACK   Well . . . may I propose to you now?

GWENDOLEN   I think it would be an admirable opportunity. And to spare you any possible disappointment, Mr. Worthing, I think it only fair to tell you quite frankly before-hand that I am fully de-termined to accept you.

JACK   Gwendolen!

GWENDOLEN   Yes, Mr. Worthing, what have you got to say to me?

JACK   You know what I have got to say to you.

GWENDOLEN   Yes, but you don't say it.

JACK   Gwendolen, will you marry me? (*Goes on his knees.*)

GWENDOLEN   Of course I will, darling. How long you have been about it! I am afraid you have had very little experience in how to propose.   *Another weird marriage proposal*

JACK   My own one, I have never loved anyone in the world but you.

GWENDOLEN   Yes, but men often propose for practice. I know my brother Gerald does. All my girl-friends tell me so. What wonder-fully blue eyes you have, Ernest! They are quite, quite blue. I hope you will always look at me just like that, especially when there are other people present.

(*Enter* LADY BRACKNELL.)

LADY BRACKNELL   Mr. Worthing! Rise, sir, from this semi-recumbent posture. It is most indecorous.

GWENDOLEN   Mamma! (*He tries to rise; she restrains him.*) I must beg you to retire. This is no place for you. Besides, Mr. Worthing has not quite finished yet.

LADY BRACKNELL   Finished what, may I ask?

GWENDOLEN   I am engaged to Mr. Worthing, mamma. (*They rise together.*)

LADY BRACKNELL   Pardon me, you are not engaged to anyone. When you do become engaged to someone, I, or your father, should his health permit him, will inform you of the fact. An en-gagement should come on a young girl as a surprise, pleasant or unpleasant, as the case may be. It is hardly a matter that she could be allowed to arrange for herself. . . . And now I have a few questions to put to you, Mr. Worthing. While I am making these inquiries, you, Gwendolen, will wait for me below in the carriage.

GWENDOLEN   (*Reproachfully.*) Mamma!

LADY BRACKNELL   In the carriage, Gwendolen! (GWENDOLEN *goes to the door. She and* JACK *blow kisses to each other behind* LADY BRACKNELL's *back.* LADY BRACKNELL *looks vaguely about as if she could not understand what the noise was. Finally turns around.*) Gwendolen, the carriage!

GWENDOLEN   Yes, mamma. (*Goes out, looking back at* JACK.)

LADY BRACKNELL   (*Sitting down.*) You can take a seat, Mr. Worthing. (*Looks in her pocket for note-book and pencil.*)

JACK   Thank you, Lady Bracknell, I prefer standing.

LADY BRACKNELL   (*Pencil and note-book in hand.*) I feel bound to tell you that you are not down on my list of eligible young men, although I have the same list as the dear Duchess of Bolton has. We work together, in fact. However, I am quite ready to enter your name, should your answers be what a really affectionate mother requires. Do you smoke?

JACK   Well, yes, I must admit I smoke.

LADY BRACKNELL   I am glad to hear it. A man should always have an occupation of some kind. There are far too many idle men in London as it is. How old are you?

JACK   Twenty-nine.

LADY BRACKNELL   A very good age to be married at. I have always been of opinion that a man who desires to get married should know either everything or nothing. Which do you know?

JACK   (*After some hesitation.*) I know nothing, Lady Bracknell.

LADY BRACKNELL   I am pleased to hear it. I do not approve of anything that tampers with natural ignorance. Ignorance is like a delicate exotic fruit; touch it and the bloom is gone. The whole theory of modern education is radically unsound. Fortunately in England, at any rate, education produces no effect whatsoever. If it did, it would prove a serious danger to the upper classes, and probably lead to acts of violence in Grosvenor Square.[6] What is your income?

JACK   Between seven and eight thousand a year.[7]

LADY BRACKNELL   (*Makes a note in her book.*) In land, or in investments?

JACK   In investments, chiefly.

LADY BRACKNELL   That is satisfactory. What between the duties expected of one during one's lifetime, and the duties[8] exacted from one after one's death, land has ceased to be either a profit or a pleasure. It gives one position, and prevents one from keeping it up. That's all that can be said about land.

6. Located in the fashionable West End of London.
7. Using the Consumer Price Index as a basis for comparison, this would be about $750,000 in 2003 U.S. dollars.
8. Taxes imposed on the estate of the deceased.

JACK　I have a country house with some land, of course, attached to it, about fifteen hundred acres, I believe; but I don't depend on that for my real income. In fact, as far as I can make out, the poachers are the only people who make anything out of it.

LADY BRACKNELL　A country house! How many bedrooms? Well, that point can be cleared up afterwards. You have a town house, I hope? A girl with a simple, unspoiled nature, like Gwendolen, could hardly be expected to reside in the country.

JACK　Well, I own a house in Belgrave Square,[9] but it is let by the year to Lady Bloxham. Of course, I can get it back whenever I like, at six months' notice.

LADY BRACKNELL　Lady Bloxham? I don't know her.

JACK　Oh, she goes about very little. She is a lady considerably advanced in years.

LADY BRACKNELL　Ah, now-a-days that is no guarantee of respectability of character. What number in Belgrave Square?

JACK　149.

LADY BRACKNELL　(*Shaking her head.*) The unfashionable side. I thought there was something. However, that could easily be altered.

JACK　Do you mean the fashion, or the side?

LADY BRACKNELL　(*Sternly.*) Both, if necessary, I presume. What are your politics?

JACK　Well, I am afraid I really have none. I am a Liberal Unionist.[1]

LADY BRACKNELL　Oh, they count as Tories.[2] They dine with us. Or come in the evening,[3] at any rate. Now to minor matters. Are your parents living?

JACK　I have lost both my parents.

LADY BRACKNELL　Both? . . . To lose one parent, Mr. Worthing, may be regarded as a misfortune; to lose both looks like carelessness.[4] Who was your father? He was evidently a man of some wealth. Was he born in what the Radical papers call the purple of commerce, or did he rise from the ranks of the aristocracy?

JACK　I am afraid I really don't know. The fact is, Lady Bracknell, I said I had lost my parents. It would be nearer the truth to say

---

9. Located in the fashionable West End of London.

1. This name was given to any member of the party formed by those Liberals who refused to support Gladstone's measure of Irish Home Rule in 1886.

2. An alternative designation for the Conservative Party. As a formal name, "Tory" was superseded c. 1830 by conservative, but "Tory" is still retained colloquially today.

3. This is a subtle form of class distinction. They may not be suitable to have in for dinner, but they can provide amusing conversation afterwards.

4. "To lose . . . carelessness" is the sentence that Wilde originally wrote. In the 1899 edition, Wilde abbreviated this line to read as follows: "That seems like carelessness." This edition follows what has become common practice in deviating from the Smithers text to retain the wittier version.

that my parents seem to have lost me . . . I don't actually know who I am by birth. I was . . . well, I was found.

LADY BRACKNELL   Found!

JACK   The late Mr. Thomas Cardew, an old gentleman of a very charitable and kindly disposition, found me, and gave me the name of Worthing, because he happened to have a first-class ticket for Worthing[5] in his pocket at the time. Worthing is a place in Sussex.[6] It is a seaside resort.

LADY BRACKNELL   Where did the charitable gentleman who had a first-class ticket for this seaside resort find you?

JACK   (*Gravely.*) In a hand-bag.

LADY BRACKNELL   A hand-bag?

JACK   (*Very seriously.*) Yes, Lady Bracknell. I was in a hand-bag—a somewhat large, black leather hand-bag, with handles to it—an ordinary hand-bag in fact.

LADY BRACKNELL   In what locality did this Mr. James, or Thomas, Cardew come across this ordinary hand-bag?

JACK   In the cloak-room at Victoria Station.[7] It was given to him in mistake for his own.

LADY BRACKNELL   The cloak-room at Victoria Station?

JACK   Yes. The Brighton line.[8]

LADY BRACKNELL   The line is immaterial. Mr. Worthing, I confess I feel somewhat bewildered by what you have just told me. To be born, or at any rate bred, in a hand-bag, whether it had handles or not, seems to me to display a contempt for the ordinary decencies of family life that reminds one of the worst excesses of the French Revolution. And I presume you know what that unfortunate movement led to? As for the particular locality in which the hand-bag was found, a cloak-room at a railway station might serve to conceal a social indiscretion—has probably, indeed, been used for that purpose before now—but it could hardly be regarded as an assured basis for a recognized position in good society.

JACK   May I ask you then what you would advise me to do? I need hardly say I would do anything in the world to ensure Gwendolen's happiness.

---

5. From the eighteenth century, when it was made popular by George III, Worthing has been a favorite seaside resort for the royal, the rich, and the fashionable. Wilde spent the summer and autumn of 1894 there writing *The Importance of Being Earnest*.
6. A county located south of London.
7. One of London's largest railway stations, located southwest of Westminster Cathedral.
8. According to Peter Cunningham's *Hand-Book of London* from 1850, the Brighton Line was "[b]egun in 1837, projected by Sir John Rennie, executed by Mr. Rastrick, and opened 21st of September 1841. Its cost up to the 31st December 1844, has been 2,640,000*l.* out of which the law expenses have been nearly 200,000*l.* The first mile and a half runs side by side with the Greenwich Railway. For the next eight miles the Croydon Railway is used."

LADY BRACKNELL   I would strongly advise you, Mr. Worthing, to try and acquire some relations as soon as possible, and to make a definite effort to produce at any rate one parent, of either sex, before the season is quite over.

JACK   Well, I don't see how I could possibly manage to do that. I can produce the hand-bag at any moment. It is in my dressing-room at home. I really think that should satisfy you, Lady Bracknell.

LADY BRACKNELL   Me, sir! What has it to do with me? You can hardly imagine that I and Lord Bracknell would dream of allowing our only daughter—a girl brought up with the utmost care—to marry into a cloak-room, and form an alliance with a parcel? Good morning, Mr. Worthing!

(LADY BRACKNELL *sweeps out in majestic indignation.*)

JACK   Good morning! (ALGERNON, *from the other room, strikes up the Wedding March.* JACK *looks perfectly furious, and goes to the door.*) For goodness' sake don't play that ghastly tune, Algy. How idiotic you are!

(*The music stops and* ALGERNON *enters cheerily.*)

ALGERNON   Didn't it go off all right, old boy? You don't mean to say Gwendolen refused you? I know it is a way she has. She is always refusing people. I think it is most ill-natured of her.

JACK   Oh, Gwendolen is as right as a trivet. As far as she is concerned, we are engaged. Her mother is perfectly unbearable. Never met such a Gorgon[9] . . . I don't really know what a Gorgon is like, but I am quite sure that Lady Bracknell is one. In any case, she is a monster, without being a myth, which is rather unfair . . . I beg your pardon, Algy, I suppose I shouldn't talk about your own aunt in that way before you.

ALGERNON   My dear boy, I love hearing my relations abused. It is the only thing that makes me put up with them at all. Relations are simply a tedious pack of people, who haven't got the remotest knowledge of how to live, nor the smallest instinct about when to die.

JACK   Oh, that is nonsense!

ALGERNON   It isn't!

JACK   Well, I won't argue about the matter. You always want to argue about things.

ALGERNON   That is exactly what things were originally made for.

JACK   Upon my word, if I thought that, I'd shoot myself . . . (*A pause.*) You don't think there is any chance of Gwendolen be-

---

9. From Greek mythology any of three females, with snakes for hair, whose gaze turned the onlooker to stone. The best known, and the only mortal, Medusa, was slain by Perseus, and her head fixed on Athene's shield. The term has come to denote a very acerbic or ugly person.

coming like her mother in about a hundred and fifty years, do you, Algy?

ALGERNON   All women become like their mothers. That is their tragedy. No man does. That's his.

JACK   Is that clever?

ALGERNON   It is perfectly phrased! and quite as true as any observation in civilized life should be.

JACK   I am sick to death of cleverness. Everybody is clever now-a-days. You can't go anywhere without meeting clever people. The thing has become an absolute public nuisance. I wish to goodness we had a few fools left.

ALGERNON   We have.

JACK   I should extremely like to meet them. What do they talk about?

ALGERNON   The fools? Oh! about the clever people, of course.

JACK   What fools!

ALGERNON   By the way, did you tell Gwendolen the truth about your being Ernest in town, and Jack in the country?

JACK   (*In a very patronizing manner.*) My dear fellow, the truth isn't quite the sort of thing one tells to a nice sweet refined girl. What extraordinary ideas you have about the way to behave to a woman!

ALGERNON   The only way to behave to a woman is to make love to her, if she is pretty, and to someone else, if she is plain.   *Funny*

JACK   Oh, that is nonsense.

ALGERNON   What about your brother? What about the profligate Ernest?

JACK   Oh, before the end of the week I shall have got rid of him. I'll say he died in Paris of apoplexy.[1] Lots of people die of apoplexy, quite suddenly, don't they?

ALGERNON   Yes, but it's hereditary, my dear fellow. It's a sort of thing that runs in families. You had much better say a severe chill.

JACK   You are sure a severe chill isn't hereditary, or anything of that kind?

ALGERNON   Of course it isn't!

JACK   Very well, then. My poor brother Ernest is carried off suddenly in Paris, by a severe chill. That gets rid of him.

ALGERNON   But I thought you said that . . . Miss Cardew was a little too much interested in your poor brother Ernest? Won't she feel his loss a good deal?

JACK   Oh, that is all right. Cecily is not a silly romantic girl, I am

---

1. A sudden physical seizure that arrests more or less completely the powers of sense and motion; it is usually caused by an effusion of blood or serum in the brain and preceded by giddiness or partial loss of muscular power.

glad to say. She has got a capital appetite, goes on long walks, and pays no attention at all to her lessons.

ALGERNON   I would rather like to see Cecily.

JACK   I will take very good care you never do. She is excessively pretty, and she is only just eighteen.

ALGERNON   Have you told Gwendolen yet that you have an excessively pretty ward who is only just eighteen?

JACK   Oh! one doesn't blurt these things out to people. Cecily and Gwendolen are perfectly certain to be extremely great friends. I'll bet you anything you like that half an hour after they have met, they will be calling each other sister.

ALGERNON   Women only do that when they have called each other a lot of other things first. Now, my dear boy, if we want to get a good table at Willis's, we really must go and dress. Do you know it is nearly seven?

JACK   (*Irritably.*) Oh! It always is nearly seven.

ALGERNON   Well, I'm hungry.

JACK   I never knew you when you weren't. . . .

ALGERNON   What shall we do after dinner? Go to a theatre?

JACK   Oh no! I loathe listening.

ALGERNON   Well, let us go to the Club?

JACK   Oh, no! I hate talking.

ALGERNON   Well, we might trot round to the Empire[2] at ten?

JACK   Oh, no! I can't bear looking at things. It is so silly.

ALGERNON   Well, what shall we do?

JACK   Nothing!

ALGERNON   It is awfully hard work doing nothing. However, I don't mind hard work where there is no definite object of any kind.

(*Enter* LANE.)

LANE   Miss Fairfax.

(*Enter* GWENDOLEN. LANE *goes out.*)

ALGERNON   Gwendolen, upon my word!

GWENDOLEN   Algy, kindly turn your back. I have something very particular to say to Mr. Worthing.

ALGERNON   Really, Gwendolen, I don't think I can allow this at all.

GWENDOLEN   Algy, you always adopt a strictly immoral attitude towards life. You are not quite old enough to do that. (ALGERNON *retires to the fireplace.*)

JACK   My own darling!

GWENDOLEN   Ernest, we may never be married. From the expression on mamma's face I fear we never shall. Few parents now-a-days pay any regard to what their children say to them. The old-fashioned respect for the young is fast dying out. Whatever

2. Referring to the Holborn Empire, an amusement hall popular in London at this time.

Her mom destroys marriage

influence I ever had over mamma, I lost at the age of three. But although she may prevent us from becoming man and wife, and I may marry someone else, and marry often, nothing that she can possibly do can alter my eternal devotion to you.

JACK   Dear Gwendolen!

GWENDOLEN   The story of your romantic origin, as related to me by mamma, with unpleasing comments, has naturally stirred the deeper fibres of my nature. Your Christian name[3] has an irresistible fascination. The simplicity of your character makes you exquisitely incomprehensible to me. Your town address at the Albany I have. What is your address in the country?

JACK   The Manor House, Woolton, Hertfordshire.[4]

> (ALGERNON, *who has been carefully listening, smiles to himself, and writes the address on his shirt-cuff. Then picks up the Railway Guide.*[5])

GWENDOLEN   There is a good postal service, I suppose? It may be necessary to do something desperate. That of course will require serious consideration. I will communicate with you daily.

JACK   My own one!

GWENDOLEN   How long do you remain in town?

JACK   Till Monday.

GWENDOLEN   Good! Algy, you may turn round now.

ALGERNON   Thanks, I've turned round already.

GWENDOLEN   You may also ring the bell.

JACK   You will let me see you to your carriage, my own darling?

GWENDOLEN   Certainly.

JACK   (*To* LANE, *who now enters.*) I will see Miss Fairfax out.

LANE   Yes, sir. (JACK *and* GWENDOLEN *go off.*)

> (LANE *presents several letters on a salver to* ALGERNON. *It is to be surmised that they are bills, as* ALGERNON, *after looking at the envelopes, tears them up.*)

ALGERNON   A glass of sherry, Lane.

LANE   Yes, sir.

ALGERNON   To-morrow, Lane, I'm going Bunburying.

LANE   Yes, sir.

ALGERNON   I shall probably not be back till Monday. You can put up[6] my dress clothes, my smoking jacket,[7] and all the Bunbury suits . . .

---

3. In the play's Victorian society, which privileged the dominant culture, this was an alternative form for designating one's first, or given, name.
4. Woolton is located in Merseyside, in the northwest of England. Hertfordshire is known for its Roman ruins, the childhood home of Queen Elizabeth I (Hatfield House), and the home of George Bernard Shaw, a contemporary of Wilde's.
5. A train timetable.
6. Pack.
7. A man's evening jacket, often made of a fine fabric, elaborately trimmed, and usually worn at home and intended to protect other clothes from the smell of tobacco smoke.

LANE   Yes, sir. (*Handing sherry.*)

ALGERNON   I hope to-morrow will be a fine day, Lane.

LANE   It never is, sir.

ALGERNON   Lane, you're a perfect pessimist.

LANE   I do my best to give satisfaction, sir.
(*Enter* JACK. LANE *goes off.*)

JACK   There's a sensible, intellectual girl! the only girl I ever cared for in my life. (ALGERNON *is laughing immoderately.*) What on earth are you so amused at?

ALGERNON   Oh, I'm a little anxious about poor Bunbury, that is all.

JACK   If you don't take care, your friend Bunbury will get you into a serious scrape some day.

ALGERNON   I love scrapes. They are the only things that are never serious.

JACK   Oh, that's nonsense, Algy. You never talk anything but nonsense.

ALGERNON   Nobody ever does.
(JACK *looks indignantly at him, and leaves the room.* ALGERNON *lights a cigarette, reads his shirt-cuff, and smiles.*)

ACT-DROP

Second Act

Scene— *Garden at the Manor House. A flight of grey stone steps leads up to the house. The garden, an old-fashioned one, full of roses. Time of year, July. Basket chairs, and a table covered with books, are set under a large yew-tree.*

(MISS PRISM *discovered seated at the table.* CECILY *is at the back watering flowers.*)

MISS PRISM[8]   (*Calling.*) Cecily, Cecily! Surely such a utilitarian occupation as the watering of flowers is rather Moulton's duty than yours? Especially at a moment when intellectual pleasures await you. Your German grammar is on the table. Pray open it at page fifteen. We will repeat yesterday's lesson.

CECILY   (*Coming over very slowly.*) But I don't like German. It isn't at all a becoming language. I know perfectly well that I look quite plain after my German lesson.

MISS PRISM   Child, you know how anxious your guardian is that you should improve yourself in every way. He laid particular

8. *Prism*: a device for breaking light into bands of color.

stress on your German, as he was leaving for town yesterday. Indeed, he always lays stress on your German when he is leaving for town.

CECILY   Dear Uncle Jack is so very serious! Sometimes he is so serious that I think he cannot be quite well.

MISS PRISM   (*Drawing herself up.*) Your guardian enjoys the best of health, and his gravity of demeanour is especially to be commended in one so comparatively young as he is. I know no one who has a higher sense of duty and responsibility.

CECILY   I suppose that is why he often looks a little bored when we three are together.

MISS PRISM   Cecily! I am surprised at you. Mr. Worthing has many troubles in his life. Idle merriment and triviality would be out of place in his conversation. You must remember his constant anxiety about that unfortunate young man his brother.

CECILY   I wish Uncle Jack would allow that unfortunate young man, his brother, to come down here sometimes. We might have a good influence over him, Miss Prism. I am sure you certainly would. You know German, and geology, and things of that kind influence a man very much. (CECILY *begins to write in her diary.*)

MISS PRISM   (*Shaking her head.*) I do not think that even I could produce any effect on a character that according to his own brother's admission is irretrievably weak and vacillating. Indeed I am not sure that I would desire to reclaim him. I am not in favour of this modern mania for turning bad people into good people at a moment's notice. As a man sows so let him reap.[9] You must put away your diary, Cecily. I really don't see why you should keep a diary at all.

CECILY   I keep a diary in order to enter the wonderful secrets of my life. If I didn't write them down I should probably forget all about them.

MISS PRISM   Memory, my dear Cecily, is the diary that we all carry about with us.

CECILY   Yes, but it usually chronicles the things that have never happened, and couldn't possibly have happened. I believe that Memory is responsible for nearly all the three-volume novels that Mudie[1] sends us.

MISS PRISM   Do not speak slightingly of the three-volume novel, Cecily. I wrote one myself in earlier days.

CECILY   Did you really, Miss Prism? How wonderfully clever you are! I hope it did not end happily? I don't like novels that end happily. They depress me so much.

9. A paraphrase of Galatians 6:7: "Be not deceived; God is not mocked: for whatsoever a man soweth, that shall he also reap."
1. An abbreviated form of the name of the circulating library opened by Charles Mudie in London.

MISS PRISM   The good ended happily, and the bad unhappily. That is what Fiction means.

CECILY   I suppose so. But it seems very unfair. And was your novel ever published?

MISS PRISM   Alas! no. The manuscript unfortunately was abandoned. I use the word in the sense of lost or mislaid. To your work, child, these speculations are profitless.

CECILY   (*Smiling.*) But I see dear Dr. Chasuble coming up through the garden.

MISS PRISM   (*Rising and advancing.*) Dr. Chasuble! This is indeed a pleasure.

(*Enter* CANON[2] CHASUBLE.[3])

CHASUBLE   And how are we this morning? Miss Prism, you are, I trust, well?

CECILY   Miss Prism has just been complaining of a slight headache. I think it would do her so much good to have a short stroll with you in the Park, Dr. Chasuble.

MISS PRISM   Cecily, I have not mentioned anything about a headache.

CECILY   No, dear Miss Prism, I know that, but I felt instinctively that you had a headache. Indeed I was thinking about that, and not about my German lesson, when the Rector[4] came in.

CHASUBLE   I hope, Cecily, you are not inattentive.

CECILY   Oh, I am afraid I am.

CHASUBLE   That is strange. <u>Were I fortunate enough to be Miss Prism's pupil, I would hang</u> upon her lips. (MISS PRISM *glares.*) I spoke metaphorically.—My metaphor was drawn from bees. Ahem! Mr. Worthing, I suppose, has not returned from town yet?

MISS PRISM   We do not expect him till Monday afternoon.

CHASUBLE   Ah yes, he usually likes to spend his Sunday in London. He is not one of those whose sole aim is enjoyment, as, by all accounts, that unfortunate young man his brother seems to be. But I must not disturb Egeria[5] and her pupil any longer.

MISS PRISM   Egeria? My name is Laetitia, Doctor.

CHASUBLE   (*Bowing.*) A classical allusion merely, drawn from the Pagan authors. I shall see you both no doubt at Evensong?[6]

---

2. A member of certain religious communities living under a common rule and bound by vows. It is not clear from the context if this title fits Dr. Chasuble.
3. Chasuble's name echoes that of a cloak-like ecclesiastical vestment worn over the alb and stole by the celebrant at Mass or the Eucharist.
4. A cleric in charge of, and who derives tithes from, a Church of England parish.
5. A goddess from Roman mythology, supposed to be the instructress of Numa Pompilius, and regarded as the giver of life. Hence, an idealized designation for an educator.
6. A prayer service usually celebrated shortly before sunset, being the sixth of the seven "canonical hours" of the Western Church. In the Church of England it is also known as the "Evening Prayer."

MISS PRISM   I think, dear Doctor, I will have a stroll with you.
I find I have a headache after all, and a walk might do it
good.

CHASUBLE   With pleasure, Miss Prism, with pleasure. We might go
as far as the schools and back.

MISS PRISM   That would be delightful. Cecily, you will read your
Political Economy in my absence. The chapter on the Fall of the
Rupee[7] you may omit. It is somewhat too sensational. Even these
metallic problems have their melodramatic side. (*Goes down the
garden with* DR. CHASUBLE.)

CECILY   (*Picks up books and throws them back on table.*) Horrid Political Economy! Horrid Geography! Horrid, horrid German!

(*Enter* MERRIMAN *with a card on a salver.*)

MERRIMAN   Mr. Ernest Worthing has just driven over from the station. He has brought his luggage with him.

CECILY   (*Takes the card and reads it.*) "Mr. Ernest Worthing, B. 4,
The Albany, W." Uncle Jack's brother! Did you tell him Mr. Worthing was in town?

MERRIMAN   Yes, Miss. He seemed very much disappointed. I mentioned that you and Miss Prism were in the garden. He said he
was anxious to speak to you privately for a moment.

CECILY   Ask Mr. Ernest Worthing to come here. I suppose you had
better talk to the housekeeper about a room for him.

MERRIMAN   Yes, Miss. (MERRIMAN *goes off.*)

CECILY   I have never met any really wicked person before. I feel
rather frightened. I am so afraid he will look just like everyone
else. (*Enter* ALGERNON, *very gay and debonair.*) He does!

ALGERNON   (*Raising his hat.*) You are my little cousin Cecily, I'm sure.

CECILY   You are under some strange mistake. I am not little. In
fact, I believe I am more than usually tall for my age. (ALGERNON
is rather taken aback.) But I am your cousin Cecily. You, I see
from your card, are Uncle Jack's brother, my cousin Ernest, my
wicked cousin Ernest.

ALGERNON   Oh! I am not really wicked at all, Cousin Cecily. You
mustn't think that I am wicked.

CECILY   If you are not, then you have certainly been deceiving us
all in a very inexcusable manner. I hope you have not been leading a double life, pretending to be wicked and being really good
all the time. That would be hypocrisy.

ALGERNON   (*Looks at her in amazement.*) Oh! Of course I have
been rather reckless.

CECILY   I am glad to hear it.

---

7. The monetary unit of India, represented by a cupro-nickel (formerly silver) coin and
equivalent to 100 paise.

ALGERNON   In fact, now you mention the subject, I have been very bad in my own small way.

CECILY   I don't think you should be so proud of that, though I am sure it must have been very pleasant.

ALGERNON   It is much pleasanter being here with you.

CECILY   I can't understand how you are here at all. Uncle Jack won't be back till Monday afternoon.

ALGERNON   That is a great disappointment. I am obliged to go up by the first train on Monday morning. I have a business appointment that I am anxious . . . to miss?

CECILY   Couldn't you miss it anywhere but in London?

ALGERNON   No: the appointment is in London.

CECILY   Well, I know, of course, how important it is not to keep a business engagement, if one wants to retain any sense of the beauty of life, but still I think you had better wait till Uncle Jack arrives. I know he wants to speak to you about your emigrating.

ALGERNON   About my what?

CECILY   Your emigrating. He has gone up to buy your outfit.

ALGERNON   I certainly wouldn't let Jack buy my outfit. He has no taste in neckties at all.

CECILY   I don't think you will require neckties. Uncle Jack is sending you to Australia.

ALGERNON   Australia! I'd sooner die.

CECILY   Well, he said at dinner on Wednesday night, that you would have to choose between this world, the next world, and Australia.

ALGERNON   Oh, well! The accounts I have received of Australia and the next world are not particularly encouraging. This world is good enough for me, cousin Cecily.

CECILY   Yes, but are you good enough for it?

ALGERNON   I'm afraid I'm not that. That is why I want you to reform me. You might make that your mission, if you don't mind, cousin Cecily.

CECILY   I'm afraid I've no time, this afternoon.

ALGERNON   Well, would you mind my reforming myself this afternoon?

CECILY   It is rather Quixotic[8] of you. But I think you should try.

ALGERNON   I will. I feel better already.

CECILY   You are looking a little worse.

ALGERNON   That is because I am hungry.

CECILY   How thoughtless of me. I should have remembered that when one is going to lead an entirely new life, one requires regular and wholesome meals. Won't you come in?

8. A term applied to one with the idealism and clouded sense of perception of Cervantes's Don Quixote.

ALGERNON   Thank you. Might I have a buttonhole[9] first? I never have any appetite unless I have a buttonhole first.

CECILY   A Maréchal Niel?[1] (*Picks up scissors.*)

ALGERNON   No, I'd sooner have a pink rose.

CECILY   Why? (*Cuts a flower.*)

ALGERNON   Because you are like a pink rose, Cousin Cecily.

CECILY   I don't think it can be right for you to talk to me like that. Miss Prism never says such things to me.

ALGERNON   Then Miss Prism is a short-sighted old lady. (CECILY *puts the rose in his button-hole.*) You are the prettiest girl I ever saw.

CECILY   Miss Prism says that all good looks are a snare.

ALGERNON   They are a snare that every sensible man would like to be caught in.

CECILY   Oh, I don't think I would care to catch a sensible man. I shouldn't know what to talk to him about.

> (*They pass into the house.* MISS PRISM *and Dr.* CHASUBLE *return.*)

MISS PRISM   You are too much alone, dear Dr. Chasuble. You should get married. A misanthrope I can understand—a womanthrope, never!

CHASUBLE   (*With a scholar's shudder.*) Believe me, I do not deserve so neologistic a phrase. The precept as well as the practice of the Primitive Church[2] was distinctly against matrimony.

MISS PRISM   (*Sententiously.*) That is obviously the reason why the Primitive Church has not lasted up to the present day. And you do not seem to realize, dear Doctor, that by persistently remaining single, a man converts himself into a permanent public temptation. Men should be more careful; this very celibacy leads weaker vessels astray.

CHASUBLE   But is a man not equally attractive when married?

MISS PRISM   No married man is ever attractive except to his wife.

CHASUBLE   And often, I've been told, not even to her.

MISS PRISM   That depends on the intellectual sympathies of the woman. Maturity can always be depended on. Ripeness can be trusted. Young women are green. (*Dr.* CHASUBLE *starts.*) I spoke horticulturally. My metaphor was drawn from fruits. But where is Cecily?

CHASUBLE   Perhaps she followed us to the schools.

> (*Enter* JACK *slowly from the back of the garden. He is dressed*

---

9. A shortened form of the term *button-hole flower*, a decorative ornament worn in the lapel of a man's jacket.
1. A variety of climbing rose introduced in 1864, bearing large, fragrant, yellow flowers.
2. A designation for the early Christian Church, with the implication that it reflected the purest level of practice.

in the deepest mourning, with crape hat-band and black gloves.)

MISS PRISM   Mr. Worthing!

CHASUBLE   Mr. Worthing?

MISS PRISM   This is indeed a surprise. We did not look for you till Monday afternoon.

JACK   (*Shakes* MISS PRISM's *hand in a tragic manner.*) I have returned sooner than I expected. Dr. Chasuble, I hope you are well?

CHASUBLE   Dear Mr. Worthing, I trust this garb of woe does not betoken some terrible calamity?

JACK   My brother.

MISS PRISM   More shameful debts and extravagance?

CHASUBLE   Still leading his life of pleasure?

JACK   (*Shaking his head.*) Dead!

CHASUBLE   Your brother Ernest dead?

JACK   Quite dead.

MISS PRISM   What a lesson for him! I trust he will profit by it.

CHASUBLE   Mr. Worthing, I offer you my sincere condolence. You have at least the consolation of knowing that you were always the most generous and forgiving of brothers.

JACK   Poor Ernest! He had many faults, but it is a sad, sad blow.

CHASUBLE   Very sad indeed. Were you with him at the end?

JACK   No. He died abroad; in Paris, in fact. I had a telegram last night from the manager of the Grand Hotel.

CHASUBLE   Was the cause of death mentioned?

JACK   A severe chill, it seems.

MISS PRISM   As a man sows, so shall he reap.

CHASUBLE   (*Raising his hand.*) Charity, dear Miss Prism, charity! None of us are perfect. I myself am peculiarly susceptible to draughts. Will the interment take place here?

JACK   No. He seems to have expressed a desire to be buried in Paris.

CHASUBLE   In Paris! (*Shakes his head.*) I fear that hardly points to any very serious state of mind at the last. You would no doubt wish me to make some slight allusion to this tragic domestic affliction next Sunday. (JACK *presses his hand convulsively.*) My sermon on the meaning of the manna[3] in the wilderness can be adapted to almost any occasion, joyful, or, as in the present case, distressing. (*All sigh.*) I have preached it at harvest celebrations, christenings, confirmations, on days of humiliation and festal

---

3. Identified in the Bible (Exodus 16) as a substance miraculously provided each day as food for the Israelites in the wilderness after their departure from Egypt. It has come to mean spiritual nourishment, especially God-given, or simply something beneficial or pleasing (originally food) appearing or being provided unexpectedly or opportunely.

days. The last time I delivered it was in the Cathedral, as a charity sermon on behalf of the Society for the Prevention of Discontent among the Upper Orders. The Bishop, who was present, was much struck by some of the analogies I drew.

JACK   Ah! that reminds me, you mentioned christenings I think, Dr. Chasuble? I suppose you know how to christen all right? (*Dr.* CHASUBLE *looks astounded.*) I mean, of course, you are continually christening, aren't you?

MISS PRISM   It is, I regret to say, one of the Rector's most constant duties in this parish. I have often spoken to the poorer classes on the subject. But they don't seem to know what thrift is.

CHASUBLE   But is there any particular infant in whom you are interested, Mr. Worthing? Your brother was, I believe, unmarried, was he not?

JACK   Oh yes.

MISS PRISM   (*Bitterly.*) People who live entirely for pleasure usually are.

JACK   But it is not for any child, dear Doctor. I am very fond of children. No! the fact is, I would like to be christened myself, this afternoon, if you have nothing better to do.

CHASUBLE   But surely, Mr. Worthing, you have been christened already?

JACK   I don't remember anything about it.

CHASUBLE   But have you any grave doubts on the subject?

JACK   I certainly intend to have. Of course I don't know if the thing would bother you in any way, or if you think I am a little too old now.

CHASUBLE   Not at all. The sprinkling, and, indeed, the immersion of adults is a perfectly canonical practice.

JACK   Immersion!

CHASUBLE   You need have no apprehensions. Sprinkling is all that is necessary, or indeed I think advisable. Our weather is so changeable. At what hour would you wish the ceremony performed?

JACK   Oh, I might trot round about five if that would suit you.

CHASUBLE   Perfectly, perfectly! In fact I have two similar ceremonies to perform at that time. A case of twins that occurred recently in one of the outlying cottages on your own estate. Poor Jenkins the carter,[4] a most hard-working man.

JACK   Oh! I don't see much fun in being christened along with other babies. It would be childish. Would half-past five do?

CHASUBLE   Admirably! Admirably! (*Takes out watch.*) And now, dear Mr. Worthing, I will not intrude any longer into a house of sorrow.

---

4. One who drives carts or wagons.

I would merely beg you not to be too much bowed down by grief. What seem to us bitter trials are often blessings in disguise.

MISS PRISM   This seems to me a blessing of an extremely obvious kind.

(*Enter* CECILY *from the house.*)

CECILY   Uncle Jack! Oh, I am pleased to see you back. But what horrid clothes you have got on! Do go and change them.

MISS PRISM   Cecily!

CHASUBLE   My child! my child! (CECILY *goes towards* JACK; *he kisses her brow in a melancholy manner.*)

CECILY   What is the matter, Uncle Jack? Do look happy! You look as if you had toothache, and I have got such a surprise for you. Who do you think is in the dining-room? Your brother!

JACK   Who?

CECILY   Your brother Ernest. He arrived about half an hour ago.

JACK   What nonsense! I haven't got a brother.

CECILY   Oh, don't say that. However badly he may have behaved to you in the past he is still your brother. You couldn't be so heartless as to disown him. I'll tell him to come out. And you will shake hands with him, won't you, Uncle Jack? (*Runs back into the house.*)

CHASUBLE   These are very joyful tidings.

MISS PRISM   After we had all been resigned to his loss, his sudden return seems to me peculiarly distressing.

JACK   My brother is in the dining-room? I don't know what it all means. I think it is perfectly absurd.

(*Enter* ALGERNON *and* CECILY *hand in hand. They come slowly up to* JACK.)

JACK   Good heavens! (*Motions* ALGERNON *away.*)

ALGERNON   Brother John, I have come down from town to tell you that I am very sorry for all the trouble I have given you, and that I intend to lead a better life in the future. (JACK *glares at him and does not take his hand.*)

CECILY   Uncle Jack, you are not going to refuse your own brother's hand?

JACK   Nothing will induce me to take his hand. I think his coming down here disgraceful. He knows perfectly well why.

CECILY   Uncle Jack, do be nice. There is some good in everyone. Ernest has just been telling me about his poor invalid friend Mr. Bunbury whom he goes to visit so often. And surely there must be much good in one who is kind to an invalid, and leaves the pleasures of London to sit by a bed of pain.

JACK   Oh! he has been talking about Bunbury, has he?

CECILY   Yes, he has told me all about poor Mr. Bunbury, and his terrible state of health.

JACK   Bunbury! Well, I won't have him talk to you about Bunbury or about anything else. It is enough to drive one perfectly frantic.

ALGERNON   Of course I admit that the faults were all on my side. But I must say that I think that Brother John's coldness to me is peculiarly painful. I expected a more enthusiastic welcome, especially considering it is the first time I have come here.

CECILY   Uncle Jack, if you don't shake hands with Ernest I will never forgive you.

JACK   Never forgive me?

CECILY   Never, never, never!

JACK   Well, this is the last time I shall ever do it. (*Shakes with* AL-GERNON *and glares.*)

CHASUBLE   It's pleasant, is it not, to see so perfect a reconciliation? I think we might leave the two brothers together.

MISS PRISM   Cecily, you will come with us.

CECILY   Certainly, Miss Prism. My little task of reconciliation is over.

CHASUBLE   You have done a beautiful action to-day, dear child.

MISS PRISM   We must not be premature in our judgments.

CECILY   I feel very happy.
        (*They all go off.*)

JACK   You young scoundrel, Algy, you must get out of this place as soon as possible. I don't allow any Bunburying here.
        (*Enter* MERRIMAN.)

MERRIMAN   I have put Mr. Ernest's things in the room next to yours, sir. I suppose that is all right?

JACK   What?

MERRIMAN   Mr. Ernest's luggage, sir. I have unpacked it and put it in the room next to your own.

JACK   His luggage?

MERRIMAN   Yes, sir. Three portmanteaus,[5] a dressing-case,[6] two hat-boxes,[7] and a large luncheon-basket.[8]

ALGERNON   I am afraid I can't stay more than a week this time.

JACK   Merriman, order the dog-cart[9] at once. Mr. Ernest has been suddenly called back to town.

MERRIMAN   Yes, sir. (*Goes back into the house.*)

ALGERNON   What a fearful liar you are, Jack. I have not been called back to town at all.

JACK   Yes, you have.

---

5. Cases or bags used for carrying clothing and other necessaries when traveling. Originally of a form suitable for carrying on horseback; now applied to oblong stiff leather cases, which open like books, with hinges in the middle of the back.
6. A case used to carry toiletries.
7. Large boxes intended to house one's hat safely.
8. A box for holding one's food; a picnic basket.
9. An open, horse-drawn vehicle with two back-to-back seats. In early versions of the cart, the seat further back shut to form a box for dogs.

ALGERNON   I haven't heard anyone call me.

JACK   Your duty as a gentleman calls you back.

ALGERNON   My duty as a gentleman has never interfered with my pleasures in the smallest degree.

JACK   I can quite understand that.

ALGERNON   Well, Cecily is a darling.

JACK   You are not to talk of Miss Cardew like that. I don't like it.

ALGERNON   Well, I don't like your clothes. You look perfectly ridiculous in them. Why on earth don't you go up and change? It is perfectly childish to be in deep mourning for a man who is actually staying for a whole week with you in your house as a guest. I call it grotesque.

JACK   You are certainly not staying with me for a whole week as a guest or anything else. You have got to leave . . . by the four-five train.

ALGERNON   I certainly won't leave you so long as you are in mourning. It would be most unfriendly. If I were in mourning you would stay with me, I suppose. I should think it very unkind if you didn't.

JACK   Well, will you go if I change my clothes?

ALGERNON   Yes, if you are not too long. I never saw anybody take so long to dress, and with such little result.

JACK   Well, at any rate, that is better than being always overdressed as you are.

ALGERNON   If I am occasionally a little over-dressed, I make up for it by being always immensely over-educated.

JACK   Your vanity is ridiculous, your conduct an outrage, and your presence in my garden utterly absurd. However, you have got to catch the four-five, and I hope you will have a pleasant journey back to town. This Bunburying, as you call it, has not been a great success for you. (*Goes into the house.*)

ALGERNON   I think it has been a great success. I'm in love with Cecily, and that is everything. (*Enter* CECILY *at the back of the garden. She picks up the can and begins to water the flowers.*) But I must see her before I go, and make arrangements for another Bunbury. Ah, there she is.

CECILY   Oh, I merely came back to water the roses. I thought you were with Uncle Jack.

ALGERNON   He's gone to order the dog-cart for me.

CECILY   Oh, is he going to take you for a nice drive?

ALGERNON   He's going to send me away.

CECILY   Then have we got to part?

ALGERNON   I am afraid so. It's a very painful parting.

CECILY   It is always painful to part from people whom one has known for a very brief space of time. The absence of old friends

one can endure with equanimity. But even a momentary separation from anyone to whom one has just been introduced is almost unbearable.

ALGERNON   Thank you.

   (*Enter* MERRIMAN.)

MERRIMAN   The dog-cart is at the door, sir. (ALGERNON *looks appealingly at* CECILY.)

CECILY   It can wait, Merriman . . . for . . . five minutes.

MERRIMAN   Yes, Miss. (*Exit* MERRIMAN.)

ALGERNON   I hope, Cecily, I shall not offend you if I state quite frankly and openly that you seem to me to be in every way the visible personification of absolute perfection.

CECILY   I think your frankness does you great credit, Ernest. If you will allow me, I will copy your remarks into my diary. (*Goes over to table and begins writing in diary.*)

ALGERNON   Do you really keep a diary? I'd give anything to look at it. May I?

CECILY   Oh no. (*Puts her hand over it.*) You see, it is simply a very young girl's record of her own thoughts and impressions, and consequently meant for publication. When it appears in volume form I hope you will order a copy. But pray, Ernest, don't stop. I delight in taking down from dictation. I have reached "absolute perfection." You can go on. I am quite ready for more.

ALGERNON   (*Somewhat taken aback.*) Ahem! Ahem!

CECILY   Oh, don't cough, Ernest. When one is dictating one should speak fluently and not cough. Besides, I don't know how to spell a cough. (*Writes as* ALGERNON *speaks.*)

ALGERNON   (*Speaking very rapidly.*) Cecily, ever since I first looked upon your wonderful and incomparable beauty, I have dared to love you wildly, passionately, devotedly, hopelessly.

CECILY   I don't think that you should tell me that you love me wildly, passionately, devotedly, hopelessly. Hopelessly doesn't seem to make much sense, does it?

ALGERNON   Cecily!

   (*Enter* MERRIMAN.)

MERRIMAN   The dog-cart is waiting, sir.

ALGERNON   Tell it to come round next week, at the same hour.

MERRIMAN   (*Looks at* CECILY, *who makes no sign.*) Yes, sir. (MERRIMAN *retires.*)

CECILY   Uncle Jack would be very much annoyed if he knew you were staying on till next week, at the same hour.

ALGERNON   Oh, I don't care about Jack. I don't care for anybody in the whole world but you. I love you, Cecily. You will marry me, won't you?

CECILY   You silly boy! Of course. Why, we have been engaged for the last three months.

ALGERNON   For the last three months?

CECILY   Yes, it will be exactly three months on Thursday.

ALGERNON   But how did we become engaged?

CECILY   Well, ever since dear Uncle Jack first confessed to us that he had a younger brother who was very wicked and bad, you of course have formed the chief topic of conversation between myself and Miss Prism. And of course a man who is much talked about is always very attractive. One feels there must be something in him after all. I daresay it was foolish of me, but I fell in love with you, Ernest.

ALGERNON   Darling! And when was the engagement actually settled?

CECILY   On the 14th of February last. Worn out by your entire ignorance of my existence, I determined to end the matter one way or the other, and after a long struggle with myself I accepted you under this dear old tree here. The next day I bought this little ring in your name, and this is the little bangle with the true lovers' knot I promised you always to wear.

ALGERNON   Did I give you this? It's very pretty, isn't it?

CECILY   Yes, you've wonderfully good taste, Ernest. It's the excuse I've always given for your leading such a bad life. And this is the box in which I keep all your dear letters. (*Kneels at table, opens box, and produces letters tied up with blue ribbon.*)

ALGERNON   My letters! But, my own sweet Cecily, I have never written you any letters.

CECILY   You need hardly remind me of that, Ernest. I remember only too well that I was forced to write your letters for you. I wrote always three times a week, and sometimes oftener.

ALGERNON   Oh, do let me read them, Cecily!

CECILY   Oh, I couldn't possibly. They would make you far too conceited. (*Replaces box.*) The three you wrote me after I had broken of the engagement are so beautiful, and so badly spelled, that even now I can hardly read them without crying a little.

ALGERNON   But was our engagement ever broken off?

CECILY   Of course it was. On the 22nd of last March. You can see the entry if you like. (*Shows diary.*) "To-day I broke off my engagement with Ernest. I feel it is better to do so. The weather still continues charming."

ALGERNON   But why on earth did you break it off? What had I done? I had done nothing at all. Cecily, I am very much hurt indeed to hear you broke it off. Particularly when the weather was so charming.

CECILY   It would hardly have been a really serious engagement if it

hadn't been broken off at least once. But I forgave you before the week was out.

ALGERNON (*Crossing to her, and kneeling.*) <u>What a perfect angel you are, Cecily.</u>

CECILY You dear romantic boy. (*He kisses her, she puts her fingers through his hair.*) I hope your hair curls naturally, does it?

ALGERNON Yes, darling, with a little help from others.

CECILY I am so glad.

ALGERNON You'll never break off our engagement again, Cecily?

CECILY <u>I don't think I could break it off now that I have actually met you.</u> Besides, of course, there is the question of your name.

ALGERNON Yes, of course. (*Nervously.*)

CECILY You must not laugh at me, darling, <u>but it had always been a girlish dream of mine to love someone whose name was Ernest.</u> (ALGERNON *rises,* CECILY *also.*) There is something in that name that seems to inspire absolute confidence. I pity any poor married woman <u>whose husband is not called Ernest.</u>

ALGERNON But, my dear child, do you mean to say you could not love me if I had some other name?

CECILY But what name?

ALGERNON Oh, any name you like—<u>Algernon</u>—for instance . . .

(CECILY) But I don't like the name of <u>Algernon.</u>

ALGERNON Well, my own dear, sweet, loving little darling, I really can't see why you should object to the name of Algernon. It is not at all a bad name. In fact, it is rather an aristocratic name. Half of the chaps who get into the Bankruptcy Court[1] are called Algernon. But seriously, Cecily . . . (*Moving to her.*) . . . if my name was Algy, couldn't you love me?

CECILY (*Rising.*) <u>I might respect you, Ernest, I might admire your character, but I fear that I should not be able to give you my undivided attention.</u>

ALGERNON Ahem! Cecily! (*Picking up hat.*) Your Rector here is, I suppose, thoroughly experienced in the practice of all the rites and ceremonials of the Church?

CECILY (Oh, yes. Dr. Chasuble is a most learned man. He has never written a single book, so you can imagine how much he knows.) *Ironic*

ALGERNON I must see him at once on a most important christening—I mean on most important business.

---

1. The bankruptcy court in London is now located in Carey Street. According to Peter Cunningham's *Hand-Book of London* (1849), "The business of the court is managed by two judges, and five commissioners. Number of Bankrupts in 1845— 1028; in 1846— 1326. The bankrupt is a trader, the insolvent not necessarily so. The bankrupt, when discharged, is discharged not only as to his person, but as to future acquired property; while the insolvent is discharged only as to his person, and not as to future acquired property."

CECILY   Oh!

ALGERNON   I shan't be away more than half an hour.

CECILY   Considering that we have been engaged since February the 14th, and that I only met you to-day for the first time, I think it is rather hard that you should leave me for so long a period as half an hour. Couldn't you make it twenty minutes?

ALGERNON   I'll be back in no time. (*Kisses her and rushes down the garden.*)

CECILY   What an impetuous boy he is! I like his hair so much. I must enter his proposal in my diary.

(*Enter* MERRIMAN.)

MERRIMAN   A Miss Fairfax has just called to see Mr. Worthing. On very important business, Miss Fairfax states.

CECILY   Isn't Mr. Worthing in his library?

MERRIMAN   Mr. Worthing went over in the direction of the Rectory some time ago.

CECILY   Pray ask the lady to come out here; Mr. Worthing is sure to be back soon. And you can bring tea.

MERRIMAN   Yes, Miss. (*Goes out.*)

CECILY   Miss Fairfax! I suppose one of the many good elderly women who are associated with Uncle Jack in some of his philanthropic work in London. I don't quite like women who are interested in philanthropic work. I think it is so forward of them.

(*Enter* MERRIMAN.)

MERRIMAN   Miss Fairfax.

(*Enter* GWENDOLEN.)

(*Exit* MERRIMAN.)

CECILY   (*Advancing to meet her.*) Pray let me introduce myself to you. My name is Cecily Cardew.

GWENDOLEN   Cecily Cardew? (*Moving to her and shaking hands.*) What a very sweet name! Something tells me that we are going to be great friends. I like you already more than I can say. My first impressions of people are never wrong.

CECILY   How nice of you to like me so much after we have known each other such a comparatively short time. Pray sit down.

GWENDOLEN   (*Still standing up.*) I may call you Cecily, may I not?

CECILY   With pleasure!

GWENDOLEN   And you will always call me Gwendolen, won't you?

CECILY   If you wish.

GWENDOLEN   Then that is all quite settled, is it not?

CECILY   I hope so. (*A pause. They both sit down together.*)

GWENDOLEN   Perhaps this might be a favourable opportunity for my mentioning who I am. My father is Lord Bracknell. You have never heard of papa, I suppose?

CECILY   I don't think so.

Gwen + Cecily both lik Ernest

GWENDOLEN   Outside the family circle, papa, I am glad to say, is entirely unknown. I think that is quite as it should be. The home seems to me to be the proper sphere for the man. And certainly once a man begins to neglect his domestic duties he becomes painfully effeminate, does he not? And I don't like that. It makes men so very attractive. Cecily, mamma, whose views on education are remarkably strict, has brought me up to be extremely short-sighted; it is part of her system; so do you mind my looking at you through my glasses?

CECILY   Oh! not at all, Gwendolen. I am very fond of being looked at.

GWENDOLEN   (*After examining* CECILY *carefully through a lorgnette.*[2]) You are here on a short visit, I suppose.

CECILY   Oh no! I live here.

GWENDOLEN   (*Severely.*) Really? Your mother, no doubt, or some female relative of advanced years, resides here also?

CECILY   Oh no! I have no mother, nor, in fact, any relations.

GWENDOLEN   Indeed?

CECILY   My dear guardian, with the assistance of Miss Prism, has the arduous task of looking after me.

GWENDOLEN   Your guardian?

CECILY   Yes, I am Mr. Worthing's ward.

GWENDOLEN   Oh! It is strange he never mentioned to me that he had a ward. How secretive of him! He grows more interesting hourly. I am not sure, however, that the news inspires me with feelings of unmixed delight. (*Rising and going to her.*) I am very fond of you, Cecily; I have liked you ever since I met you! But I am bound to state that now that I know that you are Mr. Worthing's ward, I cannot help expressing a wish you were—well, just a little older than you seem to be—and not quite so very alluring in appearance. In fact, if I may speak candidly—

CECILY   Pray do! I think that whenever one has anything unpleasant to say, one should always be quite candid.

GWENDOLEN   Well, to speak with perfect candour, Cecily, I wish that you were fully forty-two, and more than usually plain for your age. Ernest has a strong upright nature. He is the very soul of truth and honour. Disloyalty would be as impossible to him as deception. But even men of the noblest possible moral character are extremely susceptible to the influence of the physical charms of others. Modern, no less than Ancient History, supplies us with many most painful examples of what I refer to. If it were not so, indeed, History would be quite unreadable.

CECILY   I beg your pardon, Gwendolen, did you say Ernest?

2. A pair of eyeglasses usually affixed to a metal, ivory, or tortoiseshell handle.

GWENDOLEN　Yes.

CECILY　Oh, but it is not Mr. Ernest Worthing who is my guardian. It is his brother—his elder brother.

GWENDOLEN　(*Sitting down again.*) Ernest never mentioned to me that he had a brother.

CECILY　I am sorry to say they have not been on good terms for a long time.

GWENDOLEN　Ah! that accounts for it. And now that I think of it I have never heard any man mention his brother. The subject seems distasteful to most men. Cecily, you have lifted a load from my mind. I was growing almost anxious. It would have been terrible if any cloud had come across a friendship like ours, would it not? Of course you are quite, quite sure that it is not Mr. Ernest Worthing who is your guardian?

CECILY　Quite sure. (*A pause.*) In fact, I am going to be his.

GWENDOLEN　(*Enquiringly.*) I beg your pardon?

CECILY　(*Rather shy and confidingly.*) Dearest Gwendolen, there is no reason why I should make a secret of it to you. Our little county newspaper is sure to chronicle the fact next week. Mr. Ernest Worthing and I are engaged to be married.

GWENDOLEN　(*Quite politely, rising.*) My darling Cecily, I think there must be some slight error. Mr. Ernest Worthing is engaged to me. The announcement will appear in the *Morning Post*[3] on Saturday at the latest.

CECILY　(*Very politely, rising.*) I am afraid you must be under some misconception. Ernest proposed to me exactly ten minutes ago. (*Shows diary.*)

GWENDOLEN　(*Examines diary through her lorgnette carefully.*) It is certainly very curious, for he asked me to be his wife yesterday afternoon at 5:30. If you would care to verify the incident, pray do so. (*Produces diary of her own.*) I never travel without my diary. One should always have something sensational to read in the train. I am so sorry, dear Cecily, if it is any disappointment to you, but I am afraid I have the prior claim.

CECILY　It would distress me more than I can tell you, dear Gwendolen, if it caused you any mental or physical anguish, but I feel bound to point out that since Ernest proposed to you he clearly has changed his mind.

GWENDOLEN　(*Meditatively.*) If the poor fellow has been entrapped into any foolish promise I shall consider it my duty to rescue him at once, and with a firm hand.

CECILY　(*Thoughtfully and sadly.*) Whatever unfortunate entangle-

funny argument

3. A popular and well-known London newspaper that ran upper-class marriage announcements.

ment my dear boy may have got into, I will never reproach him with it after we are married.

GWENDOLEN   Do you allude to me, Miss Cardew, as an entanglement? You are presumptuous. On an occasion of this kind it becomes more than a moral duty to speak one's mind. It becomes a pleasure.

CECILY   Do you suggest, Miss Fairfax, that I entrapped Ernest into an engagement? How dare you? This is no time for wearing the shallow mask of manners. When I see a spade I call it a spade.

GWENDOLEN   (*Satirically.*) I am glad to say that I have never seen a spade. It is obvious that our social spheres have been widely different.

> (*Enter* MERRIMAN, *followed by the footman. He carries a salver, table cloth, and plate stand.* CECILY *is about to retort. The presence of the servants exercises a restraining influence, under which both girls chafe.*)

MERRIMAN   Shall I lay tea here as usual, miss?

CECILY   (*Sternly, in a calm voice.*) Yes, as usual. (MERRIMAN *begins to clear table and lay cloth. A long pause.* CECILY *and* GWENDOLEN *glare at each other.*)

GWENDOLEN   Are there many interesting walks in the vicinity, Miss Cardew?

CECILY   Oh! yes! a great many. From the top of one of the hills quite close one can see five counties.

GWENDOLEN   Five counties! I don't think I should like that; I hate crowds.

CECILY   (*Sweetly.*) I suppose that is why you live in town? (GWENDOLEN *bites her lips, and beats her foot nervously with her parasol.*)

GWENDOLEN   (*Looking round.*) Quite a well-kept garden this is, Miss Cardew.

CECILY   So glad you like it, Miss Fairfax.

GWENDOLEN   I had no idea there were any flowers in the country.

CECILY   Oh, flowers are as common[4] here, Miss Fairfax, as people are in London.

GWENDOLEN   Personally I cannot understand how anybody manages to exist in the country, if anybody who is anybody does. The country always bores me to death.

CECILY   Ah! This is what the newspapers call agricultural depression, is it not? I believe the aristocracy are suffering very much from it just at present. It is almost an epidemic amongst them, I have been told. May I offer you some tea, Miss Fairfax?

---

4. In this context, the term refers to something of inferior quality, and by extension to people who are low-class, vulgar, or unrefined.

GWENDOLEN   (*With elaborate politeness.*) Thank you. (*Aside.*) Detestable girl! But I require tea!

CECILY   (*Sweetly.*) Sugar?

GWENDOLEN   (*Superciliously.*) No, thank you. Sugar is not fashionable any more. (CECILY *looks angrily at her, takes up the tongs and puts four lumps of sugar into the cup.*)

CECILY   (*Severely.*) Cake or bread and butter?

GWENDOLEN   (*In a bored manner.*) Bread and butter, please. Cake is rarely seen at the best houses now-a-days.

CECILY   (*Cuts a very large slice of cake, and puts it on the tray.*) Hand that to Miss Fairfax.

   (MERRIMAN *does so, and goes out with* FOOTMAN. GWENDOLEN *drinks the tea and makes a grimace. Puts down cup at once, reaches out her hand to the bread and butter, looks at it, and finds it is cake. Rises in indignation.*)

GWENDOLEN   You have filled my tea with lumps of sugar, and though I asked most distinctly for bread and butter, you have given me cake. I am known for the gentleness of my disposition, and the extraordinary sweetness of my nature, but I warn you, Miss Cardew, you may go too far.

CECILY   (*Rising.*) To save my poor, innocent, trusting boy from the machinations of any other girl there are no lengths to which I would not go.

GWENDOLEN   From the moment I saw you I distrusted you. I felt that you were false and deceitful. I am never deceived in such matters. My first impression of people are invariably right.

CECILY   It seems to me, Miss Fairfax, that I am trespassing on your valuable time. No doubt you have many other calls of a similar character to make in the neighbourhood.

   (*Enter* JACK.)

GWENDOLEN   (*Catching sight of him.*) Ernest! My own Ernest!

JACK   Gwendolen! Darling! (*Offers to kiss her.*)

GWENDOLEN   (*Draws back.*) A moment! May I ask if you are engaged to be married to this young lady? (*Points to* CECILY.)

JACK   (*Laughing.*) To dear little Cecily! Of course not! What could have put such an idea into your pretty little head?

GWENDOLEN   Thank you. You may! (*Offers her cheek.*)

CECILY   (*Very sweetly.*) I knew there must be some misunderstanding, Miss Fairfax. The gentleman whose arm is at present round your waist is my guardian, Mr. John Worthing.

GWENDOLEN   I beg your pardon?

CECILY   This is Uncle Jack.

GWENDOLEN   (*Receding.*) Jack! Oh!

   (*Enter* ALGERNON.)

CECILY   Here is Ernest.

ALGERNON (*Goes straight over to* CECILY *without noticing anyone else.*) My own love! (*Offers to kiss her.*)

CECILY (*Drawing back.*) A moment, Ernest! May I ask you—are you engaged to be married to this young lady?

ALGERNON (*Looking round.*) To what young lady? Good heavens! Gwendolen!

CECILY Yes! to good heavens, Gwendolen, I mean to Gwendolen.

ALGERNON (*Laughing.*) Of course not! What could have put such an idea into your pretty little head?

CECILY Thank you. (*Presenting her cheek to be kissed.*) You may. (ALGERNON *kisses her.*)

GWENDOLEN I felt there was some slight error, Miss Cardew. The gentleman who is now embracing you is my cousin, Mr. Algernon Moncrieff.

CECILY (*Breaking away from* ALGERNON.) Algernon Moncrieff! Oh! (*The two girls move towards each other and put their arms round each other's waists as if for protection.*)

CECILY Are you called Algernon?

ALGERNON I cannot deny it.

CECILY Oh!

GWENDOLEN Is your name really John?

JACK (*Standing rather proudly.*) I could deny it if I liked. I could deny anything if I liked. But my name certainly is John. It has been John for years.

CECILY (*To* GWENDOLEN.) A gross deception has been practised on both of us.

GWENDOLEN <u>My poor wounded Cecily!</u>

CECILY My sweet wronged Gwendolen!

GWENDOLEN (*Slowly and seriously.*) You will call me sister, will you not? (*They embrace.* JACK *and* ALGERNON *groan and walk up and down.*)

CECILY (*Rather brightly.*) There is just one question I would like to be allowed to ask my guardian.

GWENDOLEN An admirable idea! Mr. Worthing, there is just one question I would like to be permitted to put to you. Where is your brother Ernest? We are both engaged to be married to your brother Ernest, so it is a matter of some importance to us to know where your brother Ernest is at present.

JACK (*Slowly and hesitatingly.*) Gwendolen—Cecily—it is very painful for me to be forced to speak the truth. It is the first time in my life <u>that I have ever been reduced to such a painful position</u>, and I am really quite inexperienced in doing anything of the kind. However I will tell you quite frankly that I have no brother Ernest. I have no brother at all. I never had a brother in my life, and I certainly have not the smallest intention of ever having one in the future.

They go from beefing to homies

CECILY   (*Surprised.*) No brother at all?

JACK   (*Cheerily.*) None!

GWENDOLEN   (*Severely.*) Had you never a brother of any kind?

JACK   (*Pleasantly.*) Never. Not even of any kind.

GWENDOLEN   I am afraid it is quite clear, Cecily, that neither of us is engaged to be married to anyone.

CECILY   It is not a very pleasant position for a young girl suddenly to find herself in. Is it?

GWENDOLEN   Let us go into the house. They will hardly venture to come after us there.

CECILY   No, men are so cowardly, aren't they?

> (*They retire into the house with scornful looks.*)

JACK   This ghastly state of things is what you call Bunburying, I suppose?

ALGERNON   Yes, and a perfectly wonderful Bunbury it is. The most wonderful Bunbury I have ever had in my life.

JACK   Well, you've no right whatsoever to Bunbury here.

ALGERNON   That is absurd. One has a right to Bunbury anywhere one chooses. Every serious Bunburyist knows that.

JACK   Serious Bunburyist! Good heavens!

ALGERNON   Well, one must be serious about something, if one wants to have any amusement in life. I happen to be serious about Bunburying. What on earth you are serious about I haven't got the remotest idea. About everything, I should fancy. You have such an absolutely trivial nature.

JACK   Well, the only small satisfaction I have in the whole of this wretched business is that your friend Bunbury is quite exploded. You won't be able to run down to the country quite so often as you used to do, dear Algy. And a very good thing too.

ALGERNON   Your brother is a little off colour, isn't he, dear Jack? You won't be able to disappear to London quite so frequently as your wicked custom was. And not a bad thing either.

JACK   As for your conduct towards Miss Cardew, I must say that your taking in a sweet, simple, innocent girl like that is quite inexcusable. To say nothing of the fact that she is my ward.

ALGERNON   I can see no possible defence at all for your deceiving a brilliant, clever, thoroughly experienced young lady like Miss Fairfax. To say nothing of the fact that she is my cousin.

JACK   I wanted to be engaged to Gwendolen, that is all. I love her.

ALGERNON   Well, I simply wanted to be engaged to Cecily. I adore her.

JACK   There is certainly no chance of your marrying Miss Cardew.

ALGERNON   I don't think there is much likelihood, Jack, of you and Miss Fairfax being united.

JACK   Well, that is no business of yours.

ALGERNON   If it was my business, I wouldn't talk about it. (*Begins to eat muffins.*) It is very vulgar to talk about one's business. Only people like stockbrokers do that, and then merely at dinner parties.

JACK   How you can sit there, calmly eating muffins when we are in this horrible trouble, I can't make out. You seem to me to be perfectly heartless.

ALGERNON   Well, I can't eat muffins in an agitated manner. The butter would probably get on my cuffs. One should always eat muffins quite calmly. It is the only way to eat them.

JACK   I say it's perfectly heartless your eating muffins at all, under the circumstances.

ALGERNON   When I am in trouble, eating is the only thing that consoles me. Indeed, when I am in really great trouble, as anyone who knows me intimately will tell you, I refuse everything except food and drink. At the present moment I am eating muffins because I am unhappy. Besides, I am particularly fond of muffins. (*Rising.*)

JACK   (*Rising.*) Well, that is no reason why you should eat them all in that greedy way.
    (*Takes muffins from* ALGERNON.)

ALGERNON   (*Offering tea-cake.*) I wish you would have tea-cake instead. I don't like tea-cake.

JACK   Good heavens! I suppose a man may eat his own muffins in his own garden.

ALGERNON   But you have just said it was perfectly heartless to eat muffins.

JACK   I said it was perfectly heartless of you, under the circumstances. That is a very different thing.

ALGERNON   That may be. But the muffins are the same. (*He seizes the muffin-dish from* JACK.)

JACK   Algy, I wish to goodness you would go.

ALGERNON   You can't possibly ask me to go without having some dinner. It's absurd. I never go without my dinner. No one ever does, except vegetarians and people like that. Besides I have just made arrangements with Dr. Chasuble to be christened at a quarter to six under the name of Ernest.

JACK   My dear fellow, the sooner you give up that nonsense the better. I made arrangements this morning with Dr. Chasuble to be christened myself at 5:30, and I naturally will take the name of Ernest. Gwendolen would wish it. We can't both be christened Ernest. It's absurd. Besides, I have a perfect right to be christened if I like. There is no evidence at all that I have ever been christened by anybody. I should think it extremely probable I never was, and so does Dr. Chasuble. It is entirely different in your case. You have been christened already.

ALGERNON   Yes, but I have not been christened for years.

JACK   Yes, but you have been christened. That is the important thing.

ALGERNON   Quite so. So I know my constitution can stand it. If you are not quite sure about your ever having been christened, I must say I think it rather dangerous your venturing on it now. It might make you very unwell. You can hardly have forgotten that someone very closely connected with you was very nearly carried off this week in Paris by a severe chill.

JACK   Yes, but you said yourself that a severe chill was not hereditary.

ALGERNON   It usen't to be, I know—but I daresay it is now. Science is always making wonderful improvements in things.

JACK   (*Picking up the muffin-dish.*) Oh, that is nonsense; you are always talking nonsense.

ALGERNON   Jack, you are at the muffins again! I wish you wouldn't. There are only two left. (*Takes them.*) I told you I was particularly fond of muffins.

JACK   But I hate tea-cake.

ALGERNON   Why on earth then do you allow tea-cake to be served up for your guests? What ideas you have of hospitality!

JACK   Algernon! I have already told you to go. I don't want you here. Why don't you go!

ALGERNON   I haven't quite finished my tea yet! and there is still one muffin left. (JACK *groans, and sinks into a chair.* ALGERNON *still continues eating.*)

ACT-DROP

Third Act

Scene— *Morning-room at the Manor House.*

(GWENDOLEN *and* CECILY *are at the window, looking out into the garden.*)

GWENDOLEN   The fact that they did not follow us at once into the house, as anyone else would have done, seems to me to show that they have some sense of shame left.

CECILY   They have been eating muffins. That looks like repentance.

GWENDOLEN   (*After a pause.*) They don't seem to notice us at all. Couldn't you cough?

CECILY   But I haven't got a cough.

GWENDOLEN   They're looking at us. What effrontery!

CECILY   They're approaching. That's very forward of them.

GWENDOLEN   Let us preserve a dignified silence.

CECILY   Certainly. It's the only thing to do now.

> (*Enter* JACK *followed by* ALGERNON. *They whistle some dreadful popular air from a British Opera.*[5])

GWENDOLEN   This dignified silence seems to produce an unpleasant effect.

CECILY   A most distasteful one.

GWENDOLEN   But we will not be the first to speak.

CECILY   Certainly not.

GWENDOLEN   Mr. Worthing, I have something very particular to ask you. Much depends on your reply.

CECILY   Gwendolen, your common sense is invaluable. Mr. Moncrieff, kindly answer me the following question. Why did you pretend to be my guardian's brother?

ALGERNON   In order that I might have an opportunity of meeting you.

CECILY   (*To* GWENDOLEN.) That certainly seems a satisfactory explanation, does it not?

GWENDOLEN   Yes, dear, if you can believe him.

CECILY   I don't. But that does not affect the wonderful beauty of his answer.

GWENDOLEN   True. In matters of grave importance, style, not sincerity is the vital thing. Mr. Worthing, what explanation can you offer to me for pretending to have a brother? Was it in order that you might have an opportunity of coming up to town to see me as often as possible?

JACK   Can you doubt it, Miss Fairfax?

GWENDOLEN   I have the gravest doubts upon the subject. But I intend to crush them. This is not the moment for German skepticism.[6] (*Moving to* CECILY.) Their explanations appear to be quite satisfactory, especially Mr. Worthing's. That seems to me to have the stamp of truth upon it.

CECILY   I am more than content with what Mr. Moncrieff said. His voice alone inspires one with absolute credulity.

GWENDOLEN   Then you think we should forgive them?

CECILY   Yes. I mean no.

GWENDOLEN   True! I had forgotten. There are principles at stake

---

5. Wilde is undoubtedly referring to a musical number by Sir William S. Gilbert (1836–1911) and Sir Arthur Sullivan (1842–1900), the famous British lyricist and composer, who lampooned him in their comic opera *Patience, or Bunthorne's Bride* (1881).

6. A broad reference to a perceived inclination to doubt the truth of some assertion or supposed fact, often extending to general mistrustfulness.

that one cannot surrender. Which of us should tell them? The task is not a pleasant one.

CECILY   Could we not both speak at the same time?

GWENDOLEN   An excellent idea! I nearly always speak at the same time as other people. Will you take the time from me?

CECILY   Certainly. (GWENDOLEN *beats time with uplifted finger.*)

GWENDOLEN *and* CECILY   (*Speaking together.*) Your Christian names are still an insuperable barrier. That is all!

JACK *and* ALGERNON   (*Speaking together.*) Our Christian names! Is that all? But we are going to be christened this afternoon.

GWENDOLEN   (*To* JACK.) For my sake you are prepared to do this terrible thing?

JACK   I am.

CECILY   (*To* ALGERNON.) To please me you are ready to face this fearful ordeal?

ALGERNON   I am!   *They are the same*

GWENDOLEN   How absurd to talk of the equality of the sexes! Where questions of self-sacrifice are concerned, men are infinitely beyond us.

JACK   We are. (*Clasps hands with* ALGERNON.)

CECILY   They have moments of physical courage of which we women know absolutely nothing.

GWENDOLEN   (*To* JACK.) Darling!

ALGERNON   (*To* CECILY.) Darling! (*They fall into each other's arms.*)
          (*Enter* MERRIMAN. *When he enters he coughs loudly, seeing the situation.*)

MERRIMAN   Ahem! Ahem! Lady Bracknell!

JACK   Good heavens!
          (*Enter* LADY BRACKNELL. *The couples separate in alarm. Exit* MERRIMAN.)

LADY BRACKNELL   Gwendolen! What does this mean?

GWENDOLEN   Merely that I am engaged to be married to Mr. Worthing, mamma.

LADY BRACKNELL   Come here. Sit down. Sit down immediately. Hesitation of any kind is a sign of mental decay in the young, of physical weakness in the old. (*Turns to* JACK.) Apprised, sir, of my daughter's sudden flight by her trusty maid, whose confidence I purchased by means of a small coin, I followed her at once by a luggage train.[7] Her unhappy father is, I am glad to say, under the impression that she is attending a more than usually lengthy lecture by the University Extension Scheme[8] on the Influence of a permanent income on Thought. I do not propose to undeceive

---

7. A cross-country train, as opposed to one making commuter stops.
8. An effort to extend the scope of the universities by offering lectures and examinations to non-resident students.

him. Indeed I have never undeceived him on any question. I would consider it wrong. But of course, you will clearly understand that all communication between yourself and my daughter must cease immediately from this moment. On this point, as indeed on all points, I am firm.

JACK   I am engaged to be married to Gwendolen, Lady Bracknell!

LADY BRACKNELL   You are nothing of the kind, sir. And now, as regards Algernon! . . . Algernon!

ALGERNON   Yes, Aunt Augusta.

LADY BRACKNELL   May I ask if it is in this house that your invalid friend Mr. Bunbury resides?

ALGERNON   (*Stammering.*) Oh! No! Bunbury doesn't live here. Bunbury is somewhere else at present. In fact, Bunbury is dead.

LADY BRACKNELL   Dead! When did Mr. Bunbury die? His death must have been extremely sudden.

ALGERNON   (*Airily.*) Oh! I killed Bunbury this afternoon. I mean poor Bunbury died this afternoon.

LADY BRACKNELL   What did he die of?

ALGERNON   Bunbury? Oh, he was quite exploded.

LADY BRACKNELL   Exploded! Was he the victim of a revolutionary outrage? I was not aware that Mr. Bunbury was interested in social legislation. If so, he is well punished for his morbidity.

ALGERNON   My dear Aunt Augusta, I mean he was found out! The doctors found out that Bunbury could not live, that is what I mean—so Bunbury died.

LADY BRACKNELL   He seems to have had great confidence in the opinion of his physicians. I am glad, however, that he made up his mind at the last to some definite course of action, and acted under proper medical advice. And now that we have finally got rid of this Mr. Bunbury, may I ask, Mr. Worthing, who is that young person whose hand my nephew Algernon is now holding in what seems to me a peculiarly unnecessary manner?

JACK   That lady is Miss Cecily Cardew, my ward. (LADY BRACKNELL *bows coldly to* CECILY.)

ALGERNON   I am engaged to be married to Cecily, Aunt Augusta.

LADY BRACKNELL   I beg your pardon?

CECILY   Mr. Moncrieff and I are engaged to be married, Lady Bracknell.

LADY BRACKNELL   (*With a shiver, crossing to the sofa and sitting down.*) I do not know whether there is anything peculiarly exciting in the air of this particular part of Hertfordshire, but the number of engagements that go on seems to me considerably above the proper average that statistics have laid down for our guidance. I think some preliminary inquiry on my part would not be out of place. Mr. Worthing, is Miss Cardew at all connected

with any of the larger railway stations in London? I merely desire information. Until yesterday I had no idea that there were any families or persons whose origin was a Terminus.[9] (JACK *looks perfectly furious, but restrains himself.*)

JACK   (*In a clear, cold voice.*) Miss Cardew is the grand-daughter of the late Mr. Thomas Cardew of 149 Belgrave Square, S.W.; Gervase Park, Dorking, Surrey; and the Sporran, Fifeshire, N.B.[1]

LADY BRACKNELL   That sounds not unsatisfactory. Three addresses always inspire confidence, even in tradesmen. But what proof have I of their authenticity?

JACK   I have carefully preserved the Court Guides[2] of the period. They are open to your inspection, Lady Bracknell.

LADY BRACKNELL   (*Grimly.*) I have known strange errors in that publication.

JACK   Miss Cardew's family solicitors are Messrs. Markby, Markby, and Markby.

LADY BRACKNELL   Markby, Markby, and Markby? A firm of the very highest position in their profession. Indeed I am told that one of the Mr. Markbys is occasionally to be seen at dinner parties. So far I am satisfied.

JACK   (*Very irritably.*) How extremely kind of you, Lady Bracknell! I have also in my possession, you will be pleased to hear, certificates of Miss Cardew's birth, baptism, whooping cough, registration, vaccination, confirmation, and the measles; both the German and the English variety.

LADY BRACKNELL   Ah! A life crowded with incident, I see; though perhaps somewhat too exciting for a young girl. I am not myself in favour of premature experiences. (*Rises, looks at her watch.*) Gwendolen! the time approaches for our departure. We have not a moment to lose. As a matter of form, Mr. Worthing, I had better ask you if Miss Cardew has any little fortune?

JACK   Oh! about a hundred and thirty thousand pounds[3] in the Funds.[4] That is all. Good-bye, Lady Bracknell. So pleased to have seen you.

LADY BRACKNELL   (*Sitting down again.*) A moment, Mr. Worthing. A hundred and thirty thousand pounds! And in the Funds! Miss Cardew seems to me a most attractive young lady, now that I look at her. Few girls of the present day have any really solid qualities,

---

9. The end of a line of a railway, or the station at that end.
1. Fifeshire is a maritime peninsular county of east central Scotland. That Cardew owned three properties bodes well for his respectability.
2. The title of a directory containing the names and addresses of the nobility, gentry, and people in "society," the theory being that it contains the names of all persons who have been presented at court.
3. Using the Consumer Price Index as a guide, this amount would translate to $13,850,958.89 in 2003 U.S. dollars.
4. Investments backed by the Bank of England.

any of the qualities that last, and improve with time. We live, I regret to say, in an age of surfaces. (*To* CECILY.) Come over here, dear. (CECILY *goes across.*) Pretty child! your dress is sadly simple, and your hair seems almost as Nature might have left it. But we can soon alter all that. A thoroughly experienced French maid produces a really marvellous result in a very brief space of time. I remember recommending one to young Lady Lancing, and after three months her own husband did not know her.

JACK   (*Aside.*) And after six months nobody knew her.[5]

LADY BRACKNELL   (*Glares at* JACK *for a few moments. Then bends, with a practised smile, to* CECILY.) Kindly turn round, sweet child. (CECILY *turns completely round.*) No, the side view is what I want. (CECILY *presents her profile.*) Yes, quite as I expected. There are distinct social possibilities in your profile. The two weak points in our age are its want of principle and its want of profile. The chin a little higher, dear. Style largely depends on the way the chin is worn. They are worn very high, just at present. Algernon!

ALGERNON   Yes, Aunt Augusta!

LADY BRACKNELL   There are distinct social possibilities in Miss Cardew's profile.

ALGERNON   Cecily is the sweetest, dearest, prettiest girl in the whole world. And I don't care twopence[6] about social possibilities.

LADY BRACKNELL   Never speak disrespectfully of Society, Algernon. Only people who can't get into it do that. (*To* CECILY.) Dear child, of course you know that Algernon has nothing but his debts to depend upon. But I do not approve of mercenary marriages. When I married Lord Bracknell I had no fortune of any kind. But I never dreamed for a moment of allowing that to stand in my way. Well, I suppose I must give my consent.

ALGERNON   Thank you, Aunt Augusta.

LADY BRACKNELL   <u>Cecily, you may kiss me!</u>

CECILY   (*Kisses her.*) Thank you, Lady Bracknell.

LADY BRACKNELL   You may also address me as <u>Aunt Augusta</u> for the future.

CECILY   Thank you, Aunt Augusta.

LADY BRACKNELL   The marriage, I think, had better take place quite soon.

ALGERNON   Thank you, Aunt Augusta.

CECILY   Thank you, Aunt Augusta.

LADY BRACKNELL   To speak frankly, I am not in favour of long engagements. They give people the opportunity of finding out each

5. Jack suggests that Lady Lancing's character so degenerated under the tutelage of her French maid that people in polite society refused to associate with her.
6. A sum of money, equal to two pennies.

other's character before marriage, which I think is never advisable.

JACK   I beg your pardon for interrupting you, Lady Bracknell, but this engagement is quite out of the question. I am Miss Cardew's guardian, and she cannot marry without my consent until she comes of age. That consent I absolutely decline to give.

LADY BRACKNELL   Upon what grounds may I ask? Algernon is an extremely, I may almost say an ostentatiously, eligible young man. He has nothing, but he looks everything. What more can one desire?

JACK   It pains me very much to have to speak frankly to you, Lady Bracknell, about your nephew, but the fact is that I do not approve at all of his moral character. I suspect him of being untruthful. (ALGERNON *and* CECILY *look at him in indignant amazement.*)

LADY BRACKNELL   Untruthful! My nephew Algernon? Impossible! He is an Oxonian.[7]

JACK   I fear there can be no possible doubt about the matter. This afternoon during my temporary absence in London on an important question of romance, he obtained admission to my house by means of the false pretence of being my brother. Under an assumed name he drank, I've just been informed by my butler, an entire pint bottle of my Perrier-Jouet, Brut, '89[8]; a wine I was specially reserving for myself. Continuing his disgraceful deception, he succeeded in the course of the afternoon in alienating the affections of my only ward. He subsequently stayed to tea, and devoured every single muffin. And what makes his conduct all the more heartless is, that he was perfectly well aware from the first that I have no brother, that I never had a brother, and that I don't intend to have a brother, not even of any kind. I distinctly told him so myself yesterday afternoon.

LADY BRACKNELL   Ahem! Mr. Worthing, after careful consideration I have decided entirely to overlook my nephew's conduct to you.

JACK   That is very generous of you, Lady Bracknell. My own decision, however, is unalterable. I decline to give my consent.

LADY BRACKNELL   (*To* CECILY.) Come here, sweet child. (CECILY *goes over.*) How old are you, dear?

CECILY   Well, I am really only eighteen, but I always admit to twenty when I go to evening parties.

LADY BRACKNELL   You are perfectly right in making some slight alteration. Indeed, no woman should ever be quite accurate about her age. It looks so calculating. . . . (*In a meditative manner.*)

7. The designation indicates that Algy has attended Oxford University.
8. A champagne produced by the firm of Perrier-Jouët of Epernay.

Eighteen, but admitting to twenty at evening parties. Well, it will not be very long before you are of age and free from the restraints of tutelage. So I don't think your guardian's consent is, after all, a matter of any importance.

JACK   Pray excuse me, Lady Bracknell, for interrupting you again, but it is only fair to tell you that according to the terms of her grandfather's will Miss Cardew does not come legally of age till she is thirty-five.

LADY BRACKNELL   That does not seem to me to be a grave objection. Thirty-five is a very attractive age. London society is full of women of the very highest birth who have, of their own free choice, remained thirty-five for years. Lady Dumbleton is an instance in point. To my own knowledge she has been thirty-five ever since she arrived at the age of forty, which was many years ago now. I see no reason why our dear Cecily should not be even still more attractive at the age you mention than she is at present. There will be a large accumulation of property.

CECILY   Algy, could you wait for me till I was thirty-five?

ALGERNON   Of course I could, Cecily. You know I could.

CECILY   Yes, I felt it instinctively, but I couldn't wait all that time. I hate waiting even five minutes for anybody. It always makes me rather cross. I am not punctual myself, I know, but I do like punctuality in others, and waiting, even to be married, is quite out of the question.

ALGERNON   Then what is to be done, Cecily?

CECILY   I don't know, Mr. Moncrieff.

LADY BRACKNELL   My dear Mr. Worthing, as Miss Cardew states positively that she cannot wait till she is thirty-five—a remark which I am bound to say seems to me to show a somewhat impatient nature—I would beg of you to reconsider your decision.

JACK   But my dear Lady Bracknell, the matter is entirely in your own hands. The moment you consent to my marriage with Gwendolen, I will most gladly allow your nephew to form an alliance with my ward.

LADY BRACKNELL   (*Rising and drawing herself up.*) You must be quite aware that what you propose is out of the question.

JACK   Then a passionate celibacy is all that any of us can look forward to.

LADY BRACKNELL   That is not the destiny I propose for Gwendolen. Algernon, of course, can choose for himself. (*Pulls out her watch.*) Come, dear; (GWENDOLEN *rises.*) we have already missed five, if not six, trains. To miss any more might expose us to comment on the platform.

(*Enter* Dr. CHASUBLE.)

CHASUBLE   Everything is quite ready for the christenings.

LADY BRACKNELL   The christenings, sir! Is not that somewhat premature?

CHASUBLE   (*Looking rather puzzled, and pointing to* JACK *and* ALGERNON.) Both these gentlemen have expressed a desire for immediate baptism.

LADY BRACKNELL   At their age? The idea is grotesque and irreligious! Algernon, I forbid you to be baptized. I will not hear of such excesses. Lord Bracknell would be highly displeased if he learned that that was the way in which you wasted your time and money.

CHASUBLE   Am I to understand then that there are to be no christenings at all this afternoon?

JACK   I don't think that, as things are now, it would be of much practical value to either of us, Dr. Chasuble.

CHASUBLE   I am grieved to hear such sentiments from you, Mr. Worthing. They savour of the heretical views of the Anabaptists, views that I have completely refuted in four of my unpublished sermons. However, as your present mood seems to be one peculiarly secular, I will return to the church at once. Indeed, I have just been informed by the pew-opener[9] that for the last hour and a half Miss Prism has been waiting for me in the vestry.

LADY BRACKNELL   (*Starting.*) Miss Prism! Did I hear you mention a Miss Prism?

CHASUBLE   Yes, Lady Bracknell. I am on my way to join her.

LADY BRACKNELL   Pray allow me to detain you for a moment. This matter may prove to be one of vital importance to Lord Bracknell and myself. Is this Miss Prism a female of repellent aspect, remotely connected with education?

CHASUBLE   (*Somewhat indignantly.*) She is the most cultivated of ladies, and the very picture of respectability.

LADY BRACKNELL   It is obviously the same person. May I ask what position she holds in your household?

CHASUBLE   (*Severely.*) I am a celibate, madam.

JACK   (*Interposing.*) Miss Prism, Lady Bracknell, has been for the last three years Miss Cardew's esteemed governess and valued companion.

LADY BRACKNELL   In spite of what I hear of her, I must see her at once. Let her be sent for.

CHASUBLE   (*Looking off.*) She approaches; she is nigh.

      (*Enter* MISS PRISM *hurriedly.*)

---

9. An usher in a church.

MISS PRISM   I was told you expected me in the vestry, dear Canon. I have been waiting for you there for an hour and three-quarters. (*Catches sight of* LADY BRACKNELL *who has fixed her with a stony glare.* MISS PRISM *grows pale and quails. She looks anxiously round as if desirous to escape.*)

LADY BRACKNELL   (*In a severe, judicial voice.*) Prism! (MISS PRISM *bows her head in shame.*) Come here, Prism! (MISS PRISM *approaches in a humble manner.*) Prism! Where is that baby? (*General consternation. The* CANON *starts back in horror.* ALGERNON *and* JACK *pretend to be anxious to shield* CECILY *and* GWENDOLEN *from hearing the details of a terrible public scandal.*) Twenty-eight years ago, Prism, you left Lord Bracknell's house, Number 104, Upper Grosvenor Street, in charge of a perambulator[1] that contained a baby of the male sex. You never returned. A few weeks later, through the elaborate investigations of the Metropolitan police,[2] the perambulator was discovered at midnight, standing by itself in a remote corner of Bayswater.[3] It contained the manuscript of a three-volume novel of more than usually revolting sentimentality. (MISS PRISM *starts in involuntary indignation.*) But the baby was not there! (*Everyone looks at* MISS PRISM.) Prism! Where is that baby? (*A pause.*)

MISS PRISM   Lady Bracknell, I admit with shame that I do not know. I only wish I did. The plain facts of the case are these. On the morning of the day you mention, a day that is for ever branded on my memory, I prepared as usual to take the baby out in its perambulator. I had also with me a somewhat old, but capacious hand-bag in which I had intended to place the manuscript of a work of fiction that I had written during my few unoccupied hours. In a moment of mental abstraction, for which I never can forgive myself, I deposited the manuscript in the basinette,[4] and placed the baby in the hand-bag.

JACK   (*Who has been listening attentively.*) But where did you deposit the hand-bag?

MISS PRISM   Do not ask me, Mr. Worthing.

1. A carriage with three or four wheels for one or two young children, pushed from behind.
2. The sector of Scotland Yard associated with the city of London.
3. From Charles Dickens, Jr.'s *Dickens's Dictionary of London*, 1879: "Bayswater lies to the west of Tyburnia, and possesses much the same characteristics. It has, however, rather a specialty for good shops at lower prices than are usual at this end of the town. There are some enormous houses about Lancaster-gate at proportionately enormous prices, but rents are here beginning to lower a little in comparison with those in Tyburnia, and a fairly comfortable house can be got for £150 to £200 a year. It is well, however, to bear in mind that this is merely a comparative drop in prices, and that good houses in this neighbourhood, as in most other parts of the West-end, are steadily rising in value from year to year."
4. This can be an oblong wickerwork basket, with a hood over one end, used as a cradle for babies, or, as in this instance, a form of child's perambulator of the same shape.

JACK   Miss Prism, this is a matter of no small importance to me. I insist on knowing where you deposited the hand-bag that contained that infant.

MISS PRISM   <u>I left it in the cloak-room of one of the larger railway stations in London</u>.

JACK   What railway station?

MISS PRISM   (*Quite crushed.*) Victoria. The Brighton line. (*Sinks into a chair.*)

JACK   I must retire to my room for a moment. Gwendolen, wait here for me.

GWENDOLEN   If you are not too long, I will wait here for you all my life.

   (*Exit* JACK *in great excitement.*)

CHASUBLE   What do you think this means, Lady Bracknell?

LADY BRACKNELL   I dare not even suspect, Dr. Chasuble. I need hardly tell you that in families of high position strange coincidences are not supposed to occur. They are hardly considered the thing.

   (*Noises heard overhead as if someone was throwing trunks about. Everyone looks up.*)

CECILY   Uncle Jack seems strangely agitated.

CHASUBLE   Your guardian has a very emotional nature.

LADY BRACKNELL   This noise is extremely unpleasant. It sounds as if he was having an argument. I dislike arguments of any kind. <u>They are always vulgar, and often convincing</u>.

CHASUBLE   (*Looking up.*) It has stopped now. (*The noise is redoubled.*)

LADY BRACKNELL   I wish he would arrive at some conclusion.

GWENDOLEN   This suspense is terrible. I hope it will last.

   (*Enter* JACK *with a hand-bag of black leather in his hand.*)

JACK   (*Rushing over to* MISS PRISM.) Is this the handbag, Miss Prism? Examine it carefully before you speak. The happiness of more than one life depends on your answer.

MISS PRISM   (*Calmly.*) It seems to be mine. Yes, here is the injury it received through the upsetting of a Gower Street[5] omnibus[6] in younger and happier days. Here is the stain on the lining caused by the explosion of a temperance beverage,[7] an incident that occurred at Leamington.[8] And here, on the lock, are my initials. I had forgotten that in an extravagant mood I had had them placed

---

5. Located in the borough of Camden.
6. A public vehicle carrying passengers by road, running on a fixed route and typically requiring payment of a fare.
7. A non-alcoholic beverage as approved by a Temperance Society, that is, a society that believes in abstinence from alcohol.
8. Located in central England in Warwickshire, Leamington was famous in the nineteenth century for its health spa, the Royal Leamington Spa.

there. The bag is undoubtedly mine. I am delighted to have it so unexpectedly restored to me. It has been a great inconvenience being without it all these years.

JACK   (*In a pathetic voice.*) Miss Prism, more is restored to you than this hand-bag. I was the baby you placed in it.

MISS PRISM   (*Amazed.*) You?

JACK   (*Embracing her.*) Yes . . . mother!   *Miss Prism = Jack's mom*

MISS PRISM   (*Recoiling in indignant astonishment.*) Mr. Worthing! I am unmarried.

JACK   Unmarried! I do not deny that is a serious blow. But after all, who has the right to cast a stone[9] against one who has suffered? Cannot repentance wipe out an act of folly? Why should there be one law for men, and another for women? Mother, I forgive you. (*Tries to embrace her again.*)

MISS PRISM   (*Still more indignant.*) Mr. Worthing, there is some error. (*Pointing to* LADY BRACKNELL.) There is the lady who can tell you who you really are.

JACK   (*After a pause.*) Lady Bracknell, I hate to seem inquisitive, but would you kindly inform me who I am?

LADY BRACKNELL   I am afraid that the news I have to give you will not altogether please you. You are the son of my poor sister, Mrs. Moncrieff, and consequently Algernon's elder brother.

JACK   Algy's elder brother! Then I have a brother after all. I knew I had a brother! I always said I had a brother! Cecily,—how could you have ever doubted that I had a brother. (*Seizes hold of* ALGERNON.) Dr. Chasuble, my unfortunate brother. Miss Prism, my unfortunate brother. Gwendolen, my unfortunate brother. Algy, you young scoundrel, you will have to treat me with more respect in the future. You have never behaved to me like a brother in all your life.

ALGERNON   Well, not till to-day, old boy, I admit. I did my best, however, though I was out of practice. (*Shakes hands.*)

GWENDOLEN   (*To* JACK.) My own! But what own are you? What is your Christian name, now that you have become someone else?

JACK   Good heavens! . . . I had quite forgotten that point. Your decision on the subject of my name is irrevocable, I suppose?

GWENDOLEN   I never change, except in my affections.

CECILY   What a noble nature you have, Gwendolen!

JACK   Then the question had better be cleared up at once. Aunt Augusta, a moment. At the time when Miss Prism left me in the hand-bag, had I been christened already?

9. A variation on Christ's admonition, recorded in the Gospel of Saint John, to those planning to stone to death an adulterous woman: "Let him who is without sin cast the first stone" (8:7).

LADY BRACKNELL   Every luxury that money could buy, including christening, had been lavished on you by your fond and doting parents.

JACK   Then I was christened! That is settled. Now, what name was
I given? Let me know the worst.

LADY BRACKNELL   Being the eldest son you were naturally christened after your father.

JACK   (*Irritably.*) Yes, but what was my father's Christian name?

LADY BRACKNELL   (*Meditatively.*) I cannot at the present moment
recall what the General's Christian name was. But I have no
doubt he had one. He was eccentric, I admit. But only in later
years. And that was the result of the Indian climate, and marriage, and indigestion, and other things of that kind.

JACK   Algy! Can't you recollect what our father's Christian name
was?

ALGERNON   My dear boy, we were never even on speaking terms.
He died before I was a year old.

JACK   His name would appear in the Army Lists[1] of the period, I
suppose, Aunt Augusta?

LADY BRACKNELL   The General was essentially a man of peace, except in his domestic life. But I have no doubt his name would appear in any military directory.

JACK   The Army Lists of the last forty years are here. These delightful records should have been my constant study. (*Rushes to
bookcase and tears the books out.*) M. Generals . . . Mallam,
Maxbohm, Magley, what ghastly names they have—Markby,
Migsby, Mobbs, Moncrieff! Lieutenant 1840, Captain, Lieu-
tenant-Colonel, Colonel, General 1869, Christian names, Ernest
John. (*Puts book very quietly down and speaks quite calmly.*) I always told you, Gwendolen, my name was Ernest, didn't I? Well, it
is Ernest after all. I mean it naturally is Ernest.

LADY BRACKNELL   Yes, I remember now that the General was called
Ernest, I knew I had some particular reason for disliking the
name.

GWENDOLEN   Ernest! My own Ernest! I felt from the first that you
could have no other name!

JACK   Gwendolen, it is a terrible thing for a man to find out suddenly that all his life he has been speaking nothing but the truth.
Can you forgive me?

GWENDOLEN   I can. For I feel that you are sure to change.

JACK   My own one!

CHASUBLE   (*To* MISS PRISM.) Laetitia! (*Embraces her.*)

MISS PRISM   (*Enthusiastically.*) Frederick! At last!

1. A publication containing the official list of all the commissioned officers of the British
Army.

ALGERNON Cecily! (*Embraces her.*) At last!

JACK Gwendolen! (*Embraces her.*) At last!

LADY BRACKNELL My nephew, you seem to be displaying signs of triviality.

JACK On the contrary, Aunt Augusta, I've now realised for the first time in my life the vital Importance of Being Earnest.

TABLEAU

CURTAIN

- She's more pressed about
  hand bag than lost baby
- Examine handbag w/care

Excised Portions of the Play

The Gribsby Episode from the Manuscript Draft†

The following sequence is transcribed from the manuscript draft of Act Two (New York Public Library), as reproduced in Sarah Augusta Dickson, *The Importance of Being Earnest . . . As Originally Written by Oscar Wilde* (New York, 2 volumes, 1956). The portion reprinted here corresponds to ff. 49–67 of the manuscript, and begins with lines 360–1 of the Second Act in the present edition.

MERRIMAN   Mr. Ernest's luggage, sir. I have unpacked it and put it in the room next to your own.

ALGY   I am afraid I can't stay more than a week, Jack, this time.

CECILY   A week? Will you really be able to stay over Monday?

ALGY   I think I can manage to stop over Monday, now.

CECILY   I am so glad.

MERRIMAN   (*To* ERNEST.) I beg your pardon, sir. There is an elderly gentleman wishes to see you. He has just co[m]e in a cab from the station. (*Holds card on salver.*)

ALGY   To see me?

MERRIMAN   Yes, sir.

ALGY   (*Reads card.*) Parker and Gribsby, Solicitors. I don't know anything about them. Who are they?

JACK   (*Takes card.*) Parker and Gribsby: I wonder who they can be[?] I expect Ernest they have come about some business for your friend Bunbury. Perhaps Bunbury wants to make his will, and wishes you to be executor. (*To* MERRIMAN.) Show Messrs. Parker and Gribsby in at once.

MERRIMAN   There is only one gentleman in the hall, sir.

JACK   Show either Mr. Parker or Mr. Gribsby in.

MERRIMAN   Yes, sir. (*Exit.*)

JACK   I hope, Ernest, that I may rely on the statement you made to me last week when I finally settled all your bills for you. I hope you have no outstanding accounts of any kind.

† Fragments of the four-act version of *The Importance of Being Earnest*. Copyright © The Estate of Oscar Wilde, 1956, 1983. Used with permission.

ALGY   I haven't any debts at all, dear Jack. Thanks to your generosity, I don't owe a penny, except for a few neckties I believe.

JACK   I am sincerely glad to hear it.
> (*Enter* MERRIMAN.)

MERRIMAN   Mr. Gribsby.
> (*Enter* GRIBSBY. *Exit* MERRIMAN.)

GRIBSBY   (*To* CANON CHASUBLE.) Mr. Ernest Worthing?

PRISM   (*Indicating* ALGY.) This is Mr. Ernest Worthing.

GRIBSBY   Mr. Ernest Worthing?

ALGY   Yes.

GRIBSBY   Of B.4, The Albany—?

ALGY   Yes, that is my address—

GRIBSBY   I am very sorry, Mr Worthing, but we have a writ of attachment for 20 days against you at the suit of the Savoy Hotel Co. Limited for £762. 14. 2.

ALGY   What perfect nonsense! I never dine at the Savoy at my own expense. I always dine at Willis's. It is far more expensive. I don't owe a penny to the Savoy.

GRIBSBY   The writ is marked as having been [served] on you personally at the Albany on May the 27th. Judgement was given in default against you on the fifth of June—Since then we have written to you no less than thirteen times, without receiving any reply. In the interest of our clients we had no option but to obtain an order for committal of your person. But, no doubt, Mr. Worthing, you will be able to settle the account, without any further unpleasantness. Seven and six should be added to the bill of costs for the expense of the cab which was hired for your convenience in case of any necessity of removal, but that I am sure is a contingency that is not likely to occur.

ALGY   Removal! What on earth do you mean by removal? I haven't the smallest intention of going away. I am staying here for a week. I am staying with my brother. (*Points to* JACK.)

GRIBSBY   (*To* JACK.) Pleased to meet you, sir.

ALGY   (*To* GRIBSBY.) If you imagine I am going up to town the moment I arrive you are extremely mistaken.

GRIBSBY   I am merely a Solicitor myself. I do not employ personal violence of any kind. The officer of the Court whose function it is to seize the person of the debtor is waiting in the fly outside. He has considerable experience in these matters. In the point of fact he has arrested in the course of his duties nearly all the younger sons of the aristocracy, as well as several eldest sons, besides of course a good many members of the House of Lords. His style and manner are considered extremely good. Indeed, he looks more like a betting man than a court-official. That is why

we always employ him. But no doubt you will prefer to pay the bill.

ALGY   Pay it? How on earth am I going to do that? You don't suppose I have got any money? How perfectly silly you are. No gentleman ever has any money.

GRIBSBY   My experience is that it is usually relations who pay.

JACK   Kindly allow me to see this bill, Mr Gribsby— (*Turns over immense folio*) —£762. 14. 2 since last October. I am bound to say I never saw such reckless extravagance in all my life. (*Hands it to* Dr. CHASUBLE.)

PRISM   £762 for eating! How grossly materialistic! There can be little good in any young man who eats so much, and so often.

CHASUBLE   It certainly is a painful proof of the disgraceful luxury of the age. We are far away from Wordsworth's plain living and high thinking.

JACK   Now, Dr. Chasuble[,] do you consider that I am in any way called upon to pay this monstrous account for my brother?

CHASUBLE   I am bound to say that I do not think so. It would be encouraging his profligacy.

PRISM   As a man sows, so let him reap. The proposed incarceration might be most salutary. It is to be regretted that it is only for 20 days.

JACK   I am quite of your opinion.

ALGY   My dear fellow, how ridiculous you are! You know perfectly well that the bill is really yours.

JACK   Mine[?]

ALGY   Yes: you know it is.

CHASUBLE   Mr. Worthing, if this is a jest, it is out of place.

PRISM   It is gross effrontery. Just what I expected from him.

CECILY   It is ingratitude. I didn't expect that.

JACK   Never mind what he says. This is the way he always goes on. (*To* ALGY.) You mean to say that you are not Ernest Worthing, residing at B.4, The Albany[?] I wonder, as you are at it, that you don't deny being my brother at all. Why don't you?

ALGY   Oh! I am not going to do that, my dear fellow, it would be absurd. Of course, I'm your brother. And that is why you should pay this bill for me. What is the use of having a brother, if he doesn't pay one's bills for one?

JACK   Personally, if you ask me, I don't see *any* use in having a brother. As for paying your bill I have not the smallest intention of doing anything of the kind. Dr. Chasuble, the worthy Rector of this parish, and Miss Prism[,] in whose admirable and sound judgement I place great reliance[,] are both of opinion that incarceration would do you a great deal of good. And I think so too.

GRIBSBY (*Pulls out watch.*) I am sorry to disturb this pleasant family meeting, but time presses. We have to be at Holloway not later than four o'clock; otherwise it is difficult to obtain admission. The rules are very strict.

ALGY Holloway!

GRIBSBY It is at Holloway that detentions of this character take place always.

ALGY Well, I really am not going to be imprisoned in the suburbs for having dined in the West End. It is perfectly ridiculous.

GRIBSBY The bill is for suppers, not for dinners.

ALGY I really don't care. All I say is that I am not going to be imprisoned in the suburbs.

GRIBSBY The surroundings I admit are middle class: but the gaol itself is fashionable and well-aired: and there are ample opportunities of taking exercise at certain stated hours of the day. In the case of a medical certificate[,] which is always easy to obtain[,] the hours can be extended.

ALGY Exercise! Good God! no gentleman ever takes exercise. You don't seem to understand what a gentleman is.

GRIBSBY I have met so many of them, sir, that I am afraid I don't. There are the most curious varieties of them. The result of cultivation, no doubt. Will you kindly come now, sir, if it will not be inconvenient to you.

ALGY (*Appealingly.*) Jack!

PRISM Pray be firm, Mr. Worthing.

CHASUBLE This is an occasion on which any weakness would be out of place. It would be a form of self-deception.

JACK I am quite firm: and I don't know what weakness or deception of any kind is.

CECILY Uncle Jack! I think you have a little money of mine haven't you? Let me pay this bill. I wouldn't like your own brother to be in prison.

JACK Oh! you can't pay it, Cecily, that is nonsense.

CECILY Then you will, won't you? I think you would be sorry if you thought your own brother was shut up. Of course, I am quite disappointed with him.

JACK You won't speak to him again, Cecily, will you?

CECILY Certainly not. Unless, of course[,] he speaks to me first[;] it would be very rude not to answer him.

JACK Well, I'll take care he doesn't speak to you. I'll take care he doesn't speak to any body in this house. The man should be cut. Mr. Gribsby—

GRIBSBY Yes, sir.

JACK I'll pay this bill for my brother. It is the last bill I shall ever pay for him too. How much is it?

GRIBSBY £762. 14. 2. May I ask your full name, sir?

JACK Mr. John Worthing, J.P., the Manor House, Woolton. Does that satisfy you?

GRIBSBY Oh! certainly, sir, certainly. It was a mere formality. (*To* MISS PRISM.) Handsome place. Ah! the cab will be 5/9 extra: hired for the convenience of the client.

JACK All right.

PRISM I must say that I think such generosity quite foolish. Especially paying the cab.

CHASUBLE (*With a wave of the hand.*) The heart has its wisdom as well as the head, Miss Prism.

JACK Payable to Gribsby and Parker I suppose?

GRIBSBY Yes, sir. Kindly don't cross the cheque. Thank you.

JACK You are Gribsby aren't you? What is Parker like?

GRIBSBY I am both, sir. Gribsby when I am on unpleasant business, Parker on occasions of a less severe kind.

JACK The next time I see you I hope you will be Parker.

GRIBSBY I hope so, sir. (*To Dr.* CHASUBLE.) Good day. (*Dr.* CHASUBLE *bows coldly.*) Good day. (MISS PRISM *bows coldly.*) Hope I shall have the pleasure of meeting you again. (*To* ALGY.)

ALGY I sincerely hope not. What ideas you have of the sort of society a gentleman wants to mix in. No gentleman ever wants to know a Solicitor, who wants to imprison one in the suburbs.

GRIBSBY Quite so, quite so.

ALGY By the way, Gribsby. Gribsby, you are not to go back to the station in that cab. That is my cab. It was taken for my convenience. You and the gentleman who looks like the betting man have got to walk to the station, and a very good thing too. Solicitors don't walk nearly enough. They bolt. But they don't walk. I don't know any solicitor who takes sufficient exercise. As a rule they sit in stuffy offices all day long neglecting their business.

JACK You can take the cab, Mr Gribsby.

GRIBSBY Thank you, sir. (*Exit.*)

The Dictation Episode (Act II) in the Licensing Copy

The following appears in the licensing copy (LC) after Cecily's speech instructing Algernon not to cough (lines 438–40 of the present edition). It is a slightly revised version of a passage in the MS draft and the Arents III typescript.

ALGERNON (*Speaking very rapidly.*) Miss Cardew, ever since half past two this afternoon, when I first looked upon your wonderful

and incomparable beauty, I have not merely been your abject slave and servant, but, soaring upon the pinions of a possibly monstrous ambition, I have dared to love you wildly, passionately, devotedly, hopelessly.

CECILY   (*Laying down her pen.*) Oh! Please say that all over again. You speak far too fast and too indistinctly. Kindly say it all over again.

ALGERNON   Ever since it was half past two this afternoon, when I first looked upon your wonderful and incomparable beauty—

CECILY   Yes, I have got that all right.

ALGERNON   (*Stammering.*) I—I— (CECILY *lays down her pen and looks reproachfully at him.*)
(*Desperately.*) I have not merely been your abject slave and servant, but, soaring on the pinions of a possibly monstrous ambition, I have dared to love you wildly, passionately, devotedly, hopelessly. (*Takes out his watch and looks at it.*)

CECILY   (*After writing for some time looks up.*) I have not taken down 'hopelessly'. It doesn't seem to make much sense, does it? (*A slight pause.*)

ALGERNON   (*Starting back.*) Cecily!

CECILY   Is that the beginning of an entirely new paragraph? or should it be followed by a note of admiration?

ALGERNON   (*Rapidly and romantically.*) It is the beginning of an entirely new existence for me, and it shall be followed by such notes of admiration that my whole life shall be a subtle and sustained symphony of Love, Praise and Adoration combined.

CECILY   Oh, I don't think *that* makes any sense at *all*. The fact is that men should never dictate to women. They never know *how* to do it, and when they *do* do it, they always say something particularly foolish.

ALGERNON   I don't care whether what I say is foolish or not. All that I know is that I love you, Cecily! I love you! I can't live without you, Cecily! You know I love you. Will you marry me? Will you be my wife? (*Rushes over to her and puts his hand on hers.*)
(*Enter* MERRIMAN.)

MERRIMAN   The dog-cart is waiting, sir.

The Conclusion of Act Two in the Licensing Copy

This extract begins at line 878 of the present edition.

JACK   Yes, but you said yourself it was not hereditary, or anything of the kind.

ALGERNON   It usen't to be, I know—but I daresay it *is* now. Science is always making wonderful improvements in things.

JACK   May I ask, Algy, what on earth do you propose to do?

ALGERNON   Nothing. That is what I have been trying to do for the last ten minutes, and you have kept on doing everything in your power to distract my attention from my work.

JACK   Well, *I* shall go into the house and see Gwendolen. I feel quite sure she expects me.

ALGERNON   I know from her extremely cold manner that Cecily expects me, so *I* certainly shan't go into the house. When a man does exactly what a woman expects him to do, she doesn't think much of him. One should always do what a woman doesn't expect, just as one should always say what she doesn't understand. The result is invariably perfect sympathy on both sides.

JACK   Oh, that is nonsense. You are always talking nonsense.

ALGERNON   It is much cleverer to talk nonsense than to listen to it, my dear fellow, and a much rarer thing too, in spite of all the public may say.

JACK   I don't listen to you. I can't listen to you.

ALGERNON   Oh, that is merely false modesty. You know perfectly well you could listen to me if you tried. You always underrate yourself, an absurd thing to do nowadays when there are such a lot of conceited people about. Jack, you are eating the muffins again! I wish you wouldn't. There are only two left. (*Removes plate.*) I *told* you I was particularly fond of muffins.

JACK   But I hate tea-cake.

ALGERNON   Why on earth do you allow tea-cake to be served up for your guests, then? What ideas you have of hospitality!

JACK   (*Irritably.*) Oh! that is not the point. We are not discussing tea-cake. (*Crosses.*) Algy! you are perfectly maddening. You can never stick to the point in any conversation.

ALGERNON   (*Slowly.*) No: it always hurts me.

JACK   Good heavens! What affectation! I *loathe* affection!

ALGERNON   Well, my dear fellow, if you don't like affectation I really don't see what you *can* like. Besides, it isn't affectation. The point always *does* hurt me and I hate physical pain of any kind.

JACK   (*Glares at* ALGERNON; *walks up and down stage. Finally comes up to table.*)
Algy! I have already told you to go. I don't want you here. *Why don't* you go?

ALGERNON   I haven't quite finished my tea yet. (*Takes last muffin.*)
(JACK *groans and sinks down into a chair and buries his face in his hands.*)

ACT-DROP

BACKGROUNDS

KARL BECKSON

London in the 1890s†

The ends of centuries have traditionally fascinated and terrified the imagination, for the sense of an ending and an irreversible but inexorable progression to the unknown (or, for Christians, the Last Judgment) have often conjured images of final decay and lingering death. In his diary for 1889, the London publisher Grant Richards recorded that the Reverend Michael Paget Baxter, the author of books of prophecy and editor of the *Christian Herald*, "holds forth that the world comes to an end in 1901 and that in 1896 144,000 devout Christians will be taken up to Heaven." No one can be certain whether such a number of the devout were in fact introduced to Paradise in 1896, but the Reverend Mr. Baxter was not entirely wrong in his other prediction, for Queen Victoria's world did come to an end in 1901, when she expired.

While the demise of a century may encourage such apocalyptic visions, ideological collapses, and exhausted psyches, the human imagination also has the capacity to create images of renewal (based on the perception of nature's rebirth). At the end of the nineteenth century, many intellectuals, having abandoned their religious faith but inspired by utopian dreams, envisioned a new age in the next century, convinced that the past—with its failures and disappointments—was a burden to be abandoned. In 1882, the positivist philosopher and advocate for social and political reform Frederic Harrison wrote: "We *are* on the threshold of a great time, even if our time is not great itself. In science, in religion, in social organisation, we all know what great things are in the air. . . . It is *not* the age of money-bags and cant, soot, hubbub, and ugliness. It is the age of great expectation and unwearied striving after better things." In his introduction to *The New Spirit* (1890), Havelock Ellis also looked forward to a future purged of previous errors: "Certainly old things are passing away; not the old ideals only, but even the regret they leave behind is dead, and we are shaping instinctively our new ideals. . . . The old cycles are for ever renewed, and it is no paradox that he who would advance can never cling too close to the past."

† From *London in the 1890s: A Cultural History* (New York: Norton, 1992). Copyright © 1992 by Karl E. Beckson. Used by permission of W. W. Norton & Company, Inc.

For many, such optimism was fueled by scientific discovery and technological innovation. Hundreds of new inventions, such as faster railroad locomotives, ocean-going steamships, photography, and electric lighting, as well as the rapid growth of such scientific disciplines as physics, astronomy, and chemistry transformed the nineteenth-century view of the world so dramatically that, by the fin de siècle, Victorians referred to their age as "modern." In 1897, J. J. Thompson, of Cambridge University, discovered the electron (the discovery of the atom's nucleus was more than a decade away); by 1900, Gregor Mendel's work in genetics had been rediscovered, and, in the same year, Max Planck theorized that "quanta of energy were involved when light was being absorbed or emitted." In 1905, Einstein's "special theory of relativity" superseded Newton's laws of motion and gravitation as well as James Maxwell's electromagnetic theory of light, thereby making possible new concepts of time, space, and mass. In effect, Einstein established the principle that energy and mass were interconvertible, as indicated in the famous equation $E = mc^2$, the theoretical basis for later nuclear fission.

In *The Idea of Progress* (1920), J. B. Bury observed that, in the nineteenth century, "the achievements of physical science did more than anything else to convert the imaginations of men to the general doctrine of progress." At the same time, however, many expressed pessimism and doubt, particularly after the publication of Darwin's *Origin of Species* (1859), which followed a series of scientific discoveries and evolutionary theories that undermined orthodox belief in creationism, unsettled religious faith, and ultimately resulted in emotional crises for many Christians. Earlier in the century, the frightening specter of entropy arose from the second law of thermodynamics, which contends that heat from the sun's radiation becomes progressively unusable as it becomes dispersed in the universe (so-called "heat death"). In the 1850s, Sir William Thompson (Lord Kelvin), who was instrumental in formulating the principle, concluded that "the earth must have been, and within a finite period to come, the earth must again be, unfit for the habitation of man as at present constituted."

In his first science fiction novel, *The Time Machine* (1895), H. G. Wells depicts such a bleak future when the Time Traveller travels into the "fourth dimension" and reaches the year 802,701. The humans then living on the earth are the degenerate Eloi, whose gender is indeterminate. Indulging in such trivial pursuits as singing, dancing, and adorning themselves with flowers in their earthly paradise, they exist in a condition of apparent uselessness. However, the "ape-like" Morlocks live in the subterranean depths with the remnants of human technology and feed on the Eloi. Journeying further into the future, the traveler discovers no sign of humanity; instead,

the earth is inhabited by giant crabs. Thirty million years later, he finds no traces of any significant life forms; he leaves when darkness descends over the earth after an eclipse of the sun. The second law of thermodynamics has achieved its ultimate triumph.[1]

A further cause of pessimism in the nineteenth century was the social and psychological effect of the Industrial Revolution, which enslaved millions of workers in gloomy "sweating" industries and created cities of "dreadful night," such as Manchester, Sheffield, and Birmingham. Moreover, the so-called "Great Depression" from the early 1870s to the mid-1890s, resulting from poor harvests, declining arable land, and lower-priced imports, accelerated the migration of almost three million farm workers to the crowded cities or to colonies abroad.[2] London's East End contained some of the worst slums in England, where disease and despair flourished. Discouraged reformers sought desperate remedies. In his influential survey *In Darkest England and the Way Out* (1890), William Booth, founder and first general of the Salvation Army, rose to exalted rhetoric while describing the degrading living conditions of the London poor: "Talk about Dante's Hell, and all the horrors and cruelties of the torture-chamber of the lost! The man who walks with open eyes and with bleeding heart through the shambles of our civilisation needs no such fantastic images of the poet to teach him horror." Such misery also distressed the socialist and poet William Morris, who yearned for the end of a moribund, corrupt society so that a genuine "barbarism" would return to the world to destroy its false "progress":

> I have [no] more faith than a grain of mustard seed in the future history of "civilization," which I *know* now is doomed to destruction, and probably before very long: what a joy it is to think of! and how often it consoles me to think of barbarism once more flooding the world, and real feelings and passions, however rudimentary, taking the place of our wretched hypocrisies. . . .

1. In 1904 at Cambridge University, Ernest Rutherford discovered, in such material as radium, the lasting power of radioactivity which creates heat within the earth's rocks. He wrote that "the radioactive elements, which in their disintegration liberate enormous amounts of energy, thus increase the possible limit of the duration of life on this planet. . . ." Rutherford's finding challenged the second law of thermodynamics (quotation from Timothy Ferris, *Coming of Age in the Milky Way* [New York, 1988], 249).
2. The economist Alfred Marshall, testifying before the Precious Metals Commission in 1887, asserted that the industrial depression had a greater impact on businessmen than on workers. The result was "a depression of prices, a depression of interest, and a depression of profits" without "any considerable depression in any other respect." Gertrude Himmelfarb has recently written that, "among regularly employed workers, there were depressed seasons and years when unemployment rose and wages fell. . . . But these conditions, however grievous, did not add up, for the working classes as a whole, to a 'Great Depression' " (*Poverty and Compassion: The Moral Imagination of the Late Victorians* [New York, 1991], 70–71).

During the final decades of the century, a widespread perception that Britain and the empire were in a state of decline found expression in the periodicals, which published articles in profusion with titles announcing the decline or decay of such phenomena as cricket, genius, war, classical quotations, romance, marriage, faith, bookselling, and even canine fidelity. There were also articles on the presumed degeneracy of the race and the startling increase in insanity and "suicidal mania." Writers pointed to the decline and fall of the Roman Empire as the analogy of the anticipated fate of the British Empire, though a writer in *Nineteenth Century* (August 1894) regarded such a view as a "dismal argument," for though the Romans were a "great nation" and "far ahead of their time," they were still "barbarians" compared to the modern British. The sensation of 1895, which appeared just before the even more sensational trials of Oscar Wilde, was the English translation of Max Nordau's *Degeneration*, which attacked the unorthodox works of such figures as Ibsen, Wagner, Wilde, Nietzsche, and Tolstoy as evidence of cultural decadence. Bernard Shaw argued that these artists were not suffering from degeneration but were indicative of the spirit of regeneration: "At every new wave of energy in art the same alarm has been raised, and . . . these alarms always had their public, like prophecies of the end of the world. . . ."

While many were deploring cultural degeneration and decay, others were hailing the new, which, like Ellis's New Spirit, was an indication of presumed liberation from the deadening hand of the past. As soon as late Victorian cultural developments appeared, they were habitually affixed with the "new" designation to elevate them to fashionable status and to ward off the pervasive pessimism of the age. Such were the New Drama, New Woman, New Journalism, New Imperialism, New Criticism, New Hedonism, and New Paganism, which appeared in William Sharp's one and only issue of the *Pagan Review* (August 1892), written under his various pseudonyms. As the critic H. D. Traill asserted in *The New Fiction and Other Essays* (1897): "Not to be 'new' is, in these days, to be nothing. . . ."

Cultural trends in the final decades of the century were thus moving in two simultaneously antithetical directions: declining Victorianism (the synthesis of moral, religious, artistic, political, and social thought that had produced the wealthiest and most powerful empire on earth) and rising Modernism (with its challenges by writers and artists to the cultural foundations of Philistine society, which habitually condemned daring innovations in the arts as "immoral" or "degenerate"). Such manifestations of Modernism were frequently described by both sympathetic and hostile critics as characteristic aspects of the fin de siècle. The term, adopted in

Britain around 1890 to indicate the end of the century, had such associated meanings as "modern," "advanced," and "decadent." The French themselves had been using the term with increasing looseness: It served, for example, to describe both a shoemaker praised "for being a traditional cobbler rather than fin de siècle" and a blackmailer who lived off his wife's prostitution—"a fin de siècle husband." A verse at the time indicated its imprecision:

> Fin de siécle! Everywhere
> . . . It stands for all that you might care
> To name . . .

Some British writers employed it for its apocalyptic foreboding, as "advanced" writers delighted in uttering oracular premonitions while inspired by an exhausted century. In *The Picture of Dorian Gray* (1890/1891), Oscar Wilde may have been one of the first in England to make use of such implications. When a dinner guest ponders the current fashion that "all the married men live like bachelors, and all the bachelors like married men," the response is characteristic:

> "*Fin de siècle*," murmured Lord Henry.
> "*Fin du globe*," answered his hostess.
> "I wish it were *fin du globe*," said Dorian with a sigh. "Life is such a great disappointment."

In a letter to a Tory journalist in 1894, Wilde identified the fin de siècle with artistic achievement as opposed to cultural decadence: "All that is known by that term I particularly admire and love. It is the fine flower of our civilisation: the only thing that keeps the world from the commonplace, the coarse, the barbarous."

In John Davidson's comic novel, *A Full and True Account of the Wonderful Mission of Earl Lavender* (1895), a poem precedes the narrative involving Lavender's "mission" to spread the gospel of the "survival of the fittest" in a plot including sexual perversity (a Beardsley drawing for the frontispiece depicts a woman flagellating a figure of indeterminate gender):

> Though our thoughts turn ever Doomwards,
> Though our sun is well-night set,
> Though our Century lotters tombwards,
> > We may laugh a little yet.

Later in the novel, a matronly Victorian woman evokes, in fractured French, her equivalent of fin de siècle to explain the chaos of modern life: "It's *fang-de-seeaycle* that does it, my dear, and education, and reading French."

The French were indeed the object of suspicion by the British,

who regarded their neighbors across the Channel as potential invaders, either by sea or through a proposed tunnel connecting the two. Far worse to those who objected to subversive influences, however, was the invasion of French literature and critical attitudes, especially Zola's Naturalistic novels, often called "decadent" by British critics, as well as the tradition of an amoral *l'art pour l'art* and fin-de-siècle Decadence, which impelled Tennyson to fulminate in verse against the "troughs of Zolaism" and against those Aesthetes who had objected to the moral teaching in the *Idylls of the King* (1869):

> Art for Art's sake! Hail, truest Lord of Hell!
> Hail Genius, Master of the Moral Will!
> "The filthiest all of paintings painted well
> Is mightier than the purest painted ill!"

To Tennyson, the doctrine of "art for art's sake" disregarded the "ideal of an integrated culture." The poet and critic Richard Le Gallienne (father of the actress, Eva) also judged the invasion of French Decadence as particularly grave. In the prefatory poem to his *English Poems* (1892), he echoed the title of Tennyson's early poem "The Palace of Art" (1833) in expressing his own anxiety over the fin-de-siècle separation of moral from aesthetic elements in art:

> Art was a palace once, things great and fair,
> And strong and holy, found a temple there:
> Now 'tis a lazar-house of leprous men.
> O shall we hear an English song again!

Such anxieties as Tennyson's and Le Gallienne's were widespread at the end of the century, an indication that the earlier cultural synthesis of Victorianism was unraveling as such common beliefs and assumptions concerning social relationships, the nature of reality, and the nature of art were subjected to attack by such groups as the New Women, the New Dramatists, the New Hedonists, the New Naturalists, as well as the Aesthetes and Decadents.

For many decades, the 1890s have been casually disposed of as the Yellow Nineties, suggestive of decay, principally because of the famous periodical, the *Yellow Book* (1894–1897), and because of a relatively small but articulate band of writers, Wilde included, who proclaimed "art for art's sake." The decade has also been called the "Decadent Nineties" or the "Naughty Nineties." But whatever those terms may mean, the fin de siècle embraced such a wide variety of literary and artistic modes of expression, including Impressionism, Aestheticism, Decadence, Naturalism, and Symbolism, that reducing the late nineteenth century to one of them and

branding it "decadent" merely because it was anti-Establishment is to inflict simplicity on complexity. The decade of the nineties was an extraordinary period of artistic activity and energy, many of the greatest figures of the twentieth century, such as Shaw, Yeats, Conrad, and Wells, in their apprenticeship years while older figures, such as Whistler, Wilde, Morris, and Hardy had completed—or were in the process of completing—their major work.

Many moved freely from one mode of expression or group to another as inclination dictated. Wilde wrote an essay still widely read, "The Soul of Man under Socialism" (1891/1895), which fused Aestheticism and anarchist socialism in an attempt to locate beauty and freedom for the artist within a radically new economic and political system. Yeats's aesthetically conceived Celtic poems, such as "A Man Who Dreamed of Fairyland" (the title changed slightly in subsequent printings), were published in W. E. Henley's *National Observer*, a periodical devoted to activist, anti-Decadent causes. Henley nevertheless regarded Yeats the dreamer as one of his "young men." In the late 1880s, Yeats was also a member of Morris's circle at the Socialist League, a short-lived association that ended when the younger man discovered that Morris's literary "dream world . . . knew nothing of intellectual suffering." Shaw, contributed to the first number of the *Savoy* (January 1896), the Symbolist/Decadent periodical that contained much of Beardsley's most daring literary and artistic work, an odd setting for a socialist who publicly expressed scorn for "art for art's sake."

This cultural history focuses on the legendary decade of the 1890s, more a symbol than a mere ten years of the calendar, for an entire age was simultaneously coming to an end as another was in the process of formation. London, also this history's principal focus, is here treated as the heart of the empire as well as the artistic and cultural heart of Britain. Between 1851 and 1901, the area of present-day Greater London had grown from 2.7 million people to 6.6 million, a progressive urbanization that concentrated artistic talent and cultural ferment more densely than in any other British city. As Malcolm Bradbury has shown, London became one of the major "cities of Modernism," closely associated in this international movement with Paris, Berlin, and Vienna. Writers and artists inevitably gravitated to London—as did Yeats, Wilde, and Shaw from Ireland and Henry James, Whistler, and Sargent from America, as well as countless others from provincial British cities. A *Yellow Book* contributor recalled that each was hoping that he might ride "on the crest of the wave that was sweeping away the Victorian tradition" with its undue restrictions in artistic expression based on an outdated conception of the world as one of stable, absolute values. As Modernism developed, the arts sought new forms of personal

expression, the new aesthetic values replacing the formerly prescribed moral values of Victorian art.

Pater might have described London as "the focus where the
greatest number of vital forces unite[d] in their purest energy."
Down from Oxford, the young but "perpetually old" Max Beerbohm
luxuriated in such energy despite his dandiacal pose of feigned indifference: "Around me seethed swirls, eddies, torrents, violent
cross-currents of human activity. What uproar! Surely I could have
no part in modern life." Henry James called London "the biggest
aggregation of human life—the most complete compendium of the
world." As a constant subject for verse in the nineties, the city assumed the aura of Romantic artifice with its "iron lilies of the
Strand" in Richard Le Gallienne's "A Ballad of London": "Ah, London! London! our delight, / Great flower that opens but at night.
. . ." The nights of London, when the city became a ghostly apparition in the faint evening light as imagination transformed ware-
houses into palaces, inspired Whistler's "nocturnes." And Arthur
Symons envisioned a magical London in which two lovers, dancer
and poet, are entwined in each other's dreams, oblivious to the in-
dustrialism, poverty, and despair of the city:

> You the dancer and I the dreamer,
> Children together,
> Wandering lost in the night of London,
> In the miraculous April weather.

*　*　*

JOSEPH·DONOHUE

Wilde and the Idea of a Theatre†

As the centenaries of Oscar Wilde's major writings for the stage occur during the present decade, the need for a new point of view on
the playwright and his plays in the broad and various contexts of
the theatre of his age has become clear. At the outset it is obvious
that the subject for reassessment extends well beyond the drama itself, taken as a literary artifact, to the professional stage of West
End and Broadway houses and of the actor-managers George
Alexander, Herbert Beerbohm Tree, Lewis Waller, and Charles
Frohman, who produced a remarkable series of Wilde's plays in
London and New York in the brief period 1892–95. In the context
of Continental avant-garde drama, however, the subject also en-

† From *Rediscovering Oscar Wilde*, ed. C. George Sandulescu (Gerrards Cross: Colin
Smythe, 1994), 118–26. Reprinted by permission of the author.

compasses the theatre of Ibsen, Strindberg, and Maeterlinck, for whose plays Wilde asked while in prison—an alternative stage, a kind of anti-theatre with respect to the commercial, featuring plays mostly unstageable in England (as the uproar over Ibsen's *Ghosts* and the failure of Wilde's own *Salomé* to pass the English censor suggest), though much in evidence on the Continent.

Connected with these two spheres of activity, yet distinct in crucial ways, was a private, radical notion of the theatre conceived by Wilde himself. This highly unorthodox idea of a theatre emerges even in his earliest dramatic efforts, *Vera, or The Nihilist* and *The Duchess of Padua*; is articulated in an intensely symbolic way in the later *Salomé*; and informs the full range of his critical writings and even his poetry (as in the sonnets to Sarah Bernhardt and Ellen Terry). Deriving certain features from Maeterlinck's 'static' theatre and the symbolist tradition exemplified by Baudelaire and Mallarmé, Wilde's idea of a theatre is nonetheless authentically his own: a theatre that conjures images of idealized emotional states and crises, an interior theatre of the heart and soul, of suffering and loss. Wilde's professional reputation grew rapidly, beginning in 1892, as the flamboyant author of the main-stream comedy-dramas *Lady Windermere's Fan*, *A Woman of No Importance*, and *An Ideal Husband* and of the 'trivial' comedy *The Importance of Being Earnest*. And yet the celebrity who, wearing a green carnation in his lapel and smoking a cigarette, sauntered onto the stage of the St James's Theatre on the opening night of *Lady Windermere's Fan* and congratulated his audience on their success was also, and simultaneously, writing for a private yet more comprehensive ideal theatre, a theatre whose idea was obscured by the scintillating wit and engaging characters of these four West End successes but was nonetheless present. As late as 1894, during the initial stages of composition of *The Importance of Being Earnest*, a scenario on a guilty love affair and an abandoned marriage sent by Wilde to George Alexander identifies that idea in its abiding concern for authentic personal feeling: '*I want the sheer passion of love to dominate everything. No morbid self-sacrifice. No renunciation. A sheer flame of love between a man and a woman. That is what the play is to rise to.*'

The clarity and singularity of Wilde's idea are typical of his approach to dramatic creation. He was comparably clear about the governing idea of *The Duchess of Padua*, whose 'two great speculations and problems', he wrote to Mary Anderson in 1883, are 'the relations of Sin and Love.' Ten years later he confided to a correspondent who had praised the New York production of *Lady Windermere's Fan* that its idea was essentially psychological:

A woman who has had a child, but never known the passion of maternity [. . .] suddenly sees the child she has abandoned falling over a precipice. There wakes in her the maternal feeling—the most terrible of all emotions. [. . .] She rushes to rescue, sacrifices herself, does follies—and the next day she feels, 'This passion is too terrible. It wrecks my life. I don't want to know it again. It makes me suffer too much. Let me go away. I don't want to be a mother any more.' And so the fourth act is to me the psychological act, the act that is newest, most true.

These are examples of a consistent, if quite complex, idea about the theatre that unifies Wilde's approach to writing for the stage and endows the great range of that writing in style and subject with a coherence and a moment that, for the most part, would seem to have gone unobserved in criticism up to the present time.

The reassessment I propose consequently looks to a wide range of topics, including the history of Wilde's involvement and sustained labor in the professional London theatre, his aspirations as a poetic dramatist, his practice as a critic and theorist of the drama, his determined bid for success in the public arenas of the theatre, literature, and journalism, and the implications of that success for his personal life. Moreover, it entails scrutiny of such major topics as Wilde's views of the nature and purpose of the theatre, the social occasions of the performed play, and the dramatist's relationship to audience and society.

At the same time, it is essential to consider the ways in which Wilde's own life and personality make their way into the broader subject, characterizing it definitely. An understanding of Wilde's personal predicament here is of crucial importance: it is fundamental to see Wilde's plays as adopting an attitude broadly reflective of Wilde's own, complex character. As Wilde himself and Wilde's dramatic characters frequently remind us, modern literature and modern life itself in this period were busily at work defining the age of the individual—an age when the artist's life was perceived to be intimately and deeply implicated in his art. Ibsen told us we could read the record of his life, hidden though it was, in his plays. Picasso said to his friend John Richardson, 'My work is like a diary. To understand it, you have to see how it mirrors my life.' Wilde's dandiacal figures, like Lord Goring in *An Ideal Husband* and Lord Illingworth in *A Woman of No Importance*, are especially well-endowed spokesmen: 'To love oneself', says Goring, 'is the beginning of a lifelong romance'; 'People nowadays are so absolutely superficial', Illingworth comments, 'that they don't understand the philosophy of the superficial.' Goring and Illingworth are conspicuous instances of authorial surrogates, but the more covert signs of

Wilde's intervention in his own works lie almost everywhere. 'I took the drama, the most objective form known to art', he explained to Lord Alfred Douglas in the long confessional letter written from Reading Prison, now known as *De Profundis*, 'and made it as personal a mode of expression as the lyric or the sonnet.' As Wilde's spokesman Gilbert puts it in 'The Critic as Artist', 'Man is least himself when he talks in his own person. Give him a mask, and he will tell you the truth.' Reading Richard Ellmann's biography *Oscar Wilde* on its appearance in 1988 underscored my conviction that analysis of Wilde's personal predicament was a crucial part of the Wildean critical enterprise. Wilde's plays should be seen as adopting an attitude deeply reflective of his own personality and of the necessarily covert relationship, as he sensed it, between objective form and subjective content.

For Wilde that relationship remained a necessary but difficult one, given his need to cultivate his keen desire for self-fulfillment in private life and his conflicting need to succeed by accepting the exigencies of professional life as a working dramatist in the public theatre—as he did in capitulating to George Alexander's insistence that the revelation of the identity of Mrs Erlynne as the mother of Lady Windermere must occur no later than the end of the second act. In her 1986 study *Idylls of the Marketplace* Regenia Gagnier characterizes Wilde's entire literary output as conditioned by the formative pressures and glittering spectacle of the capitalistic bourgeois marketplace. Gagnier's rejection, for purposes of her argument, of any notion of Wilde's autonomous personal life is directly countered, in effect, by Ellmann's blithe assumption of a coherent, autonymous psychological makeup fueling intense intellectual and emotional drives. Ellmann and Gagnier have thus, to a considerable extent, effectively set the terms of further discussion.

And yet neither Gagnier nor Ellmann appears to take any substantial interest in the theatre of Wilde's time, let alone in Wilde's own manifest fascination with the stage. Indeed, Ellmann's dismissive attitude toward the contemporary theatre of his subject—both the West End theatre of Pinero, Jones, Grundy, and their fellow playwrights, and the avant-garde Continental theatre of Maeterlinck, Ibsen, Strindberg, and their iconoclastic and symbolist brothers—leads him to what I believe is a biased and superficial reading of Wilde's career as a dramatist. The essential conclusion that Ellmann reaches is that, after a false start in the poetic drama, Wilde abandoned it and, with measured cynicism, began writing charming and witty but ultra-conventional plays for a philistine upper-middle-class audience. To be sure, George Alexander's offer to the struggling dramatist of £50 against royalties to write a modern comedy did not fall on deaf ears, and the resultant series of suc-

cessful comedy-dramas between 1892 and 1895, culminating in
the brilliant farce of *The Importance of Being Earnest*, might in itself indicate that Wilde had abandoned the manner of those early,
seemingly false starts. But the reputation as a comic dramatist that
those four sumptuously produced plays established for Wilde has
served to obscure the more fundamental fact that in writing them
he changed only his artistic *métier*, not his sense of the way he conceived of human nature and how to represent it in dramatic art;
changed his stylistic strategies and their verbal manifestations, but
not his conviction of the necessity for representing human passions, needs, and desires on the stage in ways that remained faithful to genuine experience as he saw it and felt it in his own, private
ways.

The problem that consequently lies still unresolved in Wilde criticism remains one of reconciling Wilde's successful 'realistic' plays
(to give them that simplistic and often misused term)—that series
of stunning successes beginning with *Lady Windermere's Fan* in
1892 and ending (all too abruptly, at the point of his trial and conviction for homosexual offences) with *The Importance of Being
Earnest* in 1895—reconciling the generic features, including familiar plot elements, and the general stylistic qualities of those four
plays with his evident continuing interest in writing other kinds of
dramatic fare altogether. Some examples: at about the time *The Importance of Being Earnest* opened in February 1895, he wrote to
George Alexander offering to read him 'the vital parts of my Florentine play', a play in blank verse that he later called '*Love and Death
— Florentine Tragedy*'. This play and *La Sainte Courtisane*, a blank-
verse tragedy whose typescript Wilde, while held in Holloway
Prison in April 1895, directed Robert Ross to retrieve from his Tite
Street house, were 'plays of a completely different type', he told
Lord Alfred Douglas in his long letter from Reading Prison. Even as
the clouds were gathering over *The Importance of Being Earnest* in
April 1895, Wilde roughed out the scenario for the poetic tragedy
The Cardinal of Avignon.

Moreover, the familiar critical explanation, repeated essentially
without variation by Ellmann, to the effect that Wilde finally abandoned the 'poetic' approach to dramaturgy in favor of a more commercial product because he couldn't live off the proceeds of poetry,
ignores the persistent presence of certain pointed ethical qualities
and experiential features lying implicit within the ostensible con-
ventionalities of the four later plays. Those qualities and features
were well obscured, it would seem, by Wilde's calculated and sometimes brilliant exploitation, as Kerry Powell's recent *Oscar Wilde
and the Theatre of the 1890s* (1990) demonstrates, of the contemporary genres of comedy-drama and farcical comedy. And, of

course, such preoccupation with West End success entirely passes over the key work, *Salome*—as does Patricia Flanagan Behrendt, unaccountably, in her otherwise interesting and useful study of sexuality in Wilde's works, *Oscar Wilde: Eros and Aesthetics* (1991).

Overall, then, criticism has neglected to set Wilde's dramaturgical efforts in contexts at once more perspicuous and more personal, and so has yet to come to terms with what remains, ostensibly, the puzzlingly ambiguous profile of the author of *Salome* and *Lady Windermere's Fan* (to identify one pair of seemingly antithetical or unconnected works) in order to clarify the vital substance it frames.

At the same time, any critical approach that aspires to the kind of reconciliation of apparent inconsistency that I have been advocating here must be wary of too great a preoccupation with the biographical and the theatrical; rather, it must be broadly enough based to address the concerns of intellectual, social, and cultural history along with those of the theatre itself. As they relate to the central presence (I take it to be central) of Wilde's own personality as it informs his writings for the theatre, these concerns lead us to scrutinize an illusionistic stage world filled out by Wilde's expansive genius and passionate dedication to art—a world enlivened also by literary and pictorial art, criticism, critical theory, and journalism; and a world that also includes Wilde's personal relationships with contemporaries such as Whistler and Shaw, his conversations, and his letters (a truly valuable resource) every bit as much as it encompasses the more private—and yet ever less so as time went on—realm of his homosexuality and his relationships with men, and boys.

What finally emerges at the centre of interest is, then, the complex identity of Wilde as a man of the theatre. The most readily accessible aspect of this issue is, as I have suggested, the public stage, the commercial theatre. There, the role adopted by the professional dramatist normally conforms in broad measure to the needs and demands of star actors, actor-managers, and paying audiences. In this arena of activity Kerry Powell's book on Wilde and his contemporary professional theatre identifies with welcome precision and full example the dramatic genres and sometimes specific plays under whose influential presence Wilde was apparently quite consciously working. Powell's sturdy, well-argued scholarship can be built upon to good effect, and it is bound to have a salutary influence on studies of this aspect of Wilde's dramaturgical activities.

Wilde's original and independent intellect, however, led him to resist and partly to subvert the role of the professional dramatist—one of the masks he so ostentatiously wore—in the interests of his own private values and ends. Ultimately, Wilde's position with respect to the theatre of his time was as ambivalent as it was com-

plex, and in certain ways unique, even though in other ways it remained completely representative of the character of the contemporary professional dramatist. Faced with this complexity, criticism must understand that coming to terms with the agenda and goals of the contemporary French symbolist theatre is of equal importance to assessing the apparent formative influence upon Wilde's writing for the theatre of the practices of the late Victorian commercial stage. Nor does this describe the practical limits of the reassessment here proposed. An additional area of influence hardly touched upon in criticism to date is the example of the post-Elizabethan poetic drama—early on, that of Webster, but most notably the Romantic drama of Shelley. The text of *The Cenci*, whose subject involves a terrible crime and its terrible revenge, lurks like a cloak-and-dagger assassin behind the often lurid and derivative verse of Wilde's *The Duchess of Padua*, but its more important influence on Wilde's play, in the example of Shelley's unorthodox central character of Beatrice Cenci and his radical ideas of human innocence, lies deeper than mere words.

The orientation of a study of the kind I propose, then, must finally point toward a more integral and holistic understanding. There are some bountiful rewards in store, I believe, for critical perseverence toward that end. For, in the process of coming to terms with the full range, style, and character of Wilde's writing for the theatre, a study of this sort may also clarify and perhaps even alter to some extent our sense of the nature of *fin de siècle* theatre, art, literature, and culture. In any case, a study of Wilde and the theatre inevitably entails a study of the late nineteenth-century theatre as a whole, as well as antecedents ancient and otherwise. The reassessment I propose thus carries the additional purpose of describing Wilde's ideal theatre both in itself and in respect to the heterodox values of *fin de siècle* artistic and cultural life. For, notwithstanding the personal, even private character of his artistic values, the impact of Wilde's writing on the theatre of his age was so striking, and his own absorption of its chief features so thorough, that any fresh scrutiny of Wilde's idea of a theatre must inevitably broaden into an inquiry into the nature of the theatre of his age and the cultural life it illuminated and itself conditioned.

And so, as we approach the one hundredth anniversary of Oscar Wilde's death in Paris, it is appropriate to reconsider the true character of the plays to which he devoted himself, early and late in his career. Undoubtedly, there will be many a centenary production of *The Importance of Being Earnest*, in both three- and four-act versions, just as there has already been, in advance of its centenary, a sparkling and very satisfying London revival of *An Ideal Husband* directed by Peter Hall that captures much of the true seriousness

lying just beyond the glittering wit and bold character outlines of that still eminently playable play. It may be too much to ask for revivals of *Vera* and *The Duchess of Padua*, dramaturgically inexpert as they are; but *Salome*, I would think, will richly repay the attentions of a director who has the wit and insight to take the play in its full dimensions of lush but ironic eroticism and simultaneous parody of a gaudy symbolist tradition. We can hope that the combined effect of persistent intelligent attention to the scripts of these plays as dramatic vehicles, and to the significance of the looming profile of the author himself that has always lain behind them, will go far toward some necessary clarifications. 'I live in fear of not being misunderstood', Wilde once said. A century later, it may be safe, and even more entertaining, to attempt a greater understanding.

REGENIA GAGNIER

Creating the Audience†

* * * Wilde's jovial contempt at the expense of the public—or at the very least the bourgeois author's awareness of the distance between writer and general readers ("the quarter-educated" as Gissing calls them in *New Grub Street*)—was especially pronounced in the 1890's, but it was a well-established tradition. Images of print as self-devouring but paradoxically infinitely reproducible had multiplied during the century, not as the potentially positive collapse of the Benjaminian "aura" but as voracious vacuities, cheap thrills, implements of crime, and finally a total environmental hazard, an ecological disaster.

In 1831,[1] Carlyle had complained about critics and reviewers who were stealing the market from authors: "At the last Leipzig Fair, there was advertised a Review of Reviews. By and by it will be found that all Literature has become one boundless self-devouring Review."[2] By the time he wrote "Shooting Niagara" (*Macmillan's Magazine*, August 1867), Carlyle was prepared to instruct the public to "leave Literature to run through its rapid fermentations . . . and to fluff itself off into Nothing, in its own way—like a poor bottle of soda-water with the cork sprung." *Culture and Anarchy*

---

† From *Idylls of the Marketplace: Oscar Wilde and the Victorian Public* (Stanford: Stanford University Press, 1986), 22–28. Copyright © 1986 by the Board of Trustees of the Leland Stanford Jr. University.

1. Thomas Carlyle (1795–1881), Scottish essayist and economic theorist. [*Editor's note.*]

2. Cited in John Gross, *The Rise and Fall of the Man of Letters: A Study of the Idiosyncratic and the Humane in Modern Literature* (London, 1969), 1. I owe many of the following quotations to the attentiveness and energy of Deidre Lynch in my seminar on Victorian lives, Stanford U, autumn 1983.

(1869) may be read as a lament for the British reading public's promiscuity: the newspapers Arnold mocks flaunt slogans as flat as Carlyle's soda-water. In 1872, in his letters to workers called *Fors Clavigera*, Ruskin associated the new reading public with thieves in a scorchingly contemptuous description of two rich American girls reading novels on a train—"cheap pilfered literature" Ruskin calls the new railroad fiction, which read like a form of rapid transit.[3] Wilde, in "The Soul of Man," coupled journalism and vandalism in describing journalists who "use the words very vaguely, as an ordinary mob will use ready-made paving-stones."

In "Fiction, Fair and Foul" (1880), Ruskin despaired over the vulgarity of fictional deathbed scenes—the drama most accessible to inhabitants of the city—tailored for the market, and he wished for audiences worthy of Scott rather than Dickens. The causes of the decline of health and dignity in literature were, of course, economic and social: "Nell, in *The Old Curiosity Shop*, was simply killed for the market, as a butcher kills a lamb," whereas Scott "never once . . . permitted the disgrace of wanton tears round the humiliation of strength, or the wreck of beauty."[4] One might recall Wilde's own bright response to the Dickensian public's sentimentality, that one would have to have a heart of stone not to laugh at the death of Little Nell, or Q. D. Leavis's correct observation that Bulwer Lytton's novels exploited each possible market: *Pelham*, novel of fashion, 1828; *Devereux*, historical romance, 1829; *Paul Clifford*, novel with a thesis, 1830; *Eugene Aram*, idealization of crime, 1832; *Godolphin*, philosophical-fashionable, 1833; *Last Days of Pompeii* and *Rienzi*, historical, 1834–35; *Ernest Maltravers*, realism and philosophy, 1837; *Zanoni*, supernatural, 1842.[5] Out of patience, Ruskin, Wilde's teacher at Oxford, simply condemns the urban public, railroads, readers, and writers and gathers "into one Caina of gelid putrescence the entire product of modern infidel imagination, amusing itself with destruction of the body, and busying itself with aberration of the mind."[6]

Print polluted the world. Literature had become litter, the very acme, as Deidre Lynch has said, of conspicuous consumption and built-in obsolescence. The narrator of *Our Mutual Friend* (1864) looks at London wondering: "That mysterious paper currency which circulates . . . when the wind blows . . . whence can it come, whither can it go? It hangs on every bush, flutters in every tree, is caught flying by the electric wires, haunts every enclosure, drinks at every pump, cowers at every grating, shudders upon every plot of

3. John D. Rosenberg, ed., *The Genius of John Ruskin* (Boston, 1980), 394.
4. Ibid., 443.
5. Q. D. Leavis, *Fiction and the Reading Public* (London, 1932), 163.
6. Ruskin, 444.

grass, seeks rest in vain behind the regions of iron rails."[7] In Ruskin's close-up of the desecrated English landscape in "Fiction, Fair and Foul," the infamy is presided over by print, like flies over excrement:

> Mixed dust of every unclean thing that can crumble in draught, and mildew of every unclean thing that can rot or rust in damp; ashes and rags, beer-bottle and old shoes, battered pans, smashed crockery, shreds of nameless clothes, door-sweepings, floor-sweepings, kitchen garbage, back-garden sewage, old iron, rotten timber jagged with out-torn nails, cigar-ends, pipe-bowls, cinders, bones, and ordure, indescribable; and variously kneaded into, sticking to, or fluttering foully here and there over all these, remnants, broadcast of every manner of newspaper, advertisement or big-lettered bill, festering and flaunting out their last publicity in the pits of stinking dust and mortal slime.[8]

Crowning it all is the image of the collapse of Mudie's circulating library in the 1890's because of the cost of storing thousands of ephemeral three-decker "latest novels" after their brief span of popularity.[9]

There were hundreds of cheap books and articles written on the problem of trashy literature. Literary dystopias from *Culture and Anarchy* to H. G. Wells's *Tono-Bungay: A Romance of Commerce* (1908) portrayed the proliferation of print for the quarter-educated with more energy and wit than had been expended on art in years. Gissing's *New Grub Street* (1891) is the most urgent treatment of a literary dystopia in all its appalling horror, and it presents the various components of the market in the 1890's. Gissing defined the quarter-educated and their subliterary wants:

> No article in the paper is to measure more than two inches in length, and every inch must be broken into at least two paragraphs. . . . I would have the paper address itself to the quarter-educated; that is to say, the great new generation that is being turned out by the Board schools, the young men and women who can just read, but are incapable of sustained attention. People of this kind want something to occupy them in trains and on 'buses and trams . . . bits of stories, bits of description, bits of scandal, bits of jokes, bits of statistics, bits of foolery. . . . Everything must be very short, two inches at the utmost; their attention can't sustain itself beyond two inches.[1]

7. Charles Dickens, *Our Mutual Friend*, ed. Stephen Gill (Middlesex, 1971), 191.
8. Ruskin, 436.
9. See T. W. Heyck, *The Transformation of Intellectual Life in Victorian England* (New York, 1982), 204.
1. George Gissing, *New Grub Street*, ed. Bernard Bergonzi (Middlesex, 1983), 496–97.

The hack writer inhabits a feverish, suppressed environment and, like his market, he suffers from a sort of consumption:

> Mr. Quarmby laughed in a peculiar way, which was the result of long years of mirth-subdual in the Reading-room. . . . His suppressed laugh ended in a fit of coughing—the Reading-room cough.[2]

Another hack writer wonders whether she might not be replaced by a machine:

> A few days ago her startled eye had caught an advertisement in the newspaper, headed 'Literary Machine'; had it then been invented at last, some automaton to supply the place of such poor creatures as herself, to turn out books and articles?[3]

She fears the insanity of the Reading-room:

> Her eye discerned an official walking along the upper gallery, and . . . she likened him to a black, lost soul, doomed to wander in an eternity of vain research along endless shelves. . . . The readers who sat here at these radiating lines of desks, what were they but hapless flies caught in a huge web, its nucleus the great circle of the Catalogue? Darker, darker. From the towering wall of volumes seemed to emanate visible motes, intensifying the obscurity; in a moment the book-lined circumference of the room would be but a featureless prison-limit.[4]

The successful hack, on the other hand, has no time for such macabre fears. He recounts his day:

> I got up at 7:30, and whilst I breakfasted I read through a volume I had to review. By 10:30 the review was written—three-quarters of a column of the *Evening Budget*. . . . At eleven I was ready to write my Saturday *causerie* for the *Will o' the Wisp*; it took me till close upon one o'clock. . . . By a quarter to two, [I had] sketched a paper for *The West End*. Pipe in mouth, I sat down to leisurely artistic work; by five, half the paper was done; the other half remains for to-morrow. From five to half-past I read four newspapers and two magazines, and from half-past to a quarter to six I jotted down several ideas that had come to me whilst reading. . . . Home once more at 6:45, and for two hours wrote steadily at a long affair I have in hand for *The Current*.[5]

This particular hack marries "the woman who has developed concurrently with journalistic enterprise":

2. Ibid., 114.
3. Ibid., 138.
4. Ibid.
5. Ibid., 213.

She read a good deal of that kind of literature which may be defined as specialism popularised; writing which addresses itself to educated, but not strictly studious, persons. . . . Thus, for instance, though she could not undertake the volumes of Herbert Spencer, she was intelligently acquainted with the tenor of their contents; and though she had never opened one of Darwin's books, her knowledge of his main theories and illustrations was respectable. She was becoming a typical woman of the new time, the woman who has developed concurrently with journalistic enterprise.[6]

As for the rest, those whom Gissing sees as artists, the stylist dies of starvation and exposure, deliriously apologizing for his relative lack of productivity to the wife who has abandoned him because of his poverty, and the realist commits suicide with the help of toxins researched in the British Museum. Moreover, in one of Gissing's better tragicomic ironies, the realist, who has devoted his life to the theory of the "essentially unheroic" embodied in a novel entitled *Mr. Bailey, Grocer*, at one point throws himself into a burning building to rescue the unpublished manuscript. Possibly the only more sinister treatment of late-Victorian letters is Arthur Machen's thriller *The Three Impostors* (1895), in which all information bears the duplicity of crime, all stories are deceptions, all professional writers are mystified, and any attempt at interpretation is fatal.

New Grub Street illustrates that we are not merely talking about one division—between artists and an inartistic public—but rather about many divisions among writers, publics, and writers and publics: the quarter-educated; the specialized popularized audience as defined above by Gissing; the new journalist; the old (amateur) man of letters; the specialists themselves, both readers and writers; and so on. Q. D. Leavis saw the eighteenth-century novelists as writing for the best—and only—reading public, at the very least the novelist's peers. In the nineteenth century, they wrote for the shopkeeper and worker as well. In some cases the writer and a public *were* peers: Leavis cites Dickens as one such case.[7] The Thackeray/Trollope/Eliot public may have had occasion to despise the Dickens/Reade/Collins public, but in any case what could conceivably be called incipient middlebrow and lowbrow tastes were represented side by side in the shilling magazines and twopenny weeklies.

Leavis was hesitant to claim more than the beginnings of a split between popular and cultivated taste in the mid-Victorian period, but most historians agree that one occurred in the 1880's, about

6. Ibid., 397–98.
7. Leavis, 157.

the time of *Treasure Island* (1882). By this time the standardizing effects of the public schools, the rise of the new journalism facilitated by the expansion of advertising, and academic specialization had divided the market and was effectively silencing the former man of letters. The biographer of the newspaper entrepreneur Northcliffe recited the differences between the old elite and the democratic new journalists:

> The props of the Old Journalism feel bewildered. Their task, they believe, is to enlighten such of the public as can profit by enlightenment on political questions, on foreign policy. Their duty, they maintain, is to guide opinion concerning matters which may affect national well-being, cause changes of Government, raise the issue of peace or war. They have nothing to do with increase of circulation. They call this "pandering to mob interest in trivialities," commercial, undignified. Their standard of importance is set by the chiefs of political parties, Foreign Office, and the Treasury; by the famous Clubs (Reform, Carlton, Athenaeum); by the great country houses, the country rectories; by the Universities, by Bench and Bar. Now the standard is to be set by the mass of the people; the New Journalism will put in the foreground whatever is of interest to them, whatever will make them "hand the paper about."[8]

The growth and splintering of the reading publics, the marketing changes of 1840–80 that resulted in the professionalization of authorship—for example, specialist readers at publishing houses, literary agents, author's royalties, the Society of Authors—and the high and low culture industries contributed to the hostility rampant in the press. Far from appreciating the new platforms for exposure and the more respectable status of authors, the traditional men of letters and great social critics more often than not felt drowned out by triviality and claptrap.[9] The new journalists, they felt, represented not democracy but demagoguery. By the 1880's, according to John Gross's *Rise and Fall of the Man of Letters*, Oxbridge produced as many journalists as philosophers, and the ambitious graduates plagued traditional men of letters like Gissing's Alfred Yule in *New Grub Street*. After a life of unappreciated scholarly toil—that is, he was never even offered an editorship—the embittered Yule goes mad and blind and must be supported until his death by a hack-writing daughter. Within the universities, research experts exposed inaccurate and insufficient information in amateur writing—of the sort that Lady Carbury produces in Trollope's *The Way We Live Now*. Sidney Colvin finally formulated the brutal choice:

8. Ibid., 191.
9. See Gross, 26.

"There comes a time when you must choose between the dispersion and fragmentariness, which is the habit of journalism and life in a hurry, and the concentration and completeness which is the habit of serious literature."[1]

Reading all that trash, however, had an effect on its critics. Arnold studied it to mock it, and the result was a work of satiric genius richer and livelier than anything he had written before.[2] The texts that make up his *Culture and Anarchy: An Essay in Political and Social Criticism* provide excellent examples of the encroachment of anarchy on Culture, for they include more anarchy than Culture. With the skill of a caricaturist, Arnold labels an unpleasant audience and attempts to construct a pleasant one. He pilfers clichés out of newspapers and parodies them with his own clichés, absorbing them with the intention of subverting them. Like his labels Barbarians, Philistines, and Populace, even his central terms Hebraism and Hellenism smack to a classicist of tags or slogans soliciting a congeries of slightly evangelical attitudes toward education and reform.

With low cunning he quotes the classes on themselves: "the great broad-shouldered genial Englishman"; "the great middle class of this country, with its earnest common-sense penetrating through sophisms and ignoring commonplaces"; "the working man with his bright powers of sympathy and ready powers of action." He parodies religions "with their so many thousand souls and so many thousand rifles" and their "Dissidence of Dissent and Protestantism of the Protestant Religion." He parodies John Bright's "commendable interest in politics." He parodies himself as he is represented in the press, "a plain, unsystematic writer, without a philosophy." Against these he shoots his own slogans—phrases that sound like advertisements: "From Maine to Florida, and back again, all America Hebraises"; "Take care that your best light be not darkness" (pilfered from Bishop Thomas Wilson). One must cultivate, Arnold reiterates, one's Best Self, Right Reason, Sweetness, and Light. Here again we find the primitive form of the spectacular society's competitive oppositions, as if Arnold's readers could choose to be Barbarian, Philistine, or Populace.

Arnold probably deliberately permitted the forms of newsprint to dominate his style: he knew his market. By depoliticizing society and proposing the impossible conjunction of hypostatized qualities like Hebraism and Hellenism, Arnold thought to create something

---

1. Sydney Colvin, "Fellowships and National Culture," *Macmillan's* (June 1876), 141; cited in Heyck, 229.
2. Critics today are only beginning to appreciate this aspect of Arnold. See Eugene Goodheart, "The Function of Arnold at the Present Time," *Critical Inquiry* 9.3 (March 1983): 451–68.

out of nothing, a solid State out of anarchy, an audience out of the public. He tried to sell Culture, and so, like most advertisers, he sloganized, reasoning by definition or tautology. Yet because his definitions generally took care to be idiosyncratic, nominal identities rather than empirical or functional consensus, he often succeeded in excluding from the definitions any ordinary (or practical) point of view. Therefore he produced rhetoric, but few sales. Thus he was able to say that culture is spiritual, therefore machinery (materialism) is not culture; or that criticism alone, "the free disinterested play of mind," rather than the practical point of view, can see the object as it really is ("The Function of Criticism at the Present Time"). The resultant slogan could be *Criticism alone sees the object as it really is*.

In a country where there is no "sovereign organ of opinion" or "recognised authority in matters of tone and taste"—that is, nothing like the French Academy—there may be poetry and genius, writes Arnold, but prose and intelligence will always bear "a note of provinciality" ("The Literary Influence of Academies"). This exemplifies reasoning by tautology, for the key roots are "centre" (the academy) and "province," which are by definition mutually exclusive. The resultant slogan could be *For tone and taste, try an Academy*.

Arnold could also write that "human nature" is the impulse to relate all knowledge to our sense of conduct and beauty, and so he could deduce that since science is only instrumental knowledge, which has nothing to do with conduct and beauty, the study of science alone can never satisfy human nature. Art, on the other hand, is one manifestation of the human relationship to beauty, and the great actions in great art refer to conduct, so literature by definition is sufficient ("Literature and Science"). The resultant slogan: *Only art can satisfy*. In *Seven Types of Ambiguity* (1947), William Empson felt that the "increasing vagueness, compactness, and lack of logical distinctions" in English journalism may "yet give back something of the Elizabethan energy to what is at present a rather exhausted language."[3] Although Empson was half-ironic here, in Arnold's case the exuberant, exploitative wordplay resulted in a sort of un-self-conscious poetry. One might even say that it resulted in his best poetry.

Of course, Arnold's word games were in the service of proclaiming that—again a slogan—"the men of Culture are the true apostles of equality," much as Wilde would claim that "the new Individualism is the New Hellenism" in the conclusion of "The Soul of Man Under Socialism." But without wit, slogans are no less than mental

3. William Empson, *Seven Types of Ambiguity* (London, 1947), 236–37.

bondage. If *Culture and Anarchy* were not so exuberant in Arnold's destruction of his adversaries' speech, the reader who accepted Arnold's pious nomenclature would suffer a sort of textual bondage. Those who do not like his slogans find themselves alienated from the text or reduced to an epithet. Those who do not share his concept of Culture and its "disinterested study" are in bondage to the Ordinary—not Best—Self.

CRITICISM

Reviews and Reactions

WILLIAM ARCHER

On *The Importance of Being Earnest*†

The dramatic critic is not only a philosopher, moralist, æsthetician, and stylist, but also a labourer working for his hire. In this last capacity he cares nothing for the classifications of Aristotle, Polonius, or any other theorist, but instinctively makes a fourfold division of the works which come within his ken. These are his categories: (1) Plays which are good to see. (2) Plays which are good to write about. (3) Plays which are both. (4) Plays which are neither. Class 4 is naturally the largest; Class 3 the smallest; and Classes 1 and 2 balance each other pretty evenly. Mr. Oscar Wilde's new comedy, *The Importance of Being Earnest*, belongs indubitably to the first class. It is delightful to see, it sends wave after wave of laughter curling and foaming round the theatre; but as a text for criticism it is barren and delusive. It is like a mirage-oasis in the desert, grateful and comforting to the weary eye—but when you come close up to it, behold! it is intangible, it eludes your grasp. What can a poor critic do with a play which raises no principle, whether of art or morals, creates its own canons and conventions, and is nothing but an absolutely wilful expression of an irrepressibly witty personality? Mr. Pater, I think (or is it some one else?), has an essay on the tendency of all art to verge towards, and merge in, the absolute art—music. He might have found an example in *The Importance of Being Earnest*, which imitates nothing, represents nothing, means nothing, is nothing, except a sort of *rondo capriccioso*, in which the artist's fingers run with crisp irresponsibility up and down the keyboard of life. Why attempt to analyse and class such a play? Its theme, in other hands, would have made a capital farce; but 'farce' is far too gross and commonplace a word to apply to such an iridescent filament of fantasy. Incidents of the same nature as Algy Moncrieffe's 'Bunburying' and John Worthing's invention and subsequent suppression of his scapegrace brother Ernest have done duty in

† Signed review in the *World*, 20 February 1895.

many a French vaudeville and English adaptation; but Mr. Wilde's humour transmutes them into something entirely new and individual. Amid so much that is negative, however, criticism may find one positive remark to make. Behind all Mr. Wilde's whim and even perversity, there lurks a very geniune science, or perhaps I should rather say instinct, of the theatre. In all his plays, and certainly not least in this one, the story is excellently told and illustrated with abundance of scenic detail. Monsieur Sarcey himself (if Mr. Wilde will forgive my saying so) would 'chortle in his joy' over John Worthing's entrance in deep mourning (even down to his cane) to announce the death of his brother Ernest, when we know that Ernest in the flesh—a false but undeniable Ernest—is at that moment in the house making love to Cecily. The audience does not instantly awaken to the meaning of his inky suit, but even as he marches solemnly down the stage, and before a word is spoken, you can feel the idea kindling from row to row, until a 'sudden glory' of laughter fills the theatre. It is only the born playwright who can imagine and work up to such an effect. Not that the play is a masterpiece of construction. It seemed to me that the author's invention languished a little after the middle of the second act, and that towards the close of that act there were even one or two brief patches of something almost like tediousness. But I have often noticed that the more successful the play, the more a first-night audience is apt to be troubled by inequalities of workmanship, of which subsequent audiences are barely conscious. The most happily-inspired scenes, coming to us with the gloss of novelty upon them, give us such keen pleasure, that passages which are only reasonably amusing are apt to seem, by contrast, positively dull. Later audiences, missing the shock of surprise which gave to the master-scenes their keenest zest, are also spared our sense of disappointment in the flatter passages, and enjoy the play more evenly all through. I myself, on seeing a play a second time, have often been greatly entertained by scenes which had gone near to boring me on the first night. When I see Mr. Wilde's play again, I shall no doubt relish the last half of the second act more than I did on Thursday evening; and even then I differed from some of my colleagues who found the third act tedious. Mr. Wilde is least fortunate where he drops into Mr. Gilbert's Place-of-Truth mannerism, as he is apt to do in the characters of Gwendolen and Cecily. Strange what a fascination this trick seems to possess for the comic playwright! Mr. Pinero, Mr. Shaw, and now Mr. Wilde, have all dabbled in it, never to their advantage. . . .

"H.F."

On *The Importance of Being Earnest*†

Oscar Wilde may be said to have at last, and by a single stroke, put his enemies under his feet. Their name is legion, but the most inveterate of them may be defied to go to St. James's Theatre and keep a straight face through the performance of *The Importance of Being Earnest*. It is a pure farce of Gilbertian parentage, but loaded with drolleries, epigrams, impertinences, and bubbling comicalities that only an Irishman could have ingrafted on that respectable Saxon stock. Since *Charley's Aunt* was first brought from the provinces to London I have not heard such unrestrained, incessant laughter from all parts of the theatre, and those laughed the loudest whose approved mission it is to read Oscar long lectures in the press on his dramatic and ethical shortcomings. The thing is as slight in structure and as devoid of purpose as a paper balloon, but it is extraordinarily funny, and the universal assumption is that it will remain on the boards here for an indefinitely extended period.

GEORGE BERNARD SHAW

On *The Importance of Being Earnest*‡

It is somewhat surprising to find Mr Oscar Wilde, who does not usually model himself on Mr Henry Arthur Jones, giving his latest play a five-chambered title like *The Case of Rebellious Susan*. So I suggest with some confidence that *The Importance of Being Earnest* dates from a period long anterior to Susan. However it may have been retouched immediately before its production, it must certainly have been written before *Lady Windermere's Fan*. I do not suppose it to be Mr Wilde's first play: he is too susceptible to fine art to have begun otherwise than with a strenuous imitation of a great dramatic poem, Greek or Shakespearian; but it was perhaps the first which he designed for practical commercial use at the West End theatres. The evidence of this is abundant. The play has a plot—a gross anachronism; there is a scene between the two girls in the second act quite in the literary style of Mr Gilbert, and almost inhuman enough to have been conceived by him; the humour is adulterated by stock mechanical fun to an extent that absolutely

---

† Notice signed "H.F." (Hamilton Fyfe) in the *New York Times*, February 17, 1895.
‡ Review signed "G.B.S." in *Saturday Review* (February 23, 1895), lxxix, 249–50.

scandalizes one in a play with such an author's name to it; and the punning title and several of the more farcical passages recall the epoch of the late H. J. Byron. The whole has been varnished, and here and there veneered, by the author of *A Woman of No Importance*; but the general effect is that of a farcical comedy dating from the seventies, unplayed during that period because it was too clever and too decent, and brought up to date as far as possible by Mr Wilde in his now completely formed style. Such is the impression left by the play on me. But I find other critics, equally entitled to respect, declaring that *The Importance of Being Earnest* is a strained effort of Mr Wilde's at ultra-modernity, and that it could never have been written but for the opening up of entirely new paths in drama last year by *Arms and the Man*. At which I confess to a chuckle.

I cannot say that I greatly cared for *The Importance of Being Earnest*. It amused me, of course; but unless comedy touches me as well as amuses me, it leaves me with a sense of having wasted my evening. I go to the theatre to be moved to laughter, not to be tickled or bustled into it; and that is why, though I laugh as much as anybody at a farcical comedy, I am out of spirits before the end of the second act, and out of temper before the end of the third, my miserable mechanical laughter intensifying these symptoms at every outburst. If the public ever becomes intelligent enough to know when it is really enjoying itself and when it is not, there will be an end of farcical comedy. Now in *The Importance of Being Earnest* there is plenty of this rib-tickling: for instance, the lies, the deceptions, the cross purposes, the sham mourning, the christening of the two grown-up men, the muffin eating, and so forth. These could only have been raised from the farcical plane by making them occur to characters who had, like Don Quixote, convinced us of their reality and obtained some hold on our sympathy. But that unfortunate moment of Gilbertism breaks our belief in the humanity of the play. Thus we are thrown back on the force and daintiness of its wit, brought home by an exquisitely grave, natural, and unconscious execution on the part of the actors. . . . On the whole I must decline to accept *The Importance of Being Earnest* as a day less than ten years old; and I am altogether unable to perceive any uncommon excellence in its presentations.

H. G. WELLS

On *The Importance of Being Earnest*†

It is, we were told last night, 'much harder to listen to nonsense than to talk it'; but not if it is good nonsense. And very good non-sense, excellent fooling, is this new play of Mr. Oscar Wilde's. It is, indeed, as new a new comedy as we have had this year. Most of the others, after the fashion of Mr. John Worthing, J.P., last night, have been simply the old comedies posing as their own imaginary youngest brothers. More humorous dealing with theatrical conven-tions it would be difficult to imagine. To the dramatic critic espe-cially who leads a dismal life, it came with a flavour of rare holiday. As for the serious people who populate this city, and to whom it is addressed, how they will take it is another matter. Last night, at any rate, it was a success, and our familiar first-night audience—whose cough, by-the-bye, is much quieter—received it with delight. . . .

. . . It is all very funny, and Mr. Oscar Wilde has decorated a hu-mour that is Gilbertian with innumerable spangles of that wit that is all his own. Of the pure and simple truth, for instance, he re-marks that 'Truth is never pure and rarely simple'; and the reply, 'Yes, flowers are as common in the country as people are in Lon-don,' is particularly pretty from the artless country girl to the town-bred Gwendolen. . . .

How Serious People—the majority of the population, according to Carlyle—how Serious People will take this Trivial Comedy writ-ten for their learning remains to be seen. No doubt seriously. One last night thought that the bag incident was a 'little far-fetched'. Moreover, he could not see how the bag and the baby got to Victo-ria Station (L.B. and S.C.R. station) while the manuscript and per-ambulator turned up 'at the summit of Primrose Hill'. Why the summit? Such difficulties, he said, rob a play of 'convincingness'. That is one serious person disposed of, at any rate.

On the last production of a play by Mr. Oscar Wilde we said it was fairly bad, and anticipated success. This time we must congrat-ulate him unreservedly on a delightful revival of theatrical satire. *Absit omen.* But we could pray for the play's success, else we fear it may prove the last struggle of its author against the growing seri-ousness of his dramatic style.

---

† Unsigned review in the *Pall Mall Gazette*, February 15, 1895, p. 4.

Essays in Criticism

E. H. MIKHAIL

The Four-Act Version of *The Importance of Being Earnest*†

It has been known to a few of the many readers and playgoers who
have delighted in *The Importance of Being Earnest* that Oscar
Wilde originally wrote this comedy in four acts. In the form in
which the play was first produced, it consisted of three acts, and it
has been played in that form ever since. The original version contained a whole scene, with one fresh character, besides a good deal
of additional dialogue, all of which Wilde cut out in revising the
script. George Alexander, the manager of the St. James's Theatre
and the producer of the play, did not like the idea of another character who appeared only in one particular scene. So, to oblige him,
the author condensed Acts II and III to form a single act, and
dropped the scene[1] with the extra character, whose name was Gribsby. That the most drastic part of the curtailment, the actual compression of the four acts in three, was done shortly before the
comedy was presented is clear from the fact that the counterfoil of
the license to perform, issued by the office of the Lord Chamberlain which is dated 30 January 1895, states that the play is in four
acts, although the actual copy deposited is in three.[2]

Wilde's early biographers do not seem to have known of the four-
act version of his play; at least they do not mention it. Nor does
there seem to be any comment on the four-act text in the collected
editions of Wilde's works. The author himself alludes to his play in
more than a dozen letters, of which five were written in 1894–1895

---

† From *Modern Drama* 11 (1968): 263–66. Reprinted by permission of University of
Toronto Press Incorporated.
1. The scene was performed for the first time in the B.B.C. Home Service on 27 October
1954 and reproduced in *The Listener*, 4 November 1954. It was performed on the stage
by the Wanstead Players in January 1955.
2. This information has been supplied by Mr. C. D. Heriot, of the Lord Chamberlain's Office. See *The Importance of Being Earnest; A Trivial Comedy for Serious People. In Four
Acts as Originally Written by Oscar Wilde*, ed. by Sarah Augusta Dickson (New York,
1956).

when he was working on it, and soon after it was first produced, and the rest in 1898–1899 at the time of its publication. In none of these letters is anything said of the important changes made in the text of the play. St. John Hankin, however, in an article for *The Fortnightly Review* in 1908,[3] mentions that the four acts had been "boiled down" into three, apparently being the first to note the fact in print. He was not aware that the original version had survived, as he expresses a wish that it might some day be found and published, saying, "If the deleted act is half as delightful as the three that survive, every playgoer will long to read it." The play is mentioned in Hesketh Pearson's *The Life of Oscar Wilde* (1946) as a four-act comedy shortened to three at George Alexander's insistence, a fact divulged to Pearson by Alexander himself. James Agate, alluding to the German translation in an essay for *The Masque* (1947), declared that "The fun in the act that Wilde deleted is better than any living playwright can do."[4] Either Robert Ross, Wilde's friend and the executor of his estate, or someone acting for him submitted a four-act typescript in 1903 to the German translator (Herman Frieherr von Teschenberg; published at Leipzig in 1903 and entitled *Ernst Sein!*). At that date Wilde's works were still ostracised in England. This publication seems to have attracted little attention beyond bibliographical listings until long afterwards a copy of the German translation came into the hands of James Agate who searched for the original English text, but could not find it.

What had happened to the manuscript is curious. It consisted of four quarto-size note-books. Somehow they got separated. In 1909, Wilde's literary executor, Robert Ross, presented a number of Wilde manuscripts to the British Museum, but only the fourth of the note-books was amongst them. The whereabouts of the other three, which included the missing scene, remained a mystery for many years. Apparently they had been borrowed by a friend of Wilde's named Arthur Clifton, who was also a business associate of Ross, and they were never returned. They came to light on the death of Clifton's widow, being discovered among her effects in an old trunk. They were sold by public auction in London in 1950. Their eventual purchaser was an American collector, Mr. George Arents, and they are now in the Arents Collection in the New York Public Library. From these sources a coherent version of an early draft was assembled and published in 1956.[5]

3. St. John Hankin, "The Collected Plays of Oscar Wilde," *The Fortnightly Review*, LXXXIX (May 1908), 791–802.

4. James Agate, "Oscar Wilde and the Theatre," *The Masque*, No. 3 (1947).

5. Montgomery H. Hyde, "*The Importance of Being Earnest*; The Lost Scene from Oscar Wilde's Play," *The Listener* (4 November 1954), 753; Vyvyan Holland, "Explanatory Foreword" to *The Original Four-Act Version of "The Importance of Being Earnest"* (London, 1957); Sarah Augusta Dickson, "Introduction" to *The Importance of Being Earnest*;

The difference between the three-act play and the four-act version is aptly summed up in the following words:

> In the original four-act play, Act I takes place in Algernon Moncrieff's rooms in London; Act II in the garden of the Manor House, Woolton; and Acts III and IV in the sitting-room of the Manor House. In the shortened three-act version, as it is always performed, Act I remains substantially unchanged, the action taking place, as before, in Algernon Moncrieff's rooms. Act II is a combination and condensation of Acts II and III of the four-act play, the whole of the action taking place in the garden. Act III is Act IV of the four-act play, though there are considerable alterations in the dialogue, necessitated by the revisions in the earlier acts; the action remains in the sitting-room of the Manor House. The three-act version is at least twenty per cent shorter than the four-act version; in the process of shortening about six hundred words were deleted from the end of the original Act II alone.

> In the three-act version, again, two of the characters in the original play were cut out: Mr. Gribsby, of the firm of Gribsby, solicitors, and Moulton, the gardener of the Manor House. The exclusion of Moulton did not affect the play, as he appeared only once and then he had only four lines to speak. But the removal of Gribsby seems to be a pity. He was an amusing character who only appeared in a short scene in the second act; but his disappearance made a great deal of alteration necessary in the subsequent dialogue, as in the four-act version frequent references were made to the object of his visit, which was to serve a writ on the mythical Mr. Ernest Worthing. These references had, of course, to be modified or deleted. In the original version, also, Lady Bracknell was called Lady Brancaster, and Algernon Moncrieff was called Montford.[6]

Dr. Sarah A. Dickson, the editor of the New York four-act edition, maintains that this is the best edition and one Wilde would have preferred:

> It is difficult to keep from believing that, if Oscar Wilde had known that the four-act version of *The Importance of Being*

A *Trivial Comedy for Serious People. In Four Acts As Originally Written by Oscar Wilde* (New York, 1956); Theodore Bolton, "The Importance of Being Earnest," *Papers of the Bibliographical Society of America,* L (1956), 205–208; "Wilde's Comedy in Its First Version," *The Times Literary Supplement* (1 March 1957), 136; "The Importance of Publishing 'Earnest'," *Bulletin of the New York Public Library,* LX (July 1956), 368–372; William W. Appleton, "Making A Masterpiece: *The Importance of Being Earnest,*" *The Saturday Review* (12 May 1956), 21; and *Oscar Wilde: The Importance of Being Earnest,* ed. by Vincent F. Hopper and Gerald B. Lahey (Great Neck, N.Y., 1959), p. 50.

6. Vyvyan Holland, "Explanatory Foreword" to *The Original Four-Act Version of "The Importance of Being Earnest"* (London, 1957), pp. vi–vii.

Earnest was still available . . . he would have preferred to publish his comedy as he had originally conceived it. By printing
the entire text of the comedy as Wilde wrote it . . . we believe
we are fulfilling what would have been the wishes of the author.[7]

Actually, the examination of the text shows that the New York four-
act edition is not a preferable or even an alternative version at all,
but merely an early draft. The organisation of the plot is looser and
the arrest of Jack for debt diffuses the action. Many of the best
lines are missing; the dialogue is less polished than in the regular
edition; certain witticisms are even repeated from act to act, showing that Wilde had not finally decided where they should go. The
theatrical qualities of the four-act version are of course untested,
but the play as it has been known to the English-speaking theater
since 1895 is surely a better play to read. The shortening of the
comedy, mainly by the compression of Acts II and III, and with the
regrettable omission of a rather amusing solicitor called Gribsby
who comes to arrest Algernon for debt, are accomplished with skill
and effectiveness. In the course of his cutting Wilde deprived us, it
is true, of some amusing moments, such as that in the last scene
when Miss Prism, leafing through a volume in search of the name
of Jack's father, the General, remarks: "To me . . . you have given
two copies of the Price Lists of the Civil Service. I do not find generals marked anywhere. There either seems to be no demand or no
supply." Despite the interesting additional material in the four-act
version, the three-act version is superior in artistic neatness and
verbal economy, the action moves more smoothly and the wit crackles a little more sharply, and the play is a little less elaborately mannered in style. However, in reading the text of the four-act version,
there is the satisfaction gained from an examination of the manuscripts presented therein. One could follow the dramatist as he
worked, almost incessantly, on what he considered his best play,
which was not "dashed off" at the seashore as some writers believe,[8] but was Wilde's chief concern and care from the summer of
1894 to the end of the January 1895, when he deposited his shortened version at the Lord Chamberlain's Office.

7. Sarah Augusta Dickson, *op. cit.*, p. xxvii.
8. Montgomery H. Hyde, "*The Importance of Being Earnest*; The 'Lost' Scene from Oscar
Wilde's Play," *The Listener* (4 November 1954), 753. Francis Winwar writes in *Oscar
Wilde and the Yellow Nineties* (p. 258) that "it was dashed off in about a fortnight."
Robert Harborough Sherard says in *The Real Oscar Wilde* (p. 363) that the play "was
turned out in about a fortnight."

EVA THIENPONT

From Faltering Arrow to Pistol Shot:
The Importance of Being Earnest†

Since 1966, the editors of the Collins *Complete Works of Oscar Wilde*, often used as a reference book, have chosen to print the reconstructed four-act text of *The Importance of Being Earnest* rather than the better-known version in three acts.[1] The authoritative French Pléiades edition (1966) followed suit, arguing, like Collins, that since Wilde converted his original four-act version into a three-acter at the instigation of George Alerander, the four-act version is the play as Wilde intended it to be. Here I should like to oppose this view, and suggest the reasons for considering the three-act version superior.

When one reads the scanty comments on the difference between the four- and three-act texts of *The Importance of Being Earnest*, it often seems as though the only change Wilde made was the deletion of the so-called Gribsby scene, in which a solicitor of that name arrives at Jack's country house to arrest 'Mr Ernest Worthing' for debt.[2] In a chapter of his book *Oscar Wilde: Art and Egotism*, Rodney Shewan explores the two texts a little further and finds that the four-act play contains more biographical and literary self-parody. Thus, the four-act text mentions debts at the Savoy, has Algernon nearly arrested and sent to Holloway prison and Cecily quote one of the *Phrases and Philosophies for the Use of the Young*, and refers to theories from *The Decay of Lying*. Shewan suggests that the play's 'status as a classic owes much to the removal of precisely those references capable of direct biographical interpretation'.[3] In this 1970 analysis, Shewan pays no attention to the impact the removal of these 'references' has on the internal logic and meaning of the text. In the meantime, scholars such as Russell Jackson and Sos Eltis have stressed that Wilde's textual changes are not to be treated lightly. For Jackson, some of them 'might seem trivial in themselves, but in a play so economical in its language and effects, they had a serious consequence'.[4] Eltis has shown that through succeeding drafts the playwright subverted the Victorian melodrama tradi-

---

† From The Cambridge Quarterly, Vol. 33, No. 3 2004. Copyright © The Editors, *The Cambridge Quarterly*. Reprinted by permission of the publisher.

1. I have consulted the 1963 Collins edition, identical to Wilde's 1899 edition, for the three-act play and the 1994 Collins edition for the four-act play.
2. Regenia Gagnier, *Idylls of the Marketplace. Oscar Wilde and the Victorian Public* (Aldershot 1986) p. 116; Norbert Kohl, *Oscar Wilde: The Works of a Conformist Rebel* (Cambridge 1989) pp. 273–4; Allan Bird, *The Plays of Oscar Wilde* (London 1977) p. 177; Peter Raby (ed.), *Cambridge Companion to Oscar Wilde* (Cambridge 1998) p. 121.
3. Rodney Shewan, *Oscar Wilde: Art and Egotism* (London 1970) pp. 188, 192.
4. Jackson, 'The Importance of Being Earnest', in Raby (ed.), *Cambridge Companion to Oscar Wilde*, p. 163, and Sos Eltis, *Revising Wilde: Society and Subversion in the Plays of Oscar Wilder* (Oxford 1996).

tion he used as a base. Neither scholar has, however, devoted specific attention to the meaningful changes between the four- and three-act texts. This article will argue that, whereas the four-act play looked like a society comedy with parodic, Gilbertian airs, the play in its final three-act form has been made more subtle and more radical at the same time. As I will show, the final rewriting of *The Importance of Being Earnest* effected a more poignant social subversion caused by a move towards absurdity, a fortification of the position of the play's women, and a heightened identification with Victorian stereotypes.

When considering the revisions Wilde made to the original four-act text of *The Importance of Being Earnest*, it is good to take note of the fact that 'revision' in this case nearly always means 'shortening'. Wilde very rarely added to the text while reworking; he changed meanings and implications mainly by taking out words, sentences and sequences from the original text.

Taking out the Gribsby scene at George Alexander's request, Wilde decided to conflate the second and third acts of his play into one, resulting in a second act distinctly longer than the other two. Proof of the fact that the three-act version of *The Importance of Being Earnest* is not simply to be dismissed as 'Alexander's version' is that he also tackled the first and fourth acts, which the actor-manager had not complained about. Here, Wilde cut considerable portions of text that slowed down the play's pace. Their deletion tightens the textual fabric and increases the swiftness of the play. However, most portions removed did create remarkable effects, and it is rewarding to take a look at what they are and what happens when they are removed.

As a rule, Wildean comedies touched upon *fin-de-siècle* social debates such as the issue of 'good' and 'bad' women (*Lady Windermere's Fan*), the inequality of the sexes (*A Woman of No Importance*) and political corruption (*An Ideal Husband*). These are plays with an undercurrent of seriousness: they call into question the Victorian stereotyped definitions of men and women, good and bad, and expose the shallowness and hypocrisy of contemporary society. In order to achieve this, Wilde mobilises—and subverts—all the machinations and conventions of the melodrama tradition he works in, because melodrama endorses the Victorian system. There is an unease in the atmosphere, even though the plays apparently end happily. Convictions, judgements, are called into question, and wit and humour go hand in hand with serious reflection.

The Importance of Being Earnest is different. At the centre of the play are two pairs of lovers who, despite complications, fall into one another's arms at the end. No moral conflict hovers over them, and the two references to social disgrace are erroneous and comical, as Jack's ending up in a handbag was *not* an attempt at hiding a 'social indiscretion', and Miss Prism very soon turns out *not* to be his mother.

In fact, much of *The Importance of Being Earnest*'s lightness of tone was established during the last round of rewriting. The four-act text featured several instances of outside reality and its troubles intruding into the play's light-hearted atmosphere. The most prominent serious item is the recurrent tension between different social classes.

So, for example, the four-act play contained the character of Moulton the gardener, a figure so small and insignificant to the plot that he could easily be dispensed with. However, in the second act the gardener served to illustrate the condescension in the attitude of the aristocracy towards their servants, as Cecily felt it necessary to point out to Moulton that 'German is the language talked by people who live in Germany'. Moulton thus provided a critical counterbalance to the witty and easy relationship of Algernon and his manservant Lane.

In the same act, Cecily shocks Miss Prism and Canon Chasuble by airing views that smack of socialism, as when she retorts to Chasuble's cheerful remark, 'It is wonderful how girls are educated nowadays. I suppose you know all about relations between Capital and Labour?' by observing: 'All I know is about the relations between Capital and Idleness.' Miss Prism's anxious exclamation, 'Cecily, that sounds like Socialism! And I suppose you know where Socialism leads to?' is parried by Cecily's 'Oh, yes! That leads to Rational Dress, Miss Prism.'

Although Cecily's remarks seem innocent rather than calculated to shock, she nevertheless touches upon several issues that disturbed Victorian society at the end of the nineteenth century, namely the rise of socialism and the birth of feminism. Socialism in the public eye was often linked with feminism and New Womanhood. Although the connection between the two movements was less close than the public assumed, New Women were indeed inspired by socialist theories.[5] The Rational Dress movement went against the grain of contemporary women's fashion by attacking light lacing and became associated with women's liberation, and feminists were stereotypically portrayed as "badly dressed', that is, as refusing to wear fashionable (male-dictated) clothes.[6]

This small dialogue in the four-act version of the play seems light-hearted and funny enough, but actually contains a rather acerbic sketch of upper-class short-sightedness. Cecily, as an exponent of her class, is not aware of the changes taking place in society, and her greatest concern is that Rational Dress, notoriously unbecoming and middle-class, may be gaining support.

5. Ann Heilmann: *New Woman Fiction: Women Writing First-Wave Feminism* (London 2000) p. 66.
6. Ibid., pp. 121–2. Oscar Wilde sympathised with the Rational Dress movement and wrote several articles supporting it. His wife Constance edited the society's magazine for several years.

Class tensions and the aristocratic fear of a proletarian revolution are also more keenly apparent in Lady Bracknell's earlier interview with Jack than in the three-act text, when the latter insists that he doesn't want 'to put the asses against the classes'.

Taking out such blatant—even if critical—references to tensions between the classes, Wilde also removes the atmosphere of unease and the threat that they entail. Lady Brackness's references remain, but views like 'to be born, or at any rate bred, in a hand-bag, whether it has handles or not, seems to me to display a contempt for the ordinary decencies of family life that reminds one of the worst excesses of the French Revolution', are statements so out of proportion that they undermine the drama they invoke and reduce it to absurdity. Lady Bracknell's awareness of lower-class attacks on the upper class is exaggerated to such a point that she seems at times comically paranoid. Reducing the four acts to three, Wilde resolutely chooses farce as a means of expression and creates a world separated from actual life by a magic veil of humorous detachment.

Related to this is the removal of another striking feature in the older text, namely the fact that the characters repeatedly seek to explain absurdities with which they are confronted. An example is the passage in the second act where Jack asks Canon Chasuble to christen him, asserting his doubts on his christening at birth, since 'There are circumstances, unnecessary to mention at present, connected with my birth and early life that make me think I was a good deal neglected. I certainly wasn't properly looked after, at any rate.' In the three-act version the response to the Canon's query whether he has 'any grave doubts on the subject' becomes the laconic 'I certainly intend to have.' The effect is entirely different. If the earlier version is conventional, submitting to the rules of ordinary life, the final version's quizzical answer renders the cleric's seriousness oddly out of tune.

Another example from the same act is the attempt to square Jack's announcement of the death of his brother Ernest in Paris, related to him in a telegram from the manager of the Grand Hotel, with the fact that Cecily comes in a few minutes later to say that Ernest is waiting for the dining room. Canon Chasuble surmises: 'That telegram from Paris seems to have been a somewhat heartless jest by someone who wishes to play upon your feelings.' In the three-act text Chasuble's reference to the telegram is deleted, and everybody seems naively uncritical or happily oblivious of the leaks and holes in Jack's manipulation of the truth.

Wilde's systematic removal of any explanatory elements heightens the atmosphere of absurdity already invoked by the plot's double lives and mistaken identities. It leads to a certain wonderful anarchy in the final version of *The Importance of Being Earnest*, situating the play in a world sufficiently like Victorian England to be

identifiable with it, but sufficiently unlike it not to coincide with it. Reason is ruled out, and the norms and decrees of Victorian society which so dominated Wilde's earlier comedies are now, if not exactly absent, at least not threatening because they work in what Robert Jordan aptly calls 'a world without evil', where 'sin and degradation . . . do not exist, except as unemotional abstractions'.[7]

Yet the absurdity does not render the play simply harmless. When Wilde reworks the four-act play into three acts, he chooses more radically to refuse the Victorian norms which he had originally supported clearly enough though what seem at first sight negligible details, such as four little words in a speech:

> When one is placed in the position of guardian, one has to adopt a very high moral tone on all subjects. It's one's duty to do so. And as a high moral tone can hardly be said to conduce very much to either one's health or one's happiness *if carried to excess*, in order to get up to town I have always pretended to have a younger brother of the name of Ernest, who lives in the Albany, and gets into the most dreadful scrapes. (italics added)

The words 'if carried to excess' make Jack's argument conventional: excess, even of morality, is bad. But take out this qualification, as Wilde did in 1895, and suddenly Jack states as a matter of fact that a moral tone is bad for health and happiness. This is exemplary of Wilde's meticulous consideration of every word in the text, and symbolic of the radicalisation of the play during the final revision. The characters' innocence despite their lack of moral sense becomes Wilde's key point.

Although these interventions moved the play further away from melodrama, Wilde at the same time reinforced the identification of his characters with the stereotypes of melodrama. Cecily and Jack, in particular undergo a distinct change of characterisation. Cecily is based on the stereotype of the Good Woman, an angelic creature and the supreme picture of Victorian femininity. A Good Woman was dependent, gentle, self-sacrificing and forgiving, and her mission was to be a guide for men who were likely to leave the path of Victorian respectability. In an early sketch found in an 1894 letter to Alexander, Wilde points out that Cecily only consents to marry her guardian's presumed wicked brother 'because she thought he was bad and wanted guidance'. When she finds out that her fiancé is not the profligate he pretended to be, she breaks off the engagement.[8]

However, in the four-act play Cecily explicitly resists qualifica-

7. Robert J. Jordan, 'Satire and Fantasy in Wilde's *The Importance of Being Earnest*', in Harold Bloom (ed.), *Modern Critical Interpretations: Oscar Wilde's The Importance of Being Earnest* (New York and Philadelphia 1988) p. 30.
8. *Complete Letters of Oscar Wilde*, ed. Merlin Holland and Rupert Hart-Davis (London 2000) p. 596.

tion as a Good Woman. When Algernon presents himself to her as Ernest in the second act and asks her to make his reform her mission, she vociferously rejects his assumption that 'every woman ha[s] a mission of some kind' retorting that 'Every female has! No woman. Besides, I have no time to reform you this afternoon.' If Cecily seems insulted, it is probably because the concept of the woman with a mission is rather middle-class and the four-act Cecily, as we have seen earlier, is very class-conscious. The three-act Cecily reacts very differently, stating simply, 'I'm afraid I've no time this afternoon.' There is nothing to suggest that she will not gladly take the task upon her later, and her tone, quite contrary to that of the earlier Cecily, is good-humoured and playful. Wilde now highlights the naivety and fun in the apparent assumption that reforming a person should take no more than one afternoon, a joke overruled in the earlier text by the harshness of Cecily's tone.

The four-act Cecily is on the whole less innocent than she appears at first sight. In a drawing-room scene between Cecily and Miss Prism at the beginning of the third act, later deleted, Cecily vents some opinions that are entirely uncharacteristic of a Good Woman, or of any young lady a good Victorian would have termed 'decent'. She tells her governess that 'it is only the superficial qualities that last. Man's deeper nature is soon found out', an epigram from Wilde's *Phrases and Philosophies for the Use of the Young*. These epigrams, published in the Oxford undergraduate magazine *The Chameleon* in 1894, were cited during the 1895 trials as indicative of Wilde's corrupting influence on the young. But Cecily goes even further by deriding so-called improving books: 'Are there ever any ideas in improving books?' she asks. 'I fear not. I get my ideas . . . in the garden.'

However, while Cecily has no qualms about expressing highly suspicious views, she tries to keep up an appearance of obedience and innocence, especially when in the company of Jack or Algernon. Thus, when the latter, who wants to see Cecily without the hindrance of Miss Prism's presence, asks her to help him concoct an excuse to make the governess leave, it is Cecily who suggests a ruse: Algernon is to tell Miss Prism that Dr Chasuble is waiting for her. Yet, though the lie is hers, Cecily explicitly denies being deceptive and wants Algernon to interpret her action as an experiment in cause and effect.

Another important manifestation of the split between the four-act Cecily's actual behaviour, and her awareness of what is socially expected of her, occurs in the third act, where she discloses to Algernon that in the imaginary world of her diary they have been engaged for several months, and that he has been regularly writing to her. When he objects that he never wrote her any letters, she says:

You need hardly remind me of that, Ernest. I remember it only
too well. I grew tired of asking the postman every morning if
he had a London letter for me. My health began to give way
under the strain and anxiety. So I wrote your letters for you,
and had them posted to me in the village by my maid. I wrote
always three times a week and sometimes oftener.

Cecily here comes up with a Victorian cliché which supposed
women to be weaker and less healthy than men.[9] She uses the
cliché eagerly to make Algernon feel guilty, not knowing that in the
first act he has already been informed by Jack that she is in the best
of health, has a capital appetite, and goes for long walks.

In the revised three-act version, Cecily is presented in an entirely
different way thanks to a tightened reply with a completely different
implication: 'You need hardly remind me of that, Ernest. I remember
only too well that I was forced to write your letters for you. I wrote
always three times a week, and sometimes oftener.' Here, Cecily is
impressively strong and determined: she immediately decides to take
matters into her own hands. She does not invoke weakness to appeal
to Algernon's manly feelings of protectiveness, but rather wins him
by her pertinence and determination. The wail and cry for attention
of the earlier text is turned into a dignified reproach.

The character of Cecily in the four-act text is an uneasy mix between a Good Woman and a more experienced, knowing woman; by
the final version, she has developed into an innocent young girl
who is nevertheless clever, self-confident and strong.[1] The four-act
Cecily seems quite dim repeatedly misreading metaphors and expressions. When in the second act Miss Prism says 'As a man sows,
so let him reap', Cecily remarks that men don't sew. In the next act
Algernon complains that he is forced to 'go back again into the cold
world', Cecily responding that 'the day, even for the month of July,
is unusually warm'. These remarks are removed in the three-act
play so that Cecily's innocence cannot be mistaken for stupidity.

Cecily's increased self-confidence in the three-act text is exemplified in an exchange with Merriman, the butler, who announces the
arrival of 'Ernest Worthing':

CECILY   (to herself). I don't think Miss Prism would like my being
alone with [Ernest]. So I had better send for him at once, before
she comes in. (To MERRIMAN) Ask Mr. Ernest Worthing to come
here. I suppose you had better talk to the housekeeper about a
room for him.

9. Deborah Gorham, *The Victorian Girl and the Feminine Ideal* (London 1982) p. 72, 87, 90.
1. As Sos Eltis, *Revising Wilde*, p. 183, points out, Wilde was not the only playwright to
   create a character of this kind. W. S. Gilbert's Azema in *The Palace of Truth* from 1870
   is devious and experienced, but poses as innocent and modest in order to ensnare the
   man of her choice.

MERRIMAN   I have already sent his luggage up to the Blue Room, Miss: next to Mr. Worthing's own room.
CECILY   Oh! That is all right.

The corresponding passage in the three-act play reads:

CECILY   Ask Mr Ernest to come here. I suppose you had better talk to the housekeeper about a room for him.
MERRIMAN   Yes, Miss.

Whereas in the first version Cecily's decision to take up the role of hostess seems more informed by schoolgirlish naughtiness and a wayward challenging of her teacher's wishes, the final version shows her naturally assuming the role of lady of the house. Her authority is reinforced by the fact that the manservant simply obeys her orders whereas in the earlier text he had anticipated them.

A final aspect of Cecily's growth to independence in the evolution from four to three acts is her behaviour in her courtship with Algernon. If, in the four-act play, she blatantly angles for his attention, in the three-act play her interest in him is first revealed to her baffled suitor by the laconic reply to his proposal: 'You silly boy! Of course [I will marry you]. Why, we have been engaged for the last three months.' Cecily has been quietly, modestly in control the whole time and accepts the proposal as her due.

By contrast, in the four-act version, Algernon is still allowed to talk disparagingly of women's cleverness, speculating to Jack that Cecily must be 'one of those dull, intellectual girls one meets all over the place. Girls who have got large minds and large feet.' The association of intellectuality in women with ugliness was of course an anti-feminist stock-in-trade to deride New Women and their plea for equality of education.[2] One is tempted to say that Algernon, who entertains such conservative opinions on women and learning, deserves no better than the Cecily of the four-act play, who, if 'excessively pretty', as Jack states, is also accordingly silly. Removing the reactionary comment, Wilde turns his dandy into a more suitable partner for the final version of Cecily Cardew.

Control of space, too, marks a significant shift between the four- and three-act versions, the very conflation of the second and third acts creating the transmutation. The original second act was situated in the garden of Jack's manor, the third in the drawing-room. After the exposure of Jack and Algernon in the third act, Gwendolen and Cecily leave the drawing-room and go into the garden. They chal-

2. As a reaction, New Woman writer took great care to depict their heroines as both clever *and* attractive, turning the war of the sexes, in Ann Heilmann's words, into a 'sexy war': *New Woman Fiction*, p. 32.

lenge the men to come after them by stating that they are too cowardly to do so. However, at the beginning of the fourth act the men have not responded to their bait and the women surrender by re-entering the house. In the three-act play, the garden setting is preserved and Gwendolen and Cecily retire into the house. This time it is the men who make an attempt at conciliation by coming after them, whereas the women are first to speak. Thus Wilde establishes an equality between the sexes that was not there in the four-act play.

Also greatly changed in the course of the final rewriting, but to different effect, is the character of Jack. If, in the earliest sketch of the play, Jack was based on the Melodrama Gentleman, the personification of Victorian ideal manliness, an honest, industrious, serious and protective male,[3] in the four-act text he is hardly recognisable as such. Instead, Jack is fully engaged in the game of the double life, confessing, for instance, to Algernon that he cannot dine at the Savoy restaurant because he owes the place a considerable amount of money, explaining, 'I must keep up Ernest's reputation. Ernest is one of those chaps who never pays a bill. He gets writted about once a week.' By the final version of the play Jack once more approximates to the original Melodrama Gentleman, inventing Ernest merely as a means to enable him to escape his responsibilities occasionally and come up to town while nothing points in the direction of his ever doing anything unconventional there.

Likewise, in the earlier text Jack participates in Algernon's game to such a degree that he acknowledges the existence of Mr Bunbury. When he wants to persuade Algernon to go back to London at the end of the second act, Jack puts forward such arguments as 'Bunbury is extremely ill, and your place is by his side.' In the corresponding passage of the final play, Jack can think of nothing better than to appeal to Algernon's more abstract sense of gentlemanly behaviour ('Your duty as a gentleman calls you back'), but this produces no effect whatsoever on the dandy.

Finally, in the earlier version Jack is much closer to Algernon in the ease with which he lies. When questioned on the subject of Cecily, the earlier Jack, like his later incarnation, denies knowing anybody of that name but, unlike the later Jack, cautiously and shrewdly adds 'as far as I remember', thus enabling himself to invoke a defective memory if necessary. Moreover, he is given a short speech in defence of the lie as an act of genius: 'To invent anything at all is an act of sheer genius, and, in a commercial age like ours, shows considerable physical courage.' The argument is clearly reminiscent of the views expounded by Vivian in Wilde's essay *The Decay*

3. In the early sketch, an incarnation of Gwendolen discovers that he is, besides being a JP, 'a county-councillor: a churchwarden: a philanthropist: a good example' (Wilde, *Letters*, p. 596).

of Lying, and is distinctly unconventional. Wildes estimation of the lie as an art to be encouraged runs counter to Victorian (and Christian) rules of decent behaviour. In making Jack repeat his own views, Wilde marks him as a dandy and a rebel against society's laws.

Reworking the text in 1895, Wilde took care to remove every one of Jack's more obviously dandiacal traits. There are no more excesses at the Savoy, no more foie gras and champagne 'diet', and no more quick partaking in the logic of Bunburying. Wilde now invites the audience to identify Jack with the stock melodrama character of the Gentleman, only to disturb its stereotyped apprehensions: Jack is in fact conservative to the core, but *as such* has to have recourse to a double life from time to time. In the final version, conservative Victorian gentlemen prove unable to live up constantly to the seriousness and truthfulness expected of them.

Truthfulness, or indeed earnestness, is Wilde's main target in the play, and he ultimately calls upon the gentleman to establish the truth of masks. In both versions, Jack thinks he has been lying when calling himself Ernest and pretending to have a brother, only to discover that his name is indeed Ernest and that he has a brother, Algernon. After his earlier endorsement of the lie, it comes as no surprise that Jack in the four-act text should state that it is terrible to find out that he has been speaking the truth. But in the three-act text Jack's statement becomes much more disturbing: in the absence of a speech in defence of lies, it is a conventional gentleman who proclaims his unease with truth, lending the play's title extra poignancy. Wilde establishes here what he has proclaimed elsewhere, namely that masterful lies are a superior truth. He undermines the very concept of 'earnestness' by which Victorian society set such high store, and his move is all the more powerful when worked by Jack the Gentleman rather than by Jack the Dandy. The rigid Victorian world, Wilde suggests, must eventually be destroyed by its own agents.

A friend once suggested to Wilde that farce should be like a piece of mosaic. He disagreed: it must go like a pistol shot.[4] Revising his play at George Alexander's request, Wilde tightened it to the speed of a bullet, though retaining, as Katherine Worth remarks, slowness and stateliness in the dialogue.[5] *The Importance of Being Earnest*, cautiously wrapped up in sublime humour and absurdity as it is in its final version, is the most radically subversive of Wilde's plays. If George Alexander had been reluctant to express his dissatisfaction with the play, Wilde would very probably not have rewritten it, and would have let it remain a faltering arrow.

---

4. Ellmann, *Wilde*, p. 423.
5. Katherine Worth, 'The Triumph of the Pleasure Principle', in Bloom (ed.), *Modern Critical Interpretations*. p. 59.

CAMILLE A. PAGLIA

Oscar Wilde and the English Epicene†

Oscar Wilde is the premiere documenter of a sexual persona which I call the Androgyne of Manners, embodied in Lord Henry Wotton of *The Picture of Dorian Gray* and in the four young lovers of *The Importance of Being Earnest*. The Androgyne of Manners inhabits the world of the drawing room and creates that world wherever it goes, through manner and mode of speech. The salon is an abstract circle in which male and female, like mathematical ciphers, are equal and interchangeable; personality becomes a sexually undifferentiated formal mask. Rousseau says severely of the eighteenth-century salon, "Every woman at Paris gathers in her apartment a harem of men more womanish than she." The salon is politics by coterie, a city-state or gated forum run on a barter economy of gender exchange.

Elegance, the ruling principle of the salon, dictates that all speech must be wit, in symmetrical pulses of repartee, a malicious stichomythia. Pope's complaint that Lady Mary Wortley Montagu and the epicene Lord Hervey had "too much wit" for him alludes to the icy cruelty of the beau monde, to which moral discourse is alien because it posits the superiority of the inner life to the outer. Sartre says of Genet, "Elegance: the quality of conduct which transforms the greatest quantity of being into appearing." The salon, like the object-realm venerated by the esthete, is a spectacle of dazzling surfaces—words, faces, and gestures exhibited in a blaze of hard glamour.

Occasionally, Pope was drawn to the idea of spiritual hermaphroditism. But he was deeply hostile to the Androgyne of Manners, whom he satirizes as the Amazonian belles and effeminate beaux of *The Rape of the Lock*, because this psychological type is ahistorical in its worship of the ephemeral. The salon is populated by sophisticates of a classical literacy, but its speed of dialogue inhibits deliberation and reflection, recklessly breaking with the past through fashionable irresponsibility. Pope might have said, had the word been available, that the salon was too chic. The Androgyne of Manners—the male feminine in his careless, lounging passivity, the female masculine in her brilliant, aggressive wit—has the profane sleekness of chic.

In the Decadent nineties, before his career abruptly ended in arrest and imprisonment, Wilde was moving towards an Art Nouveau

† From *Raritan: A Quarterly Review* 4.3 (Winter 1985): 85–109. Used with permission from *Raritan*. Bracketed page numbers refer to this Norton Critical Edition

esthetics. Art Nouveau, then at its height of decorative popularity, is a late phase in the history of style, in many ways analogous to Italian Mannerism. Kenneth Clark says of one of Giambologna's streamlined Mannerist bronzes:

> The goddess of mannerism is the eternal feminine of the fashion plate. A sociologist could no doubt give ready answers why embodiments of elegance should take this somewhat ridiculous shape—feet and hands too fine for honest work, bodies too thin for childbearing, and heads too small to contain a single thought. But elegant proportions may be found in many objects that are exempt from these materialist explanations—in architecture, pottery, or even handwriting. The human body is not the basis of these rhythms but their victim. Where the sense of chic originates, how it is controlled, by what inner pattern we unfailingly recognize it—all these are questions too large and too subtle for a parenthesis. One thing is certain. Chic is not natural. Congreve's Millamant or Baudelaire's dandy warn us how hateful, to serious votaries of chic, is everything that is implied by the word "nature."

Smoothness and elongation, the Mannerist figure is a series of polished ovoids hung on a mannequin's frame. Lord Henry Wotton, with his "long, nervous fingers," is an ectomorph, an undulating ribbon of Mannerist Art Nouveau. The ectomorphic line is a suave vertical, repudiating nature by its resistance to gravity, but the Mannerist figure, overcome by worldly fatigue, sinks back toward earth in languorous torsion. The Androgyne of Manners may be seen in complete effete collapse in Henry Lamb's painting of Lytton Strachey turning his back to a window, his long denatured limbs draped over an armchair like wet noodles. Because of its swift verbal genius, however, the Androgyne of Manners is best represented as sleekness and speed. Count Robert de Montesquiou, the decadent model for Huysmans's Des Esseintes and Proust's Charlus, was once described as a "greyhound in evening dress," a phrase we might readily apply to Lord Henry Wotton.

Sleekness in a male is usually a hermaphroditic motive. Cinema, the cardinal medium of modern sexual representation, evokes this theme in its topos of the well-bred English "gentleman," a word of such special connotations that it cannot be perfectly translated into any other language. From the thirties through the fifties, movies used actors of this type to illustrate a singular male beauty, witty and polished, uniting sensitivity of response to intense heterosexual glamour: Leslie Howard, Rex Harrison, Cary Grant, David Niven, Michael Wilding, Fred Astaire. The idiomatic representational qualities here are smoothness and elongation, smooth both in manner

and appearance, long in ectomorphic height and cranial contour. I think, for instance, of the astounding narrowness of Cary Grant's shiny black evening pumps in *Indiscreet*. The smoothness and elongation of figure are best shown off by a gleaming tuxedo, which signifies a renunciation of masculine hirsutism. The cinematic "gentleman" is always prematurely balding, with swept-back hair at the temples. His receding hairline is sexually expressive, suggesting hermaphroditic gentility, a grace of intellect and emotion. His sleek head is a promise of candor and courtesy, of eroticism without ambivalence or suffering. Smoothness always has an exclusively social meaning: it is nature subdued by the civil made second nature.

In *The Importance of Being Earnest*, the English gentleman, in whom the crudely masculine has been moderated by courtesy, may be seen turning into the Androgyne of Manners, in whom smoothness has become the cold glossiness of a bronze surface, like the "armored look" (*Panzerhaft*) of Bronzino's Mannerist portraits. Meeting and finally mating with their counterparts, the Art Nouveau androgynes of the play speak Wilde's characteristic language, the epicene witticism, analogous to their formal personae in its hardness, smoothness, and elongation. The Wildean epigram, like a Giambologna bronze, is immediately identifiable by a slim spareness, an imperious separateness, and a perverse elegance. Speech in Wilde is made as hard and glittering as possible; it follows the Wildean personality into the visual realm. Normally, it is pictorialism that gives literature a visual character. But there are few metaphors in Wilde and no complex syntactical units. Vocabulary and sentence structure are amazingly simple, arising from the vernacular of the accomplished raconteur. Yet Wilde's bon mots are so condensed that they become *things*, artifacts. Without metaphor, the language leaps into concreteness.

Language in Wilde aspires to an Apollonian hierarchism. His epigrams turn language from the Dionysian Many into the Apollonian One, for as an aphoristic phrase form and conversation stopper, the epigram thwarts real dialogue, cutting itself off from a past and a future in its immediate social context and glorying in its aristocratic solitude. It is the language of the Apollonian lawgiver arbitrarily assigning form, proportion, and measure. A character in Wilde's *An Ideal Husband* declares, "Women are never disarmed by compliments. Men always are. That is the difference between the sexes." The iron rod of classification is thrust before us—even if it does not fall where expected. In form and in content, the Wildean epigram is a triumph of rhetorical self-containment. No one in English, or probably any other modern language, has produced a series of utterances more mysteriously delimited. The epigram, as practiced in the Renaissance, was a poem of sharply ironic or sententious con-

cluding verses. But the *epigramma* of antiquity was literally an inscription, as on a tombstone. Wilde may therefore be said to have restored the epigram to its original representational character, for his language has a hieroglyphic exactitude and cold rhetorical stoniness, separating itself from its background by the Apollonian incised edge.

In *The Importance of Being Earnest* the courtship of youth and maiden, at the traditional heart of comedy, loses its emotional color in the Wildean transformation of content into form, of soul into surface. Jack Worthing and Algernon Moncrieff, idle gentlemen-about-town, and Gwendolen Fairfax and Cecily Cardew, the well-bred objects of their affections, are all Androgynes of Manners. They have no sex because they have no real sexual feelings. The interactions of the play are governed by the formalities of social life, which emerge with dancelike ritualism. The key phrase of the English fin de siècle was Lionel Johnson's axiom, "Life must be a ritual." In *The Picture of Dorian Gray* Wilde says: "The canons of good society are, or should be, the same as the canons of art. Form is absolutely essential to it. It should have the dignity of a ceremony, as well as its unreality." In *The Importance of Being Earnest* the ceremony of social form is stronger than gender, shaping the personae to its public purpose and turning the internal world into the external.

The play's supreme enforcer of form is Lady Bracknell, who remarks with satisfaction, "We live, I regret to say, in an age of surfaces." In a stage direction to another play, Wilde says of a lord's butler: "The distinction of Phipps is his impassivity. . . . He is a mask with a manner. Of his intellectual or emotional life, history knows nothing. He represents the dominance of form." An optimal performance of *The Importance of Being Earnest* would be a romance of surfaces, male and female alike wearing masks of superb impassivity. The Anthony Asquith film, made in 1952, though it shortens and questionably edits the text, comes close to achieving this. Joan Greenwood's entranced and nearly somnambulistic performance as Gwendolen—slow, stately, and ceremonious—is the brilliant realization of the Wildean esthetic. But the effort to make Dorothy Tutin's Cecily sympathetic at Gwendolen's expense is sentimentally intrusive, a misreading of the play disordering the symmetry between the two young ladies, twin androgynes who fight each other to a standoff.

Productions of *The Importance of Being Earnest* are often weakened by flights of Forest of Arden lyricism which turn what is sexually ambiguous in Wilde into the conventionally heterosexual. The hieratic purity of the play could best be appreciated if all the women's roles were taken by female impersonators. Language, per-

sonality, and behavior should be so hard that the play becomes a spectacle of visionary coldness. The faces should be like glass, without gender or humanity. *The Importance of Being Earnest* takes place in Spenser's Apollonian "world of glas," a realm of glittering, sharp-edged objects. Chapman says of the goddess Ceremony, "all her bodie was / Cleere and transparent as the purest glasse." Gwendolen and Cecily are the goddess Ceremony conversing with herself, her body transparent because she is without an inner life. That Wilde may well have thought of his characters in such terms is suggested in *The Picture of Dorian Gray*, where Lord Henry Wotton longs for "a mask of glass" to shield one from the "sulphurous fumes" of life.

Gwendolen is the first of the women to enact a drama of form. Soliciting Jack to propose to her, she announces in advance that she will accept him but still insists that her bewildered suitor perform the traditional ritual, on his knees. Gwendolen's thoughts never stray from the world of appearances. At the climax of their romantic interlude, she says to Jack, "I hope you will always look at me just like that, especially when there are other people present" [16]. This voyeuristic series of observers is a psychosexual topos of Decadent Late Romanticism, first occurring in 1835 in Gautier's *Mademoiselle de Maupin*. Gwendolen imagines Jack looking at her while she looks at others looking at *them*. As a worshipper of form, Gwendolen craves not emotion but display, the theater of social life.

Gwendolen's self-observing detachment is exhibited by Cecily in precisely the same situation. When Algernon ardently declares his love for her, Cecily replies, "If you will allow me, I will copy your remarks into my diary" [35]. Emotion is immediately dispatched into a self-reflexive Mannerist torsion. Going to her writing table, Cecily exhorts her suitor to continue his protestations: "I delight in taking down from dictation" [35]. Intimacy is swelled into oratory, and poor Algernon is like Alice grown suddenly too big for the White Rabbit's house. Despite their impending marriage, Cecily declares it quite out of the question for Algernon to see her diary. Nevertheless, it is "meant for publication": "When it appears in volume form I hope you will order a copy" [35]. The Sibylline archivist, with professional impartiality, grants no special privileges to her sources of data.

Never for a moment in the play are Gwendolen and Cecily persuasively "female." They are creatures of indeterminate sex who take up the mask of femininity to play a new and provocative role. The dandified Algernon and Jack are simply supporting actors whom the women boldly stage manage. Gwendolen and Cecily are adepts of a dramaturgical alchemy: they are Cerberuses on constant guard to defend the play against encroachment by the inter-

nal, which they magically transform into the external. *The Importance of Being Earnest* is one long process of crystallization of the immaterial into the material, of emotion into self-conscious personae. In Shakespeare's volatile Rosalind and Cleopatra, automanipulation of personae arises from a Renaissance abundance of emotion, which flows into a multiplicity of psychodramatic forms. But Wilde's Gwendolen and Cecily inhabit a far more stringently demarcated world, the salon of the Androgyne of Manners, and their personae are radically despiritualized, efflorescences not of psyche but of couture.

Lady Bracknell, too, ruthlessly subordinates persons to form. If Algernon does not come to dinner, "It would put my table completely out" [13], and Lord Bracknell will be exiled upstairs. In one of Wilde's most wonderful lines, Lady Bracknell rebukes Jack for being an orphan: "To lose one parent, Mr. Worthing, may be regarded as a misfortune; to lose both looks like carelessness" [18]. Matters of form are uppermost, in death as in life. The emotional intensities of Victorian bereavement are cancelled. Nothing is of interest but the public impression. Once again there is the Late Romantic stress upon visual cognition: "may be *regarded* as a misfortune;" "*looks* like carelessness." Every event occurs with naked visibility on a vast, flat expanse; life is a play scrutinized by a ring of appraising eyes. This illustrates one of Wilde's central principles, as cited by Dorian Gray: "To become the spectator of one's own life is to escape the suffering of life." Late Romantic spectatorship is an escape from suffering because all affect is transferred from the emotional and tangible into the visual: no wounds can pierce the glassy body of the Wildean androgyne. The self is without a biological or historical identity. Self-originating, it has no filial indebtedness. A parent is merely a detail of social heraldry. To lose both parents, therefore, is not tragedy but negligence, like tipping the tea service into the trashbin.

The liturgy of the religion of form of which Lady Bracknell is a communicant, and in which she has instructed her daughter Gwendolen, is determined by fashion, whose bible is any one of "the more expensive monthly magazines." Lady Bracknell declares, "Style largely depends on the way the chin is worn. They are worn very high, just at present" [51]. The chin is imperiously "worn" like an article of clothing because the human figure is merely decorative, like the mummy's foot which serves as a paperweight in a Gautier tale. There is a latent surrealism here, for once the chin, like the eyebrow of Gautier's hieratic Cleopatra, has been detached from the body by Decadent partition, there is no reason why it cannot be worn elsewhere—on the shoulder, perhaps, or hip. Gwendolen, requesting Cecily's permission to examine her through a

lorgnette (Cecily graciously makes the expected Late Romantic reply, "I am very fond of being looked at"), boasts that her mother
"has brought me up to be extremely short-sighted." The body is
sculpted at the whim of fashion, responding to its commands with
plastic ductility.

At the tea table, Gwendolen declines Cecily's offer of sugar: "No,
thank you. Sugar is not fashionable any more" [42]. To the choice
of cake or bread and butter, she replies ("in a bored manner"),
"Bread and butter, please. Cake is rarely seen at the best houses
nowadays" [42]. For Gwendolen, tastiness is irrelevant, since the
body has no needs in the world of form. Sugar and cake are items
of decor, marks of caste by which one group separates itself from a
lower group. Personal preference is renounced for hierarchical conformity. And note that cake is "rarely *seen*," not eaten—its status is
visual and not gustatory. Gwendolen is an Androgyne of Manners
rapidly approaching the android. She is so completely the product
of fashion that she is a machine, seeing myopically by maternal
edict, eating, drinking, hearing, thinking, and speaking by prepro-
grammed desire. Mallarmé says, "Fashion is the goddess of appearances." Fashion is the divinity of this world of form, which Lady
Bracknell and Gwendolen uphold with apostolic fervor.

The literary term "high comedy" is often rather loosely applied to
any comedy of manners that does not descend to broad verbal or
physical humor. I would argue that the most advanced high comedy
is a ceremoniously mannered "presentation of self," the style of *The
Importance of Being Earnest*, as most splendidly exemplified by
Gwendolen. Indeed, in Gwendolen Fairfax, Wilde has reached the
generic limit of high comedy. Gwendolen's self-hierarchization is so
extreme that other characters are virtually dispensable, for they impinge on her only feebly and peripherally. But without at least two
characters, drama as a genre cannot exist. When Gwendolen
speaks it is not to others as much as to herself or to some abstract
choir of celestial observers. Like the picture of Dorian Gray, which
is not content to remain in its assigned place and rejects its ent-
elechy, she seems ready to abandon drama for some extrageneric
destination. Here is Wilde's greatest departure from the Restoration
dramatists, for he detaches the witticism from repartee, that is,
from social relationship. The Wildean witticism is a Romantic phenomenon in its proud isolationism. In this mode of high comedy
there is an elaborately formal or ritualistic display of the persona,
indeed a brandishing of it, like an aegis. The practitioner is in a
double relation to the self, acting and also observing. But more importantly, there is a distinct trace of Late Romantic "connoisseur-
ship": the self is the subject of Decadent studiousness and
scholarship.

Let us examine several of Gwendolen's incomparable utterances, with their unyielding uniformity of tone. Late in the play she says, "I never change, except in my affections" [57]. This could serve as a darkly ironic caption to Walter Pater's Decadent "Mona Lisa." But what Gwendolen means is that, just as one might expect, she is rigidly punctilious in formal and external matters, while emotional events are beneath notice, flotsam and jetsam aimlessly adrift. Observe how she "brandishes" her personality, flaunting her faults with triumphant self-love. Her speech always has a hard, even, relentless, and yet rhetorically circumscribed character, as in her first words in the play:

ALGERNON   Dear me, you are smart!
GWENDOLEN   I am always smart! Am I not, Mr. Worthing?
JACK   You're quite perfect, Miss Fairfax.
GWENDOLEN   Oh! I hope I am not that. It would leave no room for developments, and I intend to develop in many directions [12].

If we were to speak of a psychodramatic "music," then in this last clause we are hearing the monody of a Gautierian contralto, the husky self-pleasuring of hermaphrodite autonomy. Identical intonations are present in two other of Gwendolen's remarks. At one point she gratuitously informs her suitor, "In fact, I am never wrong" [14]. And in the last act, as Jack struggles to regain her alienated affections, she says to him, "I have the gravest doubts upon the subject. But I intend to crush them" [47]. Such lines must be properly read—with slow, resonant measure—in order to appreciate their intractable severity. "I intend to develop in many directions": there is an extraordinarily distinctive sound to this in British diction, flat, formal, and sonorous, forbidding with self-command. Note the way personality is *distributed* throughout the sentence, filling the narrow channel of its syntax with a dense silvery fluid, acrid and opaque. Gwendolen's willful, elegantly linear sentences fit her like a glove. Smooth with Mannerist spareness, they carry not an extra ounce of rhetorical avoirdupois. There is no Paterian mistiness in Gwendolen. She overtly relishes her personality, caressing its hard edges, which are echoed in the brazen contours of her sentences. In this doyenne of Art Nouveau worldliness, Wilde has created a definitively modern selfhood, exposed, limited, and unsentimental, cold as urban geometry.

Above all his characters, it is Gwendolen whom Wilde has charged with creating an Apollonian dramatic language. Her speech, like Wilde's epicene witticisms, has a metallic self-enclosed terseness. She spends her words with haughty frugality for the same reason that Spenser's Belphoebe dashes off in the middle of

sentences: the Apollonian is a mode of self-sequestration. The bon mot in general is jealous of its means, prizing brevity above all. It is a kind of sacramental display, permitting the self to be seen only in epiphanic flashes, like the winking of a camera shutter. These spasms of delimitation are attempts to defy the temporal character of speech or narrative, turning sequences of words into discrete *objets*. Ideas are never developed in the Apollonian style because of its antipathy to internality. Instead, as we find in Gwendolen and in the classic maliciously witty Androgyne of Manners of the salon, language is used confrontationally, as a distancing weapon, like a flaming sword. Gwendolen's self-exhibiting utterances follow the principle of *frontality* in painting and sculpture, which, as Arnold Hauser observes, is intrinsic to "all courtly and courteous art." Abjuring the modesty of the unmarried maiden, the potent Gwendolen turns herself full-face to her suitor, bathing him with a rain of hierarchical emissions.

Admiration of *The Importance of Being Earnest* is widespread, but discussion of the play is scarce and slight. Critics seem to have accepted Wilde's own description of it—"exquisitely trivial, a delicate bubble of fancy." Scholarship has never distinguished itself in studying this kind of high comedy, with its elusive "sophistication." Frye-style myth criticism, for example, can do little with *The Importance of Being Earnest*. From the point of view of Decadent Late Romanticism, however, there is scarcely a line in the play which fails to yield rich implications.

Here are two examples. In the midst of her dispute with Cecily, Gwendolen declares, "I never travel without my diary. One should always have something sensational to read in the train" [40]. The latter sentence comes as a surprise, for ordinarily one travels with a diary not to read but to write in it. Gwendolen, however, as an Apollonian androgyne, does not keep a journal for self-examination—inwardness always being distasteful—but for self-display. To read one's diary as if it were a novel is to regard one's life as spectacle, which Wilde of course advocates. Gwendolen contemplates her life with appreciative detachment, acting both as objet d'art and Late Romantic connoisseur. Reading is normally a medium of expansion of personal experience; one reads to learn what one does not know. Here, however, reading is an act of Romantic solipsism: Gwendolen reads not to enlarge but to condense herself. Far from Emily Dickinson's mobile frigate, a book has become a mirror in which one sees only one's own face. The diary is a self-portrait. Hence Gwendolen reading her diary in a train compartment is exactly like Dorian Gray standing before his picture in the locked room. Both are performing their devotions to the hierarchized self.

The life which this diary records is, according to Gwendolen,

"sensational," a source of public scandal and eroticized fascination. But to find one's own life sensational is to be aroused by oneself. The eyes, as always in Late Romanticism, are sexual agents: Gwendolen reading her diary is lost in autoerotic skeptophila, a titillation of the eye. If books can corrupt, and we know from *The Picture of Dorian Gray* that they can, then it is possible to be corrupted by one's own diary. To be corrupted by oneself is a perfect pattern of sexual solipsism, like Goethe's twisting Venetian acrobat Bettina, self-delectating and self-devirginizing. Gwendolen is an uroboros of amorous self-study, an Art Nouveau serpent devouring herself. Train reading is casual reading, a way to pass time with minimal effort. The life recorded and contemplated in the diary is therefore reduced in significance, trivialized: it is simply a series of sensational incidents without moral meaning.

Reading one's diary like a novel implies that one has forgotten what is in it. It demonstrates a lack of moral memory characteristic of the Decadent in general. In Wilde's *A Woman of No Importance*, Lord Illingworth declares, "No woman should have a memory. Memory in a woman is the beginning of dowdiness." The internal erodes the perfection of surfaces. In *An Ideal Husband*, Sir Robert Chiltern says of an antagonist, "She looks like a woman with a past," to which Lord Goring replies, "Most pretty women do." But as we see from Gwendolen's relations with her diary, the person with a past has no past. The self is a tabula rasa open only to sensationalized Paterian "impressions." There is no moral incrementation; experience corrupts, but it does not instruct. In *The Picture of Dorian Gray* Lord Henry Wotton reflects, "Experience was of no ethical value. It was merely the name men gave to their mistakes." Reading one's diary is a diversion of the "late" phase of culture. Memory is inhibited precisely because one has done *too much*, like Pater's "Mona Lisa," fatigued by history. Her information retrieval system blocked by sensory overload, the robotlike Gwendolen is a stranger to herself, a stranger-lover.

Gwendolen never travels without her diary because it is her familiar, the inseparable escort which enables her to keep herself in a state of externalization. This is one of many traits she shares with Cecily, who uses her diary to similar effect, as we saw in the proposal scene, where Cecily instantly petrifies Algernon's sentiments midair, as if engraving them upon stone tablets. Gwendolen's diary, again like the picture of Dorian Gray, is a repository of the soul which she is able to carry about with her like a hatbox, preserving her soulless Apollonian purity. The diary is also a chronicle, the testament of her cult of the self. For both the High and Late Romantic, a diary is a personal cosmogony, a book of first and last things.

Hence it can be seen that Wilde's witticisms contain a wealth

of unsuspected meaning. Even his most apparently nonsensical *boutades* are Late Romantic gestures. For example, Lady Bracknell attempts to terminate the stormy scene at the Manor House by declaring to Gwendolen, "Come, dear, we have already missed five, if not six, trains. To miss any more might expose us to comment on the platform." These bizarre lines have that air of skewed lunatic certainty we know from Lewis Carroll, who I believe strongly influenced Wilde. What is Lady Bracknell saying? Missing a train, even "five, if not six" (a studied Decadent enumeration) normally has only private and not public consequences. In the Looking-Glass world of form, however, failure to adhere to plan is an affront to natural law, bringing murmurs of complaint from passersby. But how do others learn of one's deviation from a train schedule? Since everything is visible in this landscape of externals, and since the mental life of these androgynes, like their bodies, has a glassy transparency, their intention may be said to precede them, like a town crier, alerting the populace to their tardiness. In its visionary materialism, *The Importance of Being Earnest* reverts to the Homeric world of allegorized psychic phenomena, in which the enraged Achilles feels Athena tugging at his hair. If we characterized Lady Bracknell's remark in naturalistic terms, we would have to speak of a megalomaniacal paranoia: she imagines a general consciousness of their every move; everyone knows what they are doing and thinking. But this is a development of aristocratic worldliness. Fashionable life, as Proust attests, does indeed take place before the unblinking eyes of *le tout Paris*.

"To miss any more might expose us to comment on the platform" [53]: Lady Bracknell exists in a force field of visual sightlines. Like Gautier's chaste Queen Nyssia, tainted by the gaze of another, Lady Bracknell fears being "exposed" to infection, in this case an infection of words. Barthes says of the sadomasochistic relations in Sade's novels, "The master is he who speaks . . . ; the object is he who is silent." Lady Bracknell will lose caste if she is subject to public "comment." Her hierarchical dominance will drain from her, like divine ichor. The scene of shame which she envisions on the railway platform is one of ritual exposure, like Hawthorne's Hester Prynne braving public scorn on the town scaffold. In Wilde's world, of course, crime is not sin but bad form.

The Importance of Being Earnest was the last thing Wilde wrote before his fall. Its opening night coincided with the initiation of the Marquess of Queensberry's most virulent campaign against him, and the play continued to be performed, to great acclaim, during his two trials. Now it is a strange fact that Wilde's passage to prison was a terrible fulfillment of this remark by Lady Bracknell. In *De Profundis*, written in Reading Gaol, Wilde recalls:

On November 13th, 1895, I was brought down here from London. From two o'clock till half-past two on that day I had to stand on the centre platform of Clapham Junction in convict dress, and handcuffed, for the world to look at. . . . When people saw me they laughed. Each train as it came up swelled the audience. Nothing could exceed their amusement. That was, of course, before they knew who I was. As soon as they had been informed they laughed still more. For half an hour I stood there in the grey November rain surrounded by a jeering mob.

For a year after that was done to me I wept every day at the same hour and for the same space of time.

Lady Bracknell's railway platform was to be the site of Wilde's greatest humiliation. Who can doubt that the imagination can shape reality to its will? So close are these two scenes of ritual exposure that one wonders whether Wilde's memory of Clapham Junction was not a hallucination, a variation on a fictive theme in the solitude and squalor of prison. But granting its truth, it is another example of Wilde's shamanistic power to bring his own imaginative projections into being. Publication of *The Picture of Dorian Gray* produced Lord Alfred Douglas, the beautiful boy as destroyer, who brought Wilde to his ruin. Clapham Junction came as the agonizing materialization of Wilde's principle of life as "spectacle." The entire Late Romantic tradition of concentrated visual experience reaches a disastrous climax on that railway platform, and it ends there, with Wilde the dizzy center of the visible world, like the Ancient Mariner the focus of cosmic wrath, here taking the unbearable form of laughter. The comedian, losing control of his genre, is devoured by the audience.

The epicene witticism has received little attention partly because it is sexually heterodox and partly because it does not fit into received critical categories. Thus Wilde's plays are suitable for explication while his conversation is not. But the Androgyne of Manners, of which Wilde was his own best example, makes an art of the spoken word. With his radical formalism, Wilde created an original language which I will call the *monologue extérieur*.

The salon dialogue of the Androgyne of Manners is a duel of "cutting" remarks. Language is used aggressively as an instrument of masculine warfare designed to slash, stab, pierce, and penetrate. Dorian Gray says to Lord Henry Wotton, "You cut life to pieces with your epigrams." It is no coincidence that terms describing a witty exchange—thrust, parry, riposte, repartee—are drawn from swordplay. The close interrelations of language and martial contention in Western culture are demonstrated by fencing parlance which speaks of a "conversation" or "phrase" of action. In other

words, a fencing match is imagined as a sequence of competitive speech. It is plain how a woman of the salon who commands this sharp, challenging rhetoric is masculinized into an Androgyne of Manners. The male Androgyne of Manners achieves his hermaphroditism by combining aggressive language with a feminine manner, graceful and languid, archly flirtatious and provocative. The persona which Wilde projects in his epicene witticisms is a conflation of masculine intimidation and attack with feminine seduction and allure.

To "cut" someone is to wound him, but it is also to sever social connections with him. This duality is the subject of a pun by Lewis Carroll, when Alice is introduced to the leg of mutton:

> "May I give you a slice?" she said, taking up the knife and fork, and looking from one Queen to the other.
> "Certainly not," the Red Queen said, very decidedly: "it isn't etiquette to cut any one you've been introduced to. Remove the joint!"

Wilde's witticisms operate by a systematic "cutting," separating the self from communality and withdrawing it into an aristocratic sequestration. In *The Importance of Being Earnest* Wilde makes language into a mode of hierarchical placement. It is a series of psychodramatic gestures, each remark asserting a caste location with regard to some other person or class of person. The speakers are constantly positioning themselves at fixed distances from others. This even occurs, as we have seen, in the marriage proposals, where the heroines of the play befuddle the heroes by ceremonial demarcations, exclamatory bulletins of incipient intimacy, which they narrate like play-by-play sportscasters. To paraphrase: "We will shortly be intimate"; "We are now being intimate"; "Pray continue to be intimate." The Wildean heroine is a hierarchical commentator, plotting the relations of personae upon a mental map.

The use of language as signs of placement is often overt, as in the tea table dispute between the young ladies.

CECILY   When I see a spade I call it a spade.
GWENDOLEN   (*Satirically.*) I am glad to say that I have never seen a spade. It is obvious that our social spheres have been widely different [41].

In this literalization of metaphor, a characteristic Wildean materialization, a spade becomes, like sugar or cake, a calibrator of caste. Gwendolen glories in her self-expanded hierarchical distance from Cecily. Such language appears everywhere in *The Importance of Being Earnest*. For example, the play opens with Algernon playing the piano: "I don't play accurately—anyone can play accurately—but I

play with wonderful expression" [5]. "Anyone can play accurately": this self-absolving and demonstrably untrue premise, like a ladder leaned against a wall, stretches a great chain of being before our eyes, with Algernon exulting over the mass of the many from a top-most rung of esthetical "sensibility." The technique is used throughout Wilde. His polemical spokesman in *The Critic as Artist* says, "When people agree with me I always feel that I must be wrong." And a character in *An Ideal Husband* says, "Only dull people are brilliant at breakfast." Rhetorical energy is entirely directed toward social differentiation and segregation. Wilde was committed to an Apollonian enterprise—to create hierarchy through wit, en-nobling himself, like the self-naming Balzac, through a magisterial personal construction.

Hence the epicene witticism is a language of hierarchical command in sexually aberrant or rather sexually denatured form. Wilde's "pointed" hierarchical style ultimately descends from the eighteenth century and in particular from Pope, whose poetry Wilde vociferously disliked. Brigid Brophy asserts: "Wilde's vehicle, the epigram, is in fact an adaptation of the logical axiom and the scientific definition. The Irish—perhaps originally theological—habit of paradox . . . is (like the paradoxical mysteries of Christian theology itself) nothing else than an exposure of the ambivalence concealed in our morality." But more precisely, Wilde's epigrams, which so impede the quickness of Restoration repartee, have acquired their substantiveness from eighteenth-century generaliza-tion. It is his power of generalization which gives Wilde's writing its permanent distinction. A modern play in the Wildean manner, Noel Coward's *Private Lives*, has only one truly Wildean line: "Certain women should be struck regularly, like gongs." And even this gener-alizing axiom is a vulgarization of Wilde, in whom contemplative-ness is never distorted by action.

It was Pope who first made poetic beauty out of philosophy, de-vising a discursive style of elegant containment and high finish. Pope's rhetorical and social assumptions were transmitted to Wilde, apparently against his will, by the conservative Jane Austen, in whom we first detect Wilde's distinctive voice, tart, bantering, and lucid. Consider, for example, the great opening sentence of *Emma*:

> Emma Woodhouse, handsome, clever, and rich, with a com-fortable home and happy disposition, seemed to unite some of the best blessings of existence; and had lived nearly twenty-one years in the world with very little to distress or vex her.

There is a delicate play of modern irony around the psychological edges of this sentence which is almost impossible to arrest and de-fine. It is a meteorological disturbance or atmospheric rippling, an

undulating vocal convection. Philosophically, Jane Austen's novels, although contemporaneous with High Romanticism, affirm the eighteenth-century world view, with its neoclassic endorsement of the sexually normative. Only in *Emma* can we find anything sexually ambivalent—in Emma's infatuation with Harriet—and even there it is slight and discreet.

Wilde diverts Jane Austen's comedy into the epicene first through his own character as a Decadent Late Romantic. Eighteenth-century wit is aligned with nature, from which Wilde makes a Late Romantic swerve. But this antinaturism enables Wilde to eliminate the sexual specificities of Restoration comedy. Human lusts no longer exist in *The Importance of Being Earnest*. Even Algernon's perpetual hunger is an angelic appetite, for the characters of the play feed on things insubstantial as manna: bread and butter, cucumber sandwiches, muffins, crumpets, and tea cake. They are like the Bread-and-butter-fly of *Through the Looking-Glass*, whose head is a lump of sugar and who lives on weak tea with cream. Wilde uses Jane Austen to *clarify* high comedy, stripping away the broad and farcical elements which had been present in it since Shakespeare. There are no longer any low-comic or crudely dialectal interludes. Even the secondary characters of *The Importance of Being Earnest* are erudite verbalists. (MISS PRISM: "I spoke horticulturally. My metaphor was drawn from fruits" [29].) Wilde has pruned and simplified high comedy by eighteenth-century standards of taste, decorum, and correctness.

But there is a second influence in Wilde's epicene transformation of Jane Austen. He is aided in this project by the one wit who stands between himself and her—Lewis Carroll. It is Carroll who detaches English comedy from the ethical (which it displays even in the bawdy Restoration plays, with their virtuous finales) and prepares it for its definitive amoralization at the hands of Wilde. After Wilde, this genre of glittering high comedy is confined to the epicene and can be practiced only by sex-crossing imaginations— Ronald Firbank, Noel Coward, Cole Porter. The sexual ambiguity in Lewis Carroll is not textually overt; that development was to be implemented by Wilde. But it is perfectly evident in his life. His friends and biographers speak of his long hair and "curiously womanish face," his fascination with little girls, his detestation of boys, which was "an aversion, almost amounting to terror." Carroll's self-identification was thoroughly feminine.

The dramatic force of the *Alice* books rests upon the stability of the Victorian social structure which invisibly supports them. Alice is an imperialist of custom. Thrust into an irrational dream world, she remains serene and self-assured, a model of well-bred composure. In her firm sense of the limits of appropriate behavior, she is twin to

that menagerie of potentates, human and animal, who chide her for transgressions of mysterious local codes of conduct. There is even a surprising cultural kinship between Alice and her chief critic, the fierce Red Queen, whom Carroll elsewhere describes as "formal and strict, . . . the concentrated essence of all governesses." But the Red Queen is a governess only insofar as the governess is the first and most immediate representative of the hierarchical in the lives of English children, ruling as a regent in the name of society.

Carroll did not, I contend, hold the Romantic or modern view that social laws are artificial and false. On the contrary, he took an Apollonian pleasure in them, admiring and cherishing them as he did the equations and theorems he manipulated as an academic mathematician. One of the first pieces Carroll published as a young man at Oxford was a list of nonsensical principles, "Hints for Etiquette; or, Dining Out Made Easy."

I

In proceeding to the dining-room, the gentleman gives one arm to the lady he escorts—it is unusual to offer both.

III

To use a fork with your soup, intimating at the same time to your hostess that you are reserving the spoon for the beef-steaks, is a practice wholly exploded.

VI

The method of helping roast turkey with two carving-forks is practicable, but deficient in grace.

VII

We do not recommend the practice of eating cheese with a knife and fork in one hand, and a spoon and wine-glass in the other; there is a kind of awkwardness in the action which no amount of practice can entirely dispel.

VIII

As a general rule, do not kick the shins of the opposite gentleman under the table, if personally unacquainted with him; your pleasantry is liable to be misunderstood—a circumstance at all times unpleasant.

It would be a typically modern error to assume that this is an essay in "debunking," that Carroll is reducing manners to the absurd in order to demonstrate the fictiveness of social custom. But everything we know about Carroll's private and public deportment shows him to be an inflexible advocate of order. A contemporary speaks of the "rigid rule of his own life," his fixed daily routine. Another says

that he was "austere, shy, precise, . . . watchfully tenacious of his dignity, stiffly conservative in political, theological, social theory, his life mapped out in squares like Alice's landscape."

The evidence suggests that the rules and manners of "Hints for Etiquette" and the *Alice* books draw much of their force from Carroll's belief in their tradition-consecrated and even a priori character. Nearly all the comedy of Carroll's work arises from a natively English love of formality and ceremony. There is a tonality of wit in Carroll which has no parallel in premodern literature but which appears throughout Virginia Woolf, particularly in her masterpiece, *To the Lighthouse*. Note the similarities of voice, for example, between Carroll's "Hints for Etiquette" and this passage from a letter to Victoria Sackville-West in which Woolf reviews the comments roused by her newly bobbed hair:

1. Virginia is completely spoilt by her shingle.
2. Virginia is completely made by her shingle.
3. Virginia's shingle is quite unnoticeable.
    These are the three schools of thought on this important subject. I have bought a coil of hair, which I attach by a hook. It falls into the soup, and is fished out on a fork.

This sophisticated comic style, with its subtlety of ironic inflection, seems to be produced in England by some unexplored interaction between language and persona.

The deep structure of such passages is as follows. An excessive or unforeseen event occurs within the strict confines of convention. The dining table is the favored locus of display, as the arena of daily domestic ritual. However, the incident elicits no reaction, or only a muted one. All personae remain in a state of dignified flat affect, restoring and preserving the rule of normality. The highest English comedy is predicated on a Wildean impassivity of countenance. One can see in the Woolf letter, in fact, how three diverse reactions are allowed to cancel each other out, cleverly effecting a return to stasis. The energy deflected from reaction flows into the social structure of the occasion, which is felt with architectural solidity, vibrating with public power.

Lewis Carroll covertly introduced an epicene element into English humor which, consolidated by Wilde, has continued in force to the present. It took immediate cultural root because of certain abiding features of upper-class English personality, foremost of which is the hermaphroditic type of the "gentleman," upon which I have already remarked. English society has also been noted for a toleration of eccentricity, a proliferation of sadomasochistic erotica, and a high incidence of male homosexuality stimulated by the monasticism of public-school and university life.

Lewis Carroll, in his two strange and inexhaustible books, synthesized several of the most potent elements in English high culture: wit, hierarchy, and spiritual hermaphroditism. After Carroll, English comedy, in literature and in educated dialogue, often tends towards the absurd and incongruous, in which there is always a shadow of the epicene. What Carroll did was first to invent a nonchthonian animism, giving Romantic nature a social voice. The *Alice* books are a din of creatures, speaking as uncompromising social hierarchs. There is no "tenderness" in Carroll's characters, save in the bumbling and ineffectual, like the feeble White Knight. All are sharp, forceful personalities, nodes of aggressive selfhood. The *Alice* books, like *The Importance of Being Earnest*, are glutted with rules of behavior, which pop up at the most improbable moments. Formality is the preeminent principle in Carroll, governing not only the narrative design (a pack of cards structures the first book and a chessboard the second), but also the psychodramatic style of the characters, a punctilious ritualism not unlike Carroll's own. The Red Queen's draconian championship of manners is merely the most blatant of the ritual formulas of Carroll's animistic world, and manners are the language of the hierarchical. Veblen remarks: "Manners . . . are symbolical and conventionalised survivals representing former acts of dominance or of personal service or of personal contact. In large part they are an expression of status,—a symbolic pantomime of mastery on the one hand and of subservience on the other."

It is the ancient history of manners as articulations of power which energizes the climactic confrontation between Gwendolen and Cecily, the center not only of *The Importance of Being Earnest* but probably of Wilde's entire oeuvre. In a tableau of brilliant formal beauty, a tea table is made the scene of a ferocious wargame, with manners the medium of ritual advance and retreat. Gwendolen and Cecily manipulate their personae with chill virtuosity. Nowhere else in the play is it more evident that the gender of the Androgyne of Manners is purely artificial, that "femininity" in the salon is simply a principle of decorum shared equally by male and female. The escalating emotion of the conversation between Gwendolen and Cecily is entirely absorbed by the ceremonial framework and by the formality of their social masks.

CECILY (*Rather shy and confidingly.*) Dearest Gwendolen, there is no reason why I should make a secret of it to you. Our little county newspaper is sure to chronicle the fact next week. Mr. Ernest Worthing and I are engaged to be married.
GWENDOLEN (*Quite politely, rising.*) My darling Cecily, I think there must be some slight error. Mr. Ernest Worthing is en-

gaged to me. The announcement will appear in the *Morning Post* on Saturday at the latest.

CECILY   (*Very politely, rising.*) I am afraid you must be under some misconception. Ernest proposed to me exactly ten minutes ago. (*Shows diary.*)

GWENDOLEN   (*Examines diary through her lorgnette carefully.*) It is very curious, for he asked me to be his wife yesterday afternoon at 5:30. If you would care to verify the incident, pray do so. (*Produces diary of her own.*) [40]

Each gesture, each rhetorical movement is answered by a symmetrical countermovement of balletic grandeur. Language becomes increasingly elaborate, in baroque convolutions of ironic restraint: "It would distress me more than I can tell you, dear Gwendolen, if it caused you any mental or physical anguish, but I feel bound to point out that since Ernest proposed to you he clearly has changed his mind" [40]. There is no hysteria, or even excitement. The immovable wills of the two young women press so fiercely against the social limits of the moment that the hierarchical structure of manners leaps into visibility, another of Wilde's characteristic materializations. Stylization and ritualism approach the Oriental. The scene is a Japanese tea ceremony in which gracious self-removal has yielded to barely concealed Achillean strife.

It was Lewis Carroll who made this greatest of Wildean episodes possible. In Carroll, manners and social laws are disconnected from humane or "civilizing" values. They have a mathematical beauty but no moral meaning: they are absurd. But this absurdity is predicated not on some democratic notion of their relativism but on their arbitrary, divine incomprehensibility. In the *Alice* books, manners are meaningless, but they still retain their hierarchical force; they are Veblen's "pantomime" of mastery and subservience. Wilde, influenced by Carroll, appropriates his view of the mechanisms of social power and sets it into a much larger system of aristocratic presuppositions derived partly from his self-identification as a Baudelairean Late Romantic (always reactionary and antiliberal) and partly from his reading of English drama, in which aristocracy is one of the leading moral "ideas."

In the century of the middle class, Wilde reaffirms aristocratic *virtù*, fabricating it out of its accumulated meanings in English literature. *The Importance of Being Earnest* is a reactionary political poem which takes aristocratic style as the supreme embodiment of life as art. Through its masquelike use of manners as social spectacle, the play seeks out the crystallized idea or Platonic form of aristocracy, which resides in rank, in the ascending gradations of the great chain of being. Wilde's bon mots bring an Apollonian world

into being: language and ceremony unite to take the hierarchical to its farthest dazzling point, until it appears as form without content, like the icy latticework of a snowflake. Thus it is that the characters of *The Importance of Being Earnest*, and especially the women, have abnormal attitudes, reactions, and customs and embark upon sequences of apparently irrational thought, for they are a strange hierarchical race, the *aristoi*.

Wilde's play is inspired by the glamour of aristocracy alone, divorced from social function. In this it is quite unlike Augustan literature, which celebrates Queen Anne for her wisdom and stability of rule. In Wilde no collective benefits flow from throne or court, where the upper class is preoccupied with fashionable diversions. No contemporary regime is eulogized, no past one nostalgically commemorated. Indeed, social order has no legal, economic, or military aspects whatever; it is entirely divorced from practical reality. Class structure in Wilde exists as *art*, as pure form. This markedly contrasts with Ulysses's sermon on "degree" in Shakespeare's *Troilus and Cressida*: in *The Importance of Being Earnest* order is admired not because it is right or just but because it is beautiful. In fact, order here makes no intellectual sense at all; in Carrollian terms, it is absurd. Hence it is an error, and a common one, to say that Wilde is "satirizing" Lady Bracknell, making her ridiculous in her haughty presumptions. Lady Bracknell is beautiful *because* she is absurd. Aristocracy in *The Importance of Being Earnest* satisfies esthetic and not moral demands. The world of the play is *kosmios*, well-ordered and comely. And that it is ruled by the chic makes perfect sense when one realizes that the etymological descent of this word resembles that of *cosmetic* from *cosmos*, for the French *chic* is apparently a version of the German *schick*, meaning taste, elegance, and order.

Outside his art, Wilde found himself in the same quandary as Coleridge and Swinburne, anxiously attempting apologia and moral revision of their daemonic poems. Thus Wilde declares in *The Soul of Man Under Socialism*: "All authority is quite degrading. It degrades those who exercise it, and it degrades those over whom it is exercised." Wilde was torn between his instinctive hierarchism as an Apollonian idealist and the liberalism to which he was impelled by the miseries of being homosexual in a Christian society. This led him into glaring self-contradictions, as in the testimony at his two trials.

The Wildean epicene unites the great English dramatic theme of aristocracy with Late Romantic Estheticism and Decadence. The first step in this process is Wilde's severance of the hierarchical social values of the eighteenth century and Jane Austen from the ideal of commonweal. The second step is his sexual volatilization of

English wit. The bantering rhetoric of the celibate Jane Austen and Lewis Carroll becomes epicene in Wilde because of his sexual experience, with its shift into decadence. Works of epicene wit are typically dominated by image—a tyranny of the visual—and by scandal and gossip. There is little scandal or gossip in Lewis Carroll because the *Alice* books have no sexual "free energy": Carroll is an annalist of aggression but not of eroticism. In Wilde, however, gossip is a primary force, intensifying the aura of glamour by which prestige is measured in the salon. The erotic excitation of scandal and gossip produces the volatility of Wildean wit, aiding its transformation into the epicene. Words cast off their moral meanings and escape into the sexually transcendental, leaving only vapor trails of flirtation and frivolity.

CHRISTOPHER CRAFT

Alias Bunbury: Desire and Termination in *The Importance of Being Earnest*†

> No living word relates to its object in a *singular* way: between the word and its object, between the word and the speaking subject, there exists an elastic environment of others, alien words about the same object, the same theme, and this is an environment that is often difficult to penetrate. It is precisely in the process of living interaction with this specific environment that the word may be individualized and given stylistic shape.
>
> —Mikhail Bakhtin, "Discourse in the Novel"

> Besides, now that I know you to be a confirmed Bunburyist I naturally want to talk to you about Bunbury. I want to tell you the rules.
>
> —Algy to Jack in *The Importance of Being Earnest*

I

A vampire's is not the only kiss to initiate a transformation in being. Consider the influential kiss both "suffered" and enjoyed by "H. C., American, aged 28, of independent means, unmarried, the elder of two children." As case history 27 in Havelock Ellis's *Sexual Inversion*, H. C.'s autobiographical narrative tells the story of what H. C. calls "my developing inversion," a process whose early stages witness his puzzlement before the dawning recognition that women are to him "as likable as ever, but no longer desirable." H. C.'s equivocation here is historically poised:

† From *Representations* 31 (Summer 1990): 19–46. Used with permission of the University of California Press. Bracketed page numbers refer to this Norton Critical Edition.

Soon after this the Oscar Wilde case was bruiting about. The newspaper accounts of it, while illuminating, flashed upon me no light of self-revelation; they only amended some idle conjectures as to certain mystic vices I had heard whispered of. Here and there a newspaper allusion still too recondite was painstakingly clarified by an effeminate fellow-student, who, I fancy now, would have shown no reluctance had I begged him to adduce practical illustration. I purchased, too, photographs of Oscar Wilde, scrutinizing them under the unctuous auspices of this same emasculate and blandiloquent mentor. If my interest in Oscar Wilde arose from any other emotion than the rather morbid curiosity then almost universal, I was not conscious of it.

Erotic dreams, precluded hitherto by coition, came now to beset me. The persons of these dreams were (and still are) invariably women, with this one remembered exception: I dreamed that Oscar Wilde, one of my photographs of him incarnate, approached me with a buffoon languishment . . .[1]

Oscar Wilde comes to this dreamer, as to his readers, neither as "himself" nor even quite as his "own" simulacrum. Situated from the beginning within (indeed, as) an oscillating exchange of representations, *Oscar Wilde* surfaces in H. C.'s narrative as a precariously overdetermined signifier. He emerges either as the dominated subject of "the Oscar Wilde case," the very public object of political subjugation, his body disciplined and his name appropriated as a new alias for those nameless "mystic vices I had heard whispered of"; or else he emerges as the volatilizing subject of those uncannily "clarifying" photographs, themselves the object of a bewildered "scrutiny" whose dreaming eye finally discloses an *agent provocateur* bringing liminal homosexual recognition to oracular crisis. In either case, each the palpable obverse or complement of the other, the signifier *Wilde* encodes not homosexual desire per se but rather a whole history of tendentious citation: "newspaper accounts," anonymous whisperings, "idle conjectures," "unctuous" explications by that "emasculate and blandiloquent mentor," those fetishized photographs. Caught in an enthralling reciprocation of repudiation and identification, desire and disgust, ignorance and "self-revelation," Wilde's discursively appropriated body circulates

---

1. Havelock Ellis, *Sexual Inversion* (Philadelphia, 1931), 175. H. C.'s narrative offers further evidence of the power of Wilde's fictions to determine the real. One evening H. C. is escorted by a fellow reader of *Psychopathia Sexualis* to "several of the cafes where inverts are accustomed to foregather." At one of these "trysting places," he meets a youth who answers some of his "book-begotten queries": "The boy-prostitutes gracing these halls, he apprised us, bore fanciful names, some of well-known actresses, others of heroes in fiction, his own being Dorian Gray. Rivals, he complained, had assumed the same appellation, but he was the original Dorian; the others were jealous imposters" (177).

in H. C.'s text as (in Michel Foucault's idiom) "the inscribed surface of events (traced by language and dissolved by ideas)" and "the
locus of a dissociated self."[2] * * * In "falling heir to inversion,"
H. C. inherits not so much the occulted truth of homosexual being
(the "incubation," as he calls it, "of my perverse instinct") as he
does access to a historically specific narrative trajectory. Soon after
his dream,

> The antipodes of the sexual sphere turned more and more to-
> ward the light of my tolerance. Inversion, till now stained with
> a slight repugnance, became esthetically colorless at last, and
> then delicately retinted, at first solely with pity for its victims,
> but finally, the color deepening, with half-conscious inclina-
> tion to attach it to myself as a remote contingency. This revo-
> lution, however, was not without external impetus. The
> prejudiced tone of a book I was reading, Krafft-Ebing's *Psy-
> chopathia Sexualis*, by prompting resentment, led me on to
> sympathy. My championing, purely abstract though it was to
> begin with, none the less involved my looking at things with
> eyes hypothetically inverted—an orientation for the sake of ar-
> gument. After a while, insensibly and at no one moment, hy-
> pothesis merged into reality: I myself was inverted. That
> occasional and fictitious inversion had never, I believe, super-
> posed this true inversion; rather a true inversion, those many
> years dormant, had simply responded finally to a stimulus
> strong and prolonged enough, as a man awakens when he is
> loudly called.[3]

This passage is remarkable for its ambivalent appeal to rhetoric and
nature as modes of identification; indeed, the work of the passage,
as of the inversion metaphor generally, is to subsume the former
under the latter. First a revisionist or "reverse" reading of dominant
discourse yields a rhetorical or tropological "inversion" that subjects "the antipodes of the sexual sphere" to a chromatic slide, a
cognitive unanchoring motivated by reason, reading, "pity," "sympathy." This political inversion, or "revolution," implicitly figures
sexual identity as tropologically grounded—and, therefore, as ab-
stractable, manipulable, traversable: "It involved my looking at
things with eyes hypothetically inverted—an orientation for the
sake of argument." But the remainder of the paragraph then dis-
mantles its own prior emphasis upon tropological inversion, dis-
placing it with a counter-fiction of authentic origination.
Imperceptibly and "at no one moment," H. C. claims, "that occasional and fictitious inversion" miraculously opens onto a deeper

2. Michel Foucault, "Nietzsche, Genealogy, History," in *The Foucault Reader*, ed. Paul Ra-
binow (New York, 1984), 83.
3. Ellis, *Sexual Inversion*, 175–76.

ontological ground, an occulted or closeted "reality": his "true inversion, these many years dormant, had simply responded . . . as a man awakens when he is loudly called." In this essentializing transition, the motility of tropological sexuality submits to the transfixing call of a new name and a singular identity: "I myself was inverted." In his analytic commentary, Ellis quickly affirms this interpretation: "A critical reading of this history suggests that the apparent control over the sexual impulse by reason is merely a superficial phenomenon. Here, as ever, reason is but a tool in the hands of the passions. The apparent causes are really the result; we are witnessing here the gradual emergence of a retarded homosexual impulse."[4]

Wilde of course did not live long enough to savor the inadvertent splendor of that "tool in the hands of the ['retarded'] passions." Had he survived to read *Sexual Inversion*, he would no doubt have rejected the dehistoricizing move that Ellis and H. C. find so reassuring, so necessary to the stabilization of inverted identity. He would have recalled to H. C. the same displacement that H. C. had stressed . . . : the displacement that "grounds" experience and identity neither in nature, nor in the disclosure of absolute origin, but rather in the dizzying oscillation of persons and representations, as when, in *The Importance of Being Earnest*, baby Jack is "quite literally exchanged for writing in the cloakroom of Victoria Station, his absent-minded governess having substituted for his person a three-volume novel which is described as being 'of more than usually repulsive sentimentality.'"[5] In this farcial exchange of self and writing, the authority of the origin is punningly abrogated, preposterously reversed, as the sober Lady Bracknell makes deliriously clear: "Until yesterday," she says as she pauses before the scandal of Jack's nonoriginary origins, "I had no idea that there were any families or persons whose origin was a Terminus" [49–50]. Like a deconstructionist before her time, a proper Derrida in late Victorian drag, Lady Bracknell exposes the irreducible secondariness of an origin that, in coming first, should but cannot authorize all that comes after. Here, as in Derrida, the nonorigin is originary: "The origin did not even disappear. . . . It was never constituted except reciprocally by a nonorigin, the trace, which thus becomes the origin of the origin."[6]

Lady Bracknell's joke (which is, as we shall see, cognate with the pun motivating the play's title) delegitimates any claim of ontologi-

4. Ibid., 179.
5. Joel Fineman, "The Significance of Literature: *The Importance of Being Earnest*," *October* 15 (1980): 79.
6. Jacques Derrida, *Of Grammatology*, trans. Gayatri Chakravorty Spivak (Baltimore, 1976), 61.

cal authority or natural reference: first because it punningly installs a death or termination at the origin of male subjectivity, as when, for instance, Oedipus murders his father at a crossroads or terminus in order thereby to inherit his plagued adulthood; and second because it insinuates into the origin neither datum nor "truth" but rather the self-conscious play of terms and terminologies, texts and palpable fictions, of which Miss Prism's triple-decker is the appropriately farcical instance. Once the origin has been terminated in this way, its grave solemnities mockingly redistributed as the "trivial" pleasure traversing a pun on death and writing, no "serious" appeal can be made to natural reference or natural ground.[7] The very possibility of a "true inversion" grounded not in trope but in nature is thus punningly dismissed by a play whose deepest insistence is that individual and collective identities are based upon, and secured by, the most arbitrary of constructs: terms, terminations, termini, terminologies.

Unlike H. C., Wilde writes against all essentialist notions of being, inverted or otherwise, and refuses to identify subjectivity and sexuality, insisting instead on the irreducible difference between. That difference *is* the object of Wildean desire. For what Wilde seeks in desire is not the earnest disclosure of a single and singular identity, the deep truth of sex, but rather something less and something more: the vertigo of substitution and repetition. "The Creeds are believed," he writes in "The Critic as Artist," "not because they are rational, but because they are repeated. . . . Do you wish to love? Use Love's Litany, and the words will create the yearning from which the world fancies that they spring."[8] Nor would Wilde curtail this plastic power of language and repetition; he actively recommended the modification of the flesh. "I do not like your lips," he told a youthful André Gide. "They are quite straight, like the lips of a man who has never told a lie. I want you to learn to lie so that your lips may become beautiful and curved like the lips of an antique mask."[9] With such false beautiful lips, Wilde explores the erotic velleities of "the secret that Truth is entirely and absolutely a matter of style."[1] Hence, I suggest, Wilde would have been thrilled to find that H. C. should experience his first flash of homosexual recognition in a dream that directly thematizes repetition, a dream in which H. C. is fellated by a labile representation—

7. The pseudo-opposition between "trivial" and "serious," with which I play repeatedly in this essay, is Wilde's own; the subtitle of *The Importance of Being Earnest* is "A Trivial Comedy for Serious People." That Wilde intended a pseudo-binarism subject to parodic reversal is emphatically indicated by the subtitle of an earlier draft: "A Serious Play for Trivial People."

8. Oscar Wilde, "The Critic as Artist," in *Intentions* (London, 1891); reprinted in *The Artist as Critic: Critical Writings of Oscar Wilde*, ed. Richard Ellmann (Chicago, 1969), 399.

9. André Gide, *Oscar Wilde: A Study*, trans. Stuart Mason (Oxford, 1905), 30.

1. Oscar Wilde, "The Decay of Lying," in *Intentions*; reprinted in *Artist as Critic*, 305.

by, we might say, the picture of Dorian Gray gone Wilde, "one of my photographs of him incarnate." Whatever the annunciatory energy of this watershed experience, the fellation itself arrives as a "buffoon" enactment of a prior description. It arrives "originally" as a figure of repetition, as a re-presentation—"an act expounded shortly before by my oracle." Years before H. C. wrote, Wilde had explicated the erotics of repetition; in the first of his letters to thematize directly "the love of things impossible," he writes: "Sometime you will find, even as I have found, that there is no such thing as romantic experience; there are romantic memories, and there is the desire of romance—that is all. Our most fiery moments of ecstasy are merely shadows of what somewhere else we have felt, or of what we long someday to feel. So at least it seems to me."[2] Thus, *pace* Walter Pater, even the most immediate shocks of sensation arrive in and as the wake of their own nativity, arrive already mediate, caught indisseverably in the dreamy interstices of power, discourse, repetition.

II

> The text is (or should be) that uninhibited person who shows his
> behind to the *Political Father*.
> —Roland Barthes, *The Pleasure of the Text*

If it goes without saying that *The Importance of Being Earnest* is straight farce, then conversely it has never been said that the object of the play's derision is heterosexual representation itself, which Wilde subjects to a fierce, irrecuperable, but almost invisible transvaluation. Positioned at the latter end of a great tradition and written (1894–95) on the precipice of what W. B. Yeats called "the catastrophe," *Earnest* is a self-consciously belated text in which the venerable topoi of comedy—the dispersion of lovers and their ultimate distribution into cross-gender couples, the confusion and then the restoration of identities, the confrontation with and the expulsion of errant desire, the closural wedding sponsored by the Name of the Father (here, specifically, Ernest John Moncrieff)—are repeated, inverted, finely perverted, set finally to spin. In the ensuing delirium, Wilde exposes these topoi as culturally empowered cyphers whose particular distribution enforces heterosexual narrative. As Wilde stages it, this narrative entails not just points of departure (a "social indiscretion" in "a cloak-room at a railway station") and termination (heterosexual conjunction under the paternal signifier) but also sidelines of pseudonymous desire, here called, preposterously, "serious Bunburyism." Bunbury, to be sure,

2. Oscar Wilde, *The Letters of Oscar Wilde*, ed. Rupert Hart-Davis (New York, 1962), 185.

will be "quite exploded" by play's end, but this "revolutionary out-rage," as Lady Bracknell calls it, will have already ensured his frag-mented dissemination throughout the text. In a parodic submission to heterosexist teleology, Wilde *does* dismiss his lovers to the pre-sumptive closure of marital bliss, but not until he has insinuated what should, by law and convention, have been exiled as *non nom-inandum*: a jubilant celebration of male homosexual desire, a trenchant dissection of the supposedly "legitimate" male heterosex-ual subject, and a withering critique of the political idea, exigent in the 1890s, that sexuality, inverted or otherwise, could be natural or unnatural at all.

That Wilde achieves these critical effects without the slightest breach in heterosexual decorum is not the least measure of a ge-nius whose wile it was to broadcast homosexual critique into the gay interspace of a pun. Here the play of occultation and display, slippage and spillage, could be conveniently housed, as is Ernest John, in two oppositional domiciles—or, as in a bedroom farce, two closets—between which a great deal of shuttling would be re-quired. Transcoding the emergent, dissymmetrical binarism hetero-sexual/homosexual into verbal play, Wilde instantiates homosexual desire as the secondary, punning other of a dominant signification, thereby simultaneously affirming and subverting the authority of the norm. The inescapable duplicity of this procedure is historical in at least two senses: first because it plays with and against the tra-dition of interdiction by which celebration of the homosexual possi-bility had been silenced; and second because, as we shall see, it redeploys contemporaneous discourses on (as H. C. puts it) "true inversion," which repeatedly formulated homosexual desire as het-erosexual desire manqué: in the case of the male, *anima muliebris virili corpore inclusa*.[3]

Recent work by Ed Cohen and Jonathan Dollimore has made it possible to discern the homosexual countervalences in Wilde's transparently heterosexual texts. In a crucial essay on *Dorian Gray*, Cohen explores the ways in which Wilde produced "new discursive strategies to express concerns unvoiced within the dominant cul-ture." Examining "Wilde's novel [as it] moves both with and athwart late Victorian ideological practices that naturalized male heterosex-uality," Cohen indicates just how an ambidextrous Wilde maintains a protective heterosexual patina even as he also "inscribes the male body within the circuits of male desire."[4] And in a parallel essay on

3. Latin: a female soul trapped in a male body. [*Editor's note.*]
4. Ed Cohen, "Writing Gone Wilde: Homoerotic Desire in the Closet of Representation," *PMLA* 102, no. 5 (October 1987): 801–13. During the writing and revising of this essay I benefited enormously from Cohen's generous conversation regarding Wilde, the trials of 1895, and the history of homosexuality.

Wilde's anti-essentialism, Dollimore explicates the transgressive power of the Wildean text, which, he asserts, operates *within* the structures of legitimation and domination in order to release deviant vectors of desire, transverse lines of critique: "Deviant desire reacts against, disrupts and displaces from within; rather than seeking to escape the repressive ordering of the sexual, Wilde reinscribes himself within and relentlessly inverts the binaries upon which that ordering depends. Inversion . . . defines Wilde's transgressive aesthetic."[5] As Dollimore suggests, Wilde deploys inversion not as an occulted sexual truth disclosing effeminated being but rather as a tropological strategy whose primary devices, reversal and repetition, could bring the most upright of heterosexual norms to preposterous conclusion.

Hence the extreme formalism of heterosexual desire in *Earnest*, its inspired submission to the rigor of the signifier. As the effect of prior performances, heterosexuality for Wilde was both the a priori and the sine qua non of dramatic representation; he could neither stage nor publish an uncloseted gay play. In *Earnest* Wilde transforms this delegitimation into a mode of enablement; for if the heterosexual alignment of desires and bodies were prerequisite to representation, then Wilde would foreground and expose it as such, as a convention whose arbitrariness excited earnest celebration. The heterosexualizing machinery of Wilde's plot is too familiar to need much diagramming; clipped synopsis will do. The play opens on two exuberant bachelors, John Worthing (the eponymous hero of the play's eponymous pun) and Algernon Moncrieff, each living a "double life" of undefined specificity. ("I hope," says Cecily to Algy, "you have not been leading a double life, pretending to be wicked and being really good all the time. That would be hypocrisy.") [27] John is Jack in the country (where he is respectable) and his own dissolute brother, Ernest, in the city (where he is not), and Algy takes curious pleasure cruises to the country to visit Bunbury, about whom we know nothing except that his "permanent invalid[ism]" elicits from Algy an heroic succoring. Our heroes are schematically aligned with respective heroines: Jack with Gwendolen, who believes him to be Ernest and will only marry a man so named, and Algy with Cecily who likewise will only marry an Ernest. "There is something in that name that seems to inspire absolute confidence" [37], as Cecily explains to a bewildered Algy. And Gwendolen's explication suggests access to a more than nominal rapture: "It is a divine name. It has a music of its own. It produces vibrations" [15]. The sheer arbitrariness of this "feminine" desire for Ernest-ness underscores the for-

5. Jonathan Dollimore, "Different Desires: Subjectivity and Transgression in Wilde and Gide," *Textual Practice* 1, no. 1 (1987): 56; reprinted in *Genders* 2 (Summer 1988): 24–41.

mality of the play's manifest heterosexuality; it requires not so much
that the heroes seek women as that they seek access to women, legitimacy, and wealth through the assumption of an overdetermined
signifier, a magical term whose power lies in its capacity to trigger
fetishistic "vibrations."

The plot works conventionally first to obstruct and then to facilitate the two impending marriages, and the securing of the marriages
turns upon the elimination of two impediments. The first is Lady
Bracknell's objection to the "romantic story" of Jack's origins and to
the consequent illegibility of the Name of the Father, and the second is John Worthing's (very patriarchal, very hypocritical) insistence that Algy relinquish the incomparable pleasures of "serious
Bunburyism." Wilde's great third act farcically achieves both conditions: in an offstage parody of tragic *sparagmos* Bunbury is "quite
exploded" ("I killed Bunbury this afternoon" [49], says Algy
murderously and casually), and the dispersions of Jack's identity are
"properly" integrated within the (splayed) unity of the paternal signifier. When Jack discovers that indeed he "naturally is Ernest," this is
a nature whose authority is grounded entirely in letters, terms, texts:
in a genealogical appeal to writing, and not just any writing, but "the
Army lists of the last forty years"—the book, very simply, of the
Names of the Fathers. Consulting this august text, and reading
there for the first time both his own and his father's name, Jack discovers his denatured nature as repetition, quotation, division:

> JACK   The Army Lists of the last forty years are here. These de-
> lightful records should have been my constant study. (*Rushes
> to bookcase and tears the books out.*) M. Generals . . . Mallam,
> Maxbohm, Magley—what ghastly names they have—Markby,
> Migsby, Mobbs, Moncrieff! Lieutenant 1840, Captain, Lieu-
> tenant-Colonel, Colonel, General 1869, Christian names,
> Ernest John. (*Puts book very quietly down and speaks quite
> calmly.*) I always told you, Gwendolen, my name was Ernest,
> didn't I? Well, it is Ernest after all. I mean it naturally is
> Ernest. [58]

In these lines Jack "naturally" inherits the very same pair of signifiers that all along had structured the oscillation of his "double
life." As if in reward for his earnest lying, Jack discovers himself to
be, as indeed he had always been, both himself and his own fictive
(br)other. No longer split between "Jack" and "Ernest," the split
"Ernest/John" now installed as the law of his being, Jack inherits
himself "after all" as his "own" difference from himself. ("But what
own are you?" Gwen astutely queries.) In thus assuming what Joel
Fineman has aptly called "the unity of his duplicity,"[6] Jack's now

6. Fineman, "Significance of Literature," 79.

"natural" being is introjected with the same oscillation that the play had just ritually expelled by "quite explod[ing]" Bunbury. Condensing these figures, and stressing their more than casual relation, we may say that the murder of Bunbury enables the pseudo-integration of an irreducibly divided male subject.

Wilde's farce thus discloses heterosexual closure as the function of two fatally interlocked figures: on the one hand, the formal expulsion of Bunbury and whatever unspeakable pleasures "serious Bunburyism" may entail and, on the other, the "integration" of the "heterosexual" male subject under the Name of the Father. At once crucial *and* arbitrary, these predicates enable the heterosexual order; they alone secure the marriages that will presumably close the otherwise open circuits of desire. (Algy, we should remember, refutes this dream of closure: "You don't seem to realize," he tells Jack, "that in married life three is company and two is none.") [12] And yet these predicates have always seemed ridiculous or, in Wilde's preferred term, "trivial." What, we now need to ask, is the meaning of this overdetermined triviality, itself finally indistinguishable from the equivocal pleasure of the play's titular pun? Who is "Bunbury" and what are his filiations—familial, erotic, conceptual—with "Ernest John"? Why must desire submit to such arbitrary terms and terminations? To begin answering these questions, we must now confront the play's phantom self, itself actually no self but rather a gnomic signifier—a name, that is, without a being. I mean of course the nonexistent but omnipresent Mr. Bunbury, upon whom (but there is no whom) so much so curiously depends.

III

Like all works of art, [*The Importance of Being Earnest*] drew its sustenance from life, and, speaking for myself, whenever I see or read the play I always wish I did not know what I do about Wilde's life at the time he was writing it—that when, for instance, John Worthing talks of going Bunburying, I did not immediately visualize Alfred Taylor's establishment. On rereading it after his release, Wilde said, "It was extraordinary reading the play over. How I used to toy with that tiger Life." At its conclusion, I find myself imagining a sort of nightmare Pantomime Transformation Scene in which, at the touch of the magician's wand, instead of the workday world's turning into fairyland, the country house in a never-never Hertfordshire turns into the Old Bailey, the features of Lady Bracknell into those of Mr. Justice Wills. Still, it is a masterpiece, and on account of it Wilde will always enjoy the impersonal fame of an artist as well as the notoriety of his personal legend.
                                —W. H. Auden, "An Improbable Life"[7]

7. W. H. Auden, "An Improbable Life," in *Forewords and Afterwords* (New York, 1973), 323. This essay, a review of Hart-Davis's edition of Wilde's letters, appeared originally in the *New Yorker*, 9 March 1963; it is also available in Richard Ellmann, ed., *Oscar Wilde: A Collection of Critical Essays* (Englewood Cliffs, N.J., 1969), 116–37.

As a character "always somewhere else at present," as a figure thus *sans figure*, Bunbury had been devised by Wilde to inhabit the erotic interstices of the double bind here represented by Auden's *volonté d'oublier*, his drive to forget: "I always wish I did not know what I do." The subtle instruction of such a double bind is not so much that knowledge be voided as that knowledge perform its work along self-blinded paths of "ignorance," nonrecognition, and misidentification. "In this light," as D. A. Miller writes, "it becomes clear that the social function of secrecy"—and Bunbury is the secret subject of an open secret—"is not to conceal knowledge so much as to conceal knowledge of the knowledge. . . . Secrecy would thus be the subjective practice in which the oppositions of private/public, inside/outside, subject/object are established, and the sanctity of their first term kept inviolate."[8] As Wilde's sly figure for this regime of knowing and unknowing, of knowing through unknowing, Bunbury remains a being or subject always otherwise and elsewhere; he appears nowhere on stage, and wherever his name is present he is not. Appeals to Bunbury yield only his absence: "Bunbury doesn't live here. Bunbury is somewhere else at present." But if Bunbury has been banished from the precincts of heterosexual representation, the need to frequent his secrecy has not, as Algy explains to Jack: "Nothing will induce me to part with Bunbury, and if you ever get married, which seems to me extremely problematic, you will be very glad to know Bunbury. A man who marries without knowing Bunbury has a very tedious time of it" [12]. Bunbury thus operates within the heterosexual order as its hidden but irreducible supplement, the fictive and pseudonymous brother whose erotic "excesses" will be manifested only by continual allusion to their absence.

Of course the gay specificity of such allusiveness was technically unspeakable: *non nominandum inter Christianos*.[9] Refusing to chafe under this proscription, Wilde inverts it by inserting Bunbury into the text behind the ostentatious materiality of an empty signifier, a punning alias whose strategic equivocation between allusion and elision had already announced, a century before Foucault's formulation, "that the world of speech and desires has known invasions, struggles, plunderings, disguises, ploys."[1] Speaking strictly, *Earnest* cannot admit or acknowledge the erotic force of the gay male body, which must therefore be staged as an atopic body, a

---

8. D. A. Miller, *The Novel and the Police* (Berkeley, 1988), 207. Miller's landmark essay "Secret Subjects, Open Secrets," from which I quote here, has informed my thinking throughout these pages.

9. Latin: not to be named among Christians. Because discussion of homosexuality was taboo in the Victorian era, law books used this expression to refer to this behavior. [*Editor's note.*]

1. Foucault, "Nietzsche, Genealogy, History," 76.

body constitutively "somewhere else at present." Hence the flickering present-absence of the play's homosexual desire, as the materiality of the flesh is retracted into the sumptuousness of the signifier, whether in the "labial phonemics" of Bunbury,[2] all asmack with death and kisses, or in the duplicitous precincts of the play's most proper and improper name, *Earnest*: a name at once splayed by a pun and doubly referential, pointing with one hand to the open secret of the double life and with the other to the brittle posturings of the Name of the Father—a figure whose delicate transmissibility has always required the strictest of heterosexual propaedeutics.

What then, more specifically, are the disguises and ploys of "serious Bunburyism"? Or, in Jack's more exasperated intonation: "Bunburyist? What on earth do you mean by a Bunburyist" [10]? But the hermeneutical rage of a Jack must be a little undone by the interpretive insouciance of an Algy: "Now produce your explanation, and pray make it remarkable. The bore about most explanations is that they are never half so remarkable as the things they try to explain" [10]. In this spirit, I offer some explanations. Bunbury represents or disseminates the following: 1) an actual person of no historical importance, Henry Shirley Bunbury, a hypochondriacal acquaintance of Wilde's Dublin youth;[3] 2) a village in Cheshire that, appropriately enough, "does not even appear on most maps";[4] 3) a tongue-in-cheek allusion to Wilde's illegal "sodomitical" practices—"not only," as Fineman puts it, "British slang for a male brothel, but . . . also a collection of signifiers that straightforwardly express their desire to bury in the bun";[5] 4) a parody of the contemporaneous medicalization of homosexual desire ("Nor do I," says Lady Bracknell of Algy's visits to Bunbury, "in any way approve of the modern sympathy with invalids. I consider it morbid. Illness of any kind is

---

2. Fineman, "Significance of Literature," 83.
3. For more on Henry Shirley Bunbury, see William Green, "Oscar Wilde and the Bunburys," *Modern Drama* 21, no. 1 (1978): 67–80. I disagree with Green emphatically on the importance and function of Bunbury, to wit: "Even allowing for the possibility that the term may have existed in the form of a private joke, Wilde had ample opportunity to avoid using it in the play if he suspected it had any homosexual connotations which might have drawn attention to him. . . . Wilde could have substituted another name for Bunbury."
4. Ibid., 71. The English colloquialism for buttocks is of course not *bun* but *bum*, but the frail consonantal difference distinguishing the two terms remains always liable to elision, especially in performance, whether in a slip of the actor's tongue or in the labyrinth of the auditor's ear. *Bun*, as I argue above, points immediately to Algy's serious overeating and mediately to Wilde's sexual practice, which, his biographers agree, was primarily oral. In this regard we should remember that Wilde was not, as is often assumed, convicted of sodomy; rather he was prosecuted and convicted under section 11 of the Criminal Law Amendment Act of 1885, which criminalized all "acts of gross indecency" committed between males, whether in public or private. For an analysis of the conceptual shifts entailed by this legislation, see Ed Cohen, "From Sodomy to Gross Indecency," *South Atlantic Quarterly* 88, no. 1 (Winter 1989): 181–217.
5. Fineman, "Significance of Literature," 89.

hardly a thing to be encouraged in others. Health is the primary duty of life"); 5) a sly, even chipper, allusion to the thanatopolitics of homophobia, whose severest directives against disclosure ensure that what finally gets disclosed will be, as in *Dorian Gray*, a corpse, homicide or suicide, upon whose cold or cooling flesh the now obvious text is for the first time made legible; 6) a pragmatics of gay misrepresentation, a nuanced and motile doublespeak, driven both by pleasure and, as Gide put it, "by the need of self-protection";[6] and, as we shall see before we end, 7) a pseudonym or alias for the erotic oscillation within the male subject, his fundamental waffling between Jack and Ernest.

But more crucially than any of these, Bunbury insists upon his "own" difference from himself and from whatever signification (as above) he may, by caprice or compulsion, assume. From his prone position just offstage (to know Bunbury is "to sit by a bed of pain"), *Bunbury* performs enormous representational work, but only by way of a disseminal passage whose first effect is to expel the referent from the neighborhood of the sign: where *Bunbury* is, Bunbury is not. It is typical of Wilde's inverting wit that he should stage this expulsion as an act of ingestion, as a buttered and material pun on Bunbury's cryptographic name. I mean the "luxurious and indolent" gluttony that, by axiomatically transposing sexual and gustatory pleasures (cucumber sandwiches, muffins, breads: buns—Banbury or Bunbury—everywhere),[7] operates as a screen metaphor for otherwise unspeakable pleasures: "There can be little good in any young man who eats so much, or so often."[8] In this displacement,

6. André Gide, *The Journals of André Gide*, trans. Justin O'Brien, 3 vols. (New York, 1948), 2:410.

7. The *OED* citation for *Banbury* reads: "A town in Oxfordshire, England, formerly noted for the number and zeal of its Puritan inhabitants, still for its cakes." Cf. also the Mother Goose nursery rhyme, "Ride a cock-horse to Banbury Cross." The phonemic and imagistic affinities between *Bunbury* and *Banbury* proved too much for at least one of the typists working from Wilde's handwritten manuscripts. In a typescript of the play dated "19 Sep. 94" by Mrs. Marshall's Type Writing Office, *Bunbury* repeatedly appears as *Banbury*. Wilde, whose careless, looping handwriting no doubt encouraged the error, patiently restored the *us*.

8. This line, spoken by Miss Prism about Ernest (whom, of course, she has not met), does not appear in the three-act *Earnest* with which most readers are familiar, but can be found in the various manuscript and typescript drafts of the so-called "original" four-act version. A brief explanation of the textual confusion surrounding *Earnest* is in order. When in 1898, *après le deluge*, M. Melmoth sought to publish Mr. Wilde's farce, his only recourse to "the play itself" was to a truncated copy text, George Alexander's prompt copy, that had provided the basis for the short-lived 1895 production. Since Wilde's own drafts and copies of *Earnest* had been auctioned off in the bankruptcy proceedings following his imprisonment, "Alexander's manuscript," as Wilde called it, was for all purposes the only extant text upon which to base the published version of 1899. The problem with Alexander's typescript is that it contained substantial cuts, some authorial and some not, including, most famously, the excision of an entire scene in which Algy is almost arrested for Ernest's outstanding debts; this cut was essential to the structural reorganization of four acts into three. That Alexander's emendations were significant there can be no doubt; upon seeing the play on opening night, Wilde (whom Alexander had dismissed from rehearsals) is reported to have remarked: "My dear Aleck, it was charm-

the obscene becomes the scenic, as that which must not be spoken is consumed, before an audience, with incomparable relish and finesse. "Well, I can't eat muffins in an agitated manner. The butter would probably get on my cuffs. One should always eat muffins quite calmly. It is the only way to eat them" [45]. The fastidious allusion to Wilde's sexual practice here is exact—from hand to mouth: as H. Montgomery Hyde reports, fondling "would be followed by some form of mutual masturbation or intercrural intercourse. . . . Finally, oral copulation would be practiced, with Wilde as the active agent [sic], though this role was occasionally reversed. It gave him inspiration, he said."[9] Inspirited by "reversed" practices and reversible tropes, Wilde adopts a polite decorum (no danger to Algy's cuffs) in order to display and displace a desire to bury in the bun. In this way, serious Bunburyism releases a polytropic sexuality so mobile, so evanescent in speed and turn, that it traverses, Ariel-like, a fugitive path through oral, genital, and anal ports until it expends itself in and as the displacements of language. It was Wilde's extraordinary gift to return this vertigo of substitution and repetition to his audience. The inspiration he derived from fellatio he then redisseminated, usually *sotto voce*, through the actor's mouth. "The ejaculation," says Lady Bracknell in a line that did not survive the revisor's knife, "has reached my ears more than once."[1]

---

ing, quite charming. And, do you know, from time to time I was reminded of a play I once wrote myself, called THE IMPORTANCE OF BEING EARNEST"; quoted in A. E. W. Mason, *Sir George Alexander and the St. James Theatre* (New York, 1969), 79. Not until the 1950s would the various working manuscripts and typescripts of the "original" four-act versions begin to surface, so that, by way of a temporal inversion that Wilde surely would have delectated, *Earnest* is a work whose lost origins *postdate* its publication by some fifty years. Throughout this essay I refer both to the familiar three-act version and to the antecedent four-act versions without worrying the issue of textual authority. Unless otherwise specified all references here to the four-act version are to *The Importance of Being Earnest: A Trivial Comedy for Serious People in Four Acts as Originally Written by Oscar Wilde*, ed. Sarah Augusta Dickson, 2 vols. (New York, 1955); Miss Prism's line as quoted above can be found in Dickson, *Earnest*, 1:77. See also *The Definitive Four-Act Version of The Importance of Being Earnest*, ed. Ruth Berggren (New York, 1987), 23–41.

9. H. Montgomery Hyde, *Oscar Wilde* (New York, 1975), 187.

1. Dickson, *Earnest*, 1:146. This line occurs during a wonderful bit of stage business in which, while Jack and Lady Brancaster (as she is called in the four-act versions) are discussing "the painful circumstances of [Jack's] origin," Algy and Cecily are hiding "behind [a] screen . . . whispering and laughing." As the good lady speaks, Algy's attempts to silence or "hush" Cecily interrupt her discourse; annoyed by these intrusions, Lady Brancaster complains: "It is clear that there is someone who says 'Hush' concealed in this apartment. The ejaculation has reached my ears more than once. It is not at any time a very refined expression, and its use, when I am talking, is extremely vulgar, and indeed insolent. I suspect it to have proceeded from the lips of someone who is of more than usually low origin." In this sadly excised tableau, Wilde compactly stages the sociopolitical operations of Bunburying representation, in which a discourse of social rectitude is interrupted by an "ejaculation" that can be heard but not seen. As the screen behind which Cecily and Algy are sporting very nicely materializes the strategy of visual occlusion, so does the transposition of "hush" and "ejaculation" make audible, as laughter, the Bunburying operations by which a secret erotics may be mouthed but not quite bespoken. We should note in passing, too, that Wilde here anticipates the more-than-audible ejaculation with which Roland Barthes closes *The Pleasure of the Text*, trans.

Oscillating between verbal and seminal emissions, Lady Brack-nell's pun enacts the rhetorical equivocation essential to serious Bunburyism: an "illicit" signification is broadcast into the text even as it is also withdrawn under the cover of a licit one. In this way, Wilde duplicitously introduced into *Earnest* a parodic account of his own double life (the public thumbing of a private nose) as well as a trenchant critique of the heterosexist presumption requiring, here statutorily, that such a life be both double and duplicitous. And that *Earnest* is a text sliding deviously between exposé and cri-tique, a text saturating its reader/viewer with blinding disseminal effusions, is simply a fact whose closeting or imprisonment we must tolerate no longer. To substantiate this claim, I adduce below a brief series of discrete indiscretions in which *Earnest* "goes Bun-burying"—in which, that is, Wilde lifts to liminality his subcultural knowledge of "the terrible pleasures of double life."[2] In providing these few examples (others are adduced in a longer version of the present essay), I have drawn freely from both the three- and four-act versions of the play.[3]

1) "It is very ungentlemanly thing to read a private cigarette case" [9] (act 1, in both three- and four-act versions). In the trials of April–May 1895, Wilde would be compelled to submit again and again to "ungentlemanly" exegesis. Cigarette cases, usually silver ones purchased in Bond Street, were part (along with cash, other jewelry, food, and drink) of Wilde's payment to the male prostitutes he frequented. As the most durable material trace of Wilde's illegal sexual practice, these cigarette cases (replete with inscriptions such as "To X from O. W.") would be repeatedly introduced into evi-dence by the prosecution throughout the second and third trials. Consider the following exchange between Solicitor General Frank Lockwood, prosecutor at the third trial, and the defendant:

> Did you ever give one [a cigarette case] to Charles Parker also? —Yes, but I am afraid it cost only £1.
> Silver? —Well, yes. I have a great fancy for giving cigarette cases.
> To young men? —Yes.
> How many have you given? —I might have given seven or eight in 1892 or 1893.[4]

Richard Miller (New York, 1975). Cinema, Barthes writes, "succeed[s] in shifting the sig-nified a great distance and in throwing, so to speak, the anonymous body of the actor into my ear: it granulates, it crackles, it caresses, it grates, it cuts, it comes: that is bliss" (67).

2. Oscar Wilde, *The Picture of Dorian Gray* (Oxford, 1981), 79.

3. See note 24 above.

4. Anonymous, *Oscar Wilde: Three Times Tried*, 2 vols. ("Paris," n.d.), 389 (the two vol-umes are consecutively paginated). This text, which appears to be a pirated edition of another book issued anonymously under the same title by the Ferrestone Press (London, 1912), claims to be the most "complete and accurate account of this long and compli-cated case. Special care, it will be seen, has been devoted to the elucidation of abstruse

These cigarette cases are remarkably rich metonyms of Wilde's sexual practice. Literally inscribed with the condescension implicit in Wilde's cross-class and cross-generational sexual activity, they suggest his ambivalent relation to the prostitution he repeatedly enjoyed: he preferred to think of the cases as "gifts" not necessarily related to the sexual services they nonetheless purchased. As evidenciary deposits purchased and distributed by a "first-class misdemeanant," as Jack describes Ernest, they also bespeak a contradictory emotionality compounded of defiance, foolhardiness, and, it would seem, a certain desire to be caught. And finally, they insistently point to the orality that was both Wilde's sexual preference and *Earnest's* primary trope of displacement. Henry Wotton, after all, had already explicated for Dorian Gray the evanescent perfection of a good smoke ("You must have a cigarette. A cigarette is the perfect type of a perfect pleasure. It is exquisite, and it leaves one unsatisfied. What more can one want?"); and Edward Shelley, one of Wilde's lovers, testified that he "had received a letter from Mr. Wilde inviting him to 'come smoke a cigarette' with him."[5] Furthermore, while reporting the events of the first (that is, the libel) trial, the London daily *Evening News* (5 April 1895) printed the following:

> The Old Bailey recoiled with loathing from the long ordeal of terrible suggestions that occupied the whole of yesterday when the cross-examination left the literary plane and penetrated the dim-lit perfumed rooms where the poet of the beautiful joined with valets and grooms *in the bond of silver cigarette cases*. (Italics added)[6]

As the effective verso to the recto of *Earnest's* gay gaming with cigarette cases, the "recoil[ing]" and "loathing" specified in these lines indicate the precarious volatility of the Victorian male bonds so deftly manipulated by Wilde on "the literary plane." A gentleman might offer his peer, or even his inferior in age or class, the benefit of a good smoke or the gratuity of a cigarette case, but only so long as the gift did not suggest a bond more intimate than "proper" gentlemanly relation or condescension. The performative success of *Earnest's* oral insouciance lay in its capacity to tease the limit of the proper without seeming to violate it seriously. Prosecutor Lockwood's "very ungentlemanly" reading of private cigarette cases re-

---

legal points. . . . The evidence of witnesses, together with the prolonged cross-examination of Wilde in each of the three trials, is given as fully as possible, with due regard to discretion."

5. *Three Times Tried*, 355.

6. I encountered this passage while reading Ed Cohen's *Talk on the Wilde Side: Toward a Genealogy of the Discourse on Male Sexuality* (Ph.D. diss., Stanford University, 1988), to which I remain indebted. I quote with permission of the author.

versed this rhetorical strategy by transforming the *glissando* of Wildean wit into that "long ordeal of terrible suggestion."

2) "Fathers are certainly not popular just at present. . . . At present fathers are at a terrible discount. They are like those chaps, the minor poets. They are never even quoted" (act 1 in the four-act versions). Spoken by Algy, these lines point underhandedly to the escalating filial warfare between the Marquess of Queensberry and Lord Alfred Douglas. This triangular narrative is too familiar to require recapitulation here, except to say that the battle was being engaged even as Wilde was composing *Earnest* and that Wilde's failure to manage the situation adroitly precipitated the debacle of the trials, during which Queensberry's charge that Wilde had been "posing as a somdomite [*sic*]" would find a decisive institutional context in which to be "quoted," at length and in detail. At the conclusion of the libel trial, the jury determined the Queensberry's charge of sodomitical "posing" had been proved and that his "Plea of Justification" elaborating this charge had been "published for the public benefit."

3) Canon Chasuble in response to Jack's concern that he is "a little too old now" to be rechristened as Ernest:

> Oh, I am not by any means a bigoted Paedobaptist. . . . You need have no apprehensions [about immersion]. . . . Sprinkling is all that is necessary, or indeed, I think, advisable. . . . I have two similar ceremonies to perform. . . . A case of twins that occurred recently in one of the outlying cottages on your estate [31] . . . I don't know, however, if you would care to join them at the Font. Personally I do not approve myself of the obliteration of class-distinctions. (Act 2 in the four-act versions; a truncated version of these lines, without "Paedobaptist" and "the obliteration of class-distinctions," appears in the three-act version)

The always serious Canon Chasuble repeatedly falls into oblique and unwilling licentious allusion, as in these lines, which insinuate an outrageous chain of gay metonyms: "Paedobaptist," "sprinkling is all that is necessary," "in one of the outlying cottages," "if you would care to join them at the Font," "the obliteration of class-distinctions." If "Paedobaptist" (or "sprinkler of boys") was too blatantly obscene to survive revision, then the more subtly insinuated "outlying cottages" was not: only an elite audience would have known that by the late nineteenth century *cottage* had currency as a camp signifier for a trysting site, usually a public urinal. The word also had a more personal reference; Queensberry's Plea of Justification claimed that Oscar Wilde "in the year of our Lord One thousand eight hundred and ninety-three [a year before the composition

of *Earnest*] at a house called 'The Cottage' at Goring . . . did solicit and incite . . . the said . . . acts of gross indecency."[7] Once these Bunburied significations are allowed to resonate through the passage, once we recognize with Canon Chasuble that "corrupt readings seem to have crept into the text," the references to "sprinkling" and "join[ing] them at the Font" assume an "obscene" valence. Similarly with "the obliteration of class-distinctions," which boisterously points to the almost pederastic, cross-class prostitution Wilde enjoyed. Just a few lines earlier, Jack had the effrontery to say, "I am very fond of children," a sentence definitely courting the bourgeois outrage of the thus "discounted" fathers who pursued Wilde through the court and into prison.

4) "The next time I see you I hope you will be Parker" (act 3 in the four-act versions). As has been "public knowledge" (however inert) for some thirty years, the most substantial revision of *Earnest* was the deletion (demanded by George Alexander, who produced the play, and unhappily submitted to by Wilde) of an entire scene in which Algy, Bunburying as Ernest, is almost arrested for dining expenses incurred by Jack, or rather Ernest, at the Savoy Hotel, the site of both Jack/Ernest's "grossly materialistic" gluttony and some of Wilde's sexual encounters. Jack, delighted that Algy should suffer for extravagances that can only be correctly charged to Ernest, counsels his younger brother "that incarceration would do you a great deal of good." Algy understandably protests: "Well, I really am not going to be imprisoned in the suburbs for having dined in the West End. It is perfectly ridiculous." Ridiculous or not, Wilde would very soon suffer an analogous imprisonment, but in "never-never Hertfordshire" (as Auden called it) this end is happily remitted when Jack, his "generosity misplaced," "pay[s] this monstrous bill for my brother."

Two aspects of this scene merit emphasis. First, Algy's pseudo-arrest for serious overeating strengthens my argument that in *Earnest* "luxurious and indolent" gluttony operates as a jubilant screen metaphor for otherwise unrepresentable pleasures. This cathexis of extravagant dining and sexual transgression refers directly to Wilde's double life; it was his regular practice to dine luxuriously with his lovers prior to sex, thereby enjoying *in camera* the same metaphor he would display on stage in *Earnest*. Often meeting his assignations in the private chambers of public restaurants (Willis's or the Solferino or elsewhere), he would dazzle them with

7. Queensberry's "Plea of Justification" is reprinted as appendix A in H. Montgomery Hyde, *The Trials of Oscar Wilde* (New York, 1962), 323–27. The 1843 Criminal Libel Act, the statute under which Wilde sued Queensberry for accusing him of "posing as a somdomite [*sic*]," permitted the defendant (i.e., Queensberry) to place before the court a document, or "Plea of Justification," supporting the allegation for which the libel suit was being prosecuted.

opulence, language, and alcohol. Here is the testimony of one prostitute:

> He [i.e., Alfred Taylor, Wilde's procurer] took us to a restaurant in Rupert Street. I think it was the Solferino. We were shown upstairs to a private room, in which there was a dinner table laid for four. After a while Wilde came in. I had never seen him before, but I had heard of him. We dined about eight o'clock. We all four sat down to dinner, Wilde sitting on my left.
>
> Was the dinner a good dinner?—Yes. The table was lighted with red-shaded candles. We had champagne with our dinner, and brandy and coffee afterwards. Wilde paid for the dinner. Subsequently Wilde said to me, "This is the boy for me—will you go to the Savoy Hotel with me?" I consented, and Wilde drove me in a cab to the hotel. He took me first into a sitting-room on the second floor, where he ordered some more drink—whiskey and soda. Wilde then asked me to go into his bedroom with him.
>
> Witness here described certain acts of indecency which he alleged took place in the bedroom.[8]

The witness in this exchange is Charles Parker, a sometime valet, whose testimony against Wilde seems alternately to have been purchased and coerced. It is the name *Parker* that brings us to the last point regarding the deleted arrest scene. The scene commences with the delivery of a calling card, which Algy reads: " 'Parker and Gribsby, Solicitors.' I don't know anything about them. Who are they?" After taking and reading the card, Jack facetiously speculates: "I wonder who they can be. I expect, Ernest, they have come about some business for your friend Bunbury. Perhaps Bunbury wants to make his will, and wishes you to be executor" [61]. With these intimations of Algy's forthcoming execution of Bunbury lingering in the air, Messrs. Parker and Gribsby are shown in by Merriman, the butler. But "they," it turns out, are not exactly a they but a he ("There is only one gentleman in the hall, sir," Merriman informs Jack), and the one gentleman is Gribsby "himself," come either to collect the debt or "remove" Ernest to Holloway Prison, one of those "suburb[an]" facilities through which Wilde would be funneled on his way to ignominy: "The surroundings, I admit, are middle class; but the gaol itself is fashionable and well-aired." (From the other side of the bars Wilde would not find it so.) As these threats of incarceration and death are being ventilated in the text, Jack first teases Algy for his (that is, Jack's) profligacy and then "generously" pays Ernest's debt, thereby forestalling the correction

8. *Three Times Tried*, 191.

that would, Jack says, have done Algy "a great deal of good." Having dispatched his serious problem, Jack then luxuriates in a little trivial banter:

JACK   You are Gribsby, aren't you? What is Parker like?
GRIBSBY   I am both, sir. Gribsby when I am on unpleasant business, Parker on occasions of a less serious kind.
JACK   The next time I see you I hope you will be Parker. [65]

("After all," Wilde writes in a letter, "the only proper intoxication is conversation.")[9] Unfortunately, the next time Wilde saw "Parker," Parker would be "on [the] unpleasant business" of a reverse, or disciplinary, Bunbury. Appearing in the Central Criminal Court under the guise of *Gribsby*, appearing, that is, as an agent of the law, Parker would testify to "acts of gross indecency" committed with Wilde in 1893 while Gribsby, apparently, was otherwise and elsewhere engaged.

It could have come as no surprise to the creator of "Parker and Gribsby, Solicitors" that he should find himself prosecuted for the same sexual practices he had been (con)celebrating just beneath the lovely pellucid "heterosexual" skin of *Earnest*. That, quite literally, his dirty linen should be "well-aired" in court he had already anticipated in this deleted arrest scene, which I have only begun to discuss here. Conversely and symmetrically, the extensive newspaper coverage of April–May 1895 would guarantee the dissemination of Lady Bracknell's also deleted line: a (somewhat expurgated) narrative of his "ejaculation[s]" would indeed reach respectable English "ears more than once." But there is nothing uncanny in any of this. No mere prognosticator foretelling the doom that was about to settle around him, Wilde was instead a prevaricator of genius, a polymath of the pleasurable lie. As a person committed to homosexual practice, he was compelled *by law* to inhabit the oscillating and nonidentical identity structure of "Parker and Gribsby, Solicitors": a structure in which transgression and law, homosexual delight and its arrest, are produced and reproduced and interlocked versions and inversions of each other.

Writing from this ambivalent and endangered position, Wilde stated with a parodist's clarity and a criminal's obscurity that the importance of being was neither X nor Y, male nor female, homosexual nor heterosexual, Parker nor Gribsby, Jack nor Ernest. Being will not be disclosed by the descent of an apt and singular signifier, a proper name naturally congruent with the object it seeks to denominate. In contrast to H. C.'s essentialist move, Wilde never heralds "a true inversion" that "respond[s] finally to a stimulus strong

9. Wilde, *Letters*, 749. *Conversation* is itself a pun, referring doubly to interlocution and intercourse.

and prolonged enough, as a man awakens when he is loudly called." Belying such notions of true being, Wilde suggests instead that identity has always already been mislaid somewhere between such culturally "productive" binarisms as those listed above. Homosexual or heterosexual? Parker or Gribsby? Jack or Ernest? Which name should be "loudly called"? "I am both, sir." (Both indeed, and therefore not quite either: Wilde emphatically does *not* imply recourse to the compromise formation of bisexuality or, in Ellis's telling contemporaneous phrase, "psychosexual hermaphroditism"; for this formation leaves undisturbed the conveniently bifurcated gender assumptions that it only seemingly fuses. The component desires that, when added together, comprise the "bi" remain after all quite distinct: shot with the masculine *or* feminine through and through.) Wildean doubling indicates instead a strategy of lexical or nominal traversal, a skidding within the code and between its semantic poles. In this vertiginous shuttle, being itself must slip on a name, or two. "But what own are you?" Gwen astutely asks of Jack just as he is about to become Ernest John. "What is your Christian name, now that you have become someone else?" [57].

IV

I love the last words of anything: the end of art is the beginning.
                                                        —Oscar Wilde

Child! You seem to me to use words without understanding their proper meaning.
                              —Jack to Cecily in the four-act *Earnest*

In lieu of "serious" closure, and as if to deride even the possibility of formal solution to the fugitivity of Bunburying desire, Wilde terminates his play, farcically and famously, with an impudent iteration of his farce's "trivial" but crucial pun; here, finally, "the confusion of tongues is no longer a punishment."[1] For *Earnest* may close only when Jack, in a sly parody of tragic *anagnorisis*, "realizes for the first time in [his] life the vital Importance of Being Earnest." At this moment, as the last words of the play swallow the first words of its title, its origin therefore dutifully assimilated to its terminus, Jack "realizes" himself in and as his "own" *double entendre*: in and as, that is, the difference between 1) himself and himself and 2) himself and the symbolic system that seeks to determine his "proper" name. Jack's punning "being," such as it is, is thus located and dislocated—located *as* dislocated—in an experience of radical *méconnaissance*, of verbal and ontological slippage, that in turn fortifies his already supercharged "perception of the extrava-

1. Barthes, *Pleasure*, 4.

gance of the signifier."[2] As he celebrates the "vital importance" of being his own pun, so does Jack embrace, even as he is embraced by, the signifier's power of perverse subsumption—by the delight it gives and takes as it incorporates "deviant" vectors under its nominally proper head.

This extravagance constitutes both the subject and the subjectivity of the play, their very sound and sense; the plot is so devised that the play closes only when Jack's "being" is absurdly assimilated to his, or rather his father's, name, a requirement that enables Wilde both to acknowledge and to deride the oedipal force of prior inscriptions. In response to the pseudo-urgent question of Jack's identity ("Lady Bracknell, I hate to seem inquisitive, but would you kindly inform me who I am?") [57], the play dutifully answers with the Name of the Father, but in doing so also insistently repeats its insistence upon the letter; in its expiring breath *Earnest* resounds with Jack's other double name and so closes with an openness to what Jonathan Culler calls "the call of the phoneme." Invoking the materiality of sound and its powers of startling conjunction, the pun's "echoes tell of wild realms beyond the [semantic] code and suggest new configurations of meaning."[3] In such wild realms, the pleasures of the homophone arrive just as the differentiae of the hetero dissolve into sound and same. Culler continues:

> Puns, like portmanteaux, limn for us a model of language where the word is derived rather than primary and combinations of letters suggest meanings while at the same time illustrating the instability of meanings, their as yet ungrasped or undefined relations to one another, relations which further discourse (further play of similarity and difference) can produce. When one thinks of how puns characteristically demonstrate the applicability of a single signifying sequence to two different contexts, with quite different meanings, one can see how puns both evoke prior formulations, with the meanings they have deployed, and demonstrate their instability, the mutability of meaning, the production of meaning by linguistic motivation. Puns present us with a model of language as phonemes or letters combining in various ways to evoke prior meaning and to produce effects of meaning—with a looseness, unpredictability, excessiveness, shall we say, that cannot but disrupt the model of language as nomenclature.[4]

Culler here efficiently formulates the duplicitous operations by which the pun opens in language a counterhegemonic or revision-

2. Ibid., 65.
3. Jonathan Culler, "The Call of the Phoneme," in Culler, ed., *On Puns: The Foundation of Letters* (New York, 1988), 3.
4. Ibid., 14.

ary space, a plastic site in which received meanings ("language as nomenclature") may be perversely turned, strangely combined, or even emptied out. Because they "both evoke prior formulations, with the meanings they have deployed, and demonstrate their instability, the mutability of meaning," puns discover in prior formulations the horizon of a fresh possibility. As a figure that itself limns the liminal, sporting on the hazy border where tongues of sound and sense intermingle as in a kiss, the pun broadcasts a faintly scandalous erotic power, a power of phonemic blending and semantic bending, whose feinting extensions Reason always does its best to reign in; as when, for instance, Samuel Johnson famously quibbles with punning Shakespeare:

> A quibble is the golden apple for which he will always turn aside from his career, or stoop from his elevation. A quibble, poor and barren as it is, gave him such delight, that he was content to purchase it by the sacrifice or reason, propriety, and truth. A quibble was to him the fatal *Cleopatra* for which he lost the world, and was content to lose it.[5]

Wilde's genius implicitly submits Johnson's critique to a dizzying inversion. Earnestly "sacrific[ing] reason, propriety, and truth," Wilde works his trade, transcoding golden apples into cucumber sandwiches and fatal Cleopatra into vital Ernest. (Indeed, gender transposition of the objects of male desire was Wilde's characteristic mode of gay figuration: "I do not interest myself in that British view of morals that sets Messalina above Sporus.")[6]

But it was not against just any gendered signifier that Wilde directed the splaying call of the phoneme. He expressly targets the most overdetermined of such signifiers—the Name of the Father, here Ernest John Moncrieff—upon whose lips (if we may borrow a figure from the good Canon Chasuble) a whole cultural disposition is hung: the distribution of women and (as) property, the heterosexist configuration of eros, the genealogy of the "legitimate" male subject, and so on. Closing with a farcical pun on the father's name, Wilde discloses, in a single double stroke, the ironic cathexis (and the sometimes murderous double binding) by which the homosexual possibility is formally terminated or "exploded" ("Oh," says Algy "airily," "I killed Bunbury this afternoon") [49] in order that a familiar heterosexualizing machinery may be installed, axiomatically and absurdly, "at last." So decisive is the descent of the father's name, so swift its powers of compulsion and organization, that (at least seemingly) it subdues the oscillations of identity,

5. Samuel Johnson, "Preface to Shakespeare," in *Poetry and Prose*, ed. Mona Wilson (London, 1970), 500; quoted in Culler, "Call of the Phoneme," 6–7.
6. Wilde, *Letters*, 594.

straightens the byways of desire, and completes—*voilà!*—the marital teleology of the comic text. All three couples, "after all," are swept away ("At last!" "At last!") in the heady and "natural" rush toward presumptive conjugal bliss: a rush so heady that it peremptorily dismisses, for instance, both Cecily's exigent desire for an "Ernest" and Algy's own earlier caution against the exclusionary erotics of heterosexist integration: "Nothing will induce me to part with Bunbury, and if you [i.e., Jack] ever get married, which seems to me extremely problematic, you will be very glad to know Bunbury. A man who marries without knowing Bunbury has a very tedious time of it" [12]. Forgetting this brief dissertation on interminable Bunburyism, Algy fairly leaps toward marriage, thereby fulfilling, as if by amnesia, the comic topos which dictates that marital conjunction, or its proleptic image, shall close the otherwise open circuits of desire.

And yet the closural efficacy of this compulsory heterosexual sweep, especially any gesture it might make in the direction of the "natural" ("I mean it naturally is Ernest [58]," as Jack assures Gwen), is rendered instantly absurd—or, as Algy puts it, "extremely problematic"—by, first, its hypertrophic textuality and, second, by Wilde's insistence upon both the sovereignity of the signifier over its signified and the signifier's "liability" to indiscreet slippage, its exorbitant appetite for signifieds. Not only must Jack seek his "natural" or "proper" identity in an antic succession of texts (he "*rushes to bookcase and tears the books out*" [58], reads the stage direction), but in an earlier version this scene of frantic reading had included, besides "the Army Lists of the last forty years," an allusion to Robert Hichens's *The Green Carnation* (1894), a contemporaneous parody of Wilde's affair with Douglas.[7] Perusing this text from her unimpeachable altitude, Lady Bracknell emits an evaluation: "This treatise, the 'Green Carnation,' as I see it is called, seems to be a book about the culture of exotics. It contains no reference to Generals in it. It seems a morbid and middle-class affair."[8] After this and other preposterous citations (Canon Chasuble, for instance, is handed a Bradshaw railway guide "of 1869, I observe"), it is of course the book with the "reference to Generals in it" that brings home the prize and so surprises Jack with his now naturally punning self.

In any case, the paternally sanctioned "being" that Jack's reading hereby secures entails a literal reinscription of the same pseudo-opposition (*Jack* versus *Ernest* or *Ernest John*) under which his double life had all along been conducted, except that the order of the

---

7. Robert Hichens's travesty of the Wilde-Douglas affair was originally published anonymously (London, 1894); for Wilde's bemused response to *The Green Carnation*, see *Letters*, 373.

8. Dickson, *Earnest*, vol. 2, facsimile typescript of act 4, p. 34; also Berggren, *Earnest*, 190.

terms has been inverted: where cognomen was, there pseudonym shall be. In this inversion, the closural move that would repair Jack's splayed identity and terminate the shuttle and slide of Bunburying desire discloses again, discloses "at last," neither the deep truth of essential being nor the foundational monad of a "real" sexuality. In contrast, for instance, to the memoirs of H. C., whose sexual identity is definitively secured once he is "loudly called" by his "true inversion," *Earnest* deploys inversion as a tropological machine, as a mode of erotic mobility, evasion, play. Hence Wilde terminates his farce with terminological play on the terms-in-us: with a punning recognition of, on the one hand, the determinative force of prior inscriptions and, on the other, the transvaluing power of substitution. Thus *Earnest* does not terminate at all but insistently relays and repeats the irreducible oscillations, back and forth, froth and buck, of very much the same erotic binarism that would soon be definitely consolidated in the violent counterframing of homo- and heterosexualities (two terms that, by the way, appear nowhere in Wilde's lexicon).

But Wilde's is a crucial, a crux-making, repetition—crucial not merely because he deploys repetition to *make* a difference, but also because the difference he makes he then *makes audible* in and as the disseminal excess with which he laves his pun, and through his pun, his audience, his readers. At once titular and closural, originary and terminal, Wilde's pun practices the erotics of repetition that Barthes, collating Sade and Freud, would later theorize so compactly: "Repetition itself creates bliss . . . to repeat excessively is to enter into loss, into the zero of the signified."[9] Because in *Earnest* the object of this zero targeting, the site of this obsessional emptying, is nothing less than the marriageable male subject (let us say, anachronistically, the integral and heterosexual male subject) whose strength and legitimacy are sanctioned by the frail transmissibility of his father's empowering names, Wilde effectively empties both name and subject of their natural content and naturalizing force. In doing so he reopens *within both* an erotic space that had been prematurely closed—foreclosed, precisely, as *non nominandum*.

Wilde opens this space through a subtle dilation upon the irreducibly ambivalent erotics of the pun. On the semantic level, puns work precisely because they presuppose and reaffirm a *received difference* between (at least) two objects, concepts, or meanings; "evok[ing] prior formulations, with the meanings they have deployed" (Culler), puns operate as the semantic conservators of the hetero; in this sense, they police the borders of difference. (It is, for

9. Barthes, *Pleasure*, 41.

instance, only because *ejaculation* may mean abruptly emitted speech that Lady Bracknell may properly ejaculate on the subject of ejaculations.) But on the phonemic level this work of differentiation is quite undone. When referred to the ear, to the waiting body of the reader/listener, punning becomes homoerotic because homophonic. Aurally enacting a drive toward the same, the pun's sound cunningly erases, or momentarily suspends, the semantic differences by which the hetero is both made to appear and made to appear natural, lucid, self-evident. Difference is repeated until difference vanishes in the ear. (The ejaculation, Lady Bracknell is right to insist, "*has* reached [our] ears more than once"; repetition guarantees a certain saturation.) And when differences vanishes the result is a correlative plosion at the mouth, the peal of laughter marking precisely the vanishing point at which good sense collapses into melting pleasure, or even bliss. This explains in part the distaste with which a homophobic critical tradition has regarded puns, an affect usually attributed to the "cheapness" of the thrills they so dearly provide. (In and out of school, it seems, serious pleasure requires still harder exactions.) No surprise, then, that heterocentric culture should disdain the linguistic process by which the very power of the hetero—the power to differentiate among signifieds, objects, beings—is, on the phonemic level at least, so laughingly disdained.

Understanding all of this precisely, Wilde harnessed the erotic ambivalence of the pun for the affined purposes of pleasure, transvaluation, critique. "I am sending you, of course, a copy of my book," Wilde wrote to a friend in 1899 after Sebastian Melmoth had received copies of *Earnest*'s first pressings. "How I used to toy with that tiger Life! I hope you will find a place for me amongst your nicest books. . . . I should like it to be within speaking distance of *Dorian Gray*."[1] "Amongst your nicest books" but still "within speaking distance of *Dorian Gray*": this ironic juxtaposition very nicely glosses the urbane duplicity with which Wilde insinuated the revisionary discourse of an "Urning"—the term of gay self-reference devised by Karl Heinrich Ulrichs some thirty years before, a term of which Wilde was very well aware—into his critical pun on Earnest, and through this pun, into the "nicest" of his texts. The intrinsic cross-switching within the pun of hetero- and homosexualizing impulses provided Wilde with the perfect instrument for negotiating an impossibly difficult discursive situation. Writing "at large" for a respectably straight (not to say heterosexist) audience whose sensibilities he could afford to tease but not transgress, Wilde necessarily penned to a double measure. While mimicking

1. Wilde, *Letters*, 778.

the dramatic conventions of heterosexual triumph, he inserted within them the "unspeakable" traces of homosexual delight: inserted them where they would be least welcome—in the vocables of the paternal signifier, itself the guarantor of heterophallic order. The *Urning*, to put it wildly, would hide in *Ernest*, thereby punburying and Bunburying at the same time. ("Everything," Derrida says, "comes down to the ear you hear me with.")[2]

Of course, as Wilde insisted, his titular pun is "trivial," and it is so in the technical, etymological—and punning—sense of the word. *Trivial* not only marks what is "common," "ordinary," and "of small account" but indicates as well a crossroads or terminus "placed where three roads meet" (*OED*).[3] Etymologically speaking, the trivial is the locus of a common or everyday convergence: a site where paths (of meaning, of motion, of identity) cross and switch, a pivot in which vectors (and babies) enter in one direction and exit in another. The text represents this notion in two ways: materially and mechanically, in Victoria Station, the terminus where the "romantic story of [Jack's] origins" begins, where with a little help from Miss Prism (whose name, by the way, refracts an ocular version of the same idea) baby Jack enters as Ernest and exits as John; and, audibly and obsessively, in the pun on *e(a)rnest*, which operates exactly in the manner of a railway terminal. There should now be no difficulty in specifying the three paths that cross and merge here to such preposterous effect: 1) a plain and proper name (ultimately disclosed as the Name of the Father) that, for obscure reasons, "produces vibrations"; 2) the esteemed high Victorian quality of moral earnestness, of serious fidelity to truth, an attribute specifically gendered as "manly" and repeatedly derided by Wilde; 3) a pun-buried and coded allusion (and here two tongues, German and English, mingle) to a specifically homosexual thematics, to the practices and discourses of the "Urning" and of "Uranian love." (That Wilde was familiar with the specialized vocabulary of the "Urning" is beyond dispute: "A patriot put in prison for loving his country loves his country, and a poet put in prison for loving boys loves boys. To have altered my life would have been to have admitted that Uranian love is ignoble. I hold it to be noble—more noble

2. Jacques Derrida, "Otobiographies: The Teaching of Nietzsche and the Politics of the Proper Name," in *The Ear of the Other*, ed. Christie McDonald (Lincoln, Neb., 1988), 4.

3. The pun thus also slyly alludes to our culture's paradigmatic instance of "trivial" meeting: the terminal convergence of father and son at the crossroads called Phokis, where Oedipus meets his father and his fate. "If I understand you," says a darkening Oedipus to his mother Jocasta, "Laios was killed / At a place where three roads meet." Trivial indeed. Against the background of these tragic resonances, we may read Wilde's earnest *and* trivial pun as a gay countersign to the murderous seriousness of oedipal heterosexuality; Sophocles, *Oedipus Rex*, trans. Dudley Fitts and Robert Fitzgerald (New York, 1969), 37.

than other forms.")[4] In this laughing inversion of propriety and authority, Wilde puts the intrinsically homophilic impulse of the pun (its drive, at the phonemic level, toward the erasure of difference) to historically specific uses; not until the 1890s would the term *Urning* have been sufficiently diffused into English to operate within Wilde's punning trivium.[5]

Thus submitting his play to the delirium of the signifier, Wilde

---

4. Wilde, *Letters*, 705.

5. It is crucial to note here that the *Ernest/Earnest/Urning* pun did not originate with Wilde; it made its literary debut two years before Wilde began work on *Earnest*, and Wilde stole—or, as literary critics like to say, "appropriated"—the pun for the transvaluing purposes of his own genius. More than a merely private joke, the wordplay first appeared in a volume of poetry called *Love in Earnest* (London, 1892) by the Uranian writer John Gambril Nicholson. A collection of sonnets, ballads, and lyrics, *Love in Earnest* included a poem of pederastic devotion entitled "Of Boys' Names":

> Old memories of the Table Round
>   In Percival and Lancelot dwell,
> Clement and Bernard bring the sound
>   Of anthems in the cloister-cell,
>   And Leonard vies with Lionel
> In stately step and kingly frame,
>   And Kenneth speaks of field and fell,
> And Ernest sets my heart a-flame.
>
> One name can make my pulses bound,
>   No peer it owns, nor parallel,
> By it is Vivian's sweetness drowned,
>   And Roland, full as organ-swell;
>   Though Frank may ring like silver bell,
> And Cecil softer music claim,
>   They cannot work the miracle,—
> 'Tis Ernest sets my heart a-flame.
>
> Cyril is lordly, Stephen crowned
>   With deathless wreaths of asphodel,
> Oliver whispers peace profound,
>   Herbert takes arms his foes to quell,
>   Eustace with sheaves is laden well,
> Christopher has a nobler fame,
>   And Michael storms the gates of Hell,
> But Ernest sets my heart a-flame.
>
>   ENVOY
> My little Prince, Love's mystic spell
>   Lights all the letters of your name,
> And you, if no one else, can tell
> Why Ernest sets my heart a-flame.

Quoted from Timothy d'Arch Smith, *Love in Earnest* (London, 1970), xviii; Smith's book, a study of the Uranian poets, derives its title from Nicholson's.

Nicholson's book did not go unnoticed among gay readers and interlocutors. I think it self-evident that Wilde knew of it; the joke quoted above about "those chaps, the minor poets [who] are never even quoted" is likely Wilde's oblique acknowledgement of Nicholson's priority, although no doubt Wilde would have happily expatiated upon the (merely belated) originality of his own deployment of the pun. And certainly John Addington Symonds, who died a year *before* Wilde began composing his farce, caught the pun's gay valence. In a letter of 2 July 1892 Symonds wrote to a friend: "Have you read a volume of sonnets called 'Love in Earnest'? It is written by a Schoolmaster in love with a boy called Ernest." That "Wilde's" pun predates his own use of it would thus seem incontrovertible.

manages to achieve what Barthes would later call *subtle subversion*, by which he means that which "is not directly concerned with destruction, evades the paradigm, and seeks some *other* term: a third term, which is not, however, a synthesizing term but an eccentric, extraordinary term."[6] In *The Importance of Being Earnest*, I am arguing, Wilde invents just such an extraordinary term: a third, ternary, and trivial term in which oppositional meanings are not synthesized or sublated so much as they are exchanged, accelerated, derailed, terminated, cross-switched. Indeed, he invents this term twice over, invents it in duplicate, so that it emerges only under alias, submitted to an originary masquerade of two farcical pseudonyms. The first of these is Bunbury, the second is Ernest John. The interchangeability of these two terms (in exile Wilde even referred to *Earnest* as *Bunbury*) suggests an irreducible isomorphism between the technically unspeakable homoerotics of interminable Bunburyism and the structural bifurcation of the nominally heterosexual male subject, a point upon which Algy exuberantly insists when he explains to Jack why "I was quite right in saying you were a Bunburyist": "You have invented a very useful younger brother called Ernest, in order that you may be able to come up to town as often as you like. I have invented an invaluable permanent invalid called Bunbury, in order that I may be able to go down into the country whenever I choose. Bunbury is perfectly invaluable" [11]. In the four-act version Algy is even more concise; responding to Cecily's claim that Uncle Jack "has got such strict principles about everything. He is not like you," Algy disagrees: "Oh. I am bound to say that I think Jack and I are very like each other. I really do not see much difference between us."[7] Given this invincible parallelism, and the obviously reversible erotics of "coming up" and "going down," Jack fully qualifies as "one of the most advanced Bunburyists I know."

And yet we recall that the hetero-closure of the plot is predicated upon the formal expulsion of Bunbury, who is consequently "quite exploded" at play's end. But even as Bunbury is eliminated from the text, his (non)being thereby formally remanded to the closet from which at least his name had emerged, so also is he posthumously disseminated into the redoubled being of Wilde's earnest hero, in whose equivocal name Bunbury may be said to succeed his own surcease. Passing away only to be passed on, Bunbury is buried, and buried alive, within the duplicitous precincts of the titularly "natural" male subject. With this irreducibly ambivalent movement—partly homicidal, partly carceral, partly liberatory—Wilde

6. Barthes, *Pleasure*, 51.
7. Dickson, *Earnest*, 1:111.

closes his great farce, submitting to the heterocentric conventions that his pun thereafter continues to exceed and deride. That pun, with its gay shuttling, constitutes Wilde's bequest to a posterity that is only now learning how to receive so rare a gift: one whose power of posthumous critique is conveyed in and as an excess of signification, pleasure, even bliss. In *Earnest*, this excess is never laid to rest. Not every explosion, however terminal, implies a death. In Bunbury's end is Ernest John's beginning.

V

None of us survive[s] culture.

—Oscar Wilde[8]

It is one of the bleaker ironies of English literary history that even as *Earnest* was brashly delighting audiences at the St. James' Theatre, where it had opened on 14 February 1895, its author would be subjected to a fierce and dogged institutional "correction," the prosecution of the famous trials of 1895. For a brief time (from 5 April when Wilde was arrested for "acts of gross indecency with another male person," until 8 May when George Alexander was compelled by public opinion to remove *Earnest* from the boards), the two spectacles ran concurrently: the one all blithe insouciance, the other pure bourgeois retribution; the one a triumph of evanescent, if not quite indeterminate, signification, the other a brutal travesty in which the author would be nailed to his "acts." So juxtaposed, the two spectacles compose an almost too ready diptych of crime and punishment, as in Auden's "nightmare Pantomime Transformation Scene in which . . . the country house in never-never Hertfordshire turns into the Old Bailey, the features of Lady Bracknell into those of Mr. Justice Wills." The very facility of these transposition—Auden's and my own—suggests the volatile reversibility of the sexual and verbal inversions that Wilde delighted in practicing and perfecting. Precariously ambivalent, Wildean pleasure had always flirted with its own disciplinary relapse, a danger that no doubt honeyed the already honed edge of Wilde's enjoyment. The advent of the trials marked an implacable shift to an institutional context in which the warm lubricities of interminable Bunburyism would be frozen less by the cold face of Gradgrindian fact than by the chilling implementation of a legal, a statutory, homophobia. This defines the difference between Wildean courage and the ease of a critic who may with impunity celebrate Bunbury at the cool distance of a hundred years. Wilde *took chances*, and Wilde paid. Neither the least nor the last of his humiliations came

8. Wilde, *Letters*, 774.

in his second year of incarceration, when his wife Constance successfully petitioned to deprive him of guardianship of his sons, Cyril and Vyvyan, and to change their surnames (along with her own) to her maiden name of Holland.[9] This irony bites. As if to chastise Wilde for trifling with the patronym in *Earnest*, the state rescinded his right to propagate the Name of the Father.[1]

MICHAEL PATRICK GILLESPIE

From Beau Brummell to Lady Bracknell: Re-viewing the Dandy in *The Importance of Being Earnest*†

Despite the sense of extravagant and exuberant ambiguity that informs the dialogue of *The Importance of Being Earnest*, readings of the play have too often tended to blend restraint and detachment to distill a tame essence of Wilde. Even among the more recent interpretive approaches (such as cultural critiques that concentrate on the ideological consequences of the influence of extratextual elements) there exists a disposition to limit the scope of inquiry by giving primacy to the exposition of a single theme. Happily, less programmatic readers, such as Kerry Powell, have moved toward a position that sees Wilde's drama as an artifact existing within society and, in that respect, amalgamated into the dominant culture.[1] I would like to elaborate upon Powell's position to explore the way that context enhances the play's multiplicity. Specifically, I believe that to develop a full aesthetic appreciation of *The Importance of Being Earnest*, one must follow the same hypostatic interpretive approach that facilitates our understanding of Wilde's earlier works: seeing the play as supported by social and artistic ambiance yet maintaining a good measure of its own integrity.

As it does in Wilde's other writings, the pluralism within *The Importance of Being Earnest* manifests itself through the personalities of its diverse characters rather than its plot. Watching these men and women replicate patterns of behavior that one finds elsewhere in Wilde's canon, one begins to derive meaning through a variety of

---

9. H. Montgomery Hyde, *Oscar Wilde* (New York, 1975), 333.
1. I am happy to acknowledge the influence and assistance of the following persons who helped along the way: Stephen Booth, Ed Cohen, Joel Fineman, Catherine Gallagher, Wayne Koestenbaum, D. A. Miller, and Alex Zwerdling. This essay is dedicated to the memory of Joel Fineman, in whose work I discovered the baffled origins of my own thinking on Wilde.
† From *Oscar Wilde and the Poetics of Ambiguity* (Gainesville, FL, 1996), 115–32. Reprinted with permission of the University Press of Florida. Bracketed page numbers refer to this Norton Critical Edition.
1. Kerry Powell, *Oscar Wilde and the Theatre of the 1890s* (Cambridge: UP, 1990), 108–39.

analogues. Like Dorian Gray, Lord Arthur Savile, and countless other characters in Wilde's writings, individuals in *The Importance of Being Earnest* do not wish to make the exclusionary choices that would commit them to one established mode of living over another. Rather, each of the central figures in this play cultivates multiplicity with an almost punctilious determination that calls to mind one of the most prominent archetypes of the age—the dandy.

By the 1890s, the term had acquired an anachronistic aura. Nonetheless, Wilde's evocation of the dandy's milieu seems unmistakable, for it recurs in scene after scene of *The Importance of Being Earnest* as Wilde's characters display the same degree of canniness that made the dandy such a significant social force earlier in the century. Time and again, individuals in the play neither completely submit to the authority of public institutions nor irreversibly defy society's jurisdiction. In this fashion, their behavior precisely replicates the protocols of the archetypal dandy's life: To gain attention—a central aim for the dandy—he must disrupt the normal pattern of events. At the same time, to sustain public approval—an equally important goal—he must keep his transgressions within the bounds of communal tolerance. Thus, while acknowledging the coercive power and the definitive linearity of the dominant social institutions of the period, the dandy forgoes complete conformity and actively cultivates the digressive relativity of pluralism. Although he embraces the most radical forms of self-indulgence, the dandy in general (and Wilde's version in particular) assiduously offers nominal submission to principles of public respectability.

This last feature stands as an important aspect of the dandy's nature, yet it gets ignored in stereotypical depictions of the figure that relegate the dandy to the role of social rebel. Dandies do not in fact act as iconoclasts. Rather, they serve as mediators between independence and conformity. In this way, they secure both the indulgence and the protection of society. Understanding this delineation of the role of the dandy greatly enhances the reader's capability for appreciating *The Importance of Being Earnest*, for it provides a crucial guide for tracing the full range of aesthetic and artistic parameters of intellectually satisfying responses to Wilde's last play.

For a full comprehension of this model, one needs not only to review the evolution of the historical dandy over the course of the nineteenth century but also to trace its artistic antecedents to understand the pattern of connotations that readers generally associate with the figure. One finds evidence of dandiacal behavior in literature as old as *The Iliad* and *The Odyssey*, and clear adumbrations of the dandy appear in Shakespeare and the picaros and cavaliers of the sixteenth and seventeenth centuries. It is the

Restoration stage, however, that heralds the dandy's first fully articulated representation—in characters created by playwrights such as Wycherley and Etherege; and from this initial appearance onward, the concept of balance always conditions depictions of the dandy's antecedents.

Consequently, although theatrical rakes such as Horner and Dorimant display enormous capacities for vicious, self-gratifying behavior, they also show a reluctance to make any direct break with society. From the early eighteenth-century beaux of Congreve and Farquhar to the later manifestations of Goldsmith and Sheridan, additional modifications occur. The beaux come to represent licentious men open to the reforming influence of virtuous, clever, and beautiful women. Despite the marked diminution in their predatory attitudes, even these late-century figures remain characterized by singular, narrow, monologic forms of action; and those traits form the reader's expectations for the analogous figures that followed.

Ellen Moers's examination of dandiacal behavior in England and on the Continent during the nineteenth century offers a valuable alternative to these either/or perceptions. Her complex and rewarding study of the social and literary evolution of the dandy convincingly shows that his existence depends on not so much a determination to place himself in conflict with society's values but an ability to stretch the limits of public tolerance and sidestep the censure of those who see him as someone whose behavior threatens to subvert established communal strictures.[2] Moers's analysis attacks the validity of reductive assumptions of the dandy as iconoclast and instead leads us toward a far more complex alternative perspective: Through its fascination with his behavior, in tacit or open approval, society incessantly affirms and defines the dandy.

Moers's chapter on the rise and fall of Beau Brummell provides a striking illustration of the coercive power of this relationship, and it offers a useful paradigm for understanding that complex and volatile association. As long as his actions—licit or otherwise—remain sanctioned by society, Brummell can maintain his position as a dandy and his influence as an arbiter of taste. Ultimately, when events spur the public to withdraw its approval, all this changes: In Brummell's case his fall from favor with the Prince of Wales leads

2. Published in 1960, Ellen Moers's *The Dandy: Beau Brummell to Beerbohm* (Lincoln, 1960) remains the most intellectually sophisticated work on the topic. Eve Kosofsky Sedgwick offers a near-antithetical delineation of the dandiacal impulse in *Epistemology of the Closet* (Berkeley, 1990). To my mind, however, the heavy-handed sexual polemics of Sedgwick's approach relies upon stereotypes to reinscribe the either/or perspective that dandyism itself disdains. Other useful studies appear in Regenia Gagnier, *Idylls of the Marketplace: Oscar Wilde and the Victorian Public* (Stanford, 1986), 51–59; Richard D. Altick, *The Presence of the Present: Topics of the Day in the Victorian Novel* (Columbus, 1991); and Rosalind H. Williams, *Dream Worlds: Mass Consumption in Late Nineteenth-Century France* (Berkeley, 1982), 111–26.

literally to a loss of credit among fashionable merchants. He is forced to flee England, giving up his status and any pretense of swaying popular opinion. As one sees from analogous accounts of the lives of Count D'Orsay, Dickens, Beerbohm, and others, Brummell's experiences delineate a paradox that governs all dandies and appears specifically illustrated in the behavior of Wilde's characters: One can sustain dandiacal notoriety by giving the appearance of living outside the power of public restraint as long as one does not in fact attempt to make appearance reality.

Lord Henry Wotton articulates this code to Dorian in dazzling detail in the opening chapters of *The Picture of Dorian Gray* when he seeks to educate the young man on the proper forms of behavior in society. Harry's remarks set him off as the fin de siècle equivalent of the dandy (although the term itself is far too vulgar for the fastidious Lord Henry to use). He sustains himself through dualities and functions in a mode that resists the impulse to displace pluralism for hierarchical homogeneity. I do not mean to say that Lord Henry or any of Wilde's other dandies embrace anarchy; rather, they inhabit a world of such formalized artifice that even in their apparently defiant behavior they manage to accommodate the rhythms of society.

As attested by the rise and fall of characters throughout *The Picture of Dorian Gray*, all skilled participants in these interchanges know precisely how far one can go. Only the uninitiated mistake the dandy for the renegade, for only the uninitiated remain unaware of the dandy's utter dependence upon society. Late in the novel, in a statement heavily tinged with unconscious irony, Lord Henry reminds Dorian of just this fact when he subtly outlines the boundaries that mark the limits of dandiacal behavior: "All crime is vulgar, just as all vulgarity is crime."[3]

True dandies know quite well the difference between the sensational, which opens possibilities for a range of responses, and the vulgar, which closes down all reactions but one. They thrive upon their ability to create and then control anomalies: capturing people's interest by inviting imaginative responses to actions or behavior but never allowing reactions to fall into antagonistic postures. Such a position repeatedly skirts the margin between pluralism and parody, but that very condition, in my view, only increases its attraction for readers seeking to draw from *The Importance of Being Earnest* as much pleasure as Wilde imbued in his discourse.

Although no one in the play ever uses the term (presumably, like Lord Henry, they would find it far too common a label), time and again characters in *The Importance of Being Earnest* consciously

3. *The Picture of Dorian Gray*: A Norton Critical Edition, ed. Donald L. Lawler (New York, 1988), 162.

employ the dandy's conflicting impulses toward isolation and amal-gamation in a witty modification of the conventions of melodrama. Through these gestures characters articulate programs of hedonism that rival any in *The Picture of Dorian Gray*, but in doing so they adopt comic rather than tragic postures. Further, just as Wilde's novel eschews the conventions of a contemporary morality tale, the norms of the play skirt those that give structure to the typical melo-drama.

Paradox, the first step toward the cultivation of ambiguity, in-forms the action of *The Importance of Being Earnest*; but the antin-omies of this play go well beyond the inversions and the dualities of popular plays such as *Charley's Aunt*, *The New Boy*, and *The Foundling*.[4] Indeed, unlike these works, Wilde's drama deftly avoids the prescriptive redemption motifs inherited from eighteenth-century dramas. Contravening conventional expectations, the plot does not turn upon bringing the dandiacal behavior of Jack and Algy into conformity with the rest of society. Rather, it involves a far more complex and witty project: convincing the two young men to abandon their asocial resistance to a pattern of dandiacal behav-ior that the others have already embraced.

To accomplish this, *The Importance of Being Earnest* initially plays upon stereotypical expectations, representing Jack and Algy in the simplistic modes of old-fashioned beaux. For most of the play they evince a singular determination to move between alternative lives either inside or outside the bounds of society, with Jack's Ernest and Algy's Bunbury giving each the means to do so. At the same time the other major characters—all of whom acknowledge their role as dandies in everything but the open use of the term—strive to convince Jack and Algy to cultivate an acceptance of the multiplicity more properly suited to dandiacal roles. This condition informs Lady Bracknell's impulse, late in the play, to take pains to remind Algy of both the benefits of comprehensive and the limita-tions of exclusionary thinking: "Never speak disrespectfully of Soci-ety, Algernon. Only people who can't get in do that" [51].

The reconfiguration of expectations that I am suggesting goes well beyond simply shaping the attitudes of the male leads. It ex-tends to the audience's fundamental interpretive reconsideration of the position of the dandy within the play. This involves overturning assumptions about the dandy's role as a figure functioning outside of society. Instead, one should delineate the dandy using the plural-istic terms characteristic of much of Wilde's writing: as one in a symbiotic relationship with the world that he or she inhabits. (An-other of Wilde's gestures to overturn conventional expectations in-

4. For a view of the parallels between these three works, see Powell, 119–20.

volves extending the role of dandy to women.) In *The Importance of Being Earnest*, as elsewhere, the true dandy provides society with a measure of excitement by skirting without ever seriously challenging its social codes. In return, society provides the dandy with a degree of protection from the consequences of his or her acts through a tolerance that does not inhibit the dandy's more flamboyant behavior.

This pluralistic image of the dandy, operating within the bounds of society and at the same time endeavoring to subvert some portion of its restrictions, addresses the concerns of critics who have sought ways to resist the premature closure of simplistic, linear options for reading. Kerry Powell, for example, uncomfortable with the thought that readers might take seriously the conventional ending of the play, rightly asserts that Jack and Algy steadfastly refuse to embrace the melodramatic practice of reconciling their behavior to that of the middle class and "do not succumb to any sudden or improbable conversion at the end. . . . Wilde's play concludes on the note of revolt with which it began, leaving its heroes in a state of clearheadedness which was unprecedented in such comedies."[5]

Powell's view of the unconventional ending of *The Importance of Being Earnest* offers a welcome break from deterministic assumptions about the drama's melodramatic affinities. At the same time, some might mistakenly assume that his reading reinforces the image of the two young men maintaining their integrity by remaining indifferent to societal pressures to conform. For those attuned to the full implications of Powell's approach, a definitive resolution of matters in such an either/or fashion ultimately proves unsatisfactory.

Algy and Jack come to embrace the both/and thinking that characterizes the play's dandies. They experience both a measure of enlightenment and a form of domestication while continuing to resist amalgamation into patterns of conventional Victorian life. Much of the action of the play revolves around their socialization, as other characters lead them to the realization that the true dandy, with the rich contradictions of pluralistic vision, represents the proper mode of behavior for them to adopt. In the final scene of the drama, each renounces the role of renegade that he has previously held and assumes the more ambivalent and hence more inclusive role of the dandy, joining the conventional structure of the melodrama with an innovative contextual variation.

Attentiveness to the operative role of the dandy has a significance that goes beyond a single work. A survey of the function of

---

5. Ibid., 139. Gagnier, on the other hand, represents a different attitude and evinces no such ambivalence. She believes that the play ends with the audience enlightened and the characters still very much in the dark. Compare *Idylls of the Marketplace*, 111.

the dandiacal character in the social dramas that Wilde wrote before composing *The Importance of Being Earnest* (*Lady Windermere's Fan*, *A Woman of No Importance*, and *An Ideal Husband*)
shows this depiction as inherently part of the structure of all these
plays. One traces repeated attempts to cultivate impressions of
dandies personifying the broad range of aesthetic attitudes that
provide the intellectual framework for artistic creation. While not
the sole or even necessarily the primary images functioning in the
earlier plays, these depictions of the dandy offer clear guidance for
interpretations of Wilde's dramatic canon. Such abbreviations of
metaphysical intent produce likenesses that offer an immediate en-
hancement of one's comprehension of the action. At the same time
Wilde's artistic modifications recast common assumptions to give a
far more complex constitution to the concepts that the dandy em-
bodies.

Admittedly, the structure of these plays encompasses more than
just Wilde's attempts to work out his representation of the dandy,
and it would be foolishly reductive to contend that everything that
preceded *The Importance of Being Earnest* served as a single-minded
effort to refine a technique that would be presented with consummate effectiveness in Wilde's final drama. (Powell's book clearly
demonstrates that a range of forces had a shaping influence upon
Wilde's process of composition, from "the specialized and self-
indulgent tastes of actor-managers" to the popular appetites of Victorian audiences.) Nonetheless, precisely because a complex interplay
of diverse intra- and extratextual features contributes to the formation of each of Wilde's plays, one needs a comprehensive yet man-
ageable method for tracing the artistic and aesthetic development
within each work. Representation of the dandy in these dramas can
form the basis for just such an approach.

Lady Windermere's Fan sketches Wilde's emerging comprehension
of the creative impact that comes out of manipulating archetypal expectations when minor male characters strive for distinction by attempting to display the wit of a Count D'Orsay. Unfortunately, these
individuals have only an imprecise sense of how the dandy figure
should function, which causes them to fall into an unconscious parody of the convention. Despite these shortcomings, the image of
the dandy hovering around the discourse delineates clearly the protocols governing their discursive behavior. The following exchange
in act 1 between the mercurial Cecil Graham and the turgid Lord
Augustus illustrates this point:

> CECIL GRAHAM   (*Bows to* LADY WINDERMERE, *passes over and
> shakes hands with* LORD WINDERMERE.) Good evening, Arthur.
> Why don't you ask me how I am? I like people to ask me how I
> am. It shows a wide-spread interest in my health. Now, tonight

I am not at all well. Been dining with my people. Wonder why it is one's people are always so tedious? My father would talk morality after dinner. I told him he was old enough to know better. But my experience is that as soon as people are old enough to know better, they don't know anything at all. Hullo, Tuppy! Hear you're going to be married again; thought you were tired of that game.

LORD AUGUSTUS You're excessively trivial, my dear boy, excessively trivial!

CECIL GRAHAM By the way, Tuppy, which is it? Have you been twice married and once divorced, or twice divorced and once married? I say you've been twice divorced and once married. It seems so much more probable.

LORD AUGUSTUS I have a very bad memory. I really don't remember which.[6]

Both Lord Augustus and Cecil Graham show an admirable defensive capability to use a clever remark to shift the direction of a conversation or deflect a stream of criticism, yet the linearity of their discourse enforces their inability to match the wit of a figure attuned to multiplicity. Neither has mastered the offhand languor of the practiced dandy, whose mere presence can dominate the action or direct the course of the dialogue. The true dandy would neither ignore the social criticism implicit in Graham's questions about divorce nor appear to accept Lord Augustus's insinuation that triviality stands as a flaw. Rather—as Lord Henry Wotton demonstrates throughout *The Picture of Dorian Gray*—the accomplished dandy always retains control of the discourse and its interpretations.

Elsewhere in *Lady Windermere's Fan*, in a more accurate evocation of the dandiacal temperament (presaging attitudes that Wilde will manifest with greater elaboration and diversity in the female leads of *The Importance of Being Earnest*), one finds this sort of control in the character of Mrs. Erlynne. She holds in equilibrium the dual features of the dandy's nature: a satirical view of Victorian foibles with an experienced respect for the power of public opinion that consistently emphasizes the value of form over content. In the final scene, answering Lord Windermere's inquiry about what course she will now follow, she declares her preference for appearance over commitment: "Repentance is quite out of date. And besides, if a woman really repents, she has to go to a bad dressmaker, otherwise no one believes in her. And nothing in the world would induce me to do that."[7]

Unlike the ideal dandy, Mrs. Erlynne bears the melodramatic

---

6. *The Complete Works of Oscar Wilde* (New York, n.d.), 15.
7. Ibid., 36.

burden, albeit "only once," of maternal concerns that compel her to privilege her daughter's reputation over her own. In the end she renounces these responsibilities, telling Lord Windermere that "[t]hey were terrible—they made me suffer—they made me suffer too much."[8] Nonetheless, this single deviation from a solipsistic preoccupation with self and her connection with society mars Mrs. Erlynne's evocation of the type and temporizes the distinctness of her character. (Even this lapse into sentimentalism, however, supports my basic thesis; for it evinces, admittedly in a fairly clumsy fashion, the monumental effort required to balance the dandy's tone somewhere between that of the conformist and that of the iconoclast.)

In subsequent works, the figure of the dandy continues to exert a pronounced influence on formal and contextual parameters of dramatic perception. It reappears in *A Woman of No Importance*—more elaborately delineated and more finely attuned to the nuances of its society—in the person of Lord Illingworth. Mrs. Allonby can also make a legitimate claim to that title.) Like Mrs. Erlynne's in *Lady Windermere's Fan*, Illingworth's discourse throughout *A Woman of No Importance* combines energy with amorality to enforce control over the world that he inhabits, not by defying its opinions but by deftly refining those attitudes to suit his own behavior. In the following exchange with Lady Stutfield, his remarks set him off as a far more formidable figure than fatuous males such as Cecil Graham or Lord Augustus because of his ability to manipulate social mores without straying beyond the limits of public tolerance.

> LADY STUTFIELD   The world says that Lord Illingworth is very, very wicked.
> LORD ILLINGWORTH   But what world says that, Lady Stutfield? It must be the next world. This world and I are on excellent terms. (*Sits down beside* MRS. ALLONBY.)
> LADY STUTFIELD   Every one *I* know says you are very, very wicked.
> LORD ILLINGWORTH   It is perfectly monstrous the way people go about, nowadays, saying things against one behind one's back that are absolutely and entirely true.[9]

As the example demonstrates, throughout most of the play Illingworth functions as a consummate dandy: He responds to the opinions of society, implicitly acknowledges the power of those views to inhibit his own behavior, yet diffuses their influence by reinterpreting them in a fashion that avoids conventional restraints and best displays his own wit.

8. Ibid.
9. Ibid., 49.

Even the cleverness of scenes like the one just quoted cannot overcome the destabilizing effect of theatrical clichés upon the delicate equilibrium that holds in dynamic tension the diverse impulses within the dandy's nature. Just as the plot demands of *Lady Windermere's Fan* make Mrs. Erlynne temporarily assume the role of the sentimental mother figure, the melodramatic features of *A Woman of No Importance* force a bifurcation of Illingworth's nature: For most of the play he charms the audience as a polished representation of the dandy. Then in the closing moments, he alternately chagrins and bores us as the papier-mâché villain—part superannuated seducer, part negligent father. Far from balancing complex attitudes, the polarity of this depiction oversimplifies the aesthetic effect. It splits our assessment of his nature through the imposition of exclusionary characterization and undermines the dandiacal brilliance and formidability built up by Illingworth in the opening stages of the play.

Wilde's efforts to refine his delineation of the dandy into the perfect evocation of the pluralistic response to social mores continue in his next play, *An Ideal Husband*. There the figure of the dandy, in the person of Viscount Goring, has become both tempered and restrained, less caustic, and burdened with moral probity not usually found among characters of this type.[1] An atavistic aura surrounds him, evoking images of the dandy's antecedents in the beaux of Goldsmith and Sheridan.

Goring's character nonetheless achieves a measure of success. While retaining the near-compulsive need, so apparent in the dandies of Wilde's earlier plays, to comment on the mores of society, Goring does so in a fashion that admits both a measure of self-deprecation and a degree of sympathy (often cloaked in irony) for conventional morality.

> That is the reason they are so pleased to find out other people's secrets. It distracts public attention from their own.
>
> * * * * *
>
> Personally I have a great admiration for stupidity. It is a sort of fellow-feeling, I suppose.
>
> * * * * *
>
> The English can't stand a man who is always saying he is in the right, but they are very fond of a man who admits that he has been in the wrong. It is one of the best things about them.
>
> * * * * *
>
> Oh, I should fancy Mrs Cheveley is one of those very modern women of our time who find a new scandal as becoming as a

---

1. John Stokes also touches upon this point in *Oscar Wilde* (London, 1978), 39–40.

new bonnet, and air them both in the Park every afternoon at five-thirty. I am sure she adores scandals, and that the sorrow of her life at present is that she can't manage to have enough of them.[2]

As it does with Goring's character, the plot draws upon conventions of eighteenth-century drama—embodied in plays such as *She Stoops to Conquer* and *The School for Scandal*—to structure its development. *An Ideal Husband* requires that Goring project the aura of an honorable and idealistic man while retaining an urbanity and cleverness that allow him to deal with equal aplomb with characters as diverse as Mabel Chiltern and Mrs. Cheveley. His combination of the personalities of a wit and a paragon comes close formally if not contextually to delineating the ideal dandiacal position: encompassing a range of alternative roles within the secure boundaries of an established social system. Once again, however, the sensationalism of melodrama (in this case the eleventh-hour release of Chiltern from the threat of blackmail) blunts the viewer's imaginative process by interposing clichéd action in the midst of evocative characterization. These shortcomings nonetheless underscore the value of the dandy as a model for character analysis, fixing the play's imaginative parameters by illuminating the opportunities for greater development that it misses.

In Wilde's final play, the dandy loses all the inhibiting features of prescriptive typing: Wilde discards its gender- and generation-based limitations and even its localized figuration in favor of a far more pluralistic exposition. Thus, *The Importance of Being Earnest* recasts not only the features of the dandy but also those of the society in which he or she exists.

Further, not one but a range of dandiacal types emerge, addressing the audience's expectations and offering imaginative alternatives. With far greater confidence than one finds in the previous dramas, the play limns a world in which the views of the dandy have become the convention and where patterns of behavior judged aberrant in other contexts have become the norm for this subsection of society. Articulating these positions in a fashion that will both acknowledge and extend the audience's expectations produces a profound creative challenge, for a world made up exclusively of dandies lacks the facet of standard middle-class mores to highlight its own features.

To create the necessary contrast, Wilde turns to the twin concepts of Earnest/Ernest to establish a benchmark for illuminating alternative patterns of behavior, and this seemingly predictable ma-

2. *Complete Works*, 102, 103, 104, and 105.

nipulation of identity goes well beyond the binary condition of conformity and deviation found in all his preceding plays. Essentially, the image of Earnest/Ernest acts as the perfect catalyst for dandiacal gestures: As different individuals go beyond the conventional limitations of duality, earnestly attempting to invent or imagine Ernest, their own actions open the discourse to multiple interpretations.

At the same time, these characters contextualize their perspectives by retaining the need to define themselves against the backdrop of order provided by conventional ethos. Conversely, when each responds to Ernest as an independent concept, the imagination of each reconstitutes his nature in terms of that individual's conceptions of the broader demands of society. With so many Ernest variations presented throughout the play, the audience does not so much choose a particular rendering as maneuver around different versions to derive the social ethos of the dandiacal world that they inhabit.

In this fashion, *The Importance of Being Earnest* embraces interpretive multiplicity through a range of dandiacal poses. Various characters embody the dandy's evolution from clothes horse, through amiable ass, beyond cynic or idealist, to a protean combination of all of the above. Further, the play encourages one to see an amalgamation of social forces shaping a number of equally plausible dandiacal representations. As a result, the drama nurtures the possibility for numerous interpretations without privileging any. This overt multiplicity combines the localized archetype, Ernest, with the universal one, the dandy, into figures that assume a cultural, intellectual, and emotional significance previously only implicitly acknowledged: Assuming the role of the dandy enables the individual characters to assert their independence to a point just short of ostracism.

Of course, readers committed to interpretation as a movement toward closure might object to viewing the characterization of Ernest as this loose and pervasive entity and might assert that a literal reading of the play shows that no Ernests emerge (beyond the fictitious office of the name) until we learn the facts of Jack's origin. That issue of signification, in fact, stands as the animating point of my argument. Limiting Ernest to a single, "right" individual presumes the efficacy of either/or choices. In actual practice, however, throughout *The Importance of Being Earnest* delimiting selections undermine themselves almost as soon as one makes them. Instead of imposing stability upon the play, their rigidity has the unsettling effect of constraining artificially a dynamic situation.

One can easily claim, for example, that Jack is no more or less Ernest at the end of the play than he was at its beginning. (Just as

he may be no more or less earnest at one point in the drama than at any other.) Jack in the country denies the Ernest that he always is, while Jack in the city pretends to be an Ernest who he never was. At the conclusion, Jack becomes the Ernest who he always was with no discernable signs of physical or psychological change. The contingency of this form of self-(mis)designation enforces the validity of a broader concept: the aesthetic insufficiency of any exclusionary response. Either/or choices cannot encompass the aesthetic potential of Wilde's drama.

Over the course of the play, application of the concept of the dandy as a model for alternative interpretive approaches lays the groundwork for far more satisfying readings. This method oscillates between sharply defined and ambiguously presented features of the discourse because it refuses to privilege any perspective. Thus, one may begin the play with fairly clearcut assumptions about the dandy that Jack and Algy, as irresponsible young men with talents for coining epigrams and running up debts, seem to personify. However, initial impressions become increasingly less reliable as one compares earlier dandies—figures who misbehaved openly, arousing but not offending society—with Jack and Algy—who live the sort of irregular lives that they can maintain only through the secrecy of a pseudonym or the invocation of a nonexistent friend.

This does not deny affinities in Jack and Algy with the image of the dandy. In fact, one could argue that the play introduces the concept of the dandy by initially inviting the audience to identify Jack and Algy as such. As the action develops, however, it clearly distinguishes between these men and the dandiacal mode, putting some portions of their lives outside the approbation of society so necessary to dandiacal existence. Further, it charts their process of education by a series of tutors who bring them within the bounds—not by transforming them into upright middle-class citizens but by changing them into model dandies. These tutors not only serve to clarify the way that the dandy figure operates within the play but also lay down interpretive guidelines for the dialogic multiplicity that various dandies provoke.

The first stage of Algy's instruction—and of the audience's—occurs near the opening of the play. Despite Algy's putative position as master, his manservant, Lane, gives us a refined sense of Algy's lack of awareness of the more precise points of the dandiacal demeanor:

ALGERNON   Did you hear what I was playing, Lane?
LANE   I didn't think it polite to listen, sir.
ALGERNON   Lane, I see from your book that on Thursday night, when Lord Shoreham and Mr Worthing were dining with me,

eight bottles of champagne are entered as having been consumed.

LANE Yes, sir; eight bottles and a pint.

ALGERNON Why is it that at a bachelor's establishment the servants invariably drink the champagne? I ask merely for information.

LANE I attribute it to the superior quality of the wine, sir. I have
often observed that in married households the champagne is
rarely of a first-rate brand.

ALGERNON Good Heavens! Is marriage so demoralizing as
that?

LANE I believe it *is* [Wilde's emphasis] a very pleasant state, sir.
I have had very little experience of it myself up to the present.
I have only been married once. That was in consequence of a
misunderstanding between myself and a young person.

ALGERNON (*Languidly.*) I don't know that I am much interested
in your family life, Lane.

LANE No, sir; it is not a very interesting subject. I never think of
it myself. [5–6]

Although the undeniable stamp of Wilde's wit and grace conditions the remarks of both men, a subtle difference nonetheless ob-
tains between the natures of Lane and Algy. Even in this short
interchange, as Algy displays the languor and the self-absorption
characteristic of the dandy, he conspicuously lacks the fine sensitivity to his cultural context that gives the dandy a social advantage.
Algy's statements reveal a naïve and juvenile solipsism, whereas
the responses of Lane show a realization that the views of the
dandy must exist in tension with the demands of the world around
him.

Algy, for example, with a type of adolescent cleverness, must put
the blame for excessive champagne consumption on his butler. The
more self-consciously urbane Lane, on the other hand, knows how
to accept yet deflect such criticism. Even when Algy tries to patron-
ize Lane, the butler's involvement with life and his consequent
world-weariness have produced a far sharper wit than one finds in
Algy's defensive disengagement.

Jack Worthing demonstrates an equally oblivious sense of the re-
quirements of true dandyism. Just as Lane introduces Algy to the
specific features of the dandiacal repartee, early in the play Lady
Bracknell—a woman who herself possesses all the essential traits of
the dandy—makes a concerned effort to enlighten Jack on the finer
points informing the dandy's general demeanor while she inter-
views him as a prospective suitor for her daughter. After settling the
usual issues of money, personal habits, and political leanings, Lady
Bracknell turns to the significance of antecedents:

Mr Worthing, I confess that I feel somewhat bewildered by what you have just told me. To be born, or at any rate bred, in a hand-bag, whether it had handles or not, seems to me to display a contempt for the ordinary decencies of family life that reminds one of the worst excesses of the French Revolution. And I presume you know what that unfortunate movement led to? As for the particular locality in which the hand-bag was found, a cloak-room at a railway station might serve to conceal a social indiscretion—has probably, indeed, been used for that purpose before now—but it could hardly be regarded as an assured basis for a recognized position in good society.

*   *   *

You can hardly imagine that I and Lord Bracknell would dream of allowing our only daughter—a girl brought up with the utmost care—to marry into a cloak-room, and form an alliance with a parcel? Good morning, Mr Worthing. [19–20]

Lady Bracknell shows a keen sensitivity to Jack's need for socialization; for she well understands that the prosaic, singleminded attitudes of rebellions against public opinion do not begin to address the complexity of the world that she, Jack, Gwendolen, and others of their set inhabit. Neither the iconoclast nor the conformist has the flexibility to take full advantage of the multiplicity of social institutions. The dandy, on the other hand, exercises a refined sense of the importance of family and other societal establishments; for only from a firm communal foundation can the dandy securely practice the calculated extravagances that set apart his or her nature.

Lady Bracknell's own behavior clearly distinguishes her mode of living from reductive roles at either end of the social spectrum that any genuine dandy would abhor. She certainly leads an irregular family life: Her relegation of Lord Bracknell to his room when not otherwise needed stands as just one example of the eccentric path that she determinedly follows. She can do this with perfect confidence because she knows that the fundamental respectability of her social position conveys the freedom to indulge her idiosyncracies with impunity. The ad hoc attitude implicit in Jack's condition, on the other hand, offers no such structural stability; and Lady Bracknell's devastating response to the ambiguity of his origins underscores the point—especially in light of the numerous other irregularities that Jack's income has heretofore allowed her to overlook.

Despite these early encounters, however, both Jack and Algy require more intense exposure to the dandiacal personality and the multiple demands that the role of the dandy imposes before they will modify their behavior. It falls to Cecily and Gwendolen—

because each insists upon having a dandified Ernest for a fiancé—
to drive home these finer points. Jack, who has moved about in
London under an assumed name, and Algy, who has roamed the
countryside as a Bunburyist, both know the value of subterfuge to
accommodate self-indulgence. Nonetheless, they still operate in a
linear either/or world: Each takes on one personality in the city
only to drop it and take up another in the country. Until the closing
scene, neither seems to understand the need to embrace the ac-
commodation afforded by multiplicity in the both/and fashion
adopted by Cecily and Gwendolen, who gracefully sustain contradictions within their own nature and effortlessly maintain their
sense of Ernest throughout the fluctuating conditions of the play.

As illustrated in the lovers' reconcialiation, quoted below, Cecily
and Gwendolen have a keen awareness of the true dandy's disposition; and, more than any other factor, their confident ability to deal
with antimonies ultimately enables the couples to reunite. After
vowing to ignore Jack and Algy, both Gwendolen and Cecily reverse
themselves (without feeling the slightest need to provide an explanation) and opt for a more pragmatic approach.

> GWENDOLEN   Mr Worthing, I have something very particular to
> ask you. Much depends upon your reply.
> CECILY   Gwendolen, your common sense is invaluable. Mr.
> Moncrieff, kindly answer me the following question. Why did
> you pretend to be my guardian's brother?
> ALGERNON   In order that I might have an opportunity of meeting
> you.
> CECILY   (*To* GWENDOLEN.) That certainly seems a satisfactory ex-
> planation, does it not?
> GWENDOLEN   Yes, dear, if you can believe him.
> CECILY   I don't. But that does not affect the wonderful beauty of
> his answer.
> GWENDOLEN   True. In matters of grave importance, style, not
> sincerity is the vital thing. Mr Worthing, what explanation can
> you offer me for pretending to have a brother? Was it in order
> that you might have an opportunity of coming up to town to
> see me as often as possible?
> JACK   Can you doubt it, Miss Fairfax?
> GWENDOLEN   I have the gravest doubts upon the subject. But I
> intend to crush them. This is not the moment for German
> scepticism. [47]

In this passage Cecily and Gwendolen operate in such a perfect
harmony of dandyism that they can instinctively complete one another's thoughts, responding with full confidence to each other's
only partially articulated ideas. In coming to a resolution of the
whole Ernest affair, they do not feel hampered by a concern for fac-

tual or logical coherence; rather, they understand the need for aesthetic balance. Gwendolen succinctly sums up their attitude: "In matters of grave importance, style, not sincerity is the vital thing."

The change in the natures of Algy and Jack manifests itself in the final lines of the play in true dandiacal fashion. The dialogue closes with a pun that emphasizes individuality rather than homogeneity while at the same time conforms to convention by invoking the programmatic melodramatic closing: "I've now realized for the first time in my life the vital Importance of Being Earnest" [58]. In fact, the major characters do not allow a single, fixed conception of Ernest/Earnest to restrain their sense of the significance of these ultimately interchangeable terms. For Jack or Algy to be Ernest—in the sense demanded by both Cecily and Gwendolen—each must become Earnest, or seriously committed. Furthermore, they must do so in the paradoxical, even contradictory, fashion delineated by the dandiacal code that stands in overt opposition to conceptions of earnestness as applied either within the ethos of conventional middle-class society or outside the pale by sincere opponents of that society.

This interplay, however, goes beyond characterizations within the play. Readers should not limit their conceptions of Ernest to the impressions derived from the perspective of a single individual or for that matter to a single social group within the work. As implied by all the characters whose tutoring contributes to the reformation of Jack and Algy, context and referentiality must influence our conceptions, but one cannot allow either to impose a form of closure upon interpretations. A variety of unrelated Ernests thus emerge from the imaginations of many different characters. Each meets a particular set of expectations informed by class values and individual experience, but no one offers a fully formed version that can displace all the others. At the same time, they all enforce approaches outside the strict limits of conventions that suggest by extrapolation a paradigm for interpretation.

I would like to take this point back to references made in the opening pages of this chapter that critiqued other interpretations of the play. As the discourse itself makes evident, a range of Ernests coexists within the imaginations of the characters of Wilde's drama. It seems contradictory, then, to acknowledge this feature of the work and then impose a single vision or version of Ernest upon our interpretation. Rather, we readers must follow the example of Algy and Jack, accept the tutelage of the other characters, and become dandiacal: embracing the both/and element of the play so as not to lose a single Earnest/Ernest interpretation.

PETER RABY

The Genesis of the Play†

The Importance of Being Earnest represented a conscious attempt by Wilde to experiment with a different kind of play. Between 1891 and 1894, he had written within two distinct genres. He had achieved success in what might be termed "social comedy," plays of modern society and high society that appeared to revolve around a problem or issue, such as the "woman with a past." *Lady Windermere's Fan* (1892) and *A Woman of No Importance* (1893) had brought him a new reputation and considerable financial success, and *An Ideal Husband*, though subject to negotiation and revision, had been effectively completed. He had also written the poetic, symbolist play *Salomé*, too advanced for its day and too controversial to be licensed for performance in England, although the technical reason given was its biblical subject. By 1894, Wilde was under intense pressure in his personal life. He was torn between the needs of his immediate family and of his private self: he had a wife and two young children to support and was also giving financial help to his mother; and he was becoming more and more embroiled in barely clandestine homosexual encounters, dominated by his relationship with Lord Alfred Douglas. Largely as a result of these demands, intensified by his habitual extravagance, he was extremely short of money. His reputation in the theater was riding high, and understandably he saw it as a potential financial lifeline.

For someone in such turmoil, Wilde's output during 1894 was astonishing. He revised *An Ideal Husband*, wrote the contrasting *A Florentine Tragedy* and most of *La Sainte Courtisane*, and finally embarked on an entirely new genre in *The Importance of Being Earnest*. He was in correspondence with a considerable number of producers and managers during the course of the year: with the English actor-managers John Hare and Lewis Waller over *An Ideal Husband*; with Charles Frohman and Albert Palmer in New York in connection with several projects, both existing and unwritten; and with Dion Boucicault, who was producing *Lady Windermere's Fan* in Australia. Frohman, who controlled the American rights to *Lady Windermere's Fan*, was negotiating for *An Ideal Husband*. The year before, he had invited Wilde to write him a new play, perhaps a "modern 'School for Scandal' style of play"; Wilde's American agent,

† From *The Importance of Being Earnest: A Reader's Companion*. Copyright © 1995, (Woodbridge, CT: Twayne Publishers, 1995), 25–40. Reprinted by permission of the Gale Group. Bracketed page numbers refer to this Norton Critical Edition.

the "brilliant delightful" Elizabeth Marbury, wrote to Wilde in July from Paris with details of Frohman's latest offer, which included an option on his next modern comedy. Albert Palmer was also angling for a new comedy "with no real serious interest."[1]

Completed plays and royalties from productions were no longer enough to keep Wilde's finances buoyant. He turned his extraordinary gift for storytelling to advantage in the form of the scenario. George Alexander, the generous and approachable actor-manager who leased the St. James's Theatre, had produced Wilde's first great theatrical success, *Lady Windermere's Fan*. He expressed an interest in the new comedy Wilde was talking about, and Wilde sent him a detailed plot outline some time in July 1894, explaining that the "the real charm of the play, if it is to have charm, must be in the dialogue." After an extremely detailed account of the "slight" but "adequate" plot, he added, "Well, I think an amusing thing with lots of fun and wit might be made. If you think so, too, and care to have the refusal of it—do let me know—and send me £150. If, when the play is finished, you think it too slight—not serious enough—of course you have the £150 back—I want to go away and write it—and it could be ready in October—as I have nothing else to do—and Palmer is anxious to have a play from me for the States 'with no real serious interest'—just a comedy."

In the three-act scenario Wilde sent, which is clearly the nucleus of *The Importance of Being Earnest*, the two young men are named Lord Alfred Rufford and his great friend from the country, Bertram Ashton. The setting of Act One is an evening party at Lord Alfred Rufford's rooms in Mayfair. Ashton tells Rufford that he has "a ward, etc. very young and pretty. That in the country he has to be serious, etc. that he comes to town to enjoy himself, and has invented a fictious younger brother of the name of George—to whom all his misdeeds are put down. Rufford is deeply interested about the ward." During the evening, the "guardian" Ashton proposes to Rufford's sister, Lady Maud Rufford, who knows him only as George. They are interrupted by her mother, the Duchess of Selby. Lord Alfred has been suddenly called away to the country and arrives at the guardian's pretty cottage in Act Two as Mr. George Ashton. The story unfolds, though without the "death" of George and with the additional complications of the arrest of Lord Alfred for debts incurred in London by George and matrimonial designs on the guardian from Miss Prism. The handbag business has not yet been invented. Wilde simply writes, "Miss Prism, who had in early days been governess to the Duchess, sets it all right, without intending to do so—everything ends happily." Perhaps the most re-

1. Manuscript letter, 9 July 1894 (Clark Library, Los Angeles).

vealing sentences refer to the antipastoral, fin de siècle values that inhabit the play. The upright guardian is reproached by Lady Maud for his respectable life in the country: he is a justice of the peace, a churchwarden, a philanthropist, and, worse still, a good example. In defense, he appeals to his life in London. She is mollified on condition that he never live in the country: "The country is demoralising: it makes you respectable." In lines that have not survived in the final draft, Lady Maud praises the urban ideal of the nineties: "The simple fare at the Savoy: the quiet life in Piccadilly: the solitude of Mayfair is what you need, etc." "Result," concluded Wilde, carried away by his creation, "Result. Author called. Cigarette called. Manager called. Royalties for a year for author. Manager credited with writing the play. He consoles himself for the slander with bags of red gold. Fireworks."[2]

Early in August, Wilde traveled down to Worthing (a seaside resort in Sussex, as Jack informs Lady Bracknell) with his family, perhaps with the help, or at least the expectation, of Alexander's £150. The day before he left he wrote to Douglas, "I hope to send you the cigarettes, if Simmonds will let me have them. He has applied for his bill. I am overdrawn £41 at the bank: it really is intolerable the want of money. I have not a penny. I can't stand it any longer, but don't know what to do."[3] During August and September, when he was staying at 5, The Esplanade, Worthing, he wrote the first version of the play. The typescript acts that survive from this phase were stamped by Mrs. Marshall's typewriting agency on 19 September. Douglas provided a major distraction, coming down twice while the whole family was there and then descending on Wilde while he was trying to finish the play by himself. * * *

Wilde had the concentration to produce great work in the midst of chaotic personal circumstances. Although he had never written a farcical comedy before, he had the ability to absorb, subsume, and finally subvert the existing tradition of stage farce. Whether Wilde had actually seen many examples is beside the point, although he was a regular and critical theatergoer. He had an instinctive feel for, and knowledge of, popular entertainment, for narrative forms such as the Gothic story, melodrama, the parable. The nineteenth-century theatrical inheritance was rich and diverse, with burlesque, travesty, parody, and farce surrounding the central core of serious drama. A. W. Pinero, who was steeped in the professional theater, had already explored the genre of farce in *The Magistrate* (1885). First-night critics competed with each other to locate sources for *The Importance of Being Earnest*, and several cited W. S. Gilbert's

2. Rupert Hart-Davis, ed., *The Letters of Oscar Wilde* (London, 1962), 359; and Ian Small, *Oscar Wilde Revalued* (Greensboro, 1993), 65–68.
3. *Letters*, 359.

1877 farce *Engaged*. There are several common incidents and motifs, notably Belinda Treherne stuffing herself with jam tarts, a
compulsive or repetitive eating joke also featured in *The Magistrate*.
However, the most striking parallel in *Engaged* is the entry of Sym-
person in deep black, prematurely in mourning for a nephew who
has announced that he intends to kill himself:

> (*Enter* SYMPERSON *in deep black; he walks pensively, with a
> white handkerchief to his mouth.*)
>
> CHEVIOT HILL   What's the matter?
>
> SYMPERSON   Hallo! You're still alive?
>
> CHEVIOT HILL   Alive? Yes; why (*noticing his dress*), is anything
> wrong?
>
> SYMPERSON   No, no, my dear young friend, these clothes are
> symbolical; they represent my state of mind. After your terrible
> threat, which I cannot doubt you intend to put at once into ex-
> ecution—
>
> CHEVIOT HILL   My dear uncle, this is very touching; this unmans
> me. But, cheer up, dear old friend, I have good news for you.
>
> SYMPERSON   (*Alarmed.*) Good news? What do you mean?
>
> CHEVIOT HILL   I am about to remove the weight of sorrow which
> hangs so heavily at your heart. Resume your fancy check
> trousers—I have consented to live.

It may be that the critics' familiarity with this visual joke, the man
in mourning for someone the audience knows is still alive, triggered
the cross-reference when George Alexander entered as Jack in deep
mourning for his fictional younger brother, Ernest, black-edged
handkerchief to his mouth, shortly after the arrival of Algy as
Ernest (wearing, as it happened, fancy check trousers). There is little verbal resemblance between the plays, as the above extract
demonstrates. But one of Wilde's most characteristic traits as a
writer was to suggest the familiar, even the formulaic, before shifting the ground of his subtle reworking and re-creating.

Kerry Powell, in his key book *Oscar Wilde and the Theatre of the
1890s*, explored in convincing detail the areas where Wilde draws
upon the genre of contemporary farce, with examples such as the
obsession with travel, the idea of escape into childhood or to the
country, the preoccupation with family relations announced by
the very titles themselves, (e.g., *Charley's Aunt, Cousin Jack*). *God-
papa*, Powell comments, even has a character called Bunbury who
is subject to an imaginary ailment, and a young girl with an imaginary brother called Ernest.[4] Bunbury, to cement the coincidence,
was played by Charles Brookfield, who had lampooned Wilde in his
travesty *The Poet and the Puppets* and was to appear as Phipps, the

---

4. Kerry Powell, *Oscar Wilde and the Theatre of the 1890s* (Cambridge, 1990), 124–27.

butler, in *An Ideal Husband*. More immediate, in terms of the composition of *The Importance of Being Earnest*, was E. M. Robson and William Lestocq's farce *The Foundling*, which opened at Terry's Theatre in London on 30 August 1894. This play, like Wilde's, has a foundling hero who has lost his parents, not in Worthing but in the seaside resort of Margate. Wilde, as Powell suggested, might have seen the play on a visit to London, though he could also have gleaned plot details from the newspaper reviews. He also had an opportunity to see the piece when it played briefly in Brighton, the seaside town near Worthing that also happened to be the setting for *The Foundling*, on 20 September.

Another strand of material and motif that Wilde drew upon came from the older English comedy of manners. The suave and sophisticated language of Congreve's Restoration comedy and Sheridan's late eighteenth-century comedy offers the closest parallels to Wilde's tone and texture within English drama, and the staging and structure also provide analogies. In early drafts of *Lady Windermere's Fan*, Wilde incorporated his own echo of the screen scene from Sheridan's *The School for Scandal*, later changed to a curtain, and the screen business resurfaced in the four-act version of *The Importance of Being Earnest*, where Algernon and Cecily conceal themselves behind a screen when Lady Bracknell is announced. Lydia Languish in Sheridan's *The Rivals* writes romantic letters to herself, like Cecily. Another motif of Restoration comedy occurs in Act One of the four-act version, where Algernon is informed that several tradesmen—his wine merchant, his tailor—have called, which echoes the opening sequence of George Etherege's *The Man of Mode*, in which Dorimant may be seen as one of Algernon's precursors. The double life, the fortune seeking, and heiress hunting in the country have long-established antecedents. But as Wilde's play developed, these parallels, echoes, and analogies became less obtrusive, subsumed beneath the texture of the original work of art that he was fashioning.

The richest source for the new play lay within Wilde's own work. The concept of the dandy was one he had explored in all three of his previous comedies, through the roles of Lord Darlington, Mrs. Erlynne, and, in a minor key, Cecil Graham in *Lady Windermere's Fan* and through the darker portraits of Lord Illingworth and Mrs. Allonby in *A Woman of No Importance*, which also includes the cameo of Lord Alfred Rufford, a character almost wholly defined by his gold-tipped cigarettes and his debts:

LORD ALFRED   They are awfully expensive. I can only afford them when I'm in debt.

LADY STUTFIELD   It must be terribly, terribly distressing to be in debt.

LORD ALFRED   One must have some occupation nowadays. If I
hadn't my debts I shouldn't have anything to think about.[5]

The joke about a man's occupation would be reworked in *The Importance of Being Earnest* and given to Lady Bracknell. There are
other premonitions within *A Woman of No Importance*, besides the
title, such as the air of leisure that unfolds in the garden setting of
the first act, under the yew tree that reappears at the Manor
House, Woolton, and the benevolent tyranny and erratic memory of
Lady Hunstanton, a prototype of Lady Bracknell. But the play that
seems most clearly to contain the germ of *The Importance of Being
Earnest* is its immediate predecessor, *An Ideal Husband*.

Here Wilde developed his idea of the dandy in Lord Goring and,
in the text prepared for publication, provided additional material in
his detailed description: "Thirty-four, but always says he is younger.
A well-bred, expressionless face. He is clever, but would not like to
be thought so. A flawless dandy, he would be annoyed if he were
considered romantic. He plays with life, and is on perfectly good
terms with the world. He is fond of being misunderstood. It gives
him a post of vantage."[6] The outline is full of "buts" and qualifications, giving Lord Goring a complexity that is not nearly so marked
in, for example, the saturnine and callous Lord Illingworth, whose
icy mask rarely slips. Lord Goring is a benevolent dandy, at such
ease with the world that he does not need to wound in order to establish his superiority. Uniquely among Wilde's younger characters,
he is shown with his father, a relationship that is portrayed as both
humorous and affectionate. He stands at the apex of the play's hierarchy of wit and functions not only as Wildean commentator and
observer but also as philosopher and judge. Wilde is so taken with
this character that he provides another commentary about him in
Act Three and equips him with clothes and accessories—silk hat,
Inverness cape, white gloves, Louis Seize cane—that are modeled
on his own. "His are all the delicate fopperies of Fashion. One sees
that he stands in immediate relation to modern life, makes it indeed, and so masters it. He is the first well-dressed philosopher in
the history of thought."[7] Lord Goring, in fact, is by far the most interesting character within the play. He manipulates events and expresses his superiority by his decision to distance himself from the
world of public affairs. He is matched by an apparently frivolous,
witty, and unsentimental heroine, Mabel Chiltern, a female dandy
who anticipates Gwendolen and Cecily just as Lord Goring prepares the ground for Jack Worthing and Algernon Moncrieff.

5. *The Complete Works of Oscar Wilde* (New York, n.d.), 48.
6. Ibid., 88.
7. Ibid., 117.

Mabel, like her successors, is shown to be firmly in control of the romantic situation. She is threatening to leave Lord Goring's company, as it is her duty to remain with him, and her duty is a thing she never fulfills, on principle.

> LORD GORING   Please don't, Miss Mabel. I have something very particular to say to you.
> MABEL CHILTERN   (*Rapturously.*) Oh, is it a proposal?
> LORD GORING   (*Somewhat taken aback.*) Well, yes, it is—I am bound to say it is.
> MABEL CHILTERN   (*With a sigh of pleasure.*) I am so glad. That makes the second today.[8]

Mabel goes on to tell Lord Goring that everyone in London knows she adores him: "It is a public scandal the way I adore you." When Lord Goring confesses that he is not nearly good enough for her, she replies, "I am so glad, darling. I was afraid you were." When he admits to being fearfully extravagant, she matches him, so that they are sure to agree. Finally, when Lord Caversham, Lord Goring's father, threatens to cut him off with a shilling unless he makes Mabel an ideal husband, she intervenes, "An ideal husband! Oh, I don't think I should like that. It sounds like something in the next world." This pair of witty lovers practice a deliberately trivial manner and an elegantly ironic form of speech, in contrast to the serious and moralistic tone that prevails with the married couple of the main plot, Sir Robert and Lady Chiltern. Unfortunately, the complexities of the plot prevent Lord Goring from spending much time on stage with Mabel. As he says at the beginning of Act Four, "I can't find anyone in this house to talk to. And I am full of interesting information. I feel like the latest edition of something or other." He almost needs to be in another play, to have the right people with whom to interact. Perhaps his classic location is the opening exchange in Act Three between him and the Ideal Butler, Phipps, who himself "represents the dominance of form":

> LORD GORING   For the future a more trivial buttonhole, Phipps, on Thursday evenings.
> PHIPPS   I will speak to the florist, my lord. She has had a loss in her family lately, which perhaps accounts for the lack of triviality your lordship complains of in the buttonhole.
> LORD GORING   Extraordinary thing about the lower classes in England—they are always losing their relations.
> PHIPPS   Yes, my lord. They are extremely fortunate in that respect.[9]

---

8. Ibid., 132.
9. Ibid., 117.

Oddly, Shaw praised the "subtle and pervading levity" of this play, while objecting to the heartlessness of its successor. In this exchange with Phipps, we hear the opening notes and rhythms of *The Importance of Being Earnest*, just as the scene between Lord Goring and Mabel is a rehearsal for the proposal of Jack to Gwendolen. Wilde built on these sequences and characters to construct a world that was purely and wholly, instead of only partially, "play" and in which every character participated in the role and stance of the dandy.

One of the artistic problems Wilde grappled with in his earlier comedies was the relationship between the dandies, the aesthetical embodiment of style, and the world to which they were opposed, essentially serious, moralistic, sincere, and, in consequence, verbally and dramatically less colorful. That opposition is an oversimplification, and it can be overcome, or concealed, by subtle acting and imaginative direction, but it helps to explain the reservations that have sometimes been expressed about the theatrical effectiveness of, in particular, *A Woman of No Importance* (a reservation triumphantly dispelled by Philip Prowse's productions in Glasgow and, in 1991, London). Wilde uses the gestures of melodrama and a language heavily indebted to biblical references and cadences for Mrs. Arbuthnot, the wronged woman of no importance, which are echoed and shared by the young American puritan, Hester. In contrast, Lord Illingworth dominates the witty discourse, and shares a common language with the corrupting female dandy, Mrs. Allonby. The conflict between the two philosophies and the two moralities is brilliantly explored. Yet, when Lord Illingworth exits at the close of the play, leaving only his gloves behind, there is a sense of imaginative loss, a diminishing of energy. When Wilde has him say, for example, "A man who can dominate a London dinner-table can dominate the world. The future belongs to the dandy. It is the exquisites who are going to rule," he makes us feel that such a world is conceivable, even desirable—as desirable, certainly, as the privileged existence of upper-class country-house England, with its snobberies and its restrictions, and at least more attractive than the nice, old-fashioned, happy English home which so appals Mrs. Allonby as she examines it, like Gwendolen, through her lorgnette. Wilde, in fact, while dramatizing two worlds, is suggesting a third, an exquisite existence that Lord Illingworth and Mrs. Allonby can indicate and imagine, but from which they are ultimately excluded, except in their speech. As Lady Hunstanton observes after listening to Mrs. Allonby's long definition of the ideal man, "How clever you are, my dear! You never mean a single word you say."[1]

1. Ibid., 55.

In *An Ideal Husband*, that exquisite existence is given more solidity by making it a part of a developing relationship and by creating
a sense of perspective through Lord Goring's previous encounter
with the femme fatale Mrs. Cheveley. The serious people, their
rigid moralities softened by experience under the tutorship of the
dandy, can be dispatched into the future, to govern England and do
good works with rather more insight than they had before (and, in-
cidentally, with the assistance of a fortune created through fraud);
the dandies are too intelligent to compromise themselves and prefer to pursue a detached and "trivial" domestic privacy. In the play's
first act, Lord Caversham accuses his son of living entirely for
pleasure, and the ending endorses his judgment.

In *The Importance of Being Earnest*, Wilde created a world in
which all the characters, with one possible exception, are dandies,
living, or seeking to live, entirely for pleasure. Algernon asks Jack
what brings him up to town, and Jack, as Ernest, replies, "Oh,
pleasure, pleasure! What else should bring one anywhere" [6]? The
alternative is to adopt, as guardian, a high moral tone, and a high
moral tone can hardly be said to conduce very much to either one's
health or one's happiness. Algernon, in pursuit of the same aims,
has invented Bunbury and warns Jack that if he ever gets married,
he will be very glad to know Bunbury: "A man who marries without
knowing Bunbury has a very tedious time of it" [12]. To be Ernest,
to know Bunbury, is to construct a life of pleasure, which is at the
same time a deception, or at least a fiction, an act of imagination. It
is an ideal to which both Gwendolen and Cecily are wholly committed. Gwendolen's pronouncement is definitive: "In matters of
grave importance, style, not sincerity, is the vital thing" [47].

Wilde did not wholly exclude the dark side of existence from his
story. Instead, he transformed it into comedy, in the black leather
handbag sequence. This is in itself a parody of the traditional
recognition scene, which is essentially concerned with relationships. There may be letters, objects, jewels, clothing, or moles involved, but the focus is on individuals and their reunion. Classic
instances include the mutual recognition between Sebastian and
Viola in *Twelfth Night* and the reunion of the brothers Antipholus
with their long-separated parents in *The Comedy of Errors*. The mechanics of the convention have been frequently satirized. Wilde
subverted it in an unusual way by making the bag itself the center
of attention. Miss Prism, who has shortly before confessed that she
once lost a baby, is wholly preoccupied by the bag itself. She identifies it, as though it is a person: "Here is the injury it received
through the upsetting of a Gower Street omnibus in younger and
happier days." Writing of the 1902 revival, Max Beerbohm criticized the actress playing Prism, Miss Laverton, for omitting "and

happier," an apparently redundant phrase that underlines the dazzling self-centeredness of this character.[2] Prism goes on to note the stain on the lining and her initials on the lock. "The bag is undoubtedly mine," she concludes. "I am delighted to have it so unexpectedly restored to me. It has been a great inconvenience being without it all these years" [56]. Only after the decorative flourish of the handbag's story does Wilde shift the focus to the abandoned baby. In *A Woman of No Importance* the abandoned mother, Mrs. Arbuthnot, and her baby, Gerald, are handled with pious solemnity. In *The Importance of Being Earnest*, Wilde finds a manner and tone in which he can even indulge in the parody of his own work.

During September and the first part of October, Wilde completed a version of the play, by this time expanded to four acts, and he then began the business of serious negotiation while still based in Worthing. (Remarkably, he had also conceived another scenario, a love tragedy of modern life, which he sent to Alexander and which was eventually written up as *Mr. and Mrs. Daventry*, by Frank Harris.) Alexander, who was planning a North American tour, wanted to secure American as well as British rights for *The Importance of Being Earnest*, while Wilde, perhaps because he was already committed to one of his American managers, wished to separate them. He wrote to Alexander, "I would like to have my play done by you (I must tell you candidly that the two young men's parts are equally good), but it would be neither for your artistic reputation as a star in the States, nor for my pecuniary advantage, for you to produce it for a couple of nights in each big American town. It would be throwing the thing away." He added, "I can't come up to town, I have no money. . . . Write me your views."[3]

The revised play, with the working title of *Lady Lancing*, was typed at Mrs. Marshall's typewriting agency and stamped "3–25 October 94." Wilde, however, was unable to come to an agreement with Alexander that satisfied them both, and Charles Wyndham, another actor-manager, secured the British rights. However, Alexander's planned winter season fell apart when he found that he had a failure on his hands with Henry James's *Guy Domville*. He knew this on the very first night, 5 January, when James, taking an ill-advised curtain call, was received with a storm of boos and hisses, whereas Wilde, two nights before at the Haymarket, had basked in praise at the opening of *An Ideal Husband*. Alexander had a large clientele of regulars, so that he could run *Guy Domville* for a month while he secured and rehearsed an alternative. He immediately approached Charles Wyndham, who agreed to concede his rights in the new comedy, with the proviso that Wilde would write

2. Beerbohm, *Saturday Review*, 18 January 1902.
3. *Letters*, 368–69.

him another original play. Wyndham had no immediate need for a replacement because of the extended success and run of Henry Arthur Jones's *The Case of Rebellious Susan*. Alexander then persuaded Wilde to compress the four-act version of *The Importance of Being Earnest* into three acts. This was, of course, the form of the scenario that he had first seen. Wilde resisted for a little. "This scene that you feel is superfluous," he later told Alexander, "cost me terrible exhausting labour and heart-rending nerve-racking strain. I assure you on my honour that it must have taken fully five minutes to write."[4]

While the four-act version contains much of interest, Alexander's instincts about the advantages of reducing it to three were undoubtedly correct. The only major cut was a scene in which a solicitor, Gribsby, arrives at the Manor House to serve a writ of attachment for twenty days' imprisonment in Holloway against Ernest Worthing on behalf of the Savoy Hotel, for £762 for a series of suppers, an episode that appears in retrospect to be unnervingly prophetic. Jack, infuriated by Algy's Bunburying, agrees with Dr. Chasuble and Miss Prism that incarceration would do him a great deal of good. Algy is appalled at the prospect: "Well, I really am not going to be imprisoned in the suburbs for having dined in the West End" [64]. Cecily intervenes on Algy's behalf, and Jack relents, on condition that Algy leave by the 3:50 train and that Cecily not speak to him again (unless he asks her a question, since it would be very rude not to answer him). Act Two is set in the morning, and Act Three follows after lunch, with the declaration of love between Algy and Cecily, Gwendolen's arrival, and the girls' discovery of the gross deception that has been practiced on them both. Act Four has a structure similar to that of the ultimate Act Three. The text is generally fuller, with more elaborations and embroideries, some of them memorable. Lady Bracknell advises Dr. Chasuble to be baptized without delay if baptism is, as he professes, a form of new birth: "To be born again would be of considerable advantage to her." Cecily arranges to meet Algy in the house: "I don't like talking seriously in the open air. It looks so artificial." But the cumulative effect of these diversions is to slow the pace and dilute the comic energy. Wilde rightly trusted Alexander's judgment, and besides, he needed the money. When he came to organize the publication of the play in 1898, the manuscript he had delivered to Alexander formed the basis of the text.

An Ideal Husband opened on 3 January to a warm public and mixed critical reception. Shaw, in the *Saturday Review*, appreciated the play's brilliance, and his comments indicate the strong links be-

---

4. Hesketh Pearson, *The Life of Oscar Wilde* (London, 1946), 254.

tween it and *The Importance of Being Earnest*: "In a certain sense Mr. Wilde is to me our only thorough playwright. He plays with everything: with wit, with philosophy, with drama, with actors and audience, with the whole theatre."[5] This review kept Shaw in Wilde's favor as one of "only two dramatic critics in London"; Archer, the other, was struck off Wilde's short list after a less than enthusiastic review in the *National Observer*, though he soon redeemed himself with his reaction to *The Importance of Being Earnest*. Wilde was eager to attend rehearsals of his latest comedy: he had been closely involved in the rehearsal process of all his previous plays. However, Douglas wanted Wilde to accompany him abroad. "I begged him to let me stay to rehearse," Wilde wrote to Ada Leverson, "but so beautiful is his nature that he declined at once."[6] Before he left, he gave an interview to Robert Ross, probably a collaboration, that appeared in the *St. James's Gazette*:

> "Do you think that the critics will understand your new play, which Mr. George Alexander has secured?"
>
> "I hope not."
>
> "I dare not ask, I suppose, if it will please the public?"
>
> "When a play that is a work of art is produced on the stage, what is being tested is not the play, but the stage; when a play that is *not* a work of art is produced on the stage what is being tested is not the play, but the public."
>
> "What sort of play are we to expect?"
>
> "It is exquisitely trivial, a delicate bubble of fancy, and it has its philosophy."
>
> "Its philosophy?"
>
> "That we should treat all the trivial things of life very seriously, and all the serious things of life with sincere and studied triviality."
>
> "You have no leanings towards realism?"
>
> "None whatever. Realism is only a background; it cannot form an artistic motive for a play that is to be a work of art."[7]

On 17 January 1895, Wilde left with Douglas for Algeria, returning alone in time for the final rehearsals. His work on cutting the play must have been completed, though at a fairly late stage, because the typescript submitted for a license to the Lord Chamberlain's office on 30 January is described still as a "comedy (4 acts)," though containing only three. When he came back from North Africa, Wilde is said to have commented, perhaps in reference to the missing act, "Yes, it is quite a good play. I remember I wrote one

5. Shaw, *Saturday Review*, 12 January 1895.
6. *Letters*, 381.
7. Robert Ross, "Mr. Oscar Wilde on Mr. Oscar Wilde," *St. James's Gazette*, 18 January 1895.

very like it myself, but it was even more brilliant than this."[8] On 12 February there was a dress rehearsal without scenery. The next day, he wrote to Ada Leverson that the rehearsals were dreary; the cast had colds. There was another, more personal source of anxiety: Douglas's father, the Marquess of Queensberry, was reported to be planning a disturbance on the first night and had sent money to secure himself a ticket. Wilde instructed the business manager to return it, and the police were called in to assist the management in refusing him admission. In the event, Queensberry had to content himself by leaving a grotesque bouquet of vegetables for Wilde at the stagedoor.

On the night of 14 February, St. Valentine's Day,[9] the audience made their way to the theater through a violent snowstorm. Ada Leverson remembered that Wilde was wearing a coat with a black velvet collar, with white gloves, a green scarab ring, a large bunch of seals on a black moire ribbon watch chain hanging from his white waistcoat; his face was a clear red-brown, and a green carnation "bloomed savagely in his button-hole."[1] He watched the play from backstage, perhaps fearing that Queensberry would slip into the theater in disguise, but joined Mrs. Leverson after Act Two in a box where Aubrey Beardsley and Beardsley's sister Mabel were also sitting. By that point, it was clear that the evening was a success, and at the final curtain the play received the most enthusiastic reception of Wilde's career. William Archer wrote in his review, "It is delightful to see, it sends wave after wave of laughter curling and foaming round the theatre." According to Allan Aynesworth, who played Algernon Moncrieff, "In my fifty-three years of acting, I never remember a greater triumph than the first night of *The Importance of Being Earnest*."[2]

RICHARD HASLAM

Oscar Wilde and the Imagination of the Celt†

In an article in *Irish Studies Review*, George Watson argued that 'the key to the intellectual strategy of Celticism is the annulment,

---

8. Pearson, *The Life of Oscar Wilde*, 257.
9. 14 February is the day on which Cecily Cardew appropriately records her engagement to Ernest.
1. Ada Leverson, *Letters to the Sphinx from Oscar Wilde and Reminiscences of the Author* (London, 1930).
2. Pearson, *The Life of Oscar Wilde*, 257.
† From *Irish Studies Review* 11 (Summer 1995): 2–5. Reprinted by permission of the author and *Irish Studies Review*.

elision or denial of history'.[1] Tracing the dehistoricising of the Celtic world in English, Scottish and Irish writing over two centuries, he concluded that the image of the Celt has been fabricated 'out of opposition to modernity'.[2] I wish to examine how Oscar Wilde's effort to modernise Celticism challenges the general tendency outlined in Watson's persuasive argument.

Wilde was acquainted with the Celticism debate in Britain, and periodically aligned himself with the movement. However, the writer who claimed in 'The Soul of Man under Socialism' that 'the only thing that one really knows about human nature is that it changes',[3] and whose protagonist in *The Picture of Dorian Gray* maintained that Dandyism was 'an attempt to assert the absolute modernity of beauty',[4] was unlikely to assimilate, without significant modification, Celticist hostility to change and modernity. Richard Fallis has observed that those three arch-Celticists, Yeats, A E and Douglas Hyde, each imposed 'on a mythical Celtic race his own desires for a different world'.[5] Wilde (an *arch* Celticist) also projected onto the movement his own images.

The parameters of Wilde's Celticism emerged in his reviews of Irish, Scottish and English poetry. He reprehended stage-Irishry, havered in his attitude to dialect, but acknowledged that 'the Celtic element in literature is extremely valuable'.[6] When revising 'The Critic as Artist' for inclusion in *Intentions*, Wilde added some sentences praising the strong 'creative instinct' of the Celt, who 'leads in art' (p. 278). As Isobel Murray has noted, he probably added the passage after perusing Grant Allen's essay, 'The Celt in English Art', which was published in the same edition of the *Fortnightly Review* as Wilde's 'The Soul of Man under Socialism' (p. 612). Placing Wilde with artistic Celts such as Morris and Burne-Jones, Allen had described him as 'a man of rare insight and strong common-sense . . . an Irishman to the core'.[7] Wilde responded with a letter proposing the inauguration of a Celtic Dinner, where Celts could 'assert ourselves, and show these tedious Angles or Teutons what a race we are, and how proud we are to belong to that race'. He praised Allen's 'superb assertion of that Celtic spirit in Art that Arnold divined, but did not demonstrate, at any rate in the sense of scientific demonstration, such as yours is'.[8]

1. George Watson, 'Celticism and the Annulment of History', in *Irish Studies Review*, vol. 9 (Winter 1994–95), p. 2.
2. Watson, 'Celticism and the Annulment of History', p. 6.
3. Oscar Wilde, *The Soul of Man and Prison Writings*, ed. Isobel Murray (Oxford, 1990), p. 31.
4. *The Writings of Oscar Wilde*, ed. Isobel Murray (Oxford, 1989), p. 144. All further references are given in parentheses in the text.
5. Richard Faltis, *The Irish Renaissance: An Introduction to Anglo-Irish Literature* (New York, 1978), p. 61.
6. Oscar Wilde, *Reviews* (London, 1908), p. 271.
7. Grant Allen, 'The Celt in English Art', in *Fortnightly Review* (1 February 1891), p. 273.
8. *The Letters of Oscar Wilde*, ed. Rupert Hart-Davis (London, 1962), pp. 286–7. Hereafter cited as *Letters*.

What were the differences between Wilde's Celticism and that of
Matthew Arnold? Arnold had identified the unifying trait of the
Celtic race as sentiment: this caused 'its chafing against the despotism of fact, its perpetual straining after mere emotion', and precluded its political autonomy, since 'the skilful and resolute
appliance of means to ends which is needed both to make progress
in material civilization, and also to form powerful states, is just
what the Celt has least turn for'.[9] Towards the start of his essay,
Allen introduced Arnoldian references to the Celt's 'touch of fancy,
of beauty, of melancholy, of pathos, of the marvellous, the mysterious, the vague, the obscure', but his argument gradually became
subversive.[1] He described 'the resurgence of the Celtic substra-
tum against Teutonic dominance', in a democratic movement 'of
Radicals, Socialists, Home Rulers, Secularists'. Allen believed the
movement restored 'all the Celtic gifts and all the Celtic ideals—
imagination, fancy, decorative skill, artistic handicraft; free land,
free speech, human equality, human brotherhood'.[2] Wilde found
Allen's analysis attractive, because 'The Soul of Man under Socialism' displayed precisely the interweaving of innovative aesthetics
and radical politics adumbrated in Allen's essay. Both Allen and
Wilde opposed sentimentality, refuting the Arnoldian equation of
Celt and sentimentalist. Instead they located the unifying trait of
the Celts in the faculty of imagination. Here they were in accord
with Ernest Renan, who also significantly influenced Arnold. Renan's 'The Poetry of the Celtic Races' had suggested that 'compared
with the classical imagination, the Celtic imagination is indeed the
infinite contrasted with the finite'.[3] Many of Renan's claims—that
'the Celtic race has worn itself out in resistance to its time, and in
the defence of desperate causes', that 'it does not seem as though
in any epoch it had any aptitude for political life', that 'it has worn
itself out in taking dreams for realities, and in pursuing its splendid
visions'[4]—formed the groundwork of the patronising Arnoldian thesis. But Renan had gone beyond Arnold, by balancing the Celts' 'invincible need of illusion' with their 'profound sense of the future':

> The hand that arose from the mere, when the sword of Arthur
> fell therein, that seized it, and brandished it thrice, is the hope
> of the Celtic races. It is thus that little peoples dowered with
> imagination revenge themselves on their conquerors. Feeling
> themselves to be strong inwardly and weak outwardly, they

9. Matthew Arnold, 'On the Study of Celtic Literature', in *Lectures and Essays in Criticism*,
   ed. R H Super (Ann Arbor, 1962), pp. 344–5.
1. Allen, 'The Celt in English Art', p. 268.
2. Allen, 'The Celt in English Art', p. 272.
3. Ernest Renan, 'The Poetry of the Celtic Races', in *Poetry and Ireland Since 1800: A
   Source Book*, ed. Mark Story (London, 1988), p. 58.
4. Renan, 'The Poetry of the Celtic Races', pp. 57–8.

protest, they exult; and such a strife unloosing their might renders them capable of miracles. . . . Israel in humiliation
dreamed of the spiritual conquest of the world, and the dream
has come to pass. . . .[5]

This Celtic imagination which protests, exults, and revenges itself
on its conqueror imbues Wilde's three society satires and the anti-
English barbs of his fiction and essays. In 1887, Wilde had declared: 'Now that the Celtic spirit has become the leaven of our
politics, there is no reason why it should not contribute something
to our decorative art'.[6] The allusion to Parnell suggested that,
rather than being neutered by an excess of imagination, Celts could
set the catalyst among the pigeons. Rhetorically asking whether his
vision of a world where machines would do all the demoralising
work was Utopian, Wilde replied that 'progress is the realization of
Utopias'.[7]

As a Celt, Wilde therefore embraced modernity; as a Celtic *artist*,
he addressed futurity: 'The past is what man should not have been.
The present is what man ought not to be. The future is what artists
are'.[8] The radical critique performed by the Wildean Celt was enabled, not disabled, by imagination. In 1893, Wilde praised George
Bernard Shaw for opposing 'the ridiculous institution of a stage-
censorship', and enclosed with his letter a copy of *Salome* (the play
which had so recently suffered under that institution), commenting
that 'England is the land of intellectual fogs but you have done
much to clear the air: we are both Celtic, and I like to think that we
are friends'.[9] When sending Shaw a copy of *Lady Windermere's Fan*,
Wilde inscribed it 'Op. 1 of the Hibernian School, London 93'; in a
subsequent letter, he thanked Shaw for 'Op. 2 of the great Celtic
School' (*Widowers' Houses*. Wilde's *A Woman of No Importance* was
Op. 3), looked forward to 'Op. 4' (*The Philanderer*), and remarked
of his own Op. 5 (*An Ideal Husband*), 'I am lazy, but am rather itch-
ing to be at it'.[1] Wilde believed that Shaw and he were Celtic soul-
mates, artists dowered with imagination revenging themselves on
their Philistine oppressors. Shaw did not demur: in an 1895 review
of *An Ideal Husband*, which anticipated the concerns of *John Bull's
Other Island*, he declared that 'Ireland is of all countries the most
foreign to England . . . to the Irishman (and Mr Wilde is almost as
acutely Irish an Irishman as the Iron Duke of Wellington) there is
nothing in the world quite so exquisitely comic as an Englishman's

5. Renan, 'The Poetry of the Celtic Races', p. 59.
6. Wilde, *Reviews*, pp. 250–1.
7. Wilde, *The Soul of Man and Prison Writings*, p. 16.
8. Wilde, *The Soul of Man and Prison Writings*, p. 31.
9. *Letters*, p. 332.
1. *Letters*, p. 339.

seriousness'.[2] Four years earlier, in a review of *Lord Arthur Savile's Crime*, W B Yeats had described Wilde's life and works as 'an extravagant Celtic crusade against Anglo-Saxon stupidity'.[3]

Grant Allen's re-imagining of the Celt gave Wilde a new focus for his aesthetic concerns, since the essays in *Intentions* were studded with paeans to imagination. The future-oriented mode of Celticism, recognised by Renan and Allen, was addressed in Wilde's claim that 'the imagination is essentially creative and always seeks for a new form' (p. 229), while the supposed phyletic dimension was asserted in the definition of imagination as 'concentrated race-experience' (p. 277). But, during and after his imprisonment, Wilde reassessed some aspects of his Celticism, particularly the relationship between imagination and sympathy. Prior to imprisonment, Wilde had maintained that for the artist-critic 'there must be no mood with which one cannot sympathize, no dead mode of life that one cannot make alive': imagination expressed in artistic creation 'could teach us how to escape from our experience, and to realize the experiences of those who are greater than we are' (pp. 276–7). The true critic was one 'who bears within himself the dreams, and ideas, and feelings of myriad generations, and to whom no form of thought is alien, no emotional impulse obscure' (p. 272). But, while advocating imaginative intellectual sympathy, Wilde dismissed 'emotional sympathy': 'It is so easy for people to have sympathy with suffering. It is so difficult for them to have sympathy with thought' (p. 279–80). This aphorism (echoed by the dandy philosopher Lord Henry in *Dorian Gray*) is quoted and developed in 'The Soul of Man', where Wilde vituperates sentimentalists, whose remedies are part of and prolong the disease they purport to cure, and declares: 'All sympathy is fine, but sympathy with suffering is the least fine mode'.[4] Imprisonment and exile led Wilde to revise this claim.

In *De Profundis*, Wilde's epistle to the source of his inspiration and his desolation, Bosie Douglas, the word 'imagination' and its cognates are used almost forty times. According to Wilde, 'love is fed by the imagination . . . by which, and by which alone, we can understand others in their real as in their ideal relations'.[5] Douglas, however, driven by hate, displays a 'terrible lack of imagination, the one really fatal defect of your character'.[6] This lack becomes an accusatory refrain in the first half of the text, anticipating Wilde's doxology to Christ, whose nature 'was the same as that of the artist,

2. *Oscar Wilde: The Critical Heritage*, ed. Karl Beckson (London, 1970), p. 177.
3. *Oscar Wilde: The Critical Heritage*, p. 111.
4. Wilde, *The Soul of Man and Prison Writings*, p. 33.
5. *Letters*, p. 445.
6. *Letters*, p. 445.

an intense and flamelike imagination'. Wilde's artist-Christ 'realised in the entire sphere of human relations that imaginative sympathy which in the sphere of art is the sole secret of creation'.[7] The 'emotional sympathy' denigrated in 'The Soul of Man' is replaced by the 'imaginative sympathy' vindicated in *De Profundis*. To the artist, 'expression is the only mode under which he can conceive life. . . . To him what is dumb is dead', but Christ, 'with a width and wonder of imagination, that fills one almost with awe . . . took the entire world of the inarticulate, the voiceless world of pain, as his kingdom, and made of himself its eternal mouthpiece'.[8]

It was in imitation of his stylised, Celtic Christ that Wilde, after his release, made himself a mouthpiece for the voiceless world of pain, and wrote two letters to the *Daily Chronicle*, indicting the British prison system for a cruelty and stupidity that stemmed from an 'entire want of imagination'.[9] Wilde thus believed the prisoners' mistreatment recapitulated on a national scale his lover's fatal character defect. The Anglo-Saxon stupidity and cruelty against which Wilde the Celt inveighed was embodied by Bosie Douglas in *De Profundis* and by the English prison system in the two letters to the *Daily Chronicle*. Though he could have forgotten the prisoners left behind, Wilde's newly found 'imaginative sympathy' compelled him to write on their behalf. In an 1898 letter, he explicitly related this campaign to his Celtic nature. Responding to praise of his advocacy, Wilde admitted that, 'aided by some splendid personalities like Davitt and John Burns, I have been able to deal a heavy and fatal blow at the monstrous prison-system of English justice'. The English prison system's inhumanity was due to 'the lack of imagination in the Anglo-Saxon race', which made them 'so stupidly, harshly cruel'; conversely, 'those who are bringing about Prison Reform in Parliament are Celtic to a man. For every Celt has inborn imagination'.[1]

Wilde's post-imprisonment Celticism, while retaining the social critique of his plays, fiction and essays, was now infused with a secret revealed to him in captivity: in an 1882 lecture, he had informed his audience that 'the secret of life is in art';[2] now he had learned that 'the secret of life is suffering'.[3] *The Ballad of Reading Gaol*, an attempt to turn that suffering into art, returned Wilde to that contentious terrain between aesthetics and ethics previously negotiated during the *Dorian Gray* controversy. In 'The Critic as

7. *Letters*, p. 476.
8. *Letters*, p. 481.
9. *Letters*, p. 569.
1. *Letters*, p. 751.
2. Wilde, 'The English Renaissance of Art', in *Aristotle at Afternoon Tea: The Rare Oscar Wilde*, ed. John Wyse Jackson (Dublin, 1991), p. 28.
3. *Letters*, p. 473.

TOMARE!

[STOP!]

You're going the wrong way!

Manga is a completely different type of reading experience.

To start at the *beginning,* go to the *end!*

That's right! Authentic manga is read the traditional Japanese way—from right to left, exactly the *opposite* of how American books are read. It's easy to follow: Just go to the other end of the book and read each page—and each panel—from right side to left side, starting at the top right. Now you're experiencing manga as it was meant to be!

A Kodansha Comics Trade Paperback Original.

Fairy Tail volume 24 copyright © 2010 Hiro Mashima
English translation copyright © 2013 Hiro Mashima

Published in the United States by Kodansha Comics, an imprint of Kodansha USA Publishing, LLC, New York.

Publication rights for this English edition arranged through Kodansha Ltd., Tokyo.

First published in Japan in 2010 by Kodansha Ltd., Tokyo
ISBN 978-1-61262-266-8

Printed in the United States of America.

www.kodanshacomics.com

9 8 7 6 5 4 3 2

Translator: William Flanagan
Lettering: AndWorld Design

My Little Monster

OPPOSITES ATTRACT...MAYBE?

Haru Yoshida is feared as an unstable and violent "monster." Mizutani Shizuku is a grade-obsessed student with no friends. Fate brings these two together to form the most unlikely pair. Haru firmly believes he's in love with Mizutani and she firmly believes he's insane.

KC
KODANSHA

SANKAREA

undying love

"I ONLY LIKE ZOMBIE GIRLS."

Chihiro has an unusual connection to zombie movies. He doesn't feel bad for the survivors – he wants to comfort the undead girls they slaughter! When his pet passes away, he brews a resurrection potion. He's discovered by local heiress Sanka Rea, and she serves as his first test subject!

SHERLOCK BONES

DEDUCTIVE DOG DETECTIVE

When Takeru adopts a new pet, he's in for a surprise—the dog is none other than the reincarnation of Sherlock Holmes. With no one else able to communicate with Holmes, Takeru is roped into becoming Sherdog's assistant, John Watson. Using his sleuthing skills, Holmes uncovers clues to solve the trickiest crimes. 🐾

NO.6

A PERFECT LIFE
IN A PERFECT CITY

For Shion, an elite student in the technologically sophisticated
city No. 6, life is carefully choreographed. One fateful day, he
takes a misstep, sheltering a fugitive his age from a typhoon.
Helping this boy throws Shion's life down a path to discovering
the appalling secrets behind the "perfection" of No. 6.

DON'T MISS THE MOST ACCLAIMED ACTION MANGA OF 2013!

"Gripping doesn't begin to describe *Vinland Saga*. 5 stars."
—ICv2

"Deeply engrossing... If you have any interest at all in Vikings, the Medieval period, or pirates, this is not a series you want to miss."
—Anime News Network

"The art is gorgeous, a combination of beautiful cartooning and realistic backgrounds. Yukimura is also a master of pacing, both in frenetic battle scenes and charged emotional moments."
—Faith Erin Hicks, *Friends With Boys*

"For those who love Berserk, you'll love this too... Worth the long wait."
—A Case Suitable for Treatment

"It will be impossible to stop watching this story unfold." —Japan Media Arts Awards jury

KODANSHA COMICS

A VIKING EPIC FROM THE AUTHOR OF "PLANETES"

VINLAND SAGA

of state omnipotence." Human experience, when compared to ideal types, or what Harold Demsetz (1969) has called Nirvana models, will always be found wanting. The proper basis for making comparisons in assessing the performance of practical experiments in human governance based on different design concepts is the realm of practical experience, not utopian ideal types, Nirvana models, or images of diabolical machines.

We thus need to recognize that many levels of analysis require explicit consideration when we think about systems of administration and their associated systems of governance in human societies. First, it is essential to distinguish between languages as symbol systems, the different uses that can be made of languages, and the events that are the referents, objects, or topics of communication. When the events that are the object of inquiry are themselves artifacts which may be based on different design concepts, a second level of complexity arises. If, further, those artifactual constructions manifest themselves in the way that people think, make choices, and act, we have added complexities about how conceptualizations, theories, and practices work themselves out at different levels of choice and are reflected in human conduct.

A theory that presumes a unitary system of government with a single center of power that has ultimate authority (the last say) in the governance of society brings all aspects of life in a society within the jurisdiction of that authority. What happens in a unitary state is internal to an all-encompassing unit of government. All other units have a subordinate and derivative status.

By contrast, a highly federalized system of governance has many autonomous units of government. To understand how such a system of government operates, it is necessary to refer to multiorganizational relationships that have the internal dynamics applicable to single organizations plus the dynamics of interorganizational arrangements. Given a system of separation of powers internal to each unit of government, it is again necessary to recognize that each unit of government is in itself a polycentric order having reference to independently operating legislative, executive, and judicial instrumentalities. All of these instrumentalities of government operate within the context of

an **open public realm** constitutionally maintained by such traditions as freedom of speech, freedom of assembly, the separation of secular and religious affairs, freedom of contract and voluntary association, and rights to property and to due process of law.

Each unit of government in a constitutional federal republic is a polycentric order operating within larger sets of multiorganizational arrangements. These orderings are maintained primarily with reference to open public realms where the law applicable to particular communities of relationships can become publicly knowable. The standards inherent in a rule of law apply alike to those who are citizens and subjects and to those who exercise legislative prerogatives of setting standards, executive prerogatives of enforcing standards, and judicial prerogatives of judging the application of standards. Citizens, in turn, judge the performance of officials in light of the basic constitutional prerogatives exercised by citizens. These constitutional prerogatives are not "private" rights. Basic constitutional rights pertain to the function of persons and citizens in an open public realm that exists for developing a critical civic consciousness about the accountability of those who exercise diverse prerogatives in the maintenance of a public order with regard to many communities of interest.

Such systems then operate in processes of cooperation, competition, conflict, and conflict resolution rather than through command and control by an overarching hierarchy of officials. These systems may have equilibrating tendencies using power to check power, as Montesquieu recognized. The basic design principle, as Madison asserted in *Federalist* 51, is to rely on "opposite and rival interests" with powers distributed "in such a manner as that each may be a check upon the other—that the private interests of every individual be a sentinel over the public rights." In federal systems of government, this principle is then extended to "the distribution of the supreme powers of the State." This was a way of resolving Hobbes's dilemma in which the sovereign who exercises the ultimate power to govern is the source of law, above the law, and cannot be held accountable to law by other human beings for the discharge of sovereign

prerogatives. Sovereigns cannot have the last say and still be accountable to others. Something is wrong with the logic we use if we want it both ways. To have it both ways is incoherent, wishful thinking.

Any such system of governance, then, depends on further distinctions in levels of analysis that apply to constitutional choice, collective choice, and operational levels of analysis. The constitutional level of analysis pertains to setting the terms and conditions of government. If constitutional law is not binding on those who exercise governmental authority, then the conduct of government is no longer subject to a rule of law. The collective choice level of analysis pertains to what a collectivity should do, as a choice of policy, within the terms and conditions specified by a constitution. This is often articulated as what "the government" should do. The policy options that should be pursued by a collectivity become the standard reference in most policy analysis. The operational level of analysis pertains to what happens in the world of action and the effects that flow from human activities. The recent emphasis on implementation indicates that the link between collective choice and collective action is problematical. An implementation gap separates collective choice from collective action. Officials may command, but subjects need not obey. Instruments of coercion can be mobilized, but activities by reluctant subordinates and subjects can neither achieve goals nor attain superior levels of performance.[1]

When policy analysts become preoccupied only with what "the government" should do, they simultaneously do two things. First, they ignore the constitutional level of analysis. Second, they presume that ultimate authority resides with "the government." Can democratic societies that are fashioned as constitutional republics tolerate such poorly conceived analyses of policy problems? Only at grave risk!

A preoccupation with management in the study of public administration neglects the whole realm of institutional analysis and how appropriate institutional arrangements might be constituted to achieve mutually productive sets of relationships among diverse elements that are involved in communities of relationships. The working of a self-governing society requires

skill in putting together enterprises that appropriately reflect diverse interests so as to achieve shared communities of understanding that serve as the basis for informed public action. Public administration is then concerned more with public entrepreneurship than with management. Managers should never forget Rousseau's generalization: "One who believes himself the master of others is nonetheless a greater slave than they" (Rousseau, 1978: 46). Masters become slave to their instruments of control rather than searching out ways to create mutually productive communities of relationships among those who serve and are being served.

Unitary structures of authority operate by systems of dominance subject to command structures characteristic of bureaucracies. By contrast, polycentric systems of governance manifest emergent properties by the way patterns of cooperation, competitive rivalry, and processes of conflict and conflict resolution yield effects that occur in the intraorganizational and intergovernmental realms. These realms are equivalent to what I have referred to as an **open public realm**. The term *res publica*—the public thing—is often viewed as the source of the word "republic." The public thing—the open public realm—is the basic core of a democratic republic. Factors pertaining to "representation" are of a somewhat lesser order of importance. A federal system of government in a compound republic acquires its operational characteristics from the emergent properties that accrue in the open public realm from the patterns of interactions among the multiplicity of organizational units operating as structural elements in interorganizational fields of effects.

The magnitude of the incommensurabilities in the two different ways of viewing systems of governance can be assessed by comparing Wilson's *Congressional Government* with Tocqueville's *Democracy in America*. Both were considering patterns of governance in American society. One looked upon Congress as the supreme authority governing American society. The other looked upon American society as self-governing. What they "saw," as a consequence, was as different as day and night. Wilson was no farther in time from Tocqueville than we in the 1980s are from the New Deal and the Roosevelt administration

in the 1930s. It is not time that makes the crucial difference; rather, it is the difference in paradigmatic perspective taken by actors and observers that creates revolutionary change. When acted upon, paradigmatic shifts in ways of thinking can transform patterns of order in human societies.

One way to achieve some degree of commensurability in the two different approaches is to recognize that the theory expounded by Wilson was also used to conceptualize efforts to undertake administrative reorganizations and governmental reforms. Efforts to do so represent the design of practical experiments to undertake reorganization and reform efforts. Comparisons might then be made between those practical experiments based on reform efforts to eliminate fragmentation of authority and overlapping jurisdictions in contrast to similar circumstances when such reform efforts were not undertaken.

Beyond these distinctions bearing upon organizational, interorganizational, and multiorganizational levels of analysis plus the constitutional, collective choice, and operational levels of analysis is still one more basic distinction pertaining to the nature of order in public economies. This is the distinction, first developed by V. Ostrom, Tiebout, and Warren (1961), between **provision** and **production** of public goods and services (see Bish, 1971; U.S. Advisory Commission on Intergovernmental Relations, 1987a). Provision is conceptualized as pertaining to the collective arrangements necessary to procure a public service. It emphasizes organizing basic aspects that have to do with **consumptive** relationships in a public economy.

The nature of public goods pertains to jointness of use and the failure of exclusion as exclusion might apply to individuals. This implies that **jointness of use** pertains to **some community of people who jointly use a good or service**. Both jointness of use and the failure of exclusion imply that the critical problems of organization have to do with those features of collective organization that bound the relevant community of users and create decision-making arrangements capable of levying taxes, articulating preferences, aggregating preferences into decisions about what quality of service to provide in relation to what costs are to be borne by users/taxpayers, and establishing appropriate

rules that apply to patterns of use. All of these aspects relate to consumption functions.

The decision of how to secure the production of a public good or service is open to several options. It can be produced by hiring employees to help accomplish what needs to be done, by contracting with other producers, or by some combination of these methods. These options can give rise to quasi-market arrangements within a public economy. So long as collective-consumption functions are competently organized in relation to collective instrumentalities with powers of taxation and collective choice and powers to enforce rules and regulations, public economies can be diversely organized.

It is a mistake to focus only on production functions and to assume that units of government are primarily production units. Users of many public services are themselves essential **coproducers** (Whitaker, 1980). Teachers cannot produce education without the coproductive efforts of students; police cannot produce public order without the coproductive efforts of citizens. Public servants help to accomplish these tasks. They rarely produce the results themselves. Units of government of varying size are necessary to take account of the diverse situations and patterns of community preferences that may exist in different and overlapping communities that make joint use of various public goods and services.

Under these circumstances, presumptions about fragmentation of authority and overlapping jurisdictions as the primary source of institutional weakness and failure in systems of governance cannot hold. Fragmentation of authority, as might apply to a constitutional separation of powers, is necessary to hold the diverse instrumentalities of government accountable to citizens as they function in an open public realm. Overlapping jurisdiction does not mean duplication of functions but allows for commensurate structuring of consumption and production functions in the absence of standard marketing arrangements. Production and consumption relationships require cooperation between producers and communities of people making joint use of what is produced. The availability of alternative production and consumption units means that alternatives are available in choosing

partners with whom to cooperate in those production-consumption relationships.

Alternative access to impartial and independent processes for articulating and resolving conflicts is important when competition is not maintained within proper limits and when cooperation breaks down or becomes collusive efforts to impose costs upon others. Conflicting interests, when mediated by appropriate rules of procedure and rules of evidence, generate the information so vital to informed choice in a democratic society. Conflict, as I indicate in Chapter 5, is also an engine that elucidates alternatives and becomes a primary source of innovation. These potentials can too easily be frustrated by the preemptive strategies that allow majorities to prevail in a political process and allow subordinates to be dominated by superiors in a system of administrative management.

As long as the appropriate structural conditions applicable to the design of the different institutional arrangements existed in similar economic, social, and cultural conditions, it should be possible to test competing hypotheses derived from different theoretical arguments, even though these arguments are derived from political theories relying on different paradigmatic approaches. Such a method is expounded in Elinor Ostrom's "Metropolitan Reform: Propositions Derived from Two Traditions" (1972).

Continuing research efforts by a number of scholars have lent plausibility to arguments that were advanced when the Alabama lectures were first presented during the fall semester of 1971. E. S. Savas (1977), for example, found in an extended study of solid-waste disposal that provision by a unit of government contracting with a private vendor for a jurisdiction, or neighborhood in a jurisdiction, yielded better performance than relying on municipal employees to collect and dispose of solid waste or private vendors independently servicing individual households and places of business. Bruno Frey and Werner Pommerehne found similar results from studies of Swiss cities (V. Ostrom and Bish, 1977: chap. 8).

Elinor Ostrom, Roger B. Parks, Gordon P. Whitaker, and other colleagues associated with the Workshop in Political Theory and

Policy Analysis have over the last fifteen years conducted a series of studies concerned with how institutional variables relate to the delivery of police services when measured with reference to various standards of performance. Much of the efficiency and economy reform movement urged consolidation of local government jurisdictions into large-scale metropolitanwide units of government. Taking size as a variable, small- to medium-sized police departments consistently achieve better performance than large police departments. In metropolitan areas that have been subject to intensive study, the largest police departments consistently respond more slowly to calls for service, face higher crime rates, and satisfy their citizens less effectively than small- to medium-sized departments serving similar neighborhoods.

The most consolidated metropolitan areas require more full-time officers on the police force to support each officer on the street actually patrolling at any given time. The more consolidated metropolitan areas on average employ 950 full-time officers for every 100 officers on patrol, compared to 658 full-time officers for every 100 on patrol in the less consolidated metropolitan areas (Parks and E. Ostrom, 1981). New York City as an extreme example employed 3,000 full-time officers for every 100 officers on patrol. It is possible for large police forces to maintain a proportionately small presence on city streets, but if they do, high incidences of street crimes can be expected.

The performance of police departments was also evaluated using the dual measures of police response capabilities (the number of police cars on the street per officer employed) and police crime performance (the number of clearances of crimes by arrest per officer employed). In a study of eighty metropolitan areas, the best departments performed better in metropolitan areas with the largest number of police departments. The best departments in the more "fragmented" metropolitan areas performed better than the best departments in the more consolidated metropolitan areas.

An in-depth analysis of the effect of structure of organizational arrangements reveals complex relationships. The best police performance is achieved in metropolitan areas where there are relatively few agencies producing radio communications and

homicide investigations, while direct services such as patrol are simultaneously produced by many agencies exercising independent responsibility for the operation of those direct services (Parks, 1985). There is, thus, no single optimal scale of organization for the supply of all police services in a metropolitan area. Rather, organizing metropolitan areas so that diverse scales of operation exist for different services enhances the overall performance level. Fragmentation and overlap can enhance performance when the characteristics of particular services and the needs and resources of diverse communities being served are taken into account. These same principles should be as applicable to federal systems of governance as to metropolitan areas.

It may seem intuitively obvious that fragmentation of authority and overlapping jurisdictions will yield perverse effects in any system of public administration. What appears to be intuitively obvious, however, need not be true. The principal task in the development of any science is to clarify both counterintuitive and counterintentional relationships that exist in human social relationships. It is only then that we can develop a science of administration to serve as a design science for engaging in the practice of the art of administration under reasonable circumstances.

Once we begin to recognize that alternatives are possible, new frontiers for further inquiry begin to open. Finding that fragmentation of authority and overlapping jurisdiction can be associated with better performance in the delivery of police services, for example, raises new questions about why that should be the case. In *The Organization of Local Public Economies* (1987a) and *Metropolitan Organization: The St. Louis Study* (1988) the Advisory Commission on Intergovernmental Relations is preoccupied with how fragmentation works in the public economy of metropolitan areas. Whether inequalities among jurisdictions yield inequities in service delivery needs serious investigation rather than presuming tautologies (E. Ostrom, 1985).

Intellectual crises are never resolved by wars of words. Such crises are usually indicative of alternatives that are available at one or another level of analysis. It is only as we extend the frontiers of inquiry that we clarify the dimensions of the problem and the

ways human beings might cope with the alternatives that become available to them.

The Intellectual Crisis in American Public Administration, thus, is not confined to the paradigm problem that arose from Simon's challenge. It also addresses the paradigm problem that arose from the basic paradigmatic challenge made by Woodrow Wilson, some of his contemporaries, and those who followed in their footsteps. Still another basic paradigmatic shift occurred in the American Revolution and the diverse experiments in constitutional government that followed. Inquiry into the character of one intellectual crisis, if pressed far enough, is likely to reveal deeper issues at other levels of analysis. As we extend the frontiers of inquiry about the intellectual crises in American public administration, we are apt to press back to basic issues that stand at the foundation of our civilization. Issues pertaining more broadly to the nature and constitution of order in human societies are usually at stake. I turn to those issues next.

A Copernican Turn?

When Tocqueville referred to a "great experiment" having occurred on the North American continent to construct "society upon a new basis" using "theories hitherto unknown or deemed impracticable" and exhibiting "a spectacle for which the world had not been prepared by the history of the past" (Tocqueville, 1945: 1: 25), he was suggesting that a development had occurred in political theory and in the governance of human societies which was of Copernican proportions. Following Gerard Radnitzky, I shall refer to such an occurrence as a Copernican turn (Radnitzky and Bartley, 1987: chap. 14). Tocqueville viewed this development as creating a society that had become self-governing: "there society governs itself for itself" (Tocqueville, 1945: 1: 57).

In the prior history of mankind, great societies had always been organized as empires. City republics had existed in ancient Greece and Rome, and numerous free cities had existed in medieval Europe. Switzerland and the United Provinces had fash-

ioned confederations of free cities and provinces which were vulnerable to serious problems of institutional failure. Alexander Hamilton had analyzed these problems of institutional failure characteristic of confederations in *Federalist* 15 and 16 and had conceptualized an alternative way to constitute a federal system of government. Hamilton relied upon the principle that each unit of government must be related to the persons of the citizens rather than presuming that governments could govern other governments. A system of compound, overlapping republics was used to design a federal system of government rather than a simple unitary republic.

If the American experiments in constitutional choice represented a fundamental Copernican turn in the governance of human societies, then the paradigmatic shift made by Woodrow Wilson, his contemporaries, and their followers might be viewed as a degenerative rather than a progressive development. The erosion of basic constitutional understandings, the nationalization of American government, and the inability of the national government to keep its own house in order can be viewed as the correlatives of efforts to eliminate fragmentation of authority and overlapping jurisdictions. How do we begin to consider such conjectures?

First, we need to recognize that systems of governance may be grounded in different concepts, which are given expression in different institutional arrangements. How conceptions and associated structures are put together create what might be referred to as a constitutional order. Richard Pipes's *Russia under the Old Regime* (1974) provides an interesting account of the organizing principles used in fashioning the constitutional order of imperial Russia. Edward Crankshaw's *The Shadow of the Winter Palace* (1986) supplements Pipes's account. Ray Huang's *1587: A Year of No Significance* (1981) and Tai-Shuenn Yang's "Property Rights and Constitutional Order in Imperial China" (1987) provide comparable accounts of the organizing principles and structures in traditional China. Different political systems can be constituted in different ways.

Harold Berman's *Law and Revolution* (1983) is a comparable effort at elaborating the conceptualizations and associated struc-

tures that have been important in the constitution of systems of governance in Western Europe. When we carefully consider what Berman has to say we can appreciate that the American experiments in constituting systems of governance did not spring full grown, like a mushroom, from the soil of the North American continent. Rather, Americans drew upon a thousand years of struggle, intellectual disputations, and inquiry about authority relationships in human societies.[2] In turn, those who carried forward these contestations about basic ideas applicable to the constitution and governance of human societies drew upon the intellectual resources of still earlier civilizations. The most prominent of these were the Roman, Greek, and Hebrew traditions.

Berman considers the critical incident setting the stage for the centuries of contestation about the proper structure of authority relationships in Western societies to be the dictate proclaimed by Pope Gregory VII in 1075. This was a critical step in establishing the independence of the church from imperial and other secular authorities. From that time onward European society has had recourse to two distinctive and independent structures of authority relationships: secular and ecclesiastical. One or the other might come to short-term dominance, but the separation of secular and ecclesiastical authority allowed for a continuing disputation about the proper order of authority relationships in Western societies that has continued to this day. We see its most vivid current manifestation in Poland.

The ancient Jewish concept of law, grounded in a covenant between God and his chosen people, is the foundation upon which the Western church presumed to judge the exercise of rulership prerogatives by secular authorities. Those same principles were in turn used within the church to judge the proper exercise of ecclesiastical authority in contestations between popes, bishops, monks, priests, and parishioners. The Protestant movement was but one of the recurring controversies about the proper constitution and exercise of ecclesiastical authority within Western Christendom. A dissenting Protestant sect, which we today identify as Puritans, dedicated itself to the belief that each congregation is the proper governing authority in spiri-

tual matters. They used the same basic principles in constituting the American system of civil governance. The concept of a covenant with God could be used to constitute political regimes in which both rulers and ruled were bound by a rule of law.

One of the early products of the papal revolution of 1075 was the development of the scientific study of law and the codification of both canon law and secular law drawing upon the antecedents of Roman law interpreted and reconstructed in light of basic methods inherent in the teachings of Hebraic law. Gratian, an Italian monk, codified canon law by seeking to create "an ordered synthesis out of the tangle of apparently conflicting laws and practices that had grown up in the church over the preceding thousand years." Gratian created his *Concord of Discordant Canons* by using a general ordering principle to resolve contradictions and anomalies and yield a coherent synthesis of the whole. He did so by relying on a methodology that was grounded in the presupposition that the "principal foundation of all law [is] the timeless principle that we should do unto others as we would have them do unto us" (Tierney, 1982: 13). The golden rule can be used as a method of normative inquiry and can serve as a law of laws (V. Ostrom: chap. 11 in Kaufmann, Majone, and Ostrom, 1986). An alternative method of normative inquiry was available to derive a unity of law apart from the command of a unitary sovereign.

The scientific study of law which was generated by the papal revolution created the foundation for Western systems of law. Western codes of law were more the product of university scholars and legal practitioners working with principles of Roman and Hebraic law than they were the commands of sovereigns. Systems of law have many sources and the viability of legal doctrine depends more upon rules being a mutually agreeable basis for ordering human relationships (i.e., with the consent of the governed) than commands imposed by sovereigns.

The distinctive quality of "a rational legal order," which Max Weber associated with bureaucracy, is only characteristic of Western societies that rely upon codifications of Roman law in accordance with Hebraic principles as the primary source of legal rationality. Neither Russian nor Chinese bureaucracies were as-

sociated with a "rational legal order" with general rules of law presumed to apply to all persons alike. European efforts to achieve a rule of law, or what the Germans call a *Rechtsstaat*, relied upon a differentiation of legislative, executive, and judicial functions even though those diverse structures were linked and ordered in different ways.

One of the basic characteristics to emerge in the evolution of European societies from the continuing contestation about the nature of authority relationships was the development of significant self-governing capabilities and efforts to hold rulers accountable to a rule of law. These diverse elements were never fully brought together so that one could think of Europe as a self-governing society in which "society governed itself for itself." Self-governing cities existed everywhere in Europe, but their liberties were always subject to the threat of imperial aggression and dominance. The destruction of the freedom of the city of Frankfurt, following the Battle of Koniggraetz in 1866, was, for example, an incidental feature of Bismarck's efforts to construct the constitutional order of the second German Empire (Crankshaw, 1983: 213–214, 229–230). But that empire, established in 1871, lasted for less than fifty years. What was never effectively achieved in Europe was a way of reiterating the processes of constitutional choice that applied to free cities and provinces to reach out to a larger society of continental proportions. Those efforts are now being considered in the fashioning of a European Community, though such crucial steps as the appointment of the members of the commission in charge of the administrative center are less than an open public process.

The principal modes for achieving peace, by placing reliance upon a system of government with a single center of ultimate authority, is by merger, consolidation, and conquest. These yield imperial solutions. In the absence of federative arrangements using covenantal methods to achieve expanding self-governing capabilities, human societies will remain locked in struggles for dominance. And so it happens that anyone who conceives oneself to be the master of others is a greater slave than they. Those who depend upon clout to accomplish their missions in life make themselves the slaves of clout.

When we begin to explore the larger intellectual horizons that have to do with the nature and constitution of order in human societies, we see the world as abounding in efforts to design more appropriate systems of governance since the end of British, Dutch, French, German, and other empires following World War II. Independence presumed a theory of sovereignty; but nothing like a Copernican turn occurred. The principal formula for constituting independent nations was presumed to be a unitary state in command of an integrated bureaucratic apparatus. Thus the hopes for achieving a free world have given way to patterns of human predation and exploitation of almost unbelievable proportions. Until we recognize the predatory character of highly centralized states and their bureaucracies, we can make little progress in what has come to be called "development administration" (V. Ostrom, Feeny, and Picht, 1988: chap. 2). Different modes of analysis are required to construct systems of order in which human beings relate to one another in mutually productive ways to improve their conditions of life. Such efforts require basic skills in achieving self-organizing and self-governing capabilities.

The first priority in acquiring and teaching such skills is **not** management. A prior order of skills has to do with the way that human beings constitute themselves into mutually respectful and productive working relationships. This is a basic aspect of what I would call entrepreneurship. What people do in constituting mutually respectful and productive working relationships pertains to the constitutional level of analysis and to constitutional choice. This is the process that is constitutive of human endeavors. Persons who function as public entrepreneurs in democratic societies can do so only when they think of themselves as citizens working with other citizens to build enduring patterns of association in which the community of persons involved achieves self-governing capabilities. This is how democracies can develop and remain viable over successive generations. Democratic societies cannot achieve long-term viability if democratic processes are viewed only as a struggle to win and gain dominance over others. Administrators who conceive of themselves as good shepherds exercising management

prerogatives can create only recalcitrant and reticent masses. Human beings are not sheep.

As we contemplate the possibility that the American experiments in constitutional choice may have involved a Copernican turn in political theory and in the governance of human societies, we need not think of that paradigmatic turn as having accomplished a "revolution" by bringing that "revolution" to immediate fruition. We could hardly expect revolutionary potentials to be brought to fruition when the theory used to design those experiments was categorically rejected at the end of the first century in the conduct of those experiments.

Although the Americans who undertook the formulation of that experiment looked upon it as having revolutionary implications for all of mankind, they also viewed themselves as fallible creatures who could only propose and initiate the first steps on a new course in human development. Such a step is what Max Weber would have regarded as a "historical starting point." The course of human history can only have "historical starting points" that are marked by theoretical innovations of major proportions.

New ideas—theoretical innovations—never come full-blown. Instead, human beings need to be prepared to learn from experience by working with new ideas. This can never be done by rejecting the guidance that can be gained from writers of acknowledged authority, to paraphrase Woodrow Wilson. Instead, one needs to give careful attention to the conceptions and explanations offered by those who participate in formulating the designs of new experiments. Close attention would need to be given to what those experiments were intended to accomplish and to conjectures about what is likely to occur. By casting these considerations aside, Wilson rejected the use of the experimental method for assessing the American experiments in constitutional choice. Instead, he fantasized that human beings could directly see and describe social reality without a conceptual and computational apparatus for doing so.

Viewing systems of governance as experiments in constitutional choice, on the other hand, can open a new realm of inquiry about the constitution of order in different human societies. Such

a method can be applied to the Russian Revolution and the Soviet experiment that followed. The theory used to conceptualize that experiment is reasonably well formulated in Lenin's *What Is to Be Done?* and *State and Revolution*. Lenin anticipated a variety of developments, including the withering away of the state to follow from that revolution. Milovan Djilas, who took a leading role in the Yugoslav revolution, observes, however: "Everything happened differently in the U.S.S.R. and other Communist countries from what the leaders—even such prominent ones as Lenin, Stalin, Trotsky and Bukharin—anticipated. They expected that the state would rapidly wither away, that democracy would be strengthened. **The reverse happened**" (Djilas, 1957: 37; my emphasis).

When the reverse happens, questions arise about the warrantability of the theory being acted upon. We may have an instance when human experience had counterintuitive and counterintentional implications that departed radically from what the experimenters envisaged. This too requires an explanation. If Hobbes were alive today he would not be puzzled by what happened in the Soviet experiment. We can, if we wish, find an explanation in Hobbes's *Leviathan* for why the leadership in Lenin's vanguard party became the new sovereign in the Soviet Union. In Richard Pipes's *Russia under the Old Regime*, one sees striking similarities between the autocracy of imperial Russia and the autocracy of the Soviet Union.

How we view the world and address ourselves to the nature of social "reality" is, then, of basic importance in the social sciences and the related social professions such as law and public administration. Unfortunately, or perhaps fortunately, I too am a fallible creature. My conception of social reality cannot be the **true** conception. Nevertheless, I should be able to draw upon the critical skills of others to arrive at a closer approximation of what we might respectively conceive as true and a better assessment of what it would mean to constitute a self-governing society. If each of us could participate in such a process of inquiry, we might develop alternatives by which human beings need not rely on states to rule over societies. We might learn how to constitute viable and responsible patterns of order among

multinational communities. When we begin to think our way through to such possibilities, we may be prepared to understand the meaning of the American experiments in constitutional choice and begin to appreciate the immense task confronting human beings in fashioning something that might appropriately be called a free world. Unless we can attain such a level of understanding, we are likely to find ourselves trapped into fashioning new forms of cryptoimperialisms and autocratic despotisms which we falsely call democracies (V. Ostrom, Feeny, and Picht, 1988).

Challenging Ways of Thinking

The adventure that we have pursued in thinking about the intellectual crises in American public administration takes us well beyond recognizing that paradigm shifts may be important to the way that scholars proceed in their intellectual endeavors and well beyond the confines of American public administration as well. Ideas are always the bases for action. Human beings, and other animals, are hard-wired so that voluntary motor facilities depend upon mental processes that occur in the central nervous system. Actions depend upon thoughts and habits grounded in thought. Patterns of order in human societies depend, then, upon shared communities of understanding about how human beings relate to one another in ordering the ways of life that are constitutive of human societies.

People who are knowledgeable about the way rules can be used to order conduct among human beings can draw upon conceptions to formulate patterns of order and thus work out the structural arrangements or forms that can be used to constitute patterns of organization in human societies. Human beings thus have potentials for fashioning their own social "realities" to some significant degree. They are never confined to only one way in formulating those patterns of order. There are some ways that rely strongly upon a determinate ordering of superior-subordinate relationships characteristic of bureaucratic command structures. There are other ways that rely more upon

covenantal relationships characteristic of self-governing communities. These yield quite different ways of life in human societies.

The difference can perhaps be best understood by the distinction in the terms *Herrschaft* and *Genossenschaft* in the German language. This was Max Weber's language of discourse. *Herrschaft* is translated as authority implying domination. The term has the intuitive meaning of lordship. *Genossenschaft* has the intuitive meaning of comradeship and is frequently translated as association. When Tocqueville indicates that the science and art of association must increase as people become more equal in human societies, he was indicating that they must know how to draw upon principles of comradeship of a covenantal character in achieving self-governing capabilities. Those who rely upon the power of command conceive themselves to be the masters of others and exercise lordship over others.

We still confront the puzzle of how we recognize when one or the other principle prevails. Tocqueville saw a society that relied on a science and art of association to achieve self-governing capabilities. This would have been the equivalent of Lenin's withering away of the state. Wilson, fifty years later, saw Congress as exercising the supreme prerogatives of government. We thus face some serious problems of what intellectual tools scholars and other professional analysts might use to inquire about the nature and constitution of order in human societies and how scholars and professional analysts think about and experience themselves in human societies. Do we see our world as we think about and experience ourselves? Do we think about and experience ourselves as masters and servants, or as comrades and colleagues? Both patterns of order prevail to varying degrees in different societies. How do we see the configurations of relationships being put together?

Americans cannot confine their intellectual vistas to American society but must also be prepared to mobilize analytical capabilities for thinking about patterns of governance and ways of life in other societies and how people might think about and experience themselves in those societies. If we assume that all societies are like American societies and all officials behave like

American officials, we are not capable of understanding what happens in the world.

A similar problem was addressed, in part, nearly fifty years ago by Walter Eucken in *The Foundations of Economics* (1951). Eucken begins his inquiry by pointing to a simple event: a stove that was heating his study. He then begins to speculate about the complex chains of actions and transactions which had to be coordinated to achieve that simple event. In his speculation, he draws upon some of the analytical capabilities that economists might use to provide a mental image of the diverse interactions of people and situations that were linked together to yield a stove heating a study.

He then raises a question about how economists address themselves to those circumstances. He finds two discrete styles of scholarship prevailing among economists. One style involves efforts to develop general abstract models of the economy. Thus we might find economists talking abstractly about "the market," or political scientists about "the state." Bureaucracies are then viewed as the key command apparatus that allows "states" to govern. Reference is then made to "states," "bureaucracies," and "markets" as the essential institutions in "capitalist" societies. In doing so, Eucken argues that these scholars increasingly distance themselves from economic and social reality. On the other hand, Eucken points to economic historians who, he says, become so immersed in the details that they simply heap facts upon facts. An insurmountable gap is created between these two traditions of scholarship. Eucken refers to this gap as "the great antinomy." Eucken could as well have been discussing scholarship in public administration: abstract models and case studies with immense gaps between theory and practice.

Eucken continues his criticism by pointing to tendencies to distinguish different types of economies and different stages of historical development that are discretely associated with particular times and places. He was referring to distinctions we might make today between "capitalist" societies and "socialist" societies or between "developed" societies and "less-developed" societies. Instead, Eucken would prefer to presume that there are underlying characteristics that might apply to all

human beings coping with problems of scarcity that recur in all human societies. We should thus be able to apply common methods whether studying life in an "ancient" society, a "modern" society, a "less developed" society, a "developed" society, a "capitalist" society, or a "socialist" society. Eucken was suggesting that if we view patterns of order in human societies, we should be able to base the study of social forms or social structures by drawing upon the foundational elements that are constitutive of the great diversity of structures in human societies.

Eucken was arguing that we need a mode of inquiry which would enable us to "penetrate" social reality, in the sense of looking into that reality, rather than increasingly distancing ourselves from reality by highly abstract general models or painting idiosyncratic word pictures while heaping facts upon facts. We need modes of inquiry that enable us to address many different levels and foci of analysis, but doing so with some basic appreciation for how studies might fit in relation to one another in configurations of relationships that are constitutive of human societies. This is why Eucken is closely identified with the development of a community of scholars concerned with a theory of order (*Ordnungstheorie*) (Kruesselberg: chap. 17 in Kaufmann, Majone, and Ostrom, 1986. See also concluding observations in chap. 37).

These issues are important to contemporary scholarship and practical efforts to constitute patterns of order in human societies. The overwhelming discourse about the nature and constitution of order in human societies still occurs by reference to such abstract universalistic concepts as "states," "societies," "bureaucracies," "markets," "capitalism," "socialism," and the like. These abstract universalistic concepts are articulated with reference to abstract principles that are presumed to operate. Development is then viewed as a process of "modernization" that requires a centralized "state" and a "bureaucracy" to transform a "society" by means of "industrialization" and associated technological transfers. All of these factors are presumed to work as gross aggregates. Such ways of thinking manifest a simple-mindedness of incredible proportions. To gain some sense of reality, we need to remind ourselves of Eucken's stove heating

his study and the extraordinary configurations of relationships that were necessary to yield that simple event.

On the other hand, we have specialists in the lore of case studies who heap facts upon facts without having any consciously held intellectual tools to sort out facts and use them to assess what may be problematical in specifiable situations. These are the people who see only particular trees. The others see only sweeping forests. Unfortunately, human endeavors often require more than seeing particular trees and their idiosyncracies or sweeping vistas of forests. Many other perspectives are of essential analytical importance in the constitution of human societies. What each of us does is to sustain a few important links in the configurations of relationships that are constitutive of human societies.

We cannot get along without theory to enable us to fit together images of the complex configurations of relationships not directly observable by individual human beings. In responding to Eucken's challenge we need to sort out the basic elements that are inherent in theoretical reasoning and use these elements to develop a heuristic that will tell us what to look for. A heuristic focusing on structure, conduct, and performance, used in the study of industrial organization (e.g., Bain, 1959), is a helpful way of orienting oneself to inquiries in economic, political, and administrative theory. Larry L. Kiser and Elinor Ostrom have also made a useful beginning in their essay "The Three Worlds of Action: A Metatheoretical Synthesis of Institutional Approaches" (E. Ostrom, 1982: chap. 7). A simple heuristic is implied in Chapter 3 when I suggest that the essential elements in institutional analysis are to (1) anticipate the consequences that follow when (2) individuals choosing optimizing strategies within the structure of a situation which has reference to (3) particular organizational arrangements applied to (4) particular structures of events (productive efforts and goods) in the context of (5) some shared community of understanding.

My reference to heuristics is analogous to what Kuhn (1964) refers to as a paradigm, Irme Lakatos (1970) refers to as a research program, or Larry Laudun (1977: chap. 3) refers to as a research tradition. I am concerned with the basic elements and assump-

tions upon which theories and theoretically informed modes of analysis are built. I assume that we can also extend the frontiers of inquiry by pressing to deeper levels of analysis in reconsidering the foundations upon which inquiry is based. Rather than dealing with "values," for example, as an undefined term, we can address the problem of normative inquiry, as I have done, to indicate how human beings might make interpersonal comparisons to establish the meaning of value terms (V. Ostrom, 1984).

By clarifying the heuristic that stands at the foundation of theoretical modes of analysis, we can be much more explicit in knowing how to take hold of a problem and proceed with an analysis. Further, we can move beyond simple universal models and recognize that the elements making up a theoretical model can be varied giving us a much wider range of permutations in theoretical analyses. If heuristics are properly grounded, we should achieve the further capability of translating from one theoretical formulation to another.

If we were to rely on such a heuristic, we could then draw upon Karl Popper's suggestion that all human inquiry is addressed to problematical situations (1964). From a choice perspective, analysts can confront problematical situations by taking first a diagnostic perspective to identify what it is that is problematical in that situation and then explore the alternatives that may be available so as to alter that problematical situation and achieve a resolution of the problem if one is conceivable. From a positive perspective, an analyst can view hypothetical actors in hypothetical action situations, postulate a likely choice of strategies given incentives and constraints, and then infer what consequences will follow from actions taken, given a choice of strategy. The more fully the structure of a decision/action situation can be specified, the closer we can come to specifying the structure of constraints and incentives that will confront actors in such situations. Once these are understood, it is possible to take a game-theoretical, or an equivalent, perspective and anticipate how actors will choose strategies and act within problematical situations.

If conditions about actors in situations can be specified and

applied to hypothetical situations, we have an abstract model. If those conditions are allowed to vary depending on the attributes of existing situations, we have the makings of a theoretical analysis applicable to empirical exigencies. So long as the human condition reflects exigencies that apply to all of mankind and human beings confront prototypical situations common to all societies (such as (1) exchange relationships; (2) teamwork; (3) the organization of teams of teams; (4) circumstances associated with communal or collective use of common-pool resources, facilities and properties, and public goods and services; (5) conflict and conflict resolution; and (6) rule-ruler-ruled relationships), we have rudimentary tools with which we can work to advance the frontiers of inquiry about the nature and constitution of order in human societies.

Such an approach is amenable to inquiry in relation to many levels and foci of analysis. Thus it affords opportunities to penetrate social "reality" viewed from different vantage points without having to distance ourselves from social "reality" or heap facts upon facts in painting idiosyncratic word pictures. Redundancy in pursuing different modes of analysis is necessary if we are to learn both how to generalize about and how to cope with great multitudes of facts. We would expect to find patterns of complexity, diversity, and complementarity. We need to have recourse to different levels and foci of analysis, which are commensurable with one another, in order to make comparisons and allow ourselves to be confronted by the puzzles and anomalies that arise in human experience and the critical assessments of others. Tolerating great gaps between theory and practice implies that we have so distanced ourselves from reality that we are no longer informed observers of human societies.

Eucken did not resolve his own challenge. I doubt that any one of us shall succeed in doing so. Rather, Eucken's challenge reminds us that ways of thinking about social reality need as much critical attention as what is being observed. These matters are contestable among reasonable human beings and must continue to be contestable so long as human beings are fallible.

I conclude, then, by drawing upon Radnitzky's and Bartley's views of the task faced by fallible observers in their *Evolutionary*

Epistemology (1987: 287–288, 309). Concepts and practices can be distinguished. So can concepts of truth and certainty. Choices in choice situations always involve uncertainties. Although the fallibilist does not presume to know the truth, any fallibilist stresses the possibility of error and thus "presupposes the concept of falsity and hence that of truth" (p. 287). The idea of empirical testing would be meaningless without an implicit concept of truth. We rely on the critical capabilities that can be mobilized by others to press onward to deeper levels and new frontiers of inquiry so that we reach a better approximation of what we might respectively conceive as being true. We make progress by listening to the contestable arguments advanced by others to improve our own intellectual tools and advance beyond the limits of the intellectual vision we had previously achieved. We learn, unlearn, and continue to learn as we extend the horizons of our inquiries. In doing so, we discard ideas we had used to think about ourselves and our world and develop new ideas to "transcend our old selves" and to function as human beings who continue to grow and develop intellectually, emotionally, and creatively (p. 451).

The scientific enterprise advances as we progressively adapt our way of thinking to extend what we can "see." Fallibilists will prefer the approach that successfully withstands criticism while appreciating that it is critics who offer the stimulus to "cognitive progress" (p. 288). We are more concerned with the viability of ideas than with the justification of ideas. Justification can be distinguished from criticism. The capacity to withstand criticism or to revise in the presence of criticism is important for the warrantability of ideas and their development in an evolutionary epistemology. From the perspective of the observer and the practitioner, the capacity to withstand criticism would enhance the warrantability of ideas and their usefulness to inform practice in the art of the possible. As both Hans Albert (1986) and James Buchanan (1975; 1979: chap. 5) have variously emphasized, the frontiers of human choice extend from the seemingly trivial choices in everyday life to choices of ways of life and ways of thinking.

All these levels of choice must be understood by human beings

as they live their everyday lives in whatever they do if they are to achieve the autonomy of first being their own governors functioning in self-governing societies. A critical aspect turns upon the question of how observers of and participants in self-governing societies think of and experience themselves as they relate to other human beings: as individuals struggling for advancement to gain positions of dominance and become masters of others; or as fellow citizens (colleagues, comrades) pursuing courses of inquiry in addressing and resolving problematical situations in human societies.

An awareness of paradigm problems is but a step along the way toward developing a critical self-consciousness of both the opportunities and constraints inherent in the human condition and the universe in which we live. How we think about and experience ourselves is an essential component in the analytical situation of both the observer and the observed. When we use the method of normative inquiry inherent in the golden rule, we learn how methodological individualism can be used to create cognitive links among observers and the observed in studying the nature and constitution of order in human societies (V. Ostrom: chap. 11 in Kaufmann, Majone, and Ostrom, 1986).

Notes

Chapter 1: The Crisis of Confidence

1. Several of the essays in Robert K. Merton et al.'s *Reader in Bureaucracy* (1952) reflect the experiences of social scientists with wartime bureaucracy. So do several of the case studies in Harold Stein's *Public Administration and Policy Development* (1952).

2. Dwight Waldo has responded to my comment here by indicating:

> But what I meant to say, and still do vigorously contend, is this: No paradigm of a *disciplinary* nature can solve the problem. This is because public administration is not a scientific discipline. It is a profession in a loose sense, a collection of related professions, which can do, and must use paradigms, techniques, and so forth, from *many* disciplines.
>
> Put another way, if we need a paradigm it should be that appropriate to a profession rather than that appropriate to a scientific discipline. My historic analogy has been to "the medical profession"; I would qualify that nowadays by making my analogy "the health professions." (Personal communication; Waldo's emphasis)

I am perfectly willing to accept Waldo's position on the assumption that problems of water-resource administration may require different bodies of knowledge from police administration, for example. Yet we are confronted with the question of whether such disparate fields of administration do face comparable organizational problems associated with externalities, common property resources, and public goods. If so, there may be a general logic of collective action which is applicable to both types of problems.

3. American Society for Public Administration, *News and Views* 20 (October 1970): 5.

4. Niskanen (1971) indicates some of the differences that voting rules

will make on the expected output of public agencies. See generally his discussion in chapter 13 and following.

Chapter 2: The Intellectual Mainstream in American Public Administration

1. In light of Daniel W. Martin's "The Fading Legacy of Woodrow Wilson" (1988), I want to emphasize that I am not asserting that Wilson's contemporaries looked to him for inspiration as the founding scholar in the study of public administration. He and Van Riper (1983) are correct in asserting that early scholars did not cite Wilson. Yet the underlying presuppositions associated with a theory of state, which presumes a unitary sovereign, pervade the work of Goodnow and other leading scholars in the field. Wilson does not share Bagehot's skepticism about bureaucracy. Siedentopf (1983) is critical of Wilson's treatment of the German cameralists, but as Toonen (1987) has demonstrated, many contemporary European scholars in public administration have reconstructed the historical antecedents of administrative theory to conform to doctrinal presuppositions, as their American colleagues have done, rather than conform to the historical facts about those antecedents.

2. Wilson also observes: "It is quite safe to say that were it possible to call together again the members of that wonderful Convention [of 1787] to view the work of their hand in the light of the century that has tested it, they would be the first to admit that the only fruit of dividing power has been to make it irresponsible" (Wilson, 1956: 187).

3. So far as administrative functions are concerned, Wilson asserts, "all governments have a strong structural likeness; more than that, if they are to be uniformly useful and efficient, they *must* have a strong structural likeness" (Wilson, 1956: 218; Wilson's emphasis).

4. Wilson refers to a three-stage pattern of political development, which he assumes to be applicable to the "chief nations of the modern world." These include (1) a period of absolute rule, (2) a period of constitutional development, and (3) a period of administrative development (Wilson, 1956: 204).

5. Weber's theory of bureaucracy did not have substantial influence on American study of public administration until after World War II, when his translated work became available to American scholars. The generality of the Wilsonian paradigm is indicated, however, by the congruence between Wilson's and Weber's formulations.

6. The "monocratic principle" also implies "monopolization of legitimate violence by the political organization which finds its culmination in the modern concept of the state as the ultimate source of every kind of legitimacy of the use of physical force" (Rheinstein, 1954: 347). The persistent definition of political authority as a monopoly over the legitimate use of force indicates a monocratic or monocentric bias in modern political theory. Can a federal system with separation of powers be properly characterized as a "monopoly" over the legitimate use of force? I think not.

7. Crozier (1964) in his chapter "The Bureaucratic System of Organization" refers to Weber's place in the "paradoxical" view of bureaucracy, which runs through much of Western political analysis. See the frontispiece for a statement of the "paradox."

8. The disparity between Weber's conceptualization of bureaucracy as an ideal type of organization necessary for efficiency and for development of a rational basis for modern civilization and the consequences he anticipates as following from its perfection in a "fully developed" form is difficult to fathom. He implies that a system of bureaucratic rule is necessarily the fate of modern man. He would thus affirm Rousseau's observation that "man is born to be free but is everywhere in bondage." Such a conclusion is consistent with a "monocratic" or "monocentric" structure of political organization based on a theory of absolute sovereignty. If all political authority resides in an absolute sovereign and if all others are equal in their state of subjection, then Weber's conclusions follow. His portrayal of a "fully developed bureaucracy" is surprisingly congruent with Tocqueville's discussion of democratic despotism in the Fourth Book of Volume 2 of *Democracy in America*.

Bendix (1960) addresses this anomaly in the concluding chapter of his biography of Weber. Bendix argues that Weber's concept of "bureaucracy under legal domination" must be distinguished from his political analysis of bureaucratization as a different intellectual exercise (p. 456). If we hold to Bendix's position, then bureaucracy as an ideal type assumes perfectly obedient functionaries. The maintenance of legal rationality does not follow except as it is postulated as a limiting condition in a logical exercise. If this is the case, Weber fails to grasp the problem of indicating the logically necessary conditions that will increase the probability that a political system will conduct its affairs in accordance with rules of law. As Bendix indicates, "Bureaucratization becomes compatible with a system of legal domination only if officials are prevented from usurping the political and legislative process" (p. 457). But what is to prevent officials from usurping the political and legislative process

when a monopoly exists over the legitimate use of force? Thus it is an open question whether bureaucratization is consistent with a rational legal order or whether bureaucratization is a prelude to human bondage. We shall return to this issue in Chapter 5.

9. Victor A. Thompson's *Modern Organization* (1961) is a major exception.

10. This characterization of research in the "mainstream" of American public administration is largely associated with the administrative survey movement. Currin Shields's (1952) article "The American Tradition of Empirical Collectivism" points to quite a different tradition of analysis, which Shields summarizes:

> The empirical collectivist assumes that collective action should be employed whenever necessary to solve public problems, but that the minimal action required to dispose of the problem should be undertaken. In considering a policy question, therefore, he concentrates his attention on the actual situation in an effort to fathom the all-important character of the problem and the conditions of its solution. His initial query is: is this a public problem? No *a priori* answer can be given to this question; the answer turns on the situation itself. If it is decided that the problem is of public concern, then his next question is: which agent of the community is best able to deal with this problem? Is a local private agency, a county board, a national private organization (such as the American Red Cross), a state bureau, or a national agency best suited? Again he must examine the problem situation to arrive at an answer. His final query is: what sort of action is required to dispose of the problem? Each possibility he must canvass, and on the basis of past experience and future expectations he must select the form of collective action which appears most appropriate. Questions such as these the empirical collectivist can feasibly discuss with his fellows. Their discussion can center on differences of opinion about actual situations, and these differences they can resolve by appeals to experience, by examining the evidence. Thus, they can arrive at propitious decisions regarding collective action, and can settle, in a democratic manner, policy questions. (pp. 117–118)

Shields also indicates the "empirical collectivists" rely on a " 'rule of economy': the minimal action to dispose of a problem—and no more—should be undertaken collectively" and "public action taken to dispose of a problem should redound to the benefit of the entire community" (p. 105).

Shields observes that "the empirical collectivist prefers voluntary to mandatory action, inducement to compulsion, restriction to prohibition. And if government action is required, he prefers public regulation of

private enterprise to governmental operation of public enterprise" (p. 106).

Finally, Shields observes that the empirical collectivist's preoccupation with the welfare of the entire community leads him to take the point of view of the consumer: "The empirical collectivist is able to espouse the public interest as it is reflected in the welfare of citizens as consumers" (p. 105).

The tradition of empirical collectivism is sharply at variance with the mainstreams of American public administration. Benjamin Franklin, Alexis de Tocqueville, and Frederick Jackson Turner reflect that tradition in their writing as do a variety of practicing administrators such as John W. Powell, Elwood Mead, and William Hammond Hall and scholars such as John Dewey and Francis W. Coker. **None** of their works has come to occupy a position of central significance in the study of American public administration.

11. The *Report* states, "In a democracy consent may be achieved readily, though not without **some** effort, as it is the cornerstone of the constitution" (p. 3; my emphasis). By contrast, "efficient management" is a matter of "peculiar significance."

Given the serious challenge to democratic government and constitutional rule being posed by the rise of totalitarian regimes during the 1930s, it is striking that the Brownlow Committee could so confidently dismiss consideration affecting "the consent of the governed" and the maintenance of constitutional rule. Such perspectives were congruent with its theory that the field of politics is outside a proper concern for administration. The commissioners apparently were not prepared to consider the possibility that a fully developed system of "efficient management" based on their "canons of efficiency" could transform constitutional rule into a problematical condition.

12. Simon (1952: 1130) clarifies his distinction of "group," "organization," and "institutions" in the following observation: "In such a nest of Chinese blocks the smallest multi-person units are the primary groups; the largest are institutions ('the economic system,' 'the state') and whole societies. We will restrict the term 'organization' to systems that are larger than primary groups, smaller than institutions."

13. Where the amount of resources and the organizational objectives are given, outside the control of the administrator, efficiency becomes the controlling determinant of administrative choice [within those constraints] (Simon, 1965a: 122).

14. See the discussion of the problems of institutional failure in Chapter 3. The tragedy of the commons, for example, can occur in the absence

of appropriate institutional constraints. Thus individualistic choice in the management of a common-pool resource in which demand exceeds supply would lead to "irrational" behavior when viewed in relation to other decision-making arrangements for the management of such resources.

Chapter 3: The Work of the Contemporary Political Economists

1. Discussions of professionalism and bureaucratic organization often make a direct association between the two sets of phenomena. Thus much of the discussion of professionalism among police is associated with centralization of authority and large-scale organization. Professionalization can also be treated as a separate variable from organizational structure. Both medicine and law are frequently practiced in the context of relatively small organizations in which relationships are organized through marketlike transactions. Other professions, such as the military, are organized predominantly in large-scale organizations. If professionalization and organizational structure are treated as independent variables, we would expect different structures of opportunities to prevail among superintendents of schools and city managers than in a highly bureaucratized structure such as the military service or the foreign service.

2. Most of the political economists are associated with the Public Choice Society and publish a journal, *Public Choice*.

3. In taking the perspective of an "omniscient observer," an economist confines his or her use of an individualist calculus only to market structures and relies on an assumption that general policies affecting social welfare can be determined by an omniscient and omnicompetent despot who can maximize social utility by taking account of all utility preferences. The assumption of perfect information used in formulating a model of perfect competition is essentially applied to the problem of collective choice made by a benevolent despot. Economists who use the analytical device of the omniscient observer find Hobbes's theory of sovereignty congenial for their purposes.

Most scholars in the Public Choice tradition prefer to apply an individualistic calculus to problems of collective choice in which individuals have access to less than perfect information. Decision-making arrangements such as elections, representation, and legislation are

mechanisms for translating individual preferences into collective choices.

4. This and the previous paragraph have drawn more fire from critics than any other portion of *The Intellectual Crisis*. The model of man is at the core of Robert J. Golembiewski's "A Critique of 'Democratic Administration' and Its Supporting Ideation" (1977). This is a critical issue because much of neoclassical price theory used extreme rationality assumptions associated with perfect information. I personally reject those assumptions; and all of my own work relies on an assumption of human fallibility. There is no place for learning when assumptions of perfect information are used. These two paragraphs do **not** rely on extreme rationality assumptions. In "Some Developments in the Study of Market Choice, Public Choice, and Institutional Choice" (1989), I more fully develop the distinctions made in different traditions of economic analysis.

5. The classical theory of administration is essentially devoid of a theory appropriate to the analysis of problematical situations. Shields (1952), in his essay on empirical collectivists, emphasizes that the structure of situations provides the context for conceptualizing policy problems. John Dewey (1927) defines a public as coming into being in an effort to control indirect consequences of actions that impinge upon persons not directly involved. His concept is closely related to the concept of externalities used by political economists.

6. This position stands in contrast to Wilson's presumption that there is but one rule of "good" administration for all governments alike, or Weber's presumption regarding the technical superiority of bureaucracy over any other form of organization (see Ashby, 1962).

7. This structure of relationships applies to air pollution, water pollution, the exploitation of fishery resources, and many types of facilities. The incentive for the individual is to take advantage of any available opportunity. If one individual does not, others will. Thus the exploitation of a common-pool resource such as the whale stock in the world's oceans may proceed to a point at which the species are exterminated. Short-term advantage deviates from long-term advantage. For people to take advantage of long-term opportunities requires a modification in decision-making arrangements so that the community of individuals involved can convert a negative-sum game into a cooperative or positive-sum game.

When the relevant field of effects includes a large number of small public jurisdictions with no overlapping jurisdiction capable of regulating the conduct of the several smaller ones relative to that field of

effects, the tragedy of the commons can occur in competition among the several smaller jurisdictions. In the case of whaling, nation-states may be too small to regulate the harvest of whales. Municipalities and counties may be inadequate units for dealing with problems of air pollution. Thus Crozier (1964) is correct in indicating that the American political system is highly susceptible to institutional dysfunctions, which he characterized as the "vicious circle of decentralization" (p. 246) and which I have followed Garrett Hardin in calling the tragedy of the commons.

A solution to such pathologies can be attained by seeking recourse to a larger jurisdiction, which will bound the relevant field of effects. Such solutions, however, need not involve the creation of only one jurisdiction to the exclusion of all smaller jurisdictions. Reliance on overlapping jurisdictions is an alternative mode of organization. Still another alternative would be to rely on the decision-making capability of the next larger unit of government. Thus reliance on states to regulate interstate commerce may engender conflicts reminiscent of a negative-sum game. Federal authority to regulate interstate commerce may be necessary to avoid destructive conflict among states. As economic relations became national in scope, increasing reliance on Federal regulation was necessary for productive relationships. As economic relations become international in scope, we can contemplate a competitive rivalry among nations, which can take on the characteristics of a negative-sum game. Appropriate solutions will require capabilities to take joint action at the international level.

8. The concept of span of control, which was used to explain hierarchical structures in the traditional theory of administration, implies a substantial limit to the capability of any one supervisor to exercise control over a number of subordinates. Tullock relies on this limit to generate a theory of institutional weakness and institutional failure associated with bureaucratic organizations. The traditional theory of public administration failed to draw such inferences even though the substantial limits on control were implied by the concept of span of control.

Simon pointed out that a loss of information and control would apply to the number of tiers in a hierarchical structure as well as the number of subordinates reporting to a single superior. Thus, increasing the number of tiers in a hierarchy would lead to a loss of information and control as between the top level of command and those at the lower echelons in any organization. Narrowing the command structure at each level of organization would lead to a loss of information and control by

increasing the number of levels in an organization. Simon's formulation (1965a: 24–28) suggests serious limits to the aggregate size of a bureaucratic organization.

The elements for formulating a theory of institutional weakness and institutional failure applicable to bureaucratic organizations were inherent in the traditional theory of public administration, but the logic of that theory was not developed until Tullock's work. Weber anticipated the consequences but failed to provide the logical connection between conditions and consequences. Tocqueville in his *Old Regime and the French Revolution* (1955) provides an extended description of bureaucratic pathologies associated with a highly centralized political regime.

9. The relationship of production of public goods and services to users' preferences implies that various decision-making arrangements for articulating voters' preferences and users' demands have an essential relationship to administrative performance. Voting, representation, legislation, and the availability of various remedies for aggrieved users of public goods and services to enforce demands have significance for administrative conduct. William A. Niskanen, Jr., (1971) has begun to explore these relationships.

Political economists would reject the presumption that public administration should be conceptualized apart from the political process inherent in the traditional dichotomy of politics and administration. Instead, they would view various forms of voting, modes of representation, and rules for legislative action as critical processes for translating individual preferences into collective decisions to secure the provision of public goods and services. Thus different voting rules will yield different outputs of public goods and services. They would in turn be concerned with the decision rules available to individual persons for invoking and enforcing demands for the provision of public goods and services. See my discussion of the "anyone rule" in *The Political Theory of a Compound Republic* (1987).

10. It is possible for an inappropriate tax policy to exacerbate rather than relieve problems of congestion in the long run. G. S. Tolley (1969) argues that the use of Federal funds to relieve congestion may have the opposite effect. He argues that in such a situation, "the receiving entity will then have incentive to overspend. If large cities succeed in overspending relative to small cities, the tendency may be away from rather than toward desirable city size" (p. 36). In addition, he argues that the "danger of overbuilding in large cities is heightened if facilities are built in response to projection of travel demands assumed to be independent

of the effect of facilities themselves on city growth." Both factors when combined lead to a **cumulative** effect, which moves in the **wrong** direction (p. 36).

11. So far as I know, no literature by political economists addresses the specific issue of authority regarding administrative reorganization. The Buchanan and Tullock (1962) analysis of decision rules implies that reliance on presidential authority to formulate reorganization plans subject only to a congressional veto is the equivalent of legislation by one-man rule subject to congressional veto.

Reference to periodic needs to "shake up" the bureaucracy presumably implies deprivation costs for those who are shaken up. How do such experiences affect the productivity of the public service? Political economists are inclined to ask such questions about the practice of administrative reorganization.

12. The possibility of diversely structured systems of ordered relationships runs through the work of many different organization theorists. Ashby (1962) distinguishes among "fully-joined systems," "iterated systems," and "multi-stable systems" and considers the relative adaptability of each. Christopher Alexander deals broadly with problems of organization and design in his article "A City Is Not a Tree" (1965) and in *Notes on the Synthesis of Form* (1964). Michael Polanyi in *The Logic of Liberty* (1951) explores the concept of polycentricity as the basis for spontaneous order as distinguished from hierarchy in a corporate order.

These different approaches to order have led to a consideration of whether an "invisible hand" operates in the public as well as the private sector. Lindblom (1959; 1965), McKean (1965), and Bish (1968; 1969) have advanced arguments on behalf of the invisible hand in government. Duggal (1966) challenged the contention. Tocqueville speaks of an invisible hand when he observes: "Nothing is more striking to the European traveler in the United States than the absence of what we term the government or the administration. Written laws exist in America, and one sees the daily execution of them; but although everything moves regularly, the mover can nowhere be discovered. The hand that directs the social machinery is invisible" (Tocqueville, 1945: 1: 70). An invisible hand can become operable in the governance of human affairs to the extent that bargaining, negotiation, and competitive rivalry can be used to regulate the conduct of diverse public enterprises in relation to one another. Thus public universities govern relationships with one another through a variety of voluntary associations, contractual un-

derstandings, and forms of competitive rivalry rather than by reference to the command of superiors in an overarching bureaucracy.

13. Daniel Elazar (1971) objects to the use of the term "decentralization" to refer to the authority exercised by smaller units of government in a federal system. He contends that decentralization implies an allocation of authority from the center by a superior authority to a subordinate set of authorities. Thus he argues that federalism implies "noncentralization" of authority. His argument is sound. A federal system necessarily implies overlapping jurisdictions and concurrent exercise of authority. Lindblom (1965) makes a similar point in contrasting central and noncentral coordination.

Chapter 4: A Theory of Democratic Administration: The Rejected Alternative

1. Tocqueville wrote of "decentralized" as against "centralized" administration to refer to what conforms to Weber's distinction between "democratic" and "bureaucratic" administration. Tocqueville's references to centralization and decentralization are apt characterizations except for one unfortunate implication. Centralization is often juxtaposed to decentralization in the sense that we sometimes speak of centralization **versus** decentralization. The terms need not be mutually exclusive in a federal political system in which several regimes coexist at different levels of government. The very structure of a federal political system implies overlapping jurisdictions and simultaneous reference to elements of both "centralization" **and** "decentralization." The characteristics that Weber identifies with democratic administration are precisely those that most impressed Tocqueville.

2. Tocqueville conceptualizes a democratic society to be one in which a strong equality of conditions exists among the people. He clearly recognizes that government in a democratic society requires radical conditions of inequality in decision-making capabilities. Thus the disparity between the power of individuals living in a mass society and those vested with governmental prerogative in a highly centralized political structure is so overpowering that he despaired for the survival of liberty or free institutions in a centralized democratic society. He saw hope in the American system of overlapping jurisdictions and fragmentation of authority as permitting a sufficient dispersion of authority

for freedom to exist in a democratic society. See especially Tocqueville's conclusions in the Fourth Book of Volume 2 of *Democracy in America.*

3. These essays in particular inspired Leonard White's historical studies in American national administration.

4. Thus politics cannot be viewed as **apart** from administration. Administrators as public servants or public employees are exposed to review and reconsideration of their decisions by other persons functioning in many different decision structures who occupy potential veto positions in relation to their decisions. An administrator selects a strategy in pursuing opportunities with an awareness that any act represents a move in a series of simultaneous games. If the game of administration is dominated by an exclusive calculus of pleasing superiors, the consequences will be different than if public administrators stand exposed to the scrutiny of common councils representing citizens, to inquiries by grand juries, to actions by citizens in courts of law, and to public scrutiny by a free press, as well as to the scrutiny of other executive officers and agencies.

5. It is essential that we recall Tocqueville's definition of a democratic society as being one characterized by a condition of social and economic equality. If we were to assume that greater social equality exists among members of Soviet society than in American society, then by Tocqueville's definition the Soviet Union would be a more democratic society than the United States. I have used Max Weber's defining characteristics for democratic administration to have the same meaning that Tocqueville used in defining "decentralized administration." Tocqueville would characterize the Soviet Union as a democratic society governed by a highly centralized administration controlled by an autocratic or self-perpetuating government.

Chapter 5: The Choice of Alternative Futures

1. Dwight Waldo in *The Administrative State* (1948: 36) observes: "Influenced by British experience and British writers, Woodrow Wilson . . . and many others had contrasted our system of separation of powers unfavorably with cabinet government, and urged the need for stronger executive leadership. Students home from the Continent were anxious to find a formula that would enable democracy to secure the manifest advantages of autocracy. The traditional separation of powers became the *bête noir* of American political science, and exaltation of the powers of the executive branch its Great White Hope."

2. John Austin in *The Province of Jurisprudence Determined* (1955) formulates the concept of positive law as that which is enforceable. He argues that constitutional law, so-called, is positive morality, not positive law. Austin's argument is consistent with that of Hobbes, but Austin does not press his analysis very far in relation to the political structure represented by what he calls a composite state. See generally his Lecture VI.

3. A strong antilegalist bias runs through the traditional study of American public administration. The problem of designing a political system that could enforce constitutional law as against those who exercise the prerogatives of government is never considered. Wilson (1887: 207) impatiently observed: "Once a nation has embarked in the business of manufacturing constitutions, it finds it exceedingly difficult to close out that business and open for the public a bureau of skilled, economical administration. There seems to be no end to the tinkering of constitutions."

The effort of other Americans to "tinker" with constitutions in the late nineteenth and early twentieth centuries could also be viewed as a critical factor in accomplishing reforms that substantially reduced the opportunities for machine politics and boss rule. Among these modifications were the introduction of the Australian ballot, direct primaries, the initiative, referendum, and recall, the popular election of U.S. senators, and other such measures.

Goodnow (1900) reflects the same bias in his reference to extralegal institutions as though any undertaking not explicitly authorized in statutory law were extralegal.

White (1948) also assumed that "the study of administration should start from the base of management rather than the foundation of law" (p. xiii). Yet paradoxically, White's writings drew heavily upon legal materials and public documents. Administration was still set on a foundation of law, but no effort was made to comprehend the relationship of administrative structures to the basic design of institutional arrangements in the American political system. Neither White, Goodnow, nor Wilson pondered the issue posed by Hamilton in the first paragraph of *The Federalist*, where he raises the question, "Are societies of men really capable or not of establishing good government from reflection and choice, or are they forever destined to depend for their constitution on accident and force?" (*Federalist* 1. I have transformed an indirect question to a direct question).

4. Quoted by Alexander Bickel in a review of Gerald T. Dunne, *Justice Story and the Rise of the Supreme Court*, in *New York Times Book Review*, May 30, 1971, p. 3.

5. The section "The Constitution of Self-Governing Public Enterprises," in Chapter 3 is relevant for a consideration of constitutional decision-making perspectives as against other political perspectives. Constitutional decision making, according to Buchanan and Tullock (1962), is based on "conceptual unanimity," and the relevant criterion for Buchanan and Tullock is "Pareto optimality." Pareto optimality implies that decision rules should be chosen that will lead to advances in human welfare in the sense that no one will be left worse off.

John Rawls (1963; 1967), in a series of articles dealing with the criterion of justice as fairness, suggests that the choice of decision rules be made on an assumption that each individual has an equal probability of being subject to decisions taken by his enemies rather than his friends. If decision-making arrangements can be devised so that one's adversaries are exposed to a structural rig of the game that leads them to make reasonably good decisions, then we can expect some degree of success in devising appropriate organizational structures for human associations.

A person who invents a new game and expects that game to be successful must make certain assumptions about the capabilities of potential players and about fairness in the play of the game. Those who play the game select their strategies in order to win. The perspectives are very different. But if some set of players reaches the conclusion that a game is structurally unfair, those who bear the burdens of unfairness would rationally prefer not to play the game if they have a choice. Peasants through much of the world have long since learned that the political game in most societies is rigged against them.

The constitutional decision maker is concerned about the essential conditions of justice and fairness that apply to the rig of the game for collective decision making. The politician playing a particular election game, for example, is concerned with winning. The test of the appropriateness of a constitutional decision rule providing for popular elections is whether winning and losing over the long run without regard to particular politicians engenders the appropriate outcomes in assuring a just or fair allocation of resources in the provision of public goods and services.

Efforts to formulate legislation for the organization of water districts in California, for example, can be understood from a constitutional decision-making perspective (V. Ostrom and E. Ostrom, 1970). One reaches different conclusions about the meaning of the California efforts using a constitutional decision-making perspective than most administrative analysts would in prescribing reorganization in accordance with the traditional principles of public administration.

6. I deliberately chose to confine these lectures to the paradigm problem in **American** public administration. A problem of vastly different proportions would be raised if this discussion were extended to a comparative analysis of political systems and their reform. The existence of common assumptions that are relevant to the design of various political institutions implies that the development of a predictive political theory applicable to the study of different administrative systems is conceivable. The evidence of institutional weakness and failure characteristic of large-scale bureaucracies is widespread. So is evidence regarding phenomena characteristic of the tragedy of the commons.

The much more difficult problem is whether reforms can be undertaken that will lead to the revolutionary transformation of one system into a different system based on a radically different design. Changes in the structure of organizational arrangements cannot occur independently of the political knowledge that is relevant to organizational practice among the persons involved. A system of bureaucratic administration cannot be transformed into a system of democratic administration except over a long period of time. Individuals in a society must acquire the knowledge, skills, and moral judgment that are necessary for undertaking joint efforts to realize common benefits. The work of Danilo Dolci is especially suggestive for students interested in this problem.

If (1) the scourge of war could be avoided on the European continent for several generations, (2) the European Community were able to negotiate a series of constitutional settlements with joint benefits (net after costs) accruing to all European peoples, and (3) appropriate European political structures were devised to permit the development of a European system of positive constitutional law, then I can imagine the gradual evolution of a system of democratic administration on the European continent.

Revolutions like the Soviet Revolution do not represent basic changes in the constitutional structure of a political system. The tzarist state was destroyed, but the Soviet state has all the attributes of Hobbes's *Leviathan* with an absolute sovereign and a new elite to function as the ruling class. The major difference is that the Soviet state has fewer symptoms of bureaucratic senility than its tzarist predecessors. Tocqueville's *Old Regime and the French Revolution* (1955) documents the continuity of bureaucracy as the central feature of the French constitution through a period of revolutionary change. Crozier's *Bureaucratic Phenomenon* (1964) substantiates its persistence to the present.

The task of fashioning political and administrative institutions for the so-called underdeveloped areas of the world is beyond the competence

of American academicians. They can contribute to a political science which others may then use in devising organizational arrangements that are appropriate to an estimate of the opportunity costs inherent in different designs. Much of the literature on administrative development grossly underestimates the costs inherent in central planning and bureaucratic organization. No organizational arrangement is cost-free.

7. See, for example, the article by Albert Sigurdson in the *Toronto Globe and Mail*, December 30, 1970. Sigurdson writes: "Security guard agencies are doing a 60 million dollar business in Canada, double the level of five years ago, and new agencies continue to open across the country." Individuals are also investing heavily in private arms. A recent estimate made by the FBI is that the "private arsenal in U.S. homes now totals 90 million weapons" (*Newsweek*, August 17, 1970, p. 15).

8. The *New York Times* in an editorial on November 11, 1969, refers to a report which disclosed that two-thirds of the abandoned buildings being torn down as "unsafe" were structurally sound and probably capable of rehabilitation. If such an assertion is true, structurally sound buildings are being destroyed for failure to devise institutional arrangements with appropriate incentives for individuals to use and maintain the available housing stock. These conditions prevail amid demands for more housing.

9. A reader of an earlier draft of these lectures raised the question: "Who are the 'individual persons' who form the 'relevant public' of a public administrator? For example, is it the duty of policemen to serve the criminals?" An answer to this question requires an evaluation of the community of persons potentially affected by "criminal" activity and a sense of moral judgment regarding the consequences following from such conduct. To judge unilaterally an act to be "criminal" is contrary to basic precepts of justice. Preliminary procedures are available to take action based on a tentative judgment about the criminality of an act. Both the person who is suspected of being a criminal and the person who is convicted of being a criminal are entitled to be treated as individual persons deserving of respect in a democratic society.

Andrei Amalrik makes the essential point when he observes in *Involuntary Journey to Siberia* (1970: 112–113):

> A court sentence ought not to be an act of vengeance but the expression of a generally accepted idea of justice. The educational value of a trial lies in convincing the defendant and everyone else that he is being judged in strict accordance with the law and with the ethical standards that mankind has arrived at during its long history; it certainly does not lie in the Judge tediously haranguing the court or in his crudely defaming the de-

fendant and witnesses. There is even less educational value in trials staged for avowedly propaganda purposes—as an object lesson to others. This is not a way of enlightening people but only of intimidating them, and it brings nothing but discredit upon the courts. When a man is charged with one thing but then accused of something else during the actual trial, this may help the police in achieving their limited aim, but it also results in still further deterioration of the whole system of justice.

If correctional administration is not oriented to the interest of individual persons who may have committed criminal acts, we can expect overwhelming failure in the administration of criminal justice. Correctional authorities require a substantial sense of moral judgment in counseling and working with prison populations. People are more than obedient cogs in machines. The only way to remind ourselves of this moral imperative is to relate ourselves to the individuality of different persons. When that condition becomes impossible, moral conduct is no longer possible.

10. As John Dewey once commented: "The man who wears the shoe knows best that it pinches and where it pinches, even if the expert shoemaker is the best judge of how the trouble is to be remedied" (Dewey, 1927: 207). He might have added that the man who wears the shoe is also the best judge of the appropriateness of the shoemaker's remedy.

Chapter 6: The Continuing Constitutional Crises in American Government

1. I capitalize Executive when referring to the personification of the executive establishment as an aggregate entity in relation to the President as Chief Executive. I also capitalize President when used to personify the "head" of the Executive establishment.

2. This is not the place to advance proposals for constitutional change (see U.S. Advisory Commission on Intergovernmental Relations, 1987). Such proposals can be appropriately formulated and considered in light of serious discussion among thinkers representing diverse points of view. Constitutional settlements can be achieved only when discussions advance to a point of substantial consensus without being preoccupied with building winning coalitions. Constructive resolutions become possible only when the constitutional level of analysis is the focus of sustained, continuing, and critical inquiry.

Unfortunately, the study of the judicial process has, in the course of

the twentieth century, become largely a preoccupation with winning coalitions as though the dominant concern were with coalition formation and what it takes to put together winning coalitions. Substantive constitutional matters were presumably "decided" by the arbitrary happenstances that generated majority coalitions. Independent standards of judgment for evaluating the performance of the judiciary were no longer considered. Judicial politics as well as congressional and presidential politics became simply a matter of who prevailed on a presumption that someone should always prevail in decisions pertaining to collective action. All aspects of political life become a struggle for dominance rather than finding ways to resolve problems in mutually productive ways that take account of diverse communities of interest consistent with a due process of inquiry and a fundamental respect for the integrity of all human beings.

The problem, then, is how to create fora for discussion, dialogue, and contestation about basic issues of constitutional importance that are not transformed into another struggle to do no more than patch together winning coalitions. There is a place for basic dialogue about fundamental issues that should not be dominated by perverse appeals to loyalties in efforts to build winning coalitions and doing everything necessary, including silence about embarrassing questions, in efforts to preserve winning coalitions. When everyone becomes absorbed in such perverse forms of political participation, a democratic society no longer has reserved capabilities for addressing questions about where such a way of life leads in the development of human civilization.

Chapter 7: Intellectual Crises and Beyond

1. Nien Cheng in *Life and Death in Shanghai* (1987: 167) observes: "Since good intentions and sympathy for others often led people into trouble, the Chinese people have developed a new proverb that said, 'the more you do, the more trouble you have; the less you do, the less trouble you have. If you do nothing whatever, you will become a model citizen.' "

2. Steven Runciman in *Byzantine Civilization* (1956: 65) makes the following assessment of the Imperial Constitution of the Byzantine empire:

> The Imperial Constitution, The Emperor, elected by the Senate, the Army and the People of Constantinople, to be the Viceroy of God but to rule

according to Roman Law, was in many ways illogical and incomplete, but it had the supreme and essential merit that it worked. Its efficiency is remarkably illustrated by the fact that while in the West innumerable writers arose to discuss the difficult problem of Church and State, of Emperors and Kings and Popes and their inter-relations, for centuries Byzantium did not produce a single political theorist. The constitution worked too well for abstract discussions to be needed.

It might be conjectured instead that the emperor as viceroy of God and autocrator left no public space for disputation and contestation to occur with reference to the proper structure of authority relationships in Byzantine society. Silence is construed by Runciman as efficiency. In the absence of intellectual debates, contestations, in shaping shared communities of understanding, Byzantium failed to generate and maintain the self-governing capabilities that had earlier been achieved in the Greco-Roman city-states. When Constantinople was conquered by the Turks, the Byzantine empire collapsed without residual governing structures to maintain the continuity of the Byzantine civilization as a civilization.

References

Albert, Hans (1986). *Freiheit und Ordnung*. Tübingen: J. C. B. Mohr (Vortrage und Aufsatze/Walter Eucken Institut, No. 109).

Alexander, Christopher (1964). *Notes on the Synthesis of Form*. Cambridge, Mass.: Harvard University Press.

—— (1965). "A City Is Not a Tree." *Architectural Forum* 122 (April): 58–62, and ibid. (May 1965): 58–61.

Altshuler, Alan A. (1970). *Community Control: The Black Demand for Participation in Large American Cities*. New York: Pegasus.

Amalrik, Andrei (1970). *Involuntary Journey to Siberia*. New York: Harcourt Brace Jovanovich.

Anderson, William (1925). *American City Government*. New York: H. Holt.

—— (1942). *The Units of Government in the United States: An Enumeration and Analysis*. Chicago: Public Administration Service.

Arendt, Hannah (1963). *On Revolution*. New York: Viking Press.

Ashby, W. Ross (1956). *An Introduction to Cybernetics*. New York: John Wiley.

—— (1960). *Design for a Brain: The Origin of Adaptive Behavior*. 2d ed. New York: John Wiley.

—— (1962). "Principles of the Self-Organizing System." In H. Von Foerster and G. W. Zopf, eds., *Principles of Self-Organization*. New York: Macmillan, pp. 255–278.

Austin, John (1955). *The Province of Jurisprudence Determined*. H. L. A. Hart, ed. London: Weidenfeld and Nicolson.

Ayres, Robert U., and Allen V. Kneese (1969). "Production, Consumption and Externalities." *American Economic Review* 59 (June): 282–297.

Bagehot, Walter (1964). *The English Constitution*. R. H. S. Crossman, ed. London: C. A. Watts.

Bain, Joe S. (1959). *Industrial Organization*. Berkeley and Los Angeles: University of California Press.

Barnard, Chester I. (1938). *The Functions of the Executive*. Cambridge, Mass.: Harvard University Press.

Beck, Henry (1970). "The Rationality of Redundancy." *Comparative Politics* 3 (January): 469–478.

Bendix, Reinhard (1960). *Max Weber: An Intellectual Portrait*. Garden City, N.Y.: Doubleday.

Berman, Harold (1983). *Law and Revolution: The Formation of the Western Legal Tradition*. Cambridge, Mass.: Harvard University Press.

Bish, Robert L. (1968). "A Comment on V. P. Duggal's 'Is There an Unseen Hand in Government?'" *Annals of Public and Co-operative Economy* 39 (January–March): 89–94.

——— (1969). "The American Public Economy as a Single Firm: Reply to Duggal." *Annals of Public and Co-operative Economy* 40 (July–September): 361–365.

——— (1971). *The Public Economy of Metropolitan Areas*. Chicago: Markham.

———, and Vincent Ostrom (1973). *Understanding Urban Government: Metropolitan Reform Reconsidered*. Washington, D.C.: American Enterprise Institute.

Blau, Peter L. (1956). *Bureaucracy in Modern Society*. New York: Random House.

Blomquist, William, and Elinor Ostrom (1985). "Institutional Capacity and the Resolution of a Commons Dilemma." *Policy Studies Review* 5 (November): 383–393.

Buchanan, James M. (1960). *Fiscal Theory and Political Economy*. Chapel Hill: University of North Carolina Press.

——— (1966). "An Individualistic Theory of Political Process." In David Easton, ed., *Varieties of Political Theory*. Englewood Cliffs, N.J.: Prentice-Hall, pp. 25–38.

——— (1967). *Public Finance in Democratic Process: Fiscal Institutions and Individual Choice*. Chapel Hill: University of North Carolina Press.

——— (1968). *The Demand and Supply of Public Goods*. Chicago: Rand McNally.

——— (1969). *Cost and Choice: An Inquiry in Economic Theory*. Chicago: Markham.

——— (1970). "Public Goods and Public Bads." In John P. Crecine, ed., *Financing the Metropolis*. Beverly Hills: Sage, pp. 51–71.

——— (1975). *The Limits of Liberty: Between Anarchy and Leviathan*. Chicago: University of Chicago Press.

—— (1979). *What Should Economists Do?* Indianapolis: Liberty Press.

——, and Gordon Tullock (1962). *The Calculus of Consent: Logical Foundations of Constitutional Democracy.* Ann Arbor: University of Michigan Press.

Caldwell, Lynton K. (1965). "Public Administration and the Universities: A Half-Century of Development." *Public Administration Review* 25 (March): 52–60.

Carey, William D. (1969). "Presidential Staffing in the Sixties and Seventies." *Public Administration Review* 29 (September–October): 450–458.

—— (1970). "Remarks on Reorganization Plan No. 2." *Public Administration Review* 30 (November–December): 631–634.

Cheng, Nien (1987). *Life and Death in Shanghai.* New York: Grove Press.

Christy, Francis T., Jr., and Anthony Scott (1965). *The Common Wealth of World Fisheries.* Baltimore: Johns Hopkins Press.

Coase, R. H. (1937). "The Nature of the Firm." *Economica* 4: 386–485.

Coker, F. W. (1922). "Dogmas of Administrative Reform." *American Political Science Review* 16 (August): 399–411.

Committee for Economic Development (1966). *Modernizing Local Government.* New York: Committee for Economic Development.

—— (1970). *Reshaping Government in Metropolitan Areas.* New York: Committee for Economic Development.

Commons, John R. (1968). *Legal Foundations of Capitalism.* Madison: University of Wisconsin Press.

Crankshaw, Edward (1983). *Bismarck.* New York: Penguin Books.

—— (1986). *The Shadow of the Winter Palace.* London: Papermac.

Crozier, Michel (1964). *The Bureaucratic Phenomenon.* Phoenix Books ed. Chicago: University of Chicago Press.

Cyert, Richard M., and James G. March (1963). *A Behavioral Theory of the Firm.* Englewood Cliffs, N.J.: Prentice-Hall.

Dales, J. H. (1968). *Pollution, Property and Prices.* Toronto: University of Toronto Press.

Davis, Otto A., and Andrew B. Whinston (1961). "The Economics of Urban Renewal." *Law and Contemporary Problems* 26 (Winter): 105–117.

—— (1967). "On the Distinction between Public and Private Goods." *American Economic Review* 57 (May): 360–373.

Demsetz, Harold (1969). "Information and Efficiency: Another Viewpoint." *Journal of Law and Economics* 12 (April): 1–22.

Dewey, John (1927). *The Public and Its Problems.* New York: Henry Holt.

Diamant, Alfred (1962). "The Bureaucratic Model: Max Weber Rejected, Rediscovered, Reformed." In Ferrel Heady and Sybil L. Stokes, eds.,

Papers in Comparative Public Administration. Ann Arbor: University of Michigan, Institute of Public Administration, pp. 59–96.

Dimock, Marshall E. (1937). "The Study of Administration." *American Political Science Review* 31 (February): 28–40.

Djilas, Milovan (1957). *The New Class*. New York: Praeger.

Downs, Anthony (1957). *An Economic Theory of Democracy*. New York: Harper & Row.

——— (1967). *Inside Bureaucracy*. Boston: Little, Brown.

Duggal, V. P. (1966). "Is There an Unseen Hand in Government?" *Annals of Public and Co-operative Economy* 37 (April–June): 145–150.

Elazar, Daniel J. (1971). "Community Self-Government and the Crisis of American Politics." *Ethics* 81 (January): 91–106.

Emmerich, Herbert (1950). *Essays on Federal Reorganization*. University, Ala.: University of Alabama Press.

Eucken, Walter (1951). *The Foundations of Economics*. Chicago: University of Chicago Press.

Feagin, Joe R. (1970). "Home Defense and the Police: Black and White Perspectives." *American Behavioral Scientist* 13 (May–August): 797–814.

Follet, M. P. (1924). *Creative Experience*. New York: Peter Smith.

Friesema, H. Paul (1966). "The Metropolis and the Maze of Local Government." *Urban Affairs Quarterly* 2 (December): 68–90.

Gerth, H. H., and C. Wright Mills, eds. (1946). *From Max Weber: Essays in Sociology*. Galaxy Book ed. New York: Oxford University Press.

Golembiewski, Robert J. (1977). "A Critique of 'Democratic Administration' and Its Supporting Ideation." *American Political Science Review* 71 (December): 1488–1507.

Goodnow, Frank J. (1900). *Politics and Administration: A Study in Government*. New York: Macmillan.

Gordon, H. Scott (1954). "The Economics of a Common Property Resource: The Fishery." *Journal of Political Economy* 62 (April): 124–142.

Graham, F. P. (1968). "The Cop's Right (?) to Stop and Frisk." *New York Times Magazine*, December.

Grodzins, Morton (1966). *The American System*. Edited by Daniel J. Elazar. Chicago: Rand McNally.

Gulick, Luther, and Lyndall Urwick, eds. (1937). *Papers on the Science of Administration*. New York: Columbia University, Institute of Public Administration.

Hacker, Andrew (1970). *The End of the American Era*. New York: Atheneum.

Hamilton, Alexander, John Jay, and James Madison (n.d.). *The Federalist*. New York: Modern Library.

Hardin, Garrett (1968). "The Tragedy of the Commons." *Science* 162 (December): 1243–1248.

Hawley, Amos H., and Basil G. Zimmer (1970). *The Metropolitan Community: Its People and Government.* Beverly Hills: Sage.

Hayek, F. A. (1960). *The Constitution of Liberty.* Chicago: University of Chicago Press.

Hirsch, Werner (1964). "Local versus Areawide Urban Government Services." *National Tax Journal* 17 (December): 331–339.

——— (1968). "The Supply of Urban Public Services." In Harvey S. Perloff and Lowden Wingo, Jr., eds., *Issues in Urban Economics.* Baltimore: Johns Hopkins Press, pp. 435–476.

Hirshleifer, Jack, James C. DeHaven, and Jerome W. Milliman (1960). *Water Supply Economics, Technology, and Policy.* Chicago: University of Chicago Press.

Hjern, Benny, and David O. Porter (1981). "Implementation Structures: A New Unit of Administrative Analysis." *Organization Studies* 2, No. 3, pp. 211–227.

Hobbes, Thomas (1960). *Leviathan or the Matter, Forme and Power of a Commonwealth Ecclesiastical and Civil.* Edited by Michael Oakeshott. Oxford: Basil Blackwell.

Hohfeld, Wesley N. (1964). *Fundamental Legal Conceptions.* Edited by W. W. Cook. New Haven: Yale University Press.

Huang, Ray (1981). *1587: A Year of No Significance.* New Haven: Yale University Press.

Jacobs, Jane (1961). *The Death and Life of Great American Cities.* New York: Vintage Books.

Kaufmann, Franz-Xaver, Giandomenico Majone, and Vincent Ostrom, eds. (1986). *Guidance, Control, and Evaluation in the Public Sector.* Berlin and New York: Walter de Gruyter.

Kiser, Larry L., and Elinor Ostrom (1982). "The Three Worlds of Action: A Metatheoretical Synthesis of Institutional Approaches." In Elinor Ostrom, ed., *Strategies of Political Inquiry.* Beverly Hills: Sage, pp. 179–222.

Knight, Frank H. (1965). *Risk, Uncertainty and Profit.* New York: Harper & Row.

Kotler, Milton (1969). *Neighborhood Government: The Local Foundations of Community Life.* Indianapolis: Bobbs-Merrill.

Kruesselberg, Hans-Günter (1983). "Property Rights Theorie und Wohlfahrtsoekonomik." In Alfred Schüller, ed., *Property Rights und oekonomische Theorie.* Munich: Verlag Franz Vahlen.

Kuhn, Thomas S. (1964). *The Structure of Scientific Revolutions.* Phoenix Books ed. Chicago: University of Chicago Press.

Lakatos, Irme (1970). "Falsification and the Method of Scientific Research Programmes." In Irme Lakatos and Alan Musgrave, eds., *Criticism and the Growth of Knowledge.* Cambridge: Cambridge University Press, pp. 91–196.

Landau, Martin (1969). "Redundance, Rationality and the Problem of Duplication and Overlap." *Public Administration Review* 29 (July–August): 346–358.

Laudun, Larry (1977). *Progress and Its Problems: Towards a Theory of Scientific Growth.* Berkeley and Los Angeles: University of California Press.

Leach, Richard H. (1971). "Federalism: Continuing Predicament." *Public Administration Review* 31 (March–April): 217–223.

Lenin, V. I. (1932a). *State and Revolution.* New York: International Publishers.

——— (1932b). *What Is to Be Done?* New York: International Publishers.

Lindblom, Charles E. (1955). *Bargaining: The Hidden Hand in Government.* Research Memorandum RM-1434-RC. Santa Monica, Calif.: RAND Corporation.

——— (1959). "The Science of 'Muddling Through.' " *Public Administration Review* 19 (Spring): 1–17.

——— (1965). *The Intelligence of Democracy: Decision Making through Mutual Adjustment.* New York: Free Press.

Llewellyn, K. N., and E. A. Hoebel (1941). *The Cheyenne Way: Conflict and Case Law in Primitive Jurisprudence.* Norman: University of Oklahoma Press.

Long, Norton E. (1952). "Bureaucracy and Constitutionalism." *American Political Science Review* 46 (September): 808–818.

——— (1969). "Reflections on Presidential Power." *Public Administration Review* 29 (September–October): 442–450.

——— (1970). "Rigging the Market for Public Goods." In William R. Rosengren and Mark Lefton, eds., *Organization and Clients: Essays in the Sociology of Service.* Columbus, Ohio: Charles E. Merrill, pp. 187–204.

Mansfield, Harvey C. (1969). "Federal Executive Reorganization: Thirty Years of Experience." *Public Administration Review* 29 (July–August): 332–345.

March, James G., and Herbert A. Simon (1958). *Organizations.* New York: John Wiley.

Margolis, Julius (1955). "A Comment on the Pure Theory of Public Expenditures." *Review of Economics and Statistics* 37 (November): 347–349.

Martin, Daniel W. (1988). "The Fading Legacy of Woodrow Wilson." *Public Administration Review* 48 (March–April): 631–636.

Martin, Roscoe C. (1952). "Political Science and Public Administration." *American Political Science Review* 46 (September): 660–676.

Mayo, Elton (1933). *The Human Problems of an Industrial Civilization*. New York: Viking Press.

McConnell, Grant (1966). *Private Power and American Democracy*. New York: Alfred A. Knopf.

McKean, Roland N. (1958). *Efficiency in Government through Systems Analysis, with Emphasis on Water Resource Development*. New York: John Wiley.

——— (1965). "The Unseen Hand in Government." *American Economic Review* 55 (June): 496–506.

Merton, Robert K., Ailsa P. Gray, Barbara Hockey, and Hanan C. Selvin, eds. (1952). *Reader in Bureaucracy*. New York: Free Press.

Millett, John D. (1959). *Government and Public Administration*. New York: McGraw-Hill.

Mishan, E. J. (1969). "The Relationship between Joint Products, Collective Goods, and External Effects." *Journal of Political Economy* 77 (May–June): 329–348.

Niskanen, William A., Jr. (1971). *Bureaucracy and Representative Government*. Chicago: Aldine-Atherton.

Olson, Mancur (1965). *The Logic of Collective Action*. Cambridge, Mass.: Harvard University Press.

——— (1969). "The Principle of 'Fiscal Equivalence': The Division of Responsibility among Different Levels of Government." *American Economic Review* 59 (May): 479–487.

Ostrom, Elinor (1968). "Some Postulated Effects of Learning on Constitutional Behavior." *Public Choice* 5 (Fall): 87–104.

——— (1971). "Institutional Arrangements and the Measurement of Policy Consequences: Applications to Evaluating Police Performance." *Urban Affairs Quarterly* 6 (June): 447–475.

——— (1972). "Metropolitan Reform: Propositions Derived from Two Traditions." *Social Science Quarterly* 53 (December): 474–493.

——— (1982). *Strategies of Political Inquiry*. Beverly Hills: Sage.

——— (1985). "Racial Inequalities in Low-Income Central City and Suburban Communities: The Case of Police Services." In Kenneth Hanf

and Theo A. J. Toonen, eds., *Policy Implementation in Federal and Unitary Systems*. Dordrecht: Martinus Nijhoff, pp. 235–265.

——, William Baugh, Richard Guarasci, Roger B. Parks, and Gordon P. Whitaker (1973). *Community Organization and the Provision of Police Services*. Beverly Hills: Sage.

——, and Roger B. Parks (1971). "Black Citizens and the Police: Some Effects of Community Control." Paper presented at the annual meeting of the American Political Science Association, Chicago, September 7–11.

——, and Gordon P. Whitaker (1973). "Does Local Community Control of Police Make a Difference? Some Preliminary Findings." *American Journal of Political Science* 17 (February): 48–76.

Ostrom, Vincent (1968). "Water Resource Development: Some Problems in Economic and Political Analysis of Public Policy." In Austin Ranney, ed., *Political Science and Public Policy*. Chicago: Markham, pp. 123–150.

—— (1969). "Operational Federalism: Organization for the Provision of Public Services in the American Federal System." *Public Choice* 6 (Spring): 1–17.

—— (1971). *Institutional Arrangements for Water Resource Development*. Springfield, Va.: National Technical Information Service.

—— (1977). "Some Problems in Doing Political Theory: A Response to Golembiewski's 'Critique.' " *American Political Science Review* 71 (December): 1508–1525.

—— (1980). "Artisanship and Artifact." *Public Administration Review* 40 (July–August): 309–317.

—— (1984). "The Meaning of Value Terms." *American Behavioral Scientist* 28 (November–December): 249–262.

—— (1987). *The Political Theory of a Compound Republic: Designing the American Experiment*. Rev. ed. Lincoln: University of Nebraska Press.

—— (1989). "Some Developments in the Study of Market Choice, Public Choice, and Institutional Choice." In Jack Rabin, Gerald Miller, and Bartley Hildreth, eds., *Handbook on Public Administration*. New York: Marcel Dekker.

——, and Frances P. Bish (1977). *Comparing Urban Service Delivery Systems*. Urban Affairs Annual Reviews, vol. 12. Beverly Hills: Sage.

——, and Elinor Ostrom (1965). "A Behavioral Approach to the Study of Intergovernmental Relations." *Annals of the American Academy of Political and Social Science* 359 (May): 137–146.

—— (1970). "Conditions of Legal and Political Feasibility." In Garrett

H. Toebes, ed., *Natural Resources Systems Models in Decision Making*. Lafayette: Purdue University, Water Resources Research Center, pp. 191–208.

——— (1971). "Public Choice: A Different Approach to the Study of Public Administration." *Public Administration Review* 31 (March–April): 203–216.

——— (1977). "Public Goods and Public Choices." In E. S. Savas, ed., *Alternatives for Delivering Public Services: Toward Improved Performance*. Boulder, Colo.: Westview Press, pp. 7–49.

———, Charles M. Tiebout, and Robert Warren (1961). "The Organization of Government in Metropolitan Areas: A Theoretical Inquiry." *American Political Science Review* 55 (December): 831–842.

———, David Feeny, and Hartmut Picht, eds. (1988). *Rethinking Institutional Analysis and Development: Some Issues, Alternatives, and Choices*. San Francisco: Institute for Contemporary Studies Press.

Parks, Roger B. (1985). "Metropolitan Structure and Systemic Performance: The Case of Police Service Delivery." In Kenneth Hanf and Theo A. J. Toonen, eds., *Policy Implementation in Federal and Unitary Systems*. Dordrecht: Martinus Nijhoff, pp. 161–191.

——— and Elinor Ostrom (1981). "Complex Models of Urban Service Systems." In Terry N. Clark, ed., *Urban Policy Analysis: Directions for Future Research*. Urban Affairs Annual Reviews, vol. 21. Beverly Hills: Sage, pp. 171–199.

Parsons, Talcott, ed. (1964). *Max Weber: The Theory of Social and Economic Organization*. New York: Free Press.

Pipes, Richard (1974). *Russia under the Old Regime*. New York: Charles Scribner's Sons.

Polanyi, Michael (1951). *The Logic of Liberty: Reflections and Rejoinders*. Chicago: University of Chicago Press.

Popper, Karl R. (1964). *The Poverty of Historicism*. New York: Harper Torchbooks.

Press, Charles (1963). "The Cities within a Great City: A Decentralist Approach to Centralization." *Centennial Review* 7 (Winter): 113–130.

Radnitzky, Gerard, and W. W. Bartley III, eds. (1987). *Evolutionary Epistemology, Rationality, and the Sociology of Knowledge*. La Salle, Ill.: Open Court.

Rawls, John (1963). "Constitutional Liberty and the Concept of Justice." In Carl J. Friedrich and John W. Chapman, eds., *Nomos VI: Justice*. New York: Atherton Press, pp. 98–125.

——— (1967). "Distributive Justice." In Peter Laslett and W. G. Run-

ciman, eds., *Philosophy, Politics and Society*. Oxford: Blackwell, pp. 58–82.

Reuss, Henry S. (1970). *Revenue-Sharing: Crutch or Catalyst for State and Local Governments?* New York: Praeger.

Revel, Jean-François (1971). *Without Marx or Jesus, the New American Revolution Has Begun*. Garden City, N.Y.: Doubleday.

Rheinstein, Max, ed. (1954). *Max Weber on Law in Economy and Society*. Clarion Book ed. New York: Simon and Schuster.

Ridley, Clarence E., and Herbert A. Simon (1938). *Measuring Municipal Activities: A Survey of Suggested Criteria and Reporting Forms for Appraising Administration*. Chicago: International City Managers Association.

Riggs, Fred W. (1968). "The Crisis of Legitimacy: A Challenge to Administrative Theory." *Philippine Journal of Public Administration* 12 (April): 147–164.

Rousseau, Jean-Jacques (1978). *On the Social Contract*. Edited by Roger D. Masters. New York: St. Martin's Press.

Runciman, Steven (1956). *Byzantine Civilization*. Meridian Book. Cleveland: World Publishing Company.

Samuelson, Paul A. (1954). "The Pure Theory of Public Expenditure." *Review of Economics and Statistics* 36 (November): 387–389.

Savas, E. S. (1977). "An Empirical Study of Competition in Municipal Service Delivery." *Public Administration Review* 37 (November–December): 717–724.

——— (1987). "Privatization: The Key to Better Government." Chatham, N.J.: Chatham House Publishers.

Shackle, G. L. S. (1961). *Decision, Order and Time in Human Affairs*. Cambridge, Eng.: Cambridge University Press.

Shields, Currin V. (1952). "The American Tradition of Empirical Collectivism." *American Political Science Review* 46 (March): 104–120.

Siedentopf, Heinrich (1983). "Reflexions sur la Science Administrative Comparée." In European Institute of Public Administration, *The Development of Research and Training in European Policy Making*. Maastricht: EIPA.

Simon, Herbert A. (1943). *Fiscal Aspects of Metropolitan Consolidation*. Berkeley: University of California, Bureau of Public Administration.

——— (1946). "The Proverbs of Administration." *Public Administration Review* 6 (Winter): 53–67.

——— (1952). "Comments on the Theory of Organizations." *American Political Science Review* 46 (December): 1130–1139.

—— (1957). *Models of Man: Social and Rational; Mathematical Essays on Rational Human Behavior in a Social Setting.* New York: John Wiley.

—— (1959). "Theories of Decision Making in Economics and Behavioral Science." *American Economics Review* 49 (June): 258–283.

—— (1960). *The New Science of Management Decision.* New York: Harper & Row.

—— (1965a). *Administrative Behavior: A Study of Decision-Making Processes in Administrative Organization.* New York: Free Press.

—— (1965b). *The Shape of Automation for Men and Management.* New York: Harper & Row.

—— (1969). *The Sciences of the Artificial.* Cambridge, Mass.: MIT Press.

——, William R. Divine, E. Myles Cooper, and Milton Chernin (1941). *Determining Work Loads for Professional Staff in a Public Welfare Agency.* Berkeley: University of California, Bureau of Public Administration.

Sproule-Jones, Mark (1982). "Public Choice Theory and Natural Resources: Methodological Explication and Critique." *American Political Science Review* 76 (December): 790–804.

Stein, Harold (1952). *Public Administration and Policy Development: A Case Book.* New York: Harcourt and Brace.

—— (1963). *American Civil-Military Decisions: A Book of Case Studies.* University, Ala.: University of Alabama Press.

Stigler, George J. (1962). "The Tenable Range of Functions of Local Government." In Edmund S. Phelps, ed., *Private Wants and Public Needs: Issues Surrounding the Size and Scope of Government Expenditure.* New York: W. W. Norton, pp. 137–147.

Sundquist, James L., with the collaboration of David W. Davis (1969). *Making Federalism Work: A Study of Program Coordination at the Community Level.* Washington, D.C.: Brookings Institution.

—— (1970). "Organizing U.S. Social and Economic Development." *Public Administration Review* 30 (November–December): 625–630.

Thompson, James D. (1967). *Organizations in Action.* New York: McGraw-Hill.

Thompson, Victor A. (1961). *Modern Organization.* New York: Alfred A. Knopf.

Tiebout, Charles M. (1956). "A Pure Theory of Local Expenditure." *Journal of Political Economy* 44 (October): 416–424.

Tierney, Brian (1982). *Religion, Law and the Growth of Constitutional Thought, 1150–1650.* Cambridge: Cambridge University Press.

Tocqueville, Alexis de (1945). *Democracy in America.* 2 vols. Edited by Philip Bradley. New York: Alfred A. Knopf.

———— (1955). *The Old Regime and the French Revolution*. Doubleday Anchor Books ed. Garden City, N.Y.: Doubleday.

Tolley, G. S. (1969). *The Welfare Economics of City Bigness*. Urban Economics Report No. 31. Chicago: University of Chicago Press.

Toonen, Theo A. J. (1987). *Denken over Binnenlands Bestuur: Theorieen van de gedecentraliseerde eenheidsstaat bestuurskundig beschouwd*. Rotterdam: Erasmus University.

Toulmin, Stephen E. (1961). *Foresight and Understanding: An Enquiry into the Aims of Science*. Bloomington: Indiana University Press.

Tullock, Gordon (1965). *The Politics of Bureaucracy*. Washington, D.C.: Public Affairs Press.

———— (1969). "Federalism: The Problem of Scale." *Public Choice* 6 (Spring): 19–29.

———— (1970). *Private Wants, Public Means: An Economic Analysis of the Desirable Scope of Government*. New York: Basic Books.

U.S. Advisory Commission on Intergovernmental Relations (1987a). *The Organization of Local Public Economies*. Washington, D.C.: Advisory Commission on Intergovernmental Relations.

———— (1987b). *Federalism and the Constitution: A Symposium on Garcia*. Washington, D.C.: Advisory Commission on Intergovernmental Relations.

———— (1988). *Metropolitan Organization: The St. Louis Study*. Washington, D.C.: Advisory Commission on Intergovernmental Relations.

United States Codes, Congressional and Administrative Laws (1971). Vol. 3. 91st Cong., 2d sess., 1970. St. Paul: West Publishing Company, 1971.

U.S. Congress, Joint Economic Committee, Subcommittee on Economy in Government (1969). *A Compendium of Papers on the Analysis and Evaluation of Public Expenditures: The PPB System*. 3 vols. Washington, D.C.: U.S. Government Printing Office.

U.S. President's Committee on Administrative Management (1937). *Report with Special Studies*. Washington, D.C.: U.S. Government Printing Office.

Van Riper, Paul (1983). "The American Administrative State: Wilson and the Founders—An Unorthodox View." *Public Administration Review* 43 (November–December): 477–490.

Vile, M. J. C. (1967). *Constitutionalism and the Separation of Powers*. Oxford: Clarendon Press.

Wagner, Richard E. (1971). *The Fiscal Organization of American Federalism: Description, Analysis, Reform*. Chicago: Markham.

Waldo, Dwight (1948). *The Administrative State: A Study of the Political Theory of American Public Administration*. New York: Ronald Press.

———— (1955). *The Study of Public Administration*. New York: Random House.

———— (1968). "Scope of the Theory of Public Administration." In James C. Charlesworth, ed., *Theory and Practice of Public Administration: Scope, Objectives, and Methods*. Philadelphia: American Academy of Political and Social Science, pp. 1–26.

Wallas, Graham (1921). *Our Social Heritage*. New Haven: Yale University Press.

Walters, A. A. (1961). "The Theory in Measurement in Private and Social Cost of Highway Congestion." *Econometrica* 29 (October): 676–699.

Warren, Robert O. (1964). "A Municipal Services Market Model of Metropolitan Organization." *Journal of the American Institute of Planners* 30 (August): 193–204.

———— (1966). *Government in Metropolitan Regions: A Reappraisal of Fractionated Political Organization*. Davis, Calif.: University of California, Institute of Governmental Affairs.

———— (1970). "Federal-Local Development Planning: Scale Effects in Representation and Policy Making." *Public Administration Review* 30 (November–December): 584–595.

Weber, Max (1978). *Economy and Society*. Edited by Guenther Roth and Claus Wittich. Berkeley and Los Angeles: University of California Press.

Wengert, E. S. (1942). "The Study of Public Administration." *American Political Science Review* 36 (April): 313–322.

Weschler, Louis F. (1982). "Public Choice: Methodological Individualism in Politics." *Public Administration Review* 42 (May–June): 288–294.

———— and Robert Warren (1970). "Consumption Costs and Production Costs in the Provision of Antipoverty Goods." Paper delivered at the sixty-sixth annual meeting of the American Political Science Association, Los Angeles, Calif., September 8–12.

Whitaker, Gordon P. (1980). "Coproduction: Citizen Participation in Service Delivery." *Public Administration Review* 40 (May–June): 240–246.

White, Leonard D. (1939). *Introduction to the Study of Public Administration*. Rev. ed. New York: Macmillan.

———— (1948). *Introduction to the Study of Public Administration*. 3d ed. New York: Macmillan.

Wildavsky, Aaron (1966). "The Political Economy of Efficiency." *Public Administration Review* 26 (December): 292–310.

Williamson, Oliver E. (1975). *Markets and Hierarchies: Analysis and Anti-Trust Implications*. New York: Free Press.

Willoughby, W. F. (1923). *The Reorganization of the Administrative Branch of the National Government*. Baltimore: Johns Hopkins Press.

Wilson, Woodrow (1887). "The Study of Administration." *Political Science Quarterly* 2 (June): 197–220.

——— (1956). *Congressional Government: A Study in American Politics*. New York: Meridian Books.

Yang, Tai-Shuenn (1987). "Property Rights and Constitutional Order in Imperial China." Ph.D. dissertation, Indiana University.

Index